1/21/10

Praise for *The Sundance Kids*

"I've never been to Sundance—however, after reading this book, it feels as if I've been there and back. James Mottram makes clear the impact Sundance and all its players have had on the so-called Hollywood studio system, while breaking down the nature and structure of storytelling, something I continually struggle with, and articulating it in a manner that will enable the average movie lover to more fully understand the metaphorical undertones a writer-director is trying to achieve. The result is an enjoyable read, full of a wealth of information that leaves us asking, 'What next?'"

—Milo Addica, Oscar-nominated screenwriter of *Monster's Ball*

"Mottram . . . clearly knows this independent filmmaking terrain inside out . . . He has a keen eye for the shared aesthetic propensities of his subjects: playing with structure; fracturing the timeline; employing cinematic self-reflexiveness, expositional voice-overs and a sophisticated pop music score . . . [He] has given us a valuable, detailed map to the newest New Wave in Hollywood."

—Phillip Lopate, *Los Angeles Times Book Review*

"[Readers will] savor the engaging, erudite voice [Mottram] brings to each film—like a friend who knows every cinematic allusion in *Kill Bill*."

—David O'Grady, *Nylon*

"Mottram's coverage, alternately thematic and historic, benefits hugely from the impressive array of original interviews with key players, most notably Soderbergh, whose perspective, as someone who goes back and forth between the mainstream and indie environments, is a vital one . . . A compelling story of challenging, determined filmmaking."

—Danny Graydon, *Variety*

THE SUNDANCE KIDS

60 FARRAR STRAUS GIROUX

by the same author
The Making of MEMENTO

THE SUNDANCE KIDS

How the Mavericks Took Back Hollywood

JAMES MOTTRAM

Faber and Faber, Inc.
An affiliate of Farrar, Straus and Giroux
New York

Faber and Faber, Inc.
An affiliate of Farrar, Straus and Giroux
19 Union Square West, New York 10003

Library of Congress Control Number: 2005937470
Paperback ISBN-13: 978-0-86547-967-8
Paperback ISBN-10: 0-86547-967-4

www.fsgbooks.com

10   9   8   7   6   5   4   3   2   1

For Julie: without you, I would be blown sideways through life. Thank you for your love, patience and understanding during the writing of this book.

Contents

List of Illustrations, ix
Acknowledgments, xii
Introduction: Pizza Knights, F-64 and The Mild Bunch, xiii

Section I: The Sundance Years

1 'It's All Downhill from Here': How Steven Soderbergh Paves
   the Way for the Next Generation, 3
2 Talk Is Cheap: Sundance After *sex, lies, and videotape*, 15
3 *Reservoir Dogs* and the Class of '92, 27
4 The Changing Face of Sundance: *Public Access* and *Spanking
   the Monkey*, 37
5 'Trespassing on Hallowed Ground': *Kafka* and
   King of the Hill, 51

Section II: Indiewood

6 Pulp Fact: The Rise of Miramax as Hollywood Embraces
   Tarantino-mania, 67
7 Austin Power: How Robert Rodriguez and Richard Linklater
   Bucked the System, 85
8 Genre I: Crime Does Pay – *The Underneath*, *The Usual Suspects*
   and *Se7en*, 105
9 The Second Wave: The Conflicts of *Citizen Ruth*, *Hard Eight*
   and *Bottle Rocket*, 125
10 Spreading Propaganda: The Rise of David Fincher and
   Spike Jonze, 149
11 Beyond the Fringe: *Schizopolis* and *Gray's Anatomy*, 169
12 Adult Entertainment: Hollywood Grows Up with
   Boogie Nights, 185
13 Genre II: School Days – *Election*, *Rushmore* and *Apt Pupil*, 203
14 Adaptation: Tarantino and Soderbergh Meet Elmore Leonard, 225

15 The Sundance Sisters: Sofia Coppola and Kimberly Peirce, 243
16 Annus Mirabilis: How 1999 Became the Year of the
    Sundance Kids, 255

Section III: The Insiders

17 King of the Hills: Soderbergh Comes Back from the Brink, 285
18 The X-Man: Bryan Singer Takes on the Blockbuster, 305
19 Being Charlie Kaufman: How One Man Tried to Debunk the
    Three-Act Structure, 317
20 Family Ties: *The Royal Tenenbaums*, *About Schmidt* and
    Punch-Drunk Love, 339
21 The Failure of F-64: Soderbergh and Fincher Face the Firing
    Line, 359
22 Top of the Bill: Sofia Coppola and Wes Anderson Find Their
    Muse, 379
23 Middle-Age Malaise: *Kill Bill* and *Ocean's Twelve*, 397
24 Lit Up by the Searchlight: *I* ❤ *Huckabees* and *Sideways*, 413

    Epilogue: Bursting the *Bubble*, 435

    Notes, 447
    General Index, 453
    Index of Films, 471

List of Illustrations

1 Life through a lens: Steven Soderbergh on set, xiv
2 Andie MacDowell as Ann in *sex, lies, and videotape*, 4
3 Martin Donovan as Jude in *Surviving Desire*, 16
4 'Let's go to work': Steve Buscemi and Harvey Keitel in
   Reservoir Dogs, 28
5 Jeremy Davies helps Alberta Watson in *Spanking the Monkey*, 38
6 Jesse Bradford as Aaron in *King of the Hill*, 52
7 Golden boy: Quentin Tarantino, 68
8 *Pulp Fiction*: Uma Thurman's Mia Wallace eats her burger
   while (9) John Travolta's Vincent Vega rolls a cigarette, 73
10 *Pulp Fiction*: Bruce Willis's Butch Coolidge wakes up from his
   recurring dream; (11) Samuel L. Jackson's Jules Winnfield
   escapes death, 74
12 Robert Rodriguez films Carlos Gallardo on the set of
   El Mariachi, 86
13 Richard Linklater, during the making of *Dazed and Confused*, 86
14 David Arquette as Dude Delaney in *Roadracers*, 91
15 Ethan Hawke courts Julie Delpy in *Before Sunrise*, 100
16 *The Usual Suspects*: 'Five Criminals. One Line Up. No
   Coincidence', 106
17 Brad Pitt and Morgan Freeman confront Kevin Spacey (centre)
   in *Se7en*, 123
18 Philip Baker Hall as Sydney in *Hard Eight*, 126
19 Gwyneth Paltrow and John C. Reilly argue in *Hard Eight*, 130
20 Wes Anderson and James Caan on the set of *Bottle Rocket*, 134
21 'The world needs dreamers': Robert Musgrave, Owen Wilson
   and Luke Wilson in *Bottle Rocket*, 134
22 John Malkovich plays himself in *Being John Malkovich*, 150
23 Catherine Keener and John Cusack meet on the 7½ floor in *Being
   John Malkovich*, 150
24 Steven Soderbergh mugs to the camera in *Schizopolis*, 170

25 Burt Reynolds and William H. Macy take stock in *Boogie Nights*, 186

26 Paul Thomas Anderson on the set of *Boogie Nights*, alongside Heather Graham, 191

27 'This is a movie about family values': the *Boogie Nights* clan, 191

28 Mark Wahlberg transforms into Dirk Diggler in *Boogie Nights*, 192

29 Jason Schwartzman as Max Fischer in *Rushmore*, 204

30 Matthew Broderick and Reese Witherspoon in *Election*, 207

31 *Rushmore*: Bill Murray (father) and (32) Jason Schwartzman (son), 215

33 Pam Grier in *Jackie Brown*, 226

34 Sofia Coppola's *The Virgin Suicides*, 244

35 Hilary Swank in *Boys Don't Cry*, 248

36 David O. Russell gets ready to shoot, 256

37 *Magnolia*: John C. Reilly questions a witness; (38) Philip Baker Hall stares into the abyss; and (39) Tom Cruise confronts Jason Robards, 259

40 Mark Wahlberg, George Clooney and Ice Cube in *Three Kings*, 269

41 Brad Pitt and Edward Norton *do* talk about *Fight Club*, 282

42 *Traffic*: Erika Christensen contemplates her fate; (43) Benicio Del Toro and Jacob Vargas do the same, 286

44 Bryan Singer during the making of *X-Men*, 306

45 Nicolas Cage as both Charlie and Donald Kaufman in *Adaptation*, 318

46 Guy Pearce as Leonard Shelby in *Memento*, 330

47 Emily Watson and Adam Sandler share a kiss in *Punch-Drunk Love*, 340

48 Wes Anderson and Gene Hackman on the set of *The Royal Tenenbaums*, 343

49 The once great Tenenbaum family, 343

50 Blair Underwood and Julia Roberts go *Full Frontal*, 360

51 Bill Murray and Scarlett Johansson in *Lost in Translation*, 380

52 Team Zissou go shark-hunting in *The Life Aquatic with Steve Zissou*, 393

53 Uma Thurman takes on the Crazy 88 gang in *Kill Bill Vol. I*, 398

54 Naomi Watts as Dawn in *I ❤ Huckabees*, 414

55 Jude Law as Brad Stand in *I ❤ Huckabees*, 418

56 David O. Russell and Jason Schwartzman, 418

57 Jason Schwartzman and Mark Wahlberg in *I* ❤ *Huckabees*, 419

58 Paul Giamatti and Thomas Haden Church enjoy a glass in
      Sideways, 433

59 Ellen Burstyn as Sara Goldfarb in *Requiem for a Dream*, 438

60 Paul Schneider in *All the Real Girls*, 440

Copyrights for the illustrations are held by the following:

Outlaw Productions (*sex, lies, and videotape*); True Fiction Pictures (*Surviving Desire*); Polygram Filmed Entertainment (*Reservoir Dogs, The Usual Suspects*); Buckeye/Swelter Films (*Spanking the Monkey*); Gramercy Pictures (*King of the Hill, Dazed and Confused*); Miramax (*Pulp Fiction, Jackie Brown, Full Frontal, Kill Bill Vol. I*); Robert Rodriguez (*El Mariachi, Roadracers*); Castle Rock/Detour Productions (*Before Sunrise*); New Line (*Se7en, Boogie Nights, Magnolia, Punch-Drunk Love*); Rysher Entertainment (*Hard Eight*); Columbia Pictures (*Bottle Rocket*); Universal Studios (*Being John Malkovich*); Touchstone Pictures (*Rushmore, The Royal Tenenbaums, The Life Aquatic with Steve Zissou*); Paramount Pictures (*Election*); American Zoetrope (*The Virgin Suicides*); Fox Searchlight (*Boys Don't Cry, Sideways*); Warner Bros. (*Three Kings*); Compulsion Inc. (*Traffic*); Focus Features (*Lost in Translation*); Newmarket Capital Group (*Memento*); 20th Century Fox (*Fight Club, X-Men, I* ❤ *Huckabees*); Artisan Entertainment (*Requiem for a Dream*); Jasmin Productions (*All the Real Girls*). Photo of Quentin Tarantino by Paul Joyce. Special thanks to the Kobal Collection.

Acknowledgments

Firstly, I would like to thank my editors at Faber and Faber, Walter Donahue and Richard Kelly, for giving me the opportunity to write this book and for their invaluable advice.

I would also like to offer thanks to the staff at the British Film Institute library, in particular to Sean Delaney for his efforts on my behalf.

I also want to acknowledge a host of colleagues and friends without whom this book would not have been possible: Jan Lumholdt, David Michael, Tom Dawson, Stephen Applebaum, Monika Agorelius, Kerstin Borner, Chris Sinclair, Matt Dornan and Michael Dillingham. I am particularly indebted to Matt 'Fella' Tench.

Many thanks to all those who gave up their time to contribute their opinions to this book – in particular to Steven Soderbergh, for allowing me to bug him for so long.

NB: The quotations from actors, directors and writers contained within this book are taken from a series of interviews conducted by the author between 1998 and 2005. Any material that is not wholly original is annotated with a footnote detailing the source article.

Introduction:
Pizza Knights, F-64 and The Mild Bunch

1 Life through a lens: Steven Soderbergh on set.

Too many people have made a couple of good movies
and burned out. The truth is, studios know how to
make a successful film, one that works at the box office.
Nobody believes in the maverick anymore.
   Rod Lurie[1]

Imagine the scene: a select club has gathered in Los Angeles to watch
a private screening of Ulu Grosbard's *Straight Time*. This 1978 story
of a burglar who attempts to reform keeps its viewers' rapt attention.
Afterwards, its star, Dustin Hoffman, is on hand to take questions and
talk about his time making it. The avid listeners are all Hollywood
filmmakers, men and women working inside the studio system. They
include David Fincher, Spike Jonze, Wes Anderson, Kimberly Peirce
and Alexander Payne. Meeting once a month, they call themselves
'Pizza Knights'. Indebted to the filmmakers who inspired them as they
grew up, they pay homage twelve times a year. They are the spiritual
descendants of the so-called maverick filmmakers of 1970s Hollywood. They still believe, even if nobody else does.

   This book centres on the question: 'Are we returning to an age
where formerly independent directors are using studio funds to further
their own idiosyncratic vision?' In other words, is this the dawn of
New Hollywood Part II? As the title of this book suggests, many of the
contemporary filmmakers under consideration here have been connected to Robert Redford's Sundance Institute. For most – like
Alexander Payne, Bryan Singer, Quentin Tarantino, Sofia Coppola,
David O. Russell or Steven Soderbergh – it is with a film at the festival. Then there is Wes Anderson, whose debut feature began life as a
short film showcased there. For others, like Kimberly Peirce or Paul
Thomas Anderson, their debuts began life in the workshops of the
Institute. Many of them flunked college and eschewed film school; it
was Sundance that gave them their education.

   That said, David Fincher and Spike Jonze have never been anywhere
near the snowy heights of Park City (at least not with a film). Both
stem from a commercials/music video background. But these two
Pizza Knights, as we shall see, are honorary Sundance Kids. Both were

involved with the development of a short-lived filmmaking collective called F-64. Together with an article entitled 'The Mild Bunch', published in *The Hollywood Reporter* in 2002, it gave the inspiration for this book. But more of that later.

A Brief History of Sundance

Formed on the cusp of 1980, the Sundance Institute was the brainchild of Hollywood golden-boy Robert Redford. His plan was to lay the groundwork for an organization that would nurture independent filmmaking talent. Based in the wilds of Utah, where he had bought some land in the mid-1960s, it was named after his outlaw from *Butch Cassidy and the Sundance Kid* (1969). Redford, positioning himself – incorrectly or otherwise – as a true Hollywood maverick, was at the forefront of a new era in American cinema. The Institute quickly became known for its June Laboratory, which brought independent filmmakers together with talent from Hollywood. As it evolved, other events included an annual producers' conference, a playwrights' lab and even a children's theatre.

The most high-profile face of the Institute was the film festival. Taking over the ailing United States Film Festival in 1984, Sundance – to call it by its abbreviated name – became the Mecca for any independent filmmaker with a dream. If its first years weren't spectacular, there were still finds – notably the Coen brothers, whose neo-noir debut, *Blood Simple*, won the Grand Jury Prize in 1985. As we will see, it was Steven Soderbergh's *sex, lies, and videotape* four years later that bolstered the Sundance profile immeasurably. As Hollywood executives began to sniff money in the pine-scented mountain air, they descended on Park City in their droves for this annual January cinematic showcase. This was the place where distribution deals could be struck and nobodies could become players overnight. It was like a funfair for the American dream.

Like any organization, as it grew, it began to swallow up cash. Peter Biskind noted that by 1991 the Institute was dogged by 'a ballooning seven-figure deficit that required the elimination of nearly half the staff'.[2] Moreover, behind its idyllic façade, the Institute had 'been torn by staff backbiting and factionalism', as well as accusations of long-term mismanagement. Sydney Pollack – who directed Redford seven times and was a founder member of the Sundance Institute – notes,

'Like anything that's good and successful, the Institute is a bit of a victim of its own success. You can't help that. Once something is terrifically successful, it's hard to hang on to the purity of what it was originally.'

Over time, the sponsors moved in. Suddenly, Starbucks was providing free coffee, socialites like Paris Hilton came to party and accusations that the festival had become an annexe of Hollywood were as frequent as the snow-showers that fell on Park City. 'It's become this monster,' Redford told me in 2001. 'Jesus, it's like going to Las Vegas. It's so exhausting, yet the heart of it is still true. The heart gets smaller and smaller every year, because the body around it overwhelms it: fashion, Hollywood, the media. The media pays more attention to the celebrity aspect of Sundance, and the celebrity aspect feeds itself. It becomes this self-perpetuating goon. At the heart is still a wonderful festival, which I have a lot of pride in. We program it the same way every year; it's not about commercial quality. It's about the originality, the diversity. The independence of the film.'

The purpose of this book is not to explore the Institute as an entity or to examine Redford's part in its successes and failures. As David O. Russell, who would arrive in 1994 with his debut *Spanking the Monkey*, says: 'People are always beating up on Sundance. It's a classic American story and they want it to follow those beats, like the beats of F. Scott Fitzgerald – talented, successful, drunken, dissolute and ruined by success. I don't think that's necessarily accurate. It's still a launching platform for some really good filmmakers. It's a market – but it's kept that alive. It's an identifiable niche that studios can point to now. It's definitely a good thing that this entity exists. I think there's an understanding that audiences have an appetite for something that's different and ahead of the curve.'

The Sundance Kids aims to look at its graduates and how they shaped American film over the past fifteen years. To do that, we must first consider their predecessors.

New Hollywood, the French New Wave and the Maverick Filmmaker

As critics, industry figures and the public increasingly celebrate 1970s Hollywood, the term 'maverick' has become more loosely used. Figures such as Martin Scorsese, Francis Ford Coppola, Robert Altman and William Friedkin are regularly termed 'mavericks', despite the fact that they all worked within the studio system. The *New Oxford English Dictionary* defines a 'maverick' as 'an unorthodox or independent-minded person' or 'a person who refuses to conform to a particular party or group'.[3] If anything, grouping these directors as part of the New Hollywood movement is surely to contradict the isolation felt by true maverick filmmakers.

It's not unreasonable, however, to treat these directors as a collective: seemingly given carte blanche at the studios as a new generation of executives swept a broom through the Hollywood closet, each was fuelled by ego, drugs or ambition – often all three. Many of them had graduated from film schools and were raised on the same diet of Italian neo-realism and French New Wave, as well as the works of Howard Hawks, John Huston and Alfred Hitchcock. Many had become friends or colleagues – George Lucas started his career as Francis Ford Coppola's assistant, for example. Much of their work was a reaction against the glossy, bloated epics that almost destroyed the studio system in the 1960s. Their films buzzed with references to the political upheavals of the time and even elevated classic American genres, like the gangster film, to a higher level. But, though critics like Pauline Kael influenced their thinking, they were not united to change the course of cinema. They were just in the right place at the right time.

The closest any of them came to being a conscious collective was in the summer of 1973 when Charles Bludhorn, CEO of Gulf and Western, the owner of Paramount, suggested that Coppola, Friedkin and Peter Bogdanovich start what would become known as the Directors Company. All three were riding on the back of glorious films – respectively, *The Godfather* (1972), *The French Connection* and *The Last Picture Show* (both 1971). The idea was simplicity itself, and appealed to their desire for creative freedom. With Paramount bankrolling the company to the tune of $31.5 million, each could make any picture he wanted for under $3 million without the need to seek studio approval. With each director sharing in the profits of the others' movies, the scheme should in principle have worked. But while Bogdanovich's *Paper Moon* (1973) was a hit, his adaptation of Henry James's *Daisy Miller*, along with Coppola's *The Conversation* (both 1974) was not. Irritated by the others' work, Friedkin got fed up and backed out, without even making a film.

All three soon fell from grace. Likewise, the careers of other New Hollywood directors would fluctuate. Altman and Scorsese both left indelible marks on American cinema, but even they – along with the likes of Arthur Penn, Hal Ashby, Bob Rafelson and Michael Cimino – lost their way as the 1970s came to a close. The era of the talent agency was ushered in as William Morris and ICM took over, packaging their actors up for the studios to flesh out the crowd-pleasing disposable fare that was now de rigueur at any studio worth its salt. Directors no longer held the reins.

Much has been written about the era of the blockbuster that followed. Two so-called mavericks, Steven Spielberg and George Lucas, have been fêted for breaking away from the pack and starting their own revolution. Or maybe, like guilty schoolboys, they stopped playing truant. Both gave the ailing Hollywood studio system what it wanted: a serious cash injection. True, Coppola's *The Godfather* and its sequel, *The Godfather Part II* (1974), had broken box office records – but it was the arrival of Spielberg's *Jaws* (1975) and Lucas's *Star Wars* (1977) that ushered in an era far more lasting than that of New Hollywood. They embodied the perfect marketing formula: high-impact mainstream product that had the potential to catch on like wildfire.

Whatever the rise of the blockbuster has subsequently done to cripple Hollywood – spiralling budgets and actors' salaries, not to mention the dumbing down of world culture – one thing is certain. Blockbusters made many nostalgic for a time when artists ruled, when they changed the direction of their medium by bucking the system. There's nothing people like to hear more than stories of individuals upsetting the status quo for the better. The dearth of auteur-driven cinema in the 1980s led to nostalgia for the filmmaking of the 1970s. The decade has become hermetically sealed and preserved, viewed with a wistful glance and spoken of with hushed reverence. With films like *Taxi Driver*, *Nashville* and *The Conversation*, genuine classics all of them, this attitude is in no way unjustified. You'd be hard pressed to find three studio products in the subsequent decade that have anything like the longevity of these masterpieces. Director Sydney Pollack puts it succinctly: 'I think it was without a doubt the best ten years of American filmmaking. In terms of consistency of interesting and original films, it was a great era. It really was.'

But there's no doubt that a mythology now surrounds these filmmakers, partly of their own creating, partly due to critical re-assessment. It comes back to this romantic idea of the maverick, the masked

Hollywood gunslinger riding into town alone. Not unlike the equally romantic notion of the auteur, it has come to mean any director who made a personal statement. Given how collaborative the filmmaking process is – and many of the directors from the 1970s regularly worked with screenwriters – the idea of one individual gunning against the system is rather misleading. Only directors such as John Cassavetes, who self-funded his work and used his family as cast members, could lay claim to such status. The rest may have argued over or lied about final cuts, drunk their budgets away, and pushed the boundaries of sex and violence – but it was all done inside the Hollywood 'party'.

Compare them to the French New Wave, the group formed by Jean-Luc Godard, Jacques Rivette, Eric Rohmer and François Truffaut. These men, bonded by their time as critics for the influential magazine *Cahiers du Cinéma*, were driven to forge a new cinema. It was in the January 1954 edition that Truffaut published his landmark essay *A Certain Tendency in the French Cinema*. A plea for more personal cinema, it attacked directors who merely churned out films without any individual vision. In the same piece he promoted what would become the auteur theory, in which he suggested that the only directors worth serious consideration were those who left their own individual signatures on each of their films. When he and his colleagues began a frantic period of activity between 1958 and 1964, they put theory into practice.

Initially, they were liberated by new lightweight equipment that released them from the shackles of the studio-bound glossy French films they loathed. Such freedom stretched to using improvised dialogue, long takes, and real-time and jump-cut editing. Influenced by American genres such as the gangster film, stars like Humphrey Bogart and directors like Howard Hawks, they also recognized the work of their fellow countrymen Jean Renoir and Jean Vigo. With their protagonists often anti-heroes and loners, French New Wave films were also united in their devotion to the existential philosophies of Jean-Paul Sartre. Replete with anarchic humour and an entrenched cynicism (about the political powers-that-be), these were the touchstone films for the New Hollywood generation.

While more 'maverick' than their New Hollywood counterparts – in the sense that they were fighting against the French studio system from the *outside* – even they did not completely fit the *New OED* definition of the word. Take Orson Welles, a true Hollywood maverick. A renegade who revolutionized cinematic techniques with *Citizen Kane* (1941), Welles never came to terms with Hollywood after *The Magnificent Ambersons* and *Journey to Fear* (both 1942) were mangled by the studio, RKO. Although well received as an actor there, his early experiences as a director prompted him to make films outside the system – notably his troubled production of *Macbeth* (1948). When his film noir *Touch of Evil* (1958) was re-cut by Universal, it would be the last time he attempted to grapple with Hollywood. A self-imposed exile in Europe followed, furthering his reputation as a maverick in the most romantic of ways.

So, you might ask, why is this book subtitled: 'How the Mavericks Took Back Hollywood'? After all, like those of New Hollywood, none of these contemporary directors are working outside the studio system. In fact, they're working hand in hand. As is indicated by the rather flippant title of his article, riffing on Sam Peckinpah's revisionist Western, *The Wild Bunch* (1969), Stephen Galloway explained that these filmmakers were not rebels like their predecessors. 'What is so striking about this current crop of young directors is . . . how seamlessly they work with the studios and how willing they are to be collaborative and open-minded.'[4]

What's more, even within their nominal ranks, there are dissenters. Sofia Coppola, perhaps the one young filmmaker working today who has a genuine connection to a filmmaking dynasty, believes that attempts to replicate a bygone era are phoney. After all, she was there, albeit as a toddler. 'There's guys in my generation who are trying to recreate that thing they thought was happening in the 1970s – let's have a filmmakers' night and all hang out, trying to make themselves into the gang they thought those guys were. But I don't know if it was what it appeared to be. It's easy to idealize that era; it seems so macho and cool. Those guys really did seem like they were putting their necks on the line and now it seems safer – nobody's marching into the jungle to make a movie.'[5]

If the word has come to lose its original meaning, there is still some validity in terming these new directors mavericks. To take the first half of the *New OED* definition of the word, all of the directors under consideration here – whether you consider them auteurs or not – are 'unorthodox or independent-minded'. They are most definitely maverick filmmakers, in that meaning of the word.

Who's In and Who's Out

What must be made clear at this point is that, rather like hip hop labels Death Row and Bad Boy, the division between East and West Coast remains distinct. The filmmakers that this study will look at are working on the latter coast. As Isabelle Huppert, the French actress who has come full circle – from Michael Cimino's 1980 disaster *Heaven's Gate* to David O. Russell's *I ❤ Huckabees* – notes: 'You have people like Paul Thomas Anderson, Spike Jonze, Sofia Coppola, Wes Anderson . . . they do the same kind of movies. These people come from the West Coast and some years earlier, they would've been independent filmmakers from the East Coast. Now you have this group of people who make studio films, but very imaginative, like an independent film would be. It's interesting how much the industry in Hollywood is aware of all the new talents, instead of rejecting them and putting them on the side as independent filmmakers. They take them into the studios, so it's just noticeable.'

Whether it's Jim Jarmusch, Todd Solondz or Hal Hartley – all Sundance graduates in their own right – they have remained camped out on the East Coast, largely avoiding entanglements with the studios. Though this, as Alexander Payne claims, has limited the size of their audience. 'No one sees Hal Hartley movies. [Solondz's] *Happiness* got out there a bit. But they're New York movies. I'm glad they're there, but it's such a drop in the bucket in terms of American production.' If these East Coast filmmakers are doing their own thing, they're also forced to look outside the U.S. for funding – usually to Europe. Unlike our Sundance Kids, they don't use A-list stars, their budgets are minuscule and they all fit the traditional definition of the auteur far better than any of the filmmakers under consideration in this book. As Russell puts it, the word 'independent' still has a meaning that can apply to both East and West Coast. 'I think if you are taking risks that are very different from standard movies, you are independently minded. But there are varying degrees of independence. If you finance a Jim Jarmusch movie completely out of Europe, that's a more extreme form of independence.'

My criteria for entry into the new band of outsiders being considered here are partly a matter of subjective taste. That's why you won't find M. Night Shyamalan included, a filmmaker who belongs to the Spielberg–Lucas brigade and whose work is pure spectacle. Some, like

Robert Rodriguez and Richard Linklater, are the subjects of only brief accounts because, while independent in spirit, they have remained distanced from Hollywood for the most part.

Some would argue that Kevin Smith deserves a place in any work that surveys the cream of burgeoning American filmmakers in the 1990s. After all, following his caustic convenience-store comedy *Clerks* (1994) – famous for costing just $23,000 – he has made five films in ten years, no mean feat for any low-budget director. On top of that, he survived the studio experience with his second film, the teen comedy *Mallrats* (1995), matured considerably with his third, *Chasing Amy* (1997), and courted controversy with his fourth, the Catholic comedy *Dogma* (1999). As if to provide cohesion to the Kevin Smith world, he then reunited many of his principal characters in the road movie *Jay and Silent Bob Strike Back* (2001), only to swap farts for fatherhood in the sickly sweet *Jersey Girl* (2004). He's a genuine auteur who has written all his films, but what stops me from including him in this book is not so much his penchant for the puerile – though that doesn't help – as the limits of his cinematic ambitions.

Although *Dogma*, for example, indicated a willingness to tackle serious subject matter, Smith's body of work has yet to make an impact on the medium of cinema in the way films by Soderbergh, Payne, Fincher or Tarantino have. And it may never do. While *Clerks*, in particular, reflects the socioeconomic problems faced by working-class American youth, Smith has no desire to be a polemicist. Pop-culture saturated – everything from *Star Wars* to *The Fresh Prince of Bel Air* – a Kevin Smith film bears little or no signature aside from his trademark acerbic dialogue. With a fanbase inspired by rabid devotion, Smith is a cult filmmaker who is happy to remain so: 'I didn't get into this business to make bigger and better movies. I got into this business to make *Clerks*, over and over and over again.'

There are also no rules here about the number of films each filmmaker needs to have made; Spike Jonze and Sofia Coppola have only made two films each; Kimberly Peirce just one. That said, with the exception of Steven Soderbergh – who began his career in 1989 with *sex, lies, and videotape* – each director under consideration began his or her professional career in the 1990s. That rules out, for example, a director like Terry Gilliam, who could easily be admitted into such a group, having made non-conformist works like *Brazil* (1984) inside the studio system.

If there is one event that points to why certain filmmakers have been chosen and others left out, it was the announcement in October 2001 that several prominent Hollywood young guns were banding together. Four of our filmmakers – Soderbergh, Jonze, Fincher and Payne – were in talks to form a cooperative venture called F-64, in which each partner pledged to direct three movies over the first five years. In existence solely for the production of their films – with Barry Diller's USA Films enlisted to market and distribute the end products – it immediately recalled the notions of the Directors Company from the 1970s.

'It's an idea that's as old as cinema, almost,' Soderbergh noted. 'The idea behind it, which is very similar to what we're doing in [his and George Clooney's production company] Section Eight, is getting a group of artists together who aren't driven by money, to try and gain greater control over their work, from the content to how it's sold. But it's complicated.' While few details were released – such as whether an executive would oversee the company, whether guidelines on ratings, budgets or length would be issued – the issue of ownership was clear-cut.

'You would own the negative after seven years,' Payne noted at the time. 'The company would actually own the film. It's kind of a financial and moral thing about owning your own creative work. We're similar in that we're all interested in making good movies. I think we have similar tastes as to what are the components of a good movie.' It was envisioned that the directors' existing development deals with the studios would be honoured, with the companies acquiring foreign distribution rights. Having recently scored a success with the distribution and Oscar campaign for *Traffic*, Diller's company was touted as the home for this quartet – who also invited the British director Sam Mendes on board – because it was not a major studio. In other words, it would not look to swallow world rights and exert control over creative content. In principle, it was a great idea: keeping the studios at arm's length and using them only for distribution where necessary. Added to which, the promised creative brainstorming sessions between the filmmakers could only have been beneficial to each member of the collective.

But whether because of a clash of egos or the inability to fully finance what turned out to be a potentially risky strategy, F-64 was not to be. As Payne points out about filmmakers' collectives, referring to the Directors Company as well, 'History shows that they're hard to sustain, but that doesn't mean they can't work.' Despite looking to gain creative control over his own work – as Payne said, a 'moral' point more than anything else – Soderbergh is in total agreement.

> My mantra has always been the same. You can go back and read interviews from the *sex, lies . . .* period where I said: 'The only delineation I make is between a good movie and a bad movie.' I don't care who's paying for it, who releases it. I felt that, in the United States at least, people who were writing about films were not being helpful, in that they tended to encourage – in the hope of supporting the auteur theory, which they felt was a more pure form of filmmaking – young filmmakers to look at studios as antagonists. I was drawing my lesson from the late 1960s and 1970s, which is when you had really interesting filmmakers working successfully in the studio system. My assumption was always that we should be trying to emulate that. All along I've been saying this is just a stupid argument. What we should all want is for the smartest directors around to have the resources that the dumb directors have.

As is noted in Galloway's piece, the expense of making a film in today's economic climate vastly dwarfs anything that could have been imagined thirty years ago. Marketing and distribution, in particular, are far more complex now than they ever were – no doubt two more factors that caused the collapse of F-64. 'You have to have people who respect each other on both sides for the marriage to work,' states Fox Filmed Entertainment chairman Tom Rothman. As Payne opines, such a union is possible:

> Whether I'm a part of an independent group, or with the studio, the world I want to live in is where studios are funding auteurist personal cinema. That's my world. That's what we can have. Not that all movies are like that. There's always *Airport 75* and *Catwoman*. You have to make these to make the smarter movies, which also make a profit. They're not huge home runs but they make money. We have to keep our costs down. I make a point of keeping our costs down and bringing them in on time and under budget. I'm a good boy.

In Biskind's assessment of the current state of Hollywood, *Down and Dirty Pictures*, he rather dismissed the notion that this new breed were gaining increasing respect from the studio executives. 'Although the studios did continue to patronize a few indie directors – Wes Anderson and Spike Lee at Disney, Russell at Warner's, etc. – their hearts lay with *Spider-Man*, *X-Men* and *The Hulk*.'[6] This may be true to an extent but, as Payne says, you need one to help fund the other. Certainly, the 1970s is not the era of artistic purity it is often painted to be: the disaster movie, for example, pandered to the mainstream crowds. In the 1990s, executives like Bill Mechanic, Mike De Luca and Lorenzo di Bonaventura were canny and creative enough to balance out their slates; after all, films such as *Titanic* (1997) were balanced by films such as *Fight Club* and *Magnolia* – movies to be remembered, movies that define a generation and capture the Zeitgeist.

'I *do* think it's a good time,' says Payne:

> It's not a great time yet, but it's the beginning of a great time. Somehow when the beast is dying, it needs new blood. It's a time creatively when Hollywood seems to be opening its gates a bit more for new, strong directors. Also, we're in heavy political times. And even in a marketplace-based era, there will be an increasing demand for human and political films: not didactic films but films that are more directly concerned with our world and not just about escapist fantasy. We go to the cinema not just to escape but to discover our world, and we really need that world. We *really* need it now!

To a certain extent this is true. If Vietnam and Watergate disillusioned a nation in the 1970s, so the September 11th terror attacks in 2001, flanked by two Gulf Wars, are having much the same effect in this new era. David O. Russell, with *Three Kings* and *I ❤ Huckabees*, tackled the subjects head on. But there are also directors like Bryan Singer who use subtext, notably in his *X-Men* films. 'I feel whenever there's unrest in the world, it does breed creative revolution of sorts,' he says. 'If on the surface merely to give someone distraction from the day to day terror of the news, on the inside it gives artists the chance to express their own point of view.' Other films, like Soderbergh's *Traffic* or Fincher's *Fight Club*, tackled contemporary social issues – respectively, the drugs trade and consumer culture – with the same zeal.

Yet with Hollywood increasingly gearing its releases to the eighteen to twenty-five age bracket, it's not as if we've reached a new age of enlightenment just yet. As the writer-director Richard LaGravenese, who helped Soderbergh with the socially aware *Erin Brockovich*, says: 'I can't believe that we are going to be able to stay in this coma we've been in for much longer. World events are going to break us down.

We're in a very juvenile state. Everybody's very interested in teenagers. Adults are interested in behaving like teenagers. So eventually artists are going to have to respond to it. Audiences will respond to more stimulating work.'

Singer, who more than the others has veered away from the Sundance film to the blockbuster, adds: 'I think studios are recognizing what was also recognized in the 1970s (during my golden era of film), that there are no definitive answers for what works. Just when you think you have a formula down pat, you realize that what people really want to see is what you least expect. People don't want to see movies they can predict the outcome of. I surely don't. I want to see films that keep me guessing.' Yet as demonstrated by the proliferation of shoddy sequels and SFX-driven summer event movies, the studio heads can be lazy when it comes to filling their slates. 'They have an easier time selling those films,' says Payne. 'But I say, "Fuck that!" Have a hard time selling them. Get some balls! Don't be weenies!'

What these directors do have, however, is the loyalty of Hollywood's legions of actors. From American character actors such as Paul Giamatti, William H. Macy and Philip Seymour Hoffman to British thespians like Sir Ian McKellen and Patrick Stewart; from comedians such as Ben Stiller, Owen Wilson and Bill Murray to crossover stars like Julianne Moore, Don Cheadle and Cate Blanchett; from new kids on the block Hilary Swank and Scarlett Johansson to bona fide paid-up members of the A-list such as George Clooney, Julia Roberts and Brad Pitt, they all want to work with these directors – and regularly cut their fees to do so. Moore, who has bridged the gap between P. T. Anderson (in *Magnolia* and *Boogie Nights*) and 1970s icon Robert Altman (in *Short Cuts,* 1993, and *Cookie's Fortune,* 1999), feels that while this new breed of filmmakers are being sheltered at the studios, they're not yet sitting at the top table:

> They're not giving these guys a fortune. None of these studios are giving these guys carte blanche and saying 'Hey, here's $70 million. Go make yourself sick.' Somebody like Wes Anderson, his movies don't cost a lot. Alexander Payne's movies are small-budget. They are making movies in the system. But they're making them at a low cost too. Someone like Fincher is a different case, because he has made stuff that's a huge box office hit. They don't give you the money unless they think they're going to get it back. They do give

[P. T. Anderson] a certain amount of money and he does have a healthy budget to work with, but it's not like they're giving out oodles and oodles of money.

As this study will hopefully show, all of these directors share a debt to the 1970s and have at least one filmmaker from that era essential to their work. With Bryan Singer, it's Spielberg; with P. T. Anderson, it's Altman. Alexander Payne admires early Coppola and Wes Anderson obsesses over Bogdanovich. Soderbergh adores Richard Lester, Fincher is as fastidious as Stanley Kubrick, and Russell unconsciously replicates Mike Nichols. Pretty much all of them owe something to Scorsese. Wes Anderson compares him to legendary silent director D. W. Griffith: 'There are so many grammatical rules that he [Scorsese] invented or discovered. You almost need them to make a movie now – anytime you're doing something set to music, especially if it involves a slow-motion effect, and also the basic thing of combining dreamy, surreal moments with acting that you want to be as realistic and documentary-feeling as possible.'

No claims can be made that these directors are working towards a common goal, other than returning Hollywood to an era when films were seen as more than mere entertainment. Certainly, their choice of subject matter differs vastly. P. T. Anderson and Wes Anderson are both interested in fractured or surrogate families. While intrigued by the dangers of technology, David Fincher and Bryan Singer are particularly drawn to deconstructing the crime genre. Spike Jonze, via the postmodern scripts of his collaborator Charlie Kaufman, is all about the medium of cinema itself. Russell is the group's political activist, while Payne is drawn to satirical studies of human folly. And Soderbergh? The unwitting godfather to all of these filmmakers, he's done all of the above and more.

As we traverse chronologically the last fifteen years of American filmmaking, I aim to achieve a number of things. Firstly, by examining the films made by each of the aforementioned directors, I will form a gradual picture of each artist, looking at the traits, as well as the trials, of their filmmaking. Secondly, by telling their individual stories I hope to capture the ever-changing landscape of American cinema over the period. Beginning with Steven Soderbergh's *sex, lies, and videotape*, we shall see how American independent cinema dovetailed into Hollywood.

At the same time, it's equally important to detail the ways in which the studios accommodated these maverick talents. This means looking at the executives signalling the green lights, as well as the rise of mini-major studios like Miramax and New Line. As LaGravenese points out, the studios all have their art house divisions now. While Warner Bros. – 'the last hold-out' – now has Warner Independent, 'Universal has Focus. Disney has Miramax. Columbia has Sony Picture Classics.' Not all the films under discussion will be studio funded – but many will be. By 2004 – a banner year for many of our directors, with *Sideways*, in particular, hailed as an outright masterpiece – all will have worked, or be working, within the studio system. The mavericks have taken back Hollywood.

SECTION I: THE SUNDANCE YEARS

'It's All Downhill from Here': How Steven Soderbergh
Paves the Way for the Next Generation

2 Andie MacDowell as Ann in *sex, lies, and videotape.*

1 EXT. HIGHWAY – DAY

GRAHAM DALTON, twenty-nine, drives his '69 Cutlass while smoking a cigarette. One could describe his appearance as punk/arty, but neither would do him justice. He is a man of obvious intelligence, and his face is amiable. There is only one key on his keyring, and it is in the ignition.

Debut films, like first novels, often have a tendency to drift towards the semi-autobiographical. While Steven Soderbergh never denied this for *sex, lies, and videotape*, even he would never have dreamt of how the script's opening paragraph (quoted above) would become so prescient in years to come. Like Graham (James Spader), the obviously intelligent and amiably faced Soderbergh arrived from nowhere – or as near as, damn it, his hometown being Baton Rouge, Louisiana. With him, a film that was the key in the ignition for the American independent film scene in a way no movie was before. When Graham pulled up in his car at a service station to change into his black shirt, announcing the story's ominous upheaval ahead, it was as if Soderbergh was doing the very same.

As prophesied by both the title and Graham's own collection of taped sexual confessions, the film almost literally ushered in a new era of the video-educated filmmaker. Compared to the elite group of film-school-educated 'movie-brats' of the 1970s, Soderbergh, and those who followed, would be self-taught and home-schooled. The video cassette would unlock a vast library of celluloid riches, affording this generation an unprecedented opportunity to study world cinema from the comfort of their armchairs. The video camera would likewise encourage more than just the privileged few to dream of becoming directors. Soderbergh doesn't quite fit this stereotype, though he's close enough. The kind of fanatic who once went to see *Altered States* (1980) eleven times in two weeks because the film's sound technician had fine-tuned the speaker system in the particular theatre where it was showing, Soderbergh was a film geek. But his sensibilities steered him away from the grindhouse B-movie culture that would inspire a

5

young video clerk named Quentin Tarantino. Instead, his favourite movies of all time include five from 1970s Hollywood (*The Godfather*, *The Conversation*, *All the President's Men*, *Jaws* and *Annie Hall*). By the time he hit fifteen, he had already paid homage to another classic of the era – Martin Scorsese's 1976 film *Taxi Driver* – in a twenty-minute short called *Janitor*.

Like so many of his peers, Soderbergh eschewed film school in favour of homespun moviemaking. His only formal film tuition came at the age of thirteen, when his father, a professor of education at Louisiana State University (LSU), enrolled him in an animation class. Soderbergh quickly grew bored – although he did visit a Super 8 tutorial where the teacher told the class they could do anything they wanted, as long as they didn't film footage at the zoo and cut it to 'that Simon and Garfunkel song'. Instead, it would be in his own backyard that Soderbergh would be most productive.

The course did, however, furnish him with his first contact. After graduating from high school, he was hired as an editor by his former LSU tutor, then working on the television show *Games People Play*. It was off the air within six months, and Soderbergh was pushed to the fringes of the industry – ironically, the same place that he would occupy in the years after the celebrated release of *sex, lies, and videotape*. Working as a freelance editor at the channel Showtime, and even as a cue card holder, Soderbergh eventually cut his losses and headed back to Baton Rouge, where he made *Rapid Eye Movement*, a short about his obsession with moving to Los Angeles and making movies.

It's a lovely irony that a man who once saw Hollywood as his Mecca made a debut that would inadvertently galvanize the American independent film movement. More so, because he would ultimately prove a driving force in merging the maverick sensibilities of the indie auteur with the considerable resources at the disposal of the major studios. Whether he likes it or not, Soderbergh has become a quasi-godfather figure for a group of directors who would join him in attempting – though not always succeeding – to reprise the notion of director-driven studio features. While not exactly the leader of the pack – simply because there is no 'pack' to speak of – he led by example. Those who trod in his footsteps would take up Soderbergh's quest for personal filmmaking inside a system geared towards crushing the life out of such movies. They may not admit to it, but David Fincher, David O. Russell, Paul Thomas Anderson, Alexander Payne, Spike

Jonze and Bryan Singer all owe Soderbergh for building the bridge they would charge over.

If Dennis Hopper's freewheeling 1969 road movie *Easy Rider* was the key in the ignition for 1970s Hollywood, there's no doubt twenty years on that *sex, lies, and videotape* was the same to the decade it was to precede. In retrospect, neither film is robust enough to shoulder such weight – but few are. Winner of the Audience Award at the Sundance Film Festival in January 1989, Soderbergh's film became a genuine sensation five months later when it walked away with the coveted Palme d'Or in Cannes. At twenty-six, Soderbergh was the youngest director ever to win the prize, joining a prestigious list of American past winners that included Martin Scorsese, Francis Ford Coppola and Robert Altman.

With the film also winning the International Critics Prize and a Best Actor award for Spader – as well as gaining Soderbergh an Oscar nomination for Best Original Screenplay the following year – it was little wonder he infamously remarked during his Cannes acceptance speech: 'It's all downhill from here.' With comparisons being made to Orson Welles – who made *Citizen Kane*, another of Soderbergh's favourites, at the same age – it's a wonder his sense of self-importance didn't inflate beyond recognition. Fielding calls from the likes of Demi Moore, Sydney Pollack and Taylor Hackford, Soderbergh was the year's hot property, a dry run for the sort of rock star celebrity status Tarantino would enjoy in the early 1990s.

Made for just $1.2 million, the film was, ironically, co-funded by RCA, the home video division of Columbia Pictures. Compared with the romantic notion of selling your body for medical research, as Robert Rodriguez would famously do to help fund his 1992 debut *El Mariachi*, it rather betrayed the very ethos of the independent movement to come. Not that Soderbergh cared one iota how the financing fell into place. 'I have never felt part of any independent cinema movement,' says Soderbergh. 'Independence to me has nothing to do with where the money comes from. Independence to me means getting to make the kind of films you want to make, when you want to make them.' While working for Showtime, he had come into contact with the group Yes, and wound up going on the road with them when he was twenty-one. The result, *9012 Live*, was nominated for a Grammy. From that he found an agent, won a contract rewriting a Disney TV movie and even began penning a musical for Tri-Star.

It was at this point that Soderbergh entered a personal relationship that would eventually spill into his screenplay for *sex, lies, and videotape*. '[At the time] I was deceptive and mentally manipulative,' he recalled. 'I was just fucking up. There was one point at which I was in a bar, and within a radius of about two feet there were three different women I was sleeping with.'[7] Lying to those he was dating, he even concealed the truth from a therapist he went to for three sessions. Like the four characters he created – whom he described as his own personality divided into quarters – Soderbergh struggled with the gulf between himself and those around him.

Administering his own self-help treatment, he wrote the script for *sex, lies, and videotape* across eight days, four of which were taken up with a road trip from Baton Rouge to Los Angeles. Production was obscenely brief by Hollywood standards; the first Sundance screening was just a year after Soderbergh delivered the script to his agent, Pat Dollard. She gave the script to Morgan Mason, son of James and husband to the pop star Belinda Carlisle. Enthused by his wife's positive response to reading the script, Mason approached the head of her record company, Richard Branson. Virgin Vision agreed to put up the other half of the budget, following the contribution of RCA, in exchange for the foreign distribution rights.

While there were some problems with agents refusing to show the script to their clients because they believed it was pornographic, this was not enough to derail the project. During the production, Soderbergh established some crucial relationships: chiefly with the composer Cliff Martinez, who would go on to score almost all of the director's more eclectic projects. While Soderbergh edited the film himself, director of photography Walt Lloyd was in charge of lensing the story (and went on to shoot Soderbergh's second film *Kafka*, before Elliot Davis – and later Soderbergh himself – took over DP duties).

The film grossed over $100 million worldwide, a figure that finally had studio executives slavering at the possible profits to be made from low-budget films. In the end, you could argue it was good old-fashioned greed that inspired Hollywood's interest in the indie filmmaker, as symbolized by the now-obligatory January exodus to Park City, Utah, where insiders look to the Sundance Film Festival to showcase the next crossover hit. Sad as it may be, to say that Hollywood nurtured filmmakers to their creative peak would be largely untrue. That's not to say it doesn't happen – but only as a by-product of the economic forces that drive the industry. What Soderbergh's film did was turn the spotlight onto Sundance, and provide a financial platform for its fledgling New York–based distributor Miramax to build upon. While the rise of Miramax will be discussed in Chapter 6, for the moment it should be noted that the company outbid ten rivals at the American Film Market a month after the film's Sundance screening. It paid over $1 million for domestic theatrical distribution rights only (with the customary – and obviously lucrative – home video rights already tied up by RCA-Columbia).

Before Soderbergh there had been a series of directors who could justifiably lay claim to having paved the way for the explosion in U.S. independent features – from John Cassavetes to John Sayles and Jim Jarmusch, whose debut *Stranger Than Paradise* almost turned the key five years before Soderbergh's film did. 'Every form of independent cinema thinks it's invented the term,' says producer Christine Vachon, who has done more than most to foster East Coast indie talent. 'It seems as if independent cinema started with *Stranger Than Paradise*, but it didn't really. There have been people making movies for years that were nontraditional. John Waters, for example. He was all about pleasure.'

At another time *sex, lies, and videotape* would've remained in the Directors' Fortnight sidebar in Cannes, where it was originally slotted, leaving Spike Lee's third film *Do the Right Thing* to win the Palme d'Or and be lionized in a way the eventual winner still is. But arriving at a time when ABC's show *thirtysomething* was at the height of its popularity, the film quenched its generation's insatiable thirst for confessional adult-angst dramas. Not since Mike Nichols made *Carnal Knowledge* (1971) had an American film so trenchantly examined the battle of the sexes. While Hollywood periodically attempted to tap the Zeitgeist, the results – from Adrian Lyne's *Fatal Attraction* (1989) to Barry Levinson's *Disclosure* (1994) – would be unsatisfactory on all but the basest of levels.

The arrival of Soderbergh in the summer of 1989 smacked as a blessed relief. As Hollywood began its inexorable march towards committee-made films, *sex, lies, and videotape* demonstrated that spectacle is not the only mainstay of modern cinema. It was released in what might be called a transitional year for Hollywood. At the tail end of a decade that saw the blockbuster put a vice-like grip on the industry, the release of Tim Burton's *Batman* by Warner Bros. was orchestrated with a marketing push that reached an unprecedented saturation point. It's not that previous so-called 'summer event' movies by Lucas, Spielberg and later the dynamic duo Simpson and Bruckheimer had been launched without fanfare – just not with such a deafening hue and cry. As Mark Salisbury noted, the film also became 'a multi media merchandising and cultural phenomenon, the hype of which had never been seen before; until the release of *Jurassic Park* in 1993, it was the blockbuster against which all subsequent blockbusters had to be measured'.[8] In a pattern that has since become depressingly all too familiar, from fast food tie-ins to tabloids screaming that it was '*Batman* week', films suddenly became brands and audiences were divided into demographics.

Batman was a juggernaut that no one, least of all Tim Burton, could stop. As he told Salisbury: 'The most interesting thing about hype is that everyone thought the studio was creating it, when in fact you can't create hype; it's a phenomenon that's beyond a studio, it has a life of its own . . . but there was no way to control it. And then you get the inevitable backlash to that.' The result? It became the biggest film in the studio's history, and the first to make $100 million inside the first ten days of its release. Easily the biggest grossing film of the year, it went on to earn more than $500 million worldwide. It was also the first in a long-running series of Hollywood disappointments, made so by the wildly inflated expectations multi-media coverage inevitably generated. Let's just say the joke(r) was on us.

Compared to Burton's highly personal *Edward Scissorhands* a year later, *Batman* – while hardly devoid of idiosyncratic touches – was shackled by the studio's demand for delivering a mass-appeal product (a factor that has haunted all of Burton's big-budget projects). Burton found the blockbuster too constrained by external (financial) factors to act as a satisfactory format for investigating themes and characters at anything more than the most superficial level. In many ways, Burton's time on *Batman* foreshadowed the troubles that would be experienced by other directors, from David Fincher (*Alien³*) to Ang Lee (*Hulk*, 2003).

Like *Batman*, with its fetish-gear costumes, *sex, lies, and videotape* titillated viewers with the promise of sex. Yet despite the lurid offer of intercourse in the title, Soderbergh's debut was far from salacious. A talk-heavy drama about masturbation, impotence, and repression, it contains barely a whiff of actual copulation. But though a chaste film on the surface, it is kept red-hot underneath. Remember Ann

(Andie MacDowell), the repressed suburbanite, substituting house-work for sex? She practically jerks off the taps. Perhaps because Soderbergh largely ignores the act itself, the film reeks pungently with the promise of sex.

But that sex is problematic. Dysfunction dominates all four protag-onists' lives. There is the philandering John (Peter Gallagher), a liar and a lawyer – making him the second- and first-lowest forms of humanity, we are told – who undertakes a lust-driven affair with his wife Ann's sister. She is the callous and sexually predatory Cynthia (Laura San Giacomo), pouting away in her knee-high boots and micro-skirt. For both, the sex – if not exactly healthy, then certainly rambunctious – goes hand in hand with the lies. To have good sex, they need to conceal the truth – a value that is forever being evaded, sought after or extracted in the film.

Compare them to Ann and Graham, both painfully honest but also painfully inadequate. Ann opens the film by admitting to her therapist that she only ever masturbated once because 'it just seemed so stupid – a dumb thing to do'. Diametrically opposed to each other, you have to wonder if Ann and Cynthia came from the same stock (though it's a more credible relationship than that between Ann and John, who are entirely mismatched). It's little wonder Ann finds Graham a kindred spirit, even if you can see Soderbergh's hand pulling the strings here. Unable to gain an erection in the presence of another, Graham remains reliant on his collection of video recordings to aid him to climax. A series of frank sexual confessions by women he has known, these show he can only find intimacy via the television screen, implying in a broader context how technology has isolated individuals both from each other and from 'real' experience.

With its very title crystallizing the era to come – from the sex and lies that surrounded the Clinton–Lewinsky affair downwards – Soderbergh's film arrived at the time when actor Rob Lowe's home-made porno hit the news and almost finished his career. It had been shot with two girls he picked up at a nightclub during the time he was attending the Democratic convention and campaigning on behalf of Michael Dukakis. Twelve months later, in 1988, Lowe became a cause célèbre when the mother of the younger of the two girls – who was revealed to be sixteen – filed for personal injury. The cassette, stolen by the girls, also did the rounds: 'Sex, Lowe and video-tape' became a phrase that burned into the public psyche. Still the most infamous of celebrity-sex videos, it was one of Lowe's better performances.

While this explains the public interest in *sex, lies, and videotape*, Soderbergh's film has little interest in public scandal. Introspective, it prefers to question the voyeuristic nature of the medium of cinema. With Graham's return, home video camera in hand – figuratively heralding Soderbergh's own arrival as a director – the use of videotape ensures we, as audience members, must confront our own voyeuristic tendencies. Soderbergh also questions his own art form, and whether the camera as a means of conveying emotion and experience contributes to our dislocation from our feelings. Recalling not only the work of Atom Egoyan – particularly *Family Viewing* (1987), with its use of video as a symbol of sexual alienation – Soderbergh's film also echoes Michael Powell's *Peeping Tom* (1960), with its emphasis on the phallic powers of the camera lens. On a structural level, Soderbergh also uses videotape as a means of shifting the narrative time-line by showing scenes that have been 'recorded' earlier than their chronological position. This experiment became a feature that would dominate certain later films, notably *The Limey* and *Full Frontal*.

As a first film, *sex, lies, and videotape* demonstrates Soderbergh's considerable confidence in constructing it, even if the camera hovers uncomfortably between being a passive observer and a willing participant. Admitting that he didn't want to let the camera dictate to the actors, Soderbergh – who rehearsed for a week with his players, and then rewrote dialogue accordingly – manages to draw at least two career-best performances from his cast. Both San Giacomo and Mac-Dowell have never been offered anything remotely as juicy since. The former headed for virtual obscurity after an appearance a year later in *Pretty Woman*: a shame, as her boisterous turn for Soderbergh safeguarded against the character becoming a stereotypical harlot. From the way she handles the barfly in the watering hole where she works, to telling John 'you can go now' after they have fucked, Cynthia is as strong-willed as she is sexual. Refuting Ann's notion that 'that stuff about women wanting it as much as men is crap', Cynthia is Soderbergh's primary effort to subvert traditional gender roles, years before the go-getting gals of *Sex and the City* would become the norm.

MacDowell, meanwhile, was to follow the film with a series of lightweight romantic leads, interspersed with the occasional bid for credibility working with the likes of Robert Altman (*Short Cuts*) and

Wim Wenders (*The End of Violence*, 1997). Her performance as Ann is a fine physical embodiment of one of the film's perennial themes: surface and undercurrent. Beneath her floral dresses and blushing cheeks lurks a tightly coiled sexuality ready to be sprung; the subtlety with which it is released is a credit to MacDowell's work. 'I was *so* ready to do that movie,' she admits, having suffered the indignity of having her thick South Carolina accent dubbed over by Glenn Close in her 1984 debut film *Greystoke: The Legend of Tarzan*. 'But I had no expectations. The only thing I expected from that movie was to be able to show it to casting directors to prove what I was capable of doing. I didn't come to Cannes, so I didn't realize what was happening with the film. When Steven called me to tell me it had won the Palme d'Or, I asked him if that meant the movie would be distributed. And he laughed. I had no idea. I was completely naive.'

Curiously, both Gallagher and Spader would be confronted with their characters, or variations upon them, in later films. Gallagher, who reunited with Soderbergh on *The Underneath* in 1995, went on to play property king Buddy Kane in *American Beauty* (1999), conqueror of Annette Bening's married real-estate agent (who, like Ann, channelled all of her sexual frustrations into cleaning a house she was trying to sell). Specializing in corporate slime – think of his turn in Altman's *The Player* (1992) as studio executive Larry Levy – Gallagher's Kane was a deftly drawn comic caricature that recalled John's smarmy arrogance as well as his lack of morals. If anything, John is the film's Republican; in his eyes, his only crime is getting caught. All about 'surface', and how things look, he has surrounded himself with the trappings – house, wife, car, job – of what he believes is a successful life. Soderbergh has admitted that he is the 'least well drawn of all the characters', though Gallagher, to his credit, is willing to appear unsympathetic in the denouement after Ann discovers his treachery, punished with the loss of his wife, his girlfriend and even his job. In the film's one overly self-conscious shot, John, holding his head in his hands, is seen silhouetted in the window of Graham's house. Having discovered that Ann wants to end the marriage, John has locked Graham out to watch the recording of his wife.

Even if Soderbergh's moralizing leaves a bitter aftertaste, it's refreshing to see a film that raps the male characters over the knuckles. Graham, too, has the tables – or more to the point, the camera – turned on him by Ann, during her interview. Already dressed in a black T-shirt and blue jeans, echoing in a rather heavy-handed piece of symbolism Graham's own dress sense, Ann confronts Graham about how his former girlfriend Elizabeth would've felt about his collection of tapes. Shocked to be the one staring at the lens, rather than through it, he admits he was a pathological liar who used to express his feelings 'non-verbally'. 'I've spent nine years structuring my life so this [being forced to verbalize his feelings] wouldn't happen,' he adds, moments before he achieves some sort of cathartic breakthrough and switches the camera off, as he and Ann kiss. As noted by Harlan Jacobson, 'Each pair starts out on different ends of the continuum that runs between appetite and hibernation, between the truthful self and the deceitful, between power and paralysis, between sex and love.'[9]

Of the four actors, Spader was the most successful coming into the film, a Brat Pack outsider who was yuppified in the likes of *Wall Street* and *Less Than Zero* (both 1987). Since his Cannes triumph, his erratic career has frequently steered him towards roles where sexuality is the language of the film, notably David Cronenberg's notorious J. G. Ballard adaptation *Crash* (1996) and Steven Shainberg's S&M love story *Secretary* (2002). Like Graham, the characters of both James Ballard and E. Edward Grey are able to connect to others only through so-called 'deviant' sexual behaviour. Spader's cool detachment was perfectly tailored to playing Graham, the character perhaps closest to Soderbergh's own (with his lack of material possessions of particular relevance). 'That film came from him,' says Spader. 'Steven was very smart in that film. He took from the best parts of his own imagination, and borrowed from the best of others' to produce this unique little story. And he made the film under a set of circumstances that is the best of that sort of tradition – whether it be John Cassavetes shooting wonderful films in the confines of his own house with his friends and family, or Soderbergh shooting in his back yard.'

It may be nowhere near as guerrilla as, say, Kevin Smith's *Clerks*. But if *sex, lies, and videotape* is to be cast as the film that kick-started the American independent revolution, and ultimately steered Hollywood back towards a more creative and fertile period, then it's because of the inspiration it would provide for aspiring film directors. Others would do it cheaper, faster, even better – but Soderbergh was the first director to open our eyes to the possibility that small-scale films could be shot on a shoestring and be embraced the world over.

CHAPTER 2

Talk Is Cheap:
Sundance After *sex, lies, and videotape*

3 Martin Donovan as Jude in *Surviving Desire*.

Causing both budding filmmakers and Hollywood suits to recalculate the potential price and profits of a low-budget film, *sex, lies, and videotape* did not just make a commercial impact on the industry. Its artistry made an immediate impression too, spearheading a series of films that came to define what people understand by the term 'American indie'. In both 1990 and 1991, the effect of Soderbergh's dialogue-driven debut would be seen in the rise of such auteurs as Hal Hartley, Richard Linklater and Whit Stillman. While Soderbergh did not directly influence these men, there's no doubt the success of *sex, lies, and videotape* gave their films more momentum. Talk is cheap after all, particularly when making a film – even more so when financiers were beginning to believe that audiences were willing to listen.

At the 1990 Sundance Film Festival, with the search on to find the new Soderbergh, both Stillman and Hartley premiered their first full-length features – respectively, *Metropolitan* and *The Unbelievable Truth*. Born in 1952 and raised in upstate New York, Stillman was the son of an impoverished debutante from Philadelphia and a Democratic politician from Washington DC who worked in the Truman and Kennedy administrations. Accepting $2,000 from his family when he graduated from Harvard in 1973, he began working in publishing before moving into journalism and later the film industry itself as a foreign sales representative for Spanish films.

Hartley, seven years Stillman's junior, was born and raised in Lindenhurst, Long Island, the area that was to become his filmmaking playground. Unlike Stillman's grand lineage – his great-grandfather helped start Citibank – Hartley's family was strictly blue collar. His father, Hal Sr, was an ironworker and crane operator famed for erecting dozens of city skyscrapers. His mother died when Hartley was just twelve, leaving him and his three siblings with their father – the resonance of which would be felt throughout much of Hartley's early work. Enrolling in a Boston art college, he took a film course during his time there but quit for financial reasons – though not before he had shot his first short. It was enough to get him into the film program at the State University of New York.

Yet if their backgrounds were far apart, their films could almost be

born of the same embryo: arch intellectual works, with rigid compositions and mannered dialogue that thrives on its own artificiality.
Revered by the college campus crowd in the early 1990s, these films
dealt with angst-ridden individuals – albeit those plagued by the
banality of suburban life in the case of Hartley, or the fear of extinction on the Upper West Side with Stillman.

Metropolitan, shot for well under $1 million with a cast of unknowns,
was a semi-guerrilla affair, with Stillman calling in favours from
distant relatives to provide the luxurious residences needed to play out
the action. Its Jane Austen–influenced tale of New York debs and
their escorts, captured with the breezy comic tone of a Salinger or
Fitzgerald novel, was partly autobiographical. Like the film's main
protagonist, the red-haired Tom (Edward Clements), Stillman wore
second-hand dinner clothes when he reluctantly attended the various
soirées on offer.

While Stillman almost invited comparison with Woody Allen (from
the black-and-white title cards onwards), his characters were a world
apart from Allen's neuroses-riddled intellectuals. As they discuss life,
love and literature, these self-styled 'UHBs' (members of the *urban
haute-bourgeoisie*) feel like a dying breed, as if they belong to another
century. One even uses the word 'queer' twice, though not in the way
it is understood today. They play bridge and strip poker, though
despite being set during 'orgy week' the film is curiously asexual.
Young, superficial, naive and even innocent, Stillman's cast are pre-
vented from also seeming obnoxious by his comic use of irony. This is
something Allen often fails to do.

Replete with lines worthy of Oscar Wilde ('the most important
thing to realize about parents is that there's absolutely nothing you
can do about them'), *Metropolitan* was a film almost too learned to
survive in today's marketplace. While the film took a healthy $2.9 mil-
lion in the U.S., Stillman did not see dollar signs in his eyes and, to his
credit, did not set out to capitalize on being flavour of the month.
'When the Spielberg–Lucas adventure thing happened in the early 80s,
I felt so relieved that cinema was returning to its roots,' he said. 'But
within a couple of years it all became endlessly repetitive and Hollywood took a nosedive. What I want to make is small commercial
films, like Spike Lee's, Jarmusch's, or Soderbergh's first features.'[10]

Hartley is much the same: quite content to paint his intimate dramas
of the mind on a small canvas. *The Unbelievable Truth* cost just

$75,000, though Hartley claimed it cost $200,000 so as not to put prospective distributors off. The story of Josh (Robert John Burke), a convicted murderer fresh from prison, and a nuclear-war-obsessed high school graduate named Audrey (Adrienne Shelly), it defined what was to become the Hartley modus operandi. Its de-naturalized, exclamatory style saw the actors play verbal ping-pong with the droll and deadpan lines. Their conversations – often a series of comic non sequiturs – are more like internal dialogues, as if they are talking to themselves rather than to others.

Yet despite the formal games Hartley plays, and the posturing of his characters, he always manages to ground his work with an emotional core. The catalyst for his debut – as for *sex, lies, and videotape* – is the return to a small town of a former resident, who in this case has reputedly killed two members of his former girlfriend's family. Josh, like Graham, is even wearing all black, in this case the uniform of the tortured intellectual (a Hartley staple). The theme of forging an identity in the shadow of your parents, which becomes even more prominent in Hartley's follow-up, *Trust*, is expressed via the capricious Audrey, torn between discussing Molière with Josh and modelling to rile her parents. Both farcical and self-aware, *The Unbelievable Truth*, like *Metropolitan*, felt at home at Sundance, where the audiences were more receptive to such experimental fare.

At the time, Hartley felt that the current trend for independent directors (and, with a huge student following, he was the trendiest) was nothing new. 'There seems to me to be a cycle in American film history; every seven to ten years, the distribution industry recognizes low-budget filmmakers doing interesting work. Distributors buy the films and those filmmakers are co-opted into the industry. The last wave were filmmakers like Jim Jarmusch and Spike Lee. Before that it was Scorsese and Coppola and Bob Rafelson. Of course, then it was on a different level but here it is again.'[11]

Producing three shorts – *Surviving Desire*, *Ambition* and *Theory of Achievement* – during this time, Hartley was as economic as he was prolific. Yet as the decade wore on, the sensitive auteur unwilling to creep from his patch and head to Hollywood became an endangered species. To look at their subsequent careers, you might think Hartley and Stillman were leading near-parallel lives. Ambitious attempts to expand their range were thwarted at various turns, to the point where both now work on the margins – largely forgotten by the Sundance crowd and plain ignored by Hollywood. Hartley's excellent *Henry Fool* (1997), the everyday tale of an inept garbage man and a pretentious novelist, barely caused a ripple commercially or critically. Despite winning the Best Screenplay award at the 1998 Cannes Film Festival, its deliberate, cocky mixture of high and low brow – art, poetry and politics meet vomiting and defecation – puzzled the few that saw it. A modern-day 'Beauty and the Beast', his flawed fairy tale *No Such Thing* (2001) – originally called *Monster* – fared even worse. With little international distribution, the film took just $62,703 in the U.S. – despite the presence of Julie Christie and Helen Mirren in the cast. However, Hartley has clawed his way back from the brink of obscurity with – as he tagged it – 'a fake sci-fi movie' called *The Girl from Monday* (2005), set in a 'culture of desire' when sex appeal can be insured and sexual harassment can damage your credit rating.

Likewise Stillman. While praised in some quarters, his film *The Last Days of Disco* (1998) was not met with quite the enthusiasm that greeted *Metropolitan* or his 1994 second film *Barcelona* – which drew on the director's time spent in Spain as a rep for foreign films. Featuring early performances from a post-*Kids* Chloë Sevigny and a pre–*Pearl Harbor* Kate Beckinsale, its nostalgic story of two Ivy League gals in 'the very early 1980s' felt, somehow, both elegant and benign. Coming in the same year as Todd Haynes's *Velvet Goldmine* – a troubled paean to glam rock which also suffered from a lukewarm response – as well as Mark Christopher's equally problematic Miramax production *54*, the misleading title of Stillman's work automatically saw it categorized alongside both. But rather than the drug-fuelled excess of the Studio 54 era, its deft script again revealed Stillman to be concerned with the youthful malaise of the privileged, and the limbo time between college and career.

After completing this unofficial trilogy, Stillman broke away from such dialogue-driven comedies of manners with an adaptation of Anchee Min's memoir *Red Azalea*, set during China's Cultural Revolution in the 1960s and 1970s. The true story of a woman who escapes life on a collective farm to become the star of a propaganda film based on an opera by Madame Mao, it was to be produced by Christine Vachon's Killer Films, and bankrolled by UK outfit FilmFour. The first of a two-picture deal, it came to an abrupt end when the company was dismantled by its parent Channel 4 in July 2002, having suffered £5.4 million in losses the previous year.

Back in 1991, as Hal Hartley was beginning to establish himself with his second feature, *Trust*, two other directors made their Sundance debuts: Richard Linklater with the micro-budget *Slacker* and Todd Haynes with his second film, *Poison*, which would edge past *Trust* and win the Grand Jury Prize. Linklater's $23,000 gem would convince others – notably Kevin Smith, beginning with *Clerks* – that shooting from the hip *and* the mouth was a viable way to make a film.

That Linklater's upbringing was far less privileged than other Sundance alumni also helped dismantle the elitism that surrounded filmmaking. 'I'm from a real working-class, white trash background – unlike most people from this industry!' he says. 'Quite often, we're all hard on ourselves, saying "I should've done more movies." But I often wake up, and go "I'm doing pretty good from where I came from." I can't complain.' Born in Houston, he was an offshore oil rig worker in the Gulf of Mexico in his early twenties. 'I always had aspirations to write and do other things, but the fact is, if you don't have any money, and your family doesn't have money, you have to work.'

Set in Linklater's adopted home town of Austin, Texas, where he moved in 1984 after his time on the rigs, *Slacker*'s free-wheeling chain-link structure shifts the narrative from one character to the next, almost indiscriminately, as if the camera's eye has been caught by something new. With its dramatis personae of obsessive losers and flakes, the film eavesdrops on a series of conversations over the course of a day. While many of the segments drift amiably over you, some are vivid – notably the sunglasses-sporting waif, who became the 'face' of the film on the poster and is seen trying to sell a Madonna pap smear. ('It's a material world and I'm a material girl,' she reasons.)

If some of the choices are obvious targets – a JFK conspiracy theorist working on a book called *Conspiracy A-Go-Go* and a John Hinckley nut surrounded by TVs – Linklater never makes it seem as if he is judging his characters. Seen riffing on *The Wizard of Oz* in the back of a taxi cab in the opening sequence, he even sets the tone himself. Pre-empting his soon-to-be-friend Quentin Tarantino's regurgitation of popular culture, the film moves from the sublime to the ridiculous, as Scooby-Doo and the Smurfs (echoed, years later, in Richard Kelly's 2001 mind-bending *Donnie Darko*) come in for some serious stoner analysis.

Like *sex, lies, and videotape*, Linklater's title became part of the lexicon, as the term 'slacker' came to define the disenfranchized tail end of the post-war baby-boomer set – those that had reached their twenties during the Reagan years and been left sorely bewildered. Coinciding with the publication of Douglas Coupland's novel *Generation X*, the film was propelled to a U.S. box office take of $1.22 million, enough to secure Linklater a $6.5 million budget for his next effort, *Dazed and Confused*. In retrospect, like Soderbergh's debut, the film is not strong enough to speak for a generation – but it undoubtedly caught the mood of confusion, discontent and cynicism that characterized the times, as America headed towards the first Gulf War conflict.

Meanwhile, Haynes's *Poison*, alongside Jennie Livingston's trans-sexual documentary *Paris Is Burning*, which won the top prize in its category the same year, ensured that a mini-wave of gay-themed films made it to the fore. Later dubbed New Queer Cinema, other early examples included Greg Araki's *The Living End* and Tom Kalin's Leopold and Loeb spin *Swoon*, both of which made their Sundance bows in 1992. Araki's film, about a hustler and a movie critic who are both HIV-positive, set the tone for his later hedonistic Generation X road movies (like 1995's *The Doom Generation*), rather than a new breed of enlightened films about homosexuality.

'It was never like a real new wave,' notes Araki:

It was never like we got in a room and said: 'We have a mission and a political agenda. This is what we want to do!' We were all just filmmakers, working our films, dealing with whatever we wanted to deal with. It was coincidental that all played Sundance around the same time. It was never anything we took seriously as a movement. I'm part of the film school generation: I grew up in film school. I have a Masters and a Bachelors degree in film. I studied auteurs. That's where I come from: auteurs like Alfred Hitchcock, Howard Hawks and John Ford. The idea that film is an art form and that the director controls it.

If Araki's involvement with New Queer Cinema was by association more than anything, Christine Vachon's was anything but accidental. She produced *Poison* and all of Haynes's subsequent features, and went on to help bring to fruition several other examples of the genre, from *Swoon* to Rose Troche's *Go Fish* (1994) and Nigel Finch's *Stonewall* (1995). Her later films dealing with transgression – notably Kimberly Peirce's *Boys Don't Cry* and John Cameron Mitchell's *Hedwig and the Angry Inch* (2001) – would no doubt have been more difficult productions were it not for her groundbreaking work in the early 1990s.

Vachon, whose father was a renowned World War II photographer, met Haynes when they were students at Brown University in the late 1970s. Her elder sister, Gail, was an experimental filmmaker but Vachon was not one for such fringe work. 'At the time, there seemed to be only two types of filmmaking,' she reflects. 'You were either making radically anti-narrative movies, or slick Hollywood stuff. There was nothing in between, accessible to us in our mid-twenties in New York.'

Vachon was hired as a production assistant on Bill Sherwood's AIDS drama *Parting Glances* in 1986, the same year that David Lynch's *Blue Velvet* was released – a film she cites as highly influential for the way in which it made art house accessible. A year later Haynes made *Superstar: The Karen Carpenter Story*, while a part of the MFA program at Bard College. Depicting the decline and fall of the eponymous singer by using Barbie dolls, the film's cult reputation grew, despite A&M Records and Richard Carpenter taking legal action to withdraw it from circulation. Vachon, who helped Haynes with the sound on the film, told him she wanted to produce his first full-length film, *Poison*.

'For a couple of years it was really fun,' she says. 'We were really doing something completely new. It was before Reaganomics had come in and cut everyone's legs off. There was arts funding, a fair amount of wealth in the country. Todd and I produced these movies together. We really learned production skills from each other, and developed a method of working that transposed itself onto *Poison*. Part of the reason we never had an adversarial relationship was because we started out together.'

Made for $250,000, *Poison* has not lost any of its potency in the intervening years. A triptych of tales inspired by the works of French criminal cum author Jean Genet, its frank depictions of homosexuality angered the religious New Right, particularly given that it was partly funded by a National Endowment for the Arts grant. Cutting between three stories, each in a different genre but all dealing with notions of the outsider in society, Haynes's work focused on a trio of victims who learn to articulate themselves and rise above their suffering. A pastiche of 1950s B movies, 'Horror' deals with a scientist who isolates the sex drive, consumes it and mutates into a murderous monster; 'Hero' is a documentary-style tale of a seven-year-old boy named Richie who shoots his father then takes flight out of the window; and 'Homo' tells the story of a petty thief sent to Fontenal prison who develops a perverse fascination with an inmate whom he knew some years before.

A provocative attempt to challenge boundaries and stir up the status quo, *Poison* differed wildly from the formally and structurally conventional Hollywood depictions of gay characters, such as those in William Friedkin's *Cruising* (1980). As Haynes himself has said, the film forces you 'to mourn a little bit', chiefly for the climate of the U.S., with its right-wing administration of the time, but also for the world at large (with the shadow of AIDS looming). Like his second movie, *Safe* (1995), in which Julianne Moore played a housewife who becomes allergic to the modern world, *Poison* is both highly contemporary and strangely timeless.

As was to be the case with Linklater – whom we will encounter in more detail further on – Haynes's individual slant would not always sit well with critics. Roger Ebert is said to have quickly withdrawn his outstretched hand when introduced to the director of *Poison*. 'All of Todd's movies confound expectation,' says Vachon. 'That I think is their greatest strength. If people don't keep making movies like that, the medium will get stagnant and die. *Safe* is one of those movies that is now canonized. But its reception – at Cannes and Sundance – was awful. Six months later it's on the critics' ten-best list. Todd's work is so rich; it takes so much time to process.'

Haynes suffered the same experience on his third film, *Velvet Goldmine* (1998), a production that left him spent. After a difficult shoot in Britain, Haynes wrangled with Miramax head Harvey Weinstein over re-cutting the film, eventually relenting and removing three minutes before the film premiered at the Cannes Film Festival. Haynes, looking for new inspiration, took up painting again and relocated from New York to the relative sanity of Portland, Oregon. 'I relaxed there in a way I hadn't for so long. I met all these amazing people and fell in love with the city, and ended up buying a house there. Everything changed. I don't think I've been happier in my life. I didn't know how much I loved having a garden and flowers. It helped keep the filmmaking in perspective – you've got to have other things in your life and I now do.'

The result of this renewal was a sumptuous homage to Douglas Sirk called *Far from Heaven* (2002) that reunited Haynes with Julianne Moore. Written in just two weeks with her in mind, it told the story of Cathy Whitaker, a suburban housewife who discovers her husband (Dennis Quaid) is gay and then strikes up a relationship, much to the shock of the community, with her black gardener (Dennis Haysbert). Deeply sincere, and without a whiff of irony, it has been described by Haynes as an 'antidote' to the emotionally guarded way in which we now conduct our lives. 'Young people are not supposed to feel strongly about things, like their parents did in the 1960s,' he says. 'It's not cool. It's a cliché to be passionate about politics, or about a rock star. That's a shame and it's dangerous and it's sad.'

Inspired by such Sirk films as *All That Heaven Allows* (1956) and *Imitation of Life* (1959), the ravishing cinematography from two-time Soderbergh collaborator Ed Lachman is as memorable as any of the film's high-calibre performances. 'Sirk was our visual reference, so I immersed myself with Todd, who is very heightened in his own visualization of Sirkian language,' says Lachman. 'I just tried to recreate it in my own interpretation. It's not purely Sirk. It was just that heightened, expressionistic, Technicolor world. It was about the artifice of that world. Their lives, in the 1950s, had a certain artifice. That's what the film dealt with. So the stylization of the film became what the film was also about.'

Like *Velvet Goldmine*, the film tested poorly – viewers were confused by the fact that it was an art-house film they could take their mothers to. Battered by his previous Miramax experience, Haynes refused point-blank for the film to be picked up by Harvey Weinstein, and took it to USA Films, a splicing of October and Universal/Polygram's Gramercy, headed up by former Weinstein favourite Scott Greenstein. The film, despite its test screenings, ultimately took a healthy $15.8 million in the U.S., and won four Oscar nominations, including Best Original Screenplay for Haynes. His executive producer was none other than Steven Soderbergh, whose production company Section Eight,[12] formed with his regular star George Clooney, was set up to shelter auteurs like Haynes while working with established stars within the system.

Unlike Hartley or Stillman, Haynes has found the key to survival, ducking in and out of the studio system where necessary. Sundance, for him, was a jumping-off point, rather than a crutch to support his whole career. Talk may be cheap, particularly in film, but you still need someone to listen. But Haynes, unlike the director who was to dominate the 1992 Sundance Film Festival, has never been an avid self-promoter. If there was one man who knew the value of talk more than anyone else, it was Quentin Tarantino.

CHAPTER 3

Reservoir Dogs and the Class of '92

4 'Let's go to work': Steve Buscemi and Harvey Keitel in *Reservoir Dogs*.

There's always a class of Sundance people, who come out
every year. I'm still very close to the filmmakers I was with
back then. Quentin has this theory that he and Robert
[Rodriguez] and Allison Anders were Sundance '92. They
fancied themselves as the Class of '92 and tried to
mythologize themselves. But it was really the class of '91 –
Todd Haynes, myself, Greg Araki . . .
   Richard Linklater

Reservoir Dogs may have left the Sundance Festival of 1992 empty-
handed, but its writer-director did not. Quentin Tarantino departed
from Park City a star in the making. Yet it was not in America that his
reputation was made but in Europe – in particular the UK, where the
film took more than double its paltry $2.8 million U.S. gross. As
Tarantino has said, 'the Americans didn't get me 'til *Pulp Fiction*',
referring to his 1994 second film that would change the landscape of
U.S. independent film beyond recognition.

   Reservoir Dogs arrived in the UK at a particularly sensitive time,
when screen violence was a hot topic and video nasties were being
blamed for influencing the killers of two-year-old Jamie Bulger in
Liverpool. In 1993, the British Board of Film Classification denied
Tarantino's debut a video certificate for several months, the same fate
endured by Abel Ferrara's *Bad Lieutenant* (1992). It meant the film
remained in cinemas, playing midnight screenings at rep houses like
London's Prince Charles, and considerably boosting its cult reputation.
Recalling the days when gangs of youths dressed up like Alex and his
Droogs before taking in a screening of Stanley Kubrick's *A Clockwork
Orange* (1971), audience members would arrive sporting shades,
black suits and pencil-thin ties. Eventually, the cult spread to the U.S.
Tim Roth, the lone British star of the film, saw it first hand. 'I was in
a bar in New York on Halloween one time – one of those bars where
you can find a quiet corner in a very loud bar – and a whole ton of people came in as those characters. A couple of guys [were playing me] –
quite handsome they were!'

   Tarantino once asked a room full of people what his influence had been. One guy summed it up: 'I'll tell you exactly what's going on. In *Bad Boys*, there's a scene where two gangsters are talking about an *I Love Lucy* episode. That would not have happened if you had never been born.'[13] On one level Tarantino's work, as refreshing as it was, would inspire only bad movies from copycat filmmakers. From Guy Ritchie's *Lock, Stock and Two Smoking Barrels* (1998) downward, low-rent crime films populated by wisecracking crooks became the norm. There was no cinematic rebirth after *Reservoir Dogs*, no movement of filmmakers banding together to change the medium as we knew it.

But from the moment Tarantino is heard speaking the opening lines of *Reservoir Dogs*, as he analyses Madonna's 'Like a Virgin', popular culture has a legitimate cinematic voice. As Graham Fuller noted: 'It's not Madonna that concerns Tarantino in this scene – but what Madonna has come to represent.'[14] Tarantino wallows in the junk of modern life, symbolized by his characters' love of fast food, revering the low brow, repackaging it for dinner-table debate. For a decade that became saturated with the cult of celebrity, Tarantino's film – and his subsequent work – was the ideal mascot. Like *Slacker* the year before, and in the work of Kevin Smith to come, dialogue no longer had to drive the plot. Whether it was cold-blooded killers or convenience-store clerks, characters mattered and their personalities were defined, in part, by their favourite TV shows, music and movie stars. To the eyes of a generation surrounded by the increasingly all-pervasive entertainment industry, this humanized the characters – even if it trivialized them as well.

It was particularly prescient that *Reservoir Dogs* should open with a discussion of one of pop's genuine icons, given that Tarantino himself became the first bona fide director-as-rock-star. Over 5,000 ticket requests were taken at London's National Film Theatre in 1994 when he was interviewed on stage. His presence was revered in a way normally reserved for boy bands. His rise precipitated the emergence of the film geek from the fringes of society to the front pages. Tarantino proved to all who would listen that being able to discuss the finer points of *Star Trek* and Sonny Chiba was an important aspect of contemporary culture.

Some of Tarantino's earliest cinematic experiences were with his mother, Connie. She took him to see *Carnal Knowledge* and a double bill of *The Wild Bunch* and *Deliverance* (1972). As borne out by a sequence in *Pulp Fiction*, the anal rape scene in the latter would stay with him. Born in Knoxville, Tennessee, Tarantino grew up in L.A.'s South Bay, dropping out of high school in his mid-teens. He worked in a porno joint, The Pussycat Theatre, for a while, but it was his five-year stint at the Manhattan Beach rental store Video Archives, beginning in 1984 when he was twenty-one, that would refine his knowledge of cinema. With access to the wealth of films that would inform his own work, he became the first in a generation of movie brats educated by their VCRs. It was here that he would cultivate a first-hand appreciation of everything from Kubrick to Chow-Yun Fat.

Although it was at Video Archives that he would meet fellow clerk and future writing partner Roger Avary, his first experience as a director was with a disaster-prone effort called *My Best Friend's Birthday*, penned by an actor friend of his named Craig Hamann. The pair had met at the James Best Acting School and decided that this story – about a thirtieth birthday party that goes awry – would be their ticket to Hollywood. Tarantino, an actor at heart, was to play the role of the party-planner Clarence. He spent many an hour polishing up the scenes with what was to become his trademark postmodern dialogue. Shot guerrilla-style, with bags of weed and bottles of liquor to power the crew, there were significant gaps in production (even a year, at one point) when cash ran out. With an accident in the lab destroying the final reel, the film was never completed – something of a relief, given its amateurish nature.

But with the encouragement of Cathryn Jaymes, a talent manager introduced to him by Hamann, Tarantino began to write what ultimately became his first professional script, *True Romance*. Inspired by Terrence Malick's seminal road movie *Badlands* (1973) – even pilfering Erik Satie's original score and female lead voice-over – it also borrowed the best elements of *My Best Friend's Birthday*, from discussions about Elvis to the lead characters Clarence and the prostitute Crystal (renamed Alabama). Originally called *The Open Road*, the script had the majority of its road-movie sequences pruned away over time. Avary helped provide some of the more romantic elements, but the politically incorrect dialogue was enough to send most suits running.

Tarantino's follow-up script, about two white-trash serial killers named Mickey and Mallory Knox, was no better received. It was not until *Natural Born Killers* – a contemporary spin on *Bonnie and Clyde* (1967) – fell into the hands of the fledgling producers Don Murphy and

Jane Hamsher that the film began to find its legs, eventually to be radically rewritten and directed by Oliver Stone in 1994. A year before, *True Romance*, which also suffered from revisions to its ending, wound up in the hands of Tony Scott, whose work – notably *Top Gun* (1986) and *Beverly Hills Cop II* (1987) – was a shining example of all that was grotesque and excessive about Hollywood in the 1980s. In the case of Scott, in particular, Tarantino's edgy fare was just what he needed to rescue his reputation as a journeyman director.

Originally meant as one third of a three-part film (alongside a Roger Avary short script, *Pandemonium Reigns*, and an undecided third section), the script for *Reservoir Dogs* eventually became feature length during the autumn of 1990. At a barbecue thrown by Scott Spiegel, longtime friend of the director Sam Raimi, Tarantino met with the former actor and dancer Lawrence Bender, who had produced Spiegel's low-budget directorial debut in 1989, a slasher movie called *Intruder*. Bender, impressed by Tarantino's youthful enthusiasm, would eventually get the script to Monte Hellman, veteran director of *Two Lane Blacktop* (1971).

Desperate to direct the script himself, Hellman conceded defeat when he realized how determined Tarantino was to see the project through – even to the point of shooting it on the hoof with the fees he had earned from *True Romance*. Pledging his help to raise funds, Hellman got the script to Richard Gladstein at the video company Live Entertainment (and would also provide the link to Michael Madsen, having collaborated with him on 1988's *Iguana*). Tarantino was eventually confirmed as director, despite concerns about his inexperience.

It was only after Harvey Keitel came on board (he and Bender shared the same acting coach), that Tarantino began to feel safe. Keitel paid for the flat-broke director and producer to fly to New York and host a casting session. This led to the appointment of the Coen brothers' regular Steve Buscemi in the role of Mr Pink (a part Tarantino had earmarked for himself before he took on the 'shit' role of Mr Brown). With the ex-con and crime novelist Eddie Bunker cast as Mr Blue and the former *Dillinger* (1945) star Lawrence Tierney hired to play Joe Cabot, the mastermind behind the robbery, Tarantino was relishing his first opportunity to resurrect his fallen pulp idols.

During these feverish few months, he was also invited to take the script to Sundance and workshop it for two weeks, shooting sequences with actors as a dry run for his impending shoot. Although one focus group savaged the resulting work, particularly for its static long shots, the other – attended by Terry Gilliam – was more sympathetic. By the time Tarantino returned from Utah, the buzz on his script was becoming audible. Roth, who had made his name as a for-hire thug in Stephen Frears's *The Hit* (1984), remembers being sent the script in a stack of others by his agent, with an intriguing note saying 'Look at Orange'. 'I was halfway through it, and I picked up the phone [and called my agent and said]: "I gotta be in this! What a laugh!" It was a brilliant script. It's pretty much as is. For an English actor to be in this . . . it's like being in a Cagney movie.'

A fan of Jules Dassin's *Rififi* (1955), the benchmark for all subsequent heist movies, Tarantino made a calculated choice designed to help make his mark when he wrote the script. 'Making the greatest Western is a pretty tall order,' he stated. 'But if you set out to make the greatest heist movie, you'll probably get in the top fifteen if you make a good one.' A fan of hip hop, Tarantino's approach to moviemaking would prove not dissimilar to the way DJs or rappers sample tracks by another artist. He deliberately set out to borrow liberally from the classics of the heist genre, plundering them for his very own compilation tape script.

Influences range from Kubrick's *The Killing* (1956) with its fractured time line, to John Huston's *The Asphalt Jungle* (1950) for the betrayal after the heist. Joseph Sargent's *The Taking of Pelham 123* (1974) inspired the colour-coded pseudonyms, Lewis Milestone's *Ocean's Eleven* (1960) the opening title slow motion stroll and Phil Karlson's *Kansas City Confidential* (1952) the suits. Ringo Lam's *City on Fire* (1987) proved an even greater source: Mexican stand-offs, an undercover cop in a gang of professional thieves, even the use of the phrase 'Let's go to work' – which became the unofficial tagline for the film. While years later Tarantino freely admitted that his fourth film, *Kill Bill*, was a 'duck-press' of the grindhouse martial arts movies he was reared on, much the same can be said for his debut in relation to the heist movie.

'*Reservoir Dogs* was a helluva movie, but I would rather watch a Peckinpah film if I had to watch one of them,' says Chris Penn, who was cast as the shell-suit-sporting Nice Guy Eddie, faithful son to Joe Cabot. '*Reservoir Dogs* was one of the best things Quentin ever did. It's definitely one of the best movies I ever had. It was instant gold. Except for one scene, it was all on the page. Quentin wrote it. It's his movie. There was only one scene that I wrote, which was the last scene of the movie.' You wrote that scene? 'I had to. Quentin couldn't get along with Lawrence Tierney. It was supposed to be between Lawrence Tierney and Harvey Keitel. Quentin said: "I can't take this guy, make something up." I wrote that whole thing . . . "I'll shoot you in the heart . . ."'

Penn also claims he 'turned the character [of Nice Guy Eddie] away from being a wimp' when he was originally written as a Daddy's Boy.

> The first day of shooting was a scene between me, Michael Madsen and Lawrence Tierney. In the script, Michael Madsen was supposed to whip my ass. I hadn't made a damn movie in three years. I was fightin', I was broke. I knew they couldn't re-hire me, because it was the first day of shooting and they had $900,000 to make the movie. Quentin got very mad at me. He still is probably. I said: 'The way it's gonna work is, whoever wins, wins.' And Madsen, to his credit – he's one of my best friends – said 'Fuckin' A. I'm gonna take you out. I like that attitude.' I whacked him out three or four times, and he goes 'Let's choreograph this thing properly!'

Drawing us into its own artificiality, Tarantino structured the film through a complex series of flashbacks, revealing White, Orange and Blonde's integration into the gang, as well as the subsequent escape after the unseen robbery by Pink and Brown/White/Orange. We see Orange rehearsing his role in front of the mirror, learning the 'rules' to be accepted into the gang. Their world, like the theatrical stage of the rendezvous warehouse (the film's chief setting), is a play enacted in front of us, recognizable and yet distanced.

Tarantino juggled with cinema's heritage, reshaping the gangster genre, its characters and concerns, for an audience brought up on *The Fantastic Four*. These are criminals shaped by their love of Lee Marvin movies, their character types refracted through a celluloid prism. The dialogue, as much as it fizzes, is scripted in a language couched in movie lore. Lines like 'Where's the commode in this dungeon? I gotta take a squirt' belong to a heightened reality – or 'the normal Quentin universe . . . [which] is more real than real life',[15] as the director puts it himself.

Like his favourite filmmakers Sergio Leone and Brian De Palma, Tarantino was interested in delivering a macho movie ride. It's an exclusively male experience, to the point where a bleeding Orange's hair is groomed by his surrogate father Mr White: watching *Reservoir Dogs* is like looking in on a locker room. Sexist, homophobic and racial slurs ping round the script, as the men verbally towel-whip each other. A film that cracked the feminist movement with the butt of its gun, it bit where most films barked – even if its men were all posturing in the end.

The remainder of Tarantino's self-titled Class of '92 – outside of honorary member Robert Rodriguez, who made his Sundance bow a year later – were two filmmakers who couldn't be more different from him. Compare *Reservoir Dogs* to Allison Anders's *Gas Food Lodging* or Alexandre Rockwell's *In the Soup*, which won the Grand Jury Prize that year, and it becomes obvious. A former production assistant on Wim Wenders's *Paris, Texas* (1984), Anders had endured a rough trailer-park childhood in Kentucky, and much of it fed into *Gas Food Lodging*, her first solo effort after co-directing a film about the L.A. punk scene, *Border Radio* (1987). Although later films, *Grace of My Heart* (1996) and *Sugar Town* (1999), focused on the music industry, Anders's early work, including girl gang drama *Mi vida loca* (1994), were inspired by personal experience rather than time sitting in front of movies.

The coming-of-age story of two sisters, played by Ione Skye and Fairuza Balk, watched over by their despairing mother (Brooke Adams), *Gas Food Lodging* is sensitively etched by Anders, the film working its magic in an almost imperceptible way. In retrospect, it acts as a lovely riposte to Tarantino's world of macho values. 'That's what men do. They walk away,' we are told, as each female protagonist undergoes her own private tragedies and triumphs with members of the opposite sex. But the work of Anders and Tarantino was linked by a passion to transcend their working-class roots and break into a profession seemingly beyond their reach. In turn, filmmaking would allow them to reflect back on their origins. Like Linklater's disenfranchized slackers, Tarantino and Anders were giving genuine voice to blue-collar boys and girls.

As Rockwell's *In the Soup* showed, making a film suddenly became a viable modern means of achieving the American Dream. Fame and fortune could follow for anyone with a story to tell, and a camera to film it with. Thanks chiefly to two winning performances, from Steve Buscemi as the would-be auteur Aldolpho Rollo and Seymour Cassel as a small-time mobster and potential investor named Joe, the film is a fine expression of the fantasy that surrounds making a film. As Aldolpho says of his mentor, who begins to infiltrate every aspect of his life after agreeing to bankroll his movie, 'Instead of making my movie, I was living in his.' The film, like Tom DeCillo's *Living in Oblivion* (1995) – his definitive comedy about a troubled indie shoot, also starring Buscemi – takes great delight in deflating the pretentious ambitions of every so-and-so with a poster of Tarkovsky's *Stalker* on his wall.

As Rockwell and Anders – who teamed up and fell out with Tarantino over the ill-conceived portmanteau hotel-set story *Four Rooms* (1995) – would discover, filmmaking in America in the 1990s was not about talent. It was about how you *marketed* that talent. Without a perpetual PR machine in motion, directors like Anders and Rockwell, who had limited commercial appeal, were quickly swept to the margins of the film industry.

CHAPTER 4

The Changing Face of Sundance:
Public Access and *Spanking the Monkey*

5 Jeremy Davies helps Alberta Watson in *Spanking the Monkey*

After the Class of '92, Sundance was ready for a new group of disciples. The festivals of 1993 and 1994 were the last two to date that produced a genuine class of filmmakers. The most significant arrivals were Bryan Singer and David O. Russell. Meanwhile, those that grabbed the headlines were Robert Rodriguez (*El Mariachi*) and Kevin Smith (*Clerks*), both of whom had made their films on a pittance. But there were others, producing more esoteric fare.

Scott McGehee, who studied Japanese Film History at Berkeley, and David Siegel, a former architecture student, brought us the audacious meta-noir *Suture* (1994). A perfect example of low-budget American independent cinema scoring a home run, it had in common with *Clerks* only the black-and-white film stock. It was wonderfully uncompromising: how many film titles in recent memory refer to Lacanian theory?

As it turns out, audiences have Steven Soderbergh to thank for helping it along. Called by a friend during post-production, when the directors were in dire need of $250,000 worth of finishing funds, he saw the film and responded to it. He told them it'd take him a week to find the cash. As it goes, it took him six months of petitioning financiers. 'He'd show up to screenings and wear a *Suture* T-shirt,' says McGehee. 'He was amazing.' By the time the film made it to Sundance, where it won a Best Cinematography award for Greg Gardiner, it had already shown at Telluride and Toronto. Picking up a distributor at the latter, *Suture* went to Sundance to generate press. 'We didn't love our first experience at Sundance,' says McGehee. 'It was a frustrating festival for us at that point: a competitive atmosphere.'

Yet the festival was 'critical' for their sophomore film, the sublime domestic thriller *The Deep End*, which sold to Fox Searchlight. 'We had a much better time at Sundance then,' notes McGehee. 'The festival felt like it was much better organized and filmmaker-friendly. There's something cyclical about it. It has its ups and downs.' Typical of the difficulties facing Sundance alumni that chose to remain outside the studio system, it took seven years for McGehee and Siegel to get *The Deep End* made. By comparison, their third film, an adaptation of Myla Goldberg's novel *Bee Season* (2005) starring Richard Gere and Juliette Binoche, arrived in half that time – thanks to a continuing relationship with Fox Searchlight. Yet, not unlike its creators, this muddled mix of Kabbalah, kleptomania and spelling contests sat uneasily within its mainstream surroundings.

Lodge Kerrigan, who made his 1994 debut with the equally distinct *Clean, Shaven*, has similarly taken a decade to release three films. An intense, subjective story of a schizophrenic desperately trying to get his daughter back from her adoptive family, *Clean, Shaven* found a novel use for Sundance. 'Two people fainted in two separate screenings,' says Kerrigan, 'so it gained a lot of notoriety right out of the gate.' Following it with 1998's prostitute tale *Claire Dolan*, Kerrigan then endured every filmmaker's nightmare, as his next project, *In God's Hands*, was scrapped after the negative suffered 'extensive negative damage' in the laboratory. Again, it was Soderbergh, an executive producer on the film, who came to the rescue. Encouraging Kerrigan to shoot another movie, it led to *Keane* (2004), a return to the tone and turf of his debut produced under the banner of Soderbergh's Populist Pictures, the production company behind his own movies *The Underneath* and *Full Frontal*.

Yet as Sundance drifted towards the new millennium, its graduates were finding it hard to maintain career momentum. It was all about branding. Unless, like Tarantino or Soderbergh, their debut had made a huge splash, studios and financiers didn't want to know. That's not to say there haven't been subsequent significant arrivals: Edward Burns's *The Brothers McMullen* (1995); Todd Solondz's *Welcome to the Dollhouse* (1996); Kenneth Lonergan's *You Can Count on Me* (2000); Karyn Kusama's *Girlfight* (2000); Henry Bean's *The Believer* (2001) and Shari Springer Berman and Robert Pulcini's *American Splendor* (2003) all won the Grand Jury Prize. But of this group, only Solondz has gone on to achieve anything nearing a career as a working filmmaker. While Bean and Lonergan have always been first and foremost writers, Burns has found more success in front of the camera than behind it. Kusama, took five years to complete her second film, comic book adaptation *Aeon Flux* (2005). Many others fell by the wayside: what, for example, has happened to Tony Bui, whose *Three Seasons* won both the Grand Jury Prize and the Audience Award in 1999?

Sundance, as a festival, still remains the first port of call for anyone keen to launch their film career. As John Sayles says:

There is a phenomenon that you see in a place like the Sundance Film Festival; somebody can go in – they can be working as a bus boy in a hotel or a production assistant at a TV station – and all of a sudden this movie they made on weekends on video gets picked up by a studio and they are transformed. The idea of overnight transformation is a very attractive one to people. If you talk to the people who run the Sundance Film Festival who probably got about 800 feature films this year, they would say about 750 of them were pretty much unwatchable. Right now American independent film is about where novel writing was when I started as a novelist in 1975; every publishing house would get thousands of manuscripts and every once in a while there would be one that was worth reading. Then – even more rare – would be one that was worth publishing. This didn't used to be the case. It just wasn't that accessible. You couldn't just plunk down your credit card and make a feature film, then get it seen by somebody low down at a distribution company.

Even if directors made it past their debut, a Sundance success did not guarantee that studios would automatically respect their vision. Just ask Boaz Yakin. His 1994 Sundance debut was *Fresh*, a tale of a smart African American boy who outmanoeuvres two rival gangs, and it was as original as the title suggested. Of Jewish origin, Yakin admits, 'there were some people who were real mad about a white guy making a black movie', but the Sundance jury saw fit to reward him with the Filmmakers' Trophy for his efforts. Produced by Lawrence Bender, then hot after the success of *Reservoir Dogs*, *Fresh* managed to distinguish itself from the crop of 'hood tales – *Juice*, *Boyz N the Hood*, *Menace II Society* – that found success in the early 1990s.

Yakin followed it with *A Price Above Rubies* (1998) – 'a fable about finding yourself again' – concerning a rebellious woman trapped in a troublesome marriage with a devout Hasidic Jew. It was a subject far closer to his own experience than *Fresh*. While his parents are non-Orthodox Jews, Yakin was educated at an Orthodox school, much to his displeasure. Yet, in a climate not always welcoming to personal vision, he has been forced to become a writer-director for hire. While Yakin started out writing genre pictures – he penned Clint Eastwood's *The Rookie* (1990) – he has come full circle, paying the bills by scripting the likes of *From Dusk Till Dawn 2: Texas Blood Money* (1999) and *Dirty Dancing: Havana Nights* (2004).

Meanwhile, he has found himself directing scripts he didn't write: a true story, *Remember the Titans* (2001) starred Denzel Washington as the first black football coach hired by a Virginia school shortly after racial segregation had come to an end. It took an impressive $115.6 million at the box office, furthering Yakin's reputation as a director interested in exploring issues of race and community. But rather than capitalize on his newfound box office kudos, Yakin directed *Uptown Girls* (2003), a flyweight socialite comedy with Brittany Murphy, that suggested he had arrived at a creative impasse. 'Every time I write a script that I feel shows all the sides of me I can show as a filmmaker, it seems to get shot down pretty quick,' he says. 'And that's very frustrating. It's the nature of American cinema – it's about large, bland, all-inclusive subject matter. Any time you start focusing on the personal – unless you happen to be one of those fortunate dudes like Steven Spielberg, whose personal vision happens to be commercial – it's very, very difficult to get your stuff out there.'

Which might be why Bryan Singer has proved so successful. More than any other director of his age, Singer, unconsciously or otherwise, has fashioned his career in the footsteps of his idol Steven Spielberg. While Steven Soderbergh was blown away when he saw *Jaws* as a twelve-year-old, a similar thing happened to Singer when he hit sixteen. Emerging from a showing of *E.T. the Extra-Terrestrial* (1982) in his hometown of Princeton, New Jersey, he realized his true calling. 'He was this Jewish kid like me. He lived in New Jersey for a while. He had a drawer full of 8 mm films like me. And I thought, "I make these films for fun – why don't I do it for a living, like Mr Spielberg?" I remember walking home to my house in the middle of the night feeling like, "Wow – if nothing else, I've decided what I want to do with my life." Even if I wasn't successful, I knew I would always make films.'[16]

His upbringing uncannily mirrored that of Spielberg. Singer, who had enjoyed taking photographs as a boy, began making 8 mm films in his teens, shot with a friend's camera. Likewise, the Arizona-raised Spielberg was designated his family's official filmmaker, since his father was not very good with their camera. As a boy scout, Spielberg worked on a merit badge in photography and shot a three-minute movie called *Gunsmog*. If one thing differs between them, it's their education. Singer, after attending the School of Visual Arts in New York, headed to Los Angeles and enrolled at the USC School of Cinema-Television, earning a degree in critical film studies. Spielberg was twice turned down entry into the same college and ultimately settled for California State University, only to drop out later.

Singer's rise through the ranks would closely emulate that of Spielberg. His 1993 debut, *Public Access*, was not unlike Spielberg's own first film, *Duel* (1971), notably in terms of the pared-down style, as well as the rapid shooting schedule (eighteen days compared to twenty-three days for Spielberg's film). Both followed their debuts with a critical – rather than commercial – success: respectively, *The Usual Suspects* and *The Sugarland Express* (1974). At this point, Spielberg experienced two monster hits – *Jaws* and *Close Encounters of the Third Kind* (1977), followed by his first flop, *1941* (1979), which took in just $34 million compared to the box office records set by the previous two films. Singer did it the other way round – *Apt Pupil* taking just $8 million before his two *X-Men* films collectively grossed over $370 million in the U.S. alone.

An atmospheric examination of the negative effects of mass media, *Public Access* is as frustrating as it is inspired. Like some of its recent Sundance predecessors, the film begins with the arrival in town of a man destined to upset the status quo. But unlike *sex, lies, and videotape* or *The Unbelievable Truth*, this is not the return of a past resident, but the advent of a stranger with no discernible history. Cut with slow-motion shots of the idyllic small town of Brewster bathed in autumnal bliss – recalling the sunny opening to the town in David Lynch's *Blue Velvet* – the low-key entrance of Whiley Pritcher (Ron Marquette) disguises the disturbing events he will set in motion. Only when he rents a room from a grizzly former mayor named Bob Hodges (Burt Williams), a man obsessed with alien activity, does the film obliquely foreshadow the changes to come. Playing on a television set in the background is a nature program detailing the evolution of the butterfly; Whiley goes through a similar transformation, albeit in reverse, as he sheds his skin to reveal something a mite uglier.

The film shared the Grand Jury Prize with Victor Nunez's *Ruby in Paradise*. Nunez might well feel aggrieved that he was not the outright winner. His coming of age story examined the American Dream with a subtlety far beyond what Singer was then capable of achieving. A seasoned, sensitive and literate Florida-set drama that gave Ashley Judd her first major lead as a runaway who seeks independence and finds it working in a beach-side store, it bears out the line from an Emily Dickinson poem read by Ruby, that 'to ache is human'. Shorn of the edgy, detached cool that was beginning to dominate U.S. independent films, its Sundance triumph was an aberration.

The other significant arrival of the time – David O. Russell – won the Audience Award the following year for his debut, *Spanking the Monkey*. Like Soderbergh, Russell drew attention to his first film with a lurid-sounding title (slang for masturbation). But shot by Michael Mayers in muted tones of blue, grey and black – a reflection of the muddied psychological states of the characters – the story is never sensationalized. Of a similar scope to *Public Access*, the film is set in a small Connecticut town. Raymond Aibelli (Jeremy Davies), a medical student, is emotionally blackmailed into passing up a summer internship at the Surgeon General's office to look after his mother (Alberta Watson), who has suffered a complex leg fracture. With his philandering salesman father (Benjamin Hendrickson) away on business, Raymond – unable to consummate a relationship with a local girl named Toni – becomes an Oedipal wreck as he and his mother edge past physical boundaries they were never meant to cross. It was as if Russell took the immortal opening line 'They fuck you up, your mum and dad' from Philip Larkin's poem 'This Be the Verse' to its logical conclusion.

Russell, in some ways, is diametrically opposed to a director like Singer. He would certainly not put Spielberg at the top of his list of mentors. Referring to Mike Nichols's *Carnal Knowledge*, Hal Ashby's *Harold and Maude* (1971), Bob Rafelson's *Five Easy Pieces* (1970) and *The King of Marvin Gardens* (1972), Russell once said his 'goal' is 'to make films like that again'.[17] With Russell desperate to fashion a return to the taboo-busting psychodramas of New Hollywood, *Spanking the Monkey* was a good start. He cites Nichols as a major influence; his film certainly examines sex in society with the same morose humour Nichols used in *Carnal Knowledge* – notably in the early scenes where Raymond is trying to masturbate but is repeatedly interrupted by the family dog. The film also shadows the plot of Nichols's *The Graduate* (1967) to an alarming degree, as youthful ambition is crushed by the older generation. 'I don't think that the parents of our generation were very interested in their kids,' says Russell. 'I think they were interested in what their kids represented in terms of potential and kudos and achievement.'[18]

Those offended by *Spanking the Monkey* should blame Gus Van Sant. Russell, who wrote the script while on jury duty, followed the Portland filmmaker's lead when deciding upon what subject to make a splash with for his debut. Impressed by the way Van Sant had delved into 'the more unseemly sides of his psyche'[19] for his own debut, *Mala Noche* (1985), Russell dared himself to do the same and write a black fantasy. He had just broken up with a long-term girlfriend at the time, and found himself in a surly mood. What spilled out of him was pure acid, a complex scenario that reflected his own upbringing, in anger if not in actuality.

Born in New York in 1958, Russell was not a film-school graduate; instead, he studied English and political science at Amherst College in Massachusetts, where he wrote his dissertation on the coup that overthrew Salvador Allende in Chile. For five years after college, following a brief spell in Nicaragua in 1981, he worked as a political activist in New England – chiefly union work and teaching literacy to labour groups in Boston – before the need to make a video documenting poor housing conditions in the area brought him to filmmaking. 'It was for better housing in a mill town in Maine, where there are a lot of tenements,' he explains. 'That's where I first used video equipment to document these tenements, then we presented it to the town council and they all got fixed up. They came down on the slumlords.'

At the same time, Russell was working on a film about an émigré from Central America and his experiences in Boston, which left him broke and heading for burnout. Returning to New York, not far from his Long Island upbringing, he attempted to make ends meet with a variety of jobs – working for a publisher, teaching and even, he claims, being a waiter at a Kennedy wedding. While admitting he had 'never intended' to be a filmmaker, following his documentary work, Russell began in his late twenties to make fictional shorts, the first being *Bingo Inferno*, about an insurrection in a bingo hall. Three years later, in 1990, he made *Hairway to the Stars*, detailing the grandiose fantasies of an old woman under a hairdryer. Both would quickly establish Russell's dry and irreverent sense of humour, but this did not fully emerge until *Spanking the Monkey*, made when he was thirty-five.

Like Russell, Singer also cut his teeth on short films. While at USC, he wrote and directed a twenty-five-minute short called *Lion's Den* for the paltry sum of $15,000. Funded by family, friends, credit cards and childhood friend/lead actor Ethan Hawke, the film was eventually shown to Hollywood insiders at an event hosted by Sam Raimi, after USC refused to admit it to their First Look screening program. Co-starring Brandon Boyce – who went on to feature in *Public Access* and later to write the script for Singer's *Apt Pupil* – the film concerns five guys who reconvene at their old hang-out after their first semester at college and realize they have grown apart. Hawke, already a teen star thanks to Joe Dante's *Explorers* (1985), agreed to feature in it during the time he was making *Dad* with Jack Lemmon. Singer, after being plied with gin from a neighbouring liquor store, also appeared on camera, a feat he did not repeat until his fan boy cameo in *Star Trek: Nemesis* (2002).

Most significantly, the project marked Singer's first collaboration with John Ottman, one of the key figures in his development as a filmmaker. Ottman, who became Singer's regular editor and composer, co-directed *Lion's Den*, as well as editing it (in his living room) and creating the sound design. The film generated enough interest to afford Singer various meetings across town, all of which were entirely fruitless. Looking abroad for funding instead, Singer came into contact with a Japanese company, the Tokuma Corporation, which had set up a program called Cinebeam to award six directors from anywhere in the world $250,000 each to make a movie. Partly due to *Lion's Den*'s casting of Hawke – now under the spotlight with the arrival of *Dead Poets Society* (1989) – Singer was one of the chosen six.

Public Access was a steep learning curve for Singer who experienced numerous problems on set, partly because he was using cheap equipment to shoot the film. Difficulties in post-production meant that the film missed the Tokyo International Film Festival, where it was due to be unveiled, though ironically this left the way open for an appearance at Sundance. Even now, Singer is well aware of the debt he owes the festival.

> I was talking to Robert Redford the other day, and I realized that while so much of my fan-ship towards him is for his work, I also owe my career to him and Sundance. Mind you, you go there and it's like a transplanting of Hollywood. It's a big business now. It's like the Academy Awards a little. Whether you agree with the selection of the films, whether you think they're over-hyped or not hyped enough, it does bring attention to films that may not get that kind of attention. It'll make some guy in Middle America say 'Oh, *sex, lies and what? The Pianist?* Hmm. Maybe I'll go see it.'

One of Singer's main problems with *Public Access* was that the composer originally hired dropped out shortly into the editing period. Ottman, already on board to cut the film, stepped in. Noting that his work on the film doomed him to a future of being hired to compose 'sinister, dark, creepy, brooding, depressing music', Ottman had already been dabbling with some second-hand music equipment he had bought when *Public Access* came about. If the film is ultimately more of a mood piece, relying on ambience rather than answers, this is thanks chiefly to the contribution of Ottman, who manages to achieve a neat symbiosis between sound and vision. Again recalling the work of David Lynch, his innovative use of sound, in particular, helped foster an eerie atmosphere of impending dread, such as in the lengthy tracking shot of Whiley in the television station which is accompanied by a shiver-inducing wind on the soundtrack.

Spanking the Monkey's production history was equally tortuous. For three months, New Line optioned the film, which put Russell under a whole new set of pressures – from numerous rewrites to finding a famous cast. This latter demand proved a virtual impossibility, given that the writer-director was unknown and the material wasn't exactly wholesome. Having touted it around unsuccessfully at other studios, it did at least open a few doors for Russell – including a writing job for Fox TV on a comedy pilot that never saw the light of day.

Ironically, after its Sundance success, the film would be distributed by New Line's subsidiary, Fine Line, but only after Russell had made it the hard way. After gaining just under $50,000 in grants from groups including the National Endowment for the Arts (NEA), Russell and producer Dean Silvers set about badgering everyone they knew for cash – asking for minimum investments of $1,500, with a maximum potential return of five times this figure. Using leftover film stock, barter deals were also struck – for example, the motel in the film was given for free in exchange for Russell making them a promotional video. Buckeye Entertainment provided $100,000 of finishing funds, once the film was in the can. The film grossed $1.3 million in the U.S., enough to keep everyone involved happy – except the NEA. On seeing the finished product, they demanded their money back – not wanting federal funds attached to something that could be perceived as anti-family.

Despite winning the Grand Jury Prize, Singer's film made even less money. In his review, *Variety*'s Todd McCarthy summed it up with typical insight: '[*Public Access*] is serious-minded and bounces around some provocative ideas, but is vague about such important matters as key story points, motivation and overriding theme. Commercial prospects look very iffy, although this will clearly lead to other work for its director.' So 'iffy' were the film's prospects in the marketplace that it only received a cursory U.S. release after the success of *The Usual Suspects*. Yet, as predicted by McCarthy, the film did act as a significant stepping stone; Kevin Spacey reputedly saw it and decided he wanted to work with Singer on *The Usual Suspects*.

The film also saw Singer's first professional collaboration with screen-writer Christopher McQuarrie, who co-wrote the script with him and Michael Feit Dougan, who had met the director at the USC Cinema-Television program. McQuarrie knew Singer from high school. They teamed up after the latter graduated, Singer initially adapting a short story by the budding writer. While Singer bounced between colleges, McQuarrie disappeared to Australia to work part-time as an assistant teacher, then returned to work for his uncle in a detective agency. Not as glamorous as it sounds: he spent most of his time guarding a cinema in New Jersey – though it did give him ample opportunity to watch audience reactions and study posters and trailers. After the job fizzled out, McQuarrie was about to join the police academy when Singer called from L.A. wanting him to collaborate on a feature-length screenplay. By this time, Singer had also met Kenneth Kokin, who was to produce *Public Access* and later co-produce *The Usual Suspects*.

As in both *The Usual Suspects* and *Apt Pupil* – with their respective stories detailing a master criminal playing a helpless cripple and a former Nazi masquerading as the old man next door – *Public Access* deals with the notion of 'people not always being what they seem', as Singer puts it. Openly gay, Singer understands this notion only too well. After settling in, Whiley heads to the local public access television station to set up a phone-in program entitled *Our Town*. Swapping his comfortable cable-knit sweaters for a dapper suit, the bespectacled Whiley asks the simple question: 'What's wrong with Brewster?' At first, callers are content to grouch about their neighbours, but it's enough to set the town awash with malicious gossip. As if lifting a stone to reveal a squirming mass of insects, Singer exposes the ugliness that simmers beneath the surface of what Whiley calls a perfect 'nuclear community'.

In what can be taken as its critique of the Reagan era, and the greed, hypocrisy and anti-humanism that it ushered into America, the film is intent on showing how the media has become a means to distort – as well as convey – the truth. As we learn from the librarian Rachel (Dina Brooks), who anonymously calls Whiley's program before later striking up a romance with him, the town is full of 'ignorant people' willing to 'look in the other direction'. The example she cites is of her former teacher Jeff Abernathy, unfairly dismissed from his position, she alleges, because he was thought to be gay. When Abernathy (Larry Maxwell) later arrives at the Founders' Day Celebrations, he interrupts proceedings with accusations that the town's current mayor, Tom Breyer (Charles Kavanaugh), is driving Brewster towards the brink of destruction, having convinced local financiers to invest in floundering company Gemini Electronics. As he later says to Whiley, in what must be a nod to Michael Moore's notorious documentary *Roger and Me* (1989): 'In six months' time, Brewster will make Flint, Michigan, look like a teeming Metropolis.'

While Singer thus obliquely tackled social politics in his debut, it was, ironically, Russell who embraced the subject fully as his career developed. But at this stage of his career, Russell was dealing with sexual rather than social politics. Compared to *Public Access*, the story of *Spanking the Monkey* was all about implosion of the family unit. Russell pushes the boundaries of taboo subject matter – though he argued that the Oedipal transgression that acts as the point of no return is just one of many taboos in the film. Washing and massaging his mother, even carrying her to the toilet, Raymond's actions are incestuous long before incest becomes a reality. They lie on the bed, watching TV, drinking vodka shots and unnervingly laugh like lovers would. Having spent his lifetime living out his mother's unfulfilled expectations, Raymond's ultimate transgression is entirely in keeping with this, as he gives his mother the husband that she doesn't have. 'Take good care of your mother,' he's told – and he does.

If anything, *Spanking the Monkey* – reminding us of the destructive nature of sex while Raymond writes a paper on current HIV policy – is an extreme rites of passage tale, dealing with the loss of innocence which occurs not because Raymond has sex with his mother but because he realizes that adulthood brings no answers. 'Can't change people after a certain age,' his mother tells him. 'What's the point in living then?' he counters. Raymond realizes what he does is wrong: he escapes from his mother's bedroom window to avoid detection; he vigorously scrubs himself, as if he feels sullied. But by the end, he is as confused an adolescent as you're ever likely to meet. 'What is weird?' he pleads. 'Tell me what is weird.'

Despite its title, Singer's film provides us less access to its lead than Russell's does. We are forced to rely on brief glimpses, such as observing Whiley's downtime, as he lies on his bed, arms behind his head, listening to the strains of a record from downstairs. As the camera crawls up his body, the sounds change into a high-pitched whine – a brief insight into Whiley's own disturbed psyche. A dream sequence soon follows, brilliantly cut together by Ottman, who knits the montage with the same dexterity he would demonstrate in the finale of *The Usual Suspects*. The spine of it is the discovery of a body by a railway line, with a silhou-etted figure moving towards us holding a flashlight. By the time this is repeated, cut with an episode of *Our Town* and bleeding into the Found-ers' Day Celebrations, we begin to suspect that Whiley is psychotic – a fact confirmed later, as he dispatches first Jeff and then Rachel.

Like the framed photograph in his room that suggests a past but does not reveal it, Whiley's reasons for arriving in Brewster are hinted at but ultimately not revealed. 'The truth – that's what I came here for,' he tells Jeff, with missionary zeal. But by the time he leaves, on the same road he came in on, we are no wiser as to why he was there. If anything, the character of Whiley is a cipher, an empty vessel with no discernible personality (embodied excellently by Marquette's unnerv-ingly bland performance). Is he an instrument of Mayor Breyer? The fact that before Whiley's departure Breyer is the final guest on his show – Ottman's score drowns out their words but we assume it's a blatant PR exercise – points to this. Or, in a society where political parties, corporations and the media work together in ugly harness, are he and his murderous actions symbolic of the ruthless capitalist ethos on show? Certainly, Singer allows the audience room to ascribe their own theories to Whiley's role in the film, a device he would repeat with the mysterious figure of Keyser Soze in *The Usual Suspects*.

What Singer and his co-writers failed to do, however, was prevent the audience from tripping over various narrative holes – such as Whiley killing Jeff with no consideration for the fingerprints he will leave in the house. Unlike *The Usual Suspects*, which only reveals itself as an elaborate shaggy-dog story in the final minutes, *Public Access* has us asking questions from the middle act. By the end, the lack of concrete answers proves more frustrating than enlightening.

But whatever your view, *Public Access*, like *Spanking the Monkey*, undeniably points to the changing face of Sundance. Like *Clerks*, an-other talk-is-cheap effort, *Spanking the Monkey* was all about pushing boundaries and buttons. Little wonder it won the Audience Award: it was just the kind of film Sundance was invented for. By taking a share of the Grand Jury Prize, however, the flawed *Public Access* reflected how often the festival would be faced with lauding the best of a bad bunch. While the jury managed to give Singer a leg-up, winning such a prize had lost its kudos – as the delayed distribution of the film showed. Just ask Steven Soderbergh: while Sundance was faltering, its original Kid was having a difficult time outside of the confines of the festival.

CHAPTER 5

'Trespassing on Hallowed Ground': *Kafka* and *King of the Hill*

6 Jesse Bradford as Aaron in *King of the Hill*.

I write by myself, for myself.
Franz Kafka, *Kafka*

'It was like being manager of The Doors in 1967,'[20] noted Pat Dollard, Soderbergh's agent, in the aftermath of *sex, lies, and videotape*. While Soderbergh was never in danger of succumbing to rock star arrogance, he had no intentions of echoing the likes of Hartley and Stillman by remaining a festival director. From the beginning, he set his sights on Hollywood. With Bryan Singer and David O. Russell following in his footsteps, Sundance was, for Soderbergh, a springboard to bigger things.

The film world at his feet, Soderbergh witnessed the great and the good knocking at his door with offers of work. Before he knew where he was, he was in the middle of a tug of war between two old friends, Robert Redford and Sydney Pollack. When a producer with a development deal at Redford's company, Wildwood, approached him, claiming that the Sundance founder wanted to work with him, Soderbergh suggested A. E. Hotchner's memoir *King of the Hill*, a book he had loved for years.

He did much the same when he met with Pollack, this time pointing to William Brinkley's novel *The Last Ship*, set aboard a destroyer in the wake of a nuclear holocaust. 'I really wanted to do it,' says Pollack. 'I thought it was a great idea. It reminded me of Stanley Kramer's *On the Beach*, when there was a submarine that surfaces after an atomic war.' While Pollack busied himself successfully pitching the apocalyptic idea to Universal, Soderbergh, as if to complicate matters, also received a call from Mark Johnson at Baltimore Pictures, Barry Levinson's company. The young director suggested they might make *Kafka*, a script by Lem Dobbs that Dollard had given him as an example of good screenwriting technique.

But, with Soderbergh intent on making the projects in the order in which he received them, *The Last Ship* – a 650-page doorstop of a book – came first. Until, that is, the Berlin Wall fell. Published just a year before, in 1988, Brinkley's book – at least as far as a movie adaptation went – suddenly felt as outdated as Communism itself. 'It seemed to be irrelevant,' remarks Soderbergh, who nonetheless claims to have been happy with the screenplay he'd written.[21] With *The Last Ship* sunk, Soderbergh turned his attention to *Kafka*, much to Redford's chagrin. The son of acclaimed painter R. B. Kitaj, Dobbs wrote the script in 1980, long before Soderbergh was on the scene. He originally intended to pen an expressionistic horror film, then got to thinking of Prague as the setting before finally settling on naming the protagonist after that city's most famous literary son.

Set in 1919, *Kafka* is not a biopic in the traditional sense. Not unlike David Cronenberg's version of William Burroughs's *Naked Lunch*, also released in 1991, it takes excerpts from the writer's life and blends them with elements of his fiction.

Wrapped inside a mystery cum horror plot are off-the-cuff references to Kafka's work such as 'In the Penal Colony' and 'The Metamorphosis'. Then there are the biographical snippets, from his ailing relationship with his father, to his abandoned engagement, to the consumption that killed him. While Soderbergh fined crew members ten Czech crowns every time they used the word 'Kafkaesque', Dobbs's script is just that. Evoking themes pertinent to Kafka's oeuvre, from alienation to the crushing of the individual by tyrannical bureaucracy, it succeeds in creating a heightened version of the oppressive atmosphere that can be sensed behind the author's touchstone novels *The Trial* and *The Castle*.

Played by an ashen-faced Jeremy Irons, who was just about to win an Oscar for his role in *Reversal of Fortune* (1990), this fictionalized version of Kafka is put at the centre of a paranoid conspiracy plot. It begins when his friend Raban receives a state summons to the ominous nearby Castle, the local government stronghold, but fails to return from the appointment. A lowly insurance clerk, but with a burgeoning reputation as a writer, Kafka is soon accosted by Raban's former lover, Gabriela (Theresa Russell), who tries to convince him to join a group of anarchists with a view to writing propaganda for them. While he refuses the offer, it sets him on a path of discovery that takes him inside the Castle and into the heart of a series of genetic experiments conducted by the ruthless Dr Murnau (Ian Holm) on luckless locals from a rural mining community.

With a budget of $11 million, much of the cash went on a series of lavish sets – such as the wall of man-sized filing cabinets in the Castle and Dr Murnau's elaborate lab – created by the production designer Gavin Bocquet. No wonder Soderbergh said it was 'the size of the toy-set' that was part of the appeal in directing the script. 'I did like the idea of working on a larger canvas. From the very beginning, I've always felt it was as important not to repeat your successes as it was to not repeat your mistakes. Absolutely, I wanted to make a movie that was in direct opposition to the one I'd just made. I've always said to some degree that whatever you're working on should annihilate what you'd done before.'

Kafka, as far removed from the psychosexual territory of *sex, lies, and videotape* as you could get, certainly did that. Shot in black and white, and partly designed to pay aesthetic tribute to a number of films from Carol Reed's *The Third Man* (1949) to Terry Gilliam's *Brazil* and those of the German Expressionism movement, Soderbergh's film was practically inviting the inevitable critical backlash for 'trespassing on hallowed ground', as he puts it. 'I knew that I was due, because the response to *sex, lies* . . . was out of proportion to what the film was, a certain amount of trimming. Why not just get it all out of the way at once by working on a piece of material that provided an opportunity for a lot of people who write about movies to show how smart they are? I just thought, "Let's get it over with. Put a big bullseye on my back and let everybody shoot, and then I can move on."'

And shoot they did, offering a reception as nightmarish as anything Kafka could have envisaged. 'An exercise in style that, unfortunately, displays more energy than inspiration,' said one of the kinder reviews, by Peter Travers in *Rolling Stone*. 'Given the film's potential, it's crushing to watch it dwindle down to a conventional horror film . . . where Cronenberg succeeds in conveying the interior mind, Soderbergh stays disappointingly on the surface.'[22] Set in the year of release of Robert Wiene's *The Cabinet of Dr. Caligari*, there's no doubt *Kafka* can be accused of playing spot the reference. The script names Holm's doctor after pioneering director F. W. Murnau, the man behind the Expressionist classic *Nosferatu* (1922), and even nods to that film's vampire, by naming a location 'Orlac'. With the vast office where Kafka works recalling a similar set in Orson Welles's version of *The Trial* (1962), itself indebted to German Expressionism, Soderbergh is, as he admits, 'aping some well-worn styles'.

Steered by Dobbs's script, Soderbergh does manage to capture the blend of the macabre and the surreal that dominated the films of Murnau and Wiene. Courtesy of Walt Lloyd's coal-black cinematography, Prague's cobbled streets and Gothic architecture are made all the more malevolent and intimidating, cloaking the film in an air of dread and uncertainty. Rather like the performances, which veer between idiosyncrasy and naturalism, the landscape sways between historical accuracy and the unreal horrors of Kafka's fiction. With its disorienting lopsided angles accentuating the sense of unease, it's a twilight world – not unlike those created by the German Expressionists – that hovers in the shadows of reality. These are streets filled with paranoia, conspiracy and suspicion. However pretentious it might be to reference the likes of Murnau, it can't be denied that Dobbs's initial intention of placing Kafka alongside an artistic movement that not only was alive at the same time as the writer but bore resemblance to his work was sound.

Just as *Schizopolis*, Soderbergh's Richard Lester–inspired comedy, deals with the notion of industrial espionage, so *Kafka* has its snitches in the workplace. With his black book to record misdemeanours, office spy Burgel (played by Joel Grey, who originally inspired Dobbs when creating the character) is the official Castle tattletale. But one could easily suspect any of Kafka's superiors – notably Alec Guinness's nicely understated chief clerk, who calls Kafka 'a lone wolf' and says his solitary nature makes him 'uneasy'. With its dark alleyways plastered with posters of watchful eyes recalling Cold War paranoia, the film chillingly reminds us of the Eastern bloc's once-strong totalitarian regime. This is made explicit when Kafka confronts Murnau. 'What will you say when the great faceless crowd comes along?' he asks. 'Oh, a crowd is easier to control than an individual,' replies Murnau.

Kafka's obsession with interest in Raban's disappearance prefigures *The Limey*, Soderbergh's next collaboration with Lem Dobbs in which Terence Stamp's gangster attempts to find out the truth behind the death of his daughter. But *Kafka* also bears relation to numerous 'missing person' thrillers, most notably Alfred Hitchcock's *The Lady Vanishes* (1938), in which Margaret Lockwood attempts to find a governess who disappears at the outset of a train journey. It also recalls the aforementioned *The Third Man*, in which Joseph Cotten's pulp writer attempts to learn the truth behind the 'death' of his friend Harry Lime in a Vienna draped in as much shadow as Kafka's Prague; there's also a nod to *Brazil* and Hitchcock's *North by Northwest* (1959) – films in which an innocent protagonist is accused of terrorist or espionage activities.

Despite the potential pitfalls of a script that obviously lacked commercial viability, such was the confidence imbued in Soderbergh by *sex, lies, and videotape* that nothing would deter him. 'I know it sounds crazy, but I thought a lot of people would go see *Kafka* when I made it,' he says. In reality, it barely scraped over $1 million in the U.S. Soderbergh was unhappy with the end result. 'The shoot on *Kafka* was difficult and the whole process was hard for me,' he says.

> I walked away from it feeling like I didn't really find the tone that I was looking for. I mean, I learned a lot. As you do, when you make things that don't turn out the way you want them to. As a piece of filmmaking, it was a good thing for me to go and do. It was a much more physically complicated movie than *sex, lies* . . . All the reasons for doing it held up. It was an important part of my development. But its lack of a consistent tone is a sign of my age at the time and my inexperience. It's something I thought about a lot, coming out of that film.[23]

Upon reflection, Soderbergh wishes he'd made the film after he reinvigorated his career with *Schizopolis*, with its madcap energy gleaned from Richard Lester's Beatles films, *A Hard Day's Night* (1964) and *Help!* (1965). 'All I can say is, I wish I'd directed *Kafka* after that break, because I think I could've made it a lot more exciting and a lot more fun. To have employed a style of shooting that was much freer, and not so classical, would've resulted in a much more interesting movie. If I'd shot *Kafka* like *A Hard Day's Night*, a lot more people would be talking about it. Black-and-white, hand-held, for a film set in 1919 would've been a really interesting choice.'

Still, there are some sublime elements of *Kafka* to enjoy, notably Cliff Martinez's Middle European–flavoured score that recalled Anton Karas's famous zither composition for *The Third Man*. Using silent-film organ music, Martinez also sampled a gypsy instrument known as the cymbalom that Soderbergh first heard in a Prague restaurant. Learning to play the cymbalom on an electronic drum kit – his time as a drummer with the Red Hot Chili Peppers coming in handy – is the perfect example of how the chameleon-like Martinez operates. 'I'll usually come in with some reference point and say, "Try this,"' notes Soderbergh. 'He'll immerse himself in whatever style you want him to approximate.'

Then there's the audacious switch from black and white into colour, as Kafka enters the Castle. Reminiscent of the switch from sepia to colour in Andrei Tarkovsky's *Stalker* (1979), as the trio of protagonists enter the forbidden Zone, it's as if our hero has opened his eyes to a wider world. Although this was not in Dobbs's script, Soderbergh notes it was 'something we knew we were going to do early on, before we'd even started designing the movie'. It remains the film's standout moment. 'I think it could be read in any number of ways,' says Soderbergh. 'I was basically following *The Wizard of Oz* model. You could make the argument that he is either awakened, in some new way, or is in fact going further into a dream.'

If the denouement, when Kafka discovers Murnau's experiments, belongs to another, altogether more mainstream film, at least their resulting fight is played out on one of the oddest playgrounds you'll ever see. The men clash on top of a gigantic microscope – made from a plexiglass lens some twenty-four feet in diameter – that magnifies a particularly gruesome sight, the top of an exposed brain ready to be experimented upon. Rather like the deformed maniac who drifts in and out of the script, even attacking Kafka at one point, it's a visual reminder of Murnau's scientific experiments. With shades of Charlie Chaplin's *Modern Times* (1936), the film is ultimately a critique of scientific engineering and mismanagement. As Murnau says to Kafka, 'You are at the very forefront of what is modern – you write about it. Unlike you, though, I have chosen to embrace it.'

Although a little too in love with its multitude of conceits and ideas, the film certainly hints at Soderbergh's potential for diversity. Setting up a theme he would return to – namely, the abuse of corporate power, as seen in *Schizopolis* and his legal drama *Erin Brockovich* – it also was an early example of Soderbergh's ability to draw together a cultured ensemble cast. Arguably, it remains one of Soderbergh's most technically accomplished and aesthetically unified films.

In retrospect, you can see why Soderbergh related to a figure like Dobbs's Kafka. With *King of the Hill* set to be his next major project, he was about to enter the Hollywood Castle, a place of paranoia and suspicion, where films and scripts are mutated and experimented upon. The lone wolf was about to witness his nightmares come true.

All the important stuff can't be taught.

Aaron, *King of the Hill*

Before starting *King of the Hill*, Soderbergh agreed to direct an episode of *Fallen Angels*, a Showtime film noir–inspired series with Sydney Pollack as executive producer and other episodes directed by the likes of Tom Cruise, Peter Bogdanovich and Kiefer Sutherland. Soderbergh's contribution, 'The Quiet Room', was taken from a Frank E. Smith short story that first appeared in the crime magazine *Manhunt* in 1953. Starring Joe Mantegna as a sadistic, corrupt cop in the LAPD, it also reunited Soderbergh with Peter Gallagher, prior to their collaboration on *The Underneath* (see Chapter 8). Buoyed by the piece's reception – co-star Bonnie Bedelia received an Emmy nomination – Soderbergh directed a second episode in 1995, in the series's second season. Called 'The Professional Man', it was again taken from a Howard Rodman adaptation of a short story – this time by David Goodis – from *Manhunt*. In yet another example of Soderbergh's love for the crime genre, in particular the theme of dissecting male relationships, it starred a young Brendan Fraser as Johnny Lamb, a hitman cum elevator attendant who has to confront his conscience when sent on a job. It was a feeling Soderbergh himself would come to know all too well, though there was little in the way of a crisis of conscience for him when it came to *King of the Hill*.

His most conventional narrative to date, it seemed in many ways like a safe option for Soderbergh after the shelling he received on *Kafka*. 'It was something that would push me but not break me,' he concedes. 'But I was trying to set challenges for myself. I'd always heard it was tough to get good performances out of kids. I thought, "Here's a great opportunity for me to work with child actors and see if that's something I'm capable of or not." Throughout this period, after *sex, lies* . . . I was realizing how many mistakes the success of a movie like that would buy me. I was very anxious to take advantage of that and try some stuff.'

Set in 1933 in Depression-era Missouri, not so far from where Soderbergh grew up, *King of the Hill* deals with a time his own father knew well, having written books on the music of the period. Just as he related to Kafka, Soderbergh – who confesses to often spending time alone in his room as a child with just his fertile imagination for company – recognized himself in the young boy at the centre of the story.

Twelve-year-old Aaron Kurlander (Jesse Bradford) – through whose eyes it is seen – is, like the quartet of characters in *sex, lies, and videotape*, estranged from his feelings. Living with his family in a dingy room at the dilapidated Empire Hotel in St Louis, he finds he is unable to connect emotionally with his salesman father (Jeroen Krabbé) or mentally fragile mother (Lisa Eichhorn).

With the threat of eviction constantly hanging over his head, Aaron does what he can to help make ends meet, whether it's creating soup for his father with water and ketchup or devising a scheme to breed and sell canaries. Yet he is soon fending for himself after his younger brother Sullivan is sent away to live with relatives, his father forced to travel out of state for work and his mother committed to a sanatorium. With just kindly street thief Lester (Adrien Brody) and fellow hotel dweller Mr Mungo (Spalding Gray) on his side, Aaron must live by his wits alone, as he tries to keep the family's remaining possessions from being confiscated by the hotel's unscrupulous bellhop. Telling his mother 'everything is fine' when he visits her, he becomes the glue that holds the family together – only finding respite in his vivid fantasies. Claiming to his school friends that his parents are archaeologists who have gone missing, his flights of fancy must've appealed to Soderbergh's inner child.

While it would be warmly received by the critics, *King of the Hill* was overshadowed by Michael Caton-Jones's *This Boy's Life*, which came out four months earlier in April 1993, just as *Kafka* suffered by comparison to *Naked Lunch*. Like Soderbergh's film, *This Boy's Life* was an unsentimental true-life memoir (by writer Tobias Wolff) seen through the eyes of a child. But *This Boy's Life* had the not inconsiderable bonus of starring Leonardo DiCaprio – opposite Robert De Niro – in his breakthrough role. Not that Soderbergh's child star, Jesse Bradford, was any chump. Only thirteen when he worked with Soderbergh, he had appeared with De Niro in his 1984 screen debut *Falling in Love*, before playing screen son to both Harrison Ford, in *Presumed Innocent* (1990), and James Woods, in the TV movie *The Boys* (1991). 'He was one of these kids who could do anything,' notes Soderbergh. 'He was so technically gifted. There were some very elaborate, multiple marks in the film that he'd have to hit, which he did with no problem.' Upon feasting his eyes on the impossibly good-looking Bradford, Hotchner famously said, 'If I'd looked like that I would have had a lot less trouble in my life.'

Like Bradford, *King of the Hill* was a handsome beast, thanks chiefly to the golden-brown cinematography by Elliot Davis, in the first of four collaborations with Soderbergh. Davis studied the paintings of Edward Hopper for inspiration, but eschewed looking at other films – with the exception of John Ford's version of John Steinbeck's *The Grapes of Wrath* (1940). However, as with *Kafka*, Soderbergh again walked away unsatisfied. 'I think it's a film other people like more than I do. I mean, I like it but I just wish it had been tougher. It's too beautiful! Elliot Davis is a very gifted cinematographer and I had a great time working with him. He has a certain style he brings to the table. I think the film is really beautiful and well-crafted. It tries to be as unflinching as possible in its portrayal of his situation, but I wish it had been more Rossellini and less me!'

In the past, Soderbergh has also noted that he wished to capture the feeling of a François Truffaut or Vittorio De Sica movie. His unobtrusive direction, building momentum via the gradual accumulation of emotional and physical detail rather than heading towards dramatic peaks, goes some way towards achieving this. But despite Soderbergh's desire to emulate some of Europe's greatest directors, the film is one of the most quintessentially American in his canon, certainly when put next to *sex, lies, and videotape* and *Kafka*. At the time, Soderbergh said this was part of the appeal, a way to strip himself of his obsession with Michelangelo Antonioni, which had dominated his debut.

If the end result superficially bears similarity to Rob Reiner's film of pubescent friendship, *Stand by Me* (1986), as well as recalling the fiction of Mark Twain, it strains against nostalgia with a succession of scenes that depict the harsh reality of both the period and Aaron's struggles. As Soderbergh puts it, 'It's a movie about survival' – although many don't make it. Illness dominates the film, from Aaron's mother's nervous breakdown to the epileptic fits suffered by Ella, the young girl who lives in the same hotel. Nearly everyone Aaron befriends meets an unhappy fate. Lester is beaten by the cops and arrested during a riot, while the eccentric burn-out Mr Mungo winds up slitting his wrists. Sandoz, another hotel occupant, is locked out of his room for non-payment, and later spotted by Aaron, now destitute and living in Hooverville on the outskirts of the town. The same fate haunts Aaron. Abandoned by those closest to him, he is reduced to eating magazine pictures of food in order to fool the hunger pangs. By the time Aaron starts hallucinating, crying in bewilderment at his situation and enduring a feverish nightmare full of the faces he has met, you are willing Soderbergh to deliver a happy ending.

This he does, unashamedly, with the return of Sullivan, quickly followed by the boys' parents. 'I knew you could take care of yourself,' smiles his father, blissfully unaware of what his son has just endured. They get a huge new apartment on the other side of town and even manage to sneak out of the hotel without paying the bill. Certainly the most humane film Soderbergh has made, its sepia-tinted aesthetic nevertheless draws the viewer into thinking it will be a far more traditional heart-warmer. We're made to work for those final feel-good emotions; unlike most Hollywood films, they don't come as given. As Soderbergh says of his adaptation, 'I think emotionally it was faithful.'

Proving Soderbergh had an eye for talent, the film boasted an impressive support cast of then-unknowns. Though not his debut, this was the first role of any significance for Adrien Brody, whose winning interpretation of the light-fingered Lester is effortlessly charming. Likewise, future Fugees singer Lauryn Hill, as the gum-chewing elevator girl, is central to one of the film's most tender scenes, when Aaron gets her to smile after thanking her for the graduation gift she gives him. Offering roles to underused actresses like Karen Allen (as Aaron's teacher) and Elizabeth McGovern (as Lydia, the prostitute who frequents Mr Mungo's room), Soderbergh also forged a relationship with actor cum monologist Spalding Gray. An avid fan, Soderbergh first met him in New York, having just read his novel about mental illness, *Impossible Vacation*. 'I said, "I really think you're perfect for this, having just read your book, because this is a guy, in my mind, who is ruled by regret." And he said, "Well, that's all I need to know! That's exactly how I feel, so if that's what you're thinking, this should really work out."' So impressed would Gray be with the young director that he would later called upon him to shoot his ocular-disease monologue for what became Soderbergh's sixth film, *Gray's Anatomy*.

Although *King of the Hill* earned Universal only a $1.2 million domestic gross, Soderbergh was aware even at this early stage that forging ties with the studio system was no bad thing. While his collaboration with Pollack on *The Last Ship* was not to be, he looked to maintaining their relationship by developing *Leatherheads* together, again at Universal. A comedy about the formation of the National Football League penned by Duncan Brantley and Rick Reilly, two writers for *Sports Illustrated*, it was what Soderbergh had hoped to follow *King of the Hill* with. But to this day, it remains unmade, despite Pollack still attached as producer, and Soderbergh's business partner and sometime star George Clooney on board as director.

One relationship that was not helped by the release of *King of the Hill* was that between Soderbergh and Redford. Perhaps irked by being third in line behind *The Last Ship* and *Kafka*, Redford had ducked out of several meetings with Universal studios over the financing of *King of the Hill*. He then demanded that his deferred payments for the $8 million budgeted project be the same as everybody else's. This Soderbergh objected to, given that it was a film he had taken to Redford's company. Revenge was sweet, swift and silent. After Soderbergh had been offered Paul Attanasio's script for *Quiz Show* (1994) – again via Mark Johnson at Baltimore Pictures – Redford hijacked the project. Churning out one of the more palatable films of his directorial career, Redford never offered a word of explanation to Soderbergh.

In fact, after Soderbergh completed the shoot of *King of the Hill* and went into post-production in the winter of 1992, Redford spoke to him just one more time. Requesting a screening of the unfinished film, Redford promised to discuss the various burning issues currently alight between the two filmmakers. Soderbergh set him up a viewing with twenty-four hours' notice, but the most he heard from Redford was that he wanted to take his name off the project. The official line was that Redford doubted the significance of his contribution to the film.

While saddened by the experience, Soderbergh had other things on his mind: he was set to return to Cannes, the film being accepted into competition. But *King of the Hill* would not win anything or glean Soderbergh anything like the industry kudos *sex, lies, and videotape* did. All in all, it was a demonstration of the fickle nature of the film industry and Soderbergh found his first brush with Hollywood a bumpy ride. With Quentin Tarantino's *Pulp Fiction* still a year away, 'Indiewood', the so-called blend of Hollywood and independent film that became prevalent in the mid-1990s, was not yet even in its embryonic form. So *King of the Hill* slipped in between the cracks, neither cool enough for the Sundance crowd nor market-driven enough for the studios. Fêted one minute, forgotten the next, Soderbergh was living proof that directors were still powerless in the studio system.

SECTION II: INDIEWOOD

CHAPTER 6

Pulp Fact: The Rise of Miramax as Hollywood Embraces Tarantino-mania

7 Golden boy: Quentin Tarantino

Let's get into character.
Jules Winnfield, *Pulp Fiction*

'Tarantinnitus', as one wag named it, was a syndrome that spread like a virus in 1994. A persistent ringing in the ears, a low barely audible drone, for anyone paying attention that year – and there were a lot of us – Tarantino's voice seemed like the only one we heard. Was it the sound of ceaseless self-promotion? The art of noise? Yes and no. Tarantino, like his characters, talks the good talk. Clint Eastwood and his jury at the Cannes Film Festival that year certainly listened, awarding *Pulp Fiction* the Palme d'Or over Krzysztof Kieslowski's much-favoured *Trois couleurs: Rouge*. Like the makeshift overdose cure administered by *Pulp Fiction*'s hitman Vincent Vega (John Travolta), it was an adrenalin shot right into the heart of American independent cinema.

Although *sex, lies, and videotape* had won the prize in 1989 – followed a year later by David Lynch's *Wild at Heart*, and then in 1991 by the Coen brothers' *Barton Fink* – this felt different. A peek into an amoral world, acts of violence are as off the cuff as the conversations that surround them. As Vincent's fellow hitman, Jules Winnfield (Samuel L. Jackson), so eloquently says, it gives us front row seats to watch 'a bunch of gangsters doin' a bunch of gangsta shit'. It's easy to see why there were as many jeers as there were cheers in the Palais de Festival that night; celluloid junk food, it was never going to appeal to the more cultured taste buds on *la Croissette*.

But it did whet the appetite of a filmgoing public that had been force-fed *Forrest Gump* that very year. Dovetailing traditional scenarios from dime novels – from the washed-up boxer who throws a fight to the mob guy who takes out the boss's wife – Tarantino made murder and mayhem seem ineffably cool. If not gratuitous or glorified, the violence is undoubtedly fetishized. This is evidenced by boxer Butch (Bruce Willis), as he gleefully selects his weapon of choice – a samurai sword is preferred over a chainsaw or baseball bat to help him wreak revenge on two hillbilly rapists who have held him and crime-lord Marsellus Wallace (Ving Rhames) captive. Likewise the drug use –

69

notably, Vincent unsheathing his needle kit from its leather case – is lionised in the same wide-eyed way.

By the time the film was unleashed in October 1994, the buzz was more of a din. Canonized by a generation of students who dug designer violence, like *A Clockwork Orange* before it and *Trainspotting* (1996) shortly after, it was the film to hang on your wall. No doubt, it richly deserved its accolades – even if now, with the passing of time, the film feels as quaint as the Jack Rabbit Slim's diner visited by Vincent and mob moll Mia Wallace (Uma Thurman). Compare it to *Reservoir Dogs*, Tarantino's Jacobean tragedy, and *Pulp Fiction* feels like a Restoration comedy, a gentle breeze rather than a force ten gale.

The film took in over $200 million worldwide, remarkable for a story that features an anal rape, a heroin overdose, a leather-clad submissive and a gold watch hidden between two butt cheeks. That the taboo subject matter of *Pulp Fiction* crossed over into the mainstream says a great deal about the liberation of our social and sexual mores. It was a triumph, even if the Academy would honour the film in just one of the seven Oscar categories (Best Original Screenplay) in which it was nominated. Just as *Reservoir Dogs* was overlooked at Sundance, so *Pulp Fiction* would be largely ignored in the awards season, though Tarantino was about to become the recipient of a much bigger prize. Embraced by *Loaded* magazine and the like, he became a mascot to a generation, spawning a host of imitators as Martin Scorsese had before him.

Unlike his hero Brian De Palma, Scorsese is a director Tarantino is rarely caught talking about. Yet he was revered with the same macho fervour otherwise reserved for the New Yorker. As Ryan Gilbey noted: 'It is also likely that Scorsese's lopsided reputation has been fostered by numerous articles in the men's magazine market celebrating the likes of *Taxi Driver* and *Raging Bull* as hymns to the savage, inarticulate male – a construct designed to flatter untapped fantasies of alienation or fury in those publications' target audience, to the detriment of the movies themselves. You can witness the same response to Tarantino . . . '[24]

With its retro soundtrack, smart-alec quips and perverse postmodern bent, what can one say about *Pulp Fiction* that has not already been said? Its creation has already passed into film folklore, having begun back in 1989 when Tarantino and Roger Avary had discussed collaborating on a crime anthology, consisting of three short films not unlike Mario Bava's horror classic *Black Sabbath* (1963). Years later, with a nearly $1 million development deal in his pocket from Danny DeVito's Jersey Films, Tarantino recruited Avary and his story *Pandemonium Reigns* – ultimately adapted into 'The Gold Watch' segment – as well as two scenes of Avary's cut from the script of *True Romance*: the backseat car murder and the hidden assassin who misses from close range. Weaving together what Avary called 'the best scenes we'd ever written', they laid them out on the floor of Tarantino's Amsterdam apartment and their 'rock 'n' roll spaghetti western' (substituting Ennio Morricone for surf music) began to take shape. 'With that film, it was in effect trying to create a time-pretzel,' Avary explains. 'Everything overlaps, in a way to throw off your expectations.'

In fact, unlike the daring structure of *Reservoir Dogs*, with its flashbacks arranged like a hall of mirrors, the majority of *Pulp Fiction* – bar the sequence entitled 'The Bonnie Situation', which bookends the film but chronologically belongs within the second quarter of the narrative – progresses in a linear fashion. Emphasizing this near A to Z progression, Tarantino even closes the story (though not the film) with Butch and his girlfriend Fabienne (Maria de Medeiros) riding off on a Chopper owned by hick cop Zed (Peter Greene). Yet as Avary recalls, this wraparound structure baffled some. 'When we first turned it in, the company [TriStar] who'd hired us said: "This is the worst thing ever written. It makes no sense. Someone's dead and then they're alive. It's too long, violent and unfilmable." That was about when I was going to production on [his 1994 directorial debut] *Killing Zoe*. So I thought "That's that!" Then Bob and Harvey [Weinstein] came along and completely believed in Quentin's vision, and they gave him the chance to make that movie unfettered.'

How could they not? To simplify Tarantino's story would have been a crime far bigger than any committed on screen. The impact of Vincent's death at the hands of Butch hinges on this 'time-pretzel design' – appropriately enough coming after he emerges from the toilet with his copy of Peter O'Donnell's *Modesty Blaise* (one of three occasions in the film when Vincent heads to the bathroom during a major event). Only when we discover in the final reel that earlier that week his partner in crime had decided to quit the life after experiencing an epiphany he calls 'a moment of clarity' do we mourn Vincent's demise. Despite Jules petitioning his peer to recognize the miracle they witness when a surprise assailant unloads a gun at point-blank range in their direction but fails to hit them, Vincent chooses to remain the blind man. He, after all, and not Jules, was the one to look inside the briefcase and gaze upon its undisclosed glowing contents: a Pandora's Box, if ever there was one.

Picking up on the themes of loyalty and forgiveness seen in *Reservoir Dogs*, Tarantino introduces salvation into the mix. While Vincent misses out, Mia (after surviving her overdose) and Butch and Marsellus (after escaping their torture) all come to experience what is voiced by Jules's executioner's song; they are 'the weak' in the 'valley of the shadow of darkness'. The biblical passage from Ezekiel 25:17 – though in fact the script splices it with some of the 23rd Psalm – comes to shift in meaning after Jules undergoes his own spiritual enlightenment. By sparing the life of Pumpkin (Tim Roth), who along with the hysterical Honey Bunny (Amanda Plummer) has the misfortune to rob a diner while he is in attendance, Jules is making his first step towards being the 'shepherd'. If he is not yet 'the righteous man', he no longer belongs to 'the tyranny of evil men'.

Laying the groundwork for his later film *Kill Bill* (an idea Tarantino reputedly hatched on the set), Jules's speech is also inspired by martial arts guru Sonny Chiba's long-running 1980s TV series *Kage No Gundan* (*Shadow Warriors*). Chiba would denounce the tyranny of evil before running a sword through an assailant at the climax of each episode. Ironically, Jules claims he will 'walk the earth, like Caine in *Kung Fu*', a reference to the 1970s show featuring Chiba's *Kill Bill* co-star David Carradine, who played a benevolent drifter with training in the ancient arts of self-defence. For the time being, these would remain oblique references (Chiba having also been name-checked in *True Romance*), years before Tarantino set about resurrecting their careers.

As befits a film about redemption, Tarantino used *Pulp Fiction* – as he had used *Reservoir Dogs* and would use his third film, *Jackie Brown* – as a chance to play the priest, granting absolution to actors for their cinematic sins. After playing second fiddle to a baby in the *Look Who's Talking* trilogy in the early 1990s – at what was arguably the nadir of his career – John Travolta's celluloid purgatory came to an end once he met Tarantino. Yet with this reminder of the effortless swagger that came with every step of his 1977 role as *Saturday Night Fever*'s Tony Manero, there was a price to pay. In a film fascinated by the ephemeral nature of pop culture iconography, as evidenced by the lookalike waiters in Jack Rabbit Slim's, Travolta was the prize possession. Tarantino even makes Travolta dance one more time. That the subse-

8 & 9 *Pulp Fiction*: Uma Thurman's Mia Wallace eats her burger while John Travolta's Vincent Vega rolls a cigarette.

10 & 11 *Pulp Fiction*: Bruce Willis's Butch Coolidge wakes up from his recurring dream; Samuel L. Jackson's Jules Winnfield escapes death.

quent glut of film roles Travolta's performance precipitated would all be anti-climactic after this, now seems pre-ordained.

While Bruce Willis had already endured his own critical disasters, namely *Bonfire of the Vanities* (1990) and *Hudson Hawk* (1991), his standing at the time of playing Butch was far greater in Hollywood than Travolta's. Yet this was primarily due to *Die Hard* (1988), a turn that barely set him apart from Jean-Claude Van Damme and his muscular peers. Without Tarantino showing Willis's brute sensitivity, it's arguable that the actor would not have been cast in Terry Gilliam's *Twelve Monkeys* (1995) or M. Night Shyamalan's *The Sixth Sense* (1999).

Samuel L. Jackson, best known at that point for his role as a quivering junkie in Spike Lee's *Jungle Fever* (1991), also received his own form of second chance. One of the New York actors Harvey Keitel had rounded up for Tarantino to look over during the casting sessions of *Reservoir Dogs*, he almost blew his audition for *Pulp Fiction*, with Tarantino veering towards Paul Calderon. It was only with the intervention of Harvey Weinstein, impressed by Jackson after watching his work on the Miramax-produced *Fresh*, that he was granted another shot. Jackson won the role, kickstarting a career that has gone from strength to strength, and relegating Calderon to a cameo as the bartender and a life of what-ifs.

Yet if anything points to the universal acclaim for *Pulp Fiction*, it would be that Tarantino covers all his bases, combining elements that appealed to a diverse range of filmgoers. With its art house narrative structure, B-movie subject matter and Hollywood cast, the film is the axis for three distinct cinematic traditions to intersect. Influenced equally by exploitation films and the French New Wave in his formative years, Tarantino would reflect both in *Pulp Fiction*, itself a tribute to the potboiler stories featured in the *Black Mask* crime magazines he soaked up in his youth. Tarantino showed, as he had with his extensive pilfering for *Reservoir Dogs*, that contemporary cinema is a constantly evolving organism; just as genres could be recycled, so could plot lines and dialogue, with Tarantino acting as curator. The ultimate fan appropriating his favourite clips and assimilating them into something new, he never desecrates but merely redecorates.

One of many examples, Marsellus's ominous line to Butch, that he will 'go to work on [Zed] with a pair of pliers and a blowtorch', is lifted from Don Siegel's Mafia story *Charley Varrick* (1973). In that, a bank president named Maynard warns a crooked colleague that when the mob catches up with him, 'they'll strip you naked and go to work on you with a pair of pliers and a blowtorch'. Call it plagiarism, call it intertextuality, but Tarantino has the ability to make anything sound his own. Explicitly aware of the cinematic heritage that precedes his work, his crimes are no different to the literary felonies that have taken place over the preceding centuries. Just as Pope 'imitated' Horace, and Milton was inspired by Spenser, who was in debt to Chaucer, and so on, so Tarantino has no qualms in paying sly tribute to his forebears.

Playing down the theft, as if to show that life and literature are made up of these repetitions, Tarantino does not quote verbatim but adjusts stolen lines often by only a word or two. This is emphasized when the characters even begin to misquote themselves – from Jules's two differing renditions of Ezekiel 25:17 to Honey Bunny's screaming rant in the diner, which is markedly different on the two occasions we hear it. Remarkably, so quickly did *Pulp Fiction*'s own lines become embedded in movie-culture that it has, as yet, been impossible for filmmakers to integrate them into their own work, except via inferior parody (something Tarantino scrupulously avoids).

Tarantino, as much a master of trivia as of black comedy, wants his audience to play a sophisticated game of spot the reference. The briefcase is a reference to Robert Aldrich's *Kiss Me Deadly* (1955), the anal rape to John Boorman's *Deliverance*. Marsellus crossing the road in front of Butch recalls the moment in Alfred Hitchcock's *Psycho* (1960) where Janet Leigh's Marion spies her boss as he passes in front of her stationary car. Musical cues are also employed – Butch's getaway is accompanied by the theme from *The Twilight Zone* – while cast baggage is played on, as in Harvey Keitel's Winston Wolf, a 'cleaner' not unlike the one he played in *Point of No Return* (1993), the U.S. remake of *La Femme Nikita* (1990).

Perhaps what separates Tarantino from his imitators is the profane, xenophobic invective that doubles as dialogue. Critic J. Hoberman noted that its modus operandi was 'Talk Talk Bang Bang', the 'language as calculatedly brutal as the action'.[25] The rat-a-tat-tat words are indistinguishable from bullet fire, as shown when Jules breaks off his speech to casually shoot Burr Steers's sofa-bound victim, only to ask his shocked cohort, Frank Whaley's Brett, 'Did I break your concentration?'

But if it's a film about the power of the spoken word, *Pulp Fiction* never manages to make us squirm in the way *Reservoir Dogs* does. Less cruel, and more chaotic, the violence is often accidental; death and injury are as liable to come from a faulty gun-trigger or a stray bullet across the street, as in a pre-meditated killing. *Pulp Fiction*, Tarantino has said, has a lot to do with real-life crime. 'I'm taking genre-characters and applying them to real-life circumstances. I guess the master of that is Elmore Leonard. And real life ends up fucking up the best-laid plans of mice and men: all the humour in my films comes from the absurdity of real life rearing its head.'[26]

While this is true, it means the film lacks the operatic, tragic grandeur of *Reservoir Dogs*. Unlike the full-blooded torture scene in his debut, Tarantino teases our imaginations in *Pulp Fiction* before stepping back from the brink, with much of the violence held off screen.

If the action, characters and language achieve one thing, it is to buffer us from the pain of violence, something *Reservoir Dogs* never shied away from. Not unlike Wes Anderson's *The Royal Tenenbaums*, the world of cinema collides headlong into contemporary life, the result as messy as Butch's crossroads car crash. Is Tarantino a latter-day Raymond Chandler, distilling his hard-boiled poetry of the streets for a modern audience? Is he a new Jean-Luc Godard, drawing attention to cinematic convention while tipping a wink to the American noir heroes? Is he the son of Brian De Palma, with his mixture of blood, black comedy and violent long takes? In *Pulp Fiction*, Tarantino manages to both be and to emulate all three, sometimes in the same scene. Whether he would become anything more than that was a question that wouldn't be answered for some time to come.

The Miramax Situation

It seems appropriate to document the rise of Harvey and Bob Weinstein's Miramax in relation to Tarantino, and in particular to *Pulp Fiction*. Named after their parents Miriam and Max, the company became subtitled 'The House That Quentin Built' after the $8 million investment in *Pulp Fiction* began to see returns beyond the Weinsteins' wildest dreams. Legend has it that Harvey read the script on a plane trip, and was so excited by what he was reading that he committed to making it before he got to the end (of both script and journey). Such is the gambler in Harvey, an instinct that has paid off time and again.

Likewise, *The English Patient* (1996), *Good Will Hunting* (1997) and *Shakespeare in Love* (1998) would all subsequently be rescued from oblivion by him and pay rich dividends, in box office grosses, Oscars or both.

Yet Miramax was no overnight success story. By the time *Pulp Fiction* was unveiled, the brothers had been in business for fifteen years. Hailing from Queens, the Weinsteins began their working lives in the music business, after acquiring a Buffalo theatre and enticing bands to play there. Screening movies in between concerts, the brothers satisfied a latent passion for cinema, initiated by their father, a diamond cutter, who took his sons to the Saturday matinees while their mother was having her hair done.

Ever the spin-doctor, the gargantuan Harvey – born in 1952, he is two years older than Bob – likes it to be known that his life changed when he was fourteen after he accidentally took in a screening of Truffaut's *The 400 Blows* (1959), thinking it was a sex film. With Miramax officially formed in 1979, the Weinsteins began to edge towards distribution when they bought up the rights to the Pythonesque Amnesty International fundraiser concert *The Secret Policeman's Ball* and its sequel and spliced them into one package. It made in the region of $6 million, and these rough diamonds were on their way.

After a disaster-strewn attempt to launch their careers as writer-directors in 1986 with a loosely autobiographical musical comedy entitled *Playing for Keeps*, the brothers returned to distribution. Bolstered by a chance meeting with the British owners of the now-defunct Palace Pictures, Nik Powell and Steven Woolley, Harvey wanted to model his company on theirs. In other words, releasing prestige European pictures in the U.S. in the same way Powell and Woolley were acquiring quality U.S. indies, such as *Blood Simple* and *Kiss of the Spiderwoman* (1985), for the UK market. Impressed by Powell and Woolley's passion for their product, Harvey adopted the same attitude.

Buying, in 1989, the American rights to Palace's *Scandal*, the story of the Profumo affair directed by Michael Caton-Jones, the Weinsteins were aware that sex, as well as notoriety, sells. They had already had their first bona fide hit two years before, with Lizzie Borden's then-radical study of prostitutes, *Working Girls*. They sold Peter Greenaway's *The Cook, the Thief, His Wife and Her Lover* (1989) – a film they picked up despite dozens of walkouts in the screening they attended – with the tagline: 'Lust. Murder. Dessert.' It grossed $7.7 million, remarkable for such a defiantly non-commercial piece. In the same year, Soderbergh's *sex, lies, and videotape* would net them $24.7 million at the U.S. box office, while *Scandal* – after a first amendment tussle with the Motion Picture Association of America over certification – would pull in a healthy $8.8 million.

Yet Harvey, in particular, was not just a businessman. A self-appointed patron of the arts, he craved recognition – in his eyes bestowed not by the critics but by the Academy. 'Harvey *loves* talking about Oscars,' says Daniel Day-Lewis, whose testy relationship with Harvey began with Jim Sheridan's *My Left Foot* (1989). The film took $14.7 million in the U.S. and almost single-handedly kick-started the home video market for fringe films, shifting over 150,000 units upon release. It also netted Miramax not only five Oscar nominations in 1990 but also its first English-language statues, for Day-Lewis and Brenda Fricker. The company had already won its first Oscar – Best Foreign Film, for Bille August's *Pelle the Conqueror* (1987) – the previous year, even gaining star Max von Sydow a Best Actor nod. With *My Left Foot* winning the acting plaudits, *sex, lies, and videotape* nominated for Best Original Screenplay and Giuseppe Tornatore's *Cinema Paradiso* (1989) ensuring Miramax picked up their second Best Foreign Film Oscar in succession, it was a breakout year.

The film business being what it is, Miramax was unable to match its growing kudos in the industry with financial stability. After the glories of 1989, the brothers faced two difficult years, with a series of releases crashing at the box office, bolstered only by the $15 million–grossing Madonna documentary *Truth or Dare* (1991). Unable to invest in films that interested them, such as Sheridan's *In the Name of the Father* (1993), the Weinsteins came within a whisker of floating the company on the stock exchange – until they thought better of it.

In 1992, Miramax released twenty-two films, reaping a total gross of just $39 million. It was as if Harvey were losing his golden touch. Already cursed with the nickname 'Harvey Scissorhands' – due to his habit of tinkering with films in the edit suite – he made a hash out of selling *Reservoir Dogs* to the American public, having pestered Tarantino to trim the notorious torture scene (which he refused to do). He even initially turned down the script for Neil Jordan's IRA-themed thriller *The Crying Game*, produced by his old Palace pal Steven Woolley, shying away from its incendiary mix of race, sex and politics.

When Miramax did acquire the North American rights for the film, they ignored it, pushing *Strictly Ballroom* as their Oscar contender.

The Crying Game had already crashed and burned in the UK, but word of mouth – spurred on by a canny marketing campaign petitioning audiences not to reveal the film's central twist – ensured its U.S. release just kept growing. The Weinsteins eventually bought out the film's investors, including British Screen, with the promise that they were planning to expand the film to a thousand theatres. *The Crying Game* would go on to gain six Oscar nominations and elevate its respectable $16 million gross to a staggering $62.5 million in the U.S. It was a watershed moment for 'independent' cinema. A film that finally outstripped the grosses of *sex, lies, and videotape*, it proved that the $25 million mark was not the limit for non-studio films.

While the East Coast dream of independence from Hollywood was alive and well in 1992, by May the following year it had all but died. The whale swallowed the minnow, as Disney bought out Miramax. In the short term, it made good business sense for both parties. The Weinsteins, who had recently sold the Whoopi Goldberg film *Sarafina!* (1992) to Disney for a tidy $3 million profit, would finally be able to wipe out their debts. Meanwhile, still in its pre-Pixar days, Disney's animation division was only just beginning to emerge from its lengthy slump with *Aladdin* (1992). The Miramax deal gave the company instant (and much needed) cachet.

The initial outlay from Disney, aside from assuming control of Miramax's debts, would be $60 million. Orchestrated by the company's then head Jeffrey Katzenberg, the deal would also see the brothers paid an annual salary of $1.5 million, giving them what they wanted most of all into the bargain: their autonomy. This might not sound like the beginning of the end; after all, the Weinsteins – who, envious of rival company New Line's success with low-budget horror flicks, had already set up their Dimension offshoot to do the same – were now in a position to produce as well as acquire.

While Miramax would continue to perpetuate the myth that it was still the riskiest distributor in town – why else would Harvey have purchased Kevin Smith's *Clerks*? – such a façade was destined to collapse. Famously, the Weinsteins dropped a Martin Lawrence in-concert show for fear of offending their adopted parents, Disney. Yet, despite the risqué subject matter, ironically it was the investment in *Pulp Fiction* that precipitated the decline of the Miramax of old. The Weinsteins' first major production was in effect a swansong for their maverick Miramax ways. Flush with success, playing it safe began to seem more appealing.

By 1995, the brothers would create a separate distribution company, Excalibur Films, to release Larry Clark's *Kids* – thus distancing Disney from the storm the film was generating. Miramax was beginning to move away from making its name with controversial cinema. Turning down the opportunity to release Todd Solondz's *Welcome to the Dollhouse*, the Weinsteins tellingly put money into David O. Russell's 1996 second film, *Flirting with Disaster*, an upscale charmer unlikely to offend the majority of audiences. A comic tale of anxiety and adoption, it sees Mel Coplin (Ben Stiller) set out on a journey of discovery to meet his birth parents for the first time.

It was, in principle, a smart move for Russell. A mid-range movie that would act as a perfect bridge between the low-budget *Spanking the Monkey* and his third film, the $48 million *Three Kings*, it steered him away from the controversy of his debut. This time, unlike in his interviews for *Spanking the Monkey*, Russell was happy to discuss the autobiographical elements of the story. His sister, who was adopted, had gone on a journey similar to the film's protagonist's, while he knew of the effects a baby could have on one's sex life.

Although the subject matter was less incendiary than masturbation and mother-love, Russell was still flirting with disaster by proposing a comedy that questioned society's obsession with biological parentage, while making light of curvature of the penis, circumcision, an armpit fetish, LSD consumption, breast feeding and gay sex. Far lighter in tone than *Spanking the Monkey*, the film is in the tradition of fast-paced dialogue-driven Hollywood comedies, from those of Preston Sturges to the work of Mike Nichols. With its cast made up of the crème de la crème of contemporary and classic American comedy, *Flirting with Disaster* made a bold statement of intent. What other recent film has dared flesh out its supporting cast with the likes of Alan Alda, Lily Tomlin and Mary Tyler Moore, while gambling on the then little-known Ben Stiller for the lead?

But it was not an easy ride for Russell. He suffered from pre-production to post – with Harvey making the experience less than pleasant. At the outset, Harvey wanted John Cusack, didn't want Janeane Garofalo, and didn't like the choice of Gus Van Sant collaborator Eric Edwards for cinematographer. During the protracted nine months of post-production, he and Russell even argued over the tail-end credit sequence. Harvey threw his weight around because he could. Said Russell, 'Miramax can in some ways be more intrusive than the average studio – that's part of the power of Harvey's personality.'[27] In the end, disaster was averted, as the film doubled its $7 million budget on its U.S. release, taking in $14.7 million in total. But it cost Harvey the loyalty of Russell.

Ironically, bar Tarantino and Rodriguez, many of Hollywood's most significant directors of the decade – Fincher, P. T. and Wes Anderson, Mendes, Singer, Jonze – have steered clear of Miramax. Payne, after a disastrous experience with his debut, *Citizen Ruth*, at Miramax, has not darkened their doors again. Meanwhile, it took Soderbergh twelve years to return there after the release of *sex, lies, and videotape*, with *Full Frontal*.

The Weinsteins may inspire fierce loyalty in the likes of Tarantino, Kevin Smith, Ben Affleck and Matt Damon (whose *Good Will Hunting* signalled a further shift in Miramax product towards a Disneyfied world view), but their legendary revolving-door policy saw employees flee in droves, often to rival companies. As Harvey once joked, he and Bob identified with the family in *The Texas Chainsaw Massacre*. No doubt, if only half the stories ever told about Harvey are true, he would make Kevin Spacey's callous executive Buddy Ackerman in *Swimming with Sharks* (1994) look like a sweetie.

Yet in an era when Hollywood is peopled by soulless corporate drones, as embodied by Tim Robbins's Griffin Mill in *The Player*, there's no doubt the film industry would be a blander place without Harvey. Stories abound of his bully-boy tactics (locking the producers of 1990's *Ju Dou* in a room until they signed, for example) and his capricious temper (notably firing an employee for screwing up in a softball game only to re-employ him). Then there's his ceaseless Oscar campaigning (most triumphantly, steering *Shakespeare in Love* to Best Picture over Steven Spielberg's *Saving Private Ryan* in 1999) and his incessant cutting (starting with Errol Morris's 1988 documentary *The Thin Blue Line*).

Brad Anderson's experience was typical. His second film, *Next Stop Wonderland*, caused a bidding war at the 1998 Sundance Film Festival. A romantic comedy made for $1 million, its distribution rights cost Harvey six times that figure. In the end, it grossed just $3.3 million in the U.S. and left Anderson with mixed feelings. 'It was great because they bought the film, and that was the first movie I ever sold,' says

Anderson. 'But my experience with them – which I think I share with a number of filmmakers – [is that] they wanted to re-shoot the ending, re-cut stuff, it was too long. It was the same old crap that you hear – based on numbers that they get from research screenings. At the time, they were really beholden to these numbers. They use those as a guide to what they were going to do to your movie.'

When test audiences reacted badly to a scene where the character of Erin (Hope Davis) stands up Andre (José Zúñiga), Anderson was forced to shoot a new ending. 'For me, it was a wake-up call, a learning experience,' he says. 'Looking back on it, I wish I hadn't fucked with my movie like I did. But what are you gonna do?' As for working with the company again, he says: 'I don't burn any bridges. You can't do that in this business. I don't even want to. If Miramax had some offer they wanted to make to me about a project, I'm open to it. But it's not a company I'm gravitating towards.'

There is no doubt Harvey was a return to the old-school-style studio mogul – the men who built Tinseltown brick by brick. Yet as much as Miramax was initially at the forefront of ensuring non-studio films flourished in both the marketplace and the end-of-season award shows, Harvey eventually underwent a transformation. A New York outsider and the champion of world cinema over Hollywood assembly line product, he somewhere along the line got the old adage 'if you can't beat 'em, join 'em' lodged in his brain. Recruiting directors such as Anthony Minghella, John Madden and Lasse Hallström, Harvey set out to shake off his image as a fringe player. For a time it was left to his rivals to rebel from within, and recruit the directors who would change the face of Hollywood.

Until that is, he decided to bankroll Michael Moore's *Fahrenheit 9/11* (2004), a $6 million documentary about the George W. Bush administration in the wake of the terror attacks. When the Disney CEO Michael Eisner refused to distribute it for fear of making waves in an election year, it was the beginning of the end for the Miramax fairy tale. Bought back from Disney by the Weinsteins, who joined up with IFC Films to release it themselves (as they did for *Kids*) via a specially formed company named Fellowship Adventure Group, the film went on to gross $119 million in the U.S. alone. For Harvey, this was a triumph against all those who said he'd lost his guts. 'For me, it was about painting with a large canvas,' Harvey noted. 'If anyone thinks I will not make small films that will make a lot of money . . . I will continue to do that.'[28]

83

With their already poor relationship with Eisner soured for good, Harvey and Bob Weinstein set about pulling the plug. After months of negotiations, which were only fully resolved in March 2005, the brothers announced they were leaving Miramax, the company they had formed twenty-five years previously. Under the new arrangement, Disney retained the Miramax name and the Miramax and Dimension film libraries. The Weinsteins took the Dimension label to a new company, dubbed 'The Weinstein Co.'. Stating that they intended to use the new outfit to pursue avenues previously blocked by Disney, such as getting involved with a cable network, the Weinsteins are back where they started. Outside of Hollywood, their maverick status fully restored.

CHAPTER 7

Austin Power: How Robert Rodriguez and Richard Linklater Bucked the System

12 Robert Rodriguez films Carlos Gallardo on the set of *El Mariachi*.
13 Richard Linklater, during the making of *Dazed and Confused*.

Miramax may be the house that Quentin built, but Robert Rodriguez was the one who paid for the repairs. Excluding his co-directed efforts *Four Rooms* and *Sin City*, the six films he has made for the company – *From Dusk Till Dawn*, *The Faculty*, the *Spy Kids* trilogy and *Once Upon a Time in Mexico* (a co-production with Columbia) – have grossed $431 million in the U.S. alone. Needless to say, they far out-strip the revenue Tarantino's films have generated.

Rodriguez, who saw his no-budget debut, *El Mariachi*, and its glossy Hollywood remake, *Desperado* (1995), released by Columbia, is – like Tarantino – one of the untouchables at Miramax. 'I've always had final cut with them,' he says. 'The more money you make, the more they just let you do what you want. Keep the budget low – if you spend more then it's harder.' His relationship with Bob Weinstein and his Dimension outfit – the Miramax offshoot that established itself with the *Scream* series – would seem to be a match made in heaven.

While Rodriguez has been offered numerous high-profile studio pic-tures over the years – most notably *The Mask of Zorro* (1998) which he eventually walked away from when the project stalled – he has yet to see one to fruition. 'The thing that turned me off about it the most, after all that [on *Zorro*], I was going to get paid like a regular director. No matter how much I invented, or how cool I made it, it would never be mine. That's why I didn't mind so much not doing it. At Miramax, I have the opportunity to make stuff and take part ownership in it. When you go make a movie for somebody else that they own . . . all that work and inventiveness, and they own it! Why waste your energy on somebody else's film?'

It's easy to see why Rodriguez became the unofficial fourth member of the Sundance Class of '92, even if *El Mariachi* would not make its bow at the festival for another year. If not quite cinematic Siamese twins separated at birth, Rodriguez and Tarantino are more than just kindred spirits. Be it through dialogue, editing or structure, both were able to put a contemporary spin on creaky genres – like the Western and the crime film – even mashing together a hybrid when they felt like it. Moreover, their movies exist in hermetically sealed universes, adja-cent to our world but governed by their own laws. By Hollywood standards their films (at least until Tarantino spent $55 million making *Kill Bill* – and even then he got two movies for the price of one) are low budget. 'Quentin is still the same way,' says Rodriguez. 'He can't believe people spend so much on movies. He makes his movies very economically. So Miramax loves us, because we're always thinking about the budgets.'

Aside from the fact that Rodriguez warrants mention in this book because of his contribution to the development of Tarantino's career, does he merit serious consideration in his own right? Rodriguez, after all, is not a director who has impacted upon Hollywood in the way Tarantino did; his admittedly inventive films are fast, cheap celluloid adrenalin rushes, as unpretentious as they are throwaway. What they don't do is hold up a mirror to contemporary society, a task Rodriguez gleefully leaves for other, more 'worthy' directors.

'I have pretty much given in to the idea that I'll always just make fantasy films,' he says. 'I think I'm still twelve years old. That was when everything came together, and I really got into fantasy, art, movies and photography. I drew before that – but that was when I started making movies. I was soaking up fantasy. It was all I was ever interested in as a kid – things that weren't real. That's why I would never make a dramatic film that's similar to real life – you get enough of that on the news.'

As Peter Jackson has proved with his *Lord of the Rings* trilogy (2001–03), fantasy can be taken seriously, but you could never imagine Rodriguez adapting something as theatrical as Tolkien. Designing his own house in Texas to look like a 'Mexican Aztec castle with secret passages' – reasoning 'if you can build anything, why make it look like everyone else's houses?' – he constructs his films in much the same way. If generic conventions are his foundations, his fertile imagination is his bricks and mortar – with which he is able to construct cinematic castles from the ground up.

'It's more fun for me to get up in the morning and do this,' he says.

I don't like to work. I change the word 'work' to 'play'. I like to play! It would be work to do something that's very realistic. I'd have to research what kind of costumes this person would be wearing, or what kind of gun he would be carrying and the number of bullets it would shoot, 'cos then he runs out after six shots . . . I don't like any restriction. I really love freedom as a moviemaker; fantasy gives you the ultimate freedom. You can just make up your own rules. That's why the movies feel so mad and crazy!

Author of *Rebel Without a Crew*, a book that detailed his experiences making *El Mariachi*, Rodriguez still embodies this maverick spirit – writing, producing, directing, editing, shooting and even scoring many of his own films. Rather than his chosen subject matter, it is his defiant do-it-all streak that sets him apart from more conventional directors. Doubtless, it's why he's based in Austin, Texas – halfway between Hollywood and the eclectic East Coast scene. His company (re-titled from 'Los Hooligans') is named Troublemaker Studios, after the style of hat he wears when he's not sporting a bandana. 'I'm a troublemaker in the movie business!' he adds. 'I don't follow the rules at all.'

Born in San Antonio, Texas, in 1968, Rodriguez was always like this. A solitary, quiet child and an underachiever at the private boarding school he attended, he admits he was 'the guy in the back of the classroom that no one was paying attention to'. Meticulously making flip-cartoon books, the young Rodriguez managed to summon up the courage to show his drawings to others, realizing it was a way to gain their approval. His father, who sold china and glassware, had an old Super 8 camera lying around, and Rodriguez experimented with it, before graduating to the Quaser camera that came with the family's new VCR. When his father bought a second machine, Rodriguez was able to crudely edit his shorts – often cast with his brothers and sisters – between the two VCRs.

As his shorts became renowned throughout his school, he met another budding filmmaker, Carlos Gallardo, and the pair spent summers in Mexico, making action comedies in the busy streets of Ciudad Acuña, where Gallardo lived. With his confidence growing, Rodriguez's grades improved and he won a scholarship to the University of Texas in Austin – only to discover his grade point average was not enough to gain him entry into the film program. It was only when his short *Austin Stories*, a trilogy shot on video and starring his siblings, won first place at the National Third Coast Film and Video Festival that Rodriguez was able to petition a professor who taught on the UT-Austin course to let him on.

After shooting *Bedhead*, an eight-minute short that cost $800 to make, in 1991 Rodriguez wrote the script for *El Mariachi*. By this point, Gallardo had returned to Mexico to assist Alfonso Arau in the making of *Like Water for Chocolate* (1992). Together, he and Rodriguez hatched a plan to shoot *El Mariachi* for around $8,000 (in the end it cost $1,000 less than that) and sell it to the Spanish video market for a small profit. Short of cash, Rodriguez decided to enter a drug study program for the company Pharmaco, who were recruiting healthy male specimens to act as guinea pigs for the princely sum of $3,000. 'It didn't seem odd at the time,' he says. 'It just felt like that's what I had to do. I had two jobs at the time, paying for school and an apartment. I didn't have money for a movie, so I had to go do something else to score money. I wasn't going to hold up the bank, so I sold my body to medical science.'

Not allowed to leave the research facility for a month, Rodriguez used the time to flesh out his idea for *El Mariachi* – the story of a guitar player (Gallardo) who gets mistaken for a ruthless criminal named Azul (Reinol Martinez). 'It was always about a musician who gets drawn into this Mafia-type world and the violence changes him,' says Rodriguez. 'He was a very peaceful guy; he cooks and plays guitar! His dreams were to be a Mariachi guitar player like his father and grandfather. I identified with that.'

Shot in August 1991, in just two and a half weeks, the film is remarkable if only because it shows what can be achieved on a minuscule budget. The sequence where the Mariachi makes his escape by landing on the roof of a bus after sliding down a telephone wire that spans a busy street is impressive, particularly given it was Gallardo who was doing the stunt. The film set the template for Rodriguez's work to come: bloodthirsty action mixed with gallows humour. From the moment the Mariachi dreams of a boy rolling a ball to him, only to see it turning into a severed head, we're made patently aware of a pattern. Domino (Consuelo Gómez), the bartender the Mariachi falls for, is described as 'the most beautiful creature of the day – next to the tortoise [seen in one of the film's opening shots as the Mariachi arrives in the town of Jimenez]'.

With hand-held camera work, crude zooms and speeded-up stock, *El Mariachi* may be technically rough but, for Rodriguez, the film set the model for how to work in the future, in terms of pacing if not of scale. 'Doing a movie is like running a marathon,' he says. 'It's an endurance test. If you gain 500 lbs before you start the race, you're going to be crawling across the finish line. So I decided to always keep it very efficient and lean, so the process of making the movie is very light, so you can run the race several times and not get tired.'

His approach to getting noticed in Hollywood was equally ad hoc. Cold-calling ICM four months after shooting the film, Rodriguez landed himself an agent and soon enough, Columbia TriStar wanted to release the film, blowing it up to 35 mm and giving the soundtrack a spit and polish. With the film touring the festival circuit – Telluride, Toronto and later Sundance (where it would win the Audience Award) – Rodriguez was reluctantly thrust into the limelight, the press fascinated by his gung-ho attitude to raising finance and shooting his movie. The result was a $2 million domestic gross.

The success of *El Mariachi* humming in his ears, Rodriguez found himself invited by the cable network Showtime to direct a film as part of its now-defunct Rebel Highway series – films inspired by classic AIP exploitation films from the 1950s. The result was *Roadracers* (1994), 'a teen angst *Rebel Without a Cause* movie set in the 1950s', as Rodriguez puts it. Shot for $1 million on 35 mm, Rodriguez considered it his warm-up movie before heading for Hollywood. Keen to keep his on-the-lam shooting style, he completed the picture in just thirteen days. 'The actors were so young, fresh and energetic that they didn't know that's not the way you're supposed to do it,' he says, 'and I liked that energy!'

14 David Arquette as Dude Delaney in *Roadracers*.

The film starred David Arquette as Dude Delaney, a no-good, rock 'n' roll–crazed drifter. He stirs up trouble in a small town run by William Sadler's power-mad lawman, partly by romancing Mexican beauty Donna (played by a young Salma Hayek, who also starred in Allison Anders's *Mi vida loca* that year). An early demonstration of Rodriguez's hyperkinetic style, it was a fast and furious effort notable for John Hawkes's turn as Arquette's geek sidekick, obsessed by *Invasion of the Body Snatchers* (1956) – a film that would in turn influence the director's 1998 film *The Faculty*.

From the moment Rodriguez signed with Columbia, it was suggested he remake *El Mariachi*. Originally called *Pistolero* until the studio changed it, the remake became known as *Desperado*. Rodriguez was keen to bring his one-man-band spirit with him and continue filling as many roles as possible. He managed to convince Columbia to let him edit the film.

> It was a studio movie and they had never done that before. They said 'We can't let you edit the movie.' Why not? 'A director never edits!' I said, 'I've already done it with *El Mariachi* and that was a studio movie, because you bought it!' So they said 'OK, we'll let you edit, but we can't let you edit in Texas! You have to edit in Los Angeles!' So I moved to Los Angeles for a year, and edited over there. They never even came by the house to see what I was doing. They just felt happier that I was near by.

A slick retread, *Desperado* took $25.4 million at the box office. It established Rodriguez as a major talent, if not quite on a par with Tarantino (the pair had formed a mutual appreciation society after meeting at the Toronto Film Festival in 1992). With Spanish hunk Antonio Banderas – hitherto known for his collaborations with Pedro Almodóvar – and Salma Hayek brought in to replace Gallardo and Gómez, the film proved if nothing else that the Columbia brass were right to let Rodriguez edit his own picture. As demonstrated by the *Desperado* trailer – one of the best-cut promos in modern cinema – Rodriguez has a feel for post-production that few other directors have. But the film was afflicted by its lack of concern for narrative, preferring to set up another shoot-out rather than advance the story in any credible direction. Like watching a slick video game, *Desperado* is a shoot 'em up that oozes style and holds back on substance.

Rodriguez's next film, *From Dusk Till Dawn* (1996), started life as a twenty-page treatment, written by Bob Kurtzman and his partner John Esposito. Kurtzman, one-third of the brains behind special-effects outfit KNB EFX, conceived the gangster cum vampire story partly as a showcase for his company's work, partly as a means to make his directorial debut. After reading Tarantino's scripts for *True Romance* and *Natural Born Killers*, Kurtzman hired him in 1990 to flesh out the idea into a fully formed screenplay for just $1,500. He, in turn, created the fake ear for *Reservoir Dogs* for a nominal fee, as a favour to Tarantino, and later some effects for *Pulp Fiction*.

Like Tarantino when he was touting his early screenplays around Hollywood, Kurtzman could not get anyone to back the script with him attached as director. But by the time *Reservoir Dogs* made a splash, interest was swelling around this unproduced Tarantino property – particularly from Rodriguez. With Kurtzman and Esposito making the shrewd decision to sell the rights to Italian producers Meir Teper and Gianni Nunnari, the project – in desperate need of a rewrite – briefly stalled when no writer dared be known as the one who worked over the words of a wunderkind. After some wrangling, it was eventually agreed that Tarantino would produce a second draft, as well as act in it, if Rodriguez committed to directing it. With Kurtzman and Esposito winding up with co-producer and story credits, KNB EFX got to provide the gore: a rare moment where everybody wins.

Their collaborations did not stop there, however. Prior to shooting *From Dusk Till Dawn*, Tarantino and Rodriguez for a time shared the same lot at Sony Pictures, as Rodriguez was in pre-production on *Desperado* and Tarantino was using the Jersey Films bungalow as a working space in the early stages of penning *Pulp Fiction*. They would hang out, swap ideas and talk about movies. Rodriguez included a juicy cameo role for Tarantino in *Desperado*, which involved him delivering a lengthy monologue in the opening sequence before being shot dead.

At the time, it was Tarantino who suggested Rodriguez make a sequel of sorts to *Desperado* – which, nine years later, he did. 'Quentin came on the set [of *Desperado*] and said: "This is great. This is your *Dollars* trilogy! No one's done this since Sergio Leone. This is your chance to do a series – but you have to do the third one more epic, and you've gotta call it *Once Upon a Time in Mexico*!"' In 2003, after *Desperado* gathered a cult audience on video and cable, that idea became a reality, with Rodriguez recalling his now-regular performers Salma Hayek and Antonio Banderas to revisit the roles.

The two directors would also collaborate on *Four Rooms* (1995), after Tarantino and producer Lawrence Bender invited Rodriguez to direct one of the four segments. The remaining two 'rooms' were directed by Allison Anders and Alexandre Rockwell, the two other members of the Class of '92. Set in the grand old Mon Signor Hotel, the four wildly different shorts – each taking place in one of the rooms – would be linked by the figure of the beleaguered bellhop Ted. Eventually played by Tim Roth, the part was initially written for Steve Buscemi, who turned it down because he felt he had already played a similar role in *Barton Fink*.

Buscemi was also disturbed by the thought of working with four directors, an intuition that served him well. The film was inevitably unbalanced, as all portmanteau movies are; only Rodriguez came out unscathed. After much deliberation, he had settled on making a family comedy for his contribution – in many ways a dry run for his later *Spy Kids* films. Entitled 'The Misbehavers', the segment saw Banderas, fresh off *Desperado*, and Chinese-American actress Tamlyn Tomita cast as the parents who pay Ted $500 to baby-sit their two little darlings while they go to a party. Havoc reigns the moment the door shuts, with the nippers wrecking the room, setting it on fire and discovering a dead body. Demonstrating Rodriguez's brilliance in the cutting room, it's the only one of the four that understands how to tell a short story on film.

'When I did *Four Rooms*, that was fun because it was like "Oh, good – boundaries!"' says Rodriguez. 'We got four walls. It can only be in one room and you have to use the bellboy on New Year's Eve. You think: "Great. I can do anything in that room now," and you can come up with more stuff because you're constricted. It was the same with *El Mariachi*. That was very easy to write because you didn't have very much – a bus, a town, a dog, a motorcycle and a ranch. It was like playing "connect the dots".'

Reputedly both Anders's and Rockwell's sections were cut back in *Four Rooms*, on the order of Harvey Weinstein, while his golden boy Tarantino was given carte blanche in his segment, 'The Man From Hollywood'. Certainly, Anders's 'The Missing Ingredient' (about a coven of witches, including Madonna, seeking a man's sperm to complete their spell) and Rockwell's 'The Wrong Man' (where Ted is mistaken by a husband for the lover of his wife) felt like insignificant doodles, dashed off during a coffee break. As for Tarantino, making his first directorial outing since *Pulp Fiction*, his arrogant joke that his segment should have been called 'The One You've All Been Waiting For' was not so far from the truth.

Influenced by 'Man from the South', the 1960 Peter Lorre/Steve McQueen episode of the long-running TV series *Alfred Hitchcock Presents* (itself based on a Roald Dahl short story of the same name), the short sees Tarantino take centre stage. He plays Chester Rush, a director whose film *The Wacky Detective* has positioned him as a Hollywood hot property. Surrounded by his ass-kissing cronies, including a near-silent and unbilled Bruce Willis, Chester bets an actor named Norman (Paul Calderon) that he can't light his Zippo on ten consecutive occasions. The stake is Chester's 1964 Chevy Chevelle versus Norman's pinkie, with bellhop Ted hired to do the severing with a hatchet, should it be required. Shot with a series of long takes (the first runs to around seven minutes) until the painful conclusion, it's a playful skit that leaves you uncertain as to whether Tarantino was mocking his own success or in full belief of the hype.

In 1995, following *Four Rooms*, both Rodriguez and Tarantino took some time off. The former spent his time on his ranch in Texas 'writing, drawing, sculpting and making babies'. Tarantino spent his time acting – on Broadway, to little acclaim, and in the nonsensical movie *Destiny Turns on the Radio*; script-doctoring – notably on Tony Scott's submarine thriller *Crimson Tide*; and setting up a distribution company, Rolling Thunder. Named after the 1977 vengeance movie starring William Devane, this Miramax-sheltered outfit was devised to bring foreign-language films (initially Wong Kar-Wai's 1994 effort *Chungking Express*) to the West.

Rodriguez would not return to directing until 1998, when he made *The Faculty* from a script by the writer of the *Scream* series, Kevin Williamson. Set in an Ohio high school, it played on the feelings of alienation and paranoia that come to most teenagers as part of growing up. 'It reminded me of my high school experience,' says Rodriguez. 'It was the chance for me to use all my high school tortures, all those terrible memories I had! It also reminded me of the movies I liked when I was in high school. All those sci-fi movies that came along in the late 1970s and early 1980s that got me interested in making movies to begin with.'

By this point, Rodriguez had already begun work on what would become his most profitable franchise, *Spy Kids*. He had pitched it to Bob Weinstein during the premiere for James Mangold's Miramax-backed

Cop Land at the 1997 Venice Film Festival. 'At that party . . . Bob Weinstein was in a particularly good mood,' remembers Rodriguez. 'I went over and pitched him the title and the concept in two sentences. He shook my hand and said "We're making it!"'

An attempt to 'try to make something that's not violent, but is still very imaginative and fun', the original *Spy Kids* (2001) began with the idea of two children (Alexa Vega and Daryl Sabara) discovering that their parents (Antonio Banderas and Carla Gugino) were espionage agents in need of rescuing. 'At the end, when [the children] become spies in the very last scene, it's the same as *El Mariachi*. At the end of that film, he becomes the guy with the guns – he takes the guitar-case full of weapons. So he's just beginning. And what's nice about this is that it gives the character a real place to go.'

Replete with enough gadgets to make Q green with envy, these pint-pot James Bonds would become as inspirational to children as those adventure-seeking tykes from such 1980s films as *The Goonies* and *Explorers*. Overrun with Rodriguez's wild imagination, the sequel – *Spy Kids 2: The Island of Lost Dreams* (2002) – would take the children to the mysterious base of an evil genetic scientist (played by Steve Buscemi). The final part of the trilogy was originally not meant to be a *Spy Kids* film; entitled *Game Over*, it was a science fiction film about some children stuck inside a computer game. Ever the innovator, Rodriguez saw his chance to round off the *Spy Kids* series as a trilogy – this time in 3-D, a method he repeated with less success in 2005's *The Adventures of Sharkboy and Lavagirl in 3-D*. Made in part 'to justify all the years I spent playing video games', *Spy Kids 3-D: Game Over*, as it became known, was another nod to the films Rodriguez grew up on – cheesy 3-D flicks like *House of Wax* (1953).

Shot in Austin almost entirely in front of a green screen with a skeletal crew, the film was markedly different from its predecessors. At times, it's a surreal mix of insider jokes (George Clooney, as the president of the United States, impersonating Sylvester Stallone, who plays five characters; hobbit Elijah Wood as a giant) and hypnotic visuals created on what Rodriguez calls 'the dream screen'. 'This movie was pure imagination,' he says. Made only two years after the original *Spy Kids* came out, it was an impressive turnaround. 'It's not as rigid as you might think an effects-driven movie would be, when you know how to do effects,' he adds. 'You're not at the mercy of storyboards laid down months before. You can be extremely flexible.'

After delving into the Western, the horror film and the action-adventure genre, Rodriguez tackled film noir for what is arguably his masterpiece to date. Once again filmed entirely in front of a green screen, *Sin City* brings Rodriguez full circle, back to his days drawing cartoons as a boy. Only this time, he's bringing someone else's work to life. Based on the acclaimed graphic novels by Frank Miller, *Sin City* lovingly translates the original panels to screen. Using them as if they were storyboards, it's undeniably the most faithful comic book adaptation of its generation. In re-creating Basin City with all its shadows and silhouettes – with the odd vivid splash of primary colour for contrast – Rodriguez can lay claim to making genuine moving pictures.

Interweaving three of Miller's stories – 'The Hard Goodbye', 'The Big Fat Kill' and 'That Yellow Bastard' – it's Rodriguez's answer to *Pulp Fiction*, with its rogues' gallery of prostitutes, waitresses, strippers, jail-birds, serial killers and pederasts. Rodriguez furthers the comparison by casting Bruce Willis as honest cop Hartigan – but, as should be clear by now, there is no rivalry between him and Tarantino. He invited his friend down to Austin to guest-direct a scene – where Dwight (Clive Owen) is driving in a car with the decapitated (and talking!) head of bent cop Jackie Boy (Benicio Del Toro) – partly as a way of showing him the possibilities of digital technology. He paid Tarantino one dollar for his work.

The film says much about Rodriguez's lack of ego. Having tran-scribed scenes word for word, he takes no screenwriting credit for his script – giving the film its full title of *Frank Miller's Sin City*. When Rodriguez originally petitioned Miller, he suggested that the comic-book maestro come on board as co-director. After much persuading Miller agreed, only for the Directors Guild of America to attempt to shut the production down a week before shooting was due to begin. Rules state that only one director may be credited per picture; Rodriguez had no choice but to resign from the Guild. 'Sometimes you have to break the rules to do something different,' he says. The maverick spirit lives on.

During the making of *Sin City*, Francis Ford Coppola visited Trouble-maker Studios and commented that this was his original dream for his American Zoetrope outfit – a place where artists could come together and experiment freely. What is truly remarkable is that even with his ninth feature film Rodriguez still has as much control as when he made *El Mariachi*. The *Spy Kids* films and *Sin City* were made with the same 'fly-by-the-seat-of-your-pants' bravura as his early films, a notable achievement for effects-driven films. If his body of work has yet to show maturity (and given his love of genre films, it may never do), his methods of production certainly embody an independent spirit that is to be applauded.

Let me tell you this. The older you get, the more rules they're gonna try to get you to follow. You just gotta keep living.
   Wooderson, *Dazed and Confused*

This same independent spirit can be found in other directors who live in Austin. The home of Mike Judge, creator of *Beavis and Butthead* and the corporate comedy feature *Office Space* (1999), it is also where Richard Linklater lives. Linklater, in particular, is responsible for spearheading the development of a filmmaking community in the city, via the Austin Film Society, which was set up in 1985. A non-profit educational organization that set out initially to present films within an artistic and cultural context (programming retrospectives with everyone from Ozu and Oshima to Pasolini and Peckinpah), this impressive arts centre has now moved into film and video production with the opening of Austin Studios in 2000. Like many others, Tarantino, who began hanging out with the Austin crowd in the mid-1990s, has presented his films to the AFS.

'It's always been way outside the industry,' says Linklater of the filmmaking community in Austin.

It's become bigger and bigger over the years. I think it's 'cos we've shaped it into something that we like. It's just big enough where you can make a movie easily, and it's still just small enough to be not an industry town at all. No one is worried about per screen averages, or opening weekend grosses . . . it doesn't permeate the culture. Robert and I, and more recently Mike Judge, we're at the froth of the industry. But really there is so much more filmmaking activity beyond us; most of it is just not as commercial. There's always a lot of interesting work going on here. It's a good community to be a part of, even if we're doing very different stuff.

If Rodriguez is the Peter Pan of American cinema, refusing to grow up, Linklater is anything but – although both took a similar studio-bound path. After *Slacker*, Linklater made the 1976-set high school graduation comedy *Dazed and Confused*. Released in 1993 for Universal, via its speciality arm Gramercy Pictures, the film remains Linklater's most autobiographical to date. A painful list of high school memories, it has, compared to most studio efforts in the genre, a nasty edge to it. Seniors torture freshman students with alarming cruelty – be it the paddle-bat spankings administered to the boys or the ketchup-coverings given to the girls. The underside of George Lucas's *American Graffiti* (1973), it eschews nostalgia and naïveté for plain speaking and pessimism. 'If I ever say these were the best years of my life, remind me to kill myself,' notes Randall 'Pink' Floyd (Jason London), the star quarterback who rebels against the coach's request to sign a pledge against drugs and alcohol.

In this film, set over just sixteen hours in a post–Vietnam and Watergate era, the youngsters reflect on their times with the lack of confidence that afflicts every generation of teenagers as they try to make sense of the world. As Cynthia (Marissa Ribisi) says: 'The Fifties were boring. The Sixties rocked. The Seventies – oh my God, they obviously suck! Maybe the Eighties will be radical . . . it can't get any worse.' Of course, with Reaganomics around the corner, we all know that for some, at least, that would not be the case.

Using long, semi-improvized takes, Linklater's freewheeling approach gradually builds a community of characters with as much skill as Robert Altman did in the same year in *Short Cuts*. With around fifty speaking roles, prudent casting gathered together a series of fledgling stars: Ben Affleck, Joey Lauren Adams, Milla Jovovich, Matthew McConaughey, Parker Posey and Nicky Katt among them. For his audition process, Linklater stipulated that overachievers were out while drop-outs were in, a quest for authenticity he would repeat when casting his 2003 studio hit *School of Rock*, where he sought kids who were primarily musicians.

'It was really just a first-time trip into studio-land,' Linklater says of *Dazed and Confused*. 'I learned on that film how to make a movie and deal with other people, like financiers. It's just gotten easier and easier over the years. A lot of the job is communication, setting the tone and making sure everyone is cool with the movie you're making.' However steep the learning curve, Linklater was not interested in compromising for the sake of harmony. The smell of marijuana permeated virtually every frame, to the point where it would prove impossible to cut out all references to drugs.

But Linklater paid the price, with the film given minimal support by the studio and recouping a moderate $7.99 million. 'Studios have a way of dumping things, if they don't think it can do a lot or if you just piss them off. Which is easy to do,' he says. 'If you insist on finishing your film – you make your movie, don't look at their notes and alienate them – their attitude is "Fine, you can have your movie, but we're not really going to run ads for it."'

15 Ethan Hawke courts Julie Delpy in *Before Sunrise*.

Subsequent to *Dazed and Confused*, Linklater continued his obsession with pursuing youth-oriented stories set over a matter of hours. Both *Before Sunrise* (1995), a two-hander romance starring Ethan Hawke and Julie Delpy as two students who meet for a night on the Budapest–Vienna train, and the Eric Bogosian–scripted *Sub-Urbia* (1996), a dark night for several souls set around a twenty-four-hour convenience store, were bankrolled by Castle Rock. While the former performed exceptionally overseas, taking in over $22 million worldwide, the latter grossed only $656,747 in the U.S. Yet

Linklater makes no apologies for seeking funds inside the system. 'I've never beleaguered Hollywood or cut down the system. To me it works. I think it's incredibly efficient and kind of beautiful. Film people are pretty smart overall, and they really do want to make good films. They just need a reason. It has to make sense – financially or whatever. You just have to not get them fired.' He questions whether the 'independent scene' even exists.

> There's no real money out there for it. The independent movie is a way to start, but you can't really do that too much. Your film shows at Sundance, and then you make your next feature for $8 million for Focus, or one of the five small companies, and then people treat you like you have denied your roots. But how can you ever do it? You can't not pay people again like that. It's good to have a budget – you can have music and take your time to do it right. People are so like 'Oh, sellout!' It's ridiculous.

This cry grew with his next film, the Western/gangster hybrid *The Newton Boys* (1998) which reunited Linklater with Hawke and McConaughey in a 1920-set story about four Texan sibling bank robbers. Made for Twentieth Century Fox, it was Linklater's highest budget film (at $27 million) until he made *School of Rock*. Recouping just $10.4 million domestic, it crashed and burned, though Linklater was more concerned with the pigeonhole in which he had been placed, having become a reluctant and unofficial spokesman for Generation X. 'People were offended when the guy that did *Slackers* made a Western/gangster movie,' he says. 'Are you kidding? I come from Texas. I grew up around horses!'

It's no surprise that Linklater recoiled from Hollywood after that, retreating to Austin to make his best two films to date, *Waking Life* and *Tape* (both 2001). 'The studios at that point were running from me. That's when I first felt I was in mid-career. Up to that point, I'd been able to do everything I wanted. That was the first time I started getting stop-signs. The industry was changing, and I didn't realize it. It has changed – I couldn't get *Dazed and Confused* made today. You can't get a $6 million film made with no stars. Things have shifted. And you can't raise that kind of money outside the studio system.'

A companion piece of sorts to *Slacker*, *Waking Life* was produced via a groundbreaking computer-generated animation process known as Rotoscoping, which uses captured video footage as a template for

3-D animation. Designed by Austin-based animator Bob Sabiston, the software lent an appropriate dream-like quality to the film. Appropriate, given that the film – like *Slacker*, made up of a series of loosely connecting vignettes – follows its unnamed protagonist (Wiley Wiggins) as if in a waking dream. Told that 'dream is destiny', he encounters a string of characters and listens to their theories and beliefs, finally to realize that it's questions, and not answers, that are important. Characters range from the fictional and the familiar – Hawke and Delpy reprise their *Before Sunrise* roles, this time in bed – to the real, from celebrated motormouth tour guide Timothy 'Speed' Levitch to Soderbergh himself.

'The people at Fox Searchlight liked it, and threw it into the world,' remembers Linklater. 'It registered and made its little mark out there, so I was lucky. People think we live in this Darwinist world, where all films are created and distributed evenly, and the ones you've heard of are the best ones. But it's really not like that. All films are not released equally. There's got to be someone who is passionate in thinking that film can make them a lot of money.'

Linklater would discover this with *Tape*, which was also shot on high-definition digital video, this time in a staggering six days. After *SubUrbia*, he once again recruited a playwright (in this case Stephen Belber) to adapt his own work. A modern morality play, it's an exuberant three-hander (between Hawke, Uma Thurman and Robert Sean Leonard) that plays out – yet again for the director – over the course of one night.

Set entirely in a Michigan motel room, it concerns a trio of former high school friends and a cassette that contains the confession of a sordid event from their past history. Articulate, witty and gripping, the film succeeds in spite of – or perhaps because of – the limitations Linklater imposes upon himself. Calculated with the precision of a chess game, but feeling spontaneous throughout, *Tape* benefits from the DV medium's flexibility. Primarily, it helps Linklater conjure an intimacy that inspires some cracking performances from the actors – notably from Hawke who bounces all over the room as if let off a leash.

The film was co-produced by Independent Digital Entertainment (InDigEnt), an innovative digital filmmaking collective financed by the Independent Film Channel to produce low-budget digital feature films. Typically, 'No one in Hollywood even saw *Tape*, as far as I can tell,' laments Linklater. 'Out here, it's such a small film it doesn't even register.

It meant nothing to anyone. Fundamentally, that film didn't even have a distributor. New York City was the only place it played well.'

But one man who did see it (and loved it) was the producer Scott Rudin. He had been sending Linklater scripts for years, in the hope of collaborating with him. Rudin, the tenacious New Yorker behind films as diverse as *Zoolander* (2001) and *The Hours* (2002) remains one of Hollywood's most maverick-minded producers. The perfect embodiment of the 'indiewood' spirit, his work has drawn him to the likes of Wes Anderson (*The Royal Tenenbaums* and *The Life Aquatic with Steve Zissou*) and Russell (*I ❤ Huckabees*). But it was an unashamedly feel-good script by Mike White that finally united Rudin and Linklater.

White, who is known for his more extreme scripts like *Chuck & Buck* (2000) and *The Good Girl* (2002), wrote *School of Rock* for his neighbour, the explosive hairball Jack Black. Perfect casting, you might say, given that the film concerns a failed musician who bluffs his way into a prep school and teaches his uptight pupils how to rock. 'In a long line of films, this is my kids film,' says Linklater, again echoing Rodriguez's path. 'I felt like this film was calling me, that it needed me in some way. When you're doing a movie, it's good to feel like no one else could do it. Obviously, a lot of other people could have directed this movie, but I felt I had something to offer. This was something I would've been afraid of a long time ago.'

Remarkably, the film proved to be the biggest hit of Linklater's career, reaping nearly $80 million at the U.S. box office. As if to pre-empt further criticisms that he had sold out, he immediately followed it with *Before Sunset* (2004) 'an anti-sequel', as he calls it, to 'a film that wasn't very successful'. Following this with a remake of the base-ball comedy *Bad News Bears* (2005), with Billy Bob Thornton, what it does show is that Linklater has managed, finally, to manoeuvre him-self into a position whereby he can be successful in both the studio arena and the non-commercial world he came from. 'I think the stu-dios are more clear on what they're doing now,' he warns, referring to the fact that within the system an obvious division between studio and art house has been made. It means 'in between' films like *The Newton Boys* – 'sort of a studio film, but just weird enough to not be' – can no longer get made.

While running parallel to Rodriguez's, Linklater's career has fol-lowed the highs and lows of Soderbergh's. An indie hit (*Slacker*), followed by studio failures (*Dazed and Confused*, *The Newton Boys*), fringe productions (*Tape*, *Waking Life*), a commercial hit (*School of Rock*) and a return to his roots (*Before Sunset*). 'I will always have this opportunity to make low-budget personal films,' he says. 'The planets have to align correctly to do a bigger studio film. But when they align, it's wonderful. I learned that from Soderbergh, who felt that way about *Out of Sight*. It was something that came along and he thought he could do something with.'

As it turns out, Linklater is now collaborating with Soderbergh's Section Eight company on an adaptation of Philip K. Dick's acclaimed novel *A Scanner Darkly*. Set in the near future, when a widespread drug called Substance D causes split personalities, it is Linklater's biggest undertaking to date. With a cast including Keanu Reeves, Robert Downey Jr and Woody Harrelson, the footage will be animated with the Rotoscoping method previously used on *Waking Life*. You might say this is his *Sin City*. Like his fellow Austin resident Rodriguez, Linklater remains a genuine innovator.

CHAPTER 8

Genre I: Crime Does Pay –
The Underneath, *The Usual Suspects* and *Se7en*

16 *The Usual Suspects*: 'Five Criminals. One Line Up. No Coincidence.'

> In the 1990s, noir's retro edge has paradoxically given it post-modern chic. 'Noir' is not only the name of a cycle of historical crime movies, it is also a come-on in promoting new crime movies . . . A kind of shorthand for sex in the big city, a place where greed and desire intersect in fatal attractions, noir has become a potent marketing tool.[29]

> Noir names a knot of feelings and intuitions – dread, uncertainty, paranoia – that won't go away . . . absorbent and surprisingly mobile, noir has continued to be a reflection of the Zeitgeist – but only up to a point and only obliquely, metaphorically. Noir is not, after all, a documentary style.[30]

Be aware: crime and punishment do not always go hand in hand here; justice is not for all. The crime genre, in its broadest possible sense, has been broached by nearly all the directors considered in this book. Some, such as Quentin Tarantino, rarely dance to any other tune. Others, like Steven Soderbergh and David Fincher, return to it frequently. Even the likes of Wes Anderson, Paul Thomas Anderson, Robert Rodriguez and Bryan Singer have dabbled. Only Alexander Payne, David O. Russell and Spike Jonze have steered totally clear of the genre, albeit to focus on other forms of social transgression.

Following the year of *Pulp Fiction*, 1995 saw the arrival of three films from this new crop of directors; like Tarantino, they set out to remodel the crime genre for the contemporary audience. Soderbergh's *The Underneath*, and in particular Singer's *The Usual Suspects* and Fincher's *Se7en*, would be key films in the revolution of the crime genre, a shift taken to its logical extreme with Soderbergh's *The Limey* four years later. With the characteristics of 'dread, uncertainty and paranoia' soaked into their very fabric, they represented a common pessimistic world view shared by their directors.

It seems highly appropriate that each falls under the bracket of neo-noir – an admittedly loose term used to describe everything from Lawrence Kasdan's *Body Heat* (1981) to David Lynch's self-dubbed '21st century horror noir' *Lost Highway* (1997). The word 'neo' implies a fresh twist on a traditional style: something you might say each of the directors in this study was striving to achieve. As if to reinforce the break with tradition, backing came from the new breed of Hollywood studio. *The Underneath* and *The Usual Suspects* were both released in the U.S. by Gramercy Pictures, while *Se7en* was bankrolled by New Line. As stated at the top of this chapter, film noir is a recognizably marketable style – and with the parameters already shifted by Tarantino, crime was back in vogue.

Rather than strictly adhering to film noir, however, these three films belong to sub-genres – the heist movie in the case of *The Usual Suspects* and *The Underneath,* and the serial-killer film with *Se7en*. It is a reflection of the fractured nature of contemporary society that the mid-1990s crime film could no longer be categorized simply. It didn't hurt that neo-noir offered these directors the chance to use the parameters of film noir to riff on their favoured themes. If *The Underneath* is less concerned with the crime genre's tropes – the femme fatale preying on the weak and confused male, for example – Soderbergh proves enamoured of noir's innate sense of fatalism and the possibilities it offers for experimenting with style and structure.

In *Se7en*, the story of two detectives on the trail of a serial killer using the seven deadly sins as his guide, Fincher uses the rain-soaked cityscape so often seen in film noir to represent the relentless erosion of morals in contemporary society. It's a theme that has reappeared in each of his subsequent works to date. Meanwhile, Singer's *The Usual Suspects* – a self-conscious shaggy-dog story that uses the noir voice-over for its own ingenious reasons – touches on the use of myth in contemporary society, something he returned to for his *X-Men* films.

All three films contributed to the acceleration of the crime journey away from traditional narrative, morals, style and/or structure. And while each would prove key in the development of its director's career, they were received with varying degrees of critical and commercial success. For Fincher, who will be explored in depth in Chapter 10, *Se7en* was the equivalent of cinematic salvation, as it unexpectedly crept its way to $100 million in the U.S., following his much-maligned studio debut film *Alien³*. Meanwhile, *The Usual Suspects* cemented Singer's reputation – even if it was Kevin Spacey and writer Christopher McQuarrie who won the Oscars. Yet listening to Soderbergh, you'd think it was his professional low point. '*The Underneath* was frustrating,' he says. 'I didn't feel like the movie worked, but I learned a lot while making it. I was really not happy with where I was going. I really felt like the films were getting increasingly controlled. I was becoming a formalist, which was not what I wanted to do.'

Now I understand the appeal of just walking away. There's something very powerful about being absent.
Rachel, *The Underneath*

A reworking of Don Tracy's novel (originally filmed in 1949 by Robert Siodmak under its actual title, *Criss Cross*), the adaptation of *The Underneath* had been written by Soderbergh under the pseudonym of Sam Lowry, a reference to Jonathan Pryce's Everyman character in Terry Gilliam's *Brazil*. He became increasingly disenchanted with the project and admits that working on set with dwindling enthusiasm was a sobering experience. 'There's something somnambulant about *The Underneath*. I was sleepwalking in my life and my work, and it shows. It offered some challenges in terms of fractured narrative that I was interested in, just not interested enough.'[31]

If anything, *The Underneath* precipitated Soderbergh's desire for cinematic purification. Part of a much needed cleansing, finally achieved via his subsequent no-budget films *Schizopolis* and *Gray's Anatomy*, it pre-empted the second, and more successful, phase of Soderbergh's career beginning with *Out of Sight*. What's more, with its complex narrative weaving the story across three time lines, it marked his first significant experimentation with structure – which would be repeated more potently in *The Limey* and *Out of Sight*. With the use of coloured filters to distinguish separate parts of the narrative – an attempt, with the use of sea-green and indigo-blue colours in particular, to evoke the visual textures of classic noir – Soderbergh would also apply a technique he later reprised to better effect for *Traffic*.

Yet one suspects Soderbergh is being unnecessarily harsh on himself. Deflated after the ambivalent reception – and commercial failings – of *King of the Hill*, his problems with *The Underneath* are more to do with his own disillusion with the realities of the film industry, after the highs of his stratospheric debut, than with the film's own flaws. While it probably is the coldest of Soderbergh's films – no doubt a product of his own personal troubles of the time – its narrative and stylistic experiments are to be applauded. If the film is half-hearted in any way, perhaps that's because it remains stranded between two genres –

noir and the existential thriller – and Soderbergh never successfully melds the two, or even wants to.

While the film uses no voice-over, it demonstrates a faithful understanding of the mechanics of film noir, even if Soderbergh deconstructed them for his own purposes. The plot is labyrinthine, full of multiple double-crosses. Set in Austin, it focuses on Michael Chambers (Peter Gallagher) arriving home after a prolonged absence. Running into Rachel (Alison Elliot), the girl he abandoned when he previously fled town, he soon becomes embroiled in a heist with her new boyfriend, a crooked, violent and possessive club owner named Tommy Dundee (William Fichtner).

At first glance, *The Underneath* is a faithful update of *Criss Cross*, which also features the return of a prodigal son who hooks up with his former lover, now married to a small-time crook (also called Dundee). Likewise, Siodmak's film saw its protagonist (played by Burt Lancaster) find a job at an armoured car company and propose a heist, only to be double-crossed by his one-time girlfriend, Anna (Yvonne De Carlo). Yet while Lancaster's Steve Thompson is besotted, Gallagher's Michael Chambers is not, instead falling – for a time – into the arms of bank employee Susan (Elisabeth Shue), whom he meets on his homeward journey.

Defined by his lack of passion, lack of commitment to others, and selfishness, Michael forgets to buy his mother a present for her wedding, and wears his dead father's suit to the ceremony. He is a man without purpose who has 'skated along' on his 'looks and charm'. As Rachel accurately notes, 'beneath the apathetic exterior there was actually a raging indifference', and we remain no more enlightened than she as to his desires – it's not even clear if *he* knows what he wants. Compare this to the other characters – Tommy wants power, money and control over Rachel; Michael's obsessed brother David also wants Rachel; Rachel wanted Michael – and by the end wants revenge; even Michael's mother desires a new husband.

Continually taunted for this indecision by the narrative, as Michael enters the local bar, he is twice given pass-out hand stamps: first 'Sucker' and then 'Loser'. In an amusing comment on the contemporary desire for self-help books, Soderbergh even has Michael reading *Self-Esteem: A User's Guide* and *Saying Hello to Yourself* – all to no avail. Self-improvement, according to Soderbergh's film, is futile, with fate and fortune governing everyone's lives. As Michael is told by his mother's partner Ed, for some people 'the planets just don't line up, and there's nothing you can do about it'. This notion of luck is reinforced by Rachel's audition, where she reads out lottery numbers, and the card games played by the armoured car crew. Michael, like a cork bobbing along in the ocean, abandons himself to forces beyond his control. In flashback, we discover he allowed his fate to be changed by the result of a football game and had no qualms about walking out on Rachel when the outcome went against him. Upon return, he now gambles with lives – including his own.

Having removed the story from the big, bad city to pleasant suburban surroundings, Soderbergh gives further evidence that he has little interest in the tropes of film noir with his dismantling of the femme fatale character. Unlike *Criss Cross*'s rotten-to-the-core Anna, Rachel shifts in her journey from devoted lover (in the flashbacks) to resentful spouse (in the present). Even her absconding with the money, when she crosses Michael, is motivated not so much by greed as by her desire to finally exercise some power in their relationship – one that has been dominated by miscommunications. As if to symbolize this, Soderbergh ensures that many of Rachel's conversations with Michael take place on the telephone, with its crackle-infested line depriving the users of a clear medium to talk by.

Like *Pulp Fiction* before it, *The Underneath* rejects linear storytelling. As indicated by the overlapping time lines, events from the past hold a grip over those in the present. One particular edit – a flashback scene of Michael in bed with Rachel, rolling over and cutting to a present-day sequence of him completing the manoeuvre with his current bedfellow Susan – emphasizes this. The narrative oscillates between these flashbacks to Michael's past with Rachel, the robbery and its aftermath (complete with precise clock readings for each scene) and events leading up to the heist, starting with Michael's return to Austin. Soderbergh differentiates between the three with a variety of methods – from the presence of Michael's beard to indicate the flashbacks to the use of the ominous green filter to represent the armoured car/robbery sequences, as well as, perhaps, Michael's murky mental state.

With the use of filters achieving an expressionist intensity in the absence of black and white, Soderbergh builds on this atmosphere of uncertainty and malaise with a series of uncomfortable and alienating camera angles. In the aforementioned sequences of Michael in the armoured car, bars on the windscreen frame him. Just as his claustrophobic surname suggests, it hints at his potential incarceration. With sets often decorated with half-open venetian blinds, it's an indication that the protagonists' actions are visible to outsiders, despite their attempts to hide them. The most potent expression of this vulnerability comes in the unsettling hospital sequence – a fine retread of the scene in *Criss Cross* – where frequent visitors induce paranoia in a bed-bound Michael, as he becomes increasingly concerned for his safety.

It can be reasonably argued that *The Underneath* is a self-conscious exercise in appropriating the noir aesthetic for an altogether different set of characters. If *Criss Cross* – like so many of its peers – was dominated by fear of the female, Soderbergh's film rejects this in favour of less tangible worries. Set in a cynical era where even the head of a security firm will rob his own company, the film shows greed to have infiltrated every level of society. As one critic suggested, Michael 'may be described as the metaphorical void at the heart of Soderbergh's existential thriller'[32] – matched by Gallagher's deliberately bland and inexpressive turn. Living a fragmented existence, he is a product of the modern world – an empty vessel, with no firm convictions, drifting towards apathy and indifference. Even the conclusion, as Michael is left wounded but alive, provides him with an ambiguous destiny.

A man can't change what he is. He can convince anyone he's someone else but never himself.
Verbal Kint, *The Usual Suspects*

It was Soderbergh who introduced Bryan Singer to production designer Howard Cummings, who would work on *The Underneath* shortly before moving on to *The Usual Suspects*, the only time to date that he would collaborate with either director. Compared to his work for Soderbergh – recreating decidedly low-key small-town locations – the world of *The Usual Suspects* was a far more sophisticated, urban environment. Reminiscent of noir terrain, its landscape is that of interrogation and line-up rooms, gutted glass office buildings, underground car parks and warehouses. While it was left to cinematographer Elliot Davis to create the atmosphere in *The Underneath*, with his grungy lighting, Cummings had more opportunity to influence the psychological landscape of Singer's film. Take the key sequence when the usual suspects themselves are confronted with their mission: set in a room bathed in a reddish hue and dominated by a pool table, it immediately spells danger before a word is said.

As if to symbolize Singer and McQuarrie's transition from Sundance Kids to Hollywood players, the writer dreamed up the idea for *The Usual Suspects* while queuing to see a rival competition entry during the year *Public Access* triumphed in Park City. At the time, he was standing in line with friend Dylan Kussman, who had appeared in *Lion's Den* and would go on to feature in a small role in *X-Men* sequel *X2*. Conceiving of the notion of five criminals meeting in a line-up, McQuarrie even found the idea for the poster, in retrospect one of the most definitive images of American cinema in the 1990s. In McQuarrie's mind, celluloid crime would look cool again, as it did in *Pulp Fiction*. Yet unlike, say, Gary Fleder's *Things to Do in Denver When You're Dead* from the same year, *The Usual Suspects* manages it without being self-conscious – aside from the fact that the gang members all hold their guns sideways, of course.

Also at Sundance that year was the British producer Robert Jones, who saw *Public Access* and was impressed by Singer and McQuarrie's evident talents. A former director of acquisitions for Palace Pictures, Jones – who would go on to co-produce Paul Thomas Anderson's *Hard Eight* – is often credited, rather incorrectly, with 'discovering' Singer. Certainly, when he received the script for *The Usual Suspects* six months later, he was wise enough not to pass up the chance to take Singer and McQuarrie to the next level – albeit on a $5.5 million budget, with the film to be shot in thirty-five days. 'The script really inspired me,' he said. 'I saw elements from films of the late 1960s and early 1970s – a period rife with crime films of a type that hasn't been touched on in any way since. I think Chris would be at home writing his machine gun dialogue in the Hollywood of the 1940s and 1950s, and Bryan is able to transpose the work into a contemporary setting and make it shine.'

As we will see, Jones's comparison of the film to crime movies made in Hollywood twenty-five years before is rather inaccurate. Yet Singer notes that his agenda in making *The Usual Suspects* was 'to bridge the gap between mainstream and independent, by doing an interesting film on a large canvas, the way it was back in the 1970s'. Such a transition was largely achieved through the casting with a group of actors who had straddled both worlds, at home in neither one nor the other. Eschewing star wattage, Singer deliberately assembled a B-list cast to play out what is a stylish B movie; actors like Dan Hedaya, Giancarlo Esposito and Chazz Palminteri would have fared well in the Hollywood of yore that Jones refers to.

As for the main players, Singer deliberately chose a heady mix of acting styles brought by actors who were recognizable but would not overshadow the film's tricky narrative. At the time, Gabriel Byrne was probably the best known of the five. He was chosen to play former bent cop Dean Keaton, in part as a self-conscious reference to his role as a 1930s gangster in the Coen brothers' *Miller's Crossing* (1990), where he wore a similar hat-and-coat ensemble. It might be hard to remember, but at the time the listless-looking Kevin Spacey, who plays cardigan-wearing con artist cripple Roger 'Verbal' Kint, was best known for his stage work. Most people thought Benicio Del Toro actually spoke in the muffled Hispanic accent that he adopted for the role of Fred Fenster. Cast as 'top-notch entry man' Michael McManus, Stephen Baldwin was, and still is, one of the more invisible members of his fraternal acting clan. Kevin Pollak, as explosives expert Todd Hockney, has never had the screen profile he deserves. Yet both injected much-needed (and misplaced) cocky self-assurance into the story.

What separates *The Usual Suspects* from a run-of-the-mill crime thriller is not its performers, good as they are. Not unlike *The Underneath*, with its experiments in how to unfurl a narrative, *The Usual Suspects* is about the art of storytelling; the difference being that it builds an entire film around the theme. It begins with a police lineup – our five felons have been brought in for a routine shakedown. Flash forward six weeks. Soon to prove himself a consummate yarn-spinner, Verbal is one of only two survivors found on a San Pedro-docked boat, where it is thought a $91 million dope deal took place. With the majority of the story told in flashback, Verbal is our guide and narrator through this dark-lit world of hijacks and heists. What is fascinating in the film is how he gets from A (the lineup) to Z (the boat raid), two events that we can be sure happened.

Forced to chew the fat with U.S. customs agent Dave Kujan (Palminteri) before he makes bail, Verbal constructs an elaborate story to fill in the gaps, mixing truth with a liberal dose of fiction. It transpires that the cargo was not narcotics but an Argentinian informer, being exchanged at a high price. Out to stop the trade was Keyser Soze, a supposedly mythical criminal of Turkish-German descent. Via his lawyer, Kobayashi (Pete Postlethwaite), he blackmails the quintet of criminals from the lineup into helping him get on board the guarded ship to kill off the informer who might bring him to justice.

The identity of Keyser Soze is a question that has jammed Internet message boards ever since. Kujan believes Soze to be Keaton, who disappeared – presumed killed in a fire – three years ago to evade a murder charge. After a brief clip of Keaton firing gunshots on the boat, Singer and McQuarrie allow us to contemplate the idea that perhaps he is Soze – something that fooled even Gabriel Byrne who left the shoot believing he played the kingpin. This is the red herring before the real revelation, beautifully shown by editor John Ottman. With Kujan smugly sipping his coffee after Verbal's departure, he casually studies the bulletin board on the interrogation room wall. Key words from Verbal's story catch his eye on posters and notices. As his cup smashes on the floor, upon the underside of the china is the word 'Kobayashi'. We cut between this and Verbal, whose name translates in Hungarian as '*szó szerinti*' or '*szó sze*', if you shorten it; in one magical below-waist shot, his limp disappears, his hand flexes and he begins to smoke a cigarette in a different way. 'And like that . . . he was gone.'

That was some performance – not least from Verbal himself. The type of narrative that forces you to reread and rethink what has gone before. When you recall Verbal's lines, you realize he was taunting Kujan with his identity. 'You think you can catch Keyser Soze?' he asks. 'You think a guy like that comes this close to getting caught and sticks his head out. If he comes up for anything, it'll be to get rid of me. After that, my guess is, you'll never hear from him again.'

As Kevin Pollak said, 'When you read this script, you realize that this is why audiences go to movie theatres, to be drawn in by the story, to follow closely, to be truly curious. It's a movie that makes you feel smart. It doesn't cater to you like so many movies do, like fast food. When was the last time you went to a film and were utterly baffled?'[33] Whether it makes you feel smart or conned – for paying attention to a story full of half-truths and fabrications – is up to you. As it's almost impossible to discern what actually happened in Verbal's story, the consequences of everyone's actions are rendered meaningless.

This, more than any other reason, is why Jones's comparison of *The Usual Suspects* to the crime films from the 1970s is largely inaccurate. As Singer says, 'I like toying with points of view, taking a mainstream genre and bending it a little.' What he and McQuarrie have created is not a crime film based around the social injustices of the day but a post-modern study about, in an agnostic age, our need for myth. Soze is repeatedly referred to as Satanic. 'How do you shoot the Devil in the back?' says Verbal. 'What if you miss?' Soze has become 'a spook story that criminals tell their kids at night', as Verbal reports, a latter-day Bogeyman present to maintain order in the absence of religious belief.

The film is also an examination of the process of acting, with a narrative that is as much a performer – if not more so – than any of the actors. The line-up scene shows the five actors helplessly break-ing into fits of laughter and almost breaking character. No doubt Singer could've eventually got them to shoot the scene straight, but keeping this take for the final edit shows he was already thinking about the nature of performance in relation to cinema. Emphasizing this, five people appear as Soze in the film – Byrne, Spacey, Singer (his foot is glimpsed), Ottman (who turns in a close-up as Soze's hand) and trainee intern Scott Morgan (who plays the long-haired younger Soze, seen in flashback). Singer has called the movie 'a self-reflexive commentary on film': about how it's a medium set to the director's pace that can be manipulated to mislead you, more so than a novel or a painting.

Quite rightly, Foster Hirsch notes that 'using genre conventions like voice-over, labyrinthine plotting, spatial and temporal ruptures in new and devious ways, *The Usual Suspects* is something of a commentary on noir resources, a cunning, masterful meta-noir. The film's very clev-erness, however, confines it to a narrow thematic zone. In the richest vein of classic and neo-noir, criminality vibrates with cultural, psy-chological and thematic resonance. Limiting characters and narrative to a celebration of skilled performance, *The Usual Suspects* ends up being about nothing other than its own admirable, if finally hollow, ingenuity.'[34]

The film's persistence in reminding us that this is a neo-noir is largely thanks to the work of Newton Thomas Sigel, Singer's regular cinematog-rapher since *The Usual Suspects*. Providing the requisite amount of shade to darken Howard Cummings's use of colour, Sigel is evidently well aware what genre he is working in. Further indication of this comes with the character of Verbal, who recalls *The Underneath*'s Michael Chambers, in that he's a cipher with no discernible personal-ity. By the end, as the man we now assume is Keyser Soze packs him away, all we have learnt about Verbal ceases to become relevant, as he is merely a fiction. Existing in a lawless world akin to the one created in *The Underneath*, the film celebrates the amoral anti-hero who manages to outplay the authorities.

Coming after *The Crying Game*, *The Usual Suspects* was not the first high profile film in the 1990s to spring a major final-act surprise on the unsuspecting audience. Nor did it – via its marketing campaign – play up the fact that a twist was coming. The tagline, 'Five Criminals. One Line Up. No Coincidence', barely hints at the fact that our quintet are meant to meet. What's more – unlike the transsexual Dil, who comes into the plot reasonably early in *The Crying Game* – the figure of Keyser Soze is barely referenced until halfway through the film. Those who claim to have guessed in the first few minutes that Verbal is Soze are either lying or remarkably perceptive. Relying on the audience not to spoil its secrets, while spreading positive word of mouth, the producers got what they wished for. After it became the unqualified must-see hit of the Cannes Film Festival that year, it captured the imaginations of filmgoers, taking it to a respectable $23.3 million domestic gross.

And with it, U.S. independent cinema and mainstream Hollywood took a step closer to each other. Singer thinks he knows why. 'All of a sudden, here was a slick-looking Hollywood movie with very sly turns of phrase and drama and revelation, and yet at the same time it came out of nowhere. I think that made people confused as to what kind of a film this was. It hadn't been done in a long time – the unreliable narrator not pissing an audience off, while actually tricking people.'

It all sums up a remarkable shift for the crime film in the mid-1990s. If the films noirs of the 1940s were veiled expressions of misogyny, fifty years on the focus changed. It is fear of the unknown, of the past and of the self that dominates these introspective noir characters. Furthermore, as suggested by the non-linear fractured narratives, the contemporary criminal underworld is no longer governed by a straightforward code of ethics. There are no more godfathers in this godless universe, merely narrators who lead us astray. And as David Fincher will show, the meltdown has already started. Sodom and Gomorrah once more, the society of *Se7en* is a rain-soaked horror show where misdeeds are perpetrated as a matter of course by everyday folk. Once-strong moral barriers have been washed away in a tide of filth.

I did not choose. I was chosen.
John Doe, Se7en

In the grand scheme of things, the impact of Kevin Spacey's arrival in *Se7en*, released shortly after *The Usual Suspects*, will be lost on future audiences. Spacey's entrance as the deranged killer John Doe is, after all, dramatic enough. In the game of chess Doe plays with detectives Mills (Brad Pitt) and Somerset (Morgan Freeman), this is the check before the mate. To this point, he has managed to evade capture, by both the cops and the camera. Walking into the police station, arms aloft, he gives himself up – a triumphant twist far more unsettling than the finale of *The Usual Suspects*. While attentive viewers may have recognized his voice from an earlier phone conversation he conducts with his adversaries, we finally get to see that the actor behind the mask – uncredited in the opening titles, at his insistence – is Spacey. For viewers who had just seen *The Usual Suspects* for the first time, the unannounced arrival of Spacey must have been a heart-trembling shock. Who was this fellow, acting his second incarnation of evil in a row?

The presence of Spacey in both films is not the only parallel. A cipher like Verbal, John Doe is also a storyteller, leaving a series of interlocking clues from one murder to the next, which he expects the detectives to piece together. His tale speaks of disgust with all forms of human excess; punishing each victim with a death that fits their own sin, 'his murders are sermons to us', as Somerset puts it. While Spacey's character in *The Usual Suspects* (assuming you believe he is Keyser Soze) operates as if he were a higher power, John Doe acts on behalf of one. Even Mills's comment 'he's not the Devil . . . he's just a man' is of little assurance.

But while *The Usual Suspects* is a film that emphasizes our lack of spiritual guidance in the modern age, *Se7en* is a critique of both the moral vacuum contemporary society finds itself in and the dangers of religious fundamentalism. Written by Andrew Kevin Walker while he was working a day job in Tower Records, *Se7en* is so disturbing for the reason that Doe acts on our behalf. A vigilante on a mission from God, he is like a twisted version of Travis Bickle's avenging angel, here to wash the scum off the streets. During his investigation, Mills even invokes *Taxi Driver*, though not by name, referring to John Hinckley and his obsession with Jodie Foster, which came from watching her rescued by Robert De Niro's Travis Bickle in the film.

Once captured, Doe takes great offence when Mills refers to him killing 'innocent' people. 'Only in a world this shitty could you say those people are innocent and try to say it with a straight face,' comes the reply. What is difficult about *Se7en* is that it's hard not to agree with him on some level. Are we complicit in his crimes? Secretly, Mills – ultimately punished for his wrath – harbours the same disgust with the world as Doe. Witness his repulsion when he interviews the pimp during his investigation, asking him if he likes what he does. 'No, but that's life, isn't it?' is the answer, the perfect example of what Mills's partner Somerset, on the verge of retirement at the end of the week, feels. 'I don't think I can continue to live in a place that embraces, or nurtures, apathy as a virtue,' he says. 'Apathy is a solution. It's easier to lose yourself in drugs than cope with life.'

While Walker wrote the script during an unhappy period he spent in New York, the anonymous and imaginary rain-drenched city of *Se7en* could be anywhere in the world. With its compact architecture recollecting the mean streets of classic film noir, it's a place where people no longer care. Awash with moral decay, this is a society where the seven deadly sins are commonplace. The literary references that Walker introduces – Milton's *Paradise Lost*; Dante's *The Divine Comedy*, chiefly the *Inferno* and *Purgatory*; and, to some extent, Chaucer's bawdy *Canterbury Tales* – speak for themselves. Over the centuries, nothing has changed. As Somerset rightly predicts, 'This isn't going to have a happy ending' – though he could easily mean the world at large, rather than this particular part of it.

A former employee of the low-budget film company Bryson, the Pennsylvania-born Walker had, prior to *Se7en*, penned a couple of little-seen horror films, with titles like *Brainscan* (1994) and *Hideaway* (1995). Yet he was canny enough to realize that what frightens audiences is the imagination; in other words, the scenes of 'turning sin against the sinner', as Doe puts it, should be kept off screen. So diabolical were Walker/Doe's punishments that the aftermath was stomach-churning enough. Certainly, with 'Lust', the sight of a prostitute being vaginally penetrated with a knife harnessed to her client would be the stuff of the X-rated video nasty. Likewise, for 'Greed', the lawyer carving out the pound of flesh from his own body would have had the censors reaching for their scissors.

But consider the others: 'Pride', wherein a woman has her nose cut off and the choice to either kill herself with an overdose or phone for help, or 'Gluttony', the opening murder, in which an obese man is forced at gunpoint to eat until he haemorrhages. Worst of all, there is 'Sloth', where a pederast drug dealer named Victor is paralysed and kept alive for a year, as he wastes away. Cinematically, discovering the aftermath of these crimes – such as the knowledge that Victor chewed his own tongue off – is far more dramatic than actually watching them go down. Both Fincher and Walker understood this implicitly: words were far more powerful than pictures. Filled with ideas that fester in the back of your brain, *Se7en* is the sort of script that gets under your skin like a tick and has to be burnt out.

From the outside, as Fincher thought when he read the first twenty pages, it is just another buddy cop movie – Mills is even called Serpico at one point by his wife. As you would expect, our heroes are polar opposites. Somerset is methodical and restrained, having never fired his gun in his whole career; Mills is the rookie hothead who has already been embroiled in a shoot-out and can't even remember the name of the fellow cop who died. While Somerset is learned and literary, Mills is more in tune with pop culture – which is why he needs CliffsNotes to get through Chaucer. Denying that Doe is like *Star Wars*' green guru Yoda 'just because he has a library card', Mills later tells the killer: 'You're no Messiah. You're a movie-of-the-week. A T-shirt at best.' If his frame of reference is trash television, he's in the wrong movie, for *Se7en* praises and rewards intellect above all else.

Half noir-inflected police procedural, half serial-killer flick, *Se7en* far outweighs its rivals, escaping its generic confines by evolving into something far more sinister by the finale. The only film close to *Se7en*'s cold-edged brutality is John McNaughton's *Henry: Portrait of a Serial Killer* (1986), so raw it felt like a documentary. Others that followed – Jon Amiel's *Copycat* (1995), Philip Noyce's *The Bone Collector* (1999) and D. J. Caruso's *Taking Lives* (2004), to name but three – take great pains to dream up an inventive modus operandi for their killers only to ensure the conclusion restores the status quo.

Se7en was not Fincher's first experience of a serial killer. When he was growing up in Martin County, California, 'for about six to eight months, the Zodiac Killer was around so we were all being followed by the California Highway Patrol in our little yellow school buses, but this was the only thing to break up the idyllic patina'.[35] If the innocence of childhood was disturbed, it evidently benefited *Se7en*. It's to Fincher's credit that he fought for the film's darker elements. But fighting on Walker's behalf was not his only contribution. His direction, in harness with Arthur Max's production design and Darius Khondji's gloomy cinematography, helps create a relentless atmosphere of dread. Until the finale, every exterior scene is overcast and often teeming with rain – so much so that the actors were forced to wear wetsuits under their clothes during the shoot.

This perpetual dreariness is echoed in the interiors, where nobody ever seems to open the curtains. Torches are the only source of light, as they enter the cluttered and claustrophobic rooms where dust hangs in the air, disturbed for the first time in years. So pungent is the film, that were it not for the dozens of air fresheners hanging from the ceiling you could almost smell the rotting flesh in Victor's apartment. As for Doe's own lodging, it's as disconcerting as they come. Dominated by a luminous red cross, it's filled with the paraphernalia of his crimes: photographs, clippings, receipts, Bibles and over 2,000 notebooks, 'his mind poured out on paper' as Somerset puts it. Even Mills's apartment, shared with his young wife Tracy (Gwyneth Paltrow), is a shoebox next to a railway line that rattles uncontrollably every time a train goes past.

A relentless piece of work, *Se7en* refuses to let you come up for air. The pre-credit sequence, as Mills and Somerset are paired together for the latter's final week on the force, sees them at a crime scene, with a corpse killed by a vengeful spouse. It's not just Doe who is out there on the loose. Look closely in the moody and unsettling credit sequence and you can see Doe cutting off the skin on his fingertips, the reason the cops cannot find any prints at any of the crime scenes he creates. There is no escape from this world of sin, even in the titles. By the end, even the law enforcers cross the line, as they – in particular Mills – become central to completing Doe's 'masterpiece'.

The final two sins in this tapestry inextricably link cop and killer. After giving himself up, Doe claims there are two more bodies still to be discovered. He will unveil them only if Mills and Somerset accompany him to an undisclosed location. Finally, it would seem, there's a gap in the clouds. As the trio drive into the desert, for the first time the sky is bright blue and the sun is shining, though it will prove to be a false dawn. Before his partner, Somerset is made aware of Doe's devious plan; it leads him, in a moment he seems ashamed of, to punch the killer, an ominous act of aggression that acts as a curtain raiser to the final showdown.

In another off-screen murder, it transpires that Doe has killed

Mills's pregnant wife, severed her head and put it in a box, to be delivered to the desert rendezvous point. As he will tell Mills, 'because I envy your normal life, it seems envy is my sin'. Goading the detective, telling him she begged for the life of her unborn child, Doe hopes to become the seventh victim by incurring Mills's wrath. 'If you kill him, he will win,' warns Somerset. Unaware his wife was with child, Mills, unable to control his anger, falls into Doe's trap. Moments before he does, a single-frame flash of Tracy's face fills the screen, crossing his mind and encouraging him to pull the trigger. Falling foul of the law while trying to uphold it, Mills is seen in Fincher's final shot sitting in the back of a police car; with the wire grille foreshadowing his fate, it mirrors the spot where Doe sat earlier.

Less celebratory than *The Usual Suspects* in its victory for the criminal, *Se7en* provides no respite for the audience, no safety net. While Keyser Soze operates in a world far removed from everyday experience, John Doe could be your next-door neighbour. Soze, from what we can tell, kills to keep his criminal activities afloat; Doe kills to punish sins we are all guilty of, even if not to the extent that his luckless victims are. If *Se7en* makes you shudder by the end, it's because it's so horribly everyday.

As with Soderbergh and Singer, using the tropes of film noir leads Fincher to push the crime movie in a new direction. To recall this chapter's opening quote by Foster Hirsch, 'noir has continued to be a reflection of the Zeitgeist'. If Singer's film reflects the mythic potency we ascribe to so-called crime lords in the absence of a deity, Fincher uses the criminal – in this case, the serial killer – as a mirrored reflection of ourselves. Likewise, *The Underneath* is less a peek inside the criminal mind, than an expression of contemporary isolation and dislocation.

In the end, Fincher was a little off with the pre-shoot assessment he passed on to the actors: 'This movie is going to be a sordid little footnote in your careers . . . it won't be a movie you'll be remembered for, but it might just be one you're incredibly proud of.' People came in droves. Maybe they could smell the risk involved. The first of several examples of Pitt bucking his pretty-boy image (something he would repeat for Fincher's *Fight Club*), it will probably be the darkest film Morgan Freeman ever works on. Spacey alone remains destined to be forgotten, if only because the anonymity of his character demands it. As Doe says, 'I'm not special. I've never been exceptional. This is, though.' It's as if Walker wrote these words about himself.

17 Brad Pitt and Morgan Freeman confront Kevin Spacey (centre) in *Se7en*.

CHAPTER 9

The Second Wave: The Conflicts of *Citizen Ruth*, *Hard Eight* and *Bottle Rocket*

18 Philip Baker Hall as Sydney in *Hard Eight*.

By 1996, the new Hollywood mavericks were beginning to find their feet. David Fincher, Quentin Tarantino and Bryan Singer were all basking in the glory of their second films, with David O. Russell set to join them with *Flirting with Disaster*. Three more were about to make their debuts: Valley boy wunderkind Paul Thomas Anderson, erudite Nebraska native Alexander Payne and genial Texan genius Wes Anderson. Their films – *Hard Eight, Citizen Ruth* and *Bottle Rocket,* respectively – were modest, unassuming features, well received but little seen. They, too, proved thematic and stylistic dry runs for their respective directors' second features, all of which fired the imaginations of critics and industry insiders alike. While this trio of movies all came to life via the Sundance Institute, albeit in different ways, the aftermath would afford their creators an invaluable, if unpleasant, lesson in the importance of retaining creative control over their work.

You walk around like Mr Cool, but you're not.
Jimmy, *Hard Eight*

Born on the first day of the 1970s, P. T. Anderson, along with his two brothers and four sisters, was raised in California's San Fernando Valley. His father, Ernie Anderson, who bought him a video camera when he was twelve, made a lasting impression. Anderson Sr created the character of Ghoulardi, a late-night host of Cleveland-based cult movie show *Shock Theater*, famed for his catchphrase 'Stay Sick'. His son would later name his production company Ghoulardi Films in the character's honour. After the show finished its three-year run in 1966, Anderson Sr headed to Los Angeles, where he became the 'golden throat' announcer on shows like *America's Funniest Home Videos*, thus condemning his children to a life in Studio City.

School was not a priority for P. T. Anderson, who was forced to leave the Sherman Oaks–based private institution Buckley School in the sixth grade because of fighting and poor results. After time at Montclair College Prep High School, he spent two semesters studying English at Boston's Emerson College before dropping out. He did the same at New York University Film School after only two days. 'The problem is when I was growing up people like George Lucas, Steven Spielberg and Martin Scorsese went to film school and they preached in its favour,' he remembers.

It made a lot of kids think that the only way you could make a movie was if you went to film school. But that's nonsense really. You basically get a lot of kids who love movies going to watch more movies. That's the last thing that they should be doing, because they're going to be watching movies anyway. I don't know if it would be different if there were great teachers there. My experience with the teachers I had was not so good, so that's what turned me off. But I also think that it's silly to make someone think that they have to go to school to do this job.

The classroom was not for him. After all, he was already a film-maker. By the time he was seventeen, P. T. Anderson – by his own admission completely immersed in watching pornography – had written a half-hour short called *The Dirk Diggler Story*. Inspired by the fictional documentary format, it followed a well-endowed would-be porn star trying to break into the industry and was the template for *Boogie Nights* (see Chapter 12). By the time he had written his next short, *Cigarettes & Coffee*, P. T. Anderson had wormed his way into low-level rank-and-file positions in the entertainment industry, on promos, game shows and TV movies. While working as a runner on a PBS special, he first met veteran actor Philip Baker Hall, the man who has become both father figure and muse to him. 'Paul was just learning about the movie business – he was a gopher, getting coffee for the director,' says Baker Hall. 'He came up to me during a break, and we had a cigarette and coffee. He told me he liked me in some obscure movie the world had never seen; then he told me he liked me in another obscure movie. And as we talked I began to think "God, this kid is a walking encyclopaedia of obscure films!"'

It was Baker Hall's dazzling performance as Richard Nixon in Robert Altman's *Secret Honor* (1984) that had galvanized the young P. T. Anderson more than anything else. A one-man show, Baker Hall's turn was full of invective, paranoia and rage. Only fourteen when Altman's film was released, Anderson did not see it until it reached television. But he immediately resolved to work with Baker Hall, who had never managed to capitalize on the kudos of working with Altman. Anderson was mystified as to why he'd been forced to make his living as a jobbing actor, in episodes of *Cheers* or *Falcon Crest*. 'This guy was so great, why wasn't he Gene Hackman or Robert Duvall? I couldn't understand it,' he noted.[36] By the time the two met, P. T. Anderson was determined to make Baker Hall a star.

'Paul said he'd written a twenty-eight-minute short called *Cigarettes & Coffee*, and he said there was a great part in it for me,' remembers Baker Hall. Cutting between three separate stories that ultimately reveal characters in common, Baker Hall's sequence centres on his relationship with a younger man who believes he has killed his wife. *Cigarettes & Coffee*, which was shot on a borrowed camera for $23,000, was acclaimed on its debut at the 1993 Sundance Film Festival and became a cult hit on the circuit. 'In effect, it was a student film,' says Baker Hall. 'But it became a sensation on the short film festival circuit, and Paul became a celebrity, being flown all over the world. He was getting prizes and recognition for this extraordinary twenty-eight-minute little movie.'

P. T. Anderson expanded on the principal idea of *Cigarettes & Coffee* to create his first full-length script. Then titled *Sydney* after its lead character, it was written, of course, with Baker Hall in mind and the first draft took him just three weeks. Michelle Satter, program director of the Sundance Filmmakers Lab, read it, liked it and invited P. T. Anderson to attend with his script. It was at the Screenwriters Lab that he got to meet writer and director Richard LaGravenese, screenwriter Scott Frank and filmmaker Todd Graff, now numbered among his closest industry friends.

With the Lab allowing him the chance to workshop and fine-tune portions of his script, P. T. Anderson was able to dry-run scenes, having secured the services of Baker Hall and John C. Reilly, who had made his debut in 1989 on the Brian De Palma movie *Casualties of War*. 'When I met Paul, at the point he wanted me to do *Hard Eight*, I was getting a lot of attention from filmmakers but only in a limited way,' says Reilly. 'Paul was one of the first who saw that I could do something more. I gave him a shot, because he hadn't done anything then. But he gave me a very big shot too. It took Paul years to get that movie put together, because he was so loyal to me and Philip. He was offered many other actors, and a lot more money to let someone else direct and star. He stuck to his guns to maddening effect.' Finally P. T. Anderson also recruited Gwyneth Paltrow, at that time known only for her role in Steve Kloves's thriller *Flesh and Bone* (1993), opposite Meg Ryan and Dennis Quaid. Despite all three actors remaining committed to the project, it still took P. T. Anderson almost two years to find funding for the film. When he finally did, courtesy of production company Rysher Entertainment, he had to contend with Paltrow's increasingly busy schedule – fitting her scenes around those she was filming for David Fincher's *Se7en*.

19 Gwyneth Paltrow and John C. Reilly argue in *Hard Eight*.

From the very first frame, *Hard Eight* is a blueprint for what would become recognizable as a P. T. Anderson film. As the credits roll, it begins with a foreboding bell toll rumbling on the soundtrack. Dubbed 'Clementine's Loop', this haunting composition by Michael Penn and Patrick Warren reverberates across P. T. Anderson's first three films like an ominous signature tune. Accompanying the scene in his second film, *Boogie Nights*, where Dirk Diggler is beaten up by gay-bashers, it can also be found in his third, *Magnolia*, when Sydney Barringer loads a shotgun.

Influenced by the downbeat mood of Jean-Pierre Melville's gambling story *Bob le Flambeur* (1955), *Hard Eight* is a disconcerting chamber piece completely free of the clichés that accompany most gambling films. It is set in Reno, where John Finnegan (Reilly) is taken under the wing of the veteran gambler Sydney (Baker Hall), who teaches him how to stack the odds in his favour when working the floors of the casinos. But what he can't teach him is how to fall in love with the right girl. After John meets cocktail waitress Clementine (Paltrow), who turns tricks when she isn't waiting tables, events spin out of control as the pair hold hostage a client of hers who refuses to pay her $300.

Drawing from such hard-boiled Reno-set films as Robert Wise's *Born to Kill* (1947) and Phil Karlson's *5 Against the House* (1955), the casinos of *Hard Eight* are half empty. Likewise, the punters are a shabby-looking bunch and hardly the high rollers Hollywood would like us to believe play in casinos: think of the bride, sporting a neck brace, and her groom playing the slot machines, or Philip Seymour Hoffman's garrulous craps player who baits Sydney, calling him an 'old timer'. P. T. Anderson is clearly not afraid to draw influences from various cinematic sources, and fans might cite numerous other filmmakers – François Truffaut, Martin Scorsese, Max Ophüls, Jean Renoir, John Cassavetes and Jonathan Demme – as influential to his work. But it is to Robert Altman that he owes the greatest debt; to date he has been unwittingly re-making Altman's films one by one. *Hard Eight* owes much to *California Split* (1974), while his next film, *Boogie Nights*, would recall the Hollywood insider story *The Player*. His L.A. epic *Magnolia* could be *Short Cuts* or *Nashville* (1975), depending on taste, while his most recent film, *Punch-Drunk Love,* is a twist on *A Perfect Couple* (1979).[37]

Age twenty-four when he shot *Hard Eight*, P. T. Anderson was the same age Steven Spielberg had been when he made *Duel* (1971), a year younger than Martin Scorsese when he made *Who's That Knocking at My Door?* (1967) and some four years younger than Quentin Tarantino when he made *Reservoir Dogs*. With *Hard Eight* reeking of the same audacious self-assurance as these debuts, Anderson's talent was plain for all to see. 'Working from his own screenplay, rookie director Paul Thomas Anderson shows off the same sort of quirky smarts that Joel and Ethan Coen did in *Blood Simple*,' said one review.[38] A genuine talent had arrived.

The world needs dreamers.

Mr Henry, *Bottle Rocket*

Like *Hard Eight*, Wes Anderson's debut, *Bottle Rocket*, is also a crime film, but not as we know it. The low-key comic story of three misfit Texan friends who embark on a haphazard career as felons, it differed considerably from the postmodern neo-noirs produced by Soderbergh, Singer and Fincher in the previous year. But as his second (*Rushmore*) and third (*The Royal Tenenbaums*) films would re-enforce, it's defiantly a Wes Anderson picture. Given that he was twenty-six when he directed *Bottle Rocket*, he already had an astonishing grasp of the aesthetic concerns and thematic issues that would drive his early work.

Anderson was born in Houston, Texas, in 1969, and his parental influences were diverse, to say the least. While his father owned his own advertising agency in Houston, his mother was an archaeologist. He remembers going on digs with his mother: 'It's interesting for a period of time, then you get sick of going on excavations. You would stand there with the screen and shake it and dirt falls through and you find a piece of pottery. It's not very exciting. We were tired and wanted to go home. Every once in a while, you would unearth something that was amazing. I remember them finding a whole skeleton on an Indian burial mound. But usually, it was more of a drag.'

That his parents divorced when he was young might also indicate why his films focus on the family and the need to belong. As he grew up, the films of John Huston, Ernst Lubitsch, Preston Sturges, Peter Bogdanovich, Roman Polanski, Michael Powell and Emeric Pressburger would be vital to him. But as a child, he spent his youth watching *James Bond* and *Pink Panther* films – though Michael Ritchie's *The Bad News Bears* (1976) was also close to his heart. 'If Truffaut was going to make a movie about a twelve-year-olds' baseball team, it might turn out like that,' he explains.

After attending St John's High School in Houston – where his classmates provided him with numerous character names, particularly the ones in *Rushmore* – he studied philosophy at the University of Texas. During this period, Anderson had begun to make short Super 8 movies in his spare time (unofficially continuing the adventures of Indiana Jones) and even some video-shot shorts for the local cable access station, where he tutored himself in the art of editing. 'They were really terrible,' he remembers. 'That was at my most pretentious age. One of them was all about philosophers. That was bad news. That's where you're in trouble. An ensemble of eight characters, all philosophers . . .'

It was at the University that he met the Dallas-born Owen Wilson, in a playwriting class. The middle brother of three – Luke is younger, Andrew older – Wilson didn't talk to Anderson for the whole class. But the following semester Anderson asked the would-be actor to star in a play he'd written called *A Night in Tunisia*. Only six months older than Anderson, Wilson found they shared the same taste in film-makers – the Coen brothers and Terrence Malick, as well as Polanski and Huston. As if to cement this simpatico, their fathers even worked in the same field, though it's doubtful if the director ever emulated Wilson's childhood rebellious streak. Expelled in the tenth grade from St Mark's School (where they would later shoot scenes for *Bottle Rocket*), Wilson was a self-confessed troublemaker, possessed of a carefree spirit that has dominated his screen performances ever since.

While at college, the pair began to exchange their stories and develop their creative-writing skills. Out of this came an idea for their screen debut – based partly on their own experiences while they were college roommates (when Anderson worked as a movie house projectionist, while Wilson toiled in a burger joint). '*Bottle Rocket* is personal because it's about the stuff we were doing right then, six months before we were shooting the movie,' noted Anderson.

Bottle Rocket was initially made as a thirteen-minute black and white film in 1994, after the pair ran out of cash trying to shoot it as a feature. It had the bare bones of the full-length film: our three stooges (and the actors that play them), as well as scenes such as the robbery of Anthony's parents' house. For Anderson, making the short meant deferring a place he had been offered at Columbia University's film school. In fact he never made it there, a biographical detail symbolic of this new generation of filmmakers' rejection of such academic institutions for their training ground. That said, Anderson might not be overly keen on being labelled a Sundance Kid. While the *Bottle Rocket* short made its bow at the festival in 1994, its full-length cousin would be mysteriously rejected two years later.

Bottle Rocket centres on three friends: Anthony (Luke Wilson), who has just been released from an Arizona mental hospital; Bob (Robert Musgrave), who is emotionally isolated from his wealthy family and tormented by his elder brother, the so-called Futureman (Andrew Wilson); and the charismatic dreamer Dignan (Owen Wilson). A

20 Wes Anderson and James Caan on the set of *Bottle Rocket*.
21 'The world needs dreamers': Robert Musgrave, Owen Wilson and Luke Wilson in *Bottle Rocket*.

childlike enthusiast with the attention span of a grasshopper, Dignan is also 'no cynic and he's no quitter', as Anthony says. He aspires to a life of petty theft and encourages his friends to do the same.

It's evident that the aimless Anthony, though fiercely loyal to Dignan, envies his laissez-faire approach to life. It's no doubt why he falls under the spell of the Paraguayan chambermaid Inez (Lumi Cavazos). She barely speaks a word of English, but for Anthony it's the chance to act in a spontaneous way. Their relationship is innocent and sweet-natured but, in an askew moment typical of Anderson, must be conducted via a translator. It inevitably leads to confusion and jealousy on Dignan's part – although when he incorrectly communicates to Anthony that Inez wants him to leave, it's not done out of malice. With Bob having already bolted, the group finally disintegrates when Dignan discovers that Anthony has left their remaining money to Inez as a tip. It leads to what would become another regular Anderson device – the expositional voice-over, here in the form of a letter Anthony writes to Grace to explain what he has been up to since splitting from Dignan.

Of course, for a film about friendship, the boys must reunite in the final act – Dignan literally riding back into our lives on a scooter. As you would expect from a caper comedy, the concluding raid – on 'Hinckley Cold Storage' – goes wrong. A stray bullet shoots Apple-jack, cohort of small-time mobster Mr Henry (James Caan), while security guards catch Dignan. But this is not a film where plot ever overshadows character: rather it meanders to the tune of the characters' flaws and strengths. We may be dealing with the tropes of the crime film – such as Bob believing Anthony and Dignan will cut him out of any spoils – but the protagonists are anything but the usual suspects. We finish with a happy ending of sorts, as an incarcerated Dignan is finally admitted into the ranks of those he aspires to be like. 'Isn't it funny how you used to be in the nut house and now I'm in jail?' he muses to Anthony. Finishing with Anderson's trademark slow-motion shot, Dignan walks away from his pals back towards the jail. He has a plan for escape, of course. As Mr Henry has already reminded us, 'the world needs dreamers'.

Bottle Rocket is infused with Wes Anderson's personality, with the laid-back vibe of co-writer Owen Wilson far less evident. A literary fellow – why else would he set one of *Bottle Rocket*'s raids in a bookstore? – he shows in his films the influence of F. Scott Fitzgerald, Edith Wharton and, in particular, J. D. Salinger. Like one of his own characters, he has trouble expressing his thoughts verbally but can pour them out on the page like liquid gold. In fact, until he changed his appearance during the shoot of his fourth film, *The Life Aquatic with Steve Zissou*, Anderson, with his prescription glasses, tufts of brown hair and tank tops, even looked like one of his creations.

Wes Anderson has called the world of *Bottle Rocket* 'five degrees removed from reality', a phrase that would also suit any of his later films. This detachment is not to everyone's taste, however. Kent Jones summed it up: 'Anderson is a filmmaker whose work you either "get" or you don't – some people express a very honest bafflement at his films, some misinterpret the work severely, and some feel outright hostility.'[39] While it's easy initially to dismiss them as cult films for the intelligentsia, on repeated viewing they ferment and improve with age. 'I've found myself going back and watching *Bottle Rocket* several times,' said Martin Scorsese.[40] Quoted in an *Esquire* magazine article asking various industry figures which filmmaker was 'the next Scorsese', the director himself chose the young Texan. 'Wes Anderson, at age thirty, has a very special kind of talent: He knows how to convey the simple joys and interactions between people so well and with such richness. This kind of sensibility is rare in movies. Leo McCarey, the director of *Make Way for Tomorrow* and *The Awful Truth*, comes to mind. And so does Jean Renoir. I remember seeing Renoir's films as a child and immediately feeling connected to the characters through his love for them. It's the same with Anderson.'

Ruth – do you like to go to the movies?
Dr Charlie Rollins, *Citizen Ruth*

Like both P. T. and Wes Anderson, Alexander Payne had an affluent and middle-class upbringing. Born in 1961 in Omaha, Nebraska, where his first three films would be set, Payne comes from 'a family of Greek restaurant owners', originally with the surname 'Papadopoulos' until they changed it. His parents were ultra-conservative and wanted their offspring to pursue a career in business, law or medicine; after all, he grew up on the street where billionaire entrepreneur Warren Buffett lived. Not encouraged 'to pursue a career in the arts', Payne nevertheless benefited from an 8 mm camera given to his father by Kraft Foods for being a loyal customer. But while he enjoyed shooting short films in his youth, the notion of making a career of it seemed as fanciful as becoming an astronaut. 'To be in Omaha, Nebraska, and think "I want to be a film director", was such a huge, ridiculous dream,' he says. The furthest he got was deciding for a time that he wanted to work as a projectionist. 'I always thought that would be the best job, to watch movies all day and touch film. It's really fun to thread up a projector.'

Admitted to Stanford University when he graduated from Omaha's Creighton Prep High School, Payne read history and Spanish literature, and spent extended periods in Spain, where he studied Spanish philology. This immersion in Hispanic culture influenced him when he later attended the graduate program in film production at UCLA Film School. Graduating in 1990, Payne's fifty-minute film *The Passion of Martin* was loosely adapted from Argentinian Ernesto Sabato's *El Tunel*, 'a kind of hilarious, stark, post-war, slim novel', as Payne puts it.

Originally entitled *Blink, If You Love Me*, Payne's film, a black study of obsession and unrequited love, starred Charles Hayward as Martin, a thirty-something photographer determined to find his life partner. After seeing a girl, Rebecca (Lisa Zane), admiring his work in a gallery, he runs into her again at a wedding. The pair hit it off, but Rebecca leaves the next morning before Martin wakes up, a decision that throws him to the point where he can't fathom why she, after one night, has not made a lifelong commitment to him. Shifting from a mundane atmosphere at the outset, the film dips into Martin's rather crazed psyche, as Payne and cinematographer David Rudd concoct a frenetic visual style for him – all quick dolly movements and wide-angle lenses to achieve distortion – that contrasts wildly to when the other characters are on screen.

Unveiled to considerable acclaim at Sundance in 1991, the film toured the world; accepted into over twenty other festivals, it won awards and gained Payne the kind of attention a young director craves. Swiftly finding an agent, he was made an offer by Universal to write a script, potentially for him to direct. The result was what would later be dusted off and spliced together with Louis Begley's novel to form *About Schmidt*, Payne's third film as director. It's the story of, in Payne's words, 'an old guy who retires and then realizes how much he's wasted his life'.[41] Universal executives were less than pleased.

Yet, by this time, Payne had already met the most influential figure in his career to date: Jim Taylor. In 1989, living in a two-bedroom apartment in Silverlake, Payne put the word out among friends that he needed a roommate. Taylor turned up and the pair became firm friends, before deciding to collaborate as screenwriters. Taylor had grown up in Seattle and studied for his BA in English literature down the coast at Pomona College in Claremont, California. After graduating, he worked for Cannon Films in Los Angeles as a production coordinator and development assistant, and in 1987 received a grant and travelled to China to study the country's film industry. When he returned to the States, he worked with director Ivan Passer – best known for his cynical neo-noir *Cutter's Way* (1981) – for three years.

After his stint living with Payne in Los Angeles – the only time the pair were based in the same city – Taylor set out to clear his debts. He did so by winning on the legendary quiz show *Wheel of Fortune* the exact amount of money needed to put him in the black. Out of debt for two days, he then headed to New York and enrolled in the graduate film program at NYU, putting himself $100,000 in the red. By 1992, he and Payne had collaborated on a segment for Playboy Video Enterprises' softcore anthology *Inside Out*, a masturbatory fantasy entitled 'My Secret Moments'. They also completed the script for what would eventually become *Citizen Ruth*, a deliriously un-PC abortion comedy initially inspired by a newspaper article.

By comparison to its release, the production of *Citizen Ruth* was a smooth, if lengthy, process. Payne spent a fruitless year-and-a-half shopping it around the studios, which all recoiled from producing a comedy that satirized the abortion debate. Ironically, Payne had already met the man who would ultimately shepherd it into production. Shortly after *The Passion of Martin* had played the festival circuit, he had been introduced to Cary Woods, the former agent responsible for discovering Gus Van Sant, who also later championed enfant terrible Harmony Korine. Impressed by Payne's thesis film, he offered the young director the chance to come and make a film for him. At the time, swayed by the Universal deal, Payne refused – but three years later, they bumped into each other and in a matter of days Woods decided to produce *Citizen Ruth*, then called *The Devil Inside*.

Yet even then it was not cut-and-dried. Back in New York, Woods had met two mid-twenties venture capitalists – one with $10 million of his father's money to invest – looking to make a foray into the film business. Originally intending to funnel the money towards Payne's film, Woods decided to switch it to bankrolling Larry Clark's *Kids*, claiming Payne's script wasn't ready. As *Kids* went into production in the summer of 1994, *The Devil Inside* was forced to wait until the spring of the following year. By this point, Woods had cultivated a relationship with the erratic Harvey Weinstein who, having passed on financing *Kids*, had decided to release it. Weinstein would bankroll Payne's script, to the tune of $3.7 million, an arrangement that had difficult repercussions for Payne.

Typically, Payne says he had no interest in entering the abortion debate – then a hot topic in the U.S., notably with the case of Norma McCorvey.[42] 'I can't help thinking that most Americans agree with the basic point of it, which is that we're sick and tired of the abortion debate,'[43] he noted. Like his second film, *Election*, which detailed dirty tricks during a high school presidential campaign, Payne was more interested in examining the absurdities that grip people when they get carried away by their political agendas. 'I see it as being real – at least real to how I perceive things,' he noted.[44]

At the black heart of the film is Ruth Stoops, a pregnant down-and-out addicted to sniffing glue and paint fumes who becomes the prize in a tug-of-war between pro-life and pro-choice campaigners. In a fearless turn, Ruth is played by Laura Dern. No stranger to extreme material, having appeared in David Lynch's *Blue Velvet* and *Wild at Heart*, Dern stumbles on screen – all lank hair, chipped nail polish and scabby lips – and from that moment you know this is no vanity project. How many Hollywood actresses would take a role that required them to slump on the sidewalk with blue dye over their mouths, following a quick bout of 'hazardous vapour inhalation'? Mixing vulnerability with acidity, Dern dominates the film every second she's on the screen.

The film begins as Ruth – who has just been kicked out by her lover and then rejected by her brother, who is looking after two of her children – is hauled into court, caught for the sixteenth time that year abusing substances on the street. Pointing out that she has been declared an unfit mother on four previous occasions, the judge threatens her with 'criminal endangerment of a fetus' but – in a bizarre twist of logic that highlights the hypocrisy of the law – offers to drop the charges if she'll have an abortion. In the first of a series of moments designed to win our sympathies, the film cuts to Ruth back in her cell, curled up on a thin mattress in a fetal position, crying her eyes out.

Initially, help for Ruth comes in the shape of four fellow inmates, all

God-fearing members of a pro-life group, the Babysavers. Chanting their mantra, 'We are the soldiers of Christ', they are led by Gail Stoney (Mary Kay Place), who is wife to the local branch chairman, Norm (Kurtwood Smith). Mocking their tacky home with its petit bourgeois furnishings ('We don't sit on *those* chairs,' notes Gail), Payne and Taylor can rightly be accused of equating class trappings with political convictions. Likewise, the home of Diane (Swoosie Kurtz) and Rachel (a very dowdy Kelly Preston), the lesbian pro-choice campaigners who spirit Ruth away from the Stoney household, is full of vegetarian slogans and ethnic decorations.

Continuing this, the film moves on to the plush hotel suite of the wealthy pro-life bigwig Blaine Gibbons (Burt Reynolds) – disturbingly accompanied by Eric, his teenage masseuse. With Gibbons like a military general plotting a strategic offensive from his HQ, it evokes the sense of escalation of this war, further emphasized with the arrival of Gibbons's pro-choice rival, Jessica Weiss (Tippi Hedren), in a helicopter. The iconic casting by Payne works in favour of the film, with both Reynolds and Hedren admirably conveying the right amount of smug self-righteousness required for their roles.

Payne has admitted that while writing the script he was influenced by the subversive anger of Luis Buñuel's *Viridiana* (1961), the Palme d'Or–winning film about a novice nun whose charitable acts backfire with serious consequences. Banned in Spain, it's easy to see why this bitter attack on the value of spiritual beliefs appealed to Payne. After believing herself violated by a lecherous uncle, who then commits suicide, the saintly Viridiana throws his former home open as a shelter for local paupers – only to witness their savagery rather than gratitude. With scenes of murder and rape cut to a booming choir singing *Hallelujah*, it may be a more savage assessment of humanity than *Citizen Ruth*, but both films view the world with a merciless gaze. In a nod to Buñuel, Payne even uses the same hymn on the soundtrack in the penultimate scene, as Ruth takes a first glance at the money she has been given.

As far as American directors go, Payne regularly cites the work of Francis Ford Coppola as influential. Having developed a close relationship with the director, he can even be found in Ted Demme and Richard LaGravenese's study of New Hollywood, *A Decade Under the Influence* (2003), interviewing Coppola. Payne may admire the gargantuan Italian American, but there seems little to connect him and his small-scale satires to Coppola's grandiose visions. 'I like *The Conversation*,' Payne explains. 'It was his version of an Antonioni film, which he said openly.' If one had to choose Payne's closest forefather, it might be the late Hal Ashby. His films – from *Harold and Maude* to *Being There* (1979) – are rich with a black humour and irony that appeals to Payne. Frequently in Ashby's films, external appearances undercut the reality of the situation. It's a device Payne favours, along with Ashby's penchant for ambiguous endings.

It is perhaps more accurate, though, to place Payne's movies alongside those of Billy Wilder – although he has a long way to go before he achieves the sheer diversity of Wilder's output. Payne's characters and set-ups owe much to Wilder. *Election*'s beleaguered teacher Jim McAllister, for example, recalls Jack Lemmon's put-upon employee C. C. Baxter, from *The Apartment* (1960), who unwisely loans his home to amorous colleagues in the hope of a promotion. Both are bewildered men in situations of their own making that career out of their control. Likewise, Payne's fourth film, *Sideways*, can be seen as a nod to Wilder's *The Lost Weekend* (1945). And *Citizen Ruth* owes much to *Ace in the Hole* (1951), Wilder's unrelenting study of media exploitation. It's one of Wilder's most sombre pictures, and the casting of Kirk Douglas in the unsympathetic yet riveting role of reporter Jack Tatum no doubt struck a chord with Payne, who does much the same with Dern. *Ace in the Hole*'s cynicism, particularly via its portrayal of the media circus that ensues when the story breaks, is also mirrored in *Citizen Ruth*.

As his surname suggests, Payne was destined to examine the darker side of human existence: 'Humour comes from the most painful situations you can think of. If comedy is not based in pain, then it's not really funny. Who laughs harder than people at a wake?'[45] To date, comedy – or, most precisely, satire – has been his means of expression. As Payne says, 'To write satire you have to take an essence of truth and then give it a little dollop of sour cream. Some people might see it as stereotypical, but it's just taking something you see in people and bringing it to the fore to have comic fun.'[46] It would be unfair to claim this is done without compassion. Payne and Taylor may lampoon individuals, but they are not misanthropes; there is a belief in humanity that runs through their films, albeit ambiguously expressed.

> **Bottom line, Sydney. No matter how hard you try, you're not his father.**
> Jimmy, *Hard Eight*

What *Citizen Ruth* shares with both *Bottle Rocket* and *Hard Eight* is a thematic concern with the importance of family. Strip it down, and *Hard Eight* is simply about a father looking for a son, and vice versa. Sydney finds what he wants in John; lost without parental figures in his life, John looks up to Sydney, copying his clothing style and even ordering the same drinks. 'I'm not going to let anything happen to you,' coos Sydney to John, in the midst of chaos. 'I love you like you were my own son,' he says later. Only able to write with his heart on his sleeve, P. T. Anderson takes the stuff of melodrama and turns it up a notch. He gives new meaning to the term 'soap opera', raising the everyday to an operatic intensity. In a twist that could come straight from *Days of Our Lives*, the flashy Jimmy (Samuel L. Jackson) reveals that Sydney mentors John because he is guilt-ridden over shooting John's father years ago.

This key theme of family would anchor each of P. T. Anderson's first four films, a reason why these films have such an unabashed autobiographical streak. *Punch-Drunk Love* deals with a man emotionally crippled by his seven sisters; P. T. Anderson, of course, has four of his own. Having dealt with his parents' break-up during his teens, which led to his estrangement from his mother, P. T. Anderson writes and relates to characters who are lost or abandoned souls, looking to create families where none exist. While this is especially true of *Boogie Nights*, *Magnolia* deals with the sorrow that can be caused within the existing family unit. Redemption, reconciliation and forgiveness feature heavily, as do infidelity, abuse and violence.

Payne also deals with the notion of family. While there is no doubt that Ruth is an unfit mother, Payne wants the audience to understand her torment. As her own mother pleads with her not to get rid of her unborn child, Ruth laments that she herself was not aborted, screaming: 'At least I wouldn't have had to suck your boyfriend's cock.' With an upbringing dominated by sexual abuse, it's little wonder that Ruth is the way she is. Perhaps this is why we finally root for Ruth to take the money and run. As unsympathetic as she is, the more we get to know her, the more we realize her personality has been shaped by the social and economic pressures she has been put under. 'All my life I never had a chance,' she says. 'If I had money my life would've been different. I'd be such a good mother.' As she sneaks away, cash in hand, Ruth finally becomes a bona fide citizen.

Wes Anderson's idea of family is somewhat different. Rarely do we see any real relatives in *Bottle Rocket* – aside from Futureman and Anthony's wise-beyond-her-years sister Grace, the film's most overtly cynical presence. Yet Wes Anderson notes that the central threesome of the film have 'either been rejected by their families or they've rejected them'. He explains that they 'huddle together because none of them are part of any community . . . they're basically nice people, wandering souls who latch onto each other and create their own strange, little world.'[47] To steal the name of the landscape gardening business belonging to Dignan's mentor, Mr Henry, these are the 'Lone Wranglers'.

Earth mother . . . We are one!
Rachel and Diane, *Citizen Ruth*

Although Wes Anderson, Payne and P. T. Anderson could easily be described as Lone Wranglers themselves, all have in fact managed to pick up a posse of like-minded friends along the way. While P. T. Anderson has written all his scripts alone, he has found himself a regular cinematographer, Robert Elswit. Between them, either Jon Brion or Michael Penn have scored all of his films to date. That said, his choice of editor and production designer has been more erratic – starting, respectively, with Barbara Tulliver and Nancy Deren, neither of whom made it past *Hard Eight*. Dylan Tichenor cut *Boogie Nights* and *Magnolia* before Leslie Jones took over for *Punch-Drunk Love*. Meanwhile, *Boogie Nights*' production designer Bob Ziembicki was replaced by William Arnold for *Magnolia* and *Punch-Drunk Love*.

Aside from his co-writer Taylor, Payne met a number of other key collaborators early on. It was during the *My Secret Moments* shoot that he employed production designer Jane Ann Stewart and composer Rolfe Kent, both of whom have worked on all of Payne's films to date. By the time it came to cutting *Citizen Ruth* he had hooked up with Kevin Tent, who has also stayed with Payne for the duration. Only cinematographer James Glennon, who shot *Citizen Ruth*, *Election* and *About Schmidt*, did not return for *Sideways*.

As for Wes Anderson, when he and Wilson were writing *Bottle Rocket* they were mentored by L. M. Kit Carson, sometime actor and writer (of 1983's *Breathless*) and a family friend of the Wilsons. Carson received the script of *Bottle Rocket* and steered it to the producer Barbara Boyle. She, in turn, took it to Polly Platt, an associate of James L. Brooks at his company Gracie Films. The writer-director of *Terms of Endearment* (1983), *Broadcast News* (1987) and *As Good as It Gets* (1997) – and also one of the main forces behind *The Simpsons* – Brooks took an interest in these young Texan upstarts, finally clinching them a development deal and offices on the Columbia Pictures lot. As Wes Anderson explains: 'He believed in it and saw to it that we got our funding. I think you just need a few people who have the right powers who are behind you.'

Aside from having the much-respected Brooks on his side, Anderson ensured – as most novice directors do – that he had a distinguished cinematographer to work with. In this case, it was Robert Yeoman, who photographed Gus Van Sant's tripped-out *Drugstore Cowboy* (1989) and has shot all of Anderson's films to date. His work was vital to the mood of the piece. To include as much background detail as possible in what is a very dialogue-heavy film, it is shot entirely with a 27 mm lens, and Anderson uses a subtle-yet-smart colour palette that distinguishes between the film's three acts. The first act is as if it's been drained of colour; Dignan wearing white, Bob wearing black. Only Anthony is given bright apparel – a red jacket that signals he is the central character of the trio. In the second act, as our boys arrive at the out-of-town motel where they lie low, the colours start to bloom. With its red doors, and vivid shades of orange, yellow and turquoise, the motel comes to express the joy that Anthony feels with Inez. The final act sees a return to more neutral, albeit sophisticated, hues: deep greens and purples, punctuated only by the signature yellow jumpsuit that Dignan wears.

As well as recruiting production designer David Wasco, who subsequently designed *Rushmore* and *The Royal Tenenbaums*, Anderson met editor David Moritz, who also cut *Rushmore* and *The Life Aquatic with Steve Zissou*. He also found the composer who has scored all of his films thus far. Mark Mothersbaugh, founding member of 1970s punk band Devo, came to a screening of *Bottle Rocket* and contacted the director afterwards about doing the score. It was the start of a relationship that has continued across all of Wes Anderson's films – understandable, given the offbeat sounds that Mothersbaugh creates to complement the gallery of oddballs that dominate the director's work.

We did it, though, didn't we?
Dignan, *Bottle Rocket*

Despite these allies, each director had to endure a baptism of fire on entering the film industry. P. T. Anderson, in particular, suffered enormously. His battles with the production company Rysher Entertainment were protracted, spanning post-production, and would prove formative for the young director. He now calls *Hard Eight* his 'bastard child', chiefly because Rysher treated it with such disdain. Executives at the company claimed P. T. Anderson's initial pitch was way off his end result. 'Clearly they hadn't read the script,' he says. 'I delivered the movie and they were really confused. All I could do was point to the script and say, "This is what I shot, this is what you paid for, this is what you agreed to." And this argument would always come up – "Well, the script is not the movie and the movie's not the script." I had the most horrendous, terrible time in the editing process.'[48]

With P. T. Anderson fired from the project during this period, Rysher re-cut the film to its liking. Furious, Anderson kidnapped an incomplete work print and – with funds donated by Paltrow and Reilly, as well as his own money – completed his own version and submitted it to the Cannes Film Festival, where it was accepted. Garnering good reviews, and with Paltrow's stock rising and the increasingly noticeable Samuel L. Jackson in the cast, it was grudgingly released by Rysher who could do little else, but on the proviso that P. T. Anderson changed the title to *Hard Eight*. Worn down, he agreed, but saw Rysher open the film with minimal fanfare. It recouped virtually nothing.

In a karmic twist of justice, Rysher no longer exists. P. T. Anderson spares no tears for the company's demise. He can still remember the day it went out of business, and the feature that ran in *Daily Variety*, which published a list of Rysher's films and what each cost. 'And at the very bottom, the lowest-grossing movie in Rysher history was my movie. So I was happy I aided their downfall in some way. My movie made ten thousand dollars [it was actually $222,559] and it cost you guys two million.'[49]

Payne fared little better at Miramax. *Citizen Ruth* marked one of the company's last controversial productions – until they took on Michael Moore's *Fahrenheit 9/11*. The film was accepted into Sundance in 1996, but a week before the festival Harvey Weinstein, at his capricious best, decided its original title – invented by Taylor – made it sound too close to a horror film. Payne suggested numerous alternatives – including *Meet Ruth Stoops* – but Weinstein rejected them all in favour of the inexplicable *Precious*. Eventually, after gauging general audience discontent with the title (as well as with the original poster, depicting Dern falling through the sky), Weinstein relented and approved an early Payne suggestion, *Citizen Ruth*. Unhappy with the downbeat ending when Ruth, having miscarried, sneaks away from the abortion clinic with $15,000 donated by the pro-choicers, Weinstein insisted that a title card finish the film hinting that Ruth wound up in California as a successful real-estate broker.

While this was removed after the Sundance screenings, the Weinsteins kept the film on the shelf for nearly a year, until after the 1996 presidential elections. Given that Harvey, an ardent Democrat all his life, had been ushered into Bill and Hillary Clinton's circle as a chief fund-raiser, it might be that he didn't want such a politically sensitive satire to embarrass his newfound friends. This aside, the film's release in late December was not by the Miramax of old, the company famed for finding innovative ways of marketing films perceived as 'difficult'. Sold as a broad comedy, the film had a new poster which saw Laura Dern striking a Statue of Liberty pose, a can of glue replacing the torch. Understandably, the film made little dent on the U.S. box office: some $285,112. 'I think it's hard to market abortion satires,' says Payne. 'Miramax's publicity materials were atrocious. They totally screwed up.'

Bottle Rocket suffered similarly, making just $560,069 in the U.S. 'The studio [Columbia] that released it didn't care about the movie,' says Wes Anderson. 'They were never into the movie – the producer [Brooks] had a deal whereby he could force them to do it. It was released very badly in America, and not at all anywhere else. It only found an audience on video.' Released in February – the traditional graveyard month in the Hollywood calendar, when studios quietly sneak out unwanted products under cover of virtual darkness – it made a measly $1 million. 'By the time there were critics that got behind the movie, it was already in the theatres. Usually they'll do screenings way in advance for magazines with long lead times – we got none of that. It never really got off the ground and had to build slowly. It was very discouraging.'

But for once the critics came to the rescue. *Variety*'s David Rooney said the film was 'full of charm, unexpected plot turns and droll characters that bounce off each other in refreshing ways'.[50] In the equally influential *Los Angeles Times*, Kenneth Turan said: '*Bottle Rocket* has just what its characters lack; an exact sense of itself . . . [it] feels particularly refreshing because it never compromises on its delicate deadpan sensibility.'[51] By December, it featured on numerous critics' end-of-year lists; by the end of the decade, it had charted at number seven on Martin Scorsese's own top ten films of the 1990s. As Brooks said, the reviews 'without exaggeration saved Wes and Owen's lives, for life can be very tough on those who find existence only makes sense if someone lets them makes movies.'[52]

In Wes Anderson's opinion, Columbia's attitude to the film was a reaction to the fact that Sundance programmers had rejected it after the full-length rewrite – despite giving the short a warm reception at the festival in 1994. 'If we'd been embraced by Sundance, the movie would have found its way much more quickly,' he says. Without a festival foothold – bar an appearance at the more esoteric Rotterdam Film Festival – the film was, like the cheap firework of its title, almost doomed to have a short lifespan.

Understandably, Anderson still smarts over the film's rejection by the independent sector. 'Once *Bottle Rocket* built up its following, we always had a good support among the studios,' he says. 'Many studios responded to the work in the way I would have expected the more independent channels to.' While many of the Sundance Kids owe their careers to Redford's festival, Wes Anderson was forced to find patronage in Hollywood. In his case it's not so much that he graduated towards painting on a studio-funded canvas but, as Brooks puts it, he 'slumbered in the belly of the beast' because he had no choice. However, as we will see, the short film/festival route was not the only way into the industry. This was the mid-1990s; and as David Fincher and Spike Jonze found out, music videos and commercials could be equally valid calling cards.

CHAPTER 10

Spreading Propaganda:
The Rise of David Fincher and Spike Jonze

22 John Malkovich plays himself in *Being John Malkovich*.
23 Catherine Keener and John Cusack meet on the 7½ floor in
Being John Malkovich.

In February 1998 *Premiere* magazine ran a headline across a picture of Michael Bay, Antoine Fuqua, Simon West, Dominic Sena and David Fincher. It said: 'Do these men represent the future of Hollywood film-making – or the death of it?'[53] Their link was the production company Propaganda, by this point a byword in some people's eyes for all that was brash and offensive about contemporary Hollywood. Based in a hangar-like warehouse full of 'dressed-down hipsters' wearing black, it was, by all accounts 'part Bauhaus, part Frat-house'. The accompanying article rounded up various influential critics, who rounded on the company that has nurtured some of Hollywood's most successful directors. 'They're not concerned with having a voice,' said the then chief critic for *The New York Times*, Janet Maslin. 'They haven't just undermined film narrative. They've demolished it.' The *Los Angeles Times* writer Kenneth Turan weighed in: 'They're cold directors. They're proficient, they're not hacks. But characters and emotional content do not seem to concern them.'

No longer in operation, Propaganda stands as one of the most influential production companies of the 1990s. But to be fair, the majority of its top guns were guilty of the accusations voiced by the critics. A quick recap of their output between 1993 and 2004: Bay (*The Rock*, *Armageddon*, *Pearl Harbor*); West (*Con Air*, *The General's Daughter*, *Lara Croft: Tomb Raider*); Fuqua (*The Replacement Killers*, *Tears of the Sun*, *King Arthur*); Sena (*Kalifornia*, *Gone in Sixty Seconds*, *Swordfish*). Only Fincher shied away from making films dominated by the sound of shell-fire and breaking glass – though Fuqua's intelligent cop drama *Training Day* (2001) also stands apart from the crowd. Their work, together with later additions to the stable, demands a re-assessment.

Begun in 1986, Propaganda was the brainchild of producers Steve Golin, an NYU Film School graduate, and Joni Sighvatsson, a former Icelandic rock star. After producing forgettable films including *American Drive-In* (1985), they joined up with record executive turned video director Nigel Dick, as well as Fincher and Sena (who chose the company name), to create a working environment for young directors to learn their trade. 'There's this place; it's a factory and you don't know what the fuck goes on there, but you put your money in one end and your cassette comes out the other,' noted Fincher.

He was the company's prize asset. The son of a *Life* magazine reporter, Fincher was born in Denver in 1962. He grew up in Marin County, California – at one point two doors away from George Lucas – and had been a fan of Lucas's *American Graffiti* since he was twelve. The idea of filmmaking for a living was immediate, and seemingly attainable to him. In high school, he produced a local television news show. By the time he was nineteen, having been bowled over by *The Empire Strikes Back* (1980), he won a job at the Lucas-affiliated special-effects house Industrial Light and Magic (ILM). His credits included assistant cameraman for the miniature and optical effects team on *Return of the Jedi* (1983) and second unit work for *Indiana Jones and the Temple of Doom* (1984).

Arriving at the tail end of ILM's initial burst of creativity, Fincher – who calls his erstwhile employers 'a particularly dysfunctional family' – learned a lot about the editorial process there. However, he quit in 1985 to direct the concert documentary *The Beat of the Live Drum*, with former *General Hospital* star and Grammy-winning artist Rick Springfield. As he began directing TV spots and music videos, the creation of Propaganda offered him shelter, a tailor-made support network designed to nurture his maverick talent. Between them, he and Ohio-born Sena notched up promos for Bryan Adams, Janet Jackson, The Rolling Stones, Paula Abdul and Madonna.

A year after Propaganda's formation, when Dick directed his first (straight-to-video) feature *P.I. Private Investigations* (1987), PolyGram bought a stake in the company. This signal to the industry that Propaganda was out to make movies was reinforced when John Dahl wrote and directed his first two features (*Kill Me Again*, 1989; *Red Rock West*, 1992) for the fledgling firm. Golin openly stated that he wanted Propaganda to be like the (now defunct) Orion Pictures. Little surprise, then, that by 1992 PolyGram owned the outfit, which now had the success of David Lynch's Palme d'Or–winning *Wild at Heart* under its belt, outright.

Yet Fincher was lured from the creative nest that was Propaganda to make his Hollywood debut. In retrospect, taking on Twentieth Century Fox's *Alien* franchise was a foolhardy move, but one that fully expressed Fincher's self-confidence. Only twenty-seven at the time, he was unwittingly about to step into a real-life disaster movie. By the time Fincher came on board, the production had already seen off Finnish director Renny Harlin and New Zealand helmer Vincent Ward. The script went through a phalanx of writers, from producers Walter Hill and David Giler's collaboration with William Gibson, to Eric Red (*The Hitcher*, 1986) and David Twohy (*Pitch Black*, 2000).

After much consideration, Fincher resolved to set the film on the weapon-free Fiorina 161, a planet dominated by a maximum security correctional institution. With an alien growing inside Ripley and another on the loose, Fincher saw an opportunity to make the polar opposite of James Cameron's gun-heavy *Aliens* (1986). But the script he and co-writer Larry Ferguson turned in was a disaster and the production was shut down for three months. Sigourney Weaver, back for a third outing as Ripley, agreed to go with a script if Giler and Hill wrote it, but by the time the truncated pre-production segued into the shoot Fincher found he had an incomplete script that needed to be patched up on a daily basis. 'I always felt that with *Alien³* initially, as a studio, we set out to make a release date and not a movie. On the way that changed, but it really set us back,' says Jon Landau, at the time executive vice president of feature production at Fox. 'All movies start with one thing – a script. And David never had that. When you go through any production it's difficult . . . it's hard. When you go through your first one without a script, it's even harder.'

Claiming *Alien³* does not embarrass him, Fincher has said, perhaps a little hopefully, that it will probably be looked on one day as his first bungled masterpiece. At the time, he said, 'It was just hellish. This is the worst thing that ever happened to me.'[54] He claimed one studio executive told him: 'Look, you could have somebody piss against the wall for two hours and call it *Alien³* and it would still do $30 million-worth of business.' It's little wonder Fincher struggled in Hollywood. Faced with accountants, lawyers and studio executives, his was just one of many voices trying to get the film made. His authority called into question, he no longer had the autonomy he enjoyed at Propaganda. Being Kubrick-like in the singularity of his vision, and his unwillingness to compromise, it must've rubbed him raw.

What's more, he was no longer anonymous, as he was at Propaganda. He was the public face for what amounted to the studio's decisions. After a hard day's shooting, Fincher found himself on the telephone to Fox personnel in Los Angeles, as seemingly arbitrary decisions were relayed to him from on high. As the crazed inmate Golic says in the film, 'In an insane world, a sane man must appear insane' – a maxim Fincher no doubt took to heart.

With a budget that rocketed to between $60 million and $80 million, depending on whom you believe, the post-production process was as excruciating for Fincher as the shoot itself. 'We didn't wrap. We stopped shooting,' says the executive producer Ezra Swerdlow, admitting that no one felt the film was completely shot when they left London for the edit suites of Los Angeles. Arguments continued in the cutting room for over a year. Weaver, complete with bald cap this time, was brought back in for reshoots. With squabbles over the ending to boot, it became the classic example of filmmaking by committee, where a movie is expected to be bigger and better than its predecessors simply because it is a sequel. Although *Alien³* eventually recouped $55.4 million, Fincher swore he'd rather have colon cancer than make another studio movie; no doubt the experience fine-tuned the dark vision of humanity that was to come with his next film, *Se7en*.

Yet Andrew Kevin Walker's script for *Se7en* won Fincher over, despite the fact that the film was to be made with burgeoning studio New Line (see Chapter 12). And while Fincher soon found himself embroiled in internal politics, at least this time he had an ally. Fresh from starring in the Propaganda co-production *Kalifornia* (1993), Brad Pitt argued for the film's eventual bleak ending, which had originally been excised from the script in favour of a more formulaic finale. Veteran producer Arnold Kopelson had told Fincher, 'Look into my eyes, this movie will never end with a head in a box.' But, in an interesting example of the increased power A-list stars were experiencing in the 1990s, Pitt threatened to leave the project if Kopelson did not capitulate. Likewise, he lobbied – wisely, in retrospect – for Kevin Spacey to play Doe, after New Line had dismissed the idea, preferring the cheaper R. Lee Emery, who would eventually be cast as the police captain.

After a relatively uneventful fifty-five-day shoot, Fincher screened the film to New Line executives. After the lights came up – on cue, despite Fincher telling the projectionist to leave the audience in the dark for ten seconds or so – one woman came up to the director and told him, 'The people who made that movie should be killed.' So began the tussle over the film's bleak conclusion. At one point, it was suggested that Tracy's head be replaced by one of Mills's dogs. To placate executives, Fincher shot the final insert – as Mills is spirited away in a police car and Somerset, quoting Ernest Hemingway, admits

the world is worth fighting for. While it reinforced the notion that justice will prevail, Fincher takes a private ghoulish pleasure in imagining
Mills being 'carted off to be gang-raped by prison inmates'.[55] With this
sour vision of humanity in line with the doom-laden atmosphere he
evoked in *Alien³*, Fincher proved that not all Propaganda graduates
were out solely to commit bigger and louder explosions to film in the
name of entertainment.

That same year, the new recruit Michael Bay became a hot property
following his surprise hit, the buddy cop thriller *Bad Boys*. 'Propaganda was an interesting place,' Bay recalls. 'I look at us as a bunch of
rebels. We came in and changed the ad business. We were the world's
largest music video company. Madison Avenue was like, "Why can't
we get our commercials to be like that?" It was a very closed, old boy
network, and we took jobs from a lot of old timers. In the 1970s and
1980s, there was the huge English wave, with Ridley Scott and Alan
Parker. But that door was closed for a long time in America. It was
impossible to get commercials and we opened the door for a lot of
young filmmakers.'

Later additions to the company included West, Fuqua, Alex Proyas,
Mark Romanek, Spike Jonze and Michel Gondry. British-born West,
who was best known for the Frosty Frogs Budweiser commercial, got
the chance to turn Nicolas Cage into an action star in *Con Air* (1997),
on the back of Bay's triumphs. 'Bay had to fight hard to do *Bad Boys*.
That was a success, and he got *The Rock*,' he says.

> So I had an easier time getting *Con Air*. You could use it to your
> advantage. If the one before you was a hit, you could say, 'I'm exactly
> like that guy.' If it wasn't, you say, 'I'm completely different.' But we
> *are* different. We have completely different backgrounds. It was
> coincidental that Propaganda recruited shrewdly from different
> places to get these people together to make commercials for them.
> But it wasn't a finishing school for action directors. It was nurturing
> because you had a lot of freedom there. The company was arrogant
> enough to treat advertising agencies like dirt; if they lost the job,
> they didn't mind. They understood that their only resource was the
> directors, who attained cult status. They built the image up. That's
> why the company's called Propaganda.

Bay admits there was 'a little bit' of rivalry between the A-list employees, and it still exists. 'I remember David Fincher goes to me at the

Sony Christmas party – he's always doom and gloom – "So, Mike, don't you feel bad doing *Bad Boys II*?" What I'm thinking is "Fuck you! How many fucking franchises do you have?" So I said, "Aren't you supposed to be doing *Mission: Impossible 3*?" – which at the time he was. David fucks with you a lot.'

But even with its A-list names, Propaganda was shortlived – despite going on to produce, among others, Jonze's *Being John Malkovich* and two Neil LaBute films, *Your Friends & Neighbors* (1998) and *Nurse Betty* (2000). Propaganda was sold to Universal in 1998. It was then sold on to Barry Diller's USA Films before being taken over by a consortium of investors. Sighvatsson left in 1995 to head Lakeshore Entertainment and Golin was fired and replaced by William Morris agent Rick Hess. Golin went on to form the production company Anonymous Content in 2000; a year later Propaganda collapsed.

While the likes of Maslin and Turan were no doubt shedding few tears for this loss to the industry, the end of Propaganda Films meant on balance that an environment that stimulated and sheltered some of the most visually creative filmmakers in Hollywood no longer existed. If the Sundance Kids owe their careers to Robert Redford and his festival, then the Propaganda alumni owe much to the company where they cut their teeth. Of course, directors like Bay, West and Sena have yet to prove they have filmmaking ambitions beyond creating visceral spectacle. But whether or not Propaganda has contributed to the demise of Hollywood fare, it has undoubtedly nurtured in its filmmakers an arrogant belief that the director rules, which in turn has infiltrated back into the studio system.

I'm pulling back the curtain. I want to meet the wizard.
Nicholas Van Orton, *The Game*

If one film can be labelled Propaganda's signature production, then it is David Fincher's third film, *The Game*. As slick as the rain-drenched streets that dominate the film's landscape, Fincher's 1997 puzzler was more surface than substance – entirely in keeping with much of Propaganda's output. Emphasising this, the film was shot by Harris Savides, a former collaborator with Fincher on various commercials and music videos. Offered the chance to lens *Se7en*, he had turned it down because he had just completed work on Phil Joanou's *Heaven's Prisoners* (1996) and had sworn never to work on a movie again.

While he eventually did do some second unit work for Fincher on *Se7en*, he only returned to shooting a full-length feature on *The Game*. Savides's visuals are sleek but hollow, matching the film's protagonist but also the end result. And while *The Game* touched on subjects that would be explored in much greater depth in Fincher's next film *Fight Club* – the need to lose everything to rediscover who you are, the soulless nature of the corporate culture – this was not enough to rescue it from being one of the director's more shallow efforts.

The Game is often described as a postmodern remake of Hitchcock's *Vertigo* (1958), but Fincher prefers to compare it to an episode of *The Twilight Zone* or Charles Dickens's *A Christmas Carol*. Though set in San Francisco – the town of *Vertigo* and *The Maltese Falcon* (1941) – it would be hard to argue that *The Game* approaches the psychological complexity of either. That said, the locale of the film is more of a dreamlike psychic space than a bricks and mortar city. Just as Ripley awoke with a jolt from her cryogenic suspension in *Alien³* and Detective Somerset lulled himself to sleep to the sound of a ticking metronome in *Se7en*, so *The Game*'s protagonist is caught up in a living nightmare that suggests he's been sleepwalking all his life.

Reminiscent of the yuppies-in-peril movies that dominated the mid-1980s – notably Martin Scorsese's *After Hours* (1985) and Jonathan Demme's *Something Wild* (1986) – the film has as its central character Nicholas Van Orton (Michael Douglas), an investment banker worth around $600 million. 'I move money from one place to another,' he later explains, in a tone that suggests he's entirely disinterested in his own work. Divorced from his wife, he lives alone in a luxurious mansion with just his housekeeper for company. Reaching his forty-eighth birthday – the same age at which his father committed suicide – his reckless brother Conrad (Sean Penn) gives him a present. It's a game, 'specifically tailored for each participant'. Visiting the organizers, Consumer Recreation Services (CRS), he is told: 'We provide whatever's lacking.' In Nicholas's case, compassion, emotion . . . you name it.

Written by John Brancato and Michael Ferris, the story was influenced by a real-life scavenger hunt played by wealthy corporate types (Microsoft's Bill Gates is said to be a benefactor). Fincher received the script during the *Alien³* debacle but waited until after *Se7en* to make it. In the intervening years, it went through a variety of rewrites; Nicholas was originally written more as a Richard Branson type, a well-loved corporate raider. Fincher preferred the idea that Nicholas was more of a Scrooge-like figure, an emotional miser cut off from the world. As Fincher noted, Nicholas 'is damaged goods . . . he's atrophied in the way that people are when they cut themselves off from each other. He behaves very much like people I know who have $600 million in the bank. You have to be so guarded, because everybody has an agenda. It's especially bad if you're born into it. All of that stuff is part of a much bigger, richer movie than we had time to get into because we had a chase movie superimposed over it'.[56]

And herein lies the problem with *The Game*. A relentless thriller, it only makes brief pit stops to sketch Nicholas's character, and then only in the most one-dimensional of ways.

As the plot unfolds, you can sense Fincher is taking a sadistic pleasure in cranking up the paranoia and putting his protagonist through a living hell. Note, for example, the scene where Nicholas enters a hotel room booked under his name, and discovers cocaine strewn over the table, pornography playing on the television and incriminating Polaroid photos spread everywhere. Both tense and disturbing, it's the first time we begin to realize the extent of CRS's powers and the malicious intent behind the game itself. Like evil sprites, their employees wreak havoc in Nicholas's life – such as when he returns home to find his house covered in ultraviolet graffiti. Cut to the hypnotic, acid-drenched sounds of Jefferson Airplane's 'White Rabbit'. As Nicholas inspects this unofficial makeover, the setting is bathed in a blue hue that adds to the surreal, and surprisingly effective, nature of the scene. Purely for its visceral impact, it's one of the best scenes Fincher has ever filmed.

While the phrase 'roller coaster ride' is often lazily used to describe any Hollywood thriller that zips along, it truly applies to *The Game* – albeit a ride that feels like the brakes have been cut. Douglas described the film as 'getting in a car in traffic with a Grand Prix race driver and all of a sudden being totally surprised'.[57] As Nicholas careers from one scene to the next, he begins to crack – to the point where he won't even drink an already opened bottle of water, believing it to be spiked. His Swiss account is drained of all its money; he is drugged and wakes up in a tomb underneath a Mexican graveyard. Hitching back home, after selling his father's watch, he discovers a notice of foreclosure on his house. Looking like a tramp, he has lost all his assets, everything that means anything to him.

Taken on a literal level, the plot is too far-fetched to work. The employees of CRS must be mind readers – or else have a vast network of resources – to anticipate Nicholas's every move. But what really grates with some critics is the film's rather glib conclusion. After he spots a commercial on TV, he realizes the CRS employee who oversaw his induction was simply an actor. Tracking him down, he forces him at gunpoint to go to the CRS building. There, in the first of a series of self-satisfied twists, he enters a lunch canteen where everyone from his game is present – be they major or minor players. He winds up shooting Conrad, who bursts through the door with a birthday cake. In a manner reminiscent of his father's suicide, Nicholas finally jumps from the building; but this time there's a giant inflatable crash mat waiting to cushion his fall. Conrad's death, like everything else, was staged. Lesson learnt, Nicholas dusts himself off, his world of privilege still intact. You might even argue its values have been reaffirmed following his ordeal.

In many ways, the film is about the process of filmmaking. As Christine (Deborah Kara Unger), the waitress who has led Nicholas through the game, says, 'What did you really see the whole time? Special effects, squibs – like in the movies.' Fincher admits that he is drawn to scripts that 'begin to dismantle the architecture, not of movies, but of the pact that a movie . . . makes with an audience'.[58] In other words, it's meant as a destabilizing, disorienting and deliberately manipulative film that rebels against logical explanation. Fincher has admitted the film used 'a lot of tricks to unbalance the expectations of the movie-going experience'. Notably, in the final scene there is no music. 'That was a very conscious decision because you expect music when it's a big moment in a film. So when there isn't, does that make it a movie or make it real?'[59]

By casting Douglas, Fincher automatically recalled some of the actor's key roles, again bringing to our attention that this is a 'movie' – much like the one Nicholas is 'starring' in. Forever associated with the city after playing Inspector Steve Keller in the 1970s TV series *The Streets of San Francisco*, Douglas's turn in *The Game* also called to mind his Oscar-winning role as Gordon 'greed is good' Gecko from *Wall Street* (1987) and his unhinged white collar worker in *Falling Down* (1993). It's a first-rate performance from Douglas, who never attempts to ingratiate himself with the audience, even if he's left floundering in the scenes where Fincher and his screenwriters attempt to show Nicholas's change of heart. Keeping faith with this new generation of directors, Douglas went on to make *Traffic* with Steven Soderbergh. Fincher, buoyed by *The Game*'s $48.3 million U.S. takings, would set out to deliver one almighty sucker punch in his next film, *Fight Club*.

Would you like to be inside my skin, Craig? Think what I think? Feel what I feel? It's better than your wildest dreams.

Craig's Maxine puppet, as voiced by Craig, *Being John Malkovich*

Just as *The Game* hit cinemas, a curiously titled script fell into the hands of Propaganda employee Spike Jonze. Though he was only twenty-eight at the time, the reputation around his iconoclastic body of work was already considerable. A master at the melting pot of popular culture, he created a Lee Jeans ad that sent up superheroes and the Levi's spot that took on *ER* and 'Tainted Love' at the same time. He cast Björk in a Busby Berkeley number for 'It's Oh So Quiet', sent Wheezer into an episode of *Happy Days* for 'Buddy Holly'; and most famously created a pastiche of cheesy 1970s cop shows, complete with rooftop chases, walrus moustaches and Aviator shades, for the Beastie Boys' song 'Sabotage'. When he teamed up with Daft Punk, the gloriously absurd result – entitled 'Big City Nights' – was a curiously moving skit that saw a man with a dog's face patrolling a soulless conurbation with a boom box, blaring out the group's tune 'Da Funk'. As photographer David LaChapelle has said, Jonze 'is *the* contemporary artist. What he does is much more valid than so much going on in galleries now.'[60]

Jonze's path into films was a given. He had already worked for eight months with David O. Russell – who subsequently cast him as the sweet-natured Private Conrad Vig in *Three Kings* – on a live-action/animated version of the children's classic *Harold and the Purple Crayon* before TriStar pulled the plug. He then received the script for *Being John Malkovich*, the story of an out-of-work puppeteer named Craig who finds a portal into the eponymous actor's mind. Written by a nervy New Yorker named Charlie Kaufman, the script had Jonze immediately intrigued. 'After I read it, I was curious to find out who exactly Charlie Kaufman was,' says Jonze. 'Since then, I've been trying to find out more about who he is. I don't know – maybe we'll get to the bottom of it.'

It's a question one could easily ask about Jonze. In 1999, when *Being John Malkovich* was released, articles in the press ran with headlines like: 'Who exactly is Spike Jonze?' And to date, he's done a bang-up job of avoiding that very question. The man critics call 'the Orson Welles of rock video', he has morphed from skater-boy to sometime stuntman; photographer to actor. For all we know, he's just an empty vessel, his strings yanked by a perverse inner puppeteer who finds it amusing that a man responsible for realizing one of the best scripts of the decade can also be found performing loopy stunts in *Jackass: The Movie* (2002). Who better than Jonze to direct a film about wanting to be someone else?

He certainly makes a mockery of celebrity. Attempts to live vicariously through the rich and famous, as the characters in *Being John Malkovich* manage to do literally, are somewhat thwarted by Jonze, a man with either multiple personas or no discernible personality, depending on your point of view. This is the man who collected his MTV award for Best Music Video, for Fatboy Slim's 'Praise You', in the guise of alter ego Richard Koufay, the leader of the fictional Torrance Community Dance Group featured in the promo. It's as if he is just one lifelong in-joke; the producers must have danced with joy when he took the project on board – what a marketing ploy! You can almost imagine Jonze gleefully picking up *Variety* and answering their ad, like the one placed by Maxine and Craig that reads: 'Ever wanted to be someone else?'

Born Adam Spiegel, grandson to Art Spiegel II and heir to the $3 billion-a-year Spiegel catalogue business, he claims to have changed his name for 'legal reasons' after his parents divorced. Yet the origin of the name Spike Jonze is as unclear as the personality behind it. Is it a reference to musical satirist and bandleader Spike Jones? Or, as is often said, a nickname riffing on his unwashed hair, bestowed upon him by peers at the dirt-bike shop Rockville BMX where he worked in his teens? Either way, the Maryland-raised Jonze – whose mother appropriately enough worked in PR – began to develop multiple masks from an early age.

By the time Spike Jonze was 'born', he was principally working as a writer and photographer for the Torrance-based *Freestylin'*, a BMX/freestyle magazine, as well as contributing to *Homeboy* magazine, a blend of music, skateboarding and BMX. An ambassador for the skate subculture, he went as far as donning a chauffeur's uniform every time he picked up any professional skater from the airport. He first assumed the identity of a director with 1991's *Video Days*, a visceral twenty-minute up-close tribute to the skateboarding team Blind, as they pulled their tricks and stunts across suburban Southern California. Co-directed by Mark Gonzales, it eschewed the usual speed metal soundtrack in favour of The Jacksons' 'I Want You Back' and became an instant cult favourite among skateboarding's elite. Jonze meanwhile found himself involved with the foundation of *Dirt*, a short-lived male version of the maverick teen-girl magazine *Sassy*.

Establishing the industry contacts that would lead him towards his next incarnation, Jonze befriended Beastie Boy Adam Yauch through a photo shoot for *Dirt* and was soon hired by Tamra Davis, wife of fellow band member Mike D (and director of 1993 rap spoof *CB4*). Impressed by *Video Days*, she recruited Jonze to film a skateboarding sequence in the Sonic Youth promo '100%', though he claims to have learnt the basics of filmmaking by loading cameras for marine scientists. On the set, Jonze met Sofia Coppola, daughter to Francis and director in her own right. Through their short-lived marriage, they formed for a time Hollywood's most reluctant power couple, though it's hard to imagine Jonze being entirely comfortable at family gatherings at the Napa Valley vineyard. When wooing Ms Coppola, Jonze once arrived at the airport dressed in a fat suit, with grease on his face and cotton wool balls in his mouth; at their wedding, he avoided having his picture taken for the *Vogue* spread.

It seems fate that *Being John Malkovich* became his first directorial effort, a film designed to be crafted by a man to whom the theme of identity runs deep and personal.

While the issues tentatively explored in Kaufman's script no doubt resonated with him, Jonze was savvy enough to realize that he would have to let the words speak for themselves in order to pull it off. Photographed by Lance Acord, who worked with Jonze on many of his videos, as well as shooting Sofia Coppola's *Lost in Translation*, the film eschewed any of the eye-catching techniques pioneered in the so-called MTV age. For the most part, the frame is filled with simple, formal compositions, with the camera loitering as a hushed observer.

Only when we reach action sequences, such as Craig's kidnap of his wife Lotte, does the film spring to life, bobbing and weaving around the protagonists. With much of the action set at night, many of the interiors – from Craig and Lotte's gloomy apartment to the Mertin-Flemmer building where Craig takes a job as a clerk – are lit as if a giant thundercloud had parked itself overhead. Jonze and Acord conjure a subtle feeling of ominous dread that cuts across the more absurdly comic moments, a feeling echoed literally in the tunnel that actually leads into Malkovich's head (every time we see it, an eerie wind more suited to a Hammer Horror movie whistles on the soundtrack).

Jonze claims his decision to shoot the film without attempting to outdo the more wacky elements of the script was partly due to the limited forty-two-day production schedule, though he rightly stated: 'I thought it worked for the movie – not to make it big, flashy and overly into technique.' With the exception of Björk's 'Amphibian' accompanying the end credits, Jonze plumps for classical pieces by Verdi and Bartók, as well as an elegant, restrained score from Carter Burwell, to fill out the soundtrack, rather than the kind of Zeitgeist-forming pop tunes you might associate him with. Like those who inhabit Malkovich in the film, it's as if Jonze was looking through someone else's eyes while he directed the script, his personality packed in a box like one of Craig's puppets.

In return for this admirable restraint, this ego-free ability to admit that he is smaller than the film's grand conceit, Jonze has been somewhat overlooked in the rush to congratulate the mad professor of screenwriting that is Kaufman. For Jonze, this was probably a blessed relief. It is telling that he chose for his directorial debut a story where, for once, the writer is revered. While he was nominated for an Oscar for Best Director, it almost felt like a nod for simply not screwing up a gilt-edged story. Ironically, with *Adaptation* – Jonze's second collaboration with Kaufman – critics have been led to speculate that he has yet to prove himself as a director without his writer. It seems shocking, and grossly unfair, to think of him as a director-for-hire. It is as if he is a victim of his own success, for consciously not over-directing. Having deliberately not put his authorial stamp on the film, he is treated as a fortunate fellow who encountered an infallible script that simply directed itself.

In fact, Jonze's skill – and this will become more apparent with *Adaptation* – is a wonderful ability to draw performances from his cast, matched only by his shrewd choice of players. Take the revelatory Catherine Keener, dressed in either ominous black or virginal white depending on her mood, who chews up every sentence she has as

Craig's bitchy colleague Maxine. And it is the long-haired aspiring puppeteer Craig, who initially finds a portal into Malkovich's head behind a filing cabinet in the offices of Lestercorp, who receives the harshest lash of her tongue. To play Craig, Jonze chose John Cusack, minus his suit-sharp, streetwise persona cultivated in films like *The Grifters* (1990) and *Grosse Pointe Blank* (1997). Cusack almost folds in on himself to play his down-at-heel character, a man obsessed by the fickle Maxine. It is a pathetic desperation that Cusack subsequently channelled into his role in *High Fidelity* (2000), but here – as a tragic figure trapped by his unrequited love for Maxine, prefigured with his street puppet performance of *Abelard and Heloise* – the actor offers a quietly moving turn.

The most cultured selection by Jonze is Cameron Diaz, who plays the dowdy pet-store assistant Lotte, wife to Craig and eventual lover to Maxine. From the moment she shimmied across the screen like an extra from a Pantene ad in her debut *The Mask* (1994) until she donned that frightening frizzy brown wig to play Lotte, Diaz was slipped into a Hollywood straitjacket by studio heads that traded on her sunny cover-girl looks. Who had ever thought that this girl-next-door from *My Best Friend's Wedding* (1997) and *There's Something About Mary* (1998) could actually act without her Californian body-armour? Jonze said he wanted to find an actress who could repress her natural effervescence – and he found it in Diaz. Hired after the funding was in place, the onus to be her usual bubbly self removed, she was allowed by Jonze to recede into Lotte like a master of disguise. In the same way that Lotte comfortably inhabits the vessel Malkovich, so in this film more than any other Diaz disappears into her character. Her transformation defies our expectations, playing with our perceptions of celebrity, a theme at the dark heart of Kaufman's work. His ingenious script deals with how contemporary western society lives vicariously through the lives of others.

From the 'Maxine action figure' Craig creates to the moment where Malkovich is accosted in a restaurant by a grateful fan praising him for playing 'a retard' with sensitivity, the need to 'celebrate' permeates the entire script. When Malkovich orders bathroom accessories, checks his teeth in the mirror or eats his breakfast while perusing a copy of *The Wall Street Journal*, we are more fascinated by this voyeuristic opportunity than by the moments where we see him rehearse *Richard III* or read aloud from *The Cherry Orchard*. His pristine private quarters, and their minimalist furnishings, are of more interest than the sight we catch of him wearing a theatrical hump mid-creation. Exploding the myth of celebrity while simultaneously explaining it, the film suggests that being anointed as one of the famous few automatically ensures that your actions transcend the mundane. Like those wishing to pay Maxine and Craig $200 to be Malkovich for fifteen minutes, we are also implicated as celebrity voyeurs.

Just why Kaufman selected John Malkovich, and not anyone else, remains an enigma best left unravelled. Jonze claims that, in pre-production, he and Kaufman 'operated as if he [Malkovich] would do it', and would 'get depressed after ten minutes' if they ever discussed what would happen if he wouldn't. 'The main reason we wanted him to do it was that there's an element in the movie that is a high con-cept – the being John Malkovich. His presence legitimized the movie, stopped it from becoming a joke. A lot of people kind of know who he is.'

His use of the phrase 'kind of' is telling. In the film, Malkovich's reputation is such that people are only dimly aware of him. To his cab-bie, he is John Maplethorpe, star of that film 'where you played a jewel thief'. The worldly wise Maxine has never heard of him, and Craig, while saying Malkovich is 'one of the great American actors of the twentieth century', can only offer that he's been in 'lots of things – that jewel thief movie, for one'. Only when Craig takes over his body, in an attempt to use Malkovich's 'notoriety' (an interesting substitution for the word 'celebrity') to further his own career, are we privy to a potted history of the actor on a television special that charts his rise as a puppeteer.

Mixing fiction with fact in this mini-documentary, we hear mention of his theatre company Steppenwolf, and see a brief shot of the poster for his breakthrough film, *Dangerous Liaisons*. Beyond this the Malkovich on screen is a fabricated one. His middle name is Horatio, whereas in reality it's the less exotic Gavin. In a beautiful moment of self-mockery, we also see Sean Penn – an actor known for publicly revealing his desire to quit the business in the past – talk about wanting to emulate Malkovich the puppeteer but fearing a backlash from critics. That Jonze can also, in the same skit, show Brad Pitt, in a two-second head shot, looking shifty outside the premiere of Craig/Malkovich's performance of *Abelard and Heloise* says something about the fleeting nature of fame. An uncredited David Fincher – playing the *Los Angeles Times*'s National Arts Editor Christopher Bing – can also be spotted.

As for Malkovich, an actor Jonze believes has 'a pretty perverse sense of humour', he originally suggested to Kaufman that he would be delighted to direct or produce the piece, as long as the focus was changed to another. In the end, he relented. 'I never thought it was strange,' he says. 'I thought it was a really hilarious, very original piece of writing in a very difficult genre.' Both Kaufman and Jonze testified to the fact that Malkovich requested their portrayal of him be made 'meaner . . . darker', which goes to show just how game the actor was to take on the role.

Aside from showing himself as an ageing Lothario, egged on by his showbiz pal Charlie (Ma) Sheen and his talk of 'hot lesbian witches', Malkovich allows Kaufman to create him a subconscious that Freud would have had a field day with. His mind is brilliantly realized as a set of rooms that interconnect via trapdoors, which Maxine and Lotte tumble through. It's a remembrance of things past as traumatic as the one that haunts Lotte's chimp, Elijah, who once failed to untie his mother and father when the hunters captured them in the jungle. From seeing his parents have sex to being taunted for wetting himself on the school bus and even sniffing some underwear, being John Malkovich is a typically sorrowful human experience.

While Kaufman has stated that he began the script with the idea of 'a married man who fell in love with somebody else', he reaches this goal by suggesting that infidelity is an act – like that of entering Malkovich's head – in which the perpetrator almost switches personality. 'It's a very confusing situation,' says Maxine, as she discovers that it is no longer Lotte she is making love to (via Malkovich, acting as a sort of human condom). At this point Craig has sneaked into the actor's head, having tied Lotte up in the animal cage in their house. It makes for the most twisted love triangle (or quartet, if you include Malkovich) ever to emerge in a Hollywood film.

The end result has been called 'confusingly moralistic' for the punishing of Craig as a 'villain' in the finale. Maxine and Lotte wind up finding happiness. And yet Craig's hellish sentence, trapped inside the vessel of Maxine and Lotte's child Emily to forever gaze on the woman his ex-wife is now making love to, is the perfect conclusion to the life of one who dares to transgress. Symbolized by its location on floor 7½ of the Mertin-Flemmer building – one-half above the number regularly associated with God – the tunnel to Malkovich's mind is like a meta-physical wormhole (or, as Craig puts it, a 'metaphysical can of worms'). It raises the possibility that one can assume the power of the Creation. As if to underline this, Lotte calls the tunnel 'a vagina'; its warm innards certainly remind us of a womb.

Correctly calling his work 'a Rorschach test', Kaufman – who puts himself under greater scrutiny in *Adaptation*, as we will see in Chapter 19 – has created a work of startling ambiguity that throws up more questions than it answers. As prefigured by the glimpse of Craig's rival puppeteer, the David Copperfield–esque Derek Mantini, and his performance with a sixty-foot-high Emily Dickinson doll, *Being John Malkovich* dextrously forges high and low culture into something quite unique. Shoehorning an investigation of 'the existence of the soul' into the romantic comedy genre (albeit one that deals in transsexuality), Kaufman has created a dance of despair and disillusion that is as contemporary as it is universal. As for the master puppeteer Jonze, one question springs to mind: would he like to be John Malkovich? 'Sure. For the same reason I'd just want to be anybody. To see how they'd think about things.' If his and Kaufman's debut is anything to go by, our minds are plagued by thoughts of greed, envy, infidelity and, above all, celebrity.

CHAPTER 11

Beyond the Fringe:
Schizopolis and *Gray's Anatomy*

24 Steven Soderbergh mugs to the camera in *Schizopolis*.

No fish were harmed during the making of this film.
  Steven Soderbergh, *Schizopolis*

Some might point to 2000–2001 as Soderbergh's Second Coming, with three $100 million hit movies and a Best Director Oscar for *Traffic*. But five years earlier, between April 1995 – the miserable U.S. release of *The Underneath*, with its gross of $536,000 – and the end of 1996, Soderbergh's resurrection was well underway. Not that it seemed like it at the time. As one critic wrote, 'It is only to be hoped that the fact he hasn't made a hit for some time and his desire to withdraw from mainstream production do not mean that he disappears from film-making altogether.'[61]

Perversely, while he was a fading blip on the Hollywood radar, he was busier than ever. A writer-for-hire for Miramax, he also, as we will see, produced two films for other directors. If that wasn't enough, he was shooting, editing and finding distribution deals for *Schizopolis* and *Gray's Anatomy*, the films that would reinvigorate his battle-damaged self-belief after his torrid time on *The Underneath*. By his own admission, this was too much. As excerpts from his journal testify, he was barely keeping himself afloat, his attentions pulled every which way. On 18 April 1996, after agreeing to rewrite the script for Guillermo del Toro's horror film *Mimic* (1997), he wrote: 'Trying to take this on suddenly seems like the dumbest thing in the world. Why is it so important to me to be the hero? . . . Why am I so attracted to this romantic idea of the guy who can do five things at once and do them all well? Who really gives a shit?'[62]

At the time, he was also embroiled with Henry Selick on *Toots and the Upside Down House*, Carol Hughes's novel about a motherless young girl who discovers an upside-down miniaturized world inside her home. Having agreed to adapt the book for Selick – the stop-motion animator famed for his work on Tim Burton's *The Nightmare Before Christmas* (1993) – Soderbergh spent the best part of the year procrastinating as best he could, just as Miramax pulled their backing from the project. 'I don't consider myself a writer,' he reflects. 'I've written by default, to either further my career or because I'm after something so specific that I'm having trouble describing it to someone else. But I'm fully aware that my best films, in my opinion, have come from working with other writers.' Selick, who would later go on to work with Wes Anderson on *The Life Aquatic with Steve Zissou*, eventually watched the project crumble before his very eyes – despite interest from Twentieth Century Fox during the time Soderbergh was involved. 'I doubt he will ever hire me again as a writer,' Soderbergh would later confess.[63]

This was also the period in which Soderbergh penned the script for *Nightwatch* (1997), Ole Bornedal's American remake of his own 1994 Danish thriller. Starring Ewan McGregor as Martin Bells, a young law student who takes a job as a night watchman in a local morgue, it was produced by Miramax offshoot Dimension Films. The company had bought the U.S. rights to Bornedal's original and kept it on the shelf, presumably to halt any unfavourable comparisons.

Soderbergh's script somewhat sanitized the original – oral sex in the restaurant was turned into a handjob; scenes of sex in the morgue and one character vomiting in a font during a church communion were removed. He was also unable to deny the thriller clichés, despite pre-empting criticism by having Bells utter self-aware dialogue such as: 'It's just like one of those movies on a U.S. network – the hero sees something and no one believes him.' Despite leaving an obvious series of markers – Bells is set up as the killer; his friend James (Josh Brolin) is made to seem like the real murderer – Soderbergh manages a nice line in creepy dialogue, most of which comes from the mouth of Nick Nolte's cop investigating the crimes. 'Explanations,' he says, referring to a killer's motives, 'are just a fiction to make us feel safe, because if it can't be explained then it's just meaningless chaos.'

Ultimately, it's the final third that's the meaningless chaos, with the script relying on gruesome gestures rather than genuine chills. How much of this can be blamed on Soderbergh it is hard to fathom. While the film was shooting in Los Angeles in early 1996, by October he was called back to provide new pages for re-shoots, a fact he was not happy with. 'I'm really at my wits' end,' he said. 'Ole keeps making changes that I think are detrimental to the picture and I keep sending out faxes chock-full of cranky opinions and reactions'.[64] As he put it, he was 'playing the oversensitive disgruntled writer to the hilt'.

So taking on *Mimic*, the story of mutant cockroaches crawling through the New York subway system, was probably not the best idea. Soderbergh was called in to beef up the two main characters, a husband-and-wife team of scientists (played eventually by Mira Sorvino and Jeremy Northam). Del Toro met him during post-production on *Schizopolis* and gave him the screenplay.

> Steven said 'Why don't we make it a mixed marriage? He's black and she's white' – which I loved. Obviously, that didn't fit well with the studio. He then proceeded to say 'I'll go away and give you a draft.' He went away for forty days or so, gave me a draft, and I read it. It was an amazing character creation, but it had nothing to do with the movie I wanted to make. I called him and said 'I really don't like anything.' The only thing I kept of his was the Chinese Priest at the beginning. That is his.

Despite his brief assistance on *Suture*, Soderbergh would also wear his producer hat in earnest for the first time in this period. Back in 1994, Soderbergh and Nancy Tenenbaum (producer of *sex, lies, and videotape*) had seen a short by the unknown director Greg Mottola. They liked it and, wanting to help Mottola get something made, advised him to write a script he could shoot cheap and fast. The result was *The Daytrippers* (1996), a beautifully observed comic ensemble about a mercy dash in a station wagon. Solid reviews and a $2 million box office total in the U.S. probably did as much to keep Soderbergh's name on the lips of industry insiders as anything else at the time. He also came on board as producer for his friend Gary Ross's *Pleasantville* (1998), which began shooting in early 1997. For this story of two teenagers trapped in a 1950s sitcom, Soderbergh was employed more as a sounding board than as anything else – although he hired himself as a second-unit director to help shoot a high-school montage.

Ross, as you would expect from a friend, leaps to Soderbergh's defence when the subject of his choice of projects is raised. 'I wish people would be more tolerant of some of his more independent investigations. I resent a lot of film journalists in the United States, critics in particular, who want to embrace Steven for being mainstream, and whack him for these very responsible, cheap investigations of more idiosyncratic, arcane material that he does with his own money. I noticed a lot of scathing reviews of *Schizopolis*. I resent the fact that a lot of people have castigated him for his more daring choices. It's laudable, that's the only thing you can say.'

Soderbergh had been planning *Schizopolis*, a postmodern Python-esque comedy about the redundancy of language, since sitting on the set of *The Underneath*, 'watching that play out', as he politely terms it. 'I realized if I was going to save myself I needed to do this,' he says more dramatically. 'With *Schizopolis*, it was a Jackson Pollock of a movie designed to shake me up and get me enthused again. It was like a second first film, in a way. Everything since then has benefited from it, from its looseness and its willingness to take chances. To me, it was a very clear demarcation before and after that film.' He may joke in the film's prologue that 'this is the most important motion picture you will ever attend', but for him it was most certainly true.

Employing a back-to-basics aesthetic, *Schizopolis* is Soderbergh's equivalent of Dogme95, the Danish movement created by Lars von Trier and Thomas Vinterberg which encouraged its acolytes to simplify the filmmaking process. Ironically, that much-celebrated movement – which demanded its followers obey ten rules as a way of paring down their productions – was being established around this time. 'It's definitely my version of that,' says Soderbergh. 'When we were shooting, we knew that von Trier and company were formalizing their ideas. I was just going strictly on instinct – which was that I needed to strip away all the mechanisms of traditional production and get back to something a little more instinctual.' Soderbergh would not force himself to take a vow of cinematic chastity as part of his purification process, but he had no need. The very nature of *Schizopolis*'s production would do this for him.

When we are told at the outset of the film that 'no expense was incurred bringing this motion picture to your theatre', there is more than a grain of truth in the gag. Costing around $250,000, it was funded in part by Soderbergh pre-selling the video rights to Universal. Shot in Louisiana over a period of nine months, *Schizopolis* was guerrilla filmmaking in its purist sense. 'There was one fairly intense couple of weeks of shooting, and then it came in dribs and drabs,' remembers Soderbergh. 'This was partially as a result of availability of certain people or locations, and partially me continuing to work on the script as we went. Part of it was that I didn't want it to necessarily work the way a normal production worked. I wanted a break from that. There were only five of us. We drove around and put all the equipment in two cars. Sometimes we'd just go out and look for a location, and find one and ask if we could shoot in there.' This on-the-hoof method continued well into post-production, when Soderbergh ran out of money and was forced to use the advance Universal had given him to work on another, ultimately aborted, project entitled *Neurotica*.

The biggest concession Soderbergh had to make was playing the central role(s), office drone Fletcher Munson and his doppelganger Dr Korchek, himself. The only time he has appeared in one of his films – aside from a brief cameo in *Full Frontal* – it was a 'purely budgetary' decision. 'There was just nobody I knew that I could make that demand of – come and work for free for nine months whenever I feel like it in Baton Rouge!' And yet, surely, the practicalities of casting himself were only part of it. After all, no doubt thousands of out-of-work actors would willingly commit themselves to a project with a Palme d'Or–winning director. At times *Schizopolis* strayed into the realm of private filmmaking, as if it were a home movie. 'It was following on the heels of my own divorce,' he notes. 'I was working through some ideas about how language breaks down in a relationship.'

Opposite Soderbergh, playing Fletcher's unfaithful spouse, Mrs Munson, was his former wife, Betsy Brantley. With their then five-year-old daughter also appearing on screen, one can only imagine the tension on set. 'It just had to be done,' Soderbergh reflects.

Everybody involved would say it was a very loaded atmosphere because I was acting with my ex-wife and it was all pretty recent. It just felt like something that needed to be done. It was probably cathartic in some way, though I didn't assume it would be and I wasn't looking for that. I was just trying to find my own language, or a new language, or something. I think at that time I was more specifically aiming at a feeling in a marriage that has lost its way and lost its spark, and you're play-acting. You're not present. You're somewhere else. You've just become an automaton.

On the scant publicity materials that came with the movie, Soderbergh joked that 'all attempts at synopsizing the film have ended in failure and hospitalization', but there is actually a fairly well-structured three-act plot, albeit obscured by the wacky vignettes that take centre stage. 'It's not as arbitrary as it seems at first,' confirms Soderbergh. 'I absolutely had a design that I followed, for better or worse.' Announced by a number – delivered on a plate, fished from a river or put in a mailbox – each segment is distinct from the others yet inextricably linked. The

film begins as Fletcher, insecure, paranoid and obsessed with masturbation, is asked by his boss, Right Hand Man (Scott Allen), to write a
speech for the company's owner, T. Azimuth Schwitters (Mike Malone), an evangelist touting a New Age religion called Eventualism. As
whispers circulate that the office is rife with industrial espionage,
Fletcher is plagued by his colleague Nameless Numberheadman (Eddie
Jemison), who is becoming increasingly concerned that he may be sin-
gled out as a spy.

At home, as Fletcher struggles with his speech, Mrs Munson
embarks on an affair with a local dentist, Dr Korchek – also played by
Soderbergh – leading to the immortal line 'I'm having an affair with
my own wife' when Fletcher spies his spouse with his exact double.
The narrative switches onto Korchek, who falls in love with a patient,
called Attractive Woman Number 2 (also played by Brantley). Meanwhile, when Mrs Munson eventually returns to Fletcher's arms, he
completes the speech and attends the oration by Schwitters. But
halfway through, former pest-exterminator turned action movie star
Elmo Oxygen (David Jensen) tries to assassinate Schwitters, who survives – only to receive get well soon wishes from Oliver Stone. Little
wonder Soderbergh admits *Schizopolis* is 'one of the weirdest movies
made by a "mainstream" director in a while'.

For Soderbergh, *Schizopolis* was about being able to rebuild his
aesthetic 'from the ground up', partly by revisiting some of his
stronger influences. One of the key figures in his development was the
Philadelphia-born director Richard Lester. During 1996, Soderbergh
made several trips to London to interview Lester for the journal *Getting
Away with It*. They had met six years earlier in Park City, a year after
Soderbergh's Sundance triumph. 'It gets harder, you know,' Lester had
told him. It didn't take too long for Soderbergh to figure out what he
meant. Although, at first, the two directors seem worlds apart, Lester's
restless career bears a marked similarity to Soderbergh's own crooked
path. Lester flirted with the mainstream (his *Musketeers* films in the
1970s; his *Superman* films in the 1980s), tapped into the Zeitgeist (his
films for The Beatles) and delivered one highly influential all-out masterpiece, *Petulia* (1968).

A dissection of middle-class mores in the midst of free love, *Petulia*
observed San Francisco in much the way John Boorman's *Point Blank*
had a year earlier. Shot by Nicolas Roeg, another big influence on
Soderbergh, the story of the freshly divorced doctor (George C. Scott)

who meets a self-styled 'kook' (Julie Christie) boasts a complex time structure that also recalls Boorman's film. In particular, it influenced Roeg's later films *Performance* (1970), *Don't Look Now* (1973) and *Bad Timing* (1980). (While Soderbergh made everyone on *Out of Sight* watch *Petulia*, its flashback mechanism would reappear most strongly in *The Limey*.)

Schizopolis mirrors the anarchic intensity found in Lester's Beatles films, with its use of mock interviews (notably with C. C. Courtney, who acts as a commentator of sorts on the film) and speeded-up action footage (such as the driver's-eye view of car trips across town). Like in Lester's films, the border between fiction and reality is also regularly crossed, notably when Elmo storms off the set leaving the camera to focus on the bewildered crew. Soderbergh showed *Schizopolis* to Lester, who was even referenced in the film as the deceased employee 'Lester Richards'. 'He was funny,' says Soderbergh. 'He appreciated the energy of it, but wished I could've lashed it to a clearer narrative. We talked about that. He said, "I kept wanting Elmo Oxygen's language, and the language that exists in that world, to eventually have some sort of logic to it and make some sort of sense." He encouraged me to take this feeling and vibe and find a solid story to attach it to.'

Elmo, when he's not playing the diva by demanding fruit for his trailer, speaks in a cryptic language that replaces common phrases. Words such as 'jigsaw' and 'sneeze' can be interpreted as 'later!' and 'cheers!' – though interpreting 'death rattle monkey callousness' is a little trickier. As Elmo says, 'language does not always require speech'. Soderbergh admits he could have taken the idea further, and employed the logic that Lester craved by being more precise about what words his oddball phrases, or 'Elmo-speak', are replacing: 'I guess my feeling was that even that was a violation of his character; it had to constantly make no sense.' As far as Soderbergh is concerned, Elmo is his comic exploration of the mindset of political assassins like Arthur Bremer and John Hinckley, who was famously inspired by *Taxi Driver* before attempting to kill President Reagan: 'By definition, their experience is so disordered compared to ours, that I didn't want to have any order in it. I wanted you to experience Elmo's world the way Elmo experienced it. For some reason, this whole thing of assassination as an expression of ideology was floating around in my head at the time. I don't know why.'

But Elmo is not the only one to communicate in an idiosyncratic manner. Fletcher and his wife speak in phrases that describe the true meaning of the bland platitudes couples on the rocks can often be guilty of exchanging. 'Generic greeting' and 'generic greeting returned', for example, is their way of saying 'Hi Honey, I'm home!' When Mrs Munson returns from a supposed trip to the cinema, Fletcher says to her, 'Obligatory question about the evening's activities.' Later on, after their reunion, many of these scenes are replayed – but in Japanese, then Italian and finally French. As Soderbergh says, 'It was an attempt to grapple with what happens when language is used to obscure instead of illuminate, which is what happens a lot with our interactions.'

A film that breaks linguistic (as well as cinematic) rules, *Schizopolis* also juxtaposes various styles of humour and comedic influences. The surreal scene that simply contains a tree with a sign pinned to it, saying 'Idea Missing', that then falls off is pure Monty Python, as is the finale of a man wearing only a black T-shirt bearing the legend 'The End' being captured by two men in white coats. Likewise, the news report that 'the price of capturing, restraining and institutionalising a naked man in a T-shirt remains stable at around $367 and 50 cents' could easily find a place in BBC current affairs satire *The Day Today*, which had first aired a year earlier. In a skit that recalls *The Day Today*'s front-man Chris Morris, Soderbergh ends *Schizopolis* by appearing in an empty auditorium, answering unheard questions in a Q&A with random answers like 'foot-long veggie on wheat'.

If one can point to a minor theme in much of Soderbergh's work, it is New Age or 'alternative' practices. Whether it's Ann's therapy sessions in *sex, lies, and videotape*, the self-help books read by Michael Chambers in *The Underneath* or the palm reader visited by Reuben Tishkoff in *Ocean's Twelve*, Soderbergh's characters are often looking to third parties for reassurance. Soderbergh calls himself 'a hardcore atheist' – no doubt as a leftover reaction to the fact that his mother used to regularly hold séances in their house – though admits he has a pair of good-luck boots that he wears when on a shoot. 'I'm interested in that stuff to the extent that I'm very curious as to how people get into a frame of mind that allows them to think this way and to design their lives around this thinking. It's something I grew up around. I'm not allergic to it. I just don't relate to it.'

In *Schizopolis*, New Age theory is examined in the form of the fictional Eventualism craze that sweeps through the film. While Soderbergh denies this was directly inspired by the fashionable religion of

Scientology, it can be seen as a catch-all cult that represents contemporary society's need for alternatives to organized religion. Although, as Fletcher notes into his tape recorder, 'Eventualism is not a cause, a course, a fashion or a religion.' What it is, judging by the meaningless rhetoric that spills from Schwitters's mouth, is utter nonsense. 'Anything that can be imagined is legitimate' is just one of many empty non sequiturs he comes out with. Not that everyone is fooled: one talking head states, 'He's the worst kind of charlatan and raconteur you can imagine.' Ironically, while it is Elmo who tries to finish off Schwitters, he too 'is not feeling fulfilled'. As he tells the couple who attempt to prise him away from the film with a more lucrative offer, 'There's a spiritual element missing.' Though it should be noted, Elmo does find something to worship, later telling us, 'I believe so strongly in mayonnaise.'

Pointing out that if it's not pseudo-religions that satisfy us, it's pornography or even the perfect smile ('You don't have to floss all your teeth. Just the ones you want to keep,' Dr Korchek reminds us), *Schizopolis* is as much about what is absent in our lives today as it is about how we fill them. Yet it also seeks an order in the universe. In many ways, Soderbergh is deconstructing the notion of cause and effect, as demonstrated by the golf ball that is hit in one scene and bounces through another much later on. Looking on the brighter side of David Lynch, the possibility of parallel universes, suggested by the use of doubles and repeated scenes, is contemplated – the natural extension, one might think, of seeking out alternative ways of looking at the world and oneself. The concept of fate is also considered. A perennial Soderbergh theme – notably seen later in *Solaris* and *Out of Sight* – it is here raised via a caption that asks, 'Do you feel outside forces control your destiny?' In true *Schizopolis* style, it might be best to end at the beginning, recalling that it is Soderbergh's 'firm belief that the delicate fabric that holds all of us together will be ripped apart unless every man, woman and child in this country sees this film'.

Sadly, that was not to be. *Schizopolis* was met with indifference among audiences, industry figures, critics and even festival programmers. When he sheepishly presented *The Underneath* to an audience at the 1995 London Film Festival, telling then-programmer Sheila Whitaker he 'wanted to make a new kind of film', she invited him to bring it to the festival. But needless to say, Whitaker rejected both *Schizopolis* and its follow-up, *Gray's Anatomy*, which had been shot during a ten-day post-production hiatus on its predecessor. Both were eventually released in the U.S. via the art-house distributor Northern Arts: 'It was frustrating,' he says. 'I felt like the films were at least energetic and lively, compared to what I'd been up to recently. They were fun to watch – and nobody really cared.'

This is just a movie. It's not my eye!
Spalding Gray, *Gray's Anatomy*

Funded for around $350,000 by the BBC (who gave the film a straight-to-TV premiere in the UK) and the Independent Film Channel, *Gray's Anatomy* was not an obvious choice for a theatrical release. Soderbergh had offered it to Fox Searchlight, until the executives ran the numbers on the previous two Gray monologues – Jonathan Demme's *Swimming to Cambodia* (1978) and Nick Broomfield's *Monster in a Box* (1991) – and figured that, while they probably wouldn't lose money, they wouldn't make enough to be worth their while. Given that it made $21,053 in the U.S. (still some $10,473 more than *Schizopolis*), they no doubt felt vindicated. Soderbergh was shattered: 'I was – as I often am – deluded about my films' commercial prospects.'

As much as this book is suggesting that the studios were willing to build relationships with maverick directors, Soderbergh is evidence that this was not always the case. Anything unconventional and difficult to market was still kept at arm's length, regardless of whether it was made by a former golden child. More worryingly, neither *Schizopolis* nor *Gray's Anatomy* fitted the Sundance model, an indictment of the sort of safe and sanitized fare that the festival was now taking. The independent movie was becoming as formulaic as the Hollywood blockbuster: all arch dialogue, quirky characters and hip soundtracks. Proving that it was too edgy for Sundance, *Schizopolis* went straight to Slamdance, the concurrent Park City festival that showcases more underground material.

Soderbergh compares *Gray's Anatomy* to 'a school art project'. With a crew not much bigger than the one used for *Schizopolis*, the film was shot in a warehouse in Baton Rouge. 'We had our offices there and this huge area where we set up all the shots. My brother [Charley] came in from Atlanta to do the hair and make-up for Spalding. It was a very fertile time. There were ideas at hand. Within the basic framework I'd set up, to work with Elliot [Davis] and the production designer [Adele Plauché] to set up these shots, and again working within this very constrained budget . . . it was a really pleasurable time.'

While it was Gray who came to Soderbergh with the project, it's easy to see why the director clicked so quickly with the material. An eighty-minute to-camera digression about the time Gray suffered a retina problem with his left eye and the angst it caused him ('It was so frightening, I thought I better forget about it,' he remarks), it returns to the theme of alternative therapies. Upon meeting a Minneapolis-based single mother who also happens to be a sorcerer's apprentice, Gray relates that she advised him to avoid having a normal operation – something that terrified him anyway – and to try an Indian Sweat Lodge instead. With a dry wit typical of Gray, he then cannot stop thinking about how his ancestors killed Native Americans before he uses his time inside to pray for his partner to get a lucrative Hollywood script job.

Gray tries other options too: an all-raw-vegetable diet; a trip to the Philippines to be treated by a psychic surgeon; a Chinese doctor who promises to 'peel' rather than scrape his eye . . . the list goes on. 'In a weird sort of a way, it's a modern version of the painfulness of enlightenment,' says Soderbergh. 'It's Spalding going through personally what the world went through a few centuries ago. Which is, "Are we going to evolve and move beyond this magical thinking and recognize things for what they are, and take them for what they are, or continue to live in a world where there are miracles?"'

Full of dexterous wit, the piece contains some unforgettable Grayisms. From one-liners like 'I cannot believe my eye!' to more satirical comments, such as the moment when he claims to see former President Richard Nixon leaving his doctor's office and it gives him 'the faith, hope and courage to have that operation', it's grimly funny stuff. But beneath the playful exterior beats a rueful heart. Raised as a Christian Scientist, and therefore in part objecting to an operation on religious grounds, Gray reminds us through his increasingly desperate actions just how scary it can be to face up to a condition for which there may be no known cure.

As for Soderbergh, he was determined to try a different tack than Demme and Broomfield, who had both offered no-frills interpretations of Gray's work. 'I felt because of the material that I was justified in abstracting the visuals and taking him out of live performance mode,' says Soderbergh. 'Nick and Jonathan had done terrific jobs of capturing him in performance, and I felt I couldn't do that again. This was about a guy coming to terms with losing his eyesight in one eye – and I thought I could really open this thing up. Again, it became a challenge of "What can I do for $350,000?" I sat down with the monologue and I edited a version of it, breaking it down into sections. I started laying out visually what would happen in each section.'

Complementing Gray's words with some appropriate images, the background behind the desk where Gray is sitting changes as the story unfolds. From a huge red eye, recalling the all-seeing eye on the poster in the street in *Kafka*, to an optician's sight chart, a cloudy blue sky and a pure white screen (during the operation he finally succumbs to), limited resources are used carefully by Soderbergh to enliven Gray's chatter. At one point, when Gray first describes his visit to the doctor to talk about his problem, he is placed behind some corrugated per-spex, signifying his increasingly blurred vision. With Elliot Davis's lighting constantly bathing Gray in various colours – from angry red to sickly yellow – Soderbergh succeeds in creating an ever-shifting canvas as a backdrop for his subject.

Splicing the narrative with black and white unrehearsed talking heads is particularly inspired. As the film opens – after a brief class-room clip discussing the importance of sight – we listen to a variety of horror stories from the interviewees concerning eye-related matters. One woman managed to put glue in her eye, while one man got a fishing hook in his. Believe it or not, Soderbergh claims these were all connected to his old pal David Jensen, who had just finished playing Elmo Oxy-gen. 'I said, "You have to go out and find me people who'd had eye problems." And he did.' It is particularly effective when the film later returns to these people, and some others, to get them to comment on Gray's various crazy therapies. As one says, 'He's obviously a very intelligent person. He's very neurotic. He certainly takes things to extremes.'

Tragically, in 2004, the body of Gray was found in the East River, two months after he disappeared from his Manhattan apartment. Having suffered a horrendous car crash three years earlier, he had sub-sequently battled depression, even attempting suicide in 2002. As it stands, Soderbergh is looking to shoot a documentary about Gray's life and times, with the assistance of his widow, Kathleen Russo, who acted as an executive producer on *Gray's Anatomy*. There's no doubt that Soderbergh feels he owes Gray, along with Richard Lester, some sort of a debt. The two films changed him irreparably. 'For me, it was an explosion that continues to reverberate,' he says. 'There's no way I could have made *Out of Sight*, the way I'd made it, if I hadn't made *Schizopolis* or *Gray's Anatomy*. They both just opened me up.'

CHAPTER 12

Adult Entertainment:
Hollywood Grows Up with *Boogie Nights*

25 Burt Reynolds and William H. Macy take stock in *Boogie Nights*.

> It's the best work I've done . . . This is the film I want them to remember me by.
>
> Jack Horner, *Boogie Nights*

After the trials of *Hard Eight*, and the enforced title change, Paul Thomas Anderson was not about to let the same thing happen again. *Boogie Nights*, Anderson's epic 1997 survey of the American porn industry in its heyday, begins with a bravura opening tracking shot, lasting two minutes forty-five seconds. It starts with the camera squarely focused on the title, glimpsed as a neon-lit sign adorning a Van Nuys Boulevard theatre. The message from Anderson was clear: hands off my title, hands off my film. Try as any executive might, there would be no way to remove it from the shot and no way to cut the shot – a dazzling introduction to all the main players – from the film. As assured and exuberant an opening as you are ever likely to see, it's a precocious statement of intent: in a cinematic Second Coming, Paul Thomas Anderson rose from the ashes of his debut feature to announce what he was capable of. As he said, 'I wrote [it] fuelled by a desire for revenge on all the people who told me I'd never amount to anything.'[65]

They were wrong. From the title, the camera swirls away to focus on the car belonging to pornographer Jack Horner (Burt Reynolds) and his wife cum starlet Amber Waves (Julianne Moore) as they arrive at Hot Traxx, a club over the road belonging to Maurice Rodriguez (Luis Guzmán). A caption tells us we are in the San Fernando Valley. It's 1977; disco sounds abound and *Star Wars* fever is in full swing. Following them inside to where the dance floor is buzzing, the camera weaves a complex jig around several of Jack's regular troupe – Rollergirl (Heather Graham), Buck Swope (Don Cheadle) and Reed Rothchild (John C. Reilly). Seconds before it finally cuts, it lands and lingers on our hero, Eddie Adams (Mark Wahlberg), working in the kitchens of Hot Traxx. Rightly drawing comparison with Martin Scorsese's audacious tracking shot through New York's Copacabana club in *Goodfellas* (1990), this proved that the wounds from the battering Anderson took on *Hard Eight* were not life-threatening.

Calling *Boogie Nights* and his third film, *Magnolia*, his 'fuck-you celebrations of the Valley',[66] Anderson has also drawn links with *Hard Eight*. He dubbed *Boogie Nights* a prequel to *Hard Eight* 'in that it follows this kid as he does things that leave him with a huge karmic debt. When the story ends, you sense that Dirk will now attempt to atone for the things he's done; in other words, Dirk becomes Sydney.'[67] He is referring to Eddie – who, after being taken under the wing of Jack Horner, re-christens himself with the porn moniker Dirk Diggler. Living proof that, in America, you can reinvent yourself and live out the Dream, Dirk soon pampers himself with the tasteless trappings of success – from an oil painting of himself to curtains monogrammed with 'DD' and the obligatory gleaming red Corvette. Frustrating the myth that men with flash cars are under-endowed, Anderson nonetheless uses it as a symbolic device; as Dirk's life hits rock bottom, he freewheels the car down a hill when it runs out of gas.

As Anderson regular William H. Macy, who plays Jack's luckless first assistant director Little Bill, notes, the film deals with 'family values' just as *Hard Eight* did: '[It's] about where you go to find solace in this life. The character of Dirk Diggler is kicked out of his own family, so he has no place to go. Therefore, he creates this new "family", which just happens to be around pornographic films, and they are as loving and as complete as any other family you can find. This is a movie about family values, trust and honouring your family.'[68] Much of this focuses on Amber, who – having lost her own child in a custody battle – enjoys an almost maternal relationship with both Dirk and Rollergirl, who even asks if she can be Amber's 'adopted' child. Yet while Dirk's real mother is seen as uncaring to the point where she kicks him out, he is never at ease with his surrogate, even telling her 'you're not my mother' in a moment of anger.

Raised in the heart of the porn industry, Anderson had his first taste when he was nine, sneaking a look at his father's copy of *The Opening of Misty Beethoven* (1976). Intrigued by the nearby anonymous cinder warehouses where he knew such fare was being shot, Anderson claims to have lived near where classic blue movie *Amanda by Night* (1982) was made. Just twenty-six when he made *Boogie Nights*, Anderson may echo Jack Horner – who wants to elevate salacious material to the level of art – but he's also driven by the same desires as the naive Dirk, desperate to prove himself. While Dirk is bestowed with Adult Film Awards for Best Penis, Anderson's Oscar nomination for Best Original Screenplay granted him the acceptance he craved.

Anderson was subsequently hailed as the new Tarantino, but the comparison is a lazy one. Scorsese would be more accurate, but if Anderson draws from the director, it is more than just by emulating his stylistic flourishes. *Boogie Nights* undeniably follows the traditional rise and fall structure of the gangster film, exemplified by *Goodfellas*. That the downfall of Dirk echoes that of Ray Liotta's Henry Hill strengthens the comparison; both are brought to their knees by their addiction to cocaine, which eventually addles their powers of judgement. Both seek out surrogate families: for Hill it is with a bunch of New York wiseguys, for Dirk, it is with a group of damaged souls at the heart of the porn business. For the climax, when a chastened Dirk gives himself a pep talk in his dressing room, the film borrows from Scorsese's *Raging Bull* (1980). Like Dirk, Robert De Niro's washed-up boxer Jake LaMotta does much the same, referencing Marlon Brando's infamous 'I coulda been a contender' speech from Elia Kazan's *On the Waterfront* (1954). Of course, neither De Niro nor Brando was ever required to whip out a thirteen-inch (prosthetic) penis, as Wahlberg does, referring to himself as 'a big, bright shining star'. Anderson times his money-shot of the organ we have been teased with – so to speak – for the whole film to perfection, unleashing the beast to create one of contemporary cinema's finest and funniest payoff lines.

But Scorsese was not the only influence on *Boogie Nights*. Robert Altman's *Nashville* was also a template. Once screening a print of *Nashville* on his birthday as a present to himself, Anderson is in awe of Altman's use of long takes, interwoven multiple storylines and overlapping dialogue. In particular, one *Boogie Nights* sequence is a direct replica of the scene where David Hayward's assassin arrives in town. Like Altman, Anderson allows the vehicles from the two alternating narrative strands we have just been watching – in this case, the pickup trucks containing the rednecks who attack Dirk and the limousine containing Jack and Rollergirl – to pass each other on the street. As they do, a third strand takes over, as Buck drives his own truck moments later along the same road and into a nearby parking lot. Anderson also admits a love for Robert Downey Sr's satire on the advertising industry, *Putney Swope* (1969). 'When I watched it, it was the first time I realized you could be really punk rock in a movie,' says Anderson. 'You could just do anything.'[69]

Naming Buck Swope in honour of the film, Anderson cast Downey Sr in a small role as the record producer who refuses to give Dirk a copy of the appalling rock track he concocts – unless he pays for it. But Anderson best captures *Putney Swope*'s anarchic spirit when he expands on its firecracker scene. It's the perfect example of what makes *Boogie Nights* a startling piece of filmmaking. Acting like a warning sign as we enter into the film's last reel, the scene where Dirk, Reed and their bouffant-friend Todd Parker (Thomas Jane) try to rip off free-basing drugdealer Rahad Jackson (Alfred Molina) jars us from the disco rhythms that have thus far ruled the soundtrack. To borrow from the name of Rahad's homemade music compilation, this is Anderson's 'awesome mix tape' – as sights and sounds combine to wake us from our lethargy. Dressed in a revolting pair of red briefs and a silver dressing gown, Rahad plays air keyboard to Rick Springfield's 'Jessie's Girl' as crackers are frequently let off in the living room by his Chinese chum Cosmo. A cacophony of noise, it preps us for the chaotic shoot-out that follows, delivering an almost operatic intensity.

Boogie Nights was a blueprint for how an independently minded director like Anderson could use studio money for a less than commercial feature. But whether the New Line executives who bankrolled the $15 million production were quite aware of what they were getting themselves into is open to debate. 'It was his blossoming as a director, going from a small controlled story like *Hard Eight* to this amazing crazy epic of a story he told in *Boogie Nights*,' says Reilly.

> I think of that time as a real golden moment for Paul, myself and all of us involved. There was very little pressure on us. We shot it before anyone realized what we'd done. The studio, they were like 'What are they doing?' They gave us the money and they had read the script, obviously, but it was like sneaking one underneath the radar . . . It was before Paul was under any scrutiny as a director. He felt very free. And with all of us as actors, there weren't a lot of preconceived ideas of who any of us were.

Echoing Dirk's own need for family, Anderson was building a loyal unit around himself. While he had already begun his troupe of regular actors on *Hard Eight*, he admitted a few new members with *Boogie Nights*. Returning after *Hard Eight* were Reilly, Philip Baker Hall, Philip Seymour Hoffman, Melora Walters and Robert Ridgley; newcomers, who have since returned for more of the PTA experience, included

26 Paul Thomas Anderson on the set of *Boogie Nights*, alongside
Heather Graham.

27 'This is a movie about family values': the *Boogie Nights* clan.

28 Mark Wahlberg transforms into Dirk Diggler in *Boogie Nights*.

Moore, Guzman, Molina, Jane, and David Mamet regulars Macy and Ricky Jay. Not that *Boogie Nights* launched anyone's career. With the exception of Hoffman and Mark Wahlberg, the entire cast had begun their film careers in the 1980s or before. The least experienced was former Funky Bunch rapper Wahlberg, who had impressed in 1995's *The Basketball Diaries* alongside Leonardo DiCaprio (who reputedly turned down the role of Dirk Diggler to take his part in *Titanic*). What the film did manage was to turn the spotlight towards this group of actors who had hitherto not quite managed to impinge themselves on the public's consciousness. The likes of Macy, Moore and Molina became chic almost overnight.

As for Burt Reynolds, you might argue that Anderson was playing a sick joke on him. With the days of *Deliverance* long since behind him, the years of Dirk's rise and fall parallel Reynolds's own journey from hero to zero. Beginning in the year when Reynolds was box office king with *Smokey and the Bandit*, the film concludes in the period when Reynolds clones like Tom Selleck, attempting to emulate his superficial charm, were ten a penny. Reynolds refused the role of Jack Horner numerous times, believing it to be an exploitation flick, before eventually caving in. After seeing a rough cut, he was reputedly so disappointed with the film that he fired his agents. He relented when his performance received rave reviews and an Oscar nomination, although it's unlikely Anderson will ever work with him again. 'If Burt Reynolds isn't there, you have no ego problems at all,' the director later noted.[70]

While the names have been changed to protect the (not so) innocent, Anderson had little interest in heavily disguising his characters' influences. Melora Walters's Jessie St Vincent was based on two porn figures: the actress Jessie St James and the producer Julia St Vincent. Marilyn Chambers, an actress who briefly went legit with David Cronenberg's *Rabid* (1977), inspired Amber Waves, who also recalls Shawna Garrett, the Iowa-born adult star who eventually got hooked on drugs and committed suicide. While Dirk Diggler mentions John Holmes and his character Johnny Wadd, allowing us to think the two actors are contemporaries, in fact Diggler's experiences are loosely based on those of Holmes. In Dirk's first film, he makes the point that he's just returned from the Navy; Holmes himself was briefly a part of the Army. As for Dirk's younger rival, Johnny Doe, he was based on Dick Rambone, who was hailed as Holmes's successor. The major coke deal that dominates the film's last chapter recalls the multiple murders in Los Angeles's Laurel Canyon in 1981 – chronicled in James Cox's *Wonderland* (2003) – in which Holmes was a key suspect.

During pre-production on *Boogie Nights*, Anderson recommended the cast watch Bob Chinn's 1977 porno *The Jade Pussycat*, which featured Holmes as Wadd searching for a stolen museum artefact while pleasuring numerous eager ladies. Anderson has called it the 'quintessential' porno movie: 'This is like Hitchcock doing a porno. It's sexy. It's got a murder-mystery and an action hero.'[71] While *Boogie Nights* does not exactly emulate this, it undeniably yearns for the days when pornography involved building sexual encounters into a competent storyline. What it does get right is the sense that, back then, pornography was a genre of its own, not a seedy parallel culture. Real films such as Gerard Damiano's seminal *Deep Throat* (1972) and *The Devil in Miss Jones* (1973) aspired to achieve a critical respectability and almost made it. The figure of Jack Horner reflects this; as deluded as he seems, he wants to craft something beyond mere titillation. 'I've got a dream of making a film that's true . . . true and right and dramatic,' he muses. In his mind, when he shoots *Angels Live in My Town*, a Johnny Wadd–style story with Dirk as sexed-up detective Brock Landers, he achieves this. 'It's a real film,' says his assistant in all earnestness.

The word 'film' is particularly significant. Video is the true villain of *Boogie Nights*. Anderson underlines this during the crucial axis-point of the film – the New Year's Eve 1979 party sequence, when Little Bill ends festivities with a bang by blowing his brains out. Horner is told by fellow pornographer Floyd Gondoli (Baker Hall) that this cheaper medium is the future, that 'videotape tells the truth'. Whether it's credible or not, *Boogie Nights* is undoubtedly a lament for a time when pornography was about more than just getting a quick fix. 'Video is a blessing and a curse,' Anderson has stated. 'It's created an assembly-line mentality. If the concept is that you're making a movie for the consumer – well, the consumer is at home with a fast-forward button.'[72]

As some critics have noted, this concern for how video changed the porn industry mirrors the subject of how 'the talkies' altered the silent film industry, as detailed in 1952's *Singin' in the Rain* (another of Anderson's all-time favourites). Given that Anderson admitted that he planned *Boogie Nights* to sit in the cinematic tradition of cautionary musical biopics – such as *A Star Is Born* (1954), *Funny Girl* (1968) and *All That Jazz* (1979) – then it makes for a useful comparison. With *Boogie Nights*' plot of a teenage dreamer desperate to make it culled from the blueprints of numerous Golden Age musicals, Anderson's soundtrack performs the function of having characters burst into song. A masterful selection, it is ironically probably the best collection of songs assembled for a film since Scorsese went to town for *Goodfellas*. In particular, the use of Andrew Gold's 'Lonely Boy' – cut to a slow motion shot of Dirk jumping in the pool – speaks volumes.

With the hardcore star Ron Jeremy on board as a consultant, Anderson visited around twenty porno sets as part of his research. To add to the authenticity, the film liberally sprinkles the supporting cast with real-life porn stars. Notably, *Amanda by Night*'s Veronica Hart plays the family court judge who takes away Amber's parental rights, a subplot that takes its inspiration from Hart's own real-life experiences. Yet the film remains riddled with inaccuracies – from Horner permitting Dirk to ejaculate inside Amber rather than film the customary 'money shot', to the fact that the camera equipment Horner's crew uses is ten years out of date. Neither does Anderson point out that it was illegal to film pornography in California in the 1970s, where many sets were regularly busted.

At the time, Anderson stated that his intention with *Boogie Nights* was 'not to make a movie about the First Amendment but to make a movie that lives inside it'.[73] Stripping away the philosophical and political context, this is not an attempt to document how pornography impacted upon society – but to show how it impacted upon the pornographers. Preferring not to lionize its protagonists in the way Milos Forman's *The People vs. Larry Flynt* (1996) did, it shows them up as hollow shells hugging onto each other for dear life. While the film may be a nostalgic view of the 1970s by someone who was just ten years old when they ended, it doesn't scrimp on the lashings of morality that such a life of excess can lead to. Dirk may not go the way of John Holmes, who died of AIDS, but the casualties around him are brutal: Little Bill dead; The Colonel imprisoned on charges of underage sex; Todd gunned down by Rahad; Amber estranged from her child . . .

With the shoot wrapping in October 1996, Anderson took a further twelve months in the editing suite. Running, initially, at three hours fifteen minutes, the film was snipped by just over half an hour, though Anderson asserts no major scenes were removed. He did, however, have to endure over half-a-dozen edits to appease the MPAA ratings board and obtain an R-certification in the U.S. Of course, Anderson is too smart to create a film about pornography too explicit to be seen in mainstream cinemas. He wants us to watch and think. If anything, *Boogie Nights* is about voyeurism, from our fascination with the twisted lives of its protagonists to our delight at being admitted into the confines of a porno shoot. When Dirk first reveals his manhood to Horner's crew, Anderson turns his camera away. Preferring to concentrate on their faces before staring down the lens of their 16 mm camera, he leaves us in an awkward position by asking us to consider our relationship as audience members to the explicit material (not) on show.

Released in October in the U.S., the film received reviews that were respectful if faintly suspicious. Janet Maslin's was typical: admitting Anderson had 'no qualms about borrowing from the best', be it Altman or Scorsese, she added: 'The film's extravagant two-hour thirty-two-minute length amounts to a slight tactical mistake. *Boogie Nights* has no trouble holding interest; far from it. But the length promises larger ideas than the film finally delivers.'[74] Whether or not this is true, like *Pulp Fiction* before it, *Boogie Nights* was a watershed moment when the taboo could be elevated to the level of art. Presented with panache, it meant Tarantino was no longer a one-off: there was a new Kid in town.

Solidly Independent: The Rise of New Line

What *Pulp Fiction* was to Miramax, *Boogie Nights* was to New Line. It may have only grossed $26.4 million in the U.S. but, like Tarantino's film three years before, *Boogie Nights* was a statement of intent, winning three Oscar nominations. It was as if the company were re-branding itself before our very eyes. Just as Miramax began to invest in middle-brow studio fare like *Shakespeare in Love*, New Line – at least for a time – looked to be the home for the Hollywood auteur.

It was a return to the company's roots. Founded in 1967 by Robert Shaye, New Line began life as a specialist art house distributor, initially peddling *Reefer Madness* (1938) and the Godard Rolling Stones documentary *Sympathy for the Devil* (1968) to college campuses. It forged its first significant relationship with the Baltimore-based king of trash John Waters at the outset of his career. Justifying the company motto – 'New Line: Solidly Independent' – it released Waters's notorious *Pink Flamingos* in 1972, making a tidy profit by effectively inventing the midnight movie. 'I came to New Line in 1971 when it was just Bob Shaye and a staff of about five people, and I've, well . . . spiritually never left,' says Waters. Three decades on, after New Line produced the likes of *Female Trouble* (1977), *Desperate Living* (1977) and *Polyester* (1981), Waters is still hanging around – even seeing the company's most successful collaboration, the 1960s-set musical *Hairspray* (1988), transfer to Broadway.

It says much that Shaye managed to build up his company by distributing niche products like Waters's films, ones that most executives wouldn't dare touch. Born in Detroit in 1939, Shaye gravitated towards a career in the movies from an early age. When he was fifteen he wrote, produced and directed a training film for employees of his father's supermarket – a harmonious marriage between art and commerce, you might think, that would prove to be a fine business model for New Line. A graduate of Columbia Law School, Shaye worked in the Museum of Modern Art's film archives before setting up New Line, initially in a less than salubrious part of New York.

If for Miramax it was Tarantino and *Pulp Fiction*, then for New Line it was the House that Freddy Built. Despite finding limited success by releasing Tobe Hooper's *The Texas Chainsaw Massacre* in 1974, it was another decade before New Line rose to prominence, unleashing one of horror cinema's most enduring icons, Freddy Krueger, on an unsuspecting public. The success of Wes Craven's *A Nightmare on Elm Street* (1984) which took in some $25.5 million in the U.S., laid out a blueprint for the company. It began backing or acquiring a series of low-cost, high-return franchises that serviced a variety of markets – notably the African American community, providing an alternative to 'hood films with the *House Party* and *Friday the 13th* movies in the early 1990s. New Line struck gold in 1990, when Shaye paid just $3 million for *Teenage Mutant Ninja Turtles*, a film that went on to gross $135 million.

In the same year, Shaye invited law school friend Michael Lynne to serve as president of New Line, after promoting himself to chairman. Pre-empting the studios' creation of art house divisions, Fine Line Features was also set up. Initially fronted by Ira Deutchman, its first major commercial success was the release of Robert Altman's *The Player* in 1992. Four years later, after Deutchman was replaced by Ruth Vitale, Fine Line enjoyed one of its finest hours – swooping *Shine*, Scott Hicks's biopic of the pianist David Helfgott, from under the nose of Harvey Weinstein, and steering it to seven Oscar nominations (including a Best Actor award for Geoffrey Rush).

By the time *Boogie Night*s arrived, New Line was already a well-established mini-major; the Jim Carrey movies *The Mask* and *Dumb and Dumber* had, respectively, taken $320 million and $246 million worldwide in 1994, followed a year later by Fincher's $100 million surprise, *Se7en*. But even before that, New Line was already in rude health. In 1993, the Atlanta-based media mogul Ted Turner, licking his wounds from a failed takeover of CBS, decided to add both New Line and Rob Reiner's Castle Rock Entertainment to his already sizable powerhouse, Turner Broadcasting Systems. With an injection of $550 million, Shaye pocketed close to $100 million and claimed a seat on the TBS board – though this was quickly overshadowed when TBS merged with Time-Warner in 1995.

Shaye was determined that his company would not end up as part of Warner Bros. He attempted to buy back at least part of New Line from Turner, who had fought to keep it an independent entity within his empire. Within days of the Time-Warner takeover, New Line shelled out $4 million for Shane Black's script *The Long Kiss Goodnight* (1996), a rather expensive way to announce that it was now a major industry player. As it stands, the company remains part of Time-Warner – but is still able to claim autonomy. As its web site notes, New Line is 'the oldest and most successful fully integrated independent film company in the world'.[75]

Like the Weinsteins at Miramax, however, Shaye and his co-CEO Michael Lynne have steered the company to the verge of being considered a major studio in its own right. Cultivating the *Austin Powers* franchise with Mike Myers set them on their way, but it was a book by an English literature professor from Oxford that completed the transformation. It was Shaye who suggested to Peter Jackson to split his adaptation of J.R.R. Tolkien's *Lord of the Rings* over three films, not two, an idea that the Kiwi jumped at. A massive financial risk that paid off in spades, its production history will remain the stuff of cinematic legend. Shot back to back over fourteen months in New Zealand, at an estimated cost of $300 million, it has recouped ten times that figure worldwide. With the final part, *The Return of the King* (2003) winning an Oscar in each of the eleven categories in which it was nominated, New Line – never a company showered with awards, given their penchant for low-brow material – was no longer just a niche player.

The acquisition of Philip Pullman's *His Dark Materials* books as New Line's first post-Tolkien event-trilogy indicates the direction the company is now heading in as it takes stock of its position in the industry. It may not have a back lot, like Paramount or Warner Bros., but that won't stop New Line from playing the studios at their own game. While Shaye always likes to warn people not to 'smoke the Hollywood crack pipe' and succumb to the glamour of the business, one has to hope that the company he began doesn't do the same. It's not as if New Line hasn't suffered the slings and arrows of Hollywood before; in one disastrous quarter in 1996, the company cumulatively lost over

$100 million on *The Long Kiss Goodnight*, Walter Hill's *Last Man Standing* and the infamous John Frankenheimer debacle *The Island of Dr. Moreau*. (Ironically, it was this fallow patch that prevented Time-Warner – then looking to reduce its debts – from selling the company, chiefly as they couldn't find a buyer.)

Undeniably, with the departure of head of production Michael De Luca in 2000 to fledgling studio DreamWorks SKG, New Line has lost its maverick dynamo. Rumour had it that he was ousted, after the Adam Sandler comedy *Little Nicky* (2000) recouped less than half of its $80 million budget. Certainly Time-Warner – by this point merged with Internet behemoth AOL – was casting a chill over spending. De Luca had already blotted his copybook by paying Joe Eszterhas $2.5 million for a story outline ultimately entirely reworked by Mike Figgis as the 1997 *One Night Stand* – although being the son Shaye never had was always an advantage. Yet by 2000, with the company also facing huge losses from the Warren Beatty vanity project *Town and Country*, the reputation of New Line's former golden boy was tarnished for good. Nevertheless, in an age of faceless executives who only bet on sure things, De Luca's legacy at New Line is testament to his willingness to risk it all on sheer gut instinct.

Born in Brooklyn in 1965 to an electrician and a bookkeeper, the half-Jewish, half-Italian De Luca was, as executives go, defiantly old school. A movie geek who went to NYU film school when he was seventeen, De Luca joined New Line in 1986, the year the company went public. Entering on an internship as a story editor (only his second ever job), he scripted the sixth part of the Krueger series, *Freddy's Dead: The Final Nightmare* (1991), and later went on to pen the adaptation of H. P. Lovecraft's *In the Mouth of Madness* (1995) for John Carpenter. By 1993, De Luca had risen to be 'the movie picker', as he called it, responsible for delivering potential productions to Shaye to greenlight.

If you believe the reports, *Variety*'s 1999 Showman of the Year is a hard-drinking, drug-fuelled womanizer in the Don Simpson mould. In an article based on a potentially damaging eight-month investigation of the company by *Premiere* magazine, De Luca was called 'an accident waiting to happen' by one unnamed source.[76] In March 1997, a widely reported incident saw De Luca ejected from an elite party at the house of William Morris Agency president Arnold Rifkin, after being caught in a compromising position with a young woman in a less than private part of the house. Hardly a major crime, you might think, but it set tongues wagging that De Luca was out of control. If the stories are to be believed, he was not the only one – with his superiors alleged to have sexually harassed female New Line executives. 'Shaye and Lynne run the place like a college dorm,' said one producer.[77]

Whatever the truth of these reports, De Luca is certainly different from most slicked-back, Armani-wearing Hollywood suits. Repulsed by the studios' predilection for formulaic studio fare, De Luca's own formula was to seek out new, bold filmmakers while propping up the slate with more mainstream material. While he missed out on M. Night Shyamalan's script for *The Sixth Sense*, he brought Paul Thomas Anderson's *Boogie Nights* – and then *Magnolia* – to life; he courted *Boys Don't Cry*'s Kimberly Peirce as well as Todd Solondz, with whom he made *Storytelling* (2001). He even recruited ad man Tony Kaye for *American History X* (1998) – though he ended up having to steer the picture to safety after the director renounced his own film in the trades.

De Luca was responsible for dragging the company from its East Coast origins to Hollywood. In an illuminating interview shortly before he left for DreamWorks, he revealed how he viewed the company he had worked for since he was nineteen. 'I flourished out in Hollywood. I never thought about us as a New York film company, even though Bob [Shaye] thinks of it that way because he founded the company in New York. New York is Miramax. I thought New Line could be kind of what Fox was to the networks when they debuted. I thought I could be the maverick studio out here, and that's what I've tried to do since '93.'[78]

Unsurprisingly, De Luca was a fan of New Hollywood's brand of filmmaking – although he refuses to mythologize the era.

The '70s are over. They've been over for a long time . . . Even in the '70s, they [the films] had to be done for a price, and they featured new talent and took risks. I just think you can't repeat the political films of the '70s today because the political climate is different. People want entertainment. They're into having a good time. If you're going to be satirical or angry today, I think you're *Magnolia* or you're [Alexander Payne's] *Election*. It's a different time . . . the '70s were about the time those artists were coming of age in, and you can't duplicate that. We are living in a very ironic, weird kind of age where nothing is shocking anymore.[79]

As far as De Luca is concerned, it was the studios that caught on to New Line's strategy, in terms of departing from tried and tested formulas.

Between New Line and Miramax, and even Disney with *Rushmore* and *Being John Malkovich*, there are studios that will take risks on provocative movies . . . when I started, it wasn't that congested a marketplace, and there were a lot of independent film companies that kind of got shaken out over the course of the late '80s and the early '90s – like Cannon and De Laurentiis and New World. Watching those companies go belly-up, and watching our company succeed, kind of validated our business plan. So when I took over in '93, I wanted to keep that going, because it seemed like it was working, and supplying a niche in the marketplace that was underserved. But now, it's more of a level playing field. I think it's actually good because the more majors that depart from decaying formulas, the more interesting films you'll see.[80]

The mould was set: Hollywood had woken up to the idea that there was room for original voices among the everyday froth on offer.

CHAPTER 13

Genre II: School Days –
Election, *Rushmore* and *Apt Pupil*

29 Jason Schwartzman as Max Fischer in *Rushmore*.

Alexander Payne once met Robert Evans, the legendary producer of *The Godfather* and *Chinatown* (1974). Payne recalls the meeting: 'I asked him what he thought of movies these days. He said, "They're just software. They're not made for the right reasons. We used to make them for their ideas. Now they're made for the presence of marketable elements."' Never a truer word spoken. In the late 1990s, as if to show that regressive executives still dominated the industry, the studios were renewing their acquaintance with the teenage audience. It had been over a decade since the demise of the so-called Brat Pack of rising young stars, and almost two since the days when *Animal House* (1978) and *Porky's* (1982) became the prototypes for what was about to be belched onto cinema screens. The gross-out comedy had been threatening for a while, chiefly thanks to the work of Peter and Bobby Farrelly with films such as *Kingpin* (1996). But it took a script from Adam Herz, and direction from Paul and Chris Weitz, to precipitate a deluge. Bringing toilet humour back to its rightful pubescent owners, *American Pie* (1999) is a coy snigger behind the bike sheds. Blushing with innocence, it presented its teenage characters as wholesome and heterosexual. Their biggest problem was how to get laid. No wonder it appealed to the teenage dollar, and spawned two sequels and a host of imitators – *Road Trip* and *Dude, Where's My Car?* (both 2000) and *Old School* (2003) to name but three.

But between 1998 and 1999, three of the Sundance Kids offered an alternative lesson in how to make a film with pubescent protagonists and a high school setting. Payne's *Election* (1999), Wes Anderson's *Rushmore* (1998) and, to a lesser extent, Bryan Singer's *Apt Pupil* (1998) stand apart from these other anodyne portraits of teenage life. As piercing as a school bell, the films smuggle ideas across the screen by the cartload, stretching far beyond the parameters the teen genre ordinarily allows. A stark reminder that school days are not always the best days of our lives, these are teen films for adults. Just as a fresh spin was put on the crime genre by Fincher, Soderbergh and Singer, the teen genre was rescued from being used as a framework for gross-out gags. All melancholy at their core, *Election*, *Rushmore* and *Apt Pupil* served to remind us that it's our early experiences in life that shape us as adults.

**It's like my mom says – the weak always try to
sabotage the strong.**

Tracy Flick, *Election*

The story of high school student government elections gone awry,
Election superficially appears like its Hollywood peers. Featuring
American Pie's Chris Klein in the cast, it was also funded by MTV (to
the tune of $8 million, just over half of what it would recoup in the
U.S.). There's also Matthew Broderick. His role as teacher Jim McAllister reads like a sly nod to his definitive part as the eponymous smart-
alec student in John Hughes's cult effort *Ferris Bueller's Day Off*
(1986) – though Payne claims he hadn't seen it when he cast the actor.
'I'm not interested in teen films,' Payne opines. 'I think it's a movie
about sad, pathetic people, doing sad, pathetic things. There are no
gimmicks, it's just about people.'

All of this collides in the opening shots of the film. As voice-over, we
hear the youthful naïveté of over-achieving pupil Tracy Flick (Reese
Witherspoon) and the earnest idealism of Jim, who teaches U.S. history,
civics and current affairs at Omaha's George Washington Carver
High. Payne initially perpetuates the idea in our minds that *Election*
will follow the tropes of the teen film. Until, almost as an aside, Jim
adds: 'Oh yes, there's one more thing you should know.' Cut to his
friend and colleague, Dave Novotny (Mark Harelik), who unwisely
undertakes an affair with Tracy that eventually loses him his job. He
tells Jim, 'Her pussy gets so wet, you wouldn't believe it.' This admission of statutory rape immediately removes any thought that we are
about to consume another slice of *Pie*.

Payne and his co-writer Jim Taylor, who won an Oscar nomination for
Best Adapted Screenplay for their work, use sexually explicit language sparingly in the film. But each example is timed for maximum value
as it sticks out from the deliberately banal dialogue that knits the rest of
the film together. The best two examples are with brother and sister Paul
(Klein) and Tammy Metzler (Jessica Campbell), the two other candidates
in the race with Tracy for student council president. Tammy is the caustic
lesbian loner, banned from the election after claiming it was she (and not
the real culprit Tracy) who sabotaged her brother's poster campaign. She
says in a montage that sees the three principal teenage characters say their
prayers: 'In spite of everything, I still want Paul to win the election
tomorrow, not that cunt Tracy.' Equally disconcerting is the earlier

30 Matthew Broderick and Reese Witherspoon in *Election*.

voice-over from Paul, the deliriously innocent Mr Popular Jock who has started dating Tammy's ex-girlfriend: 'That spring was perfect . . . the weather was so nice. And every day after school, Lisa and I would go to her house to fuck and have a hot-tub.'

Reading this in print neither conveys Klein's happy-go-lucky tone, nor the punctuating use of the word 'fuck'. Spring is in the air, and Payne is keen to show that, at a base level, human beings are no different to the animals that inhabit the natural world. At one point the two meet, as Jim is stung by a bee in the back garden belonging to Linda (Delaney Driscoll), the former wife of Dave and friend to his own spouse Diane (Molly Hagan), with whom he is now enjoying a brief affair. A reminder that nature is cruel, the resultant mark left on Jim's eye is like a scarlet letter.

Like the gross-out teen comedies of the time, sex is the engine that drives the characters (with the exception of the childlike, almost asexual, Tracy who channels her urges into her political ambitions), but in no way is it shaded with a sense of wide-eyed discovery. Rather, it is seen in all its warped glory. Sex can become either painfully sterile – as endured by Jim while his wife is trying to get pregnant, uttering 'good boy' as he ejaculates. Or it can head in the other direction. This is shown by the pornography used by Jim, shortly after he has told us 'after nine years of marriage, we were closer than ever', and the lurid fantasies of Dave (and later Jim, as he imposes first Linda and then Tracy's head on Diane's during a sex session). Unable to conceive with his wife Diane, everything mocks Jim's barrenness – be it Tracy alluding to this in her argument with him, Linda's garden with its birds and bees, the motel sign that says 'Welcome, Seed Dealers', or even the shot of the sprinkler jet that opens the film. Sexual temptation is also all around, symbolized by the apple motif that runs through the film. The fruit is often glimpsed on Jim's desk and, as his life collapses, he's seen to consume an apple pie – a more wholesome use than is found in *American Pie*.

Election was adapted from the novel by Tom Perrotta, who partially based the story on an incident in which a conservative high school principal invalidated a prom queen election because the winner was pregnant. Payne and Taylor play down the notion that everyone in school wanted to sleep with Tracy, as expressed in the original source. Removing the sexual tension between her and Jim, although we see Tracy sleeping with a teacher, Payne resists turning her into the teenage femme fatale. Instead she is more the innocent victim, yanked into the bedroom (to the sound of The Commodores' 'Three Times a Lady') by Dave. Payne shows us that not every pubescent girl is a vixen, as is so often depicted in Hollywood teen films. As the director told executives in early discussions, the film *Election* would most resemble would not be *Clueless* (1995) or *Fast Times at Ridgemont High* (1982) but his own debut, *Citizen Ruth*.

Labelled as satire upon its release, Payne prefers to see it as 'just a comedy'. Relocating the story from New Jersey, Payne and Taylor stripped down the political overtones of Perrotta's novel set around the 1992 U.S. election between George H.W. Bush, Bill Clinton and Ross Perot. In Perrotta's mind Perot was represented by Tammy, the wild card who enters to upset the race by announcing that if she is elected, she will abolish the student council. Uninterested in topical references – primarily, for fear of dating the movie – Payne has admitted that he and Taylor were not keen on suggesting 'things in a larger political arena'. If they thought in political terms at all, it was of Paul as Ronald Reagan. His naïveté is an echo of the U.S. president's demeanour, which 'made him a destroyer', as Taylor puts it. But as we see from the finale, when Jim spots Tracy in Washington DC getting into a limousine some years after teaching her at school, politics does overshadow the film.

There is something chillingly pre-destined about Tracy's arrival on Capitol Hill – where else could a manipulative schemer go but towards Congress? Whether or not it pleases Payne and Taylor, who deny she is a direct reference to Monica Lewinsky, the film ultimately overtakes their intentions and heads towards that larger political arena, hinting at how ambition and unscrupulous behaviour go hand in hand.

By this point, the juxtaposition of voice-over and image has reached such an ironic level that the two are in direct conflict. Already, we have seen how self-deluded the characters are. Tammy denies she is gay, saying, 'It's just that all the people I've been attracted to have been girls.' Tracy says of her affair with Dave, 'It was the first time anyone saw the real me. The me no one knows' – just as he pushes her out of sight in the passenger seat of his car while returning to his house. But it is with Jim that the greatest incongruity exists. After Diane divorces him for his infidelity with Linda, taking everything bar the car, Jim loses his job for rigging the election in favour of Paul. His notoriety as 'a corrupt teacher' spreads beyond Omaha, forcing him to leave for New York City. 'That's what's great about America. You can always start over,' he says, his tone full of chipper optimism. Yet working in a museum as a glorified guide, he is evidently in denial, calling himself 'an educator'. When he spies Tracy in the car, he claims he 'just felt sorry for her', until he explodes in anger on screen and throws his soft drink cup at the back windscreen. Nothing has changed and never will.

Payne prepares us visually for this repetition with circle imagery, from the design of Jim's tie to the lap he does on the athletics track at the outset. Most potently, just before he is uncovered as a cheat, the camera tracks him as he does a loop around the school office before heading to discover his destiny has changed. Tracy has already told us that: 'You can't interfere with destiny. That's why it's destiny. And if you try and interfere the same thing's going to happen anyway, and you'll just suffer.' Jim, whom we glimpse irritating the school's janitor in an early scene by carelessly dropping a carton of food on the floor, is ultimately exposed by the same man, who finds evidence of vote rigging disposed of in a wastebasket. This is also prefigured with frequent shots of bins, garbage trucks and rubbish littering the film.

Is this karmic destiny, or the result of an individual's actions? 'He is responsible for his own downfall,' thinks Payne. 'What I liked about the novel is that he's a guy in complete denial about how unhappy he is with his own life. Unconsciously, he's creating all of these situations, which he is ultimately going to break out of. He rigs the elections and he's a porno addict who ends up fucking his wife's best friend. All of it will come to light, and he even wants to get caught. People who do bad things often play with fire. He's like a lobster who needs to mould out of his shell.'

Payne prepares us early on for Jim's behaviour. As Tracy says, 'Ethical conduct is the most important thing – just ask Mr McAllister,' a phrase loaded with double meaning. In another example of action undercutting voice-over, Jim tells us he is readying his pupils 'for the tough moral and ethical decisions that they'd face as adults'. But before he is able to explain to either his pupils or Dave what the difference between the two is, Payne pointedly cuts away to the next scene. Encouraging Paul to rival Tracy in the election to prevent a 'dictatorship', Jim may be a Democrat to Tracy's Republican but he's no less ruthless for it. Both he and Tracy act as the perfect counterpoint to the likes of Paul or Larry, the upstanding pupil in charge of the vote count.

Klein, who was discovered by Payne while the director was location-scouting a different Omaha school from the one that ultimately appears in the film, sees his character as almost unique in teen films. 'As the high school quarterback, he is a very, very competitive young man, and has a lot of power with the student body, and a lot of pull. The girls like him and the boys like him – a kid like that could have a lot of power. But he just doesn't get it. The first note that I got, that Alexander gave me about Paul Metzler, was that there's truly not a bad bone in his body. He just wants to do good. Not only could Paul do no wrong, but by his standards nobody else can do wrong.' Some of the film's finest comic moments come from Klein, who invests the God-fearing Paul with a likeable and earnest charm.

The Coke to Paul's Pepsi, Tracy, dressed in diamond-patterned tank tops and preppy navy skirts, is far more complex. During a voice-over by Jim, as the screen freezes on her face, she is made to look a monster with her contorted facial expression. Yet as the film goes on, we discover she grew up without a father, and her mother, a former air hostess turned paralegal secretary, is the driving force behind her desire to succeed (even offering her one of her 'pills' when she is upset). By the time Tracy's crying in her bedroom, surrounded by the mocking rosettes of her past achievements, she looks every bit the little girl she still is.

Echoing these real-life dilemmas, *Election* sets out to achieve an authentic, less artful look. On his DVD commentary, Payne speaks of studying the ebb and flow of pupils wandering in and out of the school where they filmed, in an attempt to infuse the background with a verisimilitude absent in most Hollywood films. Real teachers and pupils are used as extras, while the production crew was forced to schedule the shoot around the ongoing lessons in the school. From Broderick's shaggy haircut, styled to represent poorly groomed teachers everywhere, to the overcast weather and fluorescent school corridors, Payne wipes the gloss off *Election* as if he were cleaning a blackboard.

He utilizes Omaha's seedy motels, malls and ugly suburban sprawls to good effect, echoing the banal, colourless voice-overs of Tracy and Jim. Yet this is no gritty socio-realist tract; Payne slices through with repeated use of freeze-frames, and even an Ennio Morricone cue from Sergio Corbucci's 1966 spaghetti western *Navajo Joe*.

'What's nice about *Election* is that there is a spirit in it that's a throwback to the 1970s,' says Payne. Ambiguous and probing, like the films Evans spoke of, *Election* is made for its ideas, not its ability to reach a certain demographic. Geoffrey Macnab summed it up in *Sight & Sound*: 'If Billy Wilder had been assigned to make a teen comedy, he might well have come up with a film as witty and sour as this.'[81]

I saved Latin! What did you ever do?
Max Fischer, *Rushmore*

A tentative Wes Anderson screened *Rushmore* for the pre-eminent critic Pauline Kael in her hometown of Great Barrington, Massachusetts. Having quit her position at *The New Yorker* and suffering from Parkinson's disease, Kael was shaky on her feet but there was evidently nothing wrong with her critical faculties. She told him *Bottle Rocket* was 'thrown together, but it had some nice parts'. When Anderson begged to differ, claiming 'it had a few good parts', she stood firm. 'It had *some* nice parts. That's better than a few.' As for *Rushmore*, she was baffled. 'I don't know what you've got here, Wes,' she said. 'I genuinely don't know what to make of this movie.'[82] It was a comment that dismayed Anderson by all accounts.

Kael's bemusement is understandable. *Rushmore* is a curious character-driven comedy funded by a studio system that normally signposts the growing pains of adolescence with clumsy directions.

Here is a film whose teenage protagonist, the irrepressible Max Fischer (Jason Schwartzman), was not cut from the same cloth as most high school students. If you are to believe John Hughes's definitive Brat Pack movie *The Breakfast Club* (1985), the system – like Hollywood – divides them into five categories: 'a brain, an athlete, a basket case, a princess and a criminal'. Max, the sort of annoying over-achiever found in every school, is none of these – not that the addition of 'geek' to the list would help classify him.

Anderson admits he understands such a description. 'He's the only kid who wears a blazer but he's not stereotypical of any one type. [Max] is someone who has his very own vision about things. He really sticks to it. He's very tenacious and resilient. He takes a lot of blows but he's blindly true to himself.' The perfect example of how Anderson and co-writer Owen Wilson frequently undercut our expectations, Max initially reminds us of a Ferris Bueller–esque guide, only to swiftly prove that he is far less in control and cocksure than his celluloid peer. This is encapsulated in his relationship with his younger chapel partner, Dirk Calloway (Mason Gamble). Making a sexually explicit comment about his mother, Max loses the boy's friendship. A loyal lieutenant who hitherto served Max's ambitions, Dirk thus deals a devastating blow that heralds Max's temporary downward spiral. Just as they were in *Bottle Rocket*, anxiety, jealousy and the exuberance of youth are the subjects of the day.

With the release of Jared Hess's nerd comedy *Napoleon Dynamite* (2004), *Rushmore* was cited in numerous reviews. *L.A. Weekly*'s Scott Foundas noted that *Rushmore* is 'a film on which Hess seems to have overdosed'. He added, 'Like Anderson, Hess is a detail fetishist, and while he lacks anything resembling Anderson's fluid sense of visual direction, he's packed *Napoleon Dynamite* with the hideous relics of his own coming-of-age: knee socks, moon boots, Velcro-sealed Trapper Keepers, top-loading VCRs.'[83] Comparisons that call *Napoleon Dynamite* a trashy Midwestern remake of *Rushmore* do Anderson's film a disservice. While Hess's deadpan comedy follows a traditional story arc, portraying a retro-geek's rites of passage, *Rushmore*'s Max Fischer undergoes a far more complex transition. As most disaffected teen movies – Hess's film included – pitch younger protagonists against the authoritarian values upheld by their elders, *Rushmore* spans the generation gap via Max's friendships, uniting humanity in the process. 'It comes from a tradition of movies, but I don't know where it slots in,' acknowledges Anderson. 'If you know what genre you're in, you know which way to turn. When Max builds the aquarium . . . well there's no "aquarium-building" genre . . .'

When pressed, Anderson reluctantly places his film alongside the likes of François Truffaut's *The 400 Blows* and *Small Change* (1976), Mike Nichols's *The Graduate* and Louis Malle's *Murmur of the Heart* (1971). But *Rushmore* can also be compared to 'angry young man' films like Lindsay Anderson's *If . . .* (1968) – consciously echoed when Max arrives at school with his rifle to fire some potshots – and Tony Richardson's adaptation of Alan Sillitoe's *The Loneliness of the Long Distance Runner* (1962). More recent examples of the genre include Terry Zwigoff's *Ghost World* (2001) and, of course, Alexander Payne's *Election*, with Tracy Enid Flick a more ruthless version of Max.

At the elite Rushmore Academy, in a world where the elders are revealed to be as immature as their juniors, Max yearns to abandon his adolescence for adulthood, a desire fraught with danger and disappointment. J. D. Salinger is often cited as Anderson's literary model, notably for his evocative assessment of the pubescent nightmare in *The Catcher in the Rye*; but only in as much as Salinger's seminal hero Holden Caulfield has influenced numerous subsequent portrayals of misfit teens. Despite being the product of a single-parent family, and raised by his widowed blue collar barber father (Seymour Cassell), Max is no delinquent. He is a noble failure, albeit one who has entered the school's hallowed precincts on a scholarship. Thus Wilson and Anderson, in their writing, circumvent the class snobbery that dogs much of Salinger's work – even if Max can frequently be caught telling others his kindly father is a neurosurgeon.

While the name of the school recalls presidential achievement, *Rushmore* itself is more a monument to optimism. As the film begins, plush velvet curtains swish back. Framing the screen as a proscenium, it hints that this is a staged version of Max's life – as put on by Max himself. Perhaps, even, the whole story is imagined by Max, a budding playwright, as Anderson once was. Cutting from the drawn curtains to a brief dream sequence – as Max imagines himself hoisted aloft by his classmates after solving a near-impossible mathematical equation – Anderson takes great delight in melding mediums of dramatic expression. (He would later provide the MTV Movie Awards with a series of skits, in the style of Max's own plays, based on some of that year's nominees – including Soderbergh's *Out of Sight*.)

'I feel the story is a fable,' says Anderson. 'It's not perfectly realistic. There's a lot of behaviour that you wouldn't get away with. It's all rather surreal.' Yet, as happens frequently in the film, reality intercedes. Headmaster Guggenheim (Brian Cox) informs the steel tycoon Herman Blume (Bill Murray) that Max is 'one of the worst students we've got'. What follows is a bravura montage showing where Max puts his energies: a born leader, at least in his own mind, his extracurricular activities range from being club president of the Calligraphy Society to founder of the Trap and Skeet Club and the Debate Team captain. These, as we learn, are distractions for Max – to take him away from his mundane existence and prepare him for the life ahead.

When Blume addresses the assembly, he delivers a rallying cry to those pupils who have not come from privileged backgrounds. As he tells them to 'take dead aim on the rich boys', Max is seen scribbling it down as a note-to-self. While Max is glimpsed briefly, as a representative of Russia in the school's model version of the United Nations, Blume's words galvanize the political notions already formulating in his mind. As shown by the film's poster, depicting him like a Bolshevik in his red beret and with his fist clenched in a 'power to the people' salute, Max is a rebel with a cause. One can imagine him, a few years down the line, standing outside a local supermarket selling the *Socialist Worker* – which makes his relationship to an entrepreneur like Blume all the more intriguing.

Their friendship becomes the central focus of the film. Max recognizes in Blume the man he wants to become, even convincing him to invest $8 million into building a school aquarium. Blume, perversely, sees Max as the boy he once was before middle age, a philandering wife and two ginger-haired, wrestling-obsessed thugs for sons put a permanent downer on his spirits. Max tells him, 'I think you have to find something you love. For me, it's Rushmore.' But Max soon transfers his allegiances, as he becomes infatuated with Rushmore grade school teacher Miss Rosemary Cross (Olivia Williams). 'Rushmore was my life,' he tells her. 'Now you are!' Denying this, she counters: 'What do you really think is going to happen between us? You think we're going to have sex?' In one crushing blow, she squashes Max's adolescent fantasies.

Rushmore: (31) Bill Murray (father) and (32) Jason Schwartzman (son).

Blume also takes a shine to her, leading Max to shout petulantly: 'I was in love with her first!' It leads to a tit for tat tiff between the pair; after Max puts bees in Blume's hotel room, Blume replies by mangling Max's bike. With Max faking an accident to win her sympathy, Miss Cross makes an accurate assessment when she says, 'You and Herman deserve each other. You're both like children.' But love, it seems, is worth fighting for, a perennial theme in Anderson's work. The joke is that it's been staring Max in the face all the time, in the shape of fellow pupil Margaret Yang (Sara Tanaka): his soul mate, though he won't realize it until it's almost too late.

Telling Mrs Blume of her husband's tentative affair (while offering her a choice of sandwiches to help her digest the information), Max finishes his war against Blume by cutting the brakes on his car, an irrational act that leads to his arrest. As Blume's wife files for divorce, Max also hits rock bottom. As demonstrated by his sartorial choices, his mind free-falls into chaos. The immaculately turned-out Max suddenly begins to wear a brown anorak three sizes too small and trousers four inches too short, leaving his white socks exposed – a sure sign of madness. Likewise, Blume – seen in the same suit throughout the film – begins to look dishevelled as his life collapses around him. 'Kids don't like it when their parents get divorced,' he says, nursing a bruise administered by one of his sons.

The timing is perfect. Just at the point when we might begin to think that Anderson and Wilson are a little too much in love with their characters, they turn on them – forcing them to experience life's downs as well as its ups. Death also casts a shadow over the film. Max visits the grave of his mother, who encouraged her son's writing by presenting him with a typewriter (its case engraved with 'Bravo, Max!'). Meanwhile, Miss Cross is grieving for her late husband, Edward Applebee, leading Blume to tactfully state she's 'in love with that dead guy anyway'. That the past has a grip on the present is a notion encapsulated in the finale with the staging of Max's *Heaven and Hell*, a Vietnam-set play complete with real dynamite and flumes of smoke. Dedicated to his mother and to Applebee, it hints at the irreparable losses suffered by both him and Miss Cross, without ever overstating it.

With references to Watergate also sewn into the narrative, *Rushmore* widens out this theme of personal tragedy to a more public dimension, reflecting the dashed innocence of the American public. Yet a play about reconciliation, *Heaven and Hell* precipitates a coming together, as Max finds common ground with various characters – even with Magnus, the Scottish bully who has been tormenting him throughout the film. As the curtains close, we watch a group of friends dance to the sound of The Faces' 'Ooh La-La', with its line 'I wish that I knew what I know now/When I was younger'. Once again, reality rudely interrupts nostalgia.

If *Bottle Rocket* was a more freewheeling cinematic experience, *Rushmore* is the aesthetically rigorous work that cemented Anderson's penchant for formal compositions. Shot in 'Scope, and using as few lenses as possible – the film frequently cuts from long shot to close-up while maintaining the same focal length – Anderson creates a visually unified world that hermetically seals its characters. Richer than *Bottle Rocket* in its use of lush colours, *Rushmore* prefigured the riotous palette used in *The Royal Tenenbaums*. 'I had always imagined that I would be the kind of person to make a movie that was highly improvised, very loose in a Cassavetes sort of way,' says Anderson. 'In actually making the movie, it was tightly scripted; the shots, I drew them; the music I figured out beforehand. I feel like I want to say, "Well, we can do anything" – but with *Rushmore* we stuck to everything.'

Continuing Anderson's homespun approach to filmmaking, the casting saw parts found for *Bottle Rocket*'s Luke Wilson (as Miss Cross's boyfriend, Dr Peter Flynn) and Andrew Wilson (as Coach Beck), while Owen Wilson makes a blink-and-you'll-miss-it appearance (in a photograph) as Edward Applebee. Roles for friends Stephen Dignan and Brian Tenenbaum – the inspiration behind two of Anderson's and Owen Wilson's most evocative name-choices – were also earmarked, as they were for *Bottle Rocket* and *The Royal Tenenbaums*. After their turns in Anderson's debut, Deepak Pallana and Kumar Pallana – who would go on to play Pagoda in *The Royal Tenenbaums* – complete Anderson's modest repertory with pitch-perfect work.

The film was shot partly at Anderson's former Houston high school, and the director also hired students from the school to play extras and even some major speaking roles. Initially, the school authorities had been reluctant to let the film crew on campus, as another alumnus had returned and burned some ivy while on a visit. 'They were always writing about us in the school newspapers,' Anderson recalls. The production scoured New England's private schools in search of the right person to play Max Fischer. 'We were basically looking for someone who was that character,' says Anderson. 'They didn't have to be Olivier. Physically, I was looking for a fifteen-year-old Mick Jagger. If you took him and combed his hair and put him in a blazer and a tie, and had him talk like Max, then that was right. I wanted someone to have that rock star underneath him. He wouldn't listen to that kind of music – on some level he wants to be headmaster, but he's also got all this teenage anger.'

This idea is reflected in Anderson's carefully selected soundtrack of British Invasion hits – not only Jagger's The Rolling Stones, but also The

Kinks, The Faces, The Who and Cat Stevens. All brilliantly collated by the music supervisor Randy Poster, it was a celluloid jukebox vastly different from the chart toppers heard in most Hollywood teen films. Anderson encapsulated this teen anger with his ultimate choice of lead. Jason Schwartzman has a rock star swagger in spades; after all, his former band Phantom Planet opened for Incubus on their 2002 tour. But it was not this alone that won him the role. While numerous actors who were tested for the role spontaneously turned up to the auditions in blazers, Schwartzman was reputedly the only try-out to bother making a fake Rushmore patch, an effort Max would have wholeheartedly approved of. Son of the actress Talia Shire and the producer Jack Schwartzman, and nephew of Francis Ford Coppola, Schwartzman's triumphant screen debut recalled the early years of his cousin Nicolas Cage.

Anderson says it was a coincidence that Coppola's *Apocalypse Now* (1978) is heavily referenced in Max's play *Heaven and Hell* – but it turned out to be a happy one. While Max also directs a *Serpico* stage adaptation (complete with the instruction 'You enter stage-left with a bag of cocaine'), Anderson is not in the business of providing knowing winks to a cine-literate audience. As indicated by the line 'borrowed' from *The Godfather* (Max: 'Can you let me off? For old time's sake?'; Headmaster: 'Can't do it, Max'), he is keen to show us how popular culture has infused into the Zeitgeist on an unconscious level, something that would be achieved to an even greater degree in his third film, *The Royal Tenenbaums*.

Like *Bottle Rocket*, the critics got behind *Rushmore*. 'We needed that; it's not like they set aside $15 million to promote the movie,' says Anderson. 'We needed word from critics.' It became one of the best-reviewed films of 1998. 'Texan director Wes Anderson and his writing partner Owen Wilson are two of the best things to happen to American film this decade,' wrote *Sight & Sound*'s Richard T. Kelly. '*Rushmore* is made to be treasured: it feels like an immediate American classic.'[84] Comparing the film to *Bottle Rocket*, *Chicago Reader*'s Jonathan Rosenbaum noted 'for all that movie's style and grace, it bears the same relationship to *Rushmore* that a watercolour bears to an oil painting. This movie goes further by creating something more than a milieu and a circle of friends, widening its span to encompass a little world to contain them.'[85]

Rushmore made a modest $17 million haul in the U.S. and went on to win Anderson Best Director at the Independent Spirit Awards, a surprise given that its $10 million budget came from Hollywood. After his disappointing experience at Columbia with *Bottle Rocket*, Anderson found a studio benefactor in the shape of Joe Roth, then head of Touchstone Pictures. Released by Disney distribution arm Buena Vista, it was a further example of how the Sundance Kids were increasingly finding footholds in the industry. 'We were able to make the movie we wanted,' says Anderson. No wonder Kael was baffled.

Do you ever wonder why people do the things they do?
  Todd Bowden, *Apt Pupil*

While both *Election* and *Rushmore* sat at the back of the classroom, disrupting the teen movie with a few well-timed potshots, *Apt Pupil* was so far removed from the genre's parameters that it was practically playing truant. Based on a story from Stephen King's 1982 anthology, *Different Seasons*, it tells of an all-American teenager, Todd Bowden (Brad Renfro), and his discovery that the former SS officer Kurt Dussander (Sir Ian McKellen) is living nearby in his Southern Californian hometown. Fuelled by a fascination for the Holocaust and the Gestapo's activities, he blackmails Dussander to regale him with tales from the concentration camps in return for not contacting the authorities. The sort of home-schooling only a writer like King could envisage, it peaks in a truly astounding scene where Dussander is forced to don a Nazi uniform and goose-step to Todd's command. 'Boy, be careful, you play with fire,' Dussander tells him, as if Todd has opened a Pandora's box unleashing an evil onto the world.

After *The Usual Suspects*, Singer was sent everything from *The Truman Show* (1998) to the IRA drama *The Devil's Own* (1997). Feeling the weight of expectation, he rejected them in favour of King's novella 'because it wasn't really supposed to be a big success. It was a very inexpensive movie [$14 million]. It was a very dark subject matter, and it was something that came from passion.' He'd read it when he was nineteen. 'If only to shoot that scene where he makes the old man march, I was going to make this movie. I was determined to . . . This was an opportunity to adapt a Stephen King movie that I have a personal interest in. I'm fascinated by the Holocaust. I have always been.'

It's an obsession that can be traced back to *Public Access* (which recalled another King novel, *Needful Things*). That film's use of 'the media against the people of the town is very [Joseph] Goebbels-esque', says Singer. As a child, the Jewish Singer remembers being intrigued by German neighbours and fascinated by Nazi iconography. 'I feel awkward even saying this, but we had a Nazi club because we thought the images were so neat. And those leather suits . . . I made a little armband and drew a swastika with a crayon and rushed off to show my mom.'[86] That said, Singer denies *Apt Pupil* is about the Holocaust. 'It's not a historical essay and I make no bones about that. Nor is the film about Nazism per se. It's about all kinds of corruption.'[87]

An aborted version of the story, directed in 1988 by Alan Bridges and starring Ricky Schroder and Nicol Williamson, collapsed three-quarters of the way through the shoot when financing was pulled. 'When I heard they were shooting it . . . I was thoroughly depressed,' recalls Singer. 'Then that movie fell apart. They shot for eight or nine weeks – so somewhere, in someone's basement, there is a cut of *Apt Pupil*.' Years later, Singer discovered that the rights were available again. Stephen King, who liked *The Usual Suspects*, sold them to Singer for the princely sum of $1. Singer brought in old friend Brandon Boyce, who appeared in *Public Access*, to write the script, with the project initially set up with Spelling and Paramount. With over $1 million paid towards pre-production costs, including set construction, Singer met his first hitch when the plug was pulled. Along with the actors, Singer's production team – editor/composer John Ottman, production designer Richard Hoover, cinematographer Newton Thomas Sigel – all stuck by him while producer Don Murphy, along with his partner Jane Hamsher, looked to refinance the film. They found a home at Columbia Pictures.

Boyce's adaptation of *Apt Pupil* made numerous changes, both superficial and significant, which suited Singer's intentions. While King's story takes place over four years and contains a great deal of violence between Todd and Kurt, Boyce condenses the time period and removes much of the bloodshed. For example, the final haunting sentence of King's story, hinting at Todd embarking on a shooting spree, is ignored. Likewise, Singer shows only one incident of Todd killing a tramp, Archie (Elias Koteas), whereas King had his protagonists slaying homeless people for fun. But while Singer toyed with the idea of following the story's second and third acts more faithfully, he wisely showed restraint, merely hinting at what Todd could become rather than showing it outright. The ending says it beautifully. Having been shooting – and missing – basketball hoops throughout the film, Todd finally gets one in. Played out on an arena so often associated with triumph over adversity in the Hollywood teen film, the clip fades into a shot of Kurt's face as he dies. A sly cut, it suggests transference of evil from Kurt to Todd, without recourse to the violence of King's finale.

The screenplay also excises the novella's misogyny which Boyce replaces with a more general expression of sexual deviance or abnormality, with the emphasis on homoeroticism (and its relationship to voyeurism) and homophobia (as an expression of monstrosity). Todd, in the novella, dreams of the schoolgirl Betty as a concentration camp inmate he can rape and torture. In the film, his erotic encounters with Betty – now called Becky (Heather McComb) – are reduced to one single moment, where he cannot perform sexually. Again, Singer uses a generic staple of teenage sexual awakening in the most chilling of ways. By cutting to Kurt attempting to roast a cat in the oven (a rather crude echo of concentration camp atrocities) it attributes Todd's impotence to his homoerotic relationship with the Nazi. To further emphasize Kurt's enduring influence over Todd, he has within a couple of scenes committed his own act of animal cruelty by squashing a bird with a well-timed strike from his basketball. Whether Singer means deviance to be a metaphor for evil or vice versa is left unclear – a fact that gives the film its unbridled tension.

The key scene that hints at these sexual power shifts is set in the school shower room. Replacing the rape-dream sequence referred to earlier, this charged scene begins as Todd is washing himself among his peers in a communal changing room facility. If this is Singer's nod to another generic high school sequence – the locker room scene – it quickly mutates to embrace a potent cocktail of homoeroticism and Holocaust imagery. As the camera closes in on Todd's face, the warm hues change to blues and greys. It pans right to reveal that emaciated Holocaust victims now surround Todd, the camera leering over their scarred bodies as it did across Todd and his naked classmates. Todd is gazed upon and put in the position of the victim by the traditionally victimized.

This is later obliquely hinted at when Todd falls off his bike in the tunnel. Landing in some water, assuming the position of victim, he looks up to see a swastika on the wall. The culmination of another expertly cut-together montage from Ottman, it resembles the 'bulletin board' sequence from *The Usual Suspects* with its overlapping dialogue and shots of Kurt in uniform impinging upon Todd's consciousness. It leads him to reject his recent deviance, with Singer offering a series of scenes that would not look out of place in a Hollywood teen movie. Passing his exams, he throws away his file on Kurt and – following another montage – makes an assertion of 'normal' heterosexuality. After playing a baseball game where Becky looks on applauding, Todd and she head out on a date to the cinema. But as if to remind us that Todd can never now fully return to the normality he craves, the sequence is cut to the song 'Das ist Berlin', while a few rows in front of them in the movie theatre is a man who resembles (and laughs like) Kurt.

The director only lets us see Kurt outside of his grimy, claustrophobic bungalow momentarily. Initially, it is with his visit to Todd's school. Here, he pretends he is Todd's grandfather and makes excuses for his deteriorating grades, an indication that Todd is now his pupil and not the school's. His only other moments away from his house are his surprise visit to the Bowden home for dinner and his entry into hospital after a heart attack. There his bedridden neighbour, Ben Kramer (Michael Byrne), whose own wife and children had been killed by Kurt back in the war, finally exposes him.

For the most part, *Apt Pupil* is a two-hander, with Singer emphasizing the proximity between male bodies by filming much of their interaction in close-up. Aside from playing up this homoerotic subtext between Todd and Kurt, the camera gazes over Todd's body in numerous shots – in one in particular hovering above him while he's lying on the bed in just his underwear. Todd, who gazes upon Kurt with the same rapt and fetishistic attention, replicates such voyeurism. When Kurt initially refuses to put on the SS uniform he has found for him, Todd explodes with anger – an adjustment from the novella, which has him pathetically pleading with the old man. This plays up one of the film's major themes – power shifts within a sadomasochistic relationship. Kurt appears to be both submissive and dominated by Todd. But Singer, as he shows in the aforementioned shower sequence, ensures that the line between victim and victimizer is much more fluid than might at first appear. 'Oh my dear boy,' says Kurt, after Todd tells him to 'fuck' himself. 'Don't you see? We are fucking each other.'

None of which helped Singer, as scandal and negative advance publicity overshadowed the film's release. Singer was thrown into the eye of a media storm when five civil lawsuits were filed against him and members of the production team of Phoenix Pictures. Allegations were made that six teenage extras were bullied into stripping naked for the aforementioned shower scene. The lawsuits alleged that the boys – including some sixteen-year-olds – were initially promised they would be wearing Speedo trunks or towels but were forced to wear flesh-coloured G-strings. While some parents had been informed the shot would require 'partial nudity', the plaintiffs alleged the boys were made to stand around naked for hours as the cameras rolled. Furthermore, one parent claimed her child was 'visually raped', while others alleged 'some or all of the defendants' were 'known homosexuals, pedophiles or pederasts' who filmed the boys for sexual gratification. It was also alleged that an 'obviously homosexual' set photographer snapped pictures of them in 'indecent positions', while the crew subjected them to 'ogling, leering and suggestive glances'.

Numerous unsubstantiated rumours, as vicious as they were ridiculous, circulated about Singer, from him being a pedophile to Gabriel Byrne actually having directed *The Usual Suspects*. The suit was quickly thrown out of court. The Screen Actors Guild conducted its own investigation, concluding that the defendants were guilty of neglecting to give 'prior knowledge' that the said minors would be called upon to act naked, as well as violating labour codes for employing a minor outside the sight and sound of his guardian. That aside, the L.A. county district attorney's office stated: 'The suspects were intent on completing a professional film as quickly and efficiently as possible. There is no indication of lewd or abnormal sexual intent.'

As Singer later told *Empire*, 'It was awful. I didn't hear about it at the very start. A couple of attorneys approached the production saying they wanted money because some people were claiming that extras had been treated inappropriately during a scene. I mean, I didn't have any contact with them, I was directing Brad. I felt sorry for the kids because I think that they were being manipulated. But I had never had scandal in my life before. I've never done anything to invite it.'[88] He added that there were no adverse effects on the production. 'I mean, there were seventy people there who *knew* that nothing inappropriate had happened. If they had thought it had, they would have left at the time and nobody did. It made me much more press-shy for a while . . . And now I'm incredibly conscious of what goes on, on my sets. There are two people in charge other than me – the set-teacher if there are minors involved, and the stunt-coordinator if we're doing action. I live by that.'[89]

By coincidence, at the end of *Apt Pupil* we see the kindly – and possibly gay – guidance counsellor, Edward French (David Schwimmer), threaten to expose Todd's interactions with Kurt, only to be told he will be accused of molestation. Repeating Kurt's earlier words, Todd ominously warns, '[A scandal like] this will never go away, not for you', an irony that must have struck Singer during the uncomfortable aftermath of filming. Given this context, Singer's transition from *Apt Pupil* to *X-Men* seems perfectly understandable. A sizeable leap in scale and budget, the Marvel Comics' series about a persecuted group of so-called 'mutants' must have struck a chord with Singer – even if, to the casual viewer, it looked as if he had simply sold out.

CHAPTER 14

Adaptation:
Tarantino and Soderbergh Meet Elmore Leonard

33 Pam Grier in *Jackie Brown*.

As we have already seen, crime is the drug for many of the directors in this book; so it made sense for them to find a dealer. Just as Raymond Chandler, Dashiell Hammett and James M. Cain provided the pulp fiction to inspire the likes of Howard Hawks, John Huston and Billy Wilder in the 1940s, Elmore Leonard became the novelist of choice fifty years later. Tarantino – for *Pulp Fiction* in particular – owes much to Leonard. It can be no coincidence that Miramax purchased the rights to three Leonard novels for their golden boy to play with in the wake of the film's success.

Born in 1925, Leonard made his home in Detroit after spending his early childhood in the Deep South. This led one wit to call him the city's original white rapper, talking the talk years before Eminem was ever on the scene. As Philip French said, 'Leonard is the last of the great pulp novelists, though unlike most of them he has lived long enough to be respected, rewarded and to feel comfortable between hard covers.'[90] While working in advertising, Leonard began his career as an author by writing Westerns, his first published novel being *The Bounty Hunters* in 1953. Four years later, he had his first brush with Hollywood, as two of his short stories – '3:10 to Yuma' and 'The Tall T' – were adapted into films. It was after the Hollywood agent H. N. Swanson brokered a deal in 1964, whereby Twentieth Century Fox paid him $10,000 to adapt his 1961 novel *Hombre*, that Leonard was able to quit his day job. It was Swanson who was largely responsible for convincing his client to switch from writing Westerns to crime fiction. In 1969 he produced his first effort in the genre, *The Big Bounce*.

Although some might point to James Ellroy as the classier writer of crime fiction from the era, his work has never managed to make the same impression on the big screen as Leonard's – the exception being Curtis Hanson's *L.A. Confidential* (1997). That's not to say Leonard has seen everything he's written turn to celluloid gold: in fact, far from it. Despite having close to forty of his novels either optioned or made into movies, for years Leonard wasn't understood by Hollywood. As one critic noted, 'There have been few writers who have been so often purloined for the movies but so badly served.'[91] With the nadir of Leonard adaptations surely being Burt Reynolds's directorial effort *Stick* (1985), filmmakers too often failed to portray the underlying hilarity of the author's stories. Even notable directors Paul Schrader (*Touch*, 1997) and Abel Ferrara (*Cat Chaser*, 1989) cannot count their Leonard efforts among their best work. It wasn't until Barry Sonnenfeld's *Get Shorty* (1995) that Leonard was given the revisionist treatment. Further re-establishing John Travolta's cool after *Pulp Fiction*, this story of a loan shark who heads to Hollywood recouped a healthy $72 million in the U.S.

What is it about Leonard – once called 'perhaps the greatest popular writer of all time' by self-confessed fan Martin Amis – that draws these filmmakers to him? 'Doing an Elmore Leonard picture is like a rite of passage,' says F. Gary Gray, who directed *Be Cool* (2005), the sequel to *Get Shorty*. 'What I like about him is the detail; really quirky situations. The worlds that he creates and the situations he put these characters in, I think are very wild and very funny. That's why a lot of directors are attracted to his material.' If anything, it is his pared-down style and rich dialogue that lend themselves to celluloid adaptation. You need look no further than Leonard's books to find a direct influence on Tarantino's popular-culture-strewn jive, especially obvious in *Pulp Fiction*. 'His books were the first books I ever read where the characters referred to other movies,' stated the director. 'You know, two black guys in the welfare office talking about the movie they saw last night – they don't think they're doing a commentary on pop culture but they are. They're having a conversation and they're talking about what they know about . . . Elmore Leonard was the one who kind of gave me license to do it.'[92] That Leonard also has a keen – and very black – sense of humour when it comes to depicting human brutality cannot have gone unnoticed by Tarantino.

Scott Frank, who adapted *Get Shorty*, has a different take. 'The most important thing in an Elmore Leonard novel are the characters. I think the voice of the characters is the essence of his point of view. The real trick of adapting any of his work is in preserving his characters. He isn't as concerned as a novelist with structure, so the work is in giving his very novelistic story a real movie structure. Because he gave you this gift of such great characters, you're able all the time to infer . . . even if it's not really there in the book to begin with.'

Frank also adapted Leonard's 1996 novel *Out of Sight*, which the then thirty-four-year-old Soderbergh directed in 1998. It was a lifeline that saved Soderbergh from sinking towards oblivion, following marginal releases for *Gray's Anatomy* and *Schizopolis*. He admits he felt the pressure. 'Even though that movie was not commercially successful, if it had been viewed as a creative failure I'd have been in big trouble. It was my first attempt at a studio movie with movie stars, and if I'd blown it, I was going to have real problems. I felt a lot of self-imposed pressure on that. Once it came out, and it was OK, then I felt like I could take off running again.' It nevertheless afforded its director the chance to test how far he could take a mainstream genre and experiment with it.

For Tarantino, adapting Leonard's 1992 novel *Rum Punch* into *Jackie Brown* in 1997 was a slick way of circumventing the hefty expectations that came with following up *Pulp Fiction* with an original script. Reputedly offered *Speed* (1994) and *Men in Black* (1997) to direct, to Tarantino's credit he had loftier ambitions than to become just another A-list director pumping out formulaic fare. But as the *Time* critic Richard Schickel noted: 'All careers built around transgressive material are difficult to sustain in Hollywood. And at a time when politicians are pressing for family entertainment Tarantino is a marked man. Though he may have been surfing on the celebrity wave, he's directed two major movies and written a great one [*True Romance*] . . . it's half a career.'[93] That said, by the time *Jackie Brown* arrived in December 1997, Tarantino, at thirty-five, was the same age as John Huston when he made his debut with Hammett's *The Maltese Falcon* in 1941. But whatever the adaptation did for Tarantino's career, Leonard was truly anointed as Hollywood's new King of Crime.

> You know anyone who's actually done one last big score and gone on to live the good life?
>
>   Jack Foley, *Out of Sight*

Soderbergh's attraction to Leonard's *Out of Sight* only reinforced this new status for the novelist, even if the director initially turned down the project. At the time, Soderbergh was attempting to get Charlie Kaufman's *Human Nature* script (see Chapter 19) made. Miramax had just rejected it when Universal's Casey Silver slipped Soderbergh a copy of Leonard's book, promising that if he made it the company would bankroll *Human Nature*. With Frank's script, as well as a star (George Clooney) and a production company (Jersey Films, who made

Pulp Fiction and *Get Shorty*) already attached, Soderbergh was presented with a ready-made package, the first of his career. By way of illustrating the post-*Schizopolis* funk he was in, Soderbergh said in his diary entry of the time, 'It's a terrific script, and all the people involved are good, so of course I called Casey the next day and turned it down.'⁹⁴ He eventually relented, though still had to await approval from all concerned. He was third in line, after Cameron Crowe and Mike Newell. Both rejected it – Newell, having just completed a crime film, *Donnie Brasco* (1997), with a more obvious reason to pass. Even then, Soderbergh was competing against Ted Demme and Sydney Pollack, an indication of his place in the pecking order at the time.

After Soderbergh was given the go-ahead, he met with Tarantino. Editing *Jackie Brown* at the time, Tarantino assured him it was nothing like *Out of Sight*. He was right. While both novels portrayed the sort of low-key hoodlums that both Soderbergh (in *The Underneath*) and Tarantino had encountered before, *Out of Sight* dealt with loyalty and honour. It told the story of charismatic bank robber Jack Foley (Clooney), who makes a break from Glades Institutional Facility. Aided by his longtime friend Buddy (Ving Rhames), he heads to Detroit for one final score, a stash of uncut diamonds owned by crooked financier Richard Ripley (an unrecognizable Albert Brooks). Jack is forced to kidnap Federal Marshal Karen Sisco (Jennifer Lopez) during his escape from Glades, and it is his uncalculated-for attraction to the long legs of the law that gives the story its tension.

Jackie Brown, meanwhile, deals with disloyalty and dishonour. Every character is out to screw everyone else, though it's thanks to Tarantino's laid-back vibe that the film doesn't emerge as a series of emotionally detached double-crosses. It begins as Jackie (Pam Grier) has been picked up at LAX, with $50,000 and a bag of drugs in her hand luggage. At forty-four, and earning only $16,000 a year in her job as a stewardess for a Mexican airline, she's facing ruin – until the Feds on her tail reveal they want her to give up arms dealer Ordell Robbie (Samuel L. Jackson), the man behind her contraband. Like *Out of Sight*'s diamonds, the story concludes with numerous interested parties attempting to get their hands on something that doesn't belong to them – in this case the $500,000 Ordell's looking to move out of the country. There is also a love story – Jackie and Max Cherry (Robert Forster), the bail bondsman she teams up with – though one with more poignancy than Jack and Karen's attraction in Soderbergh's film.

Despite the differences, that didn't stop Soderbergh crafting some deliberate links with Leonard's other adaptations. Michael Keaton reprised his role of the well-meaning cop Ray Nicolette from *Jackie Brown* for a cameo in Soderbergh's film – the first time two unrelated movies have shared a character played by the same actor. Samuel L. Jackson was cast as the convict Hejira in the final scene – recalling Tarantino's film. And to complete the circle, Dennis Farina, who plays Karen's father, was previously seen in *Get Shorty*. (In a bizarre twist of fate, Forster later won a lead role in *Karen Sisco*, ABC's 2003 TV spin-off of *Out of Sight*, in which he replaced Farina as the law enforcer's father.) Yet Soderbergh denies Tarantino or Sonnenfeld was an influence:

> The commonality has more to do with Godard than Tarantino . . . There's a freedom of style and an attitude that I think is especially present in the early Godard films, but also in the works of Elmore Leonard. Quentin's influence has been so significant, because *Pulp Fiction* has been so hugely successful, and he'd be the first to admit that his influences are films and writers of the past, as they are for all of us. Honestly, if you look at *Get Shorty*, *Jackie Brown* and *Out of Sight*, Barry, Quentin and I have a very different aesthetic that happens to coincide with Elmore Leonard's voice but we're very different filmmakers. My aesthetic is very different from Quentin's. I think he's more emotional than I am. I'm more repressed! And it shows in the film [*Out of Sight*] – it's quieter. Though *Jackie Brown*, which I liked a lot, was a very gentle piece, in a weird sort of way.

While Soderbergh's encounter with Leonard was more of a happy accident, Tarantino and the novelist were always destined to meet. As a teen, he had been busted for trying to shoplift a copy of Leonard's 1978 novel *The Switch* from a K-Mart in the South Bay area of Los Angeles (where he would relocate the action of *Rum Punch*). As Tarantino tells it, he later went back and successfully stole the book. Just after *Reservoir Dogs* came out in 1992, Leonard wrote *Rum Punch*, reprising three of his characters from *The Switch*, including Ordell and his associate Louis Gara (played by Robert De Niro in *Jackie Brown*). Meanwhile, the director Tony Scott called Tarantino's script for *True Romance* 'an Elmore Leonard novel that he didn't write'.

Leonard embraced Tarantino's appropriation of *Rum Punch*. Not only did Tarantino christen his film with a new title, he also switched location from Florida to California. Changing the ethnicity of Jackie from a Caucasian to an African American, he also gave her a different surname, changing it from Burke. Its replacement recalled star Grier's classic blaxploitation role in *Foxy Brown* (1974). Leonard was again generous: 'You're the filmmaker – use what you want and make your movie,' he eventually told Tarantino, after the director deliberately avoided calling Leonard, too scared to explain away his modifications.

Initially, Leonard was less welcoming to Scott Frank's changes to *Out of Sight*. He disagreed with the screenwriter bringing the off-stage character of Richard Ripley into the story. He also disliked the more hopeful ending. Leonard said to Frank, 'You've got to remember it's *her* story' (referring to Karen Sisco). Arguing in favour of Jack, Frank countered: 'No, it's *her* book, but it's *his* film.'[95] In good grace, when Leonard saw the finished film he realized Frank's choices worked in the film's favour. That Soderbergh filmed the finale in the same Detroit locations as the novel also placated Leonard.

Soderbergh managed to find numerous concerns of Leonard's that dovetailed into his own. The novel's fatalistic view (as Sisco warns, 'This is not going to end well. These things never do') is certainly tailor-made for him, as are Leonard's circuitous narratives: 'I'm not an Elmore Leonard obsessive the way, say, Tarantino is, but I certainly felt his very specific, ironic tone was one I understood and could cast for.'[96] Like Soderbergh, Leonard regularly shows as much interest in the colourful supporting cast as in the main players. According to Soderbergh, the author also demonstrates a 'non-reductive view of people', where 'the characters don't change'.[97] This is certainly under-lined in *Out of Sight*. As Foley reminds us, 'most bank robbers are fucking morons'. When they are searching for Richard's diamonds in his mansion, one even looks under a mattress, readily expecting them to be stashed there. Foley may not be quite that dumb, but his mag-netic attraction to crime will be the end of him – and he knows it. 'If you don't, somebody else will,' he tells Karen, when she points a gun at him in the final shoot-out.

Soderbergh certainly saw Leonard's characters as anti-heroes, in the tradition of American cinema from film noir to the maverick movies of the 1970s, 'when a new generation of actors came in – Dustin Hoff-man and Jack Nicholson and Al Pacino – and played a darker version of the male movie star, and it became more prevalent. That period of filmmaking was very attractive to me, and Elmore Leonard likes protagonists who are not successful or powerful. He goes for people who aren't very ambitious or smart, but he's drawn to real life-sized characters that are not "big wheels". I think it's more interesting to make movies about these characters. It's more distinctive.'

The characters in *Jackie Brown* demonstrate this. Take De Niro's impressive turn as Louis. As the script dictates, Louis has spent over half his life in penal institutions meaning, 'in the real world his timing is thrown'. Sporting inky tattoos, sprawling facial hair and Hawaiian shirts, he looks, the script says, like he shops at the Salvation Army. De Niro admirably conveys this through his hunched-over body language and half-speed responses, correctly portraying Louis as dazed and confused – particularly next to Ordell's speedy patter. You can almost see the cogs turn in his brain. As with the well-meaning Ray, Ordell's beach-bunny girlfriend Melanie (Bridget Fonda) and the chattering hoodlum Beaumont (Chris Tucker), it is the attention paid to sketching out minor characters that makes *Jackie Brown* a more than satisfactory Leonard adaptation.

Unsurprisingly, then, *Jackie Brown* is more about finding unsung character actors who carry the weight of years in their faces than Tarantino's now-obligatory career resuscitations. Casting Grier and Forster didn't have quite the same cultural impact as when he resurrected John Travolta's fortunes with *Pulp Fiction*. Eschewing the swagger of her roles in the 1970s, Grier's Jackie is a more fragile creature. Like Louis, she's had a run-in with the authorities before, after she was caught carrying drugs on behalf of her pilot husband who wound up in jail while she walked. With this in mind, Grier carries with her a dignity in the face of adversity as Jackie grips tenuously to the tatters her life is left in.

With Max's love of The Delfonics symbolizing his affection for Jackie, his story arc is made poignant by Forster's world-weary turn. Described as 'a regular-Joe-type' in the script, it is spot-on casting. Given that most critics dubbed this Tarantino's most 'mature' work, the irony is that its central theme reflects this. Jackie, at one point, asks Max if he's bothered about getting older. 'It's not really something I think about,' he replies, before admitting he 'did something about' his hair falling out a few years ago. But Tarantino ensures this theme is more than skin deep. At the end, when Max has helped Jackie steal Ordell's money without alerting the authorities, leaving Ordell dead in the process, they finally share a fleeting kiss. Jackie is heading to start a new life in Spain. 'I didn't use you, Max,' she says. 'And I never lied to you.' As they part, their faces are full of regret. They are left with the knowledge that they must continue their lives alone.

It's a far more downbeat ending than the conclusion of *Out of Sight*. Jack finishes the film where he began, about to serve another prison term. But with Karen deliberately hooking him up with Samuel L. Jackson's Hejira, who happens to specialize in busting out of jails, it's evident his confinement will be short-lived. Having called Jack 'Clyde Barrow' when they first met, it looks like Karen will soon be his Bonnie Parker. As Clooney says of Jack:

> This guy has got bad luck and he is a bit of an idiot and a bit of a romantic. And at the end of the day he is right back in jail and his world isn't any different at all. Except that he met this girl that he likes along the way. There are no good guys [in *Out of Sight*]; there are just different degrees of bad guys, which I love. It is like when we used to make movies in Hollywood, when we made them before we had to relegate character pieces to independent films. You know, there was a period of time in the 1970s that was so character-driven.

Out of Sight truly benefits from Soderbergh's preceding cinematic outings, *Schizopolis* and *Gray's Anatomy*. 'If I'd made *Out of Sight* right after *The Underneath* I would have ruined it,' he says. Unlike in *The Underneath*, Soderbergh's rearranging of the script's linear chronology and his use of colour-coded sequences to define specific time periods no longer feel like laboratory experiments conducted at arm's length. Shot by Elliot Davis in his last collaboration with Soderbergh to date, *Out of Sight* is distinctive. The bright hues of the Lompoc jail sequence (notably the inmates' yellow jumpsuits) contrast to the more muted, monochrome colours of Glades prison, just as Miami's summer tones are at the opposite end of the spectrum to Detroit's chilly blues and greys.

Influenced by the work of Nicolas Roeg on *Don't Look Now*, notably with the Jack/Karen love scene which recalled the Donald Sutherland/Julie Christie coupling in Roeg's film, Soderbergh principally decided to juggle with the timeline to ensure that the audience is introduced to Karen a lot earlier. This further emphasizes that beating at the heart of *Out of Sight* is a relationship drama. After Karen's father gives her a gun for her birthday, we soon find ourselves inside the trunk of Jack's escape vehicle. In the film's signature scene, Jack is tucked behind Karen (a symbolically sexual juxtaposition if ever there was one), having captured her during his breakout.

Scott Frank had originally intended the scene to be shot in pitch black, which Soderbergh quickly found to be impractical. The director hit upon the idea of Jack finding a flashlight next to him to provide illumination, its light casting an erotic glow over these prospective lovers. But what's sexy, aside from their obvious proximity, is how it feels like they're on a first date, even in such unusual and extreme circumstances. They make light chat before Jack, admitting he's divorced, discusses how his marriage lacked 'that spark'. He clicks his fingers – which he repeatedly does to light his Zippo – to illustrate the point.

Tarantino's stylistic and structural devices are not so far removed from Soderbergh's. Using deliberately dated techniques like split-screen – for example, when we see Max returning to his bail bonds office – Tarantino reminds us that *Jackie Brown* owes much to a bygone era of 1970s blaxploitation movies. In the opening, the ever-modest Tarantino even set out to create 'the greatest Pam Grier opening sequence of all time'.[98] As he rightly pointed out, many of her movies began with Grier strutting her stuff and 'letting you behold the glory that is Pam'.[99] Seen in profile, dressed in her stewardess uniform, Jackie walks – and then runs, as she realizes she's going to be late – through the airport, accompanied by Bobby Womack's soulful track 'Across 110th Street' (from the 1972 New York gang war film of the same name). For a film that has the self-confidence to dictate its pace on its own terms, it's the last time anyone will feel rushed during the leisurely 151 minutes that follow.

As for the structure, while *Reservoir Dogs* and *Pulp Fiction* were marked by temporal disruption to the narratives, *Jackie Brown* proves a more linear experience – though Tarantino is unable to resist the chance to emulate the novel's multi-perspective climactic scene. He uses a suitably bland patch of Americana as a stage, exchanging the diners and dive bars of his previous films for Torrance's Del Amo Mall. A shimmering shrine to consumerism, and the 'largest indoor mall in the world' as the caption tells us, where else could a scene titled 'the money exchange' take place? Seen from three perspectives – Jackie's, Max's, and Louis and Melanie's – it is an audacious sequence, halting the forward momentum of the narrative to take us, almost in slow motion, through the pursuit of the shopping bag full of Ordell's cash.

Tarantino has compared the structure to, of all things, a pencil. For the first hour, you spend time getting to know the characters (the pencil's outer shell) while a plot is quietly put in place. As the story grows in importance – though never more than its protagonists – we get to the lead in the pencil. As Tarantino notes, this is the final close-up on Louis just as Ordell, who believes Louis has swindled him, shoots the man dead. 'Then you get to the point at the end of the pencil, and that's the final close-up on Pam. The whole movie is about those two close-ups. Everything that happens in the movie happens so that you'll feel what these people have done together when you see them at the end.'[100]

Jackie Brown is a more muted affair than either *Pulp Fiction* or *Reservoir Dogs* and feels less like a Tarantino film. Ironically, *Out of Sight* is actually more Tarantino-esque, particularly reminiscent of *Pulp Fiction*. Notably this comes across with *Out of Sight*'s cut-up structure and its film-savvy dialogue, when Karen and Jack discuss New Hollywood films such as *Network*, *Bonnie and Clyde* and *Three Days of the Condor*. But the 'real-life-sized' characters could also have been lifted straight from *Pulp Fiction*. The Schubert-hating Maurice 'Snoopy' Miller (Don Cheadle), one of Jack's former inmates also planning to heist Richard's diamonds, could well be a cousin to Jules Winnfield, while Jack's stoner chum Glenn Michaels (Steve Zahn) is a more laid-back version of Eric Stoltz's Lance. Even Jack's hold-up at the Sun Trust bank at the beginning, where his weapons are words rather than bullets, recalls the story told by *Pulp Fiction*'s Pumpkin about a heist with a mobile phone (as does Jack's recollection of a robbery with a bottle of nitroglycerine).

Another reason *Jackie Brown* feels least like a Tarantino film is the dialogue. Despite both Leonard's and Tarantino's penchant for zippy exchanges, it's not the lines that linger in the memory of the audience. The quintessential Ordell moment comes as he shows Louis a video of 'Chicks Who Love Guns', informing him that since the arrival of John Woo's *The Killer* (1989) the demand for the .45 has increased. Enter the AK-47 – or, as Ordell tags it, 'When you absolutely, positively, gotta kill every motherfucker in the room, accept no substitute.' Undoubtedly the most quoted line of the film, it felt like Tarantino's first lapse towards self-parody, written in order to satiate his acolytes.

Aside from his oblique nod to John Woo, as well as a mention of Rutger Hauer, cinematic references are thin on the ground. We briefly glimpse a shot of Peter Fonda – father of Bridget – on television in *Dirty Mary Crazy Larry* (1974), John Hough's film about the titular lovers who go on the lam with an ace mechanic, robbing supermarkets for pleasure. But when Max comes out of the cinema, and Jackie asks him what he saw, we never get to find out. Given that Rob Reiner's *The American President* (1995) is the most prominent poster on display, maybe he's too embarrassed to say – but it's more likely Tarantino deliberately held back from riffing on popular culture for the umpteenth time.

As for the violence, it feels toned down – even if Tarantino believes he was just replicating what he found in the book. Take the murder by Ordell of Beaumont. In a highly self-conscious one-take crane shot, the camera turns away from Ordell's car, lifts above the nearby fence and turns to focus on the waste ground on the other side. Cut to the Brothers Johnson's wistful 'Strawberry Letter 23', the car slowly goes around the corner and parks up on the ground, whereupon Ordell gets out and shoots Beaumont in the middle distance. Two flashes in the dark are enough to signal the murder, a bold answer from Tarantino to those who criticized his glorification of violence. In the parking lot of the Del Amo Mall, Melanie's murder, at the hands of Louis, is equally coy. His gun casually pointed at her from the side, with her out of frame, her death is as quick as the killer's earlier sexual encounter with his victim.

Tarantino was attacked for his extensive use of the word 'nigger' in *Jackie Brown*. Spike Lee led the charge, accusing him of being infatuated, adding, 'I want Quentin to know that not all Afro-Americans think the word is trendy or slick.' Is it merely a contemporary example of blaxploitation? Tarantino says not, even if it's difficult to argue against the fact that he's the natural successor to the white directors making films for black audiences in the 1970s. Like Eminem, perhaps the director's closest ally in the music world, Tarantino's argument was that he grew up around black culture, even inexplicably claiming he went to an all-black school. As Samuel L. Jackson noted, 'He's like my daughter's little white hip hop friends. They're basically black kids with white skin.'[101] As if to emphasize how black culture has seeped into the mainstream, when Jackie buys a suit at one point the white female assistant says, 'You wear that suit in a business meeting – you'll be the bad-ass in the room.'

It's no coincidence that Tarantino and Soderbergh remain among the few directors to have cracked Leonard. Two subsequent adaptations, George Armitage's *The Big Bounce* (2004) and Gray's *Be Cool* (2005) – fell way short of the mark. While Hollywood tends to over-plot Leonard, Tarantino and Soderbergh (with the help of Scott Frank) innately understood that his novels are less about story than about character. While neither *Out of Sight* nor *Jackie Brown* would quite hit the $40 million mark at the U.S. box office, both were hailed by critics as adult works. Perhaps the last great crime films of the 1990s, *Jackie Brown* and *Out of Sight* set their respective directors on vastly different paths. Tarantino went into hibernation once again; by the time he emerged in 2003 with *Kill Bill*, Soderbergh had completed a further six films, won an Oscar and enjoyed three $100 million hits.

Tell 'em I'm coming!
Wilson, *The Limey*

If *Out of Sight* was Soderbergh's way of re-establishing himself in Hollywood by delivering 'one for them', his next film, 1999's *The Limey*, was most defiantly a crime film for him. Written by Lem Dobbs, it sees Terence Stamp play Wilson, a Cockney career criminal on a mission in Los Angeles to find out the truth behind the death of his daughter Jenny. In post-production, Soderbergh described the $9 million movie, bankrolled by Artisan Entertainment, as 'Alain Resnais meets *Get Carter*'. In other words, mixing the vengeance plot of Mike Hodges's seminal 1972 British gangster film with the feel of Resnais's work, such as *Last Year at Marienbad* (1961), 'because of their ease of moving backwards and forwards in time', as Soderbergh puts it. With its merging of the past, present and future into one single moment, *The Limey* is a tour de force in narrative bravura from Soderbergh, who said it was his attempt to tell a simple tale in a complicated way. About as far removed from Leonard as you can get, it nevertheless could not have been made without Soderbergh's experience on *Out of Sight*.

Soderbergh wanted to start work on the film immediately after *Out of Sight*, which had inspired him to dream up a variety of 'cinematic ideas' he felt were inappropriate to try in such a mainstream context.

While I was shooting, for example, the cross-cutting cocktail lounge/hotel room sequence between George Clooney and Jennifer Lopez, I began to think 'What if you took a dialogue scene and shot it in two or three different locations?' And that's where the idea in *The Limey* comes from, when Terence Stamp and Lesley Ann Warren are walking and talking, and we go from the diner to the pier to the apartment. It's all one linear audio track, but we keep going back and forth. And I'm stunned that people don't just spin out of their seats. From a logical standpoint, it's completely crazy, but you see it in the movie and you don't even blink.

After the character study that was *Out of Sight*, *The Limey* is a plot-driven affair, albeit a plot that has to be pieced back together, and may only exist in one man's mind. Twice Soderbergh pulls off the fractured conversations he refers to above, the other time being when Stamp and Luis Guzmán, who plays Jenny's friend Eduardo Roel, first meet.

Moreover, the film's first ten minutes must rank as the most disorientating in contemporary American film, as Soderbergh wilfully shuffles the chronology of a set of scenes like a deck of cards, while still managing to invest the film with a narrative logic all of its own. Providing a link to *The Limey*'s experimental predecessor *Schizopolis* – as well as its successor, the equally non-linear *Full Frontal* – was the editor Sarah Flack, who has tellingly worked on all three but on none of Soderbergh's more conventional films. 'She very quickly fell into the weird rhythms that I was trying to create,' says Soderbergh. 'It was a tough balance. The first cut of the film – it was absolutely incomprehensible to everyone who worked on the film. It was completely unanchored! But I slowly started to bring it back, and try and find a balance.' The opening montage includes a clip of Wilson looking dreamily out of an aeroplane window. It's a pivotal shot, anchoring the whole film (or setting it adrift in time and space, given that we cannot be sure whether he's travelling to Los Angeles or back to London). Recalling John Boorman's dream-like revenge fantasy *Point Blank*, it's the first suggestion that this could all be in Wilson's mind, as we begin to witness a series of elliptical and seemingly disparate events. As evidenced by Soderbergh's use of stock saturation, Wilson's mind colours the truth – from the subtle blue tinge lent to his memories of Jenny's Super 8-shot childhood to a more menacing and darker hue used when she and Ed are arguing with 'some bad people' in a warehouse.

Film defines Wilson, not least because his memories of Jenny are seen as battered old home movie clips. A young Stamp is glimpsed in various excerpts from Ken Loach's *Poor Cow* (1967), in which he played a petty thief who gets sent to prison, while memories of Stamp's iconic Swinging London status remain as pungent in *The Limey* as the aroma of Wilson's Old Spice. Soderbergh wants to remind us that our perception of Wilson is shaped by our knowledge of cinema. As viewers, we are forced to confront the artificial nature of film – which, rather like memory, is a subjective construct that 'directs' us in a certain way.

Wilson's investigations lead him to bohemian record producer Terry Valentine (Peter Fonda), who had an affair with Jenny. But revenge is only a surface knee-jerk reaction. Despite being set in the context of the crime genre, *The Limey* is much more a film about one man's reckoning with his past rather than the present. Wilson watched his daughter grow up 'in increments' and, like *Schizopolis* and *King of the Hill*, *The Limey* deals with the notion of family slipping away from the protagonist's grasp, although in this case she has already gone. Wilson is left clutching at memories, reduced at one point to stealing a photograph of Jenny from Terry's wall. An overriding sense of loss, regret and melancholy pervades the film or, more specifically, Wilson's mind. 'The central premise was this man who was trying to make up for all this time he stole from himself and stole from his daughter by avenging her death,' says Soderbergh.

The lid is lifted on Los Angeles, as it was by Elliott Gould's Philip Marlowe in Robert Altman's *The Long Goodbye* (1973), to expose an underlying distaste with what the city throws up – be it the music industry types at Terry's party or the extras on a film set. The Leonard-like support characters bear witness to Soderbergh's time on *Out of Sight*. Eduardo's T-shirts of Che Guevara and Mao Zedong would suggest a political conscience uncommon among former jailbirds; while Nicky Katt and Joe Dallasandro invest their roles as Stacy and Uncle John (two thugs hired to whack Wilson) with a poetic dignity rarely bequeathed to such minor characters. 'Who gives a shit about you? Not even God,' Stacy is told – yet it's clear Soderbergh does.

One of the most telling moments in the film is Terry's speech to Adhara (Amelia Heinle), his doe-eyed replacement for Jenny, who believes the 1960s must have been 'a golden moment'. Feeling nostalgic and wistful – maybe it's the Santana poster in the background – Valentine elusively refers to this golden period as 'just '66 and early '67 – that's all it was'. He goes on to compare the era to 'a place you never recall being before, a place that maybe only exists in your imagination . . . but you knew the language, knew your way around'. In many ways, defining the decade as this hazy Eden of the mind recalls the film's approach to presenting the present day, as filtered through Wilson's vengeful consciousness. Be it his recollection of events or Valentine's love letter to his days of innocence, the mind has a habit of shaping memories to suit the heart.

A story of counter-culture gone awry, *The Limey* specifically recalls how Watergate doused the spirit of the 1960s. Terry's ruthless security chief Jim Avery, as played by Bob Newman, reminds us of the Nixon era, while Valentine himself stands for the loss of innocence and sinister cynicism that crept into America's consciousness in the early 1970s. Laundering money for the mob, he is reduced to becoming a petty crook – no doubt why Soderbergh chooses The Hollies' 'King Midas in Reverse' as Terry's signature tune on the soundtrack. 'I think the tipping point happened when big business realized that the youth movement was an economic force that was not going to go away,' says Soderbergh. 'Once that happened, the co-opting of a lot of the imagery of the Zeitgeist began. Everyone I talked to said that late '66 was the last time it was all clean and pure. By the time '67 rolled around, the drugs were harder, people were more cynical – you'd have lawyers driving to San Francisco, stopping in their cars to change from their three-piece suits to bell-bottoms to be hip.'

Though recouping just $3.2 million, *The Limey* was, like *Out of Sight* before it, critically well received. It was also a significant milestone in Soderbergh's filmmaking. Uniting the experimental urges he re-discovered while making *Schizopolis* and *Gray's Anatomy* with the commercial vibe he uncovered on *Out of Sight*, it laid the groundwork for his emergence as one of contemporary Hollywood's most celebrated directors. *The Limey* is also the finest expression yet of Soderbergh's intent. In many ways he is Wilson, roaring through Hollywood with a message on his mind: I'm coming!

CHAPTER 15

The Sundance Sisters:
Sofia Coppola and Kimberly Peirce

34 Sofia Coppola's *The Virgin Suicides*.

Until now, the Sundance Kids have been an exclusively male posse; if not commendable, this is at least understandable, given that female writer-directors are a scarce hybrid in Hollywood. This changed in 1999 with the arrival of two startling debuts, both films about death, sexual awakening and youth that were showered with awards and acclaim. Both dropping anchor at Sundance in one way or another, Kimberly Peirce's *Boys Don't Cry* and Sofia Coppola's *The Virgin Suicides* were, as maiden voyages go, smooth sailing all right, even if the captains couldn't have been more different. One was an unknown with a couple of 16 mm shorts to her name; the other belonged to a filmmaking dynasty as gargantuan as its patriarch.

Not that Coppola bears much resemblance to her father (Francis Ford, referenced from here as Coppola Sr) – just as *The Virgin Suicides* has little in common with his work. Like its creator, it was a modest waif of a film, shy and sunlit. Coppola may have celebrated her fifth birthday on the set of *Apocalypse Now*, but judging by this adaptation of Jeffrey Eugenides's novel, she had picked up none of her father's visions of grandeur. An evocation of teenage growing pains to rank alongside Peter Bogdanovich's elegiac *The Last Picture Show*, this story of the suicide of five golden-haired sisters bore no traces of the two ill-fated collaborations with her father that had blighted her early years.

In 1988, aged seventeen, she co-wrote *Life Without Zoe*, her father's segment of the portmanteau movie *New York Stories*. The story of a pampered princess living in the lap of luxury, it was, compared to Woody Allen's and Martin Scorsese's shorts, amateurish at best. Coppola Sr was rightly slammed for his contribution. While critics sniffed at Daddy's Little Girl playing at filmmaking, this was nothing compared to the savaging meted out to her two years later. Sofia Coppola was roped in as a replacement for Winona Ryder in *The Godfather Part III*, after the actress pulled out on the first day of shooting on medical grounds. As far as her father was concerned, who else could play Mary Corleone, the only daughter to Michael and Kay, but his own offspring? The right age (she was eighteen at the time), she was also the right look – half-Italian, half-WASP. And if you think of the Coppola clan as the living embodiment of the Corleones, then it made perfect sense to cast the only girl of the family.

Except for the fact that Coppola couldn't act, as she found out to her cost. From playing Michael's infant son in *The Godfather Part II*, to taking small roles in numerous Coppola family productions – *Rumble Fish*, *The Outsiders* (both 1983), *The Cotton Club* (1984), *Peggy Sue Got Married* (1986) – under the single stage name Domino, she had grown up on film. But this was different. The critics rounded on her lack of charisma. 'I can't say it wasn't painful,' she would later admit. 'It was hard [to be attacked publicly].'[102] It taught her that she didn't want to be in front of the camera again. She preferred to try on different identities off-screen.

At the instigation of her mother, Coppola went to art school to study painting. She taught herself photography and even started Milk Fed, a casual clothing company, with her childhood friend Stephanie Hayman. Hanging out with designers like Marc Jacobs, musicians like Sonic Youth's Thurston Moore and, of course, Spike Jonze, her life was far removed from the 1,700 acre Napa Valley vineyard estate where she had spent much of her sun-kissed youth. That is doubtless why she found herself drawn to Eugenides's serio-comic novel, set in the strictly Catholic Lisbon household in suburban Michigan in the mid-1970s. Manicured lawns, high school proms, curfews: this was as exotic as it got for Coppola.

Like any youngster, entering the family business is often a route taken reluctantly. Hence her older brother Roman was forging a career in music videos (though he would later receive a similar drubbing for his own feature debut, 2001's *CQ*). It was filmmaking by default, if you like. And it was a far cry from Kimberly Peirce's traditional route. Like Coppola, she had developed an early interest in images – after her degree in English and Japanese literature from the University of Chicago took her to Japan for two years, where she worked as a stills photographer. Again like Coppola, who also spent time in Japan before penning her second film *Lost in Translation*, Peirce split from Tokyo as soon as she arrived: 'I wanted to find samurai Japan, so I got on a train and travelled until I got lost. It was my first anonymous moment.'[103]

Moving to New York upon her return, she enrolled in the film course at Columbia University and began making shorts, notably *The Last Good Breath*, about two lovers who take turns sacrificing themselves to survive a war. Also honing her skills as an editor at the time, it was in 1994 – while still in film school – that she came across the story of Brandon Teena, a young Nebraskan who had been raped and murdered on New Year's Eve the previous year. Born Teena Brandon, (s)he was genetically a female but had been dressing as a male. Fascinated by women who passed themselves off as men, Peirce felt her interest piqued. At the time, she had been writing a script about a cross-dressing woman in the American Civil War who was hired as a spy. But when she came across Brandon's story in *The Village Voice* she abandoned her former script, initially making a short film about Brandon while still in college.

In their own ways, both Coppola and Peirce wanted to take ownership of the stories they had found. Given Eugenides's novel at art school, Coppola was immediately intrigued by its title and the original cover picture – simply of blonde hair. After falling in love with the book, she learnt to her disappointment that the rights were already owned and another company was intending to make a film. 'I read a few pages of their script and then I put it down, because it was so annoying,' she says. 'You know when you feel very protective of a book, you feel that it belongs to you. And I felt *The Virgin Suicides* captured that sense of being a teenager. It had a great sense of humour and wasn't at all condescending.' Instead of complaining, she immediately set about writing her own screenplay – 'but I didn't really tell anyone about it apart from Spike'. The further she got, the more she realized she should finish it. 'I thought if nothing else, I'll learn how to adapt a book into a screenplay. Eventually I gave the script to a producer at my dad's [American] Zoetrope company. She gave it to the people who owned the rights to the book. They had somebody else in mind to direct, but that fell through, so they asked me if I wanted to do it.'

Likewise Peirce faced numerous obstacles in bringing Brandon's story to the screen – notably several other versions in development, the most prominent of which involved Drew Barrymore. Harmony Korine, on-off boyfriend to Chloë Sevigny – who wound up playing Brandon's lover Lana Tisdel for Peirce – also toyed with the idea of filming the story. But it was Peirce who devoted her life to the project, playing journalist cum detective in her quest for authenticity. Inspired by such prose works as Truman Capote's *In Cold Blood* and Norman Mailer's *The Executioner's Song*, Peirce covered every angle as she researched the story and refined her script over a five-year period. She travelled to Falls City, near to where John Lotter and Thomas Nissen – ex-cons and friends of Lana – ended Brandon's life. Peirce held a vigil with a group of transsexuals; she hung out with the real Lana and her mother; she attended Nissen's murder trial and saw him testify against Lotter, as well as ploughing through court transcripts; she talked to the police and even met with kids at the local Qwik Stop to catch the local vibe.

35 Hilary Swank in *Boys Don't Cry*.

Invited to the 1997 Sundance Institute Filmakers' Lab with her writing partner Andy Bienen (when the script was called *Take It Like a Man*), Peirce tried every which way to tell the story. She eventually settled on leaving the murder until the end. Defining from the outset that this is a film about sexual orientation, and not a salacious true-crime thriller, the film begins as Teena Brandon becomes Brandon Teena. Receiving a boyish hair crop, Brandon completes the transformation with a pair of rolled-up socks stuffed in the crotch and heads out for a night on the town. Much the same happened to Hilary Swank, the virtual unknown Peirce cast to play the role four weeks before filming was due to start. Already blessed with an androgynous face, Swank went the whole hog, getting the buzz cut and working with a voice trainer before heading out into Los Angeles, on Peirce's behest, to try to pass as a boy. It evidently worked, for Swank won a Best Actress Oscar for her courageous performance. Sevigny was also nominated, though beaten by Angelina Jolie for *Girl, Interrupted* (1999). Perhaps it was just as well. The real Lana Tisdel, who resented being portrayed as a lesbian, wound up trying to sue for invasion of privacy and the use of her name and likeness without permission. It was thrown out of court.

Coppola's task was a mite easier. Her characters were fictional, after all. What's more, she had the connections to gather in an esteemed supporting cast. Danny DeVito turned up as a bald, moustachioed therapist, Scott Glenn as a priest and, playing wildly against type, James Woods as the Lisbon sisters' ineffectual father, with Kathleen Turner as their zealot of a mother. Rather than plump for an unknown, she chose a Hollywood golden girl to play Lux, the second youngest of the ill-fated Lisbon sisters, and the catalyst for their tragedy. Unlike Swank, Kirsten Dunst had been in the spotlight ever since she played opposite Brad Pitt and Tom Cruise in Neil Jordan's *Interview with the Vampire* (1994) when she was twelve. A precocious talent even at that young age, by the time she came to *The Virgin Suicides* she had blossomed to the point that Coppola's film almost feels like a love letter to Dunst. The sunlight glints in her honeydew hair and Ed Lachman's cinematography worships the ground she walks on, while the other sisters melt into the background, an interchangeable mass of blonde innocence.

While Peirce did the puzzling in *Boys Don't Cry*, Coppola's film is a riddle for its narrator (Giovanni Ribisi) and his four compatriots, all local lads in love with the Lisbons. The girls' tragedy is viewed through their eyes. As Ribisi's voice-over tells us, for the past twenty-five years they have been trying to figure out why it happened: 'Everyone dates the demise of our neighbourhood from the suicides of the Lisbon girls.' Eschewing the nostalgic *Boogie Nights* depiction of the decade – flared trousers and long hair are scarce – Coppola prefers to etch the visuals like a series of fading memories, hazy and out of reach, as if it was all a dream. Judging by the wistful narration, it's as much about male pubescence as anything else: 'We felt the imprisonment of being a girl . . . we knew that the girls were really women in disguise, that they understood love and even death.'

After the suicide of Cecilia, the youngest and most introverted of the Lisbon sisters, at the outset of the film, it is Lux who becomes the centre of attention (after all, she's now the youngest). It is she who is asked on a date to the school dance by local heartthrob Trip Fontaine (Josh Hartnett). Organizing a gaggle of fellow suitors to escort the remaining three girls, Trip – in a scene of haunting loneliness – deflowers Lux on the school playing field that very night, only to abandon her. When she wakes up in the morning, shivering from the frost that has settled – in a scene not in the novel – she has lost not only her virginity but also her freedom. Mrs Lisbon immediately grounds the four sisters indefinitely, even pulling them out of school. 'They were all living in the dead, becoming shadows,' says the narrator. Cut off in their prime, they are led to their suicide pact.

'Don't let her die a virgin,' jokes one of Trip's friends, about his date. Little does he know: as the narrator and his friends enter the house on the fateful night, each of the four remaining sisters has chosen a different, and equally grisly, way to die. 'I saw the deaths of the girls as a metaphor for the end of the boys' innocence and their youth,' says Coppola. 'I didn't want to explain the suicides. All these years later the boys are pining over them and piecing things together. The memory of these girls is more perfect than the reality. That's why the party scene towards the end is important. It represents the boys going out into adult life and meeting the sort of people they would end up marrying in the grown-up world. But they still cling on to their memories of the girls.'

If sex and death are inextricably linked in *The Virgin Suicides*, the same can be said for Peirce's film. Set against the industrial backdrop of America's heartland, the film pre-empts its almost surreal sex scene with an ominous warning. 'They hang faggots down there,' Brandon is told. As (s)he later orally pleasures Lana's vagina, Peirce cuts from this to the sight of Brandon and friends driving through the night in a truck cab. With the sex scene shot in slow motion, the groans of Lana's orgasm melt into the noise on the soundtrack. Prefiguring Brandon's screams when (s)he is raped, it's a violent, head-spinning moment and a tour de force of filmmaking. A scene that almost got the film rated in the U.S. as NC-17 (despite the fact it's not really explicit in any way), it represents, as Peirce notes, 'every girl's orgasm, because in her mind everybody in the world is coming. All the girls who never came are coming.'[104]

Both films are defined, to some extent, by music. That the Cure song from which *Boys Don't Cry* takes its title features at the crucial moment when Brandon reveals all to Lana is both ironic and uplifting at the same time. Meanwhile, Coppola's principal use of the French pop band Air, a year on from the release of their seminal *Moon Safari* album, fitted the mood of the film to a tee. 'I was listening to some of Air's music while I was writing the script,' she recalls. 'It had that dreamy, ethereal feeling, which the book had, as well as a sense of melancholy. And because the book is about memory, and how you remember things, rather than being about reality, I thought the Air music would give the spectator a sense of distance, a feeling of looking back.' Her use of the 1970s band Heart, and in particular the use of 'Magic Man' to introduce Trip, is a nice counterpoint to this.

While Coppola was inspired by Sam Haskins's photography for *Playboy*, Peirce's influences were more austere. Also based on a true story, Terrence Malick's *Badlands*, with its episodes of violence punctuated by images of rural America, is the obvious comparison. But there are others: the speeded-up cloud formations recall Gus Van Sant among others, and there is a fantastical element to the film that Michael Powell would have appreciated. Jarring against what Peirce calls a neorealist style – with its rough-hewn lighting and photography courtesy of Jim Denault chosen to represent the harsh nature of the characters' lives – these moments, such as the orgasm, are flights of internal fantasy.

You might even call *Boys Don't Cry* a fairy tale, a *Cinderella*-like story of transformation. Peirce was careful not to make statements surrounding Brandon's sexuality – notably, whether (s)he wanted to first and foremost be a boy or sleep with women. 'I was born with this weirdness,' Brandon tells Lana, having admitted (s)he is 'a person who has both girl and boy parts'. Yet does she make love to Lana (using a concealed dildo) as a boy or a girl? Does it even matter? Just as Peirce discovered, when interviewing Lana, that Brandon's orientation went back and forth in her mind minute by minute, so it does in the film. Having pleasured Lana (in fact, Brandon is the only one who gives and does not sexually receive in the film) seemingly as a man, Brandon is stripped of his/her male identity in the final scenes by Tom (Brendan Sexton III) and John (Peter Sarsgaard). 'Are you a girl or not?' screams the latter, before they rip her clothes off in one of the most terrifying scenes in contemporary American cinema. 'Looks like no sexual identity crisis to me,' adds Tom, before they drive Brandon to a wasteland to be raped. But Peirce turns this back on itself one more time before Brandon dies. Escaping from the clutches of both men, Brandon flees to Lana's house and the couple make love. While it's a scene that could be questioned, given there was no evidence for this final union, it means Brandon's masculine sexuality has been restored in a beautifully dignified moment.

At times like an anthropological study, with Peirce's interest in the tribal behaviour of Tom and John, *Boys Don't Cry* is not so far from Coppola's own vision of the Lisbon girls. As many critics have noted, *The Virgin Suicides* – despite its deft comic touches – can be read as a reaction by the director to the death of her brother Gio when she was just fifteen. The eldest in the family, he left school early to help his father, even acting as a second unit director on *The Cotton Club*. Tragedy struck when he was killed in a boating accident in 1986, when he was twenty-two. The automatic impact on the family was that Roman immediately left college to take over the family business. While Coppola told one interviewer that 'death shifts everything', she added, 'I'd always been the baby girl, the youngest. As the only girl, I retained my spot.'[105] Given that Coppola has used words like 'celebratory' and 'innocence' to describe *The Virgin Suicides*, the film appears to be her way of dealing with the gender divide that she lived through as the only female Coppola offspring. If *The Godfather* was her father's assessment of family, this was hers. That's not to say death and disappointment do not soak through the film's very fabric, from the vision of Trip's dishevelled future right down to the disease-ridden elms that are being hacked down in the neighbourhood. As sick as the joke is, the debutante ball with its asphyxiation theme, prefiguring Lux's own suicide, shows just how Coppola appears to have a gallows humour when it comes to terminal matters.

As you would expect, both films were made for nominal sums – *Boys Don't Cry* cost just $2 million; Coppola's film roughly $4 million more. While *The Virgin Suicides*, launched at the 1999 Cannes Film Festival, made just $4.9 million back in the U.S. on its theatrical release, *Boy's Don't Cry* netted a profitable $11.5 million. Picked up and released by Twentieth Century Fox on the back of a twenty-minute trailer, it evidently hit a nerve, arriving at the time of the murder of gay student Matthew Shepherd in Wyoming. (Unlike Brandon, Shepherd became a martyr of sorts – symbolic of the homophobic and/or racist violence going on every day in Middle America, which was less recognized in Brandon's lifetime.)

With Peirce and Coppola leading the way, it was a good time for female directors. At the 2000 Sundance Film Festival, where *The Virgin Suicides* played out of competition, Valerie Breiman, director of the romantic comedy *Love & Sex*, exclaimed: 'Forty percent of the filmmakers here this year have breasts!' That year, more women than ever submitted their films to Sundance and more than ever were selected. Karyn Kusama's *Girlfight*, a film about a teenage girl's struggle to become a boxing champion, shared the Grand Jury Prize in the dramatic competition with Kenneth Lonergan's *You Can Count on Me*. Mary Harron followed up *I Shot Andy Warhol* (1996) with the much-anticipated and long-gestating version of Bret Easton Ellis's touchstone novel *American Psycho*.

But while the sisters were doing it for themselves, let's not get too excited. The studio doors were only just creaking open for the male directors under consideration here. Heaven forbid that female auteurs should get a foothold in Hollywood. Let's leave that to the French, to an industry that reveres the likes of Claire Denis and Catherine Breillat as a matter of course. To date, five years on from making *Boys Don't Cry*, Peirce has yet to follow it up, though Coppola has at least managed a second film, the well-received *Lost in Translation* (see Chapter 12). Meanwhile, as noted in Chapter 4, it's taken Kusama five years to launch her second film, the comic-strip adaptation *Aeon Flux*, and Harron a similar period to make *The Notorious Bettie Page* (2005), the story of a 1950s pin-up model subjected to a Senate investigation. Just as ethnic filmmakers remain in the minority, so too do women.

Yet there have been others: former production designer Catherine Hardwicke (who worked on David O. Russell's *Three Kings*) has been carving out a name for herself as a director. Well entrenched in the burgeoning Hollywood new wave (she and Peirce are the two female members of the Pizza Knights film club), her two films, *Thirteen* (2003) and *Lords of Dogtown* (2005) have reflected this. Dealing with the disintegration of the relationship between teenage rebel-in-the-making Tracy (Evan Rachel Wood) and her mother (Holly Hunter), *Thirteen* was co-written by Hardwicke with the then thirteen-year-old

Nikki Reed, who co-stars in the film as the troublesome girl Evie who leads Tracy astray.

A more fruitful piece of juvenilia than Coppola's *Life Without Zoe*, the warts-and-all portrait of teen life reflected Reed's own experience (perhaps just as Coppola's life of privilege was shown in her effort). Scenes of self-mutilation, huffing gas and three-way sex feature in the film. Aside from drawing gutsy performances from all three female leads, Hardwicke's connections led her to crew up with some old favourites. Wes Anderson's regular composer Mark Mothersbaugh provided the score, while Steven Soderbergh's one-time cinematographer Elliot Davis gave the film a queasy look that recalled his work on *The Underneath*.

Hardwicke followed this with skateboard movie *Lords of Dogtown*, featuring Heath Ledger. Written by former skate icon Stacey Peralta, who made the definitive documentary of skate culture *Dogtown and the Z-Boys* (2001), it tells a fictionalized version of the same story, as the eponymous crew perfect their craft in the empty swimming pools around Los Angeles' Venice Beach, pioneering a new sport. Rewritten by Roger Avary, at one time David Fincher toyed with directing it – until, as Hardwicke puts it, he 'left because the budget got too big'. Based in Venice Beach herself, Hardwicke – a surfer with connections to Peralta's crowd – was brought on board. A continuation of her interest in youth culture, the film also represented a step up for Hardwicke in directing a studio-funded star-driven picture. Again with Mothersbaugh and Davis involved in the core creative team, Hardwicke has, like her male peers, managed to anchor her own idiosyncratic interests into the mainstream. But as we will see, the real turning point for her and her fellow Pizza Knights was 1999.

CHAPTER 16

Annus Mirabilis: How 1999 Became the Year of the Sundance Kids

36 David O. Russell gets ready to shoot.

You could, if you like, call it a matter of chance. But as the narrator says in P. T. Anderson's *Magnolia*: 'This is not just "something that happened".' Like an alignment of the planets, timed to arrive as we trod with trepidation towards the new millennium, a celluloid renaissance occurred, as a series of films were released that caused audiences to awaken from their slumber and rub their eyes in disbelief. They might have already been prepped along the way – from *Se7en* to *The Usual Suspects*, from *Boogie Nights* to *Rushmore* – but this year felt like no other. The Hollywood mavericks were, if not yet bestowed with the power of their 1970s forefathers, finally seen as their rightful successors. It was as if the baton passed hands. In particular, David Fincher, David O. Russell and Paul Thomas Anderson took it and ran with a brazen confidence.

In a curious way, this seamless changeover was heralded by the arrival of films by a trio of directors who had impacted upon the 1970s but since managed just one film between them. The return of Terrence Malick (*The Thin Red Line*), Stanley Kubrick (*Eyes Wide Shut*) and George Lucas (*Star Wars: Episode I – The Phantom Menace*) caused ripples of excitement, even if the end results caused bemusement, unable to sustain the hype. Other established directors also released new movies in this year, most of which caused little enthusiasm. Consider the following: *Summer of Sam* (Spike Lee); *The Insider* (Michael Mann); *Cookie's Fortune* (Robert Altman); *Bringing Out the Dead* (Martin Scorsese); *Sleepy Hollow* (Tim Burton); *The Hurricane* (Norman Jewison). With perhaps the exception of Mann's tobacco whistle-blower story, it felt like these directors were on cruise control, no longer at the cutting edge of their profession.

Compare to these Fincher's *Fight Club*, Anderson's *Magnolia* and Russell's *Three Kings*. Respectively, a devastating social critique, a multi-narrative melodrama and a Gulf War action-adventure, all were linked by a desire to portray how politics, big business and the media have negatively affected contemporary society. Each would mark a considerable step up from the previous work of its director, be it in terms of scale, ambition, power or risk. Each would also be infused with a bravura – both thematic and stylistic – the like of which suggested that finally the auteurs of the 1970s could rest in the knowledge that their legacy had not been forgotten.

Notably, two of the three came from major studios (Twentieth Century Fox and Warner Bros.), while the third came from New Line. Working from the lower end to the higher echelons of the mid-budget Hollywood film, these directors were now commanding the respect of A-list actors, such as Tom Cruise, George Clooney and Brad Pitt. It was as if the tried and tested Hollywood formula of filmmaking by committee evaporated before our very eyes. These films were true collaborations, working towards realizing a director's very singular vision. While only Anderson's *Magnolia* was an original screenplay and story written by him, each movie was shaped towards serving character and narrative rather than the external pressures of commercial moviemaking. Fresh, dark and provocative, their arrival was not just something that happened. It was much more than that.

And the book says: 'We may be through with the past, but the past ain't through with us.'
Jimmy Gator and Donnie Smith, *Magnolia*

Shortly after the release of *Boogie Nights*, Warren Beatty invited P. T. Anderson to dinner. Eating at Los Angeles's fashionable Chinese restaurant Mandarette, they were joined by Francis Ford Coppola. He recognized the position the young director was in. 'This is the one moment when you have it, when you can do whatever you want to do,' he advised. 'It's the one moment when you have a clean slate, with no stigma attached. And even if your next movie makes $400 million and gets eight Oscars, you'll still have to fight battles that you'll never have to fight right now. So, whatever you want to do, do it now.'

Anderson heeded that advice. Wearing its heart on its sleeve, *Magnolia* is a tearful paean to life, death, loss and, above all, love. Characters do not so much speak as recite arias of pain. A mosaic of contemporary life as complex as anything his hero Robert Altman ever achieved, it is directed by Anderson with such gusto, such exuberance, you'd think it was the last film he was ever going to make. While *Boogie Nights* stretched across two decades, *Magnolia* plays out its action across one day, once again in Anderson's own back lot, the San Fernando Valley. Epic in neither time span nor setting, *Magnolia* relies on the emotional journey taken by each of the nine

37, 38 & 39 *Magnolia*: John C. Reilly questions a
witness; Philip Baker Hall stares into the
abyss; Tom Cruise confronts Jason Robards.

principal characters to class it as such. Both intimate and apocalyptic, it's also a profound meditation on the nature of chance and coincidence, an attempt to address the very secrets of the universe itself. 'My idea was that generally three-hour epic movies are reserved for war films or films of important social topics,' says Anderson. 'I thought it would be an interesting idea to take small relationships – Will I fall in love? Can I go to the bathroom? Will my father talk to me? – and put them in the context of an epic.'

Where does one start with a film as vast as *Magnolia*? Let's try the final shot, of the coke-addled Claudia (Melora Walters) breaking into a smile, after a protracted scene in which a male figure – whom we assume is her recent suitor, the LAPD officer Jim Kurring (John C. Reilly) – talks gently to her while remaining mostly inaudible to us. Anderson claims this enigmatic smile, which suggests there's hope for us all, was the first image he had in his head for the film. Then again, he also claims that the film was built around the perverse line, 'Now that I've met you, would you object to never seeing me again?' Lifted from Aimee Mann's song 'Deathly', it is spoken by Claudia as she attempts to repel Jim's earlier advances on their first date.

Certainly, Aimee Mann's music is *Magnolia*'s guiding light, despite Anderson also noting that the film was inspired by the shifts in tone heard on The Beatles' track 'A Day in the Life'. 'The music really came first,' he says. 'After *Boogie Nights*, I wasn't sure what I wanted to write and I had a lot of ideas in my head. Aimee Mann had some music – she's a close friend of mine – and what I set out to do was adapt her music into a movie, like you would adapt a novel or a play. And the music really dictated the movie. Not just the themes, but the structure of the movie.'

Like *The Graduate* (with Simon and Garfunkel) and *Harold and Maude* (Cat Stevens), *Magnolia* employs one musical voice to articulate the feelings of the characters – notably in the montage where each sings along to Mann's beautiful ballad 'Wise Up'. A moment of epiphany for each character, this is typical of the risks Anderson takes with his audience, who might easily dismiss the scene as whimsy. But *Magnolia* is a film that endeavours to show how, in times of emotional upheaval, we cling to things – drugs, religion and even music – to help us connect to a wider world. The scene rings true, and not just because Anderson, during an early morning scriptwriting session, saw a woman sitting in her car in the parking lot with the door open, crying her eyes out and singing along to Whitney Houston's 'I Will Always Love You'.

The film is structured in three acts, bookended by a prologue and epilogue (entitled 'So Now Then'). Each act is marked at the start by a change in weather conditions. An indication that the omnipotent Anderson is playing god with his characters, the climate builds to a biblical deus ex machina that rains a torrent of frogs upon the unwitting protagonists.

Right from the prologue, Anderson works ferociously hard to establish his themes – notably chance and coincidence. The film begins with three vignettes, the third of which deals with the suicidal seventeen-year-old Sydney, who jumps to his death off the Los Angeles building where his family lives. But it is not the pavement that kills him. Landing in a safety net erected for window cleaners, he is shot dead by his own mother as he sails past their window. She is aiming at the husband she has argued with for years, the gun only loaded because Sydney had loaded it in the hope that one would kill the other. As the narrator says, 'This cannot be "one of those things". This, please, cannot be that . . . this was not just a matter of chance. These strange things happen all the time.' In other words, the universe is made up of chance events. Human life is accidental – or, in the case of Sydney's story, we live in a world where human actions have meaning and consequences, for better or worse.

As Aimee Mann breaks in over the title sequence, singing that 'One is the loneliest number / That you'll ever do', Anderson cranks up a gear, introducing us to the poor unfortunate souls who populate his story. In a staggeringly audacious montage, he sets out both to capture the essence of each character and to place them in a structural chain-link that suggests our lives inextricably connect. The order is as follows: a clip from an infomercial by sexual self-help guru Frank T. J. Mackey (Tom Cruise) is seen on a television in the bar where Claudia picks up a middle-aged stranger; back at her apartment within seconds, as she's having sex, the camera pans up; reflected in the glass of a picture frame is another television set, featuring a documentary about the man we will learn is her father, Jimmy Gator (Philip Baker Hall), about to record his 12,000th hour in broadcasting on America's longest-running quiz show *What Do Kids Know?* Anderson then cuts to reveal this upstanding citizen cheating on his wife, Rose (Melinda Dillon); from this we switch to schoolboy Stanley Spector (Jeremy

Blackman), the quiz show's brightest current spark, as he prepares for his day, all the while being hassled by his father; this links us to 'Quiz Kid' Donnie Smith (William H. Macy), a washed-up former child contestant from the show, whom we see at the dentist before he crashes his car into a 7/11 window. Anderson then breaks the chain, cutting to a seemingly unconnected plot strand – that of the cancer victim Earl Partridge (Jason Robards), his nurse Phil Parma (Philip Seymour Hoffman) and his trophy wife Linda (Julianne Moore). This finally brings us, in what again seems an unconnected strand, to Jim, whom we see praying, showering and weight-lifting.

For inspiration, Anderson drew from his own life – from his days as a production assistant on the now-defunct show *Quiz Kid Challenge* to the tragic sight of watching his father die of cancer around the time of *Boogie Nights*. Baker Hall remembers: 'Another close friend of Paul's dad died soon afterwards, and Paul called me up, and told me, "You can't die. You're the only dad I've got left."' Anderson even called Baker Hall when agonizing over whether or not to include the frog sequence, only to find the actor had experienced a similar episode in real life. 'It happened to me while I was in Europe in 1957. We were driving over the Brenner Pass in a new VW at night, and my car suddenly started sliding all over the place. The fog became so thick that I could only drive by holding the door open and looking down at the white line. And for fifteen minutes it rained frogs. Though they weren't as big as the ones in the film!'

While such phenomena have been recorded in the last century, Anderson knew that including such a scene as the binding event of a final act was dangerous. As if to pre-empt audience disbelief, the camera moves in during the plague to the bottom corner of a painting on Claudia's wall. A legend reads: 'But it did happen' – a fuck-you to anyone ready to criticize such a random occurrence late on in the narrative. He similarly prepares the audience for the scene where Phil is trying to get through on the phone to Frank, on behalf of the dying Earl, who reveals that the sex guru is his estranged son. 'This is the scene in the movie where the guy is trying to get hold of the long-lost son . . . this is that scene . . . and I think they have those scenes in movies because they're true. Because they really happen.'

Anderson, raised like many of his peers on a diet of movies, freely admits that the all-pervasive influence of the silver screen taught him how to react to certain life situations. 'Movies are in my DNA. I grew up watching movies, and doing what movies told me to do. Now that I have the opportunity to make them, it would be a lie if I didn't factor that in. I have lived enough real life, but I've also been so informed by movies, that it has to be a part of the movie. It's the weird confusion when things really do happen in your life that you've only seen in movies.'

Stylistically, Anderson rarely draws breath over 188 minutes. Repeated use of dolly-shots, whip-pans and complex steadicam shots (notably through the television studio) create the feeling that we're crashing headlong into the new century. Orchestrated in perfect harmony with Jon Brion's symphonic score, it may smack of arrogance, but it's exhilarating in the extreme. For Brion, regular producer to Aimee Mann, this was his first composition for orchestra. Full of ominous repetitions – including a forty-minute sequence based on one rhythm – it was composed on a keyboard as Brion watched Anderson respond to a screening of the film. 'Paul wanted this sense of sensory overload; he wanted people to struggle to hear certain dialogue . . . There aren't themes for individual characters. The idea with the music in *Magnolia* is more that it's like a central clock. It's this universal clock that's part of what unites all these different stories.'

Set close to the heart of America's entertainment industry, the first two acts are dominated by television and commercials. Either side of *What Do Kids Know?* – which acts as the narrative thread for the middle act – comes Frank's 'Seduce and Destroy' routine, prefigured by the infomercial in the prologue. While its overlapping and interconnecting narratives have led many to compare the film to Robert Altman's *Nashville* and *Short Cuts*, Sidney Lumet's prophetic examination of a television news organization, *Network* (1976) – a film Anderson screened for his crew before shooting started – is just as influential. Nearly every character has, in some way or another, been adversely affected by the power of the moving image. Even when Frank, wearing just his briefs, struts around yelling, 'I'm Batman. I'm Superman. I'm a fucking action hero,' you know it's just an illusion.

As the credits roll on *What Do Kids Know?* – taken quickly off the air after Stanley wets his pants and refuses to continue – the film's two separate strands are brought together. It's a blink-and-you'll-miss-it moment. As a tearful Claudia watches the show at home, the camera moves in to her TV set, focusing on the credit: 'A Big Earl Partridge Production'. In its own way, this moment is as shocking as the fall of frogs. The bedridden Earl, with his cancer, confessions of sexual mis-demeanours and estranged son, is revealed as the mirror image of his successful employee Jimmy Gator, who likewise is suffering from cancer, confesses his infidelities to his wife and has alienated his daughter by sexually abusing her.

Karma is a very important part of Anderson's universe. The philan-dering Earl is dying of the same disease that killed his first wife. To turn the screw, he is also being cheated on by Linda, who in turn is just as guilt-ridden over her own infidelities to the point where she is driven to attempt suicide. Meanwhile, Jimmy will be driven to putting a gun to his head, only for one of the tumbling frogs to smash through his skylight and knock him unconscious – though not before a stray bul-let fires into the television causing an electrical fire. As the narrator wryly says: 'Well, if that was in a movie I wouldn't believe it.'

The film's title refers to the main Valley thoroughfare Magnolia Boulevard, which acts as a geographical spine for the film's action. But Anderson validated his choice when he discovered that eating the bark of a magnolia tree is rumoured to help cure cancer – the disease eating its way through the elder characters. Anderson also became aware of Magonia, in his words 'a mythical place above the firmament where shit just goes and hangs out before it falls from the sky'. It echoes the work of the scientific sceptic Charles Fort, whose 1919 work *The Book of the Damned* theorized the existence of Genesistrine, a kind of sky-borne Super-Sargasso Sea above the earth from which living things were dumped every so often.

Given that *Boogie Nights* took just $24 million domestic, Anderson manoeuvred himself into the perfect position for directing *Magnolia*, cajoling New Line's Michael De Luca into giving him final cut on a $35 million budget. The film would ultimately return just $22.4 mil-lion in the U.S., despite the presence of Tom Cruise. No doubt far more concerned with his investment in Peter Jackson's *Lord of the Rings* trilogy, De Luca was nevertheless pleased to have a genuine ground-breaker on his books. Calling it 'a cinematic wake-up call illustrating what ails us at the end of the century', he set aside $150,000 for Anderson to create alternative posters and trailers for the film, and gave him approval over the film's web site design. This was Anderson's film and nobody was going to mess with it; the paranoia from his time on *Hard Eight* lingered on.

Anderson wrote the film over eight months, though the majority was done in the final fortnight (with one week spent locked inside William H. Macy's cabin in Vermont). It would eventually earn him the second Best Original Screenplay Oscar nomination of his career. As ever, he wrote characters with specific actors in mind, returning to work with several actors from his rapidly expanding troupe. 'In the case of this movie, the actors dictated the form,' he says. 'It was my desire to be around them that led to so many stories, so many characters.' He and Reilly had already co-created Jim, having come up with his character a couple of summers before (even working out some of his character arc by filming several spoofs of the reality show *Cops*).

Anderson had a definite plan for each actor. He wanted Hoffman 'to play a really simple, uncomplicated, caring character'; he wanted to see Moore 'explode'; he wrote a 'big, tearful, emotional part' for Macy. As for Jimmy, Anderson and Baker Hall sat down together and watched old game shows from the 1950s onwards. The character became a composite of the likes of the iconic former radio personality Arthur Godfrey, who pioneered the musical variety format, and Bob Barker, host of *The Price Is Right* – both of whom were not as clean cut as their television images suggested. 'We watched hours of these guys – going all the way back,' says Baker Hall. 'We watched to get a flavour of who these guys were. How these guys were adept at presenting a certain public image.'

One of the film's genuine revelations is Tom Cruise, who was rightly awarded a Golden Globe and an Oscar nomination for his work. Impressed by *Boogie Nights*, the actor had called Anderson when he was in London, and invited him to the set of *Eyes Wide Shut*. Anderson saw Kubrick's swansong during post-production on *Magnolia*. 'When I saw *Eyes Wide Shut*, I realized what had appealed to Tom [about the role in *Magnolia*]. Two years doing that movie, such a repressed character, he holds so much in. This part is 180 degrees opposite. I think he was anxious to do something different.'

It is Cruise's character of Frank who falls prey to the notion that the past will eventually catch up with you, a feeling that reverberates through the film. During his interview with the inquisitive journalist Gwenovier (April Grace), he claims 'the most useless thing in the world is that which is behind me'. Yet within the space of a few hours, he will – having been exposed as a liar in attempting to cover up his family history – be confronted face to face with his past. A father he hasn't seen for years, a man he hates for cheating on his mother and deserting her as she sunk to her deathbed: by the end of the film he is kneeling by him, tears in his eyes.

If we hadn't already guessed, the bond of father and child is a central preoccupation for Anderson. While vomiting in the toilet, Donnie remembers that 'the sins of the father laid upon the children' comes from both *The Merchant of Venice* and Exodus 20:5, lending the film the classical weight of tragedy. Frank and Claudia suffered, respectively, at the hands of Earl and Jimmy, while Donnie has been treated as a meal ticket by his parents. Donnie's life obviously foreshadows the fate of Stanley, also treated as a commodity by his father.

But just as *Boogie Nights* finished on a tender note of reconciliation, so *Magnolia* follows suit. After the rain – and it has, unusually for Los Angeles, been torrential for most of the film – a gap in the clouds appears. Jim gives Donnie the benefit of the doubt after capturing him breaking and entering; Stanley confronts his father – even if he is told to 'go to bed'. Frank has reached some sort of understanding with his father, while Linda survives her overdose. Claudia and her mother are reunited, even if Jimmy is now dead. For the Catholic-raised Anderson, sin, guilt and redemption are almost black and white. As the return of Jim's mislaid gun proves, there is an order to the cosmic chaos in Anderson's universe. Its inhabitants may not understand it – but it's there. These are misguided souls, looking for any way to survive at the end of the millennium.

You all think America is Satan, right?
Private Conrad Vig, *Three Kings*

While P. T. Anderson was contemplating life, the universe and everything, David O. Russell was more interested in pricking patriotic Americans into re-examining the decade's most prominent international conflict. Given the incendiary subject matter – four U.S. soldiers decide to steal from Saddam Hussein's illicit gold reserves – that *Three Kings* ever got made was something of a miracle. By comparison to the small-scale *Spanking the Monkey* and *Flirting with Disaster*, it was a major step up for Russell. With three bona fide (and at the time, rising) stars in the shape of George Clooney, Mark Wahlberg and Ice Cube, as well as major studio backing from Warner Bros. to the tune of $48 million, *Three Kings* eventually grossed $60.6 million in the U.S. But, right from the beginning, there was dissent in the ranks, the conflicts on screen mirrored by the war of attrition behind the scenes.

Chief among the mutineers was Clooney, who objected, in his own words, to Russell 'humiliating, yelling and screaming at crew members who weren't allowed to defend themselves'.[106] Their on-set altercation came during the shooting of the film's climactic scene, after Clooney spied Russell knocking an extra to the ground, by way of demonstrating how he wanted a scene to be played out. It was an act that led an irate Clooney, who would later accuse Russell of 'homogenizing' the political tone of the piece to make it more studio friendly, to intervene. The director replied: 'He never said anything about that to me the entire time we were shooting. I don't know what the fuck he is talking about . . . I think George is super-invested in making himself look like a good guy all the time. I think George will be president.'[107]

Stemming from an article in *Vanity Fair*, this was the first time Russell spoke on the subject. As he told me, 'For five years, I just thought, "This is ridiculous." I couldn't believe he was still talking about it. It still astonishes me. The only reason I said something in *Vanity Fair* was because I couldn't believe he was still saying something after five years. I finally said, "Well, that's enough. I'm going to have to tell him to go fuck himself." I'll say something if it's on my mind. I'll call a spade a spade. But if you don't get along, what's the big deal? Why do you have to turn it into a jihad?'

Not unlike the two wars in the Middle East and their media coverage, Hollywood feuds rarely happen as they are reported. The subterfuge offered up by studios' publicity departments rather recalls *Three Kings'* NBS journalist Adriana Cruz (Nora Dunn), as she cries despairingly, 'I've been managed by the military' – something that no doubt appealed to that master of spin, Warner Bros. executive vice president Lorenzo di Bonaventura, when he greenlit the script. But for once, director and star had no wish to repress their feelings, even if rumours, gossip and embellishments clouded events out in the field.

'They really don't like each other,' confirms Catherine Hardwicke, Russell's production designer. 'David is an amazing person. He's really focused and has a unique brain that George didn't exactly appreciate or get. I didn't get it at first either, but gradually I started to figure out how his mind works, and it's definitely not the same way that everybody else's mind works. Which is probably why he doesn't make movies like everybody else. He's a special person – you can love him, you can hate him. But he really tries to push it – testing you and doing some outrageous things.'

But shots were being fired at Russell from all sides. The core of Russell's screenplay came from a script written by John Ridley, entitled *Spoils of War*. Inspired by John Huston's *The Treasure of the Sierra Madre* (1948), Ridley's effort was devoid of the political content that would eventually dominate Russell's work, preferring to concentrate on the themes of greed and betrayal. Ridley, according to Russell, 'started playing the jilted writer', quibbling over his credit (he eventually received 'story by' and 'co-producer' before it was taken to a WGA arbitration). The director was typically blunt in his response. 'I don't understand what his whining is about because it's the most common experience in Hollywood. You write a script, you sell it and get paid. Goodbye. You're lucky you're not rewritten 700 times. If he wants to direct his own scripts, he should control them a little bit.'[108]

It's this ballsy, gung-ho attitude of Russell's that fed into the bloodstream of *Three Kings*. A heist thriller with a political conscience, it prefigured the likes of Gregor Jordan's *Buffalo Soldiers* (2001) with its satirical missiles aimed squarely at Uncle Sam. 'I thought it was deeply ironic that Saddam was left in power and allowed to crush a democratic uprising in his own country,' Russell has stated. 'It was one of the things that captured my interest for the story . . . leaving the dictator in place – it seemed strange to me.' Whether or not Russell homogenized the story as Clooney suggested, it undeniably acts as a critique of the U.S. government, and how it sends its soldiers into a situation they have little hope of understanding. 'I don't even know what we did here – can you tell me what we did here?' says Archie Gates (Clooney) – the world-weary Special Forces Major just two weeks from retirement. Surveying the destruction around him, Archie infers that this is not 'a good war' (as World War II is often called).

It therefore makes perfect sense that Archie and his mercenary peers should attempt to raid Saddam's stolen gold. What they find – aside from the Kuwaiti bullion – is a civil war, in which the Republican Guard is wiping out Shi'ite rebels, misled into thinking the American military will back their rebellion. It makes less sense, however, that Gates and his posse should jettison their greedy ambitions for the chance to help the rebels, a narrative turn Russell was no doubt advised to take in order to get the film made.

40 Mark Wahlberg, George Clooney and Ice Cube in *Three Kings*.

While the protagonists may not be as morally ambiguous as those in, say, Robert Altman's Korean War–set *M*A*S*H*, (1972), *Three Kings* remains a veritable high-wire act, Russell balancing the generic constraints of an action-adventure film with moments of absurdist comedy. It's a world where Bart Simpson dolls are tied to the front of U.S. Army–issue jeeps, and maps to $23 million worth of Kuwaiti gold are found in someone's arse crack. The population of a town cries over (a tanker of) spilt milk, while an Iraqi soldier watches the Rodney King beating on TV.

With easy-listening classics like Chicago's 'If You Leave Me Now' blaring from tape decks, and stashes of denim jeans and Mercedes cars, Russell demonstrates just how far Western culture has bled into the Middle East (and vice versa, with Ice Cube's Sgt Chief Elgin praying alongside the Muslims). As if to emphasize this, Carter Burwell's score – far more free-form than his almost classical composition for *Being John Malkovich* – fuses Asian, Middle Eastern and Western influences into what sounds like a half-demented jazz riff. Meanwhile, as the U.S. grunts party hard to the sound of Public Enemy's 'Can't Do

Nuttin' for Ya Man', former (white) rapper Wahlberg is seen to sing along, reminding us that ethnic culture has been appropriated in all sorts of ways.

Much of the film is designed to deflate cultural stereotypes, be they Iraqi or American, and force us to consider the conflict from multiple angles. 'She looks much shorter in person,' comments one Iraqi soldier to another when they see Adriana on TV, a line that does as much to humanize the 'enemy' as any wartime woe we hear. Russell takes care to show us that the U.S. grunts are regular Joes, blue and white collar workers with wives and daughters just a phone call away. And just as Elgin points out that the redneck attitudes of Private Conrad Vig (Spike Jonze) are not universally held by all American soldiers, and it's not part of their training to kill every Arab, so we glimpse frightened Iraqi civilians spitting on images of Saddam. Later on, as two fathers from opposing sides – Troy Barlow (Mark Wahlberg) and Captain Said (Saïd Taghmaoui) – come face to face, Russell underlines the indiscriminate cruelty of war. 'We're both fathers,' pleads Troy. 'I'm not a father anymore,' spits Said, as we cut to a shot of an Iraqi child caught in a blast.

Nothing is black and white out in the sun-bleached deserts; we are all creatures 'in God's country', as U2's Bono opines over the closing credits. It's a theme that rains across the whole film like shell fire. Take the early scene where Conrad, Elgin and Troy argue over the correct racial termi-nology to use when talking about Arabs. Objecting to the use of 'dune coon' and 'sand nigger', the black Elgin instructs Conrad – confused over the 'pro-Saudi, anti-Iraqi language' – to limit his racial slurs to the less offensive (in his hypocritical eyes) 'towel head' or 'camel jockey'. Race, like the army, has a rank and file. The soldiers are like ignorant tourists, communicating with the locals via cartoon instructions they have been issued with, that patronisingly demonstrate in gaudy graphics how the captives will be given food and shelter if they surrender.

Most potently – and prophetically, given the subsequent invasion of Iraq in 2003 – American imperialism is shown as the dominating force. 'Everything you stole from Kuwait belongs to us now,' announces Archie, in an uncomfortable moment that speaks volumes about U.S. involvement in the Middle East. It is lines like this, almost throwaway on delivery, that are Russell's most powerful weapons. Amir Abdulah (Cliff Curtis), one of the Shi'ite rebels rescued by the U.S. contingent from a gruesome torture contraption, mentions he was 'nearly in the black' until his cafés were all bombed by the U.S., while another Iraqi explains that all he wants to do is start a salon. Such moments resonate far harder than the sequence where Troy is tortured by his captors by being made to swallow oil, clumsily symbolising what the war was really fought over.

Despite being shot in the Arizona desert, everything about the film reeks of authenticity. From the opening desert drive (shot in Mexico), these are not the golden sand dunes of *Lawrence of Arabia* but a dusty and cracked de-saturated landscape that simply serves to disorientate us (as the camera's initial panic-stricken movements suggest). In fact, the only colour not drained in that sequence is the bright yellow of the button badge worn on Troy's helmet, showing us the one thing that is important to him – his baby daughter. While Wahlberg reputedly took a real electric shock in the torture scene for the sake of realism, far more impressive was the fabulous detail in Hardwicke's production design. From the images of Saddam on everything from walls to tea towels, to the tubular bunkers (taken from plans bought by the Iraqis from European designers), there is a great sense in the film of opening our eyes to a world that we could previously only imagine.

It's made all the more remarkable by the lack of information that was available to Hardwicke. 'I got on the Internet,' she explains.

I found refugees from Iraq that were living in Arizona, and I got them to show me their scrap books! I've been in a lot of Third World countries – and I just tried to piece it together the best I could. It turned out to be pretty damn accurate. I figured out that some bunkers would be in existing buildings, old buildings. The Kuwaiti embassy gave me a lot of books of photographs – one called *The Evidence*, had no words, just photos of shit they did over there. Now we know a lot more about what Iraq looks like, but four years ago, we didn't know that much, and it was really hard to get information. During the second Gulf War, David and I are calling each other going, 'Did you see that on the TV? It looked just like what we did!'

Ironically, it's a computer-generated sequence that stands out as the film's most shocking scene. Early on, as Conrad complains to Archie how neither he nor his fellow soldiers have seen any action, he is given a demonstration of just how damaging one bullet can be. Pointing two cocked fingers, he 'shoots' Troy, and an imaginary bullet travels into his innards. 'The worst thing about a gunshot wound, providing you survive the bullet, is something called sepsis . . . it creates a cavity of dead tissue,' explains Gates. 'It fills up with bile and bacteria and you're fucked.' As we watch the green liquid spill into the cavity, this is Russell's warning shot – one to say that every bullet counts in this film, and they're going to hurt.

With Conrad – a man evidently raised on 'movie culture', as Russell has said[109] – pictured blasting off a shotgun on his shooting range back in America, the film demonstrates how desensitized we have become to screen violence. Cinematographer Newton Thomas Sigel's stylish rendering of bullet fire – all swish-pans, slow shutter speeds and snap-zooms – is designed to suspend in time the moment when a shell is fired, thus magnifying the emotional as well as physical impact. If anything, Russell attempts to make the link between the act of warfare and news coverage (and, by inference, filmmaking). The point is made right from the opening line of the film. 'Are we shooting . . . are we shooting people or what?' yells Troy, before proceeding to shoot down a gun-carrying Iraqi with a bullet to the neck.

With Russell being the first major Hollywood director since Oliver Stone to tackle a contemporary international conflict, only Ed Zwick's *Courage Under Fire* (1996) had previously used Operation Desert Storm as a backdrop to its story. To be fair, there was little objection from Warner Bros. executives to the political content of *Three Kings*. 'I think Warner Bros. understood from the get-go that it was a provocative film critical of the United States,' said Russell to the press corps at the Berlin Film Festival in February 2000. 'There was one attempt, by a high level executive, to pull the plug on it when we were in pre-production . . . But they never tried to make it more patriotic than it was. I think that most Americans in their gut feel that the war was not as it was presented; that there was something about it that was compromised and not quite the big celebration that was presented in 1991.' But this was pre-9/11, pre-Bush Mark II, a freewheeling period in American history when oral sex in the Oval Office was the most newsworthy topic of the day. As Russell discovered when it came to the DVD release of *Three Kings* (see below), the climate changed drastically at the company. 'I don't think they'd even make *Three Kings* today, quite honestly. Since they were acquired by AOL, they've become far more conservative.'

That said, it wasn't as if the studio first announced the film to the masses as a stringent anti-war statement. The trailer, for example, cut to an infectious Beach Boys vibe, plays up the action sequences and comic elements of the film, the narrator announcing that, 'Three soldiers want to go home . . . rich!' As one-dimensional as this is – Russell himself felt the campaign was 'too rock 'n' roll' – it was no doubt this strategic marketing that took the film past the $60 million mark at the U.S. box office. 'An unpatriotic anti-war statement . . . coming soon to a cinema near you' just wouldn't have worked.

But as you would expect, Russell is in full belief that that's exactly what *Three Kings* – from its ironic title downwards – is.

> I think there are many things in it that are deeply disturbing about the nature of war – a war that was presented as an antiseptic war and a computer-chip war was, in fact, much messier and much less successful than it was presented. Is it a political film? Yeah – mostly it's an action-adventure that has political textures to it. There's something of a political exposé to it. I don't think most people realized what really happened at the end of that war. We showed this in the White House to President Clinton and he said he thought it was an important film for the American people because they need to know how that war really ended, because that was not how that war was presented to them.

Whether the people took any notice or not, *Three Kings* remains a landmark effort, proving political satire can score at the box office. An occupation of territory previously ruled by the likes of Billy Wilder (*Stalag 17*, 1953), Stanley Kubrick (*Paths of Glory*, 1957) and Robert Altman (*M*A*S*H*, 1970), it indicated the importance of Russell's role in contemporary American cinema. It may hinge on a moral note of selfless gesture, as the U.S. soldiers decide to help the rebels in an awkwardly upbeat narrative switch, but between such conventional Hollywood parameters, *Three Kings* is as subversive as they come.

In 2004, Russell contacted executives at Warner Bros., suggesting they re-release *Three Kings* theatrically in the run up to the 2004 U.S. elections. With the idea of re-packaging the film for a Special Edition DVD, Russell suggested he shoot a documentary to supplement the DVD and the film's second run. He proposed a no-frills set of interviews with a variety of talking heads concerning the 2003 Gulf War, ultimately to be entitled *Soldiers Pay*.[110] Given $200,000 and five weeks to turn it round, Russell duly did this with the help of docu-mentarian friends Tricia Regan and Juan Carlos Zaldívar. 'We did this like a fire drill,' says Russell, though he was unable to douse the blaze the film would cause.

It was reported in *The New York Times* that Russell wanted *Soldiers Pay* to be screened before the 2004 U.S. election. As Russell notes, 'that set off all these alarm bells at Warner Bros. and they disassociated themselves from it'. The studio's lawyers argued that the Federal Election Committee might call the documentary 'soft-money' – in other words, unofficial support for a candidate outside of the 'hard money' each party is allowed to receive. After retrieving the rights from Warner Bros., Russell managed to get independent distributor Cinema Libre to put it into theatres. The Independent Film Channel also aired it the night before the election.

The interviews included perspectives from all sides – from robotic Republican senator David Dreier towing the party line, to a number of Iraqis who acted in *Three Kings*. Divided into a series of topics, the main focus winds up being on the U.S. military. Major General Michael Myatt, of the U.S. Marine Corps, states that by going into Iraq 'we have, in fact, made the situation worse'. Two interviewees explain how. In the section entitled 'Requisitions', Sergeant Matt Novak, a veteran of the Desert Storm conflict, states how he was told to loot anything they needed, from computers to VCRs and even cars. 'What-ever we needed, we took,' he notes, adding that he'd also been told that when he returned to the U.S. he'd need counselling, or else he'd walk into a department store and automatically take what he wanted.

In a segment called 'The Money Find' – 'which so mirrored *Three Kings*', as Russell put it – Novak and his fellow soldier Jamal Mann came across millions of dollars in new and used bills. As Mann tells us, 'It felt pretty good finding that money . . . I wanted everything.' They walked away with $4 million – but were caught, with Novak con-demned by his superiors for not controlling the situation and given a dishonourable discharge. American soldiers have been trained to regard the Middle East as a supermarket, according to Russell. 'We don't really care who owns the supermarket or how they treat their employees.' As he points out, American soldiers 'were told to requisi-tion like a conquering army, which is not what you do if you want to win hearts and minds'.

Self–improvement is masturbation. Now self-destruction . . .
  Tyler Durden, *Fight Club*

While *Three Kings* tempered its opinions with humour, *Fight Club* didn't bother. An ode to anarchy, David Fincher's film delivers a relentless visual and verbal battering that leaves you punch-drunk with its power. The cinematic equivalent of a back-alley bare-knuckle scrap, it's a film that just doesn't play by the rules. Like a bruise that has yet to discolour the skin, its full importance – not only as a film with its finger on the pulse of a generation's pre-millennial angst, but as a touchstone in contemporary filmmaking – has yet to be determined.

At the 1999 Venice Film Festival, where it received its world premiere the same year as *Being John Malkovich*, it caused a furore loud enough to wake the dead. Tyler Durden, the agent provocateur who organizes the eponymous underground boxing matches in the film, may implore that you 'do not talk about fight club', but nobody listened in the clamour to denounce it. 'I think we have another *Crash* on our hands,' declared Alexander Walker. He would later call it 'an inadmissible assault on personal decency . . . in line with the current but threatening revival of Nazism'.[111] He also noted that the film was 'anti-capitalism, anti-society and, indeed, anti-God' – though the impish Fincher would later reply that he'd have loved to put that quote on the poster. As reactionary as Walker was, when you have lines like, 'In all probability God hates you . . . we are God's unwanted children', you can see why it would rile some critics: *Fight Club* put you in either the red corner or the blue.

Since its disappointing box office (in the U.S. it took in $37 million, recouping just over half its $68 million budget), it has become one of the largest selling DVDs in Twentieth Century Fox's history. It's a vindication in particular for the former Chairman-CEO of Fox Filmed Entertainment, Bill Mechanic, who greenlit the project. A former Disney executive who joined the company as president in 1993, he became chairman in 1996. In his time he steered James Cameron's potential disaster *Titanic* to a safe port, with Fox taking the lion's share of the $1.8 billion gross (split with Paramount). With films like *The Phantom Menace* and *Independence Day* (1996) also financial hits, you could be forgiven for thinking his tenure was an unmitigated success. But Hollywood – or in this case Mechanic's bosses at News Corporation, Rupert Murdoch and his underling Peter Chernin – had a short memory. That Edward Norton's character in *Fight Club* uses the pseudonym of Rupert while attending a group therapy session probably didn't go down well either.

A well-liked, down-to-earth guy by all accounts, Mechanic was one of the few studio executives willing to take risks on projects that were not obvious commercial successes. He helped lure Terrence Malick out of hiding for *The Thin Red Line*, and signed the cheque for Warren Beatty's political satire *Bulworth* (1998). But *Fight Club* was the last straw. It flopped just as *Anna and the King* (1999) and the animated sci-fi story *Titan AE* (2000) lost money for the studio. At the same time, Mechanic was renegotiating his contract. Industry insiders had it that Chernin broke off talks, essentially firing Mechanic. While later confessing *Fight Club*'s budget was excessive, Mechanic felt the $17.5 million paid to Pitt, who plays Tyler, was justified. 'I thought the movie should have been made for less. David [Fincher] had a bigger vision of the movie. The only commercial way the movie could get made was with Brad. In truth, maybe I should not have made the movie or waited for the price to go down.'

As miraculous as the Virgin Birth, the production of *Fight Club* made the go-ahead for *Three Kings* look like Warner Bros. were writing a check for a Jim Carrey comedy. It was distributed by a company owned by the arch-exponent of the very capitalist system the protagonists of the film aim to dismantle, which was also the organization that Fincher clashed with during the making of *Alien³*. The incorrigible producer Art Linson – who had met Fincher while he was editing *Alien³* and called him 'somebody whose ambition is to maul and excite' – remembers the film's legendary first screening for Fox executives. Not unlike Fincher's first screening of *Se7en*, it left the audience white-knuckled and numb. 'I figured [Mechanic] was already privately rehearsing how to explain this time bomb to Murdoch and Chernin. This left him even more preoccupied. When he finally spoke to Fincher, he muttered something brave like, "Powerful, very powerful . . ."'[112]

Mechanic had no idea. Edward Norton, who plays the nameless narrator, a corporate drone who comes to reject his comfort zone for a life less ordinary, summed up the film's cultural impact with typical perspicacity. 'It's the kind of movie that made me want to get into movies – in league with *Dr. Strangelove*, *A Clockwork Orange*, *Taxi Driver* or *Raging Bull*. All of which were, in some ways, too intense, and too pointed in terms of their analysis of things that were dysfunctional in the culture of the time, for people to take in at the moment. None of those films were commercially successful, and all got a certain reactionary response from narrow-minded people. But all became hallmarks of the Zeitgeist, and I can feel that happening already for people of my generation with *Fight Club*.'

Despite effectively losing his position, Mechanic remains convinced of the film's longevity. 'You'll still watch *Fight Club* in twenty years. *Fight Club* has a life. If you go back in time, *Citizen Kane* and *It's a Wonderful Life* failed but they were important movies.'[113] The film's title has since entered into the modern lexicon, an event that may not be particularly significant but nevertheless goes some way towards indicating how pervasive the film's potency is. Articles about real-life fight clubs – from the so-called teenage 'Backyard Wrestling' fanatics who practise violent acts on each other across Britain's council estates to more adult underground groups – have littered the media, as journalists persistently attempt to link Fincher's film to copycat groups.

Little wonder it has been dubbed *A Clockwork Orange* for its generation. Considerably boosting the cult appeal of its source novel (by Chuck Palahniuk) just as Kubrick's film did for Anthony Burgess's novella, all it needed was for Fincher to withdraw the film for fear of threats to his family and the parallels would be complete. For the record, Fincher claims he's not that familiar with Kubrick's film. During *Fight Club*'s release, the accusations that it promoted fascism became hysterical, with cries against the film's cynical opportunism. Comparisons to Nazi Germany were cited: that Tyler sells soap made from bags of fat stolen from liposuction clinics to department stores recalled the Holocaust; that his Fight Club minions, the Space Monkeys, were like Hitler's Brown Shirts. Even Fincher himself has compared the assembly to the Nuremberg Rally. But surely this was missing the point. Unlike the horribly black and white *American History X*, which cast Norton as a neo-Nazi who reforms after a spell in prison, *Fight Club* is slippery in its discourse.

In an era that has seen the extreme right wing on the march again, particularly in Europe, it may be a reminder that such movements can form with frightening speed. But as Tyler watches his juvenile pranksters evolve into the nihilistic faction that puts his so-called Project Mayhem into practice, it becomes obvious that those involved are no more liberated than in the days when they wore a shirt and tie.

If fascism is a political movement formed to lead us in a new direction, the drones of Project Mayhem – with their mantra-like chanting and their adherence to secrecy – have no direction at all. In Project Mayhem, you do not ask questions, you have no identity and, it would seem, you have no solutions.

From the point where Jack (the name Norton's character gives himself) blackmails his boss to get computers and 'corporate sponsorship', to the revelation that Tyler has been criss-crossing the country setting up Fight Club 'franchises', Fincher and screenwriter Jim Uhls underline the point that big business and terrorism are interchangeable. If *Fight Club* is an apology for fascism, then it's only because we are all already in its grip – albeit of a corporate kind. If it's violent, then it is about the violence in us all, our penchant for 'self-destruction', as advocated by Tyler and demonstrated by Jack as he beats himself up in his boss's office.

The film is far more concerned with the plight of men in the late twentieth century. At the time of its release, the feminist author Susan Faludi's book *Stiffed* was published, arguing that men are the new oppressed gender. Stripped of his role as sole breadwinner, yet still supplanted in the house, the 1990s man, according to Faludi, is 'invited to fill the void with consumption and a gym-bred display of his ultra-masculinity'. She compares the contemporary emasculated man – no longer appreciated in the home or able to earn a reliable wage – to the women of the mid–twentieth century who filled their void with such vacuous activities as shopping.

Fight Club touches on similar themes. As Tyler tells Jack at one point, 'We're a generation of men raised by women.' In a particularly cruel visual representation of Faludi's point, *Fight Club* gives us Bob (Meat Loaf) – a man who has developed 'bitch tits' from hormone treatment after losing both his testicles. Indeed, a fear of castration runs through the entire film. As Jack bemoans the loss of his condo, Tyler recalls the painful real-life case of Lorena and John Wayne Bobbit: 'It could be worse. A woman could cut off your penis while you're sleeping and toss it out of the window of a moving car.' Relationship anxiety also resonates at the film's heart: Jack muses that the whole story began 'with a girl named Marla Singer' (Helena Bonham Carter), leading to a love triangle with Tyler and Jack as perverse as the one seen in *Being John Malkovich*.

With unswerving brilliance *Fight Club* depicts how soulless and disposable society has become. Emotional catharsis, from the support groups attended by Jack, is as convenient as the single-serving sachets he is given while shuttling between JFK and LAX. Like Lindsay Anderson's *O Lucky Man!* (1973), this is Fincher's state-of-the-nation address, as he fills his landscape with the depressing debris of contemporary living. Technology has overtaken us and the workplace has depersonalized us, as suggested by Jack's nomadic existence as a recall coordinator (inspecting accidents for an automobile company, surely in a nod to J. G. Ballard's novel *Crash*).

Following *Alien³* and *The Game*, the film completes an unconscious trilogy about the dangers of corporate capitalism. Though unlike the fictional 'Company' or Consumer Recreation Services, the targets here seem to be more pointed – the 'IBM stratosphere, the Microsoft galaxy, Planet Starbucks', as Jack notes. Modern life is rubbish and, as Tyler rightly claims, we are 'consumers . . . the things you own end up owning you'. His impassioned speech to Jack – 'a slave to the IKEA nesting instinct', as he admits – says volumes about a society spinning out of control. 'What concerns me is celebrity magazines, televisions with five hundred channels, some guy's name on my underwear . . . I say stop being perfect. I say let's evolve!'

While Russell was attempting to smuggle political rhetoric inside a formulaic Hollywood film, Fincher made no attempt to hide his social vitriol in a similar 'comfortable' framework. Ensuring the film veers between satire, farce and black comedy, leaving the audience bewildered as to where they stand in relation to what's on show, Fincher *is* Tyler, pissing in the Hollywood soup tureen from a great height. From mangling the pretty-boy looks of actor Jared Leto (who plays the aptly named Angel Face) to perverting Bonham Carter's cherubic Merchant-Ivory image by casting her as Marla, Fincher is a cinematic terrorist. Unlike in the French director Gaspar Noé's work, however, the subversion is surreptitious. Why else would Fincher insert a subliminal full-frontal shot of a man's penis right at the end of the film – echoing Tyler's night-time profession as a projectionist who wilfully splices pornographic images into children's cartoons?

Fincher plays with the notion that images can corrupt, while at the same time simultaneously deconstructing film language, notably in the hilariously postmodern moment when we are informed about the 'cigarette burns' (the white dots glimpsed in the corner of the cinema screen denoting a reel change) – done to remind us that what we are watching is an artificial construct. A man often quoted as saying 'I just try to do my work and live it down,' Fincher may not wish to incite a people's revolution, but he surely wants to plant a nail bomb inside the Hollywood system. As good as Pitt is in the film (a role prefigured by his unhinged revolutionary in Terry Gilliam's *Twelve Monkeys*), it's the glee with which Fincher tarnishes his actor's airbrushed image in those 'celebrity magazines' that is truly captivating. The sight of his glistening six-pack, which has probably never looked better, smeared with the blood of another is hardly likely to have bolstered his female fan base.

Just as Jack notes that 'even a hummingbird couldn't catch Tyler at work', the same could be said of Fincher. He spent much of the production sneaking stuff past the suits at Fox. According to Linson, producer Laura Ziskin wanted the giant nipples removed from Meat Loaf's fat suit with its oversized breasts; Fincher refused and won. As another example, Fincher cites a line by Marla: 'I want to have your abortion.' Neither executives nor preview viewers took too kindly to it. 'They wanted me to change that, but it was in the script and that had been approved,' says Fincher. 'So I said "If I change it, I'm going to shoot something and whatever goes in, has to stay." So I shot the line that says "I haven't fucked like that since grade school." They begged me to take it out!'

No doubt *Fight Club* looks and sounds like a Fincher film. Shot by Jeff Cronenweth – who graduated from camera operator on *Se7en* and second unit DOP on *The Game* – the drab, bleached-out look is an aesthetic we're more than used to from Fincher. The visual set-pieces are among the most memorable of his career to date: the multi-storey plunge taken by the camera to the basement car park housing a transit van of explosives; the aeroplane savagely ripped apart; the living IKEA catalogue Jack walks through; the visual swan-dive behind his kitchen cooker and fridge; Jack shooting his own head off (and leaving a see-through hole in Tyler's). All are the work of a director at the cutting edge, proof that Fincher is one of cinema's greatest current manipulators of the moving image.

Set, like *Se7en*, in an unspecified metropolis, events take place either at night or in dreary, lifeless interiors. Alex McDowell's production design has a deathly quality to it that matches the sallow skin of the insomniac Jack. In sickly shades of green and beige, we witness a world that feels as unhealthy as a cancerous lung. Only following the car crash – the point in the narrative immediately prior to the shock revelation that Jack *is* Tyler – does this change. A city of shadows and musty light finally sees the sun break through the clouds, as if we have reached a new dawn. Emphasizing the point, Jack's voice-over muses, 'Was I asleep?'

But does this metaphysical twist ending, like the finale in *The Game*, serve to undo what has gone before it? On closer inspection, it becomes apparent that Fincher has subliminally prepared the viewer for the revelation that Tyler and Jack are one and the same. In the opening sequence, in the high-rise building, Jack's voice-over reflects upon his and Tyler's anarchic actions: 'Think what *we've* become.' Later, upon meeting Tyler on the plane, he comments that they both own 'exactly the same briefcase'.

On at least three occasions, Fincher slices in a single frame shot of Tyler in the background – as Jack meets the doctor in the hospital corridor, behind the leader of the group therapy session and, initially, next to an office photocopier (suggesting he is a facsimile of Jack). And, of course, there's the sequence in which Jack awakens from a feverish dream in which he imagines Marla being made love to by a faceless well-toned torso – only to find that she has wormed her way into Tyler's bed next door. If that wasn't enough, as Jack checks Marla's breast for a lump, we see them looking into a cracked mirror, a heavy-handed symbol of his split personality.

By the time we see Jack punching his own face in a car park, the film lapses into swampy narrative territory as Fincher begs us not to think too hard. 'You want to forget about what you know . . . especially about you and me,' says Tyler, as if he's speaking to us. Asking an audience to buy into the 'change-over', as Jack puts it, stretches credibility. But Fincher's gamble is undoubtedly based on the fact that, by this point, we've been beaten into submission anyway, so what's one more punch to the face?

On a metaphorical level, however, this revelation has some validity. Disgusted and disillusioned by contemporary life, Jack conceives of Tyler, a Devil sitting on his shoulder, as a means of much-needed expression. Inside Everyman Jack rages the debate: bloody revolution, as prompted by Tyler, or not? Is terrorism the answer? By Jack's rejection of Project Mayhem, it would appear not. But, adding fuel to the fire, the film climaxes as Jack and Marla both watch the bombs detonating and society returning to Ground Zero, as Tyler earlier unnervingly called it. Fincher and Uhls changed the ending of the novel (which had Jack incarcerated in a mental home) to close the film on this note of moral ambiguity. Where does it leave us? Has terrorism triumphed anyway? Is such radical upheaval an inevitable consequence of any evolving society?

Fight Club asks more questions than it answers – and this is no doubt why so many critics have read the film as an irresponsible recipe for anarchy. But just as Lindsay Anderson's pipe dream *If . . .* did not precipitate the overthrowing of the public school system, so the most Fincher's film will ever inspire is a drunken punch-up in a pub parking lot. Even a film packing the wallop of *Fight Club* would do well to inspire a revolution in this apathetic age. Yet, as *Magnolia* and *Three Kings* also hinted, a Hollywood insurrection was underway. Lucas's *The Phantom Menace* may have topped that year's U.S. box office – its $431 million gross suggesting that the blockbuster was still king – but, like Tyler's Space Monkeys, the Sundance Kids were forming their own Project Mayhem from the inside.

41 Brad Pitt and Edward Norton *do* talk about *Fight Club*.

SECTION III: THE INSIDERS

King of the Hills:
Soderbergh Comes Back from the Brink

42 & 43 *Traffic*: Erika Christensen contemplates her fate; Benicio Del Toro and Jacob Vargas do the same.

For the first time in my life, I got people respecting me.
Erin Brockovich

Sunday, 25 March 2001: Oscar night. Packed to the bursting point, Los Angeles' Shrine Auditorium is shaken to its very foundations as Steven Soderbergh is awarded Best Director for *Traffic*. Mounting the podium, warmly greeted by the dazzling smile of presenter Tom Cruise, he looks shell-shocked. 'Suddenly, going to work tomorrow doesn't seem like such a good idea,' he utters. Beating Ang Lee (*Crouching Tiger, Hidden Dragon*), Ridley Scott (*Gladiator*) and Stephen Daldry (*Billy Elliot*), he defied the odds and even beat himself. The first director to be nominated twice in the same year since 1939, when Michael Curtiz was up for *Angels with Dirty Faces* and *Four Daughters* – and lost – Soderbergh was expected to split the vote. As it turned out, it was the drugs epic *Traffic*, and not the legal drama *Erin Brockovich*, that won him the prize.

It had already been a great ceremony for Soderbergh's two productions. *Traffic* had won Best Supporting Actor for Benicio Del Toro, Best Editing for Stephen Mirrione and Best Adapted Screenplay for newcomer Stephen Gaghan. *Erin Brockovich* had brought Julia Roberts her first Oscar for Best Actress; Albert Finney was in the same category as Del Toro; Susannah Grant lost out – to Cameron Crowe for *Almost Famous* – for Best Original Screenplay. Both movies also lost out to *Gladiator* in the Best Picture stakes. But back from the brink, it was Soderbergh's triumph that was most significant. His speech was easily the most gracious of the night: 'I want to thank anyone who spends part of their day creating,' he said. 'I don't care if it's a book, a film, a painting, a dance, a piece of theatre, a piece of music. Anybody who spends part of their day sharing their experience with us . . . I think this world would be unlivable without art.'

Without doubt, as an artist, Soderbergh was in his green period. From 14 March 2000 and the release of *Erin Brockovich*, via the December opening of *Traffic* that year, to the unveiling of *Ocean's Eleven* twelve months later, Soderbergh was under a lucky star. Collectively, in the U.S. alone, this trio of films grossed $432 million. He'll probably never experience anything like it again. 'Success,' he says, 'is like this mysterious person you meet at a party. You feel like you have this connection, you spend the night together, and you wake up the next morning and they're gone. Failure is like the house guest that won't leave. As a result, you can learn more from it. Success just feels like lightning struck. You could stand on the roof with a rod for the next two years and lightning wouldn't strike. You just can't conjure it.'

While it was no shock that *Ocean's Eleven*, Soderbergh's A-list remake of Lewis Milestone's so-so 1960 Rat Pack caper, should score highly, the other two were not quite the home-bankers they now seem. *Erin Brockovich* may have starred the indefatigable Roberts as the eponymous single mother-of-three – but despite the fairy-tale ending, the film was as far removed from *Pretty Woman* territory as you could wish. 'Despite how we felt about the movie – and I felt pretty good about it – I also knew it was slightly outside what Julia had done before,' says Soderbergh. 'It wasn't a romantic comedy. It was a drama and she had a foul mouth. I felt there was absolutely a possibility that people would say "I don't want to see her do that."'

Likewise *Traffic*, with its multiple plot lines (some of them subtitled) and tough subject matter, was not an obvious hit-in-the-making – though it took $124.1 million domestically, just $1.5 million shy of *Erin Brockovich*'s U.S. haul. Despite the presence of newlyweds Michael Douglas and Catherine Zeta-Jones, who don't even appear in the same story, most of the now-recognizable names were either drawn from the Soderbergh stable (Don Cheadle, Luiz Guzmán), or plucked from obscurity (Topher Grace, Erika Christensen) or history (Dennis Quaid, James Brolin). 'It was a film I wanted to get on as many screens as possible and I knew the subject matter needed to be neutralized in a way,' says Soderbergh. 'For a lot of people in America, the subject was going to be a turn-off, but if I could put enough movie stars in the movie, then maybe I could get them to come. I thought it would be interesting to see movie stars in this sort of aesthetic, which you don't normally see them in.'

After his years in the wilderness, despite admitting, 'I'm not prone to feelings of invincibility', Soderbergh must have met this trio of back-to-back home runs with a mixture of triumph and relief. Twelve years on from *sex, lies, and videotape*, he was once again the hottest director on the planet. But this time around, at least in the case of *Traffic*, the hype did not outweigh the project. If *Erin Brockovich* and

Ocean's Eleven were more about Soderbergh's ability to stay afloat in the mainstream, *Traffic* represented the biggest achievement of his career to date. With over 100 speaking parts, it was certainly his grandest undertaking. An urban epic that sets out to view the drugs supply chain from all angles, it opened up a debate by distilling the techniques honed on films like *Schizopolis* and *The Limey* into a narrative form palatable to a mainstream audience. 'Part of my whole career plan', says Soderbergh, 'was to pretend it's 1974 and that you can make movies for adults and they'll show up.'

Erin Brockovich never quite achieves this, feeling like a dry run for *Traffic*, with its social conscience worn more blatantly on its sleeve. Telling the true story of the inhabitants of Hinkley, many of whom were stricken with severe illnesses after the Pacific Gas and Electric Company allegedly contaminated the local water supply, *Erin Brockovich* is arguably Soderbergh's least interesting film. If the credits were stripped away you'd be unlikely to recognize it as part of his canon. His most conventional narrative – even more so than *King of the Hill* – it tells one subplot-free story without recourse to multi–time lines. Despite strong performances from Finney, who plays Ed Masry, the lawyer who hires Erin, and Aaron Eckhart, as Erin's dignified biker neighbour who becomes her boyfriend cum babysitter, the novelty of watching Julia Roberts stomp and swear her way through such a David and Goliath biopic soon wears off.

In retrospect, however, it's easy to see what attracted Soderbergh. 'It was again a test to see if I could step back, after having made two films that were much more obviously demanding,' he says. 'Put it this way, *Out of Sight* and *The Limey* are two movies where you're standing in front of the audience and waving your arms. *Erin* . . . is a movie in which I felt the director should take a seat behind the audience and shut up. Especially coming out of *The Limey*, I was desperate to do something that moved, in narrative terms, in one direction. Jersey Films had pitched the idea to me as I was finishing *Out of Sight*, and I hated it. Then, smartly, they persisted and called me up and sent me the script while I was cutting *The Limey*. Then suddenly it just seemed like the perfect thing for me to do.'

When Soderbergh came on board, the writer-director Richard La-Gravenese had been brought in to do an uncredited rewrite of Grant's sassy script. Soderbergh immediately immersed himself in the details of the PG&E case that Erin takes on, after she worms her way into Masry's law firm as a file clerk. You might easily imagine he became like the obsessive Erin, who, in the stand-out scene of the film, proves how dedicated she is to the case by randomly reciting any telephone number of any plaintiff. As Roberts testifies, 'Steven gave me a lot of stuff, a lot of transcripts of interviews he'd done with Erin and a lot of the people involved in the case. He shared a lot of that stuff with me.'

Not that Soderbergh knew it while *Erin Brockovich* was in production, but its release followed the tail end of a huge storm of controversy whipped up by Norman Jewison's *The Hurricane*, the true story of the wrongly imprisoned boxer Rubin Carter. It was widely believed that claims over the film's inauthentic depiction of events ensured its exclusion from many of the principal Oscar categories that year. 'There were a lot of charges of fabrication and distortion,' remembers Soderbergh. 'I was very sensitive to that; I did not want that argument to pull people off the point of the movie. My goal was that nobody from either side of this issue comes out of the woodwork and says "That was fabricated." I'd seen that happen. It was too public a case for me not to know that it was going to be scrutinized. I wanted to be even-handed about it.'

While the film includes such heartstring-tugging moments as the sight of a child suffering from leukemia or a woman recounting the loss of her uterus and breasts, Soderbergh maintains that he could have cranked up such scenes. 'Worse things went on that I didn't show. It was awful. I was trying to maintain a certain balance. I was trying to be fair and I wanted to be accurate. Fortunately, when the film came out, PG&E smartly made no comments whatsoever about the film. And most of the characters portrayed are sort of amalgams of real people . . . nobody popped up and said it didn't happen like that. People who were involved saw the movie and felt it was pretty close to what happened.'

For what could have easily descended into a 'disease-of-the-week' film, Soderbergh managed to steer it away from mawkish and maudlin sentimentality, while remaining compassionate towards the protagonists. With the inclusion of Sheryl Crow's 'Redemption Day' and 'Every Day Is a Winding Road' on the soundtrack, it's a feminist feel-good movie, the kind of story where the man plays house husband. In this lighter side of *sex, lies, and videotape*, Erin asserts her authority and independence, chirping, 'I don't need pity. I need a paycheck! I'm smart. I'm hard-working and I'll do anything.' Dressed in her short skirts, low-cut tops and industrial-sized earrings, Erin may not suggest female emancipation by her appearance but, as Roberts explains, her apparel is positive. 'I think she dresses the way she dresses because she thinks she's pretty and she thinks she packs a punch. And I quite agree. But I don't think she does it be overly sexual or manipulative. She doesn't give a fuck what anybody thinks, which I think is a great commentary on her self-esteem.'

Given that Roberts was already attached when Soderbergh came on board, it seems fitting that he took a back seat. As her Oscar underlined, this was her film, not his. Spitting out insults like an M-60 – 'That's all you got, lady. Two wrong feet and fucking ugly shoes!' – she relished the chance to ditch her Hollywood princess image. 'It was a case of "turn the camera on" and let her go,' says Soderbergh. 'She knew exactly what she was doing. In many ways, she was very close to that character. Having sensed that, purposely, I kept them apart. I didn't want her to imitate Erin and I felt like Julia's energy was already pretty close.'

While Soderbergh was forced to reshoot one scene 'because the ending wasn't working', he claims it's the most pleasure he's ever had making a film. 'I could shoot that movie for the rest of my life,' he says. But thematically speaking, what did it do for him? There is the idea of betrayal, which had arisen in a personal capacity in films like *sex, lies, and videotape* and *Schizopolis*, and would resurface in future efforts like *Full Frontal* and *Solaris*. Here, it emerges in the form of a $28 billion corporation's actions against a whole community, a theme already explored in *Kafka*.

This reuniting with Ed Lachman, who had shot *The Limey,* would be the last time to date that Soderbergh employed a cinematographer before taking over the duties himself. Like the direction, Lachman's work is unfussy and in no way self-conscious. Resisting the temptation to dabble with filters, as Soderbergh would for *Traffic*, Lachman also avoided the cinema verité look that an investigative biopic such as this might easily go for. As evidenced by Soderbergh's choice of veteran composer Thomas Newman to pen the uplifting score, every creative decision was made to service the story rather than make the audience aware of the filmmaking process.

Poverty-stricken in the beginning – to the point where she takes her children to a hamburger restaurant but cannot afford to buy her own meal – by the end, Erin's a millionaire. After PG&E settled the case for

$333 million – the largest settlement ever awarded in a direct-action lawsuit in the history of the United States – Erin was given $2 million by her boss. Without relying on a 'raised-fist courtroom scene at the end', it's the closest Soderbergh has ever come to giving us the American Dream.

We played the game like we had nothing to lose.
Danny Ocean, *Ocean's Eleven*

That is, until he delivered *Ocean's Eleven* – with its askew vision of his nation as the land of opportunity. It's set in Las Vegas, the symbolic hub of the Dream, and the gang of thieves who set out to procure $150 million from three of the city's most lucrative casinos are – in a subtle gag in the graceful finale – seen to be made of the right stuff. The sequence by the fountain as the gang drift away – set to Claude Debussy's luminous composition 'Claire de Lune' – is a direct echo of a scene in Philip Kaufman's 1983 depiction of the U.S. Mercury astronauts, when they all watch a dance sequence cut to the same tune. As in *The Right Stuff*, the gang all glance at each other with much the same sense of satisfaction. Soderbergh's crooks may not have won the space race, but their nefarious achievements are celebrated as if they have.

While the film may have 'no social value whatsoever', as Soderbergh puts it, it sets out to show what the gambling capital of the world has come to represent in this day and age, not unlike Martin Scorsese's *Casino* (1995). While Lewis Milestone's 1960 original documented the increasing significance of Las Vegas in America, Soderbergh allows his *Ocean's Eleven* to reflect the subsequent changes to the city. No longer the mob hang-out it used to be (though Andy Garcia's casino owner Terry Benedict seems to operate beyond the law), as Sam 'Ace' Rothstein explains in Scorsese's film, 'today it looks like Disneyland'. With the plot hinging around a Lennox Lewis fight – probably the most bloodshed in a very non-violent script – the film shows Las Vegas to have become the entertainment capital of the world. Why else would you find a dozen-odd movie stars kicking back and playing it cool? With David Holmes's funky score – including a forgotten Elvis Presley B-side 'A Little Less Conversation' – serving to further remind us of the calibre of performer to grace the city in the past, Soderbergh's film is nostalgic in a way. You can almost hear the cries of 'Viva Las Vegas!'

Made so that Frank Sinatra, Sammy Davis Jr and their cronies could gamble and give Milestone the high hand (often turning up to work at 3:00 p.m. and leaving three hours later), the 1960 version was, pretty much everyone agreed, a worthless vanity project. As Garcia notes: 'It doesn't really hold up that well. It's great to watch those guys in the movie. They're always great. You could watch them make coffee. For them, *Ocean's Eleven* was just an excuse to get together while they were hanging around. But as a movie it doesn't really hold up.' Just as John McTiernan's *The Thomas Crown Affair* (1999) remake improved on the original, Soderbergh's film managed the same. Paradoxically, though, this new millennium take on the story didn't have a chance of establishing the mythic legacy around its stars that the original achieved for the so-called Rat Pack. For starters, the likes of Brad Pitt, George Clooney and Matt Damon are too clean cut. Practical jokes on set were more the order of the day than carousing around the city with as many floozies as they could get their hands on. 'We're never gonna be as cool as those guys,' said Clooney, and he was right.

Ted Griffin, who had impressed Soderbergh with his script for the murky film noir *Best Laid Plans* (1999), kept only the bare bones of the Milestone film. That is, multiple casino robberies in Vegas undertaken by an eleven-strong gang, led by the suave crook Danny Ocean (Clooney). But even their coming together was vastly different. While Griffin's criminals are recruited from all across the underworld, Sinatra et al. had all known each other from their time in the 82nd Airborne Paratroopers – a fact that guarantees loyalty in the gang. Soderbergh did reference the original, however. A house of cards, for example, is constructed by Chinese acrobat Yen (Shaobo Qin) on the swimming pool diving board at the home of fellow gang member Reuben Tishkoff (Elliott Gould), a reference to the same party trick pulled by Joey Bishop and Akim Tamiroff in the 1960 film. But by keeping the title and Danny's name intact, it's evident that Soderbergh and his band of merry men wanted to announce that, while the film would be a mite slicker than its counterpart, the same easy-going spirit was the order of the day.

Of course, part of the reason for making the film was to gather together an A-list cast, the likes of which had not been seen since the days of films like *The Dirty Dozen* (1967) and *The Longest Day* (1962). After the script was sent to Clooney and Soderbergh by the legendary producer Jerry Weintraub (the man who handled Elvis Presley's comeback concert years before), word quickly got round. Pitt was cast as 'Rusty' Ryan, the man with the plan who is rarely seen without a bite to eat in his hand. Damon replaced Mark Wahlberg – who foolishly headed off to re-imagine *Planet of the Apes* (2001) for Tim Burton – as Linus Caldwell, the small-time pickpocket whose father was well respected by the criminal fraternity. Soderbergh's *Schizopolis* collaborator Eddie Jemison was cast as the tech-head Livingston Dell. Comedian Bernie Mac was brought on board to play Frank Catton, the inside man who has previously been working as a dealer in Atlantic City. Though Luke and Owen Wilson were originally cast (before they quit to make *The Royal Tenenbaums*), young guns Scott Caan and Casey Affleck were hired to play the bickering Malloy brothers, Turk and Virgil – who provide the group's mechanical muscle. And as the film's only Achilles heel, Don Cheadle was asked to play the explosives expert Basher Tarr, with a Cockney accent about as authentic as Guy Ritchie's.

With a gag that summed up the childlike humour of the piece, the film also included the credit 'introducing Julia Roberts', something her agent reputedly found less than funny. Roberts, with her hair piled high like Angie Dickinson in the original, plays the only significant woman in the film, Danny's ex-wife Tess. Currently Benedict's lover, she is one of the principal motivations for Danny to attempt to screw over the casino owner. Before she agreed to take the role, Roberts was sent a $20 bill by Clooney and Soderbergh, with a letter saying 'we heard you get 20 a picture'. While she was no doubt paid a little more than $20 for her role (particularly after back-end participation), this summed up how the cast members were willing to take drastic pay cuts to make the project happen.

Much of *Ocean's Eleven* is about showmanship. There are Yen's circus stunts, as he contorts himself into tiny spaces and back-flips across the vault to avoid setting off the alarm. Meanwhile, led by the veteran con-artist Saul Bloom (Carl Reiner), the final gang member who disguises himself as a Middle Eastern businessman to access the casino safe, several of the group are not themselves, taking on roles to assist the scam.

The art of the con, we learn, is like the discipline of acting; Rusty even teaches a group of young Hollywood actors (including Joshua Jackson and Topher Grace) to play poker. As he says, 'Today's lesson – how to draw out the bluff.' As we see, the robbery is all about bluffing Benedict. Building an exact replica of the Bellagio casino vault, the gang fool its owner into believing the real version is being robbed. Decoys – such as the remote-controlled van full of dummy money or the SWAT uniforms the gang use to get the real cash out – also litter the script. It's all about sleight of hand, with the Lennox Lewis boxing match and the power cut orchestrated by Basher to divert everyone's attention.

Not to be left out, Soderbergh ensures his direction is as slick as the suits in Rusty and Danny's wardrobes. Aside from achieving the near impossible, by making Las Vegas look beautiful rather than tacky, he pulls a number of narrative cons in time with the gang. Reuben's anecdote about the three most successful casino robberies in the city (all failed) is classic Soderbergh; cut to his voice-over and the sound of Berlin's 'Take My Breath Away' (rather apt, given the deft nature of the film), we see a rapid succession of three flashbacks. The first is in black and white, the second in colour (set in the 1970s) and the third filmed in colour and slow motion, as one robber actually manages to get out of the front door before being pegged back. Not forgetting the split-screens and flashy dissolves, there's also the beautiful moment where Basher watches on television the razing to the ground of Reuben's casino; as it crumbles, we see it collapse for real behind Basher, who happens to be in an apartment in a nearby skyscraper.

As Soderbergh explains, *Ocean's Eleven* provided a different sort of challenge to the films he'd made in the past. Like 'a very precise wind-up toy', the highly choreographed plot-driven script could not be improvised on the day. 'You can't decide, in the middle of a scene, that you want to do it a different way, or the whole thing will collapse.' As far as he was concerned, this was his version of *The Sting* (1973) or *The Hot Rock* (1972), an earlier Robert Redford film concerning a museum-set diamond heist. Rather than emulate the narcissism of the Milestone film, Soderbergh successfully sought to recall the 'sly humour' of these later caper films. As one critic put it, the director 'has contrived a circus-stunt *Rififi* with a robotic *Mission: Impossible* backbeat'[114] – presumably a reference to the sight of Clooney and Damon sliding down a metallic lift shaft in the casino like two Navy SEALs.

Perhaps with the exception of *Out of Sight*, this was the first time Soderbergh had to pay heed to the construction of full-on action sequences.

I was just trying to teach myself to think in visual terms in a way that I hadn't before. I was studying the work of certain directors that I felt knew how to lay things out. I was watching Fincher. I was watching McTiernan. And I was watching Spielberg stuff. To break down and analyse how they laid out their shots . . . those three guys, when they're shooting physical sequences, are just impossible to beat. Their gift for creating chronological imagery is really pronounced. I was trying to study the cutting patterns, and the composition and the movement. And I realized, when these guys get into an action sequence, they never fucking repeat a shot. Yet, no matter how fast they cut, you always know where you are. The geography is always clear. You're never confused. I find it really frustrating when I watch an action sequence and I don't know where I am. These guys really know how to do it. I kept watching their stuff, again and again, trying to pick that language up. And it was hard. I never felt comfortable with it, or fluent. I kept this mantra going of 'Don't repeat your shots.' They have to link from one to the next. I just tried to follow that train of thought through to the end.

It was something he more than achieved. In many ways, *Ocean's Eleven* is the perfect mainstream movie. Shallow it may be, but its unpretentious nature meant it delivered right on cue. Entirely focused on the heist – far-fetched but not enough to throw you off the scent – it is pared-down filmmaking. Like in *Erin Brockovich*, subplots were stripped away. Even the side story of Danny courting Tess winds up becoming central to the robbery. Like a double dose of Alka-Seltzer, *Ocean's Eleven* fizzes across the screen, nursing away your cares with its A-list sheen. Yes, it's a guilty pleasure – but one that reminds you of what you love about the movies.

Your government surrendered this war a long time ago.
Eduardo Ruiz, *Traffic*

In between *Erin Brockovich* and *Ocean's Eleven* came *Traffic*. It was Soderbergh's first remake, prior to *Ocean's Eleven* and *Solaris* – though perhaps 'adaptation' is a more accurate description. The film is based on the 1989 British Channel Four mini-series called *Traffik*, written by Simon Moore. Soderbergh had been thinking of making a film about drugs for a couple of years when he bumped into the producer Laura Bickford, who had acquired the rights to the series years before. They made contact with young writer Stephen Gaghan, who had worked on shows like *NYPD Blue* and *The Practice*, as well as the script for William Friedkin's jingoistic thriller *Rules of Engagement* (2000). As it turned out, Gaghan – who had struggled with drug addiction himself in his twenties – was already working on a drug-based script for director Edward Zwick and producer Marshall Herskovitz.

Zwick's project was partly based on an article he had read about the drug wars, where three competing law enforcement agencies absurdly ended up in a running gun battle. They decided to combine the two, initially taking the project to Bill Mechanic at Twentieth Century Fox, where it stalled. While Soderbergh busied himself with *The Limey* and then *Erin Brockovich*, *Traffic* eventually found its way to USA Films – 'one of the few independent film companies left in America', as Soderbergh put it. Despite 'the conventional wisdom in the United States' that 'political . . . or issue-oriented films are not commercial', USA Films set about raising the $48 million budget.

By the time it came out, *Traffic* was unanimously hailed by the critics, particularly those from America. As so often happens, Soderbergh's film automatically suffered by comparison to its source material. It's simple mathematics: 315 minutes into 147 just doesn't go. The complexities of the original series were largely lost, although the superficial changes were perfectly acceptable. The film transferred the action from Britain and Pakistan to the U.S.–Mexico border and Ohio, and also changed the drug of choice from heroin to cocaine. As Soderbergh explains, '70 percent of the cocaine that's consumed in the States comes through Mexico. It's the balloon effect – we've squeezed Colombia, and now it's all going into Mexico.' But while the mini-series contained a sympathetic portrait of a poppy farmer named Fazal, there was no equivalent coca grower in Soderbergh's film. The chain stops in Tijuana with the cartels who distribute the drugs; the closest the film delivers to Fazal is Javier, the compromised cop expertly realized by Benicio Del Toro.

The rather one-dimensional villain in Soderbergh's film is the corrupt Mexican general Salazar (Tomas Milian), who commands the National Drug Force but is revealed to work for the Juarez cartel, who are hoping to bring down their rivals, the Obregon brothers. His equivalent in *Traffik* is an Islamic Karachi billionaire named Tariq Butt (Talat Hussain). Soderbergh argues that the Pakistan segment 'didn't work for us when transplanted to the United States', and thus the Mexican segment was created from scratch. 'Almost all of the threads from the Mexico story were pulled from newspaper headlines. Either situations or characters were based on real incidents.'

Traffic is undeniably a film from a white, western, middle-class point of view. Erika Christensen's Caroline, daughter to the Ohio judge Robert Wakefield (Michael Douglas), descends into depravity in three easy moves. After smoking pot with her friends, she is soon snorting cocaine and inhaling crack. Before you can say 'road to hell', she is prostituting herself for a fix with a black dealer in the seedier side of Cincinnati, a development that comes across like the urban yuppie nightmare. It can be inferred that this violation of the white man's daughter is justice for all. As Seth (Topher Grace), the school friend who initially supplies Caroline with drugs, explains to her father, 100,000 white people are cruising the black neighbourhoods asking for drugs. 'What do you think that does to the black psyche?' he says. Addiction, it would appear, is at the root of society's collapse. Soft drugs lead to hard drugs, in what must be the most morally unambiguous film of Soderbergh's career. Little wonder it fared so well with the Academy.

As didactic as the film can be, one can't deny Soderbergh went into it with the best of intentions. As he announced during a press conference at the 2001 Berlin Film Festival, where Benicio Del Toro picked up a Best Actor award, after two-and-a-half years' worth of research his feelings about the U.S. war on drugs were more complicated than when he started.

At the end of the day, the film is basically asking the question 'Is this the best we can do?' I don't think you'd find many people on either side of the issue in the United States who would think it is the best we can do. The net effect of our policies over the past ten years has just been to fill up prisons at an incredible rate. Whether or not the United States can begin to look at drug addiction as a health care issue rather than a criminal issue, I don't know . . . Nobody's talking. One of the great things, though, about the film coming out when it came out in the United States, people have been confronting politicians, microphone in hand, saying 'Have you seen *Traffic*? And if you have, what do you think about the war on drugs?' Which is exactly what we were trying to accomplish, which is just to get people talking.

At the time, with George W. Bush recently elected for his first term, the U.S. was without a drug czar, after the departure of General Barry McCaffrey. One of the film's most powerful sequences comes when Robert Wakefield – a borderline alcoholic himself, as the scene proves with his demands for Scotch – first takes on the job. Surrounded by real-life U.S. senators such as Orrin Hatch, Barbara Boxer, Don Nickles and Chuck Grassley, Wakefield listens to various opinions – the purity of drugs has gone up, the prices for cocaine and heroin have gone down, and so on. Wakefield appears overwhelmed, later telling his daughter that the politicians of Washington are like the beggars of Calcutta, 'only these beggars wear $1500 suits and don't say "please" and "thank you".' Rather like Soderbergh, as Wakefield progresses, he finds the subject more and more complicated. When he meets Salazar, he is told 'Addicts treat themselves. They overdose and there's one less to worry about.' By the end, he must reject the job. It gives Douglas, an actor never happier than when he's orating his scenes from a podium, a climactic climb-down scene. 'I can't do this. If there is a war on drugs, then many of our family members are the enemy. I don't know how you wage war on your own family.'

Benicio Del Toro, who speaks much of his part in Spanish, notes that his role takes his 'character through different stages of what it takes to do the right thing'. Recruited by General Salazar, he later watches his partner Manolo (Jacob Vargas), who has been selling information to the DEA on Salazar, shot dead in front of him. 'I feel like a traitor,' he says, before he is spurred into action. 'It's a bookmark of our times, especially here in America with the problem of drugs,' says Del Toro. 'It has a message without saying it, and that's the beauty of it. You can feel it. It's important to educate kids and parents of what it is to be on the "demand" side. Whatever we're doing to stop wars, without the education of what it is to be on this "side" means nothing. If you just fight without educating people that drugs are no good – or that they are a symptom of something, like what's happening at home, or at school, or with the community – it means nothing. In that way *Traffic* is very successful.'

Soderbergh (under the pseudonym Peter Andrews) shot the film himself – much of it with hand-held cameras, suggesting a faux-documentary style. One of its more memorable aspects was its colour scheme: furthering Soderbergh's earlier experiments with filters on *The Underneath*, while eschewing the use of artificial light as much as possible, cold steel-blues defined the Ohio sections and tobacco-yellow the Mexico parts, with natural whites for San Diego. 'That, to me, was just a very simple way to keep people geographically oriented,' says Soderbergh. 'I knew there was a great risk that they might not know what they were watching, but at least if they knew where they were, I thought that would be a great help. While we were preparing the film, I did some experimentation with film stocks and filters, and thought it would be a good idea that each time we went to one of the stories, before you even saw a character, you knew which story you were in. It was really that simple.'

That many of the White House scenes were shot on the set of the TV drama *The West Wing* rather sums up the successes and failures of *Traffic* as a film. The replica interiors suggest an authenticity that Soderbergh strives for throughout the picture, be it through aesthetic or dramatic choices. As an attempt to turn a social issue into main-stream entertainment, it works. The film is as thought-provoking as it is engrossing, open-ended enough to allow the audience room to think. As a return to the era of films Soderbergh so admires, it's not quite there, however. One suspects Friedkin, Coppola or Scorsese would never have been so paternally moralistic in their approach. The success of *Traffic* lies elsewhere. With the Oscars as icing, the true reward came with the industry muscle Soderbergh now found himself flexing, affording him the chance to form his own production company, Section Eight, aptly named after the 'insanity' discharge that cross-dressing Corporal Klinger kept seeking on *M*A*S*H*. Soderbergh's master plan was about to be put into action.

Our goal is to make mainstream films more interesting and take independent filmmakers and either match them with a genre or an actor that gives them an audience. George and I can create an environment for them where they'll get to make their movie and no one will bother them.
  Steven Soderbergh

It made perfect sense. Housed at Warner Bros., where Soderbergh and Clooney had just made *Ocean's Eleven*, Section Eight had a simple mandate: produce non-formulaic films with independent directors that use recognized stars to draw in the crowds. It was a model Soder-bergh had successfully employed time and again in his own films.

Moreover, it was an attempt to forge the sort of intelligent mid-budget movies Hollywood studios made back in the 1970s. Clooney, in particular, is obsessed by directors from New Hollywood; he openly admits to stealing from Mike Nichols and Alan J. Pakula for his directorial debut, the early Section Eight production *Confessions of a Dangerous Mind* (2002), which will be discussed in Chapter 19. 'Steven and myself are fighting to get films we're proud of, and we like and think are smart, made,' he says. 'We want to be involved in the entire creative process. It's a good thing to do – it makes you feel better.'

Soderbergh began the enterprise by cold-calling a number of directors with whom he hoped to collaborate. Those on the receiving end included Kimberly Peirce, Harmony Korine and James Gray, who directed *The Yards* (2000), all uncompromising artists who have found it difficult to find consistent backing for their work. One such filmmaker was John Maybury, whose 1998 debut *Love Is the Devil* was widely acclaimed. He had spent years trying to follow up his debut with a film about playwright Christopher Marlowe for Natural Nylon, the sluggish UK production outfit set up by Jude Law, Ewan McGregor and their Primrose Hill pals. When it failed to materialize, Maybury was left at his lowest ebb until he received an unexpected phone call from Soderbergh.

'I was astonished,' says Maybury. 'I thought it was one of my friends having a laugh.' Soderbergh made him an offer he couldn't refuse. 'He was looking to people like myself, Todd Haynes, Harmony Korine . . . filmmakers who are or were on the fringes of mainstream cinema.' The deal, Maybury explains, is about 'giving us access to the Hollywood power structure and actors, but also simultaneously offering some degree of protection from what that can mean. There are enough people who have had bad experiences.'

Soderbergh's call to Maybury eventually came to fruition as they collaborated on *The Jacket* (2005), the story of a Gulf War veteran incarcerated in a Vermont mental asylum for a murder he didn't commit. Earlier successes for Section Eight included Haynes's *Far from Heaven* (see Chapter 2) and Christopher Nolan's *Insomnia* (2002), a remake of Erik Skjoldbjærg's 1997 thriller about a cop who kills his partner. 'We were really pleased with *Insomnia*. And that's a really good example of what we're trying to do,' says Soderbergh. 'The biggest thing we did on that film was browbeat Warner Bros. into hiring Chris Nolan. They wanted to hire the traditional A-list director. I knew Chris a little bit and knew he wanted to do it. So I went in and said "You have to hire this guy." And they did, and everybody was happy.' The film took $67.3 million and marked star Al Pacino's third highest grossing film in the U.S. (after *Any Given Sunday* and *Heat*) since 1990's *Dick Tracy*.

But, more often than not, Section Eight's early productions barely made a dent in the U.S. box office. Their first production, *Welcome to Collinwood* (2002) – which featured the Soderbergh regular Luis Guzmán as well as Clooney – is a fine example. Soderbergh first encountered writer-directors Anthony and Joe Russo while he was screening *Schizopolis* at the Slamdance Film Festival in 1996. Their debut *Pieces*, a black comedy about three Italian brothers in the hairpiece business, was also showing in Park City. A week after seeing it, Soderbergh called the brothers and asked them what they wanted to do next. 'They showed me a series of scripts they had written which were really interesting but I thought we couldn't get made,' he says. 'They were physically pretty large. Finally, they came up with this adaptation of [Mario Monicelli's 1958 petty heist film] *Big Deal on Madonna Street*, which I thought was hilarious. So we took our producing fee from *Insomnia* and put it into *Collinwood* and got it made.'

If the end result, taking a meagre $333,620 box office in the U.S., didn't quite make it a profitable exercise, it set the template for what was to come. It further enhanced the idea that Soderbergh, in the wake of his Oscar, was trying to put something back into the industry. An unofficial godfather for the Sundance Kids, his own experiences told him that survival in the film business is very difficult on the fringes. As Joe Russo says: 'Steven's rise was very inspirational to us. The way he started working within the industry and the studio system shows you can make very artistic, intelligent films with studio money.'

As you would expect from a director who regularly works with the same people, Section Eight is run like an extended family. *Traffic* scribe Stephen Gaghan directed CIA film *Syriana* (2005), with Clooney taking the lead role; meanwhile, *Ocean's Eleven* writer Ted Griffin penned *Rumor Has It* (2005) though was replaced as director by Rob Reiner. Section Eight also afforded Greg Jacobs, Soderbergh's first assistant director since *King of the Hill*, the chance to make his directorial debut with *Criminal* (2004). For this remake of Fabián Bielinsky's *Nine Queens* (2001) – a con-artist caper set in Buenos Aires – Jacobs co-wrote the script with Soderbergh, who again used the pen name of Sam Lowry which he had previously used for *The Underneath*.

'Thank God for Section Eight,' exclaims John C. Reilly, who played the lead in *Criminal*. 'Section Eight is subversive in the best sense of the word. They're able to operate on their own terms with the protection of this appropriate entity. They're dream producers; they got us the money and believed in Greg, and let him cast whom he wanted. Which I was very happy about, because I'm sure the studio might have had other ideas. They were in touch, watching dailies and talking to Greg, but I never felt like it was this shadow government working on the film.'

Criminal made little more than *Welcome to Collinwood*, just $929,233. More hopes were pinned on *The Jacket*, particularly given that it cost $19 million and starred Adrien Brody, Keira Knightley and Jennifer Jason Leigh. As Maybury notes, 'The first films they produced – like *Welcome to Collinwood* – didn't really hit the mark, as far as they were concerned and certainly as far as the whole Warners machine were concerned.' Sadly, neither did his, recouping just $6.2 million in the U.S., with Maybury reputedly unhappy about the way the film was marketed as a horror movie.

Whatever the grosses, Section Eight is certainly allowing talent to blossom. George Clooney's sophomore film, *Good Night, and Good Luck.* (2005), was a considerable step up from his debut. Co-written by Clooney and Grant Heslov, this taut black-and-white study of renowned CBS newscaster Edward R. Murrow (a flawless David Strathairn) and his legendary on-air battle with Senator Joseph McCarthy proved both timely and timeless. As Soderbergh notes, 'To make a movie about Murrow and never have it feel like a history lesson or didactic, that's hard to do. But this one is perfectly modulated. Every element is unified.'

Arguably, Soderbergh is capable of buying Section Eight time while the company evolves by delivering Warner Bros. the occasional gilt-edged hit. As he did in 2004 with the first sequel of his career, *Ocean's Twelve*. While the film will be considered in the context of Soderbergh's career in Chapter 23, it's undeniable that a film grossing $125.4 million in the U.S. buys a lot of good will. As Soderbergh explains, 'On one level you could say, "They made *Ocean's Twelve* because all these other movies that they're making aren't performing and they need to make a hit to finance all these other mistakes." That's partially true. But I made *Ocean's Twelve* because I wanted to make it. Nobody asked me to make it. I wanted to make it and I made it the way I wanted and was totally left alone by the studio. But it so happens that it does buy us a lot of "mistakes" – or at least smaller movies that may not become profitable.' As he knows only too well, reputation alone will not guarantee you survival in Hollywood.

CHAPTER 18

The X-Man:
Bryan Singer Takes on the Blockbuster

44 Bryan Singer during the making of *X-Men*.

Mutation is the key to our evolution.
Magneto, *X-Men*

It is an historical fact – sharing the world has never been humanity's defining attribute.
Professor Xavier, *X2*

As Steven Soderbergh played Hollywood at its own game, Bryan Singer followed suit. After *Apt Pupil*, the announcement that Singer was taking on a summer blockbuster was initially a surprise. The fiendish showman behind *The Usual Suspects* was switching roles; from Keyser Soze to the more mundane Dave Kujan, if you like. Directing *X-Men*, an adaptation of the Marvel Comics series that began in 1963, sounded like a sell-out. 'Anytime you're making a film at the $100 million level, and yet you've had unique artistic success with earlier pictures, there will always be that opinion,' he notes. He's right, but it didn't feel like it at the time.

When *X-Men* rolled before the cameras in September 1999, comic book adaptations were not the money-spinners they have since become. The *Superman* franchise had long since died, despite Tim Burton's best (but aborted) efforts to revive it with Nicolas Cage in the lead; Burton's own *Batman* films also seemed like they belonged to another era, tainted by Joel Schumacher's two later entries. Only Stephen Norrington's *Blade* (1998), based on the minor Marvel Comics tale about a vampire hunter, had any bite to it. For Singer to take on *X-Men* meant he risked being ostracized, like the mutants of the story. If it went wrong, he'd be left to ponder the error of his ways in the ashes of his career.

After all, it's not as if *Apt Pupil* had been such a hit. With the rights to the *X-Men* adaptation held at Twentieth Century Fox, Singer recalls an early conversation with its chairman, Bill Mechanic. *Apt Pupil* having sunk like a stone, he said to Mechanic, 'I don't know if it's going to be successful. Do you still want me to do your *X-Men* movie?' In another example of his bravery, post–*Fight Club*, Mechanic replied: 'Yeah! That's not supposed to make money! I like your eye, your style!' Nevertheless, leaping from the arena of *Apt Pupil* to *X-Men* – a ninety-one-day shoot sometimes requiring up to four units shooting simultaneously – was a trial by fire for Singer.

Little wonder Fox hedged their bets, capping the budget at $75 million. With somewhere between 300 and 400 visual effects shots gobbling up 20 percent of this sum, it meant the cast was distinctly B-list. Only Patrick Stewart, known for playing Jean-Luc Picard in the 1990s television series *Star Trek: The Next Generation*, was a name. At the time, Halle Berry was not an Oscar winner; Sir Ian McKellen had yet to play Gandalf in *Lord of the Rings* and Hugh Jackman was just an Australian stage actor who replaced Dougray Scott at the last minute, when commitments to the never-ending shoot for John Woo's *M:I-2* (2000) kept Scott in Sydney.

Yet the Fates were with Singer; he was watched over by the godfather of comic book movies, Richard Donner, who had directed the ground-breaking *Superman* (1978) and here took an executive producer credit. Following his idol Steven Spielberg into the annals of Hollywood folk-lore, Singer was realizing his childhood dream. Of his defection to the blockbuster, he argues, 'It's like when Steven Spielberg had such tremendous artistic success with *Sugarland Express*, and then decided to go make *Jaws* – this big action-adventure film.' *X-Men* is Singer's *Jaws* – even if it isn't half as good or half the cultural phenomenon that Spielberg's shark film was. But what it did do, just as *Jaws* did in 1975 for the summer event movie, was open the floodgates.

Slow-witted studio executives began to realize that there is a market for super-villains and superheroes: that patrons of the Forbidden Planet shop or the Los Angeles Comic-Con had money to burn. The comic book blockbuster became a Hollywood superpower all of its own: Hulk, Daredevil, Elektra, Spider-Man, Blade all got their own shows and more besides. 'I see the ripple-effect that it had,' admits Singer of his film. 'Since Richard Donner did the first *Superman*, we've seen that comic book adaptations can be taken seriously. And we've seen with a lot of good science fiction and fantasy that when it's taken seriously, we can learn a lot about ourselves.'

You might say that Singer, along with the Wachowski Brothers and their sci-fi epic *The Matrix* (1999), paved the way for other indepen-dent directors to be trusted by the studios with the big bucks. Steven Soderbergh on *Ocean's Eleven* and its sequel, Ang Lee on *Hulk* (2003) and Christopher Nolan with *Batman Begins* (2005) all bucked the blockbuster blueprint. Is it a good thing? If, as in the case of Singer's

X-Men and its 2003 sequel *X2* (subtitled *X-Men United*), the big-budget format can be used to smuggle across a few ideas in keeping with the director's oeuvre, then why not? As Singer says of the *X-Men* films, 'What better way to address issues of tolerance and those kind of socio-political issues, than in a big summer event movie? What better way to move people, than move them in such a grand way?'

Originally created during the height of the Civil Rights movement, *X-Men* revolves around the titular group of superheroes – so-called 'mutants' – shunned by society for being different. In Singer's *X-Men*, a Mutant Registration Act is being pushed through Congress. Gathered together by the benevolent Professor Charles Xavier (Stewart), and housed at his School for the Gifted, the X-Men, as they're nicknamed, are forced to intervene in a war brewing between mutants and the rest of mankind. It's a conflict spurred on by the rebellious Magneto (McKellen), Malcolm X to Xavier's Martin Luther King.

No doubt, *X-Men* starts where *Apt Pupil* left off. The prologue, set in a rain-drenched World War II concentration camp, sees a young Jewish boy separated from his parents. Beaten to the ground, he stares at the gate that divides them as the metal railings start to buckle. As we later realize, this is Eric Lehnsherr – or Magneto – who has the power to manipulate metal. By the time *X2* rolls around, with the introduction of the German-born blue-skinned mutant Nightcrawler (Alan Cumming), the transition is complete. 'I've had fun with the notion of having a German hero and Jewish villain in my two *X-Men* films – just to play with the norms a little,' says Singer. It must be noted that the films are not about the Nazis and the persecution of the Jews – but how such bigotry has since soaked into the very fabric of the free world. Made, of course, before 9/11 and the 2003 U.S. invasion of Iraq, it feels particularly prophetic when Magneto notes in *X-Men*: 'America was going to be the land of tolerance, peace.' Welcome to the future, indeed.

Ironically, for a franchise that seemed tailor-made for him, Singer was initially reluctant to climb on board. While he always had an interest in science fiction and fantasy – ever since his father took him to see a 16 mm print of *The Day the Earth Stood Still* (1951) in the basement of his local library – he was unfamiliar with the *X-Men* comic book. It was his producing partner Tom DeSanto, an *X-Men* fan since childhood, who urged him to meet with the Marvel Comics honcho Stan Lee, who was a big fan of *The Usual Suspects*. When Singer finally met with Marvel executives, he had an epiphany as to how he could open the film – with the mutants discovering their superpowers at puberty.

In the resulting movie, after the Magneto prologue, this is chiefly shown with the introduction of Rogue (Anna Paquin) in 'the not too distant future'. Kissing a boy at home in her bedroom, she suddenly leaves him gasping for air as his veins begin to protrude from under his skin. Able to suck the life force or abilities from any being, even taking on their memories or secrets, she is incapable of having a normal relationship for fear of killing any potential lover. As she says, 'the first boy I ever kissed ended up in a coma for three weeks'. Dressed in these early scenes in a green hooded cloak, to symbolize her withdrawal from society as she runs away from home, she's like Little Red Riding Hood wandering through the forest. And, yes, she meets her wolf – or Wolverine (Jackman) to be precise.

Another mutant – and the fans' favourite – Wolverine has already been through his pubescence. But rather than sprout hairs on his knuckles, it's claws – made from the indestructible metal admantium – that spring from his hands. With a violent nature and a murky background that has only been hinted at in the first two films, Wolverine represents the orphaned child, stymied by his lack of roots. Both he and Rogue are taken in by Xavier to learn more. 'For me it was interesting because I'm adopted, and I don't know who my biological parents are,' says Singer. 'So I thought it was fun to beg the question, "Where does one come from and is it relevant to where one is now?"' In Wolverine's case, the green-tinged nightmares that come to him (showing him operated upon by a series of shadowy figures) are the only clues to his past.

The presence of General William Stryker (Brian Cox) in X2 furthers this mystery while developing a strong theme concerning fathers and sons. A Vietnam veteran who developed the plastic prison that incarcerates Magneto after he is captured at the end of *X-Men*, Stryker holds the key to Wolverine's background, hinting that he knew him fifteen years ago. Accompanied by his own female version of Wolverine, known as Lady Deathstryke (Kelly Hu), Stryker taunts Jackman's character: 'You are just a failed experiment. You were an animal then. You're an animal now. I just gave you claws.'

While Stryker is a surrogate father to Wolverine, it emerges that his own son Jason, now lobotomized and wheelchair-bound, was a former pupil of Xavier's whom he was unable to help. Resenting his parents, Jason projected visions into their heads, causing Stryker's wife to drill a hole in hers. Now determined to resolve the 'mutant problem', as Magneto puts it, Stryker learns of Xavier's Cerebro device, the machine that enables the Professor to connect to the inner psyche of every living soul. Attempting to rebuild Cerebro to turn it against the mutants, Stryker is a more extreme version of *X-Men*'s Senator Kelly (Bruce Davison), who looked to outlaw the creatures via the Mutant Registration Act. Like Kelly, Stryker is not a megalomaniac out for world domination; rather, he's a tortured soul pursuing a crusade he believes is right.

In *X2*, the theme of the difficulties of puberty (already well covered by Singer in *Apt Pupil*) also continues, with the characters of Bobby Drake (Shawn Ashmore) and Pyro (Aaron Stanford). While Pyro proves to be a maniac, so to speak, with his ability to set things on fire, Bobby – or Iceman, as he becomes known – can cool things down with one jet of frozen H_2O. Pyro, taken under Magneto's wing by the finale, is the archetypal teen rebel, whereas Bobby – like Rogue, who befriends him – can be seen as the pubescent struggling to come to terms with his sexual awakening. Bobby's parents believe Professor Xavier's establishment is 'a prep school', not knowing anything of their son's powers. When Bobby, along with Rogue, Pyro and Wolverine, escapes to his family home – after General Stryker and his men attack Xavier's school – he goes through what is tantamount to a 'coming out' confession. As his well-meaning mother says, 'Bobby? Have you tried not being a mutant?' Substitute 'gay' for 'a mutant' and you get the idea. No wonder the storyline appealed to the openly gay Singer. 'There's a lot of subversive things happening in *X2*,' Singer notes. 'Some of them are not so under the surface. You have sociopolitical issues happening, you have analogies to 'coming out'. I love leaving them as subtext. If I felt I was equipped to make *Schindler's List* or *The Pianist*, I would – but I don't. Yet there are issues of tolerance that are of great concern to me.'

As McKellen, a well-known activist in the gay community, noted at a press conference for *X2*:

Bryan told me the story of *X-Men* entirely in terms of the ongoing argument between two friends – Professor Xavier and Magneto.

That is, what do you do if you are a leader in a mutant community, a community that is on the whole rejected by straight society? Do you accommodate people's fears, and try and understand them and integrate and fit in? Is that the focus of what you do with your life – educate young mutants? Or, as with Magneto's view, do you take on the world, even if that leads to a violent confrontation? I know within the gay communities, that argument is a constant. Do you make your case, talk to your MP and write to the newspapers? Or do you go out on the streets and cause a fuss, throw yourself in front of the horses? And as much as I admire that method, it's not one that I feel I'm suited to follow. It was presented not as a comic fantasy and a bit of escapism, but as something rather gritty and crucial not just to the lives of a gay film director and actor . . . I know in talking to Marvel that they're very proud. It's one of their favourite publications, because it appeals to young gays, and young blacks and young Jews. They all identify themselves as mutants.

This does not sound like the work of a studio blockbuster. While *X-Men* undeniably felt like a set-up movie – introducing a series of characters and ideas for a sequel but not bothering with much of a plot of its own – the seeds it sowed truly bloomed in *X2*. It is, after all, a story about evolution more than anything, as hinted at with the nod to T. H. White's Arthurian retelling *The Once and Future King*. Published in 1958, this quartet of tales dealing with the life of King Arthur ties into various character arcs in *X2*. Both Magneto – who believes he *is* the once and future King – and Xavier are seen reading the book in the film. *X2* continually emphasizes the links between Magneto and Xavier – from the fact that both have chess sets in their studies, suggesting a battle of the minds between these two former friends, to the discovery that Magneto helped Xavier build Cerebro. But it is through White's book that this is most strongly underlined.

It also connects to Dr Jean Grey (Famke Janssen), the svelte leather-clad mutant with the abilities of telepathy and telekinesis. One of Xavier's chief assistants, in *X-Men* – together with her lover Scott Summers, aka Cyclops (James Marsden) – she spent her time readying newer mutants for battle. In *X2* her role changes dramatically. Troubled by voices in her mind, and a dulling of her powers, by the finale she sacrifices herself – aware that, like the hero of White's book, her future may be very different from her present. As anyone au fait with the comic books will know, Dr Jean Grey becomes seduced by her power to the point where she evolves again. It's not for nothing she's also called Phoenix – her resurrection a continuation of the religious theme that runs through both films, notably via Nightcrawler's continual recital of the Lord's Prayer.

Singer, who admits he was much happier with X2 than its predecessor, compares the tone of the two films to George Lucas's first two *Star Wars* films, *A New Hope* and *The Empire Strikes Back*. 'Sometimes the Death Star explodes and sometimes two people have a sword fight and there are revelations,' he shrugs. 'The set piece is not necessarily important.' By which he means the original *X-Men* finishes with an ill-conceived scrap between Magneto and the other mutants at the Statue of Liberty, whereas X2 concludes with the defection of Pyro and the 'death' of Dr Jean Grey. The biggest explosion comes as the dam where the characters wind up finally bursts. 'In the case of the dam, water is more representative of evolution and things changing,' says Singer. 'There's all this farce, then suddenly it's new life. It's more subtextual than, "Wow, what's the big explosion at the end?" The issues are more character-driven.'

As it happens, Singer – not overly familiar with visual effects before making *X-Men* – visited the set of Lucas's *Star Wars* prequel *The Phantom Menace* to glean some much-needed experience in the way of the force. If neither *X-Men* film boasts the groundbreaking visual effects of, say, *The Matrix* franchise, Singer still uses CGI to memorable effect. Think of the shapeshifting antics of Mystique (Rebecca Romijn-Stamos) or the emergence of a slime-covered Senator Kelly – turned into a mutant by Magneto – from the sea. Or the metal bridge that builds itself in front of Magneto square by square and his later escape from the exquisite plastic prison that holds him, via pellets of iron placed inside his guard's body. Then there's Nightcrawler's ghostly invasion of the White House and the cyclones conjured by weather-controlling mutant Storm (Halle Berry) and so on . . .

Singer claims, 'there was almost no pressure from the studio' to deliver the requisite firework finale for X2, despite an increase of $45 million in the budget. 'They recognized very early on, from my first treatment, that this would be a character-driven story with some serious shades of grey. Your villains are not necessarily truly evil, your heroes are not perfect and there are human conflicts and revelations and romances.'

He maintains that 'some of the more subversive, serious and tragic aspects of the movie' were among the studio's favourite ideas. 'So in that way, they've grown bold. They may not have originally thought of the *X-Men* universe being treated that way. I brought that sensibility to the first movie. They saw that it was successful, and had faith in that. Now any ideas and impact they have is more celebratory of my point of view.'

With *X2* opening on 11,000 simultaneous screens globally – at the time, the largest release of a film on a single date in the history of cinema – it was a faith that was repaid. Taking in a whopping $85 million on its opening weekend in the U.S., the film grossed close to $215 million there – even better than its predecessor, which took a healthy $157 million. While the comics provided a built-in audience, Singer maintains that these fans accounted for only a small portion of the overall takings. 'Unlike the characters of Superman, Batman and Spider-Man, which all had prime-time television series, and are all part of the mass public lexicon, *X-Men* has a very large and specific fan base. Outside of that, there was an animated series, more for kids, then ignorance. There was a large education that had to occur. It was a formidable task.'

Part of the success of both films comes from Singer's continuing desire to work with writers who are close friends and/or relative newcomers. 'I find I get the most enthusiasm [from new writers],' he notes. 'They approach a project as if it's their first and last film, which is what I do.' While numerous writers were brought on for uncredited rewrites – including James Schamus and Singer's frequent collaborator Christopher McQuarrie – it was newcomer David Hayter who took sole credit for the eventual *X-Men* screenplay. Likewise, *X2* saw Singer gamble on two Young Turks, Dan Harris and Michael Dougherty, respectively aged just twenty-three and twenty-eight at the time, who joined Hayter in penning the script. 'Between Chris and Brandon Boyce, who wrote *Apt Pupil*, we're just a bunch of young guys that have devoted ourselves to the movie industry,' says Harris. Both short-filmmakers (Harris in live-action; Dougherty in animation) who moved from New York to Los Angeles, the pair teamed up on a speculative horror script for Phoenix Pictures before Singer came calling. 'We'd casually known Bryan for a few years, through friends of friends,' adds Harris. 'He's got a reputation of working with young writers, outside of the system of normal writing – with one draft at a time. He prefers having a collaborative team, working on the script in constant development.'

Both writers were kept on call during the shoot of X2 to refine the script. Notes Dougherty: 'Bryan's not a fan of that Hollywood mentality, of "Let's get him out and get someone in to punch up the dialogue." He treats a big budget film as a small independent thing, which is why he writes with writers closely every day. We worked from his trailer. Every day was the great unknown – we'd just wake up in the morning and work out what we had to do. You could turn up to the set, and no matter what they were shooting something huge or small could change.' The attack on Xavier's school, for example, was rewritten the day before it was shot. 'You have the stunt guys, visual effects guys and the extras on hold, and you think there's no way they could change it. But there is – all the other teams were just as willing to accommodate Bryan when he wanted to change something.'

The film also reunited Singer with trusted editor cum composer John Ottman, who had been forced to duck out of working on X-Men as he was directing, editing and scoring his own feature film, Urban Legends: Final Cut (2000). While Singer had brought in Michael Kamen to score X-Men and a trio of editors to cut it, it was clear he relished the chance to team up with the man who had been instrumental in helping choreograph his first three films. As Singer told Starburst, 'I know that while he's cutting he's thinking about the score, and he's also creating a decent temp-score to articulate how things will ultimately work.'[115]

But the final testament to the films must be how they passed the muster of obsessive X-Men fans, despite altering a variety of the characters and the colours of their costumes. Rogue, for example, is an amalgam of Kitty Pryde, Jubilee and Rogue from the Marvel Comics. Pyro, meanwhile, was a minor henchman who has been beefed up considerably. As for Wolverine, he was far more mean-spirited in the comic books. While major characters Beast (removed at the last minute from X-Men), Angel (ditto X2) and Gambit have yet to make an appearance, there have been brief glimpses of minor players like Colossus. But Singer, it seems, can do no wrong. 'The beauty of what Bryan did with the first film, is that he captured the heart and soul of the X-Men,' says Dougherty. 'And was faithful without it being ridiculous. I think the reason why X-Men became so popular, and breathed new life into the comic book genre, is because it respected its source material, so we all took it seriously.'

Yet just as the *X-Men* story was beginning to get interesting, Singer jumped ship – well, studio, comic house and franchise. For in 2004, the same year that Christopher Reeve died, Singer announced plans to resurrect DC Comics' hero in *Superman Returns*. Heading to Warner Bros. with his key *X2* crew – including Harris and Dougherty, Ottman and DP Newton Thomas Sigel – Singer cast a virtual unknown, Brandon Routh, as the Man of Steel. In retrospect, it's easy to see why such a project appealed to Singer. After all, Spielberg had Indiana Jones; now Singer had got his own iconic hero to play with. Not that he'll care, but Singer is fast becoming the Sundance Kids' resident nerd. Quite why he abandoned the X-Men in their hour of need, just as the series was heating up, is a mystery. No doubt a few executives in the Fox boardroom were left wishing they could strap a block of Kryptonite around Singer's neck, after his departure left the *X-Men* franchise in difficulties. The British producer-director Matthew Vaughn flirted with directing the third installment only to quit weeks before shooting commenced. Then, ironically, Brett Ratner – a one-time candidate to direct *X-Men*, he was also attached to *Superman Returns* before Singer – came on board the project. While the *X-Men* series could be viewed as an episodic franchise, like the James Bond or *Star Trek* films, as Sir Ian McKellen notes: 'Without Bryan Singer at the helm, what would the films be like? It's all unknown territory.'

CHAPTER 19

Being Charlie Kaufman: How One Man Tried to Debunk the Three-Act Structure

45 Nicolas Cage as both Charlie and Donald Kaufman in *Adaptation*.

> I've written myself into my screenplay . . . it's self-indulgent,
> it's narcissistic, solipsistic, it's pathetic. I'm pathetic. I'm fat
> and pathetic.
>
> Charlie Kaufman, *Adaptation*

Raymond Chandler once said 'Good original screenplays are almost as rare in Hollywood as virgins.' Perhaps he should have changed that to 'good original screenwriters', as he obviously never read a script by Charlie Kaufman. After the success of *Being John Malkovich*, the fiercely unique Kaufman reassured us he was no one-hit wonder: *Human Nature* (2001), and more particularly *Adaptation* (2002) and *Eternal Sunshine of the Spotless Mind* (2004), are worthy successors to his debut. Only *Confessions of a Dangerous Mind* – Kaufman's one straight-up adaptation, of Chuck Barris's delusional 1984 'unauthorized autobiography' in which the former king of TV trash claimed he was also a CIA hitman – failed to impress in quite the same way. A script Singer seriously considered making after *Apt Pupil*, only to drop out just six weeks before shooting was due to begin, its failure could be put down to the fact that first-time director George Clooney played script doctor, one role he was perhaps not qualified to take on.

After *Adaptation* – Kaufman's second collaboration with Spike Jonze, in which Nicolas Cage played both Charlie Kaufman and his fictional twin brother Donald – he became the most recognizable screenwriter in Hollywood, unwittingly or otherwise. It seems remarkable, yet somehow wholly appropriate, that such a publicity-shy figure as Kaufman should become as near to a household name as a screenwriter can get. As critic Peter Bradshaw noted, Kaufman is 'one of the very few screenwriters in Hollywood – perhaps the only screenwriter – whose authorial identity supersedes the director's'.[116] If nothing else, it signified a shift from the time when Shane Black (*The Long Kiss Goodnight*, 1996) and Joe Eszterhas (*Basic Instinct*, 1990) were celebrated for being paid seven-figure sums for their shallow, high-concept scripts.

Kaufman is on a different page from the host of A-list screenwriters who keep studios in the material to which they are accustomed: men like John Logan (*Gladiator*, 2000), Steven Zaillian (*Schindler's List*, 1993), Ron Bass

(*Rain Man*, 1988) and David Koepp (*Spider-Man*, 2002), who live and die by the three-act resolution and champion the heroic protagonist. These are assembly-line writers, Hollywood craftsmen bereft of the daring of their forefathers – mavericks like William Goldman (*Butch Cassidy and the Sundance Kid*, 1969), Robert Towne (*Chinatown*, 1974), Waldo Salt (*Midnight Cowboy*, 1969) or Paddy Chayefsky (*Network*, 1976), whose cynical works reflected America's post-Vietnam/Watergate malaise.

In an ideal world, the rise of Kaufman would signify the promotion of the screenwriter from the position of lowest amoeba in the Hollywood food chain. Undeniably, the likes of Alan Ball (*American Beauty*, 1999) and Kevin Williamson (*The Faculty*, 1998; *Scream*, 1996) were already promoting the notion of writer-as-auteur, no doubt aided by the success of their respective television shows, *Six Feet Under* and *Dawson's Creek*. But in the new millennium, it is Kaufman, along with Mike White, whose star is in the ascendancy. White, the former *Dawson's Creek* writer discussed in Chapter 7, does not believe screenwriters are any more valued than they ever were. 'I think in Charlie's case, and in my case, we are weird exceptions,' he says. 'I think the reason I get attention is because I am in the movies, and anonymity never helped anyone in this town, that's for sure. And I think Charlie Kaufman, while he doesn't act in his films, he – at least in *Adaptation* – puts himself in them. There's certainly an effort to put himself out there and make sure he is associated with his material. I think, generally, screenwriters are still anonymous; their faces aren't connected to the material. They still have trouble finding seats at the premiere.'

It would be rash to even think that the days of the commercial screenwriter are gone. Let's be clear here. *Being John Malkovich* was arguably the last great script of the twentieth century, a beacon of light that blinded us all with its postmodern mix of philosophy, celebrity and psychology. But Kaufman is an alchemist of unparalleled skill. You won't find his work being used as a template by screenwriting guru Robert McKee (even if Kaufman pays homage to the man by awarding him a significant role in *Adaptation*). 'I just admire people who think about what they do,' says Kaufman. 'Their goal is not to manipulate people into liking them or their product. Someone really trying to look at something or say something, that's what I admire.'

Born in 1958, like his comedic heroes – the Marx Brothers, Lenny Bruce and Woody Allen – Kaufman is of Jewish descent. He once played the lead in a high-school stage production of Allen's *Play It Again, Sam*

(1972), and it's tempting to find something of the Marx Brothers' lunacy, Bruce's anarchy and Allen's neuroses in Kaufman's scripts – though they remain diluted enough not to feel derivative. Living in Massapequa, Long Island, Kaufman maintains his upbringing was untroubled. When he moved with his parents and older sister to West Hartford, Connecticut, in his mid-teens, he began his interest in the arts as a performer, contributing to community plays and even an improv group called Upscene. Graduating with a scholarship for achievement in dramatic arts, he headed to Boston University before transferring to NYU to study film. As *Being John Malkovich* hinted, Kaufman followed his college years with a host of McJobs: filing (naturally), selling theatre tickets, working in a warehouse, an art museum and the circulation department of the Minneapolis *Star Tribune*.

In 1991, Kaufman moved to Los Angeles to tout himself as a writer, having won himself an agent. After almost returning to Minneapolis – to take up his one job offer, on the Fred Willard–fronted show *Access America* – he was eventually awarded a stint writing two episodes for the second season of the Fox sitcom *Get a Life!* TV work continued steadily – shows like *The Dana Carvey Show* and *The Trouble with Larry* received the Kaufman touch – while he tried to launch his own pilots, with little success. Given that one, *Rambling Pants*, was about a travelling poet called Pants, this is understandable.

Do you know what truly separates us? Civilization.
Nathan Bronfman's father, *Human Nature*

Kaufman finished *Being John Malkovich* in 1994 but it was more than two years before it fell into the hands of Spike Jonze. His second script *Human Nature* found its way to Steven Soderbergh in late 1996, a project the director toyed with to the point that both David Hyde-Pierce and Marisa Tomei were considered for the principal roles. 'I'm not sure how to describe *Human Nature*, except to say it's very weird and hysterically funny,' noted Soderbergh in his diary, before dropping the project in favour of the Elmore Leonard adaptation *Out of Sight*.[117]

A comic parable concerning nature vs nurture, *Human Nature* is described by Kaufman as a story about 'four people who are victims of their biology and/or their upbringing, who meet and have their moment together'. The film finally went into production in the spring of 2000, helmed by French promo king (and friend to Jonze) Michel

Gondry. During the publicity crawl for *Being John Malkovich*, Kaufman felt the advance word on *Human Nature* had 'misrepresented' the story. 'It's very hard to summarize – in the same way that it's hard to sum up *Malkovich* without making it sound silly,' he said. To be fair, the end result showed that it was Gondry who misrepresented the script more than the press.

Gondry's work with such artists as the Foo Fighters, The Rolling Stones, Massive Attack, Kylie Minogue and The White Stripes has led him, like Jonze, to be recognized as one of the most innovative music video directors of his generation. With his grandfather, Constant Martin, credited as creating one of the earliest synthesizers, the Clavioline, Gondry's future in the arts was assured. His father, who ran a shop in Versailles selling musical instruments, provided Michel and his younger brother with a drum kit and bass guitar, respectively, and the pair formed a punk-rock band for a time. After heading to art college in Paris, he and a few close friends established rock outfit Oui Oui, with Gondry on drums and providing the pioneering visuals (often far more interesting than the songs themselves).

Blending often-crude animation techniques with live-action footage, as on the Escher-inspired promo for 'La Ville', Gondry soon caught the attention of the Icelandic singer Björk. In particular, his video for Oui Oui's 'Ma Maison', which featured a man dressed as a yellow and blue beetle crawling through the undergrowth, set the pattern for his breakthrough promo with Björk, 'Human Behaviour' in 1993. Set in a magical artificial forest, their first collaboration was a visually extravagant study in the quirks of humans as expressed through various species of the animal kingdom. It made perfect sense, then, for Gondry to make his feature film debut with *Human Nature*, which shares some similar preoccupations.

The story is pure whimsy; like *Being John Malkovich* it is overtly obsessed with behaviour, the body and the nature of 'being'. Repressed scientist Nathan Bronfman (Tim Robbins), a man driven to teaching mice table manners, undertakes a relationship with a novelist named Lila Jute (Patricia Arquette), author of the best-selling book, *Fuck Humanity*. While Nathan is cursed with 'an incredibly small penis', Lila has suffered from an excessive amount of body hair since puberty. After a time as a circus freak, she entered a self-imposed exile, living in the woods with the animals before re-emerging into society after subjecting herself to painful electrolysis. While on a stroll in the woods one day, the pair stumble upon a man raised as an ape – later to be named Puff (Rhys Ifans). Against Lila's better judgement, Nathan decides to spirit their find to his lab to try and civilize him.

Narrated, in turn, by all three protagonists from a late point in the story – Puff at a congressional hearing; Lila in prison; Nathan, complete with bullet-hole in his head, in a white-room afterlife – *Human Nature* has at its core the notion that the sex drive is an all-powerful base instinct that civilization sets out to control. Deriving much of the one-dimensional humour from Puff's initial inability to control his urges – humping a waitress, and so on – the film also plays on the fact that the civilized Nathan is equally unable to control his desire for his French assistant Gabrielle (Miranda Otto).

Of course, there is bitter irony when Puff, having quickly switched from reading Yeats and singing show tunes to drinking and whoring, reflects that he has been snatched 'from the depths of depravity and taken to the heights of culture'. According to him, as he addresses Congress, the moral of this tale seems to be that in our pursuit of intellectual preoccupations we have become detached from our baser instincts; that we are living in a state of paradise lost, 'totally out of touch' with our 'surroundings'. As Nathan tells him, 'when in doubt, don't ever do what you really want to do'.

As summed up by the oxymoronic title, our very existence is a fundamental philosophical dilemma – though both Nathan and Lila appear too rigid and single-minded as characters to reflect this. With nowhere to go, they are robbed of their humanity and the social satire fizzles into unfunny farce. This reflects the inadvertent tug of war between the logical Kaufman (who could easily be Nathan) and the childlike innocent that is Gondry (at one with nature, like Lila), the latter ultimately winning out. His storybook aesthetic dominates the film to its detriment; with two-thirds of the hyper-stylized film shot on a soundstage, his use of rear-screen projection and in-camera optical effects (notably for Lila's forest song) give the impression of a Technicolor musical from Hollywood's Golden Age.

This might explain why the film garnered middling reviews ('an overemphatic, would-be wacky, ultimately tedious sex farce', noted one critic[118]) and a U.S. box office tally of $705,308. Both Gondry and Kaufman, predictably, blame the marketing by distributor Fine Line. But Otto sheds some light on why *Human Nature* equals less than the sum of its parts. 'There were things in there [in the dialogue] of mine that I pushed a little too far. But what's very clever about it – you can play it very realistically. I think, sometimes, I was a little too aware of how funny it was. I adored the script so much, and sat with it for so long, that I think I became aware of how clever it was. In some ways, you have to stop thinking about that.'

It's a fair piece of self-criticism, and something that could easily be levelled at Gondry – who thankfully manages not to fall into the same trap of admiring the brilliance of Kaufman's conceit from afar on their second collaboration, *Eternal Sunshine of the Spotless Mind*. Maybe he took a long look at Jonze's collaborations with Kaufman. As with *Being John Malkovich*, Jonze manages not to become lost inside Kaufman's maze of ideas on *Adaptation*, instead nurturing them to fruition. Restricting his own visual flourishes to moments such as the time-lapse day-to-night sequence that closes the film, Jonze realized that Kaufman's words are strong enough to speak for themselves, without recourse to pyrotechnics.

'On *Adaptation*, the visual approach was to keep it simple and real, and leave us room to focus on the performances, the characters and the relationships,' says Jonze. 'We knew way before we shot that when we got into editing, that would be the time when the movie would come together. I wanted to keep it as modular as possible. We constantly moved stuff around in editing; it was almost like editing a documentary. The first two-thirds are not plot driven; it's more interior. What drives the movie are the internal thoughts and feelings of the characters. There's a lot of jumping around in time and locations.'

In this sense they [the insect and the flower] show us how to live, how the only barometer you have is your heart. When you spot your flower, you can't let anything get in the way.
John Laroche, *Adaptation*

As audacious as the concepts for both *Adaptation* and *Eternal Sunshine of the Spotless Mind* are, it's their manner of execution that leaves a lasting impression. Constructed with architectural care, the shape and structure of these two Kaufman screenplays emulates the very themes central to the stories being told. First *Adaptation*, a story that literally grew out of Kaufman's own struggles to bring *The New Yorker* journalist Susan Orlean's 1998 book *The Orchid Thief* to the screen. The result – which blends excerpts from Orlean's 'unfilmable' story with scenes of Kaufman's writer's block – is a meta-film about the process of creation that unfolds like a flower shot by time-lapse photography. As Kaufman says of his screen alter ego, 'You're watching a movie he's writing as he writes it.' (For the sake of clarity, the author will be referred to here as 'Kaufman', while his screen version will be 'Charlie'.) Not unlike Woody Allen's *Deconstructing Harry* (1997), this trick is not truly unveiled until the final act when Charlie begins to comment on events as they happen, such as the ending, where he drives out of the parking lot, claiming this would make a suitable conclusion to his work.

'It came out of desperation,' notes Kaufman:

I really couldn't deal with the project anymore. I didn't know what to do with it. I struggled with it for four months. I became more and more depressed. When I started thinking about this idea, it seemed to answer a lot of questions about how to proceed. Then things opened up for me. It was a eureka moment tinged with, 'Oh my God, what am I doing?' I was concerned with how I'd represented Susan, and the fact that I'd put myself in a script. I was mostly concerned with that. It felt self-indulgent and a bit embarrassing. But I take a certain kind of thrill in doing that too. I felt like I was being honest and was therefore taking a risk, which I like to do.

Returning to the themes of *Human Nature*, *Adaptation* is a film about evolution, but on a far grander scale. It begins, as it should, with the birth of mankind. This is prompted early in the narrative when Charlie, outside the studio where *Being John Malkovich* is being shot, asks rhetorically, 'How did I get here?' Cue a crash course from Jonze in the history of the natural world, 'the journey we all take', as a series of images detailing the evolutionary process skitter across the screen, leading us back to the beleaguered figure of Charlie.

But *Adaptation* is not just an exploration of Darwinian theories. Kaufman's characters, like his screenplay, evolve organically as the film progresses. As the subject of Orlean's book, the indefatigable John Laroche (Chris Cooper), will later say: 'Adaptation is a profound process. It means you figure out how to thrive in the world.' A survivor whose life has been beset by tragedy – losing his front teeth, wife, mother and uncle in a car accident, and later his hothouses in a hurricane – Laroche has figured out how to 'thrive'. His willingness to drop his passions – such as tropical fish – at will symbolizes this to perfection. Compare him to Orlean (Meryl Streep) who, hermetically sealed in her smug Upper West Side existence, admits to herself: 'I want to know what it feels like to care about something passionately.' But as her obsession with Laroche grows, in tandem with her addiction to the green Ghost Orchid extract she has taken to sniffing, it shows she is unwilling, or unable, to change her life for the better.

As for Charlie, obsessed with Orlean in much the way she is with her subject, he may fail in trying to 'dramatize [and] . . . show the flower's arc' but, by the end of the film, he has evolved as a person. As he cracks his script, he is 'for the first time filled with hope', shedding the self-loathing that has dogged him throughout the story and his life. His own evolution mirrors the evolution of the screenplay – which no longer resembles the radical work Charlie tries and fails to complete in the first two acts. The key axis point in the film comes when he concedes he is getting nowhere, and takes up twin brother Donald's advice of attending a seminar held by Robert McKee.

On the plane to New York, he reads a pivotal sentence from Orlean's book – 'Life seemed to be filled with things like the Ghost Orchid . . . fantastic, fleeting and out of reach' – just seconds after we have heard the same line from her. As we reach the film's final third, source and screenplay begin to merge. Sitting in the attentive audience thinking he's a sell-out – spoken as voice-over just before McKee on stage admonishes the use of such a device – Charlie is given the kernel of an idea for his conclusion. 'Find an ending but don't cheat,' McKee tells him. 'Your character must change but it must come from them.'

This happens, as not only does Laroche come to realize that his relationship with Orlean must end, as she is ashamed of him, but Charlie comes to appreciate the brother he has always spurned. With the conclusion also featuring a car chase in the Florida swamps, gun-play and even the death of Laroche in the jaws of an alligator – elements of Hollywood convention Charlie has thus far derided – it's little wonder this schizophrenic screenplay is credited to both Charlie and Donald. Quite what this self-reflexive masterstroke means is open to numerous interpretations. Is *Adaptation* a dramatization of the eternal Hollywood struggle between author and screenwriter? Or, more specifically, is it a reaction by Kaufman to the difficulty of following up a film as original as *Being John Malkovich* in an industry where odious agents champion ludicrous screenplays like Donald's serial killer script *The 3*? As Donald notes, quoting McKee, 'we all write in a genre', and despite its resistance to this in the first two-thirds – in an attempt to write something refreshing – Charlie's screenplay ultimately succumbs to McKee's principles of story structure.

Like McKee, the gregarious Donald proves unexpectedly influential over Charlie. Not only does his advice allow his sibling to finish his screenplay: he also teaches him how to live, how to open himself up to life. 'You are what you love – not what loves you,' he tells him. Lesson learnt, Charlie (or perhaps, by now, Kaufman) has no more need for Donald's happy-go-lucky commercial instincts, and the script necessarily kills him off (via a speeding car, naturally). While Donald and Charlie represent two sides to Kaufman's artistic leanings, as he wrestles with the very notion of what makes a good screenplay, he has already lampooned his own 'split-personality' device. This is done via Donald's script, which revolves around the notion that a killer, a victim and a cop are all the same person – a concept not so far removed from James Mangold's 2003 thriller *Identity*.

It's a slippery final third, as Kaufman both mocks and embraces his own ideals and those of McKee. In the end, they find some sort of harmony, a coexistence on the page, as expressed in The Turtles' song 'Happy Together' that reverberates through the film. And so at the very end, as Charlie finally makes a move on the cute cellist Amelia (Cara Seymour), only to be rebuffed as she has found love with another man, Kaufman is fully in control of the screenplay. As Orlean has already noted of her own time with Laroche, 'the relationship ends when the book ends'. It may not be a happy Hollywood ending – after all, Donald is dead and Charlie doesn't get the girl – but it's a hopeful one.

Come the 2003 Oscars, it was the same story. While Chris Cooper rightfully won for Best Supporting Actor, both Cage and Streep were overlooked, beaten in their respective categories by *The Pianist*'s Adrien Brody and *Chicago*'s Catherine Zeta-Jones. Although both have been recognized previously in their careers by the Academy, it was a shame that the most nuanced and most playful performances of, respectively, Cage's and Streep's bodies of work were ignored. More important, Kaufman lost in the Best Adapted Screenplay category to *The Pianist* scribe Ronald Harwood (three years after losing the Best Original Screenplay award to *American Beauty*'s Alan Ball). With 'Donald' sharing Kaufman's nomination, evidently Hollywood wasn't quite ready to embrace such a radical departure from the McKee-blighted screenplays that dominate the marketplace.

Blessed are the forgetful, for they get the better even of their blunders.
  Friedrich Nietzsche, *Beyond Good and Evil*

Like *Adaptation*, *Eternal Sunshine of the Spotless Mind* ends on a muted but positive note: even if we fall into repeat patterns in our relationships with lovers, we should never give up on finding unbridled happiness. Ironically, Kaufman was commissioned to write the script – the idea for which was inspired by a dinner conversation between Michel Gondry and the artist Pierre Bismuth – within days of winning the job of adapting *The Orchid Thief*. And like *Adaptation*, Kaufman's eventual screenplay proved to be a cryptic and playful piece of work, thematically and structurally unified, but one that resonates with human emotion.

For some critics, it represents his most mature work to date: 'Say what you will about previous Kaufman efforts . . . none of them exhibits the sensitivity and romantic longing that envelops *Eternal Sunshine* like a soft blanket on a chilly night . . . as an affirmation of the power and meaning of love – sharing experiences, memories and risks – in its concluding moments *Eternal Sunshine* achieves a touching and unexpected epiphany.'[119] It was also the most successful, reaping $34.1 million in the U.S., compared to the $22 million that both *Adaptation* and *Being John Malkovich* took.

Divorced from the self-referential, celebrity-intoxicated worlds of *Being John Malkovich* and *Adaptation*, or the 'paradise lost' state that envelops *Human Nature*, this is certainly Kaufman's most universal script – particularly given the subject matter, the erasure of a relationship from the minds of the two participants. But that's not to say this was the first time he successfully dealt with matters of the heart. Like *Eternal Sunshine of the Spotless Mind*, previous outings have focused on the nature of obsession and love, but in a more darkly comic way. Compared to the odd couplings of *Human Nature*, the self-love (and loathing) of *Adaptation* or the bizarre love triangles of *Being John Malkovich*, a story dealing with the breakdown of a straightforward relationship would always resonate with more people. That Kaufman won his first Oscar in the Best Original Screenplay category at the 2005 ceremony went some way towards indicating this.

The film's title comes from a line in Alexander Pope's poem 'Eloisa to Abelard', based around the thwarted twelfth-century paramours celebrated for their correspondence who were also featured in Craig's street-based puppet show in *Being John Malkovich*.

> How happy is the blameless vestal's lot!
> The world forgetting, by the world forgot.
> Eternal sunshine of the spotless mind!
> Each pray'r accepted, and each wish resign'd;
> Labour and rest, that equal periods keep;
> 'Obedient slumbers that can wake and weep;' [120]

While the reference to the poem once again signals Kaufman's thematic obsession with love gone awry, the title itself sums up the very crux of the film: is it better to have loved and lost, than never to have loved at all?

In an everyday story of boy-meets-girl, boy-loses-girl, girl-has-boy-surgically-wiped-from-her-memory, Kaufman – as he did with the portal in *Being John Malkovich* – uses technology as the starting point for his story. The lengthy opening sequence that we assume is the prologue introduces us to our main protagonists: the shy and retiring cartoonist Joel Barish (Jim Carrey, complete with facial hair) and the vivacious librarian Clementine Kruczynski (Kate Winslet, complete with various shades of hair dye). Setting the film over Valentine's Day – as Joel says, 'a holiday invented by greeting card companies to make people feel like crap' – Kaufman makes his intentions explicit from the outset. This is an anti–Valentine's Day card, free of the commercialized and cynical schmaltz that blights such tacky expressions of feeling (a staple of the Hollywood romantic comedy and, one might say, something Kaufman was unable to resist venturing towards in *Adaptation*).

In this sequence, as Joel ditches work for the day and encounters Clementine on a train bound for the Long Island seaside town of Montauk, the dialogue is pregnant with double meaning. 'Do I know you?' asks Clementine, before later telling Joel: 'You don't know me, so you don't know.' Of course, they do know each other. This is their second 'first' meeting. We have already discovered that the last two years' worth of entries in Joel's diary have been removed. By the finale, we will know why. Clementine, via the specialist company Lacuna, run by Dr Howard Mierzwiak (Tom Wilkinson), has had all traces of her failing relationship with Joel removed from her memory. Inconsolable, Joel has decided to do the same.

The bulk of the film is taken up with this procedure, as Lacuna tech-

46 Guy Pearce as Leonard Shelby in *Memento*.

nicians Stan (Mark Ruffalo) and Patrick (Elijah Wood) spend an evening at Joel's apartment frying his brain. In fact, from the moment Joel begins to look for the Lacuna building shortly after the credits, we have actually been 'inside' the process – the scenes of him applying to have his memory wiped being the first to be deleted. By the time this is made explicit, as we cut to Stan and Patrick in his bedroom, we get to view first hand just why Joel and Clementine have split, as memories from their time together are played out in reverse.

It begins, naturally, at its most unpleasant: 'I assume you fucked someone tonight. Isn't that how you get people to like you?' accuses

Joel, after he discovers she's wrecked his car. As their relationship gets younger, the arguments become less serious and more mundane – from whether they should have children to hair being left in the soap. With these conversations being something we all recognize, the conceit comes as Joel realizes he no longer wants to forget his darling Clementine. It transpires that his unhappiness over her is part of his identity: a conscious presence inside his mind. Joel decides to spirit the Clementine of his memories into a part of his brain where the Lacuna technicians won't be able to find her. This means giving Clementine a front row seat in the show that was his childhood – from baby baths in the sink to being caught masturbating by his mother.

Ironically, these are the scenes where Gondry excels while Kaufman lapses into self-indulgence. As memories begin to collide, converge and collapse, Gondry delivers a rush of surreal images: the double bed on the beach, a faceless Patrick in the library where Clementine works; a fence disappearing post by post; a house being erased; a car crashing from the sky. With the narrative at a standstill, it's fair to say this is territory Kaufman has explored before. Recalling the trapdoor-linked 'memory rooms' in *Being John Malkovich*, in which characters crawl from one embarrassing Malkovich childhood recollection to another, it feels like Kaufman's repeating himself. Then again, maybe that's the point.

The film plays out like Christopher Nolan's *Memento* (2000) – but not, as you might think, because we are viewing events from end to beginning. In *Memento*, we learn that the reverse-played excerpts of vengeance-obsessed Leonard Shelby's attempts at retribution are, in fact, part of a much bigger structure; a perpetual loop, enabled by his short-term memory, that leaves him in a desperate and never-ending cycle of violence as he hunts for the killer of his wife. With *Eternal Sunshine of the Spotless Mind*, superficially, once we are in the recesses of Joel's memory, his relationship with Clementine *is* viewed in reverse, also recalling Harold Pinter's backwards-plotted analysis of a couple's union in *Betrayal*. But ultimately, it transpires that – like Leonard – these star-crossed lovers are destined to exist in a patterned cycle of behaviour and to repeat the same mistakes. Like *Memento*'s reverse time-shifts, which allow the audience to experience first hand what it's like to have Leonard's short-term memory loss, so the cyclical structure of *Eternal Sunshine of the Spotless Mind* puts us inside Joel's mind. As Dr Mierzwiak says, 'Technically speaking the procedure *is* brain damage,' and the film hints, via its narrative zigzags, that Joel might be suffering from some form of mental illness.

As we reach the final memories inside Joel's mind, we return to the beach. Briefly referenced when Joel is giving an account of their pairing to Dr Mierzwiak early in the film, this is the location for the real 'first' meeting between him and Clementine some two years ago, confirmed by the fact that he sings, much to her annoyance, 'Oh my darling Clementine' – a song he claimed not to know in the film's prologue. We now know that this was a post-Lacuna Joel. With his final words about Clementine – 'She was just a girl' – wiped from his mind, it's time for him to wake up. The film returns to the sequence, seen at the outset, which we now realize is the epilogue.

Kaufman also brings a secondary relationship into the film – Dr Mierzwiak and his young secretary Mary Svevo (Kirsten Dunst) – which mirrors that of Joel and Clementine. With Mary's surname recalling the writer Italo Svevo, Kaufman alludes to Svevo's 1923 book *Zeno's Conscience*, a first-person account of the protagonist's failed attempts to quit smoking. Frustrated by his psychoanalyst, who won't allow him to forget his past, Zeno – like many of Kaufman's characters, Mary included – finds true progress impossible. As Kaufman hints, one must cultivate the art of forgetting if the transition from one lover to the next is to be managed.

Mary, ironically, recites the Nietzsche passage – quoted at the top of this section – about how some are fortunate to be able to forget their failures. Infatuated by Dr Mierzwiak, Mary is reminded that she and he already 'have a history', as the good doctor delicately puts it. That Mary chose to wipe her mind of it leaves her in the same unenlightened position as Joel. Collecting all the confidential taped interviews between Dr Mierzwiak and his clients, she mails them all back to those it may concern. As a narrative device, this allows Joel and Clementine – who have, of course, just met for the second 'first' time – to realize they too have a 'history'. With the tapes full of invective from each about the other, they now know their last stab at making a go of it was a failure.

In what is probably Kaufman's most self-referential line in the film, Clementine notes, 'I'm not a concept, Joel. I'm just a fucked-up girl looking for my own peace [or should that be 'piece'?] of mind.' It is here that Kaufman achieves what he has struggled to do in the past: to transcend the conceptual nature of his story and achieve a universal resonance, thus affirming the value of romantic couplings. Joel and Clementine decide to have another go at their relationship, despite being aware that they have already split once and that they may be destined to repeat the same mistakes. As Kaufman's circular structure has already hinted, Joel and Clementine are caught in a behavioural cycle they may never break. Like the conclusion to *Adaptation*, it's a pathos-drenched finale; hope and melancholy are blended with equal measure. Maybe they will fail, maybe they won't. Either way, the fact that they are going to try adds up to the most deliriously romantic moment in Kaufman's oeuvre so far. After all, as Beck croons on the song that accompanies the credits, 'Everybody's got to learn sometime.'

I am responsible for polluting the airwaves with mind-numbing puerile entertainment. In addition, I have murdered thirty-three human beings.
Chuck Barris, *Confessions of a Dangerous Mind*

While both Gondry and Jonze involved Kaufman at every stage of the production during the making of the four films he bequeathed them, the same cannot be said about George Clooney on *Confessions of a Dangerous Mind*. By the time it went into production in late 2001, Kaufman's script had been in existence for over six years, having already been in development with numerous directors, including Curtis Hanson, David Fincher and Bryan Singer. Originally a Warner Bros. project, it was put into turnaround and picked up by New Line Cinema.

With actors such as Mike Myers and Jim Carrey mentioned to play Chuck Barris, *Entertainment Weekly* named it one of the ten-best unproduced screenplays of the time. 'I think what fascinated me about the Barris story is that he claims he's an assassin in a very straightforward way,' says Kaufman. 'I didn't quite believe it, so I was curious. The question of whether anything is true or not always interests me – if it weren't true, why would he make up this fantasy? It seemed like an odd fantasy for an adult to attach himself to.'

Pre-production costs were already standing at $5 million by the time Clooney, who was attached to play CIA operative Jim Byrd from the beginning, took the reins. With the budget heading towards $40 million, and with Miramax on board as backers, the actor-turned-director called in some favours. Recruiting Julia Roberts, as a mysterious femme fatale, and Drew Barrymore, as Chuck's on-off hippie girlfriend Penny, to work for scale, Clooney also dropped Johnny Depp in favour of the relatively unknown Sam Rockwell to play Chuck. In the end, it wasn't enough; *Confessions of a Dangerous Mind* recouped just $16 million in its native country.

More significantly, Clooney played around with Kaufman's screenplay. He later told journalists at the 2003 Berlin Film Festival: 'Charlie Kaufman is a great screenwriter, and dialogue is probably what he's best at. Most of the time, you just had to sit back and let his work speak for itself. There weren't a lot of Clooney-isms there.' What Clooney seemingly failed to realize is that while Kaufman's dialogue is strong, it's his ability to structure a screenplay that remains his true forte. The finished film falters in the final third, for no other reason than Clooney being unable to disguise the fact that this is a one-joke movie. From the outset, we know that Chuck is a con man, as a flashback to his childhood shows him attempting to convince a girl he has a strawberry-flavoured penis. He is the archetypal unreliable narrator, with Clooney's CIA operative the superego to his id. But as the realisation dawns upon us, so does the notion that what we are watching is an illusion. Despite the presence of Roberts and Rutger Hauer, the Berlin sequences – where Chuck chaperones the winners of his game show as a cover for his espionage work – leave the narrative in neutral.

As was reported during the release of *Eternal Sunshine of the Spotless Mind*, Kaufman was less than pleased with the end result. 'I was unhappy with the fact that he took the movie from me and then cut me out after that. I'm unhappy with the end result. And I'm unhappy with George Clooney. I had a movie that I wrote and that isn't it. Clooney just rewrote a bunch of the stuff, took a load of things out and restructured it. And I know that's what happens when movies are made, but I've always been involved in the process with Spike and Michel. If there's any rewriting to do, I do it . . . I mean, Clooney went on forever about how my *Confessions* . . . screenplay was one of the greatest scripts he'd ever read. But if someone truthfully felt that way then they'd want the person who wrote it to be onboard, offering their thoughts and criticisms. But Clooney didn't. And I think it's a silly way to be a director.'[121]

In Clooney's defence, he undeniably made the film his own. He recruited his principal crew from projects he was close to: cinematographer Newton Thomas Sigel (Bryan Singer's regular DP since *The Usual Suspects*), Clooney worked with on *Three Kings*; while editor Stephen Mirrione (who won an Oscar for Soderbergh's *Traffic*) had cut together *Ocean's Eleven*. Flexing his muscles as a director, Clooney – who storyboarded every shot with the Coen brothers' regular artist J. Todd Anderson – delivered one of the most visually original films of the year. Not unlike Gondry, Clooney eschewed the use of computer effects, preferring to use revolving sets and costume changes to enable the actors to move seamlessly from one scene to another (thus emulating techniques used in the early days of television).

In many ways Clooney was a perfect choice to direct a script about television's corrosive influence. Nephew of actress Rosemary Clooney (name-checked during the film) and son of newscaster and talk-show host Nick Clooney, the Kentucky-born actor would make his name on the medical drama *ER* as television's most desirable doctor, Doug Ross. As the film's opening scene shows – in which a bearded Chuck decides to pen his story – Clooney fully understands the themes under consideration: clinically depressed, Chuck is holed up in his musty hotel room, strewn with symbolic garbage. Barris, after all, was responsible for low-IQ game shows like *The Dating Game* and *The Newlywed Game*, as well as the dire 'talent' vehicle *The Gong Show*.

'Certainly it's about the dark side of pop culture,' says Clooney. 'It's more an indictment of popular television at the time. Chuck gets blamed for being the father of the Jerry Springers of the world. In some ways it's fair. He should get some of the blame. But not all of it. I decided to make his double life a metaphor for the assassination of the American viewing audience. I loved the idea of comparing bad television to the CIA. That made me laugh out loud. I wanted to change the line on the trailer for the film to, "There's One Business Like Show Business!"'

By the end, Clooney and Kaufman make the link explicit: television, a device designed to humiliate and degrade, is far deadlier than an automatic weapon. Cut to a shot of the real Barris, we hear his idea for a new game show: three guys with loaded guns look back at their lives to see what they've accomplished and how close they got to their dreams. 'The winner is the one who doesn't blow his brains out,' says Chuck. 'He gets a refrigerator.' It's a resonant moment, one of the film's precious few. Gone is the wide-eyed youngster, full to the brim with (misguided) ideas and optimism. Returning full circle, here is a dreamer shorn of his dreams: 'When you're young, your potential is infinite . . . then you get to an age where what you might be gives way to what you have been. You weren't Einstein. You weren't anything. That's a bad moment.'

It's easy to see why Kaufman was attracted to adapting Barris's book. Set to the backdrop of the entertainment industry (as both *Being John Malkovich* and *Adaptation* are), Barris' story blends fantasy and reality in much the same way as Kaufman's earlier films, portraying real-life figures with a degree of dramatic license. Likewise, it deals with the issue of failure and how it can affect the psyche. Following Craig in *Being John Malkovich*, Joel in *Eternal Sunshine of the Spotless Mind* and Donald and Charlie in *Adaptation*, Chuck is someone who seeks approval, is beset by a degree of self-loathing and hits rock bottom.

Like those who enter the Malkovich portal, or *Adaptation*'s John Laroche, pondering who should 'play' him, craving the spotlight is at the centre of *Confessions of a Dangerous Mind*. It even afflicts Chuck himself. During his *Gong Show* years, as the cane-twirling, top-hat-sporting ringmaster, he takes centre stage, like a celebrity Pied Piper. His acolytes from the show, the Unknown Comic and Gene-Gene The Dancing Machine, are proof positive of the depths people will sink to. Pre-dating the explosion of reality television, when anyone wishing to be embarrassed for the sake of viewing figures is allowed on the box, these are characters desperate to feel the warm glow of the cathode ray tubes.

Kaufman treads a fine line, playing with our perceptions of a personality, as filtered through the media – as he does with Malkovich and himself, respectively in *Being John Malkovich* and *Adaptation*. Complicating the portrait of Chuck, one of the most innovative aspects of the film is its use of to-camera interviews with Barris' associates, providing multiple perspectives on the man. Dick Clark, the host of the ABC show *American Bandstand*, notes, 'I wouldn't want to live his life because he hasn't been happy all of his life.' The *Gong Show* panelist Jaye P. Morgan says, 'He was a good guy, even though he was a prick.' Jim Lange, host of *The Dating Game*, reasons, 'He obviously had the common touch because he knew what people wanted to watch.'

In many ways, just as Kaufman wrestled with the problems of adapting a book in *Adaptation*, so he considers the difficulties of the biopic in *Confessions of a Dangerous Mind*. How can a writer-director convey a life other than theirs with any degree of accuracy? In this case, by inserting documentary-style footage of real-life associates. But can we trust them? And for that matter, given that Barris's autobiography is 'unauthorized', can we trust him? As evidenced by the lengthy fantasy Cold War sequence, the film comments upon our ability to rewrite our own histories. At the same time, it notes that as audience members, we are willing to accept lurid fantasy in place of ugly reality. For Charlie Kaufman, it's a theme that dominates all of his work to date.

By morning, you'll be gone. The perfect ending to this shit story.
Joel Barish, *Eternal Sunshine of the Spotless Mind*

Arguing that the modern Hollywood screenplay will always be taken from the writer and reworked, because filmmaking is 'a collaborative process', *The Observer*'s Mark Morris stated, 'scriptwriters – already well paid, now even better paid and getting a bit more recognition in the business – should be happy as they are. The only real stars in Hollywood are the ones up on the screen.' Yet he conceded, 'Nevertheless it can only be a good thing when people like Charlie Kaufman, or *Election* writer-director Alexander Payne, or the *Rushmore* team of Wes Anderson and Owen Wilson, are getting attention. All have genuinely startling ideas, the kind that can't be cobbled together by committee. If Hollywood wants more films like *Being John Malkovich* and fewer sequels, no one is going to complain.'[122]

Kaufman, who for a long time was left on the fringes of Hollywood, now knows this to be true. Yet as his screenplays show, he distrusts Hollywood. As is reflected particularly in *Adaptation* and *Confessions of a Dangerous Mind*, Kaufman is obsessed with whether the entertainment industry contributes to the dumbing down of contemporary culture. But he freely admits the glamour is seductive, as symbolized when his alter ego in *Adaptation* – desperate for the approval of Valerie Thomas (Tilda Swinton), the female executive who commissions him to adapt *The Orchid Thief* – masturbates to the thought of her. Kaufman's self-disgust manifests itself with his portrayals of male executives as misogynists. In *Being John Malkovich*, Malkovich's arrogant agent repeatedly apologizes to his client 'for the cunt at reception'. Meanwhile in *Adaptation*, Charlie's agent Marty (Ron Livingston) muses, out loud, about which female co-workers he'd like to sodomize.

Inspired in part by his real-life agent, UTA star Marty Bowen, Marty (both the character and his real-life counterpart) is, Kaufman admits, separated from 'the feeling of falseness and sharkiness in [most] agents' in that 'he seems to be who he is and says what he thinks'.[123] However much he might be having fun at the expense of Bowen – a man with a reputation for partying hard – Kaufman clearly respects a straight shooter in a town full of crooked gunslingers. It was Bowen who really pushed for *Being John Malkovich* to be made, after Kaufman's previous agent at William Morris had stalled on the project. In turn, just like in the film, Kaufman really did visit Bowen when he found adapting Susan Orlean's *The Orchid Thief* an impossible task. Rather than tell Kaufman quitting the job would be bad for his career, as his screen version does, Bowen simply said, 'Whatever you need to do.'

Like Jonze and Gondry, and the executives such as Thomas who dared to believe in Kaufman's vision, Bowen needs to be congratulated for nurturing the considerable – and unique – talent of this fragile genius. Were Kaufman to direct, it would enable him to join the likes of Quentin Tarantino, David O. Russell and Paul Thomas Anderson as one of contemporary cinema's genuine auteurs. Such a move from the typewriter to the camera could bestow upon Kaufman the responsibility of spearheading the next generation of mavericks. He would probably recoil at the thought, but his singular quest for originality is a shining example to any budding filmmaker.

Hollywood, at least, has recognized this. Studios have begun to make room, among their summer popcorn films and their winter heavyweights, for good writing. Aside from the scripts of Kaufman and Mike White, and in addition to the work of the aforementioned writer-directors included in this study, writing partnerships – rather than scripts-by-committee – are back in vogue. As we have already seen in previous chapters, the collaborations of directors Alexander Payne, Wes Anderson and Bryan Singer, with their respective partners Jim Taylor, Owen Wilson and Christopher McQuarrie, have all born fruit. Meanwhile, David Fincher and Steven Soderbergh are, in their own way, cultivating a stable of reliable writers to work with.

It would be naive to think that Hollywood studios will entirely lean towards such a creative pool. There will always be films – particularly those with enormous budgets – that are written and repeatedly rewritten by a half-dozen or more writers who never get to meet, have to arbitrate for a credit and wind up feeling disenchanted. As detrimental to a project as this is, it's perfectly understandable. A sign of desperation on the part of the executives banking their reputations and jobs on the scripts in question, it's only, as Kaufman knows so well, the result of human nature.

CHAPTER 20

Family Ties: *The Royal Tenenbaums*, *About Schmidt* and *Punch-Drunk Love*

47 Emily Watson and Adam Sandler share a kiss in *Punch-Drunk Love*.

Early December 2001 saw the U.S. release of Wes Anderson's majestic third film, *The Royal Tenenbaums*. The following May, at the Cannes Film Festival, both Alexander Payne's third film, the droll *About Schmidt* and Paul Thomas Anderson's fourth, the giddy *Punch-Drunk Love*, were unveiled. By now, it was six years since all three directors had made their feature film debuts and each had firmly established himself among the elite of contemporary U.S. filmmakers. These new works were as keenly anticipated as any other movie of the time – with the exception, perhaps, of Martin Scorsese's long-gestating *Gangs of New York*.

Each reaped just rewards for its creators, a sure sign these Sundance Kids were now regarded as major players. Despite a modest $17 million haul in the U.S., *Punch-Drunk Love* won P. T. Anderson a share of the Best Director prize at Cannes with Korean grand master Im Kwon-taek (for *Chihwaseon*). Meanwhile, Payne and co-writer Jim Taylor won a Golden Globe for their screenplay of *About Schmidt*, while the film grossed $65 million domestic. As for *The Royal Tenenbaums*, the cover of *Film Comment* heralded it as the film of 2001. Winning a Best Original Screenplay Oscar nomination for Wes Anderson and Owen Wilson, it took $52.3 million at the U.S. box office.

Once again all three directors were dealing with the subject of the family dynamic, and each film was also a textbook example of how the Sundance Kids set about making movies. With the scripts written free of outside interference, the resulting films were all mid-budget pictures funded by the studio system – Touchstone Pictures/Disney for *The Royal Tenenbaums*; Sony Pictures for *Punch-Drunk Love* and newcomers New Line for *About Schmidt*. Payne and Taylor, in particular, were now true insiders. The pair had already begun to carve out a niche for themselves as Hollywood script doctors, having reshaped both Joe Johnston's *Jurassic Park III* (2001) and Jay Roach's *Meet the Parents* (2000). In the latter, for which they remain uncredited, the sequence in which Robert De Niro forces Ben Stiller to take an ad hoc lie detector test at the airport was entirely their invention. 'It's a sideline,' says Payne. 'Normally it takes us six months to write a screenplay for something I'm going to direct, so it's nice to be forced to do something with a deadline – and something that we don't care deeply about.'

Can't somebody be a shit for their whole life. And then try and repair the damage?
Royal Tenenbaum, *The Royal Tenenbaums*

While *Punch-Drunk Love* upturns the romantic comedy and *About Schmidt* uses the road movie by way of investigating the theme of family, *The Royal Tenenbaums* actually sets itself up as a household melodrama. Following in the footsteps of Orson Welles's saga *The Magnificent Ambersons* and Jean Renoir's country house drama *La Règle du jeu* (1939), it also appropriately recalls J. D. Salinger's Glass family stories. For while *Rushmore* is framed by its stage curtains, suggesting its theatrical origins, *The Royal Tenenbaums* is presented to us as a dusty volume pulled from the shelves of a library.

The very first shot, of a book bearing the film's title, confirms this. Borrowed by an unseen user, the cover is rather old-fashioned – not some gold-embossed dust jacket but one that looks as if it were printed years ago. Likewise, its method of removal – stamped with ink rather than its bar code scanned – hints that we are entering into a rather quaint world devoid of contemporary trappings. As we will discover, modern technology has been pushed to the side; vinyl records, not CDs, are the preferred format for listening to music. The closest we come to electronic gizmos will be a portable television crudely strapped to a bathroom radiator. A remembrance of things past, without feeling like a retro time capsule, the very fabric of Wes Anderson's film is drenched in a wistful nostalgia, entirely fitting for a story about the once-great Tenenbaum family who have all fallen on hard times.

The film is divided into a prologue and eight chapters, the start of each shown as a page from this fictional Tenenbaum biography complete with etchings illustrating the characters as you might once have seen them in a Victorian novel. There are even a few words glimpsed from the beginning of each chapter, describing the early action of the scene that follows. With Alec Baldwin narrating in the authoritative, hushed tone of the omnipotent novelist, we are led into a protracted meet-and-greet with the characters. Briefly, Royal Tenenbaum (Gene Hackman) and his wife Etheline (Angelica Huston) have three

48 Wes Anderson and Gene Hackman on the set of *The Royal Tenenbaums*.
49 The once great Tenenbaum family.

over-achieving children: Chas, an entrepreneur who made a fortune from breeding Dalmatian mice; Richie, his tennis-ace brother; and Margot, their adopted sister – as Royal keeps reminding her – who found success as a young playwright. In tribute, Etheline even writes a book entitled *Family of Geniuses*, as a way to show other parents how to nurture prodigious talents. As Wes Anderson says, 'That's probably what I wish my formative years were like. It probably sounds weird, as the characters don't really have good experiences. But I like characters who are aspiring to something beyond their grasp and are not reluctant to try to achieve something.' But it was not to last. As the narrator tells us: 'In fact, virtually all memory of the brilliance of the young Tenenbaums had been erased by two decades of betrayal, failure and disaster.'

With the exception, perhaps, of P. T. Anderson's establishing sequence in *Boogie Nights*, there has not been a better introduction to the main players in any ensemble film of the era than this. In an opening often compared to that of François Truffaut's *Jules et Jim* (1962), just as Baldwin completes the sentence quoted above – the end to this breathless and breathtaking set-up – Wes Anderson literally lifts us into the air as Richie lets go his pet falcon Mordecai from the rooftop. Set to an instrumental version of The Beatles' 'Hey Jude', it's like a hymn to the Tenenbaums' former glories, these final words timed to coincide with the song's concluding mantra-like chant, mainlining a celluloid rush that most films find themselves hard pressed to provide over ninety minutes, let alone ten.

After the prologue comes the cast of characters, reintroducing each one twenty-two years later in much the same manner. Ben Stiller, Luke Wilson and Gwyneth Paltrow are billed as Chas, Richie and Margot, while Owen Wilson is Eli Cash, Richie's neighbouring friend from their childhood who has since published his second novel – a sub–Cormac McCarthy tome called *Old Custer* – to great acclaim. Margot, now married to the Oliver Sachs–like writer and neurologist Raleigh St Clair (Bill Murray), has not completed a play in seven years, preferring to lock herself in the bathroom for hours and secretly smoke cigarettes. Richie, always the favourite with Royal, much to the others' chagrin, still holds a candle for Margot, lit the day they ran away from home and camped out in the African wing of the public archives. Recalling Björn Borg, who retired at the top of his profession, Richie quit tennis after he suffered a meltdown in his last game – the day after his sister married Raleigh. Wearing a beard, sunglasses and head-band, he has for the past year remained adrift on an ocean liner (inspired by Anderson's own experience travelling to Europe to promote *Rushmore* on the QE2).

In fact, the apparel worn now by the Tenenbaum children is more or less what they wore in their youth, indicating just how stunted they are. Margot is glimpsed as a child in a zebra costume, performing one of her early plays. As an adult, she is rarely seen without her fur coat, as well as the blue and white horizontal-striped Le Coste dress and black loafers. With her hair worn in exactly the same style as seen in her childhood years (complete with red plastic clip), her panda-like eye shadow completes the wildlife-themed ensemble. Chas, of course, can be seen in the same-style business suit he sported as a teenager. While still a successful tycoon, his loss is more personal; the one with the most contempt for Royal, he has become increasingly paranoid about the safety of his two sons, Ari and Uzi, after his wife/their mother died in a plane crash. All three wear matching red track suits, so they can spot each other in a crowd. Chas also regularly puts them through fire drills in their sparsely furnished apartment, the only space in the film that looks in any way contemporary.

Kicked out of the house by Etheline after ten years of marriage, Royal has been lodging in the Lindbergh Palace hotel; we discover that in the 1980s he was disbarred and briefly imprisoned, partly down to Chas's efforts. Etheline, now an archaeologist, has not had sex with another man since Royal left – although Henry Sherman (Danny Glover), her business partner with whom she teaches people how to play bridge, wants to change that. When Royal discovers that Henry has plucked up the courage to propose – added to the fact that he has a pile of unpaid bills at his hotel – he decides action is needed. Claiming he has cancer, he returns to the family home to right some wrongs, just as Chas, Margot and Richie all independently of each other descend on the house too. 'I want this family to love me,' mumbles Royal, the film's central arc laid bare for all to see.

The problem – if, indeed, it is that – is how easy it is to stand back and admire *The Royal Tenenbaums*, without ever feeling moved by it. The crux of the story – aside from the discovery by Henry that Royal has been faking his illness – comes down to the odd love triangle between Richie, Margot and Eli that eventually leads to a suicide attempt by Richie. Yet whether you're soaking up the fact that Richie lives in a tent inside his old room or marvelling at the mocked-up album cover for the (fictional) Jamaican musical outfit – the Desmond Wilson Manchester XI – that Margot once joined, the densely detailed universe can distance you from this very sad tale about a family shattered by failure.

Is it a heavy layer of irony, laid on thick by Anderson and Wilson, that prevents you from crying tears of sadness as well as laughter? No. Rather, it's because the characters are emotionally sterile themselves, isolated from each other and unable to properly articulate their feelings, that they feel detached from us. As Royal tells Ari and Uzi, in just one example, 'I'm very sorry for your loss. Your mother was a terribly attractive woman.' The progression in Anderson's films seems to be one from innocence to experience. While in *Bottle Rocket* death was never a possibility, in *Rushmore* it was mentioned (with Miss Cross a widow). In *The Royal Tenenbaums* characters are aware of their own mortality. Both Chas and Henry are widowers; Richie tries to end his life, and the film concludes with Royal's funeral after he dies from a heart attack.

Anderson's regal, almost symmetrical style, eschewing the use of the Steadicam, may lend the film a rigid formality that sucks out the spontaneity – but it would be unfair to say that Anderson is not lacing the script with personal details. In interviews he has stated that he relates to Margot – as he, too, was a middle child and a budding playwright – and to Eli, as he often felt the need to belong to other families around him (no doubt why the communal nature of filmmaking appeals to him). His mother and Etheline share the same profession, while after his parents split when he was young his father left home, albeit to move just down the road. 'There's a lot more of my mother in the Angelica Huston character than of my father in Royal,' says Anderson. 'Her approach to raising the children, and the household that that character runs, are connected to my mother. My father was worried because the mother is so much like my mother that he felt this was my take on him, which was totally wrong. It was hard to convince him otherwise.'

At least for some of the cast, the notion of playing characters from an over-achieving family had some personal resonance. 'Ben Stiller's, Gwyneth Paltrow's, certainly Angelica Huston's . . . all those families are real achievers,' says Anderson. 'And fame is an issue for their whole families. For Angelica Huston, I think there are definitely things for her to relate to, in terms of people in her own life.' The director admits he didn't know much about Hackman's background until he saw an episode of *Inside the Actor's Studio* after the shoot was over.

> He did it while we were filming, and he talked about his father. That stuff caught me so much off guard, but it seemed to really relate to what he'd been playing in the movie. There was no dialogue between us about it. It was just clearly something he couldn't have helped but tap into. His father left his family when he was thirteen. And he just described this moment when his father was driving down the street, and Hackman and his friends were playing outside, and his father drove by and waved from the window but didn't stop the car. That was the last he saw of him for ten years. Hackman got really choked up when he was telling it. It was very moving – particularly since he was playing a father who abandons his family.

If *The Royal Tenenbaums* has personal relevance for Anderson and his cast, it's also a love letter to New York, albeit a fictitious, romanticized version of the city. There is no 375th Street, nor is there a Green Lines bus service or the run-down Gypsy Cab Company that he shows here. 'I've always had this fascination with New York,' says Anderson. 'I'm from Texas. There are so many New York novels and movies that are among my favorites, and so I had this not quite accurate idea of what New York was like.' Aside from Salinger, Edith Wharton and F. Scott Fitzgerald made an impression on Anderson, along with numerous New York–set films ranging from Walter Hill's *The Warriors* (1979) and William Friedkin's *The French Connection* to Frank Capra's *You Can't Take It with You* (1938).

Then there's Anderson's literary Bible, *The New Yorker*; in particular, the work of the magazine's regular cartoonist Roz Chast is reflected with Richie's sketches of Margot reading a variety of literary classics. In general, the written word is treated as sacred. Think of the rows of folders containing Chas's collection of *Fortune* magazine or the bunker of spy novels belonging to Royal in the hotel. Then there are the literary achievements of the characters: Raleigh's *The Peculiar Neurodegenerative Inhabitants of the Kazawa Doll*, Henry's *Accounting for Everything: A Guide to Personal Finance* and Margot's plays, *Nakedness Tonight*, *Static Electricity* and *Erotic Transference*.

In the end, *The Royal Tenenbaums* is saturated with set-up and texture to the point that the plot becomes secondary. While the first reel is all exposition, the pattern is set throughout the film; from the account of Margot's lovers by the private detective Raleigh hires to the final reel, dominated by the stunning shot that pans across the characters during the disrupted wedding of Henry and Etheline, Anderson wants us to hang with these characters, observe them in the minutiae of their lives. Although there are some dramatic moments – Richie's suicide attempt, Royal's death, Eli crashing his car into the house during the wedding – they seem to matter less than the everyday resolutions that are framed in miniature: Chas, for example, acknowledging Royal, after he saves Ari and Uzi from Eli's car. Rather than a novel, *The Royal Tenenbaums* feels like a photo album, full of snapshots of family life.

I am weak and I am a failure. There is no getting around it. Relatively soon, I will die.
  Warren Schmidt, *About Schmidt*

A sensitive yet scabrous look at the human condition, *About Schmidt* deals with old age with the same degree of wincing accuracy as *Election* dealt with pubescence. Like their previous efforts, Payne and Taylor walk a thin tightrope, the film frequently leaving you uncertain as to whether its creators like their characters.

Warren Schmidt (Jack Nicholson) is a retired insurance actuary who undertakes a 'futile road trip of non-discovery', as Payne puts it. Filled to the brim with the disappointments and denials that come with reaching your sell-by date in the family dynamic, it reads like a Midwest mixture of Akira Kurosawa's *Ikiru* (1952) and Yasujiro Ozu's *Tokyo Story* (1953). Old age, of course, is hardly a sexy topic in Hollywood. But *About Schmidt* joins that rather exclusive group of films – Ingmar Bergman's *Wild Strawberries* (1957), Jack Lemmon's *Kotch* (1971) and Hal Ashby's *Harold and Maude*, to an extent – that deal sympathetically with the subject.

The genesis of *About Schmidt* was serendipitous, to say the least. Partly based on the novel by Louis Begley, the resulting script also comprehensively plundered an unproduced screenplay entitled *The Coward*. Written by Payne during the period he first met Taylor, it dealt with a man enduring his retirement, even boasting the voice-over-as-letters gimmick that eventually worked its way into the film. Begley's novel, meanwhile, followed a character named Schmidt, a wealthy Harvard-educated New York lawyer. After his wife dies, he determines to stop his daughter, an advertising executive, from marrying 'an idiot', the Jewish son of two Manhattan shrinks. While Payne and Taylor removed the novel's mild strain of anti-Semitism to replace it with general misanthropy, the mechanics of the plot provided the narrative engine missing from *The Coward*, a rather formless script by all accounts.

Payne says *About Schmidt* 'came from, "Wouldn't it be funny if there were a guy, and he were sixty-six and he really fucked up all of his decisions and now he's paying for it?"' If the film is about retirement, it's only in as much as it's a starting point for the story. Like anyone, Warren hates the notion of being passed over, of being forced to come to terms with the fact that he is now surplus to requirements. Unable to let go of the routine he has clung to for most of his working life, he returns to his old office the day after his retirement to see if his 'cocky bastard' replacement needs any help. Needless to say, this oily upstart has it all under control, but when Warren returns home he tells his wife: '[He] needed my help with a couple of loose ends.' Not unlike *Election*'s Jim McAllister, Warren is a man who lives in denial; it's his defence mechanism, a place to salvage his inane pride.

To recall George and Weedon Grossmith's novel, *The Diary of a Nobody* is a more apt title than *About Schmidt*. Payne notes that Warren's ranting letters to Ndugu, the Tanzanian orphan he sponsors for $22 a month, are 'like a diary'. More than just an expositional device, they provide an insight into his psyche. 'He's not really writing to Ndugu, he's writing to himself. At the beginning of the film, he's shown to be extremely laconic. He could speak to nobody – even to himself. And it's only through this odd, epistolary relationship with Ndugu that he is able to say things, even to himself. It's not entirely incredible that he might be brought to a point that he could speak aloud.'

A portrait of an asshole as an old man, *About Schmidt* is relentless in wringing its comedy from the misfortunes of this crumpled heap of a chap. As Vicky, the occupational therapist Warren meets on his travels, tells him, 'inside you're a sad man'. She glimpses 'anger and . . . fear, loneliness' in him. You might add 'bitterness'; after forty-two years of marriage, the best he can say of his wife, Helen, is: 'Who is this old woman living in my house?' He hates the way she sits, smells and cuts him off in conversations. He hates the way she spends money on collections of thimbles and the fact that she forces him to urinate while sitting down on the toilet, his masculinity well and truly neutered. When she collapses and dies, Dustbuster in hand in a domestic swansong, he even buys her the cheapest-but-one casket from the funeral parlour, much to the disgust of his daughter Jeannie (Hope Davis).

Not above emotional blackmail – 'Who's gonna take care of me?' he whines to Jeannie – he's a pathetic creature at times. In yet another moment where Warren undercuts his speech via his actions, he tells Ndugu 'life is short . . . and I can't afford to waste another minute' just as he's dozing off in his chair watching ice hockey. When he wakes up, the television still on but playing a different program, he looks dishevelled from an uncomfortable night's sleep. But what's funny is not that he's wasted an evening snoozing. As he wanders around the house, we realize that Payne has installed the subtlest of jump cuts: it's now weeks later, the house is a mess, the cupboards are bare and he's living off frozen foods.

It's only when he discovers a pile of ancient love-letters from his best friend Ray to Helen, hinting at a brief affair they had years before, that he is finally motivated to leave his hometown of Omaha and head to Denver, on a crusade in his new Winnebago. He wants to stop Jeannie – set to marry Randall (Dermot Mulroney), a 'nincompoop' waterbed salesman with a mullet and a goatee – from making the same mistake he did. Echoed by the moody skies and windswept Nebraskan plains on his journey (shot by Payne's regular DP, James Glennon), this is not – as Payne makes it abundantly clear – a story heading towards some form of reconciliation.

Warren is a father who carries no pictures of his daughter in his wallet; as Jeannie hints, his concern about her marriage is the first time he's ever had an opinion on her in his life. His interference, it would seem, is more about absolving himself from guilt. Likewise, as he looks up at the stars, he asks the departed Helen: 'Was I really the man you wanted to be with . . . or were you disappointed?' And while he buys some 'exquisitely crafted' collectibles in memory of his wife, who loved them, he manages to carelessly leave them behind after his nighttime vigil. 'Nicholson likes that scene because it shows you what a fraud he is,' says Payne. 'He [Warren] is sincere but I'm not sure how sincere he is in the film.'

Notably, when Warren visits various museums, he does seem to represent the narrow-minded viewpoint of Middle America in relation to its history, culture and politics. 'Those people got a raw deal,' he reports to Ndugu, with surprise in his voice, when he learns about the plight of the Native Americans. Not unlike in *Citizen Ruth*, Payne dramatizes the conflict between traditional American values and New Age consciousness, here represented by Randall's ex-hippie mother, Roberta (Kathy Bates). Randall himself is caught somewhere in between, a mixture of his mother's touchy-feely way and a Reaganite salesman.

As Payne told one writer: 'Many of the films of the 1970s were a mirror to our society. Our human concerns, our political concerns. Few films are political anymore, either overtly or covertly. I just think it's a time where we're hungry, especially after twenty years of Reaganized hypnosis, and whatever the 1990s were. I haven't seen too much in American cinema that mirrors how Americans are living because we're not making American films. We're making comic books or films that can be easily digested around the world in many forms. It's all about the contrived story, not the human being.'[124]

Can Payne lay claim to achieving this mirror on contemporary society? His former UCLA classmates, according to Taylor, used to accuse the pair of making 'terrarium films', whereby they would set characters loose in a cage and observe them, as if they were scientific experiments. Payne recounts that 'one time Jim was writing a script on his own – it was more of a straight movie and he was having a hard time of it. He said, "I realized unless I'm making fun of people, I really don't have anything to say."' While there is a certain level of ironic detachment in Taylor's work with Payne – more so, say, than in Wes Anderson and Owen Wilson's writing – *About Schmidt* supersedes mere mockery. 'I don't just want to make fun of people,' says Payne. 'As long as it's not done in a superior way . . . if it's in a way that implicates yourself as well, and the pathetic side of life, I think it's cool.'

By the end of the film, Payne and Taylor present a humane and sympathetic picture of a man in emotional turmoil. As Warren receives a letter from a nun, writing on behalf of Ndugu, he learns that his regular donations have brightened up the boy's life. Tears roll down Warren's cheeks. But why? Does he cry because he's finally helped someone? Or because it's the only decent thing he's ever done in his life? Is Ndugu the son Warren never had? It's a sweetly struck note of ambiguity.

Long before Taylor came on board, while editing *Election,* Payne had been sent Begley's novel by the producer Harry Gittes. An old friend of Jack Nicholson's (even inspiring the naming of the actor's *Chinatown* gumshoe), Gittes felt Warren was a perfect role for the star. He was right: Nicholson's restrained turn won him a Golden Globe and his twelfth Oscar nomination. With Nicholson's wolfish screen persona all wrapped up in a straitjacket, the only time he wriggles free is when Warren arrives for the wedding and is put up by Roberta. Staying at her house, he discovers he is sleeping on a bouncy waterbed. Cue some agile physical comedy from Nicholson, as he rolls around and cricks his neck. 'That's the one little section where he could be playful, with respect to showing Warren Schmidt,' says Payne. 'I told him early on that I needed him to play a small man and he heard that and did it. There were a couple of times when we were shooting, when I said make it bigger. And he was hesitating to do that because he was so much in the vibe of this small man with very suppressed and repressed emotions and reactions to things.'

With a similarly brave (and Oscar-nominated) turn from Bates, as she slips into the hot tub with her guest and comes on to him, it's these scenes where we truly get to see how stunted Warren is. Admittedly, as Roberta explains about her hysterectomy, that she had her first orgasm when she was six and how Jeannie and Randall will stay together because they have a 'white hot' sex life, the comedy at Warren's expense is a little cheap. Yet these scenes serve a purpose beyond humour. With Warren holed up in bed, being fed like a baby, Payne and Taylor gleefully highlight how regressive old age can be. With Roberta the optimist to Warren's pessimist, we are also reminded that hitting retirement age need not mean it's the end of your life. While Payne may believe this, his camera leering over a naked Roberta's ample figure suggests a certain horror at turning old, amplified by Warren's earlier revulsion with Helen's aged body.

If anything sums up the mood of *About Schmidt,* it's Rolfe Kent's score. A composer Payne credits for having a gift with melody, he was asked by the director to consider the work of *The Godfather*'s Nino Rota. An avowed fan of Italian film music – think of the Ennio Morricone influence running through *Election* – Payne wanted Kent to create a melancholic piece in the vein of Rota.[125] Or, as Payne puts it, music to help prop up one's smile. The resulting jaunty work reflects Warren's own propensity to do this, while finding time to express his inner sadness (via a haunting piano strain). Indeed, you might see the whole film as a requiem. As he reflects upon his impending death, Warren notes it will be like 'I never existed'.

I'm looking at your face and I just want to smash it.
Barry Egan, *Punch-Drunk Love*

Compared to Wes Anderson, who stepped up a gear, and Payne, who stayed in neutral, P. T. Anderson deliberately shifted down a notch with *Punch-Drunk Love*. After *Magnolia*, critics said he couldn't make a movie that ran under three hours. At a brisk ninety-five minutes, this '$25 million Adam Sandler art house movie', as he called it, sure showed them. While *Boogie Nights* and *Magnolia* were expansive ensembles, this surreal, twisted, nervy romantic comedy (and never has that generic label felt so inappropriate) seemed like a doodle by comparison.

'It's harder to do a stripped-down, straightforward story like this,' P. T. Anderson admits. 'That's what I found anyway. What it does is help focus in on what you really want to say, on what your real point is. That can get a bit muddled in three hours. I wish I could take ten or fifteen minutes out of *Magnolia*. I don't know where from, but it might help pinpoint what it was saying a bit better. But in ninety minutes you have to get to it, say what you've got to say and get the hell out of there.'

In this case, his focus was Barry Egan (Sandler), a sad-sack businessman battered by years of verbal abuse from his seven sisters. It's only when he meets Lena (Emily Watson) that his life changes, but not before he has dealt with some Utah-based extortionists, who have been menacing him for money after he called a phone sex-line. Bizarrely, the starting point – which worms its way into the story – was a *Time* news article P. T. Anderson had read. It concerned David Phillips, a University of California civil engineer, who stumbled upon a lucrative frequent-flyer promotion. By purchasing 12,150 cups of Healthy Choice pudding for just $3,000, he accumulated 1.25 million air miles – a stunt Barry tries to pull throughout the movie.

A distillation of the themes and obsessions that circulate through every P. T. Anderson film, *Punch-Drunk Love* was also a chance for the writer-director to step outside the darkness that had enveloped his first three films. 'I did want to make a lighter movie,' he admits. 'It's a bit like if you've been in your house all day, you just want to go outside. It's like that kind of feeling. Wherever you were last you generally want to go somewhere else next. And there are so many stories to tell, I wanted to try to make a real love story, a romantic picture. I certainly don't want to repeat myself.'

Despite the Technicolor titles, to expect a chocolate-box romance from P. T. Anderson is wishful thinking, for this is a confection with a very hard centre. *Punch-Drunk Love* is like a red rose, full of beauty and pain in equal measure. A 'romantic dream', as Philip Seymour Hoffman, who plays the leader of the Utah crew Dean Trumbell, calls it, the title says it all. Few films have captured better the crazy, exhilarating feeling of falling in love. Recall the scene where Barry and Lena head to Hawaii, and share a kiss in an archway looking out onto a tranquil ocean as passers-by stream past. A swoon-inducing moment, it's even more beautiful than their first kiss – after Barry races back through an endless series of corridors to find Lena's apartment and they lock lips at her door. If it's more of a dreamy, fantasy-driven film than P. T. Anderson's earlier work, the passion that runs through it is no less real.

'I certainly remember the experience of punch-drunk love,' says P. T. Anderson:

> So many of the emotions in this movie are personal. I come from a large family too, so I know very well the insanity and craziness that goes on there. They're not all sisters in my family though, thank god. That would be a nightmare, to have the situation that Barry has in the film. The 'smack you and kiss you' thing would really screw you up. But a lot of big families are like that, the tendency that siblings have on each other to have that push and pull thing going on all the time. Being completely aggressive toward each other but then completely protective from any outsiders. It's a crazy dynamic.

Recalling Melora Walters's Claudia in *Magnolia*, P. T. Anderson continues his obsession with characters psychologically scarred by their family. 'I don't freak out very often,' Barry tells Lena when they share their first kiss, transparently attempting to disguise the truth. Prone to spontaneous bouts of violence – from smashing his sister's patio windows to busting up a restaurant bathroom – Barry is like a pressure cooker ready to boil over. Desperate for help, he even petitions his sister Elizabeth's husband, Walter, to put him in touch with a therapist – seemingly oblivious to the fact that his in-law is a dentist. 'I don't like myself sometimes,' he explains, in a heartbreaking moment of honesty. With his siblings calling him 'gay boy' and 'retard', Barry is steeped in self-loathing.

If the tough love of a family can prove destructive, P. T. Anderson underlines the emotion's redemptive powers. As Barry falls for Lena, he grows in strength. The first sign comes as he travels to Hawaii to hook up with her. Calling Elizabeth to retrieve Lena's phone number, he unleashes a torrent of abuse when she isn't automatically forthcoming. 'You're killing me,' he screams. 'Give me the fucking number or I'll fucking kill you!' On return from Hawaii, when Lena's car is rammed by the pick-up belonging to the Utah thugs, Barry comes out fighting, crowbar in hand. When he decides to put an end to the war, heading out to find his adversaries, the force is with him. 'I have so much strength in me, you have no idea,' he states. 'I have love in my life. That makes me stronger than anything you can imagine.'

P. T. Anderson has no qualms about confessing his influences on *Punch-Drunk Love* – his perennial favourites Blake Edwards and the Frenchman Jacques Tati, two masters of physical comedy. Like P. T. Anderson, both men implicitly grind out humour from the most painful of situations. In particular, while writing, P. T. Anderson re-watched Edwards's *Pink Panther* movies; he stated that the former *Saturday Night Live* star Sandler has a Peter Sellers quality about him. Edwards's work even inspired him to use long shots and keep a lot happening within the frame. P. T. Anderson also freely admits to ripping off Vincente Minnelli musicals, such as *The Band Wagon* (1953), and anything starring Fred Astaire and Ginger Rogers. 'I tried to steal a bit of that and wondered how they did it,' he says. 'Even though they were musicals, they're really romances more than anything else.' Of course, the nearest Barry gets to being Fred Astaire is his dance in the supermarket, as he skips down the aisles with a trolley collecting dozens of Healthy Choice puddings.

P. T. Anderson's thefts are rarely referential, the film finding a pitch all of its own. The opening scene, delivering as much impact as *Boogie Nights*' initial tracking shot or *Magnolia*'s breakneck prologue, sets the tone straight away. We fade in to a warehouse where Barry – wearing a loud blue blazer and white shirt that complements the room's repugnant decor – is talking on the phone. After he finishes his call, he takes his giant coffee cup and heads outside. It's dawn in the Valley, though with eerie, alien noises filling the soundtrack, we could just as easily be on Mars. As Barry heads towards the road, the camera takes over, sliding onto the quiet street. In the distance, a car approaches. Out of the blue, it rams into the back of a parked car, corkscrewing over with an almighty bang. Before we've had time to draw breath, a red Checker Cab Co. van pulls up, the side door slides open and a harmonium is unceremoniously dumped on the pavement next to the understandably startled Barry. As with the rain of frogs in *Magnolia*, P. T. Anderson offers no explanation. It merely warns us we're about to see the world through his eyes again.

Punch-Drunk Love is a film more in synch with its score than most other movies. While *Magnolia* might be the closest thing P. T. Anderson has done to a musical, *Punch-Drunk Love* feels more like a one-man concert film, thanks to the work of Jon Brion. The title music, used also when the two lovers kiss, may be a traditional, swooning score for a Hollywood romance, full of lush sounds that wash over you. But this only serves as contrast to what must be one of the most unconventional pieces of film music ever created. Employed principally in the scenes where Barry is in his warehouse, being harassed by phone calls from his sisters, it's a freewheeling score dominated by bleeps, beats, pulses, tics and rattles – the perfect external expression of Barry's inner turmoil.

Both P. T. Anderson and Brion were fascinated by the work of the legendary composer John Williams – particularly the instantly recognizable two- and five-note tunes used, respectively, in *Jaws* and *Close Encounters of the Third Kind*. In particular, P. T. Anderson wanted to use the harmonium to recreate Williams's alien sound from the latter. Brion, in turn, felt it must be woven together with Barry learning to play the instrument. You might say Barry is entering alien territory as he begins his affair with Lena. If so, he's not on his own. As Lena hugs him in the final scene, she whispers, 'So here we go.' These lovers have only just begun their fine romance.

The two Andersons, along with Payne, were now Hollywood royalty; if not untouchable, then they were directors whose work had to be treated as art and revered as such. By comparison with the trials each filmmaker experienced back in 1996 with their debuts, these new films were smooth sailing. Why? Put it down, in part, to star power. As this trio of films showed, via a broken-down Gene Hackman, a rage-fuelled Adam Sandler and a browbeaten Jack Nicholson, the Sundance Kids were all capable of subverting the screen images of A-list actors. In turn, the stars – repeatedly pigeonholed by studios – were now willing to cut their salaries to join these extended families. For the likes of Nicholson and Hackman, after years wasting their talents on formulaic fare, this was a godsend, a return in spirit to the days of New Hollywood.

CHAPTER 21

The Failure of F-64:
Soderbergh and Fincher Face the Firing Line

50 Blair Underwood and Julia Roberts go *Full Frontal*.

After the success of *Erin Brockovich*, *Traffic* and *Ocean's Eleven*, you could be forgiven for imagining that Steven Soderbergh would simply light a fat cigar with a $100 bill, watch his Hollywood stock shoot through the roof and retire to the Caribbean. Following years spent on bended knee, for the first time since *sex, lies, and videotape* Soderbergh could walk tall. Once again, the studios were willing to take his calls; and 2002 was his year for getting away with it. Neither *Full Frontal* nor *Solaris*, despite the presence of Julia Roberts and George Clooney respectively, were overtly commercial vehicles. It was as if the studios involved – Miramax and Twentieth Century Fox – were looking to find favour with Soderbergh, so that he would return to make more lucrative projects with them at a later date.

But Soderbergh had other ideas. As discussed in the introduction, it was during this period that he – together with Spike Jonze, David Fincher and Alexander Payne – was planning the birth of F-64. The company would afford directors sole ownership of their product. And by early January 2002, it emerged that Jeff Korchek, the former head of business affairs at Universal, was the most likely candidate to run the company. Negotiations were under way with Barry Diller's USA Films – the company that helped steer *Traffic* to Oscar glory – to act as the distributor for F-64. But it was a turbulent time in the world of independent film, as the Hollywood whales were swallowing the minnows wholesale.

The mighty Universal had purchased October Films back in 1997. This so-called 'anti-Miramax', started by Bingham Ray and Jeff Lipsky in 1990, was one of the most successful independent companies of the era, steering films like Mike Leigh's *Secrets and Lies* and Lars von Trier's *Breaking the Waves* (both 1996) to Oscar nominations, if not huge box office success. By 1999, Universal rid itself of the company – having clashed with the art house arm over the release of Todd Solondz's controversial pedophile portrait, *Happiness* (1998), the year before. It was sold to former Paramount Pictures chairman Diller, who renamed the company USA Films, merging it with his Gramercy Pictures and other assets. Aside from *Traffic*, Diller's fledgling company produced Robert Altman's *Gosford Park* and the

Coen brothers' *The Man Who Wasn't There* in 2001, a statement of intent that suggested Diller was, indeed, the right man for F-64.

As if to complicate matters, just as F-64 was getting off the ground, Universal bought Diller's company in December 2001. Now under the banner Vivendi Universal Entertainment, by early 2002 the former October Films was merged with another linchpin of the New York independent scene, Good Machine, which Universal had also purchased. The company had been set up by the regular Ang Lee collaborator James Schamus along with Ted Hope in 1990; in its time it had sired four Sundance grand jury winners, as well as Lee's *Crouching Tiger, Hidden Dragon*. Renamed Focus Features, with Schamus and fellow Good Machine man David Linde in charge, the company has been responsible for some of the finest films in the first years of the twenty-first century – *Eternal Sunshine of the Spotless Mind* and *Lost in Translation* included. But there's no doubt, the demise of USA Films meant that F-64 was out of focus even before it started.

At the time, Soderbergh and his fellow directors were attempting to see if existing projects – in his case, the *Solaris* remake with Fox – could be included under the F-64 umbrella, with the offer of foreign rights distribution to whichever studios were involved. As it turned out, the dream died and F-64 never came to pass. At the time, Soderbergh's three compatriots all had projects, in one way or another, with Sony Pictures. Jonze's *Adaptation* was released via the studio and Payne's *About Schmidt* was originally meant for the company to produce. Recalls Payne, 'They read the script and said, "No way, this is too much of a bummer." We said, "We've got Jack Nicholson." They said, "Oh, you mean an expensive bummer? We don't want to make it." But bless their hearts, they said, "We won't obstruct your beliefs to make it elsewhere."' As for black sheep Fincher, he set out to make *Panic Room* with the studio, partly as a way of quelling the hysteria around him after *Fight Club*. But just as he found with *Se7en* at New Line, and *Alien³* and *Fight Club* at Fox, his way was not the studio's way.

Echoing Paul Thomas Anderson's desire to make a small-scale movie after *Magnolia*, *Panic Room* is set in a single location over the course of one night with just a handful of actors – the sort of slick high-concept tale one has come to expect from David Koepp, the writer of *Spider-Man* (2002) and *Mission: Impossible* (1996). It tells the story of Meg Altman (Jodie Foster), a recent divorcee who takes up residence in a New York brownstone with her teenage daughter, Sarah (Kristen Stewart). The house is equipped with the titular safe room – 'a castle keep in medieval times' as the estate agent calls it, complete with thick steel door, surveillance monitors and food supplies. Three intruders arrive, intent on removing $3 million in bearer bonds, hidden under the floor of the panic room by the previous owner. Brought together by the cocky Junior (Jared Leto) are Burnham (Forest Whitaker), who works for a security company that specializes in building such impregnable bunkers, and Raoul (Dwight Yoakam), who provides the muscle. As Meg and Sarah install themselves in the room, it becomes a game of cat and mouse between them and the robbers, replicating Fincher's own battles with the studio.

As with *Alien³* and *Se7en*, Fincher faced problems during the preview process. As he says, 'You find out more about the people who have supposedly been watching your back for the last year, during the preview process, than you do at any other point in the movie-making process. You begin to see their inherent insecurities.' Just over eight weeks into post-production, the film was shown to an audience. It ends as Burnham has a change of heart and returns to the house to shoot the psychotic Raoul dead, thus condemning himself to certain capture by the authorities. According to Fincher, the preview audience 'weren't confused by anything'; 78 percent loved Jodie Foster and 79 percent loved Forest Whitaker. 'So the studio started asking if Forest could get away at the end of the movie. I said it was sort of amoral; he does break and enter. It is an illegal act. He's given at least three opportunities to leave. His whole moral dilemma at the end, as to whether or not he goes back over the fence to save these people, is that he's probably going to get caught. I didn't think that was a good idea. I think the script they bought for $3 million was right about the end.'

Nevertheless, Sony executives petitioned him to try an alternative ending. An old pro by now, the wily Fincher reasoned with them in a language they could understand – money. The budget had already escalated from $42 million to $48 million.

I said, 'I would love to [reshoot]. But the set, which cost $6 million, has been torn down, and it'll cost $3 million to rebuild the section we need, and take eight or nine days of shooting, at $150,000 a day. I will have to postpone the editorial process while we're prepping this, plus with five or six extra weeks of post-production at

$100,000 a week . . .' The grand total was about $6 million. I said, 'I'll happily re-shoot the ending, and I'll take a look at it, and if I think it's better, I'll use it.' And they said, 'We like the way the movie ends.'

While the finished film was a hit – grossing $95 million in the U.S., it became the second most lucrative of Fincher's career to date, after *Se7en* – it was an uphill struggle for Fincher. He had already endured the loss of his cinematographer Darius Khondji, who had shot *Se7en*, though the studio's part in this remains less than clear. The age-old excuse 'creative differences' was offered at the time, with reports suggesting Fincher and Khondji had reached an impasse over the visual style of the film. Given that, at one point, Fincher had wanted the film to be shot in complete darkness, with just the whites of the characters' eyes showing in the gloom, this would seem unlikely. 'As a cameraman, I love darkness a lot,' says Khondji. 'David is the only person I know that likes it sometimes more than I do. I'd rather be a DP of the dark, than a DP of over-lit movies. There is always light in darkness.' It was an ominous aesthetic that matched the characters' moods.

Somewhat cryptically, Khondji hints that a spat between him and Fincher was not the case. 'I was fired by the studio, by Sony. It was not David Fincher. He defended me up to a certain extent, where probably his right to "final cut", which is very rare on studio pictures, [was under threat]. I wouldn't have defended my DP over my final cut.' Over what, Khondji refuses to say – though suggestions that he was sacked for his Fincher-like perfectionism may be closer to the truth. 'It was a true nightmare shooting my half of it,' he says. 'I was very frustrated because I saw it coming alive, I saw the baby coming alive, while I was watching the dailies every evening. On a movie that takes place behind closed doors, when you start, most of the soul of the movie is already there. It was some of my best work as a DP. It was very exciting. So when someone pulls this baby out of you, that's frustrating.'

You know how this is going to end.
Raoul, *Panic Room*

According to Forest Whitaker, *Panic Room* 'was supposed to be the easiest and quickest shoot that he [Fincher] was ever going to do, because it was so planned out. But all the plans went awry'. It might be easier to list what went right, rather than detail the numerous calamities Fincher and his team endured. Broken bones, blackouts, flooded sets, walkouts, equipment failure, pregnancy . . . it was more dramatic than the film itself.

Panic Room originally starred Nicole Kidman as Meg Altman. Fincher had intended for her to play the role of Marla Singer in *Fight Club*, but when that didn't pan out, he hired her for *Panic Room*. During January 2001, three weeks into filming, Kidman aggravated a recurring knee injury she had sustained during the arduous shoot for Baz Luhrmann's musical *Moulin Rouge!* (2001) and was forced to pull out under medical advice.[126] Her departure left the film in 'a moment of uncertainty', as Whitaker notes with typical understatement. Suspended for two months, while the producers scouted around for another lead, the film teetered on the brink of collapse, with the then-imminent actors' strike in 2000 meaning most A-list actresses were already booked up in projects hastily being rushed before the cameras.

By a bizarre chance, Jodie Foster was also suffering on her directorial project, the circus story *Flora Plum*. Two-and-a-half weeks before it was due to roll, star Russell Crowe injured his shoulder during rehearsals, leaving the film in limbo. Having been a late replacement once before, when she took over from Meg Ryan and paired up with her longtime friend Mel Gibson on *Maverick* (1994), Foster was a welcome saviour for Fincher's film, even if her own was simultaneously shelved. It also proved there were no hard feelings between her and the director, after the actress wound up leaving *The Game* at an early stage, having been set to appear as Nicholas Van Orten's sister (the role that eventually mutated to the one played by Sean Penn).

With the arrival of the actress most famous for playing FBI rookie Clarice Starling in *The Silence of the Lambs* (1990), Fincher admits, the tone of *Panic Room* changed considerably from that of the footage shot with Kidman. 'Originally, it was more of a Hitchcockian studio picture,' says Fincher. 'It's a different thing when Clarice Starling walks into this set-up. She can take care of herself. I think there's something glamorous about Nicole; more of a Grace Kelly damsel in distress. What Jodie Foster brings to it is what she's been building for thirty-five years of her life and career. She's smart and capable; she's not going to be anybody's fool.' However, five weeks into shooting, Foster dropped a bombshell. She was pregnant with her second son, Kit. When Dwight Yoakam heard the news, he echoed the feelings floating around the set. 'It seemed like the movie was cursed or doomed. Like these characters, there was a disregard for the signs along the way, that maybe they should turn back or leave. They just kept going forward [and so did we].'

With the departure of Darius Khondji, it got worse. His replacement was Conrad W. Hall, son of the legendary DP Conrad L. Hall (who was lensing Sam Mendes's *Road to Perdition* at the time). Under Khondji, Hall Jr had been a camera operator on *Se7en* and Second Unit DP on *Alien: Resurrection* (1997), Jean-Pierre Jeunet's fourth entry in the franchise after Fincher's own effort. While Hall Jr accepted the job, he evidently didn't know what he was letting himself in for. From out-of-focus footage to faulty motion-control cameras, everything that could go wrong did. Shot principally on a Hollywood sound stage, frequent electricity blackouts also hampered the production, as did waterlogged sets.

Even when things were going right, the complexities of the shoot caused major headaches. With the script making Meg watch the intruders laying into her home with sledgehammers on video surveillance monitors, most scenes had to be shot twice – for security camera footage as well as for the audience. 'The continuity had to be so rigorous because you are seeing the fruits of all of their actions on the camera,' says Fincher. 'It was a very procedural movie.' This meant shooting chronologically, to ensure the images remained consistent, with each actor's hair, weight and complexion required to stay the same – not helpful when Foster was pregnant. But as Whitaker testifies, Fincher entered into Kubrick territory at times. 'He'd really want his frame to be right, so he'd just do it until he felt like it was right. I don't know what the average number [of takes] was – twenties, thirties, forties, maybe more.'

Undeniably, the film is a meticulously planned exercise in style. Out-gunning even the stunning sequence in *Fight Club* that sees the camera descend through floors of a skyscraper to its basement and into a van full of explosives, the film's 'big shot', as Fincher calls it, comes early. Floating like a spectre, the camera glides from Meg's bedroom and twists down the stairs to glimpse the robbers outside as they arrive. Panning across a bay window, it dives into the front door lock, before reversing out and heading through the kitchen (even spiriting itself through the handle of a coffee pot) to witness the crooks trying to force entry at the back door. 'It's showing you the cat arriving from the point of view of the goldfish,' says Fincher. 'You're inside looking out; they're outside looking in.' With the camera rising through the floors – as the trio all climb a ladder to the rooftop – it's a seamless piece of CG-aided work and a bravura flourish from Fincher. But in a film with no real establishing sequences, it also works as 'a real important geography lesson', a guided tour acquainting the audience with the layout of the house.

It would be harsh to suggest *Panic Room* is a film devoid of substance. Not unlike *Punch-Drunk Love* and *About Schmidt*, it deals with the destructive nature of the family dynamic. Shattered by an acrimonious divorce from Stephen Altman (Patrick Bauchau), a wealthy pharmaceutical tycoon, Meg must also deal with the void it's created between her and her cynical, surly daughter. 'She's lost her confidence,' says Foster:

> She doesn't know if she can take care of herself anymore. It doesn't help that her daughter is at the stage where she spends her whole day trying to make her mother look bad. So that also erodes her confidence. She gets talked into this house that she didn't want to move into in the first place. She gets talked into this panic room she didn't want, and doesn't listen to her own instincts and make her own decisions. It's through the conflict and the drama that she learns to grab back her own confidence and identity and fight back.

With Stephen alerted by the distress call from his ex-wife and daughter, his arrival at the house leads to a change in the shape of the family unit. Strapped to a chair by the robbers, his arms broken, he must leave it to Meg to defend their child. After stealing into the bedroom to collect the phone, she makes a second mercy dash to retrieve the diabetic Sarah's medicine. She calmly prevents two policemen from entering her house, when Burnham and Raoul are locked into the panic room with Sarah, in order to keep her daughter safe. Trapping Raoul's hand in the door, she even smashes the surveillance cameras, prompting a dumbfounded Raoul to ask: 'Why the hell didn't we do that?' She will knock him for six again, this time with a sledgehammer: an empowering act if ever there was one.

Without doubt, Burnham is the film's moral centre. As he states, his reason for participating in this robbery is down to the custody problems he is facing after a divorce – a fact that ties him emotionally to Meg. In many ways, *Panic Room* becomes less about Meg's survival than it does about his change of heart. 'He's probably the most con-flicted of the characters,' says Whitaker. 'He doesn't really want to cause any problems. He's just trying to take care of himself and his family. He just keeps getting sucked in deeper and deeper and all of a sudden it's too late.' As he tells Sarah, after delivering her a vital insulin shot, 'I wish I coulda put my kid in a place like this. It's not that I didn't try. Sometimes things, they don't work out the way you want them to.'

Having saved her life, it's no surprise that he returns to save Meg from Raoul. If he does achieve one act, it is to reunite Meg with Sarah and Stephen: parents and child bloodied but briefly bonded. We don't know what will happen when the credits roll; in all probability Stephen will go back to his girlfriend. But this feels like a victory for the victim; the woman scorned has had her day. And it was all thanks to a divorced man with a moral conscience; Burnham may not have been able to keep his own family together but he makes up for it with his selfless act for the Altmans.

While Fincher admits he talked about Alfred Hitchcock's *Rear Window* (1954) and Sam Peckinpah's 1971 home invasion film *Straw Dogs* in pre-production, he denies there is 'much of a straight line from those to this'. That said, Koepp's script is no conventional beast. Self-aware, it plays with the parameters of this 'yuppies-in-peril' sub-genre. While Sarah learnt morse code from watching *Titanic*, Junior states to Raoul: 'Don't start spouting some Elmore Leonard bullshit you just heard, because I saw that movie too.' These are movie characters living in a world where they have learnt to talk and act by watching movies. It's no accident that Meg and Sarah 'watch' much of the film on video monitors. It may not be a trenchant attack on cor-porate or consumer culture, like *The Game* or *Fight Club*, but *Panic Room* is a very postmodern thriller. A metaphor for the isolation we increasingly feel in modern society, the panic room is, as Fincher shows, a very contemporary state of mind to be in.

Am I alive or dead?
Chris Kelvin, *Solaris*

In many ways, *Solaris* is anything but a studio product – despite its $47 million price tag. It is, of course, based on the 1961 novel by the Polish science fiction writer Stanislaw Lem, famously filmed nine years

later by the Russian director Andrei Tarkovsky into a 165-minute monster of a movie. What was for Tarkovsky a riposte to Stanley Kubrick's
2001: A Space Odyssey (1968) was for Soderbergh 'a cross between
2001 and *Last Tango in Paris*'. It plays out on board the space station
Prometheus, orbiting the mysterious ocean planet of Solaris. The widowed psychiatrist Chris Kelvin (George Clooney) arrives after receiving
a distress signal from his old friend, the ship's commander Gibarian
(Ulrich Tukur). Upon boarding, he discovers Gibarian is dead; the two
remaining survivors are Snow (Jeremy Davies), a gibbering stoner type
slowly losing his mind, and the frosty Dr Gordon (Viola Davis). 'A
mirror that reflects part of your mind', as Gordon puts it, Solaris is
able to plug directly into the memories, desires and guilt of each
human being that comes within its range. True to form, Chris is
reunited with his wife Rheya (Natascha McElhone), who committed
suicide seven years ago after she had an abortion without telling her
spouse.

Like in *Panic Room*, at the core of *Solaris* is a relationship gone
sour. A chamber piece, it's Soderbergh's most intimate and psychologically probing film since *sex, lies, and videotape* (with perhaps the
exception of *Schizopolis*). As he says:

> I think that what's being explored in *Solaris* is really the idea of
> choice. You have two characters in a situation that they suspect can
> only end one way. The issue becomes, 'How much freedom of
> choice do you have about emotional issues?' The relationship
> [between Chris and Rheya] begins to mimic the trajectory that it did
> on earth. They both feel like they can't stop it from doing that; and
> their awareness of it isn't helping. The question the film poses is:
> 'Can you exert free will in this specific emotional situation, or are
> you bound to repeat the same thing again and again?' That's what
> the movie is about.

The film was co-produced by Section Eight with James Cameron's
Lightstorm Entertainment. 'I bought the book, and I was going to
develop it myself, but Steven called me one day and asked if he could
direct it,' notes Cameron. 'That was a no-brainer.' He eventually took
a producer credit. It's easy to see why Cameron was attracted to Lem's
story; after all, the idea of an 'intelligent ocean' was used, to some
extent, in his 1989 film *The Abyss*. As he tells Soderbergh on the DVD
commentary, his version 'would have been much more literal, not as

metaphysical, not as spiritual. Probably more emotional, in that I'm always a sucker for a good love story, which is part of what attracted me to it.'

From the first, Soderbergh distanced himself from Tarkovsky's film, preferring to base his script – the first he had written for himself to direct since *Schizopolis* – on the original source material. With 'so many things in the book . . . you could make two films', Soderbergh narrowed it down to two themes. These are the degree to which we project onto other people in our relationships, and what it means to be human. In other words, what defines being human? Should Rheya, the psychological construct, be extended the same considerations as a human being? As the director puts it, 'When you have someone who's been created but, unlike the rest of us, is not unique, what does that mean? Do we define them the same way we define ourselves?' In a departure from Tarkovsky's approach, he leaves it for his audience – rather than his characters – to debate such questions. As Gibarian says, 'There are no answers, only choices.'

Yet neither did he ignore the Tarkovsky version – even if his colour scheme of blues and greys strove for more melancholy than the reds and creams used by the Russian. Casting the British actress Natascha McElhone, with her long hair and saucer eyes, was a deliberate visual reference to Natalya Bondarchuk from the original. As for Rheya's resurrection scene, after she kills herself by drinking liquid oxygen, Soderbergh filmed it backwards to give it an eerie quality, a trick he confesses to stealing directly from Tarkovsky. 'I didn't think we were in a competitive situation [with Tarkovsky], because I had a very different approach to the book,' says Soderbergh. 'If I have any regrets to do with the film, it's whether I went far enough. This film is designed to divide people.'

And divide people it did, critics either falling for its mysteries or finding themselves bored rigid. As Soderbergh has advised any potential viewer, if you think the opening ten-minute sequence on Earth dull you should leave the auditorium. 'The script was only seventy-five pages long,' he adds. 'I wanted to sketch what it felt like to be Kelvin, and avoid traditional scenes of setting up a character. I just wanted to show you glimpses of this guy's life on earth, and how isolated he has made himself.' Removing the lengthy black and white discussion on earth about Solaris, as watched on television by Kris Kelvin in Tarkovsky's original, Soderbergh's snapshot opening is anything but tedious. Philip Messina, production designer on all Soderbergh's high-budget films, does a marvellous job in conveying the isolation Chris, and the rest of humanity, now exist in. His low-key apartment, decked out with videophones and flat-screen hologram televisions, backs up the statement made by the Muslim woman in his group therapy session. 'I see the TV,' she says. 'I see the Internet. I see those T-shirts and I feel nothing. The more I see those images, the less I feel, the less I believe that it's real.'

By the end, we will feel the same – even down to the act of cutting a finger on a kitchen knife. With just a handful of shots, Soderbergh establishes a near-future world that reflects Chris's own state of mind. The very first is a tight angled close-up on a rain-washed windowpane; inside, the only voice Chris can hear is that of Rheya. On the street, as pedestrians pour past him, Chris is made to appear insignificant, Soderbergh emphasising this with the drone of aircraft noise – a direct echo of the protracted traffic sequence in Tarkovsky's version – engulfing him. Even future fashions are sad and grey; everyone dresses in charcoal mackintoshes with Nehru collars, even the messengers who bring him Gibarian's video SOS.

When the narrative returns to Earth in the finale, nothing except Chris has changed. 'Earth – even the word sounded strange to me now,' he notes. Immediately preceded by Chris staring into the increasingly angry red mists of Solaris, we soon learn that this is a created version of home in Chris's mind. As we cut back to the *Prometheus* – Chris now being deafened by white noise – Soderbergh leaves the conclusion shrouded in as much mystery as it is religious imagery. The child on board the ship, who we have previously been led to believe is Gibarian's now-fatherless son, reaches out his hand to Chris, as if he were an angel leading him to Heaven. We return to Chris's apartment, with Rheya now present. 'Am I alive or dead?' he asks. 'We don't have to think like that anymore,' she replies. 'We're together now. Everything we've done is forgiven. Everything.' They hold each other, as the shot fades into a last look at the enigmatic force that is Solaris.

Evading all the clichés of science fiction – right from not showing Chris's blast-off into space – Soderbergh's film takes place around tables, as the characters pontificate and puzzle their way through the narrative. It is deliberately devoid of tension; if there's any anxiety, it comes from Soderbergh's concern about the fact he is neither a poet nor a philosopher in the way Tarkovsky was. In the original script he wrote 'I am not a poet' as the opening snatch of dialogue – a line also used by Tarkovsky. He later has Chris attempting to bluff his knowledge of the literary form with Rheya, during one of the flashbacks to the early part of their time together on earth, quoting Dylan Thomas's 'And Death Shall Have No Dominion' and then confessing his lack of interest in poetry. Much the same could be said for Soderbergh, who had to e-mail Mike Nichols (with whom he had just done a DVD commentary for the director's 1970 version of *Catch-22*) to ask for a 'transcendent death poem' to include in the film. As the real Rheya dies, a torn page showing the poem can be found in her hand; it's one of the few times the film stumbles, as it strains for meaning.

Editing a film for the first time since *King of the Hill* (under the name Mary Ann Bernard), Soderbergh also once again shot the film himself, as Peter Andrews. 'Being on the set of the *Prometheus* with George and Natascha, and holding the camera, connects me directly to the first sensation I had when I held the camera when I was thirteen,' he says. 'I'm willing to trade the fact that I'm not a world class cinematographer for the momentum that I get from not having to have an extra layer of conversation. Also the intimacy I have with actors. I can literally whisper to them while we're shooting. I think for them it creates a level of comfort.' Such control over the project even extended to influencing Cliff Martinez's understated and hypnotic score, asking him to research how the composer György Ligeti used note clusters to structure his music for Kubrick's *2001: A Space Odyssey*. At one point considering using cues such as Pink Floyd, Beck and the Velvet Underground for the trip into space, Soderbergh wisely restrained himself, opting to fully employ what is Martinez's ninth – and perhaps finest – score for the director.

The film was rushed through post-production for a late November release in the U.S. It backfired spectacularly, recouping just $14.9 million. In a schizophrenic publicity campaign – one trailer attempting to play up the action-adventure/science-fiction elements, the other highlighting the film's romantic entanglements – neither spot conveyed the true psychological core of the movie. 'In retrospect, people needed more preparation for that,' Soderbergh notes on the film's DVD commentary. 'The fact that the film wasn't finished until very, very close to the release date meant that maybe we should have pushed, maybe we should have had more time to screen the film, and come up with a campaign that gave people a sense of the experience they were about to have. It was a difficult movie to encapsulate in a poster or a trailer or a TV spot. I don't think we ever quite solved it.'

Publicists at Twentieth Century Fox ended up stirring up a storm around the fact that George Clooney's naked rear featured in the film, 'trivializing' the work, as the actor noted. At one point, Soderbergh found himself in a battle with the MPAA, who planned to slap an R rating on the film (it eventually got PG-13 after the director appealed) because of these intimate shots. 'Have you seen *Black Hawk Down*? That movie is an R,' fumed Soderbergh. 'How do you fit these two films in the same category? I didn't understand it. It hijacked the dialogue about the film at the moment when we were trying to define it for people. I think the people thought it would have more sexually explicit material than it did. The timing of it was unfortunate for us.'

If you ever left me, I would die.

Lee Bright, *Full Frontal*

Sandwiched between the March 2002 release of *Panic Room* in the U.S. and the unveiling of *Solaris* eight months later was *Full Frontal*. Given the protracted negotiations over F-64, it seems highly appropriate that the film is the closest Soderbergh has come to a Hollywood satire. Even more so since Fincher can be glimpsed in a cameo role as the director of a buddy cop movie, starring one Brad Pitt (dressed rather like his character from *Se7en*). With 'f64' seen on Fincher's cap, we can view one sequence of rushes – bearing the legend 'Property of f64' in the right-hand bottom corner – as an in-joke laced with a dose of wishful thinking.

Written by the poet and playwright Coleman Hough, *Full Frontal* was previously called *How to Survive a Hotel Room Fire* (until post-9/11 sensitivity quashed that). It was then given the equally bizarre moniker *The Art of Negotiating a Turn*, before finally settling on its explicit-sounding title. Based on a short play called *Shipping and Receiving*, Hough says the idea for the film began after she had a conversation with a friend a year after giving her a present that had offended her on her fortieth birthday (an idea that remains in the final film). Soderbergh's first production for Miramax since *Kafka*, it was shot for $2 million in a mere eighteen days.

When the script was sent out to prospective cast members, a note detailing ten rules that they must obey during the shoot accompanied it. 'It's our mutated version of a Dogme movie,' says Soderbergh. It said that all sets were to be practical locations and no craft service or trailers would be available. While 'holding areas' might be provided, it warned, 'if you need to be alone a lot, you're pretty much screwed'. The actors would also choose and maintain their own wardrobe, hair and make-up and be required to drive themselves to the set or 'become the subject of ridicule'. Improvization would be encouraged, and the actors would be interviewed about their own and other characters – material that 'may end up in the finished film'. Rule number ten ominously stated: 'You will have fun whether you want to or not.' While most were designed to direct the actors, Soderbergh also derived some informal guidelines for himself. To represent the 'real' segments of the movie – as opposed to the glossy film-within-a-film called *Rendezvous* that weaves in and out of the story – the scenes would be shot on digital video using only natural light. Likewise, these scenes would be completely without score or Foley-achieved sound effects – lending such sequences a documentary-like feel.

As experimental as the film's aesthetic would prove, that was nothing compared to its narrative. Meshing together numerous plot lines of Los Angelenos gathering for the fortieth birthday party of the Hollywood producer Gus Delario (David Duchovny), it piles layer upon self-reflexive layer. The film begins with a series of title cards introducing the principal characters: the movie stars Francesca Davis (Julia Roberts) and Calvin Cummings (Blair Underwood); the executive Lee Bright (Catherine Keener); her masseuse sister Linda (Mary McCormack); her screenwriter husband Carl (David Hyde Pierce) and his writing partner Arthur 'Arty' Dean (Enrico Colantoni). As we discover, Arty has a low-budget play about Hitler (played by Nicky Katt), called *The Sound and the Führer*, in rehearsal.

The credits arrive – not for *Full Frontal* but for *Rendezvous*, a Gus Delario production written by Arty and Carl (and directed by one Constance Alexander). A Hollywood romantic drama, it stars Francesca and Calvin as, respectively, Catherine, a magazine journalist, and Nicholas, an actor she is profiling. Adding to these layers of fiction, one scene in *Rendezvous* shows Nicholas and Catherine chatting on the set of his latest film, the aforementioned cop movie being directed by Fincher and co-starring Pitt. Nicholas then performs his scene opposite Pitt, who delivers the immortal line, 'like the back of my big ten-inch' when he is asked if he thinks differently to the adversary they're chasing.

Where things really start to get complicated, however, is when we return to Nicholas and Catherine hanging out on set. After walking outside and finishing their dialogue together, they 'break' character, wondering if 'cut' has been said. Outside of the party scene that concludes the film, this is one of the rare times we see Francesca and Calvin as themselves, not playing their screen roles. Switching to the grainy film stock that sets apart the 'real' sequences from *Rendezvous*, we then see Francesca take off her wig. At this point, the director of *Rendezvous* – clearly Soderbergh himself, despite the fact that his face is blacked out – arrives to take charge. Casting himself as (we assume) Constance Alexander adds further spin to this headache-inducing mix of fiction and reality. Even Brad Pitt seems confused, with Fincher explaining to him about their film-within-*Rendezvous*: 'This is the only movie. As far as he's concerned, it's the only movie.'

Despite what this might suggest, as far as Soderbergh is concerned *Full Frontal* is not a movie about the making of a film in the manner of François Truffaut's *Day for Night* (1973) or Federico Fellini's 8½ (1963). 'Those movies are explorations of the creative process – and this movie really isn't,' he says. 'This movie isn't really about making movies. It has two characters that are actors, but it is more about how we watch movies than how they are made. It's exploring the idea of a contract between the filmmaker and the audience. I guess, in some ways, we were trying to push the boundaries of that contract. Even at the end of the day, if the movie was too nuts for audiences to wrap their minds around, then fine – at least now we know where that line is.'

Dealing with the theme of the erosion of the barriers between fiction, celebrity and reality – a pertinent theme given the increased obsession with reality TV shows – Soderbergh continues with this theme to the very last inspired shot. Arthur and Linda coincidentally meet on a plane heading to Tucson, where unbeknown to each other they are about to be formally introduced, having met via an Internet chat room. Improvised by Soderbergh on the day, he backs the camera away as the scene plays out, taking it out of the fake plane innards and into a darkened studio. As he has noted on the DVD commentary for the film: 'It is as much a construct as the *Rendezvous* portion of the film, and you shouldn't necessarily take either one more seriously than the other. Ultimately this is not life, this is a movie.'

There's no doubt this experiment wraps itself up in knots. Part of what makes the film either interesting – or insufferable, depending on your point of view – is the proliferation of in-jokes. Jerry Weintraub, the legendary producer of *Ocean's Eleven*, plays Carl's boss at (the real-life) *Los Angeles* magazine. Terence Stamp reprises his role as Wilson from *The Limey*. Seen in *Rendezvous* in the back of the plane Nicholas and Catherine are on, he is glimpsed with Nancy Lenehan, with whom he shared the equivalent scene in *The Limey*. Nicholas also raps to Catherine about the experience of being a black actor in Hollywood. 'Can even Mr Washington briefly be seen kissing a pretty woman under a pelican moon?' he says, in reference to the widespread reported incident on the set of *The Pelican Brief* (1993), where Washington balked at a sex scene with Roberts for fear of offending his black female fans.

'I was aware of the fact that the film wasn't providing any of the handrails that a normal movie provides to keep your equilibrium,' says Soderbergh. 'The point of the movie was: can I get rid of all of these crutches that we use to tell stories? Coleman and I talked about it, and she wondered if there should be a murder or mystery to be solved. And I said: "If we do that, then we're hypocrites, because I'm trying to purposefully strip all that stuff away."' The closest they come to this is when Lee discovers Gus's corpse in his hotel room, after a spot of erotic asphyxiation goes wrong, but even the aftermath of this is not the disruption of his party but the sobering effect it has on Lee. 'I was trying to strip out all false incidents that you normally put in a movie to create drama. At the same time, contrasting it with *Rendezvous* – the film – which is all made up of chance encounters.'

It is Catherine Keener, as Lee – in her first role for Soderbergh since *Out of Sight* – who provides the emotional centre. The portrait of a marriage on the brink she creates together with Hyde Pierce is the most moving examination of a relationship in crisis Soderbergh has achieved since *sex, lies, and videotape*. A deranged control freak who likes nothing better than intimidating her employees, Lee is, it becomes clear, having an affair with Calvin – unbeknown to Carl, who is 'afraid his wife finds him boring', as his opening title card tells us. As her story begins, she has decided to leave her husband. While Soderbergh explores, via Katt's sympathetic portrait of Hitler, the idea of whether one can ever view such historical figures as anything more than an abstraction, Lee is the expression of the monster that can emerge in all of us when in a relationship. Likewise her sister, despite looking for true love on the web, succumbs to her own monster when she accepts Gus's offer of $500 to masturbate him during his massage.

The film took in $2.5 million in the U.S., after it had what could be described as a limited engagement at the cinemas. After the trio of $100 million–hitters he'd just experienced, critics called it Soderbergh's penance. Which was incorrect. *Full Frontal* fulfilled a similar function to *Schizopolis*; it may screen like a lab experiment gone wrong, but for Soderbergh it was all about the science behind it. 'Part of me thought, "Let's make something that'll really piss people off,"' he says. 'Nobody was encouraging me to make this. Most people would prefer that I didn't. All I can say is, for the people who would prefer that I make things more coherent or palatable, the only reason that I'm able to make those films is that every once in a while I get to shoot off a little steam. Making *Full Frontal* and *Schizopolis* informs those other films, in ways that can only be understood if you make movies.'

For Soderbergh, this was a year to remember artistically, if not financially. Be it with the narrative experiments of *Full Frontal* or the philosophical challenges of *Solaris*, he embraced difficult material wholeheartedly. As he approached 2003 – during which he aimed to take some time off – it would be the first year he had not had a film released since 1997. 'It seemed to me like the first phase of my career was coming to a conclusion. It felt to me like the end of a chapter. It was about a lot of things I was interested in personally. I sweat these things out. I want these things to be good, to stand up in ten or fifteen years. I always agonize.'

CHAPTER 22

Top of the Bill:
Sofia Coppola and Wes Anderson Find Their Muse

51 Bill Murray and Scarlett Johansson in *Lost in Translation*.

Just as the Sundance Kids keep the same crew members, so time and again they return to their favourite actors. By *Punch-Drunk Love*, Paul Thomas Anderson had worked with Philip Seymour Hoffman four times while Bryan Singer, after completing *X2*, had worked with Ian McKellen on three occasions. Soderbergh, as we know, is a frequent collaborator with George Clooney, Julia Roberts and Don Cheadle; likewise, Tarantino favours Samuel L. Jackson, Uma Thurman and Michael Madsen.

While such loyalty is nothing unusual, these directors seem less keen on casting an actor once he or she has worked for one of their peers. There are exceptions: Soderbergh and David Fincher have both used Brad Pitt. Meanwhile, Ben Stiller went from David O. Russell's *Flirting with Disaster* to Wes Anderson's *The Royal Tenenbaums*, playing a neuroses-riddled character in both. In a reversal of this, Jason Schwartzman went from Anderson's *Rushmore* to Russell's fourth film, *I ❤ Huckabees*, playing a rebel-of-sorts twice over. Russell also cast Mark Wahlberg as a wide-eyed innocent in *Three Kings*, after his similar turn in P. T. Anderson's *Boogie Nights*. And then there's Bill Murray, the actor who has benefited more than most from this new breed of filmmaker.

Murray has become an unlikely muse off-screen, as well as an on-screen embodiment of the misery middle age can bring. Sofia Coppola cast him for the first time in her second film, *Lost in Translation* (2003), as she left behind the sun-drenched Michigan suburbs of *The Virgin Suicides* for the bustle of Tokyo. Meanwhile, Wes Anderson made it three times in a row with his fourth film, *The Life Aquatic with Steve Zissou* (2004). 'He's the one man I'm most likely to describe as a genius,' says Anderson. 'I don't mean that necessarily as the highest compliment; more as a description of him. He can be very surprising, the way he'll come up with something. His thought process is something I can't quite put my finger on at all.'

Before he and Anderson met for *Rushmore*, Murray was lost in transition. The former *Saturday Night Live* alumnus had become one of Hollywood's highest grossing comedians in the 1980s with a succession of hits – *Caddyshack* (1980), *Stripes* (1981), *Ghostbusters* (1984) and

Scrooged (1988). But with the arrival of Jim Carrey and many other younger *Saturday Night Live* graduates, Murray's box office star began to fade. With the exception of a brief cameo for Tim Burton in *Ed Wood* (1994) and his seminal re-teaming with *Ghostbusters* co-star Harold Ramis for *Groundhog Day* a year earlier, Murray was too often found squandering his talents in films that did not merit them. The nadir was his turn as Bosley in the *Charlie's Angels* (2000) remake, a shoot where he reputedly clashed with co-star Lucy Liu.

But, by this point, he had also appeared in *Rushmore*, reputedly a script Murray liked so much he offered to do it for free. The role of Herman Blume was tailor-made for him, with his saggy, craggy face expressing the character's mid-life crisis to perfection. Likewise with his brief turn in *The Royal Tenenbaums*, as the emotionally detached Raleigh St Clair. By the time he took the lead as oceanographer Steve Zissou, written by Anderson specifically for him, Murray was fast usurping Owen Wilson as Anderson's pet player. 'There's some of him in the role,' admits Anderson. 'I have known him for a long time and there are things about him that I wanted to be a part of the character. Then there are things that have nothing to do with Bill Murray. But I do think he brings a wildness into it that's not on the page; it's just something in him that's tragic.'

A close friend of Anderson, Sofia Coppola was impressed by Murray's turn in *Rushmore* and similarly wrote the role of crumpled heap Bob Harris with the actor in mind. 'I thought he could add a lot to this story,' she says. 'So I sent him the script, and after many months of leaving messages and trying to reach him, he reached me.' At the time, she had a director friend who had spent six months trying to contact the elusive Murray and eventually gave up. Coppola refused to think of any other actor in the role. When Murray finally contacted her, he didn't even sign a contract but just gave his word he'd arrive in Tokyo – and he did. The resulting film now usurps even *Groundhog Day* as the work he loves the most.

Winning his first Golden Globe for *Lost in Translation* in 2004, aged fifty-three, Murray's career profile received a much-needed adrenalin shot. Calling it his 'blue period', he quips: 'I'm just lucky that I've had these two gifted people find me in the Yellow Pages.' Hip once more, he immediately struck up a relationship with Jim Jarmusch, collaborating on the anthology movie *Coffee and Cigarettes* (2003) before taking the lead in *Broken Flowers* (2005), the story of a singleton who revisits four former girlfriends to find out if one sired him a son twenty years ago. As co-star Angelica Huston says of the mercurial and mysterious Murray, he is 'brilliant, volatile [and] has fantastic comic timing', a statement that sums up just why both Coppola and Anderson have been drawn to him. It's as if his personality sums up the very filmmaking of the Sundance Kids en masse.

Yet Murray is uncertain whether the work of Anderson, Coppola or any other hipster signals a significant shift in studio tastes. 'Is it a new movement? God, let's hope it's a new movement, and let's hope it catches on. It probably won't.' As he notes, 'The studios don't seem to foster good writing. They're not so interested in that, but they're more interested in what worked most recently. They're definitely very serious about making money, and that's not a wrong thing, but you don't have to make money the same way all the time.'

I just don't know who I'm supposed to be.
Charlotte, *Lost in Translation*

If we weren't already convinced by her debut, *Lost in Translation* cemented Coppola's reputation as a filmmaker worthy of the family name. Just as her father had picked up a Best Original Screenplay Oscar, for *Patton* (1970), at the outset of his career, so did she. Though given how much of Murray's own unique brand of improvisation pads the film out, it's little wonder he pulled such a scowl when he lost out to Sean Penn for Best Actor at the 2004 Oscars, the first such nomination of his career.

Murray only met with Coppola two days before the twenty-seven-day shoot – filmed largely in sequence on locations in Tokyo – but they evidently enjoyed an intimate communion. 'I read the script, but I don't generally over-prepare,' says Murray. 'But because the script was so spare, and because there was so little dialogue, I had to really be emotionally available for everything that happened. So I really tried to get myself out of the way and just be available for the tone that the boss set in every scene. In a way, I had to accept everything she gave me as a person and an actor. It works the same way it works in the story. I responded naturally, because I wasn't cluttered.'

At first glance, Murray does not appear to be the focus. In a continuation of the style – if not subject matter – of *The Virgin Suicides*, it would be easy to say Coppola simply swapped Kirsten Dunst for

Scarlett Johansson as her alter ego cum muse. *Lost in Translation* even begins with a brief shot of Johansson's rear, in a pair of translucent pink panties, reminiscent of those hidden under Dunst's party dress. It's the perfect image with which to open a film that teases us with intimacy. But while Lux from *The Virgin Suicides* is an unobtainable fantasy, seen through the eyes of the neighbouring boys, Johansson's Charlotte is Coppola's viewfinder onto the Orient, sitting on the window sill of her hotel room gazing across the city like an ethereal spirit.

Charlotte is a listless philosophy graduate stranded in Tokyo's Park Hyatt hotel as her feckless photographer husband, John (Giovanni Ribisi), busies himself with his career. Murray plays faded movie star Bob Harris, entrenched in his mid-life crisis as he arrives in Japan to endorse Suntory whisky – as Coppola Sr once did – for a neat $2 million. Both marooned in a sea of discontent, they cling to each other for a few days before going their separate ways.

Coppola admits it was during conversations with her brother, Roman, that the notion of Bob arriving in the country to advertise a product arose. 'You see those campaigns when you walk down the street and you can't help but think of the story behind them,' she says. A common trick of Hollywood stars, this strategy is one Murray is well aware of among his peers. 'Both Sofia and I have witnessed – and obtained, or possess – American movie stars huckstering. She has an advert of Kevin Costner for canned espresso, and I have one of Harrison Ford selling beer that I brought back from Japan. They both have the same face on, as they're holding up the product. It's pretty much the face I use in the movie, "When is this over? When do I get paid? And don't tell anyone I'm doing this!"'

As the limo-bound Bob glides through the cityscape upon his arrival, he is immediately confronted with his own satanic pact – a billboard of himself, nursing a tumbler of scotch, haunts the skies. Later, another Suntory poster, pasted to the side of a lorry, will slip past him and Charlotte. Even the waiter in the hotel bar knows the infamous 'For relaxing times, make it Suntory times' tagline that Bob is made to repeat ad infinitum during the humiliating shoot he endures. Worse still, he is made to see his own appearance on the real-life talk show *Matthew's Best Hit TV* – where the host, 'the Johnny Carson of Japan', prances around in a candy-coloured suit leaving Bob bemused. Catching a clip on TV back in the hotel room is his punishment for delaying his return to his family in the U.S. in order to spend more time with Charlotte.

For Murray fans, there's much to enjoy: Bob's troubles with the cross-trainer in the hotel gym; his 'conversation' with a Japanese man and his walking stick in the hospital waiting room; his enjoyment of a gymnastic stripper; and, of course, the Suntory photo shoot where he delivers a series of impressions – from Frank Sinatra, Dean Martin and Joey Bishop to Roger Moore. In a moment that blends reality with the film's fiction, Bob even catches an old clip of himself (or rather Murray) performing a sketch on *Saturday Night Live* – complete with chimpanzee.

But while these moments raise a smile, it's the resignation etched in Murray's face that elicits the most resonance. He slips into Bob's tux perfectly – even if he requires the aid of a few bulldog clips to tuck him in. 'I'm completely lost,' he tells his wife, in a moment that makes you want to reach out and comfort him. 'Every line in this film I truly believed,' says Murray. 'There was nothing that made me squirm. There was nothing that made me uncomfortable. I think Sofia's movie puts a smile on your face. You walk out with self-respect – "Goddamn, I'm a member of that same human race."'

Much of the film's dreamy jet-lagged atmosphere comes from Coppola's own experience of hotel malaise during her time in Japan. She regularly stayed at the Park Hyatt while on Milk Fed business. Such is her warm and impressionistic evocation of the place, you'd think you were drunk on sake while watching it. A *Brief Encounter* for the jet-set crowd, with its postage stamp–sized plot, *Lost in Translation* is more a series of sketchbook moments with a tender cumulative effect. 'After *The Virgin Suicides*, I felt sad so I was in the mind for something funny – and a bit romantic,' says Coppola. 'And also because that story had a lot of characters, I wanted to do something intimate between two people.'

Coppola also wanted the relationship between Charlotte and Bob

. . . to be that kind of romantic friendship that falls between a completely platonic friendship and a love affair. It's just a brief encounter that never turns into something else. There is all of this tension and anticipation of it becoming something. You can have an intimate brief moment without it becoming an affair. That can leave an impression on you as strong as someone you've known in your life for five years. I've had moments in my life where I've met people who are not part of my life, and they've left an impression on me. But I didn't have what Bob Harris experienced.

While critics said her debut was a reaction to the death of her brother, many suggested that this delicate May-to-September romance hinted at the demise of Coppola's marriage to Spike Jonze. The *Adaptation* director's own street style has even been compared to John's 'rumpled schleppiness', by one commentator.[127] Given that Jonze was much more present than John, filming much of *Lost in Translation*'s behind-the-scenes footage glimpsed on the DVD, such comparisons are misplaced. It is, after all, hard to imagine Coppola as the sort who listens to self-help tapes (as Charlotte does, with *A Soul Search: Finding Your True Calling*). Yet it's tempting to read biographical detail into the lines of dialogue, if only because Coppola's vision is such a personal one. 'What about marriage? Does that get any easier?' asks Charlotte of Bob. 'That's hard,' he replies, as if he were Coppola's own sounding board.

In the subsequent scene, Charlotte visits a temple in Kyoto and spies on a traditional marriage ceremony, before tying an 'offering' to a tree. Rather like Bob's enigmatic whisper in Charlotte's ear at the end, we never discover the content of this offering. Coppola lets us speculate that it could be a prayer for Charlotte's own ailing union. Earlier she juxtaposes an X-ray of the character's foot (damaged after an accident in her hotel room) with the sight of her leafing through Polaroids of her and John; a move that subtly prompts you to wonder which of the images is the more transparent. Less is more for Coppola once again: just as *The Virgin Suicides* revealed little about the girls' suicide pact, so *Lost in Translation* is as coy and chaste a work as you are ever likely to come across. By the finale, Bob learns that a quick fix with a young-ster is no way to solve his relationship: 'I think they go back to their lives but they've taken something from the experience,' says Coppola. 'That's what I think.' And who are we to argue?

At one point, Bob and Charlotte watch Federico Fellini's *La Dolce vita* (1960) while lying on the bed. As they listen to Italian dialogue with Japanese subtitles, it sums up the confusion and isolation these characters feel, both geographically and spiritually. Rather like the redhead American singer in the bar (whom Bob winds up bedding) with her rendition of 'Scarborough Fair', everything is out of place.

Here is an alien world where the razors, beds and showerheads are designed in miniature, for another race of people; where Bob towers above everyone in the lift. Even Charlotte is a blonde vision, hermetically sealed from the sea of brunettes on the street by the bubble of her clear plastic umbrella.

If much of the film's humour is derived from misunderstandings during the process of translation from Japanese to English (the call girl sent to Bob demanding he 'lip my stocking' being a classic example), much of its soul comes from the misunderstandings between characters – even when they're speaking the same language. Charlotte's tearful telephone call back home; Bob's weary conversations with his wife Lydia, where she asks, 'Do I need to worry about you, Bob?' Even Kelly (Anna Farris), the Hollywood starlet friend of John's also staying in the hotel, is registered at the desk under the pseudonym 'Evelyn Waugh' – which Charlotte is quick to point out was a man's name.

Although it's true the film derives some of its laughs at the expense of the Japanese language, there's enough mockery of the Americans, and specifically Hollywood, to make it an even split. Much of this comes via Farris's hilarious turn as Kelly, in town to promote a *Matrix*-sounding action film with 'Keanu' called *Midnight Velocity*. Rumoured to be based upon Coppola's experience of meeting Cameron Diaz during Jonze's shooting of *Being John Malkovich* (though she has gone on record to deny this), the character of Kelly comes across as the archetypal Californian airhead. Devoted to 'power cleanses' to rid her body of toxins, like John – who expresses an interest in Buddhism – Kelly claims in the press conference for *Midnight Velocity* that it was her interest in reincarnation that drew her to the project. It's the sort of empty appropriation of Eastern culture that gives Westerners a bad name.

Coppola is also careful not to let her principal pair come across as too superior. Bob admits he is seriously considering buying a Porsche when Charlotte suggests he's having a mid-life crisis; likewise, she confesses she's been through the common phases every aspiring artist (including Coppola) goes through, from writing to photography. Bob forgets his son's birthday, and his wife, for all her faults (expressed perfectly as she sends him nine burgundy-coloured carpet samples to choose from with the note 'I like the burgundy'), is evidently having a tough time rearing their children while he frolics through the pachinko arcades of Tokyo. If Coppola's depiction of the Japanese is primarily

387

backdrop cliché (bowing and serene, colourful and excitable), she at least allows them the upper hand in the karaoke scene. After Charlotte's friend Charlie Brown (Fumihiro Hayashi) delivers a gutsy version of The Sex Pistols' 'God Save the Queen', we're treated to Bob's God-awful version of Roxy Music's 'More Than This'. Even he admits, 'This is hard.' Just like his marriage, it needs working on.

If the music that spills from this scene recalls the generation when Bob was still making movies, Coppola's inspired collaboration with music supervisor Brian Reitzell is achingly contemporary. 'We talked about how the music could make this dreamy atmosphere,' she recalls. Tracks by such bands as the Chemical Brothers ('The State We're In'), Death in Vegas ('Girls') and Air ('Alone in Kyoto') haunt the hazy visuals, beautifully captured by Lance Acord. By the time we reach the finale, cut to The Jesus and Mary Chain's 'Just Like Honey', you have to wonder if the lyrics – 'Listen to the girl / As she takes on half the world' – are talking about Coppola herself. Only someone with her kudos could have enticed My Bloody Valentine's reclusive genius Kevin Shields to provide the bulk of the music that washes over Charlotte and Bob as they drift through the neon-lit night.

At times boasting the exuberance of Jean-Luc Godard's lovers-on-the-run in *À bout de souffle* (1960), as Bob and Charlotte gleefully flee from a bar, chased by the owner with a weird laser gun, the film is just as slight. Burdened with the pressure of terrific advance word after the film made its debut at the 2003 Venice Film Festival, it's not a movie that necessarily holds up to a repeat viewing, if only because the film has as little momentum as the relationship between Bob and Charlotte. As over-hyped as it was, following a glut of favourable reviews it nevertheless rode its wave to become one of the toasts of the season. Costing $4 million, it made $44.9 million in the U.S., won three of the five Golden Globes it was nominated for and even scored a Best Picture nod at the Oscars. Scarlett Johansson, receiving a Golden Globe nomination for her performance, became the year's must-see actress and the film wound up on numerous critics' top-ten lists for the year. Judging by the line snaking from the Carlton Hotel at the 2004 Cannes Film Festival, where interested parties jostled to get a piece of the action on Coppola's next film – a biopic of Marie Antoinette reuniting her with original muse Kirsten Dunst – the film, at least, lost nothing in translation.

Obviously, people are going to think I'm a showboat and a bit
of a prick – but then I am those things!
  Steve Zissou, *The Life Aquatic with Steve Zissou*

Visiting some old friends, including Bill Murray, Coppola spent some
time on the set of Wes Anderson's *The Life Aquatic with Steve Zissou* in
the little Italian town of Anzio. 'There's something fun about putting Bill
in pathetic situations and watching him crawl to safety,' she told *Premiere* magazine.[128] Like Coppola, for his fourth film Anderson set out to
examine middle age and the incumbent crisis of confidence it can
induce, using a withered and washed-up Murray. Only this time it was
Murray, and not his character, who was suffering.

Filming for six months took its toll on Murray, who was unhappy
about the conditions he endured on location. When he picked up his
Golden Globe for *Lost in Translation*, he referred to working on 'the
death ship'. As he told one interviewer, 'This is by far the hardest film
I've ever done, the most physically demanding, the most emotionally
demanding, personally and professionally.'[129] Upon his return, he
added, 'I was gone so long people didn't think I was coming back. It was
terrible: a sickening, anxiety-provoking experience. The actual job was
extraordinary but the pain of being away for so long was deep. And I'm
still scarred by it. My family is scarred by it.' Was it worth it? To a
degree, Steve Zissou is an echo of better past performances by Murray.
Following just a year after *Lost in Translation*, Anderson's eponymous
marine man feels a little too close to Bob Harris. A half-hearted father
dealing with a troubled marriage and a struggling career, Murray's wistful melancholy feels more about the role than the character.

Perhaps the difference is that Zissou is too close to Anderson, by now
in the most introspective stage of his career to date. Coppola, still in her
twenties while making *Lost in Translation*, viewed Bob – and the acting
profession she once flirted with – with an amused detachment. She evidently related more to the confused Charlotte than the cynical Bob, more
concerned with the trials of finding your path in life than regretting the
one you've taken. But Anderson, thirty-five by the time this fourth film
was complete, had reached a point in his career where the onset of middle-age mediocrity was haunting him like a ghost – as perhaps it did Murray
in the mid-1990s. As evidence for this, after becoming good friends with
Peter Bogdanovich, Anderson became intrigued with the director's career
trajectory. After the low-key *Targets* (1968), Bogdanovich's triple-shot

of success – *The Last Picture Show*, *What's Up, Doc?* (1972) and *Paper Moon* (1973) – wildly inflated critical expectations. Beginning with his Henry James adaptation *Daisy Miller* (1974), he was never able to recapture the glories of his early forays into Hollywood.

Like Bogdanovich, Anderson had experienced increasing adulation with every film, to the point where *The Royal Tenenbaums*, a film about failure, perversely became his greatest success. Anderson admits he has discussed this topic with Bogdanovich. 'I think about him sometimes,' he says. 'He is interesting because in terms of directing movies, he hasn't been able to do what he wanted lately. It's been a while. I think he will direct more good films . . . but he also has this second career as a scholar and movie historian, and he's written these great books that are irreplaceable. He talks to groups at the Museum of Modern Art, so he has this second career that is enough for one person. But he also has this glory that he experienced before.'

It seems that Anderson is dissecting the role of the director; after all, Zissou is a filmmaker and *The Life Aquatic with Steve Zissou* is Anderson's answer to Fellini's 8½. While Anderson admits, 'when somebody makes a movie about a filmmaker it can feel self-important', his film is not this. It's not indulgent – at least, no more than any of his other films. Yet again it's a study in failure, a topic it has become clear Anderson is obsessed with. 'I think, for me, failure has always been much more interesting [than success]. It's not like I ever had any intention to write about failure or focus on it, but I feel like I have – utterly. Every movie I make is just about someone who can't fit in or make things work, and is dealing with failure. *The Royal Tenenbaums* – the whole movie is about everyone's disappointment in their lives. To me, it's a more complex subject than success – and more moving.'

Anderson claims to already be au fait with failure in other parts of his life. 'Even if I've had success with my movies, there are so many other things that haven't worked out. That's where that stuff comes from. But also there are certain elements of all these characters that come from the people around me.' Indeed, as Zissou asks, 'What happened to me? Did I lose my talent?' this could be either Bogdanovich talking or Anderson fretting. This is furthered when Zissou, in a brutal moment of self-reckoning, describes himself as 'a washed-up old man with no distribution deal', perhaps the biggest fear of any filmmaker.

If nothing else, the film underlines that Anderson is intrigued by the lightning-in-a-bottle nature of the creative process. After all, *The Royal Tenenbaums* featured a blocked playwright, while Zissou is reminded that he hasn't 'made a hit documentary in nine years'. Inadvertently, by investigating this very subject, Anderson suffers accordingly – almost predictably. As *Sight & Sound* noted, Anderson 'used the fourth film to inspect with even greater thoroughness territory already mapped out in earlier work',[130] a polite euphemism for saying he's treading water. The film barely broke even, taking $1 million less than its $25 million budget in the U.S.

While Paul Thomas Anderson (*Punch-Drunk Love*) and, as we will see, David O. Russell (*I ❤ Huckabees*), managed to take leftfield turns for their fourth films, Anderson retreated into a world even more idiosyncratic than that of *The Royal Tenenbaums*: David Bowie songs, performed in Portuguese by the Brazilian actor and pop star Seu Jorge; an underwater world animated by Henry Selick; characters called Oseary Drakoulias and Vladimir Wolodarsky . . . the list goes on. As inventive as these individual elements are, the fact that *The Life Aquatic with Steve Zissou* is full of anticipated trademarks rather supports the idea that, not unlike Team Zissou with its specially designed Adidas sneakers, pinball machines and pyjamas, Anderson has become a brand.

Like Tarantino's, Anderson's hermetically sealed celluloid universes are, by now, instantly recognizable. Beginning with a stage and its plush red curtains as he did for *Rushmore*, and concluding with a slow-motion shot, as he does for every film, Anderson once again packs his story with luscious detail. When an autograph hunter asks Zissou to sign posters of his past films – including *Island Cats* – we are reminded of Anderson's technique in *The Royal Tenenbaums*, with the inclusion of posters, book dust jackets and paintings to spell out the characters' past achievements. This time, it's not Salinger who provides the literary template but Herman Melville with *Moby-Dick*, while *National Geographic* and the conservationist Jane Goodall are equally important influences.

Thematically, he once again explores the notion of family. Like Royal Tenenbaum, Zissou is a reluctant father trying to make amends. He tells Ned (Owen Wilson), his Air Kentucky pilot son who turns up unannounced, that he never contacted him 'because I hate fathers and I never wanted to be one'. Zissou's real children are the crew of his ship, notably the German first mate, Klaus (Willem Dafoe), who – in reference to Zissou and his late business partner Esteban (Seymour

Cassel) – says, 'I've always thought of you two as my dads.' pregnant journalist Jane Winslett-Richardson (Cate Blanchett), on board to write an article about Zissou, must also contend with becoming a mother – without the father (her editor) to help raise the child.

If the film is chiefly about absent fathers, it's also about jealous husbands. As with *The Royal Tenenbaums*, Angelica Huston plays the wife of the main character – in this case 'rich bitch' Eleanor Zissou, reputedly 'the brains' behind the outfit. Once married to Zissou's former roommate, the suave fellow oceanographer Alistair Hennessey (Jeff Goldblum), Eleanor abandons Zissou to reunite with her ex-spouse. Zissou apologizes, saying, 'I know I haven't been at my best this past decade' – yet another example of his protracted mid-life crisis given extra pathos by Murray's hangdog expression. It points to the fact that all the characters are lost and looking for something, as symbolized by Zissou's quest to find the elusive Jaguar Shark – the creature that killed Esteban at the outset, and the hunt for which bookends the film.

As Zissou pursues the shark like a latter-day Captain Ahab, his search takes on a metaphorical significance. 'It's this guy who's been dealing with his own sense of failure through the whole story. He had this glory at one point, and it's all faded,' says Anderson. 'He's been hunting something that probably doesn't exist. No one really wants to believe him anymore but they're following him, anyway, because they love him I think. At the end, he does find something. It's real and there is something there to connect to. It's a basic optimism that I feel. If, say, Terrence Malick had made this story, the shark would not show up at the end. He has a darker view and I don't think he could have that optimistic moment.'

The scene, with the principal characters all crammed into Zissou's miniature sub, is the highlight of the film – but we're forced to endure some rather amateur moments to get us there. In particular, the invasion of the pirates aboard the Belafonte and the subsequent rescue of the kidnapped bail bondsman Bill Ubell (Bud Cort) from Ping Island are so ham-fisted in their execution, you almost suspect Anderson is doing it deliberately. At least production designer Mark Friedberg, marking his first collaboration with Anderson, was full of invention. Take the cutaway doll's house–like shot of Zissou's boat, showing it as a hive of activity as the camera pans from one cabin to the next. Or Ping Island, with its VW Beetle half-buried in the sand, and the dilapidated and waterlogged Hotel Citröen, with birds and monkeys the only remaining residents. Like Selick's enigmatic Jaguar Shark, these are moments of beauty that rescue Anderson from wallowing in introspection.

Initially written as a short story while Anderson was in college – with the character then called Steve Cocteau – it was fleshed out into a screenplay in response to Wilson's intermittent encouragement. But with Wilson's increasingly busy schedule as an actor, it meant that by the time Anderson came to do this the pair were unable to collaborate on the script for the first time in their careers. Instead, Anderson asked his friend the filmmaker Noah Baumbach to assist, after the two had worked together on Baumbach's directorial debut *The Squid and the Whale* (2005), a Brooklyn-set story about two young boys dealing with their parents' divorce. 'Our way of working together is very

52 Team Zissou go shark-hunting in *The Life Aquatic with Steve Zissou.*

similar to the way Owen and I worked together, which was conversations and trying to entertain each other as we invent the movie,' says Anderson. 'Then I would write everything down in a notebook, go home, type it and bring in the pages the next day. The difference is that Noah and I could meet every day and work all day. And with Owen, I would be just working on my own a lot of the time because he had so many offers. And for an actor, they have to do it when their chance is there.'

Anderson liberally borrows from Jacques Cousteau's life and times to construct the narrative, notably the death of his son which is echoed by Ned's demise in Zissou's helicopter. The textual details – from the red caps that Zissou's crew wear, to him casting them in his films – also match up. 'That's somebody who is thinking as an artist as much as he is thinking as a scientist,' says Anderson. 'He was very aware that his work was going to be on camera and that he was going to record this stuff. A lot of his ideas were for how he was going to present this. He wanted his work to be seen all over the world. He wanted to be huge – and he was huge.' Of course, it wouldn't be a Wes Anderson film without an obscure reference. 'Zissou' is the nickname of the brother of the French photographer Jacques Henri Lartigue, a favourite of Anderson's. Like Cousteau/Zissou, Maurice Lartigue was a daredevil inventor who built airplanes and racing cars.

Reinventing his own image after *The Royal Tenenbaums*, there's no doubt Anderson sees something of himself in Zissou. Not just because he made films but also because he explored rich, untapped worlds. When Bowie's 'Rebel Rebel' is strummed on board the *Belafonte*, it may be directed not just at the captain of the boat but at his creator too. Are his films rebellious statements against Hollywood confection? 'I don't really think I'm particularly rebelling against anything. I'd rather have $50,000 to do what I wanted to do than $40 million to do something I wish I didn't make or feel no connection to. Maybe when I have a mortgage sometime later in my life, I'll feel differently about that. It's less about something to rebel against and more about something to get inspired by.'

A Henry James–like figure, Anderson is now the intellectual American abroad. Shooting at the famed Cinecittá sound stages in Rome and employing Luchino Visconti's former hair guru Maria Teresa Corridoni (who also styled for Fellini) – as well as using Oscar-winning costume designer Milena Canonero – Anderson has entered his Italian period. He even allowed his hair to grow, began to wear contacts and started buying all his shirts from a particular Parisian tailor. 'I think he's more handsome since we made *The Life Aquatic with Steve Zissou*,' says Angelica Huston. 'He seems to fill out his suits more. He was thinner before and a little more nerdy. I think he's looking more sexy and somehow directorial.'

If he is more certain of his image now, Anderson is less sure-footed about his fourth film. 'I don't know how to present it to people,' he says. 'It's not a traditional adventure movie. It's not a comedy or a drama, specifically. It's hard to know exactly what it is.' Such uncertainty is entirely appropriate, of course. Alongside *Lost in Translation*, as well as Alexander Payne's *Sideways* and David O. Russell's *I ❤ Huckabees* – two other 2004 efforts dealing with men-in-crisis that will be examined in Chapter 24 – *The Life Aquatic with Steve Zissou* is preoccupied with the discontent middle age can bring. No longer Kids, it was a topic that was becoming increasingly pertinent to our Sundance alumni.

CHAPTER 23

Middle-Age Malaise:
Kill Bill and *Ocean's Twelve*

53 Uma Thurman takes on the Crazy 88 gang in
   Kill Bill Vol. I.

> Revenge is never a straight line. It's a forest. And like a forest,
> it's easy to lose your way.
>
> Hattori Hanzo, *Kill Bill*

After a six-year absence, you would expect Quentin Tarantino to return with a bang. And he didn't disappoint. *Kill Bill: Vol. 1* and *Vol. 2* were undeniably two of the most hotly anticipated films of late 2003 and early 2004, generating acres of press coverage. Like the films' heroine, the sword-wielding assassin known as The Bride, it was as if Tarantino had woken from a coma to avenge himself upon those who thought he was finished.

After his stint on Broadway, Tarantino remained in New York to begin work on an epic World War II story, *Inglorious Bastards*. A Nazi-occupied-France version of Sergio Leone's *The Good, the Bad and the Ugly* (1966), by all accounts it began to sprawl wildly into three scripts, none of which had an ending. This was temporarily abandoned after a glut of war movies – from Steven Spielberg's *Saving Private Ryan* to Terrence Malick's *The Thin Red Line* – had stolen Tarantino's thunder. Rumours that he was also planning a prequel to *Reservoir Dogs* and *Pulp Fiction* entitled *The Vega Brothers*, that would see Michael Madsen and John Travolta reprise their roles from their respective films, also began to circulate.

Then, in 2000, Tarantino bumped into Uma Thurman at a Miramax Oscar party. She reminded him of an idea she'd suggested on the set of *Pulp Fiction* about a deadly female assassin. 'I do remember the whole conversation,' says Thurman. 'It was just between the two of us . . . the concept of a female assassin, a wedding chapel massacre, a road to revenge, this assassin trying to quit the business and being dragged back by her colleagues. And in that same conversation he invented the character of [The Bride's former lover/boss] Bill and called the film *Kill Bill*.' At the time, Tarantino penned, according to Thurman, 'nine pages' of the script. When it was finally announced that *Kill Bill* was his next film, the speculation around this martial arts spectacular began in earnest. Cast as The Bride, Thurman promptly became pregnant, holding up the shoot for almost a year. She had just

eight weeks to recover before going into an intense three-month training period, where she was taught Kenjutsu samurai sword skills by the
legendary Japanese star Sonny Chiba, whom Tarantino had cast as
Hattori Hanzo, the retired sword-maker who provides The Bride with
her weapon of choice.

Then Warren Beatty, originally set to play Bill, dropped out, and the
role expanded beyond what was a glorified cameo. David Carradine,
in yet another 1970s career resurrection by Tarantino, was cast as a
replacement. 'I've always considered David Carradine – when it comes
to wild actors of Hollywood – one of the great mad geniuses,' says the
director, who had been reading the actor's autobiography *Endless
Highway* shortly before casting him. 'To read about this guy's life, and
imagine him as the Shakespearean actor John Carradine's son in Hollywood, was quite a fascinating journey. As I was reading it, I was like,
"God, this could be Bill's story!" It would be different but just as
inventive and just as character-filled. So that went a long way towards
me casting David.'

Following a lengthy eight-month shoot in Beijing, Tokyo, Mexico
and Pasadena, that overran by 155 days and wound up $16 million
over budget, Tarantino was subjected to the sort of scrutiny Martin
Scorsese endured over *Gangs of New York* (2002). In league with Harvey Weinstein, he deflected the hype with all the dexterity of a samurai
swordsman. After months in the editing room, only someone with the
gall of Tarantino could get away with scything the 220-page script for
this martial arts epic in twain. It had been done before – from Richard
Lester's *Musketeers* movies to Claude Berri's *Jean de Florette* and *Manon
des Sources* (both 1986). For Weinstein and Miramax, this was a no-
brainer. Getting two films for the price of one, they knew that Tarantino's
fan base was such that audiences would pay a second time to see the
completion of the story. Both parts went on to individually out-gross the
$55 million budget, recouping $136 million in the U.S. alone. A sound
business decision though it may have been, artistically it was anything
but, even if Tarantino claims this was his plan all along.

'If I could have done it as two movies from the get-go, I would
have,' he says:

But to bring it up to Harvey Weinstein from the beginning, saying
'Hey, I've got an idea, let's make it two movies!' – that would have
set up a warning sign right off the bat, which might not have been

prudent. But when it actually happened, Harvey Weinstein came on the set, in the last weeks of shooting, and said, 'Y'know, Quentin, I'd hate like hell for you to lose anything. Why don't we make it two movies!' And I'm like, 'That's a great idea, Harvey! *Genius!*' Then I went back to work for the next hour, and figured it all out. This would happen here, the second one would start here, the first would end here.

Undeniably, the splice between the two volumes comes at a dramatic point. In *Vol. 1*, The Bride, left for dead at her wedding rehearsal, comes to from her four-year coma and resolves to track down Bill and the gang she once belonged to – the Deadly Viper Assassination Squad (or DiVAS), the ones responsible for the massacre. After our heroine dispatches with her one-time colleagues Vernita Green (Vivica A. Fox) and O-Ren Ishii (Lucy Liu), also leaving the latter's assistant Sofie Fatale (Julie Dreyfuss) minus a limb or two, the unseen (at this point) Bill reveals that The Bride's 'daughter is still alive'. For those listening carefully at *Vol. 1*'s opening black and white clip, flashing back to the massacre, they will have heard this child is Bill's. An emotional cliffhanger, it is the perfect bridge from the martial arts mayhem of the first volume to the heady mix of film noir and spaghetti western in the second.

As the posters emphasized, Tarantino had lost none of his own sense of cinematic genius. This second comeback of his career, after *Jackie Brown*, was advertised on the striking yellow and black one-sheets as 'the fourth film by Quentin Tarantino'. A statement of vast self-importance, it was nevertheless entirely in keeping for a man who turned filmmaking on its head with *Pulp Fiction*, as well as being a typical piece of Miramax marketing. What was entirely unexpected was to see the same phrase woven into the opening credits, rather than the usual 'a film by', an astonishing slice of arrogance that demonstrated just how much Tarantino had bought into his own hype.

Was it all worth it? The critics were divided. 'I felt like the director himself had cacklingly jammed his hypodermic into my throbbing arm. Really, no one delivers that sheer, aneurysm-inducing rush with the same intravenous efficiency as Tarantino,' wrote Peter Bradshaw in *The Guardian*.[131] He was similarly enthusiastic about *Vol. 2*. 'Once again, with an insouciant blaze of energy and style, Tarantino has seen off the imitators, detractors and condescenders . . . *Kill Bill* just seems to bypass the rational filters which impede the respectable films and attacks the endorphin centres of the brain.' Others were distinctly underwhelmed: 'This smells like the work of an ageing enfant terrible incarcerated in his malodorous living room, scrabbling among the empty pizza boxes for fresh ways to shock,' noted Jenny McCartney of *Vol. 1*.[132]

While not quite on the scale of *Reservoir Dogs*, Tarantino still had to face criticism about his use of violence in this post-9/11 world. 'Sure *Kill Bill* is violent,' he told *Empire*. 'Sure it's fucking intense. But it's a Tarantino movie. You don't go to a Metallica concert and ask the fuckers to turn the music down.'[133] To be fair, any anger was fairly muted, given the presentation of the bloodshed. Be it shooting a battle scene in black and white, or fleshing out O-Ren Ishii's violent back-story via a stunning anime sequence from the Japanese company Production IG, Tarantino deliberately distances us from the violence. He also tempers it, as ever, with humour. The funniest moment in the two volumes must be when the black-suited Crazy 88 gang ('I think of them as *Reservoir Dogs* with less cool sunglasses,' says Tarantino), are all rolling around in puddles of blood, groaning in pain, after The Bride's single-handed victory. 'I've done violence before but I've never done it in such an outrageous way,' says Tarantino. 'It's using a lot of Japanese filmmaking influences. It's a standard staple in Japanese cinema to cut somebody's arm off and use water-hoses for veins. Pshhh! I've kept that tradition a lot.'

The stand-out set piece of the two volumes, this so-called Showdown at the House of Blue Leaves was chiefly responsible for delaying the production, taking eight weeks instead of the scheduled two to film. 'It took me a year to write that fight sequence,' says Tarantino. 'I was trying to think of every inventive, most entertaining way I could to dismember, disembowel and put an end to those bastards! I was out there trying to create one of the greatest, most exciting sequences in the history of cinema.' He admits he often borrowed from other films for inspiration while writing the scene. 'Over the course of a year, I would constantly rewrite it, until all those scenes I'd taken from other movies had gone, until I was all filled with original stuff.'

But as ever with Tarantino, there was more than an element of spot-the-reference. Announcing as much in the opening shot – of the logo for 1970s Hong Kong production company Shaw Brothers – this was, after all, what he called a 'duck-press' of the grindhouse B movies that he had gorged himself on over the years. The yellow-and-black jumpsuit worn by The Bride in *Vol. 1* alludes to Bruce Lee's outfit in *Game of Death* (1978), while the Kato masks worn by the Crazy 88 gang are referring to Lee's 1960s TV series *The Green Hornet*. Casting nineteen-year-old Chiaki Kuriyama as the deadly Gogo, complete with schoolgirl uniform, recalled her role in Kinji Fukasaku's *Battle Royale* (2000). Playing dual roles – Crazy 88 leader Johnny Mo in *Vol. 1* and The Bride's cruel tutor Pai Mei in *Vol. 2* – is the former Shaw Brothers star Gordon Liu, who appeared in one of the studio's biggest earners, *The 36th Chamber of Shaolin* (1978).

Perhaps most influential upon Tarantino was Chang Cheh, the director chiefly responsible for the Shaw Brothers' pre-eminence in action cinema, who died during pre-production for *Kill Bill*. 'He is to old school kung-fu films what John Ford was to Westerns,' notes Tarantino. The fight sequence with the Crazy 88 gang is a blatant nod to Cheh's 1972 film *The Boxer from Shantung*, right down to the use of hatchets. 'Any time we put the camera up in the ceiling and looked down, I called it "Chang Cheh's POV" [point of view],' notes Tarantino, who even confesses to a spiritual experience with the late director once on the shoot. Frustrated with the hydraulic-assisted technique for jetting out blood from one of The Bride's victims, it was suggested he use a Chinese condom, as Chang Cheh once did. But with the blood not spurting out in the direction he wanted, Tarantino grew more irritated. 'But I swear to goodness, I felt like Chang Cheh talked to me. He came to me and said "Hang in there Quentin! It's going to work out. It's bound to explode the right way once." Sure enough, four times later, it did it perfectly. And to this day, I'm almost positive that Chang Cheh came to me.'

Websites such as www.tarantino.info have unearthed over eighty movies referenced in the two films. Daryl Hannah's DiVAS member, Elle Driver, walking down the hospital corridor in a nurse's whites, recalls a scene in Alfred Hitchcock's *Marnie* (1964). Her eye patch refers back to a Swedish movie (banned in its own country) called *Thriller: En Grym Film*, in which a heroin-addicted prostitute has her eye poked out after she tries to quit her profession. Made by Bo Arne Vibenius, this was one of four films made between 1972 and 1974 featured in a tribute to *Kill Bill* programmed by London's ICA in 2004. Two others from Japan, Toshiya Fujita's *Lady Snowblood* and Shuyna Ita's *Female Convict Scorpion: Jailhouse 41*, also featured females seeking vengeance. Inspired by the women-in-prison and rape-revenge sub-genres, *Lady Snowblood* followed a nineteenth-century swordswoman tracking down the killers of her mother's husband; Ita's film sees a convict wreak revenge on the warden who locks her up. The fourth, from the U.S., was Ted V. Mikel's *The Doll Squad*, with its female assassin team an evident influence for the DiVAS. Putting them all through his press, Tarantino, to his credit, once again managed to squeeze out something that feels fresh rather than derivative.

Tarantino further emphasized that this was a martial arts remix by hiring the Wu-Tang Clan's creative heart, The RZA, to compose the music for *Vol. 1* (with his old pal Robert Rodriguez working on the follow-up). A huge fan of the kung-fu genre himself, The RZA's contributions included his 'Ode to O-Ren Ishii' and a mix of Charles Bernstein's 'White Lightning'. In what must be Tarantino's best compilation tape yet, the score for *Vol. 1* in particular is a blistering blend of Japanese surf-pop, Southern rockabilly and flamenco, spliced with soundtrack steals from the likes of Bernard Herrmann, Isaac Hayes and Ennio Morricone. Particularly memorable is the use of the Quincy Jones title track from *Ironside*, while the opening Nancy Sinatra cover of the Sonny and Cher classic 'Bang Bang' reminds us that artists borrowing from artists has been going on for years.

If the films don't make quite the cultural impact of *Pulp Fiction*, both were certainly at the forefront of bringing together Hong Kong and Hollywood cinema. As if to symbolize this, martial arts adviser Yuen Wo-Ping – who worked on the other influential films in this movement, *The Matrix* and *Crouching Tiger, Hidden Dragon* – was hired to teach the cast 'wire work' stunts. Underlining the fact that spaghetti westerns have often been influenced by Asian cinema – Akira Kurosawa's *The Seven Samurai* (1954) remade by John Sturges as *The Magnificent Seven* (1960) for one – Tarantino's two films are like a head-on crash between East and West. Of course, he had been doing this for years; *Reservoir Dogs*, borrowing from Ringo Lam's *City on Fire*, was a yakuza movie transplanted to modern day Los Angeles. But here, we can glimpse Tarantino's intent in his dialogue, a curious mixture of American slang and stately samurai-style lines: for example, in the fight between The Bride and Vernita Green, who alternate 'bitch' with 'I beseech you'. As The Bride tells Green's daughter, who finds her mother's knifed corpse, 'It was not my intention to do this in front of you. For that I am sorry.'

While both volumes were largely shorn of Tarantino's usual dialogue riffs, his trademark references remained. Lucky Charms cereal, women's feet, Red Apple cigarettes (advertised by Sofie Fatale on a poster), trunk shots, self-referential lines (*Reservoir Dogs*' 'kill crazy rampage' pops up, as does the phrase 'natural born killer') and scenes arguing over nicknames (à la *Reservoir Dogs*) all weave their way into this world. Comic book references even get a look in, notably via Bill's speech about the difference between the alter egos of Superman and Spider-Man. The DiVAS snake-inspired nicknames – Copperhead (Vernita), Sidewinder (Budd), Cottonmouth (O-Ren Ishii), Black Mamba (The Bride), California Mountain Snake (Elle) – were also the names of Captain America's enemies.

As you would expect, Tarantino's macabre sense of humour also lingered – from The Bride squashing Elle Driver's remaining good eye between her toes to the pubic-hair-infested tub of Vaseline supplied by Buck, the hospital orderly, for paying customers to lube up the comatose Bride before sex. Tarantino also hasn't lost his uncanny ability for 'putting his finger on those horrifying universal fear-factors', as Thurman puts it; in this case being buried alive (as The Bride is by Budd), losing an eye or being bitten by a snake (as Elle and Budd experience).

On more than one occasion, Tarantino has stated that *Kill Bill* falls into his 'movie-movie' universe, as opposed to the normal world to which *Reservoir Dogs*, *Pulp Fiction* and his screenplay for *True Romance* belonged. Others in this 'movie-movie' category would be his scripts for *Natural Born Killers* and *From Dusk Till Dawn* (emphasising the link, Michael Parks – who also plays Bill's associate Esteban Vihaio in *Vol. 2* – reprises his role of Sheriff Earl McGraw, originally killed by the Gecko brothers). Set in a world where an assassin can park her sword next to her on a plane, *Kill Bill* was the first film Tarantino had directed inside this hyper-referential, movie-saturated cosmos. 'The most accurate way to describe the differences between the two universes is to say that when the characters in *True Romance* or *Reservoir Dogs* or *Pulp Fiction* go to the movies, these are the movies they see.'[134] Which might account for why *True Romance*'s devout kung-fu movie fan Clarence Worley wears the same Elvis-style glasses as Buck. Certainly, creating films for your characters to watch is a good indication of how much effort Tarantino puts into creating his universes.

But as some critics mumbled, after the maturity of *Jackie Brown* Tarantino seemed to have taken two steps back, with *Kill Bill: Vol. 1* in particular pandering to his core audience of motorbike-and-martial-arts-loving teenagers. While *Vol. 1* is all about action rather than arcs, storytelling rather than story, *Vol. 2* attempts to fill in the blanks – with superficial success. 'There's a personality change that happens between *Vol. 1* and *Vol. 2*,' says Tarantino:

> If you see *Vol. 1*, at the end of it, when Sonny Chiba gives that little parable – when he says 'Revenge is never a straight line. It's a forest, and like a forest, it's easy to get lost, lose your way and forget where you came in.' *Vol. 1* is the straight line – *Vol. 1* is the straight-ahead, heart-pumping, sit-on-the-edge-of-your-seat, 'wow – that was a night at the movies!' The resonance is in *Vol. 2*. It's not straight ahead. Now, it's the forest, and easy to get lost, as far as The Bride's journey is concerned. We slow down a little bit, we get to know the characters a little bit more. Things aren't one-two-three anymore. Real life rears its ugly head into its journey and then she must deal.

You have to ask if The Bride's reunion with her daughter, coming at the end of *Vol. 2*, delivers the resonance he talks about. Preparing for her transition to motherhood, The Bride exchanges her garish yellow tracksuit for jeans and hooded tops. Her name, amusingly bleeped out every time it's spoken until this point, is finally revealed as Beatrix Kiddo – although Bill throughout has said her surname as if it were a term of endearment. She also becomes much more vocal in the second film, after being 'held very close, very shielded and very silent for huge sections', as Thurman says, in the preceding part. 'I think once Quentin split the movie, it gave him the ability to completely allow them to embrace their own tone,' she adds. 'And truly the character is much more revealed and stripped down in the second half of the one story, so it has a much more emotional focus. The camera becomes closer, the scope narrows. It becomes very, very intimate. It ends in a conversation. If you look at the two films together, it's like a giant frame that narrows and narrows.'

This split personality can certainly be seen in the work of two of the film's collaborators. David Wasco, Tarantino's production designer since *Reservoir Dogs*, outdid himself, in particular with his lavish House of Blue Leaves set, with its snow-bound garden complete with water feature. But as we progress through the second volume, the sets become less grand and more sordid – from the strip bar to Budd's trailer and winding up at the nondescript villa belonging to Bill. As Thurman has already hinted, the cinematography – shot by the legendary Oliver Stone DP Robert Richardson, who had even filmed *Natural Born Killers* – took a similar tack. While *Vol. 2* begins with a black and white noir-inflected scene, where The Bride recaps the story while driving in an open-topped car, such flourishes give way to a simplistic, near-still presentation by the end.

In returning to the question of the film's emotional centre, it's fair to say The Bride is the finest female creation of Tarantino's oeuvre to date. 'Usually women don't get to play that type of anti-hero,' says Thurman, 'the type of person who takes a beating and comes back with so much courage, ferocity and energy.' Watching her mature into a parent – 'Mommy' is her final alias, added by Tarantino in the end credits – we witness the lioness reunited with her cub. One of *Vol. 2*'s most effective scenes comes as a flashback to the moment in a hotel room when The Bride discovers she is pregnant, while about to assassinate the red-jacketed Karen (Helen Kim). 'I'm the deadliest woman in the world,' The Bride tells her. 'Right now, I'm just scared shitless for my baby.'

With Thurman sucking the rhythm out of her lines, it is Bill who 'narrates' the final scene, almost speaking stage directions such as 'the smirking killer advanced'. As he explains how their daughter deliberately killed her pet goldfish – gasping for breath on the floor, it is 'the perfect image of life and death', he says – he then tells The Bride how she's an assassin, not a mother. 'You're not a worker bee. You're a renegade killer bee.' But *Kill Bill* – which ends with The Bride doing just that, with the Five Point Palm Exploding Heart Technique taught to her by Pai Mei – is ultimately about female empowerment. Vengeance satisfied, The Bride reclaims her identity as Beatrix, a single mother now, and an assassin no more.

I was once in a vault while it was being robbed.
  Danny Ocean, *Ocean's Twelve*

While Tarantino was busy regressing, Steven Soderbergh was basking in the reflected glory of his coterie of famous friends. There's no doubt *Ocean's Twelve* (2004) is a reflection of just how much of a Hollywood insider he now is. His fourteenth film in fifteen years –

a tremendous work rate matched by few English-language directors bar Michael Winterbottom – it represents a fascinating pit stop in his career. Veering from overnight independent sensation to fringe player to comeback king to Oscar winner, he's now in a position with Section Eight to be benefactor to a whole new generation of filmmakers.

While Soderbergh previously noted that *Solaris* was the beginning of a new era in his career, you could be forgiven for thinking *Ocean's Twelve* was a step backwards – or at least, as discussed in Chapter 17, a way of paying the rent for Section Eight at Warner Bros.

Recalling films such as Alfred Hitchcock's *To Catch a Thief* (1955), with Cary Grant as the retired cat burglar on the Riviera, Soderbergh makes no grand claims for *Ocean's Twelve*. 'At the end of the day, it's almost criminal to talk about either this, or *Ocean's Eleven*, in anything but the most superficial terms, because they're literally meant to party.' Like the hologram of the Fabergé Egg, used by the gang to replace the real thing, *Ocean's Twelve* may contain nothing of substance, but it's a jewel-encrusted wonder to behold. Just as much of the novelty of the 2001 film came about through watching half a dozen A-list stars larking about, so the sequel ups the ante – notably with the inclusion of Catherine Zeta-Jones.

The idea of continuing the story came to Soderbergh when the press tour for the original film hit Rome. Impressed by the city, he had already been formulating the film's key idea – that three years on, the gang are forced to reunite and head to Europe to pay back Terry Benedict, the Las Vegas casino owner they shafted in the original. So the story goes, he has managed to track them all down, giving them two weeks to pay back what they stole – with interest. As we discover, each has been spending varied amounts of the cash, in accordance with their personality: Rusty, now a hotel owner, has blown $25 million while Livingston, now a stand-up comic, has barely spent a cent as he's been living with his parents. As Reuben – the only one to have invested his money (in the stock market) and increased it – quickly calculates, they collectively owe around $190 million.

The notion of a sequel took a further step forward when the producer Jerry Weintraub encountered a script by the newcomer George Nolfi entitled *Honor Among Thieves*. Originally conceived as a possible project for John Woo to direct, it told the story of the greatest thief in America being confronted by his European equivalent. It added the ideal ingredient to spin the story in a different direction. As the gang discovers, it is the rich playboy François Toulour (Vincent Cassell) – a stealthy cat burglar also known as the Night Fox – who has made their whereabouts known to Terry. Peeved that their Vegas heist has demoted him from being regarded as the world's finest active thief, he has lured them to Europe to challenge them to steal the Fabergé Coronation Egg, currently in transit from Paris to Rome. While *Ocean's Eleven* was all about how the gang manages to swindle the loot with barely a hitch, the sequel is all about problems that keep getting in their way. Aside from the Night Fox's cunning, they have the Europol investigator Isabel Lahiri (Zeta-Jones) on their tail, with the added twist that she's Rusty's old flame.

As Soderbergh says, 'It's more emotional, it's more character-driven and it's more complicated on a narrative level.' But it might be more appropriate to call the film 'plot-heavy' – unlike Bryan Singer's *X2*, which took the chance to expand on the themes of the original; merely increasing the scale of the project and density of the story achieves very little.

The introduction of the love story between Isabel and Rusty does give the film the extra 'emotional' dimension Soderbergh talks about, by mirroring the romance between the remarried Danny and Tess. At one point Danny asks Rusty if Isabel was worth all the hassle and he replies sharply, 'Was Tess?'

The film's central twist, of course, is when Tess is called to Rome to pose as an actress to whom she bears a passing resemblance – one Julia Roberts – to help get access to the Fabergé Egg. Following *Full Frontal*, and its industry asides – in particular surrounding Roberts's early career – such territory is not alien to either Soderbergh or Roberts. Just as Soderbergh's version of *Ocean's Eleven* equated con-artistry with acting, so the idea is furthered here. As Tess says, when asked to play Roberts, 'I am apparently playing a real person.' She admits she has a problem playing a real-life person, crying: 'You want me to speak for someone who's out there?' It's as if Roberts as Tess as Roberts – who played a real person in *Erin Brockovich*, of course – is asked to question the very validity of her own profession. With Tess told that playing Roberts means 'you're like an image', the film appears to contain a subtle commentary on the superficial nature of stardom – entirely apt for a film packed with Hollywood stars. As Soderbergh says, such a device was a natural extension of having such a top-drawer cast. 'To me I felt like it's in everybody's mind. You're watching a film like this and you are aware that you're watching a lot of movie stars cavorting, because you just don't see that many together that often anymore.'

While it's not unusual to quote directly from other films, *Ocean's Twelve* is the most blatant of Soderbergh's canon in doing so. Linus's mother says to him, referring to the riddles of the Amsterdam-based contact Matsui, 'Let me guess – he pulled a "Lost in Translation" on you' – a firm indication of how the title of Sofia Coppola's film has seeped into collective consciousness. Likewise, Rusty casually asks Danny and Reuben if they remember the 'Look into Your Heart' scene in *Miller's Crossing* with John Turturro, a question that lays the groundwork for another of the film's stars, Albert Finney, to arrive in a cameo later on. And the beautifully staged sequence where the Night Fox evades numerous security laser beams to get to the Fabergé Egg, contorting his body under and over them like a ballerina cum limbo dancer, can only be a reference to co-star Zeta-Jones's similar scene in Jon Amiel's *Entrapment* (1999).

Numerous lines and scenes seem to carry double meanings in regard to the performers. 'I'd really like to play a more central role,' says Linus to Rusty during the flight to Europe. He is, of course, referring to his part in the caper they're about to set up – but this could easily be Matt Damon himself wanting to assume more weight in the film, barging out Pitt and Clooney. As for Clooney, a lovely streak of self-mockery comes into play in the scene at the French railway station, where he asks the Malloy brothers, and then Basher, whether they think he looks fifty. It's a concern that could easily be read as his own. Indeed, as Reuben tells Terry at the end, in reference to the Night Fox, 'The competition; it's worse than our business. Some young punk always trying to prove himself.' Shut your eyes and this could be Soderbergh talking.

To be fair, Soderbergh's ego is not on a par with that of Tarantino, despite the excessive Hollywood references. Both men, by this point, had turned forty-one. Likewise, David Fincher – whose *Panic Room* two years before was equally entrenched in the mainstream – was now forty-two. Can it be that these men were entering a Bill Murray–like mid-life crisis? That, suddenly, the studio was a place to run to for safety, rather than shake to the foundations? As we will see, given that Alexander Payne is a year older than Fincher and David O. Russell is three years older still, it seems unlikely that age is the cause. More than likely, this was a period where Fincher, Tarantino and Soderbergh temporarily rested on their laurels. It didn't matter; the spirit of the Sundance Kids was more than alive in 2004. Payne and Russell were about to strike a blow with their respective fourth films, *Sideways* and *I ♥ Huckabees*. Both produced by studio art-house arm Fox Searchlight, they are the final proof that the crossover was complete.

CHAPTER 24

Lit Up by the Searchlight:
I ❤ Huckabees and *Sideways*

54 Naomi Watts as Dawn in *I ❤ Huckabees*.

Almost thirty years after Spielberg's *Jaws*, the blockbuster is stronger than ever. As nervous executives pace their offices on opening weekends, the hype that surrounded Tim Burton's *Batman* in the year of *sex, lies, and videotape* is now commonplace. Unveiling the five U.S. box office champions between 1999 and 2004 makes for depressing reading: *How the Grinch Stole Christmas* (2000); *Harry Potter and the Sorcerer's Stone* (2001); *Spider-Man* (2002); *The Return of the King* (2003); and *Shrek 2* (2004). Of this quintet, three of the five were aimed at children, to encourage the broadest market appeal; the remaining two – *Spider-Man* and *The Return of the King* – tapped into adult fantasy to bring out the inner child in all of us.

Yet following 1999 – the year of *Fight Club*, *Magnolia* and *Three Kings*, to name but three – Hollywood had woken like a giant from its slumber, rubbing its eyes with curious wonder. In a time when executives give the go-ahead to $200 million movies like *Troy* (2004) that haven't a hope in hell of making their money back, alternative ways of balancing the books are being sought out. The Sundance Kids – who, perhaps with the exception of David Fincher, practise low-budget filmmaking – are now the ideal cowboys to come in and remind the studios just how possible it is to make mid-budget movies. As Alexander Payne puts it, 'They're not huge home runs but they make money.'

As noted by Richard LaGravenese in the introduction to this book, each of the major studios is now equipped with an art house division, overpopulated with zealous acquisitions executives who scour the festivals – notably Sundance – to snap up a bargain and turn it into the next break-out hit. If the Weinsteins' Miramax led the way at Disney, the other studios were quick to follow suit. Sony Picture Classics, Paramount Classics, Universal's Focus Features and now Warner Independent – with the added bonus of Soderbergh's Section Eight as a supply line – dominate the horizon.

But if there was one that led the way in 2004, it was Fox Searchlight. Turning Sundance successes *Napoleon Dynamite* and *Garden State* into U.S. hits, the films grossed $44.5 million and $26 million, respectively. This was followed with a triple-shot of films most other companies refused to touch: Bill Condon's *Kinsey*, David O. Russell's *I ♥ Huckabees* and Alexander Payne's *Sideways*. The previous year, the company released Catherine Hardwicke's *Thirteen* in the U.S. while other distributors ran scared. As Condon says, it's 'just doing completely original movies, movies that don't fit into categories'.

Founded by Tom Rothman in 1994, the company has been successfully run, since English-born Peter Rice took over in 2000, on a series of guiding principles. These include releasing no more than twelve movies a year, producing half and acquiring the rest. As it stood in 2003, an imposed budget cap of $15 million was implemented to help keep losses down and profits up. Period movies are out, while edgy contemporary scripts that attract stars and encourage them to take a pay cut are in. And it works: in 2002, Fox Searchlight saw seven films collectively grossing over $135 million, including the Propaganda alumnus Mark Romanek's *One Hour Photo*, which grossed a chunky $60 million. With all the benefits a corporate parent can bring, the company is a shining light as it shows its rivals just how it is possible to make quality films that don't cost the earth. David O. Russell is well aware of the irony that Fox Searchlight is owned by Rupert Murdoch's media empire. 'I can't figure it out. Searchlight is very independent right now; they're making some great films. I can't imagine that Murdoch's not going to do something about it!'

Originally, Russell hoped to launch *I ♥ Huckabees* with a co-production between two of his former collaborators, Miramax and Warner Bros. At the latter, he had gained incredible goodwill after the success of *Three Kings*, which afforded him the opportunity to 'take a risk' with his next film. But even though both companies were on board, they refused to produce it for more than $15 million – meaning the film would have to be shot in Canada. Russell wanted a budget some $5 million higher than that figure, and the deal collapsed. 'There were all these people who told me they were dying to make movies with me over the years, and I would go to them and they were all freaked out by this project,' he says. 'It wasn't like people were lining up to make it.'

Rejected by New Regency, DreamWorks, Paramount and even New Line, it didn't help Russell's mood that during the same period, he was helping the rising comic genius Will Ferrell and the director Adam McKay get their script *Anchorman: The Legend of Ron Burgundy* (2004) off the ground. 'I lost respect for a lot of the studio guys, because

I saw the choices they made, and how they chose to use their money,' says Russell. 'They would spend $45 million on an Angelina Jolie–Ed Burns comedy [2002's *Life, or Something Like It*] – that's what we spent on *Three Kings*! This is a romantic comedy about two people, and they wouldn't make Will Ferrell's movie or my movie!'

Like his friend David O. Russell, Alexander Payne reports that many executives are still gutless when it comes to experimenting. '[They say] "We love that film you made. It's so new and different. What do you want to do next?" You show them and they say, "Oh, no, that's too new and different!" That's a constant. They are who they are. I still get my films made. One of the prices I pay is time. It takes time to get financing for my film, and maybe I don't work in the most ideal way.' That said, *Sideways*, at around $14 million, cost the same as *About Schmidt* without above-the-line costs for the stars like Nicholson. Following Russell to Fox Searchlight, Payne reports *Sideways* was one of his easier projects to get off the ground. As we will see, it was to prove another milestone in the journey of the Sundance Kids.

How am I not myself?
Brad Stand, I ❤ Huckabees

In 2004, commentators were incessantly reminding us that we were living in a post-9/11 world. Hanging over us like a shadow, George W. Bush's crusade against terror saw to this. Just as filmmakers from the 1970s reacted to the Vietnam War, it was inevitable that those working in the new millennium would follow suit. Given the second Gulf War that followed its release, *Three Kings* was becoming more prescient by the day. It meant that *I ❤ Huckabees* emerged as its companion piece, a spiritual reflection of our times in the wake of 9/11.

That an overtly political director like Russell should wrestle with 'the big September thing', as one character coyly puts it, is no surprise. 'I think we're living in strange times,' agrees Russell. 'It's like [Mark] Wahlberg says in the movie: "Why do people only ask deep questions when something bad happens?" Then they forget all about it later. And I think that did happen after 9/11.' But considering Fox Searchlight's umbrella company, it's even more remarkable that it co-produced this so-called 'existential comedy', together with ex–Polygram head Michael Kuhn's British-based company Qwerty Films. Despite recruiting an A-list cast that included Wahlberg, Jude Law and Naomi Watts, Russell's script

55 Jude Law as Brad Stand in
    I ❤ Huckabees.

56 David O. Russell and
    Jason Schwartzman.

must be one of the most leftfield to ever have surfaced via the main-stream. Invoking everything from the Belgian surrealist Magritte to Shania Twain and the Dixie Chicks, this is Russell's attempt to scratch underneath the surface of life's big questions: something he thinks is rarely done in most American independent films.

There's no doubt this is Russell's most personal film in an already highly personal body of work. Compare him to the film's lead char-acter, beleaguered environmental activist and leader of the Open Spaces Coalition, Albert Markovski (Jason Schwartzman). Often dressed in a suit, striped shirt and trainers like Albert, whose shoulder-length hair is styled in the same cut as Russell's. Given his own days as a poetry-spouting political activist, it's fair to say Albert is the character closest to Russell in his canon so far. 'I know what it's like to stand in a parking lot and have teenage kids spit gum at you,' says Russell. 'All these people in the movie are my heroes. They go beyond the conventional pursuit of a question or a position.' Yet, as a middle-class intellectual young man, Albert stands out – alongside Ray in *Spanking the Monkey* and Mel in *Flirting with Disaster* – as Russell's favourite archetype.

57 Jason Schwartzman and Mark Wahlberg in *I ❤ Huckabees*.

As Alexander Payne – who, with Russell, was honoured in New York's Museum of Modern Art in a series called 'Works in Progress' – has said, this is Russell's 'cry from the heart'. His alter ego Albert hires a pair of existential detectives, Vivian (Lily Tomlin) and Bernard Jaffe (Dustin Hoffman). Loosely inspired by Dashiell Hammett's martini-swigging detectives from his 1933 novel *The Thin Man*, they learn that Albert wants them to investigate a series of coincidences he has experienced with a lanky African autograph-hunter cum doorman, ultimately revealed to be Sudanese refugee Steven Nimieri (Ger Duany). With Vivian observing Albert's every move, right down to his bathroom habits, they swiftly conclude that at the core of their young client's problems is his relationship with the slick Brad Stand (Jude Law).

A rising executive with the department store Huckabees – based, says Russell, on the upmarket Target chain – Stand is trying to muscle Albert out of the Open Spaces Coalition's campaign to fight 'suburban sprawl' and save some nearby forest and marshland. As part of his therapy, the Jaffes pair Albert with Tommy (Mark Wahlberg) as his 'other'. A firefighter whose obsession with the petroleum crisis has driven away his wife and young daughter, Tommy introduces Albert to the nihilist philosophies of Caterine Vauban (Isabelle Huppert), a rebellious former pupil of the Jaffes. Authoress of *If Not Now*, she theorizes that nothing is connected, the polar opposite to the Jaffes' beliefs. While their business card reads 'Crisis. Investigation. Resolution', Caterine's states 'Cruelty. Manipulation. Meaninglessness'. As Albert falls under her spell, even entering into a brief sexual liaison with her much to Tommy's disgust, the Jaffes take on Brad, whose perfect veneer begins to crack as the story progresses.

Rather like Paul Thomas Anderson following *Magnolia* with *Punch-Drunk Love*, David Fincher shooting *Panic Room* after *Fight Club* and Steven Soderbergh making *Full Frontal* subsequent to *Ocean's Eleven*, Russell was of a mind to make something smaller after *Three Kings*. 'It wasn't like I did that and said, "Let's go make another $48 million movie with a big canvas." I came away from it with the opposite feeling, saying, "Let's make a $20 million movie."' He eventually hooked up with producer Scott Rudin, who took the project to Fox Searchlight. The film was finally up and running.

While Rudin has twice collaborated with Wes Anderson, on *The Royal Tenenbaums* and *The Life Aquatic with Steve Zissou*, Russell also poached a number of other key collaborators who had made their reputations with some of the other Sundance Kids. The production designer K. K. Barrett had worked with Sofia Coppola on *Lost in Translation*, as well as on Spike Jonze's *Being John Malkovich* and *Adaptation* and Michel Gondry's *Human Nature*. Meanwhile, costume designer Mark Bridges and composer Jon Brion had both collaborated with Paul Thomas Anderson, while Brion also worked for Gondry on *Eternal Sunshine of the Spotless Mind*. With the editor Robert K. Lambert returning after his time with Russell on *Three Kings*, the director also recruited the David Lynch DP Peter Deming to shoot the film.

For the first time, Russell also took on a writing partner, Jeff Baena, a recent NYU graduate with an enthusiasm for the great philosophers. Russell had hoped to make a film about philosophical matters since 1990, when he received some money to fund a short film he'd written. It was 'about a guy in a Chinese restaurant who had planted microphones on every table, so he could write insanely personal fortunes for everybody – and he got involved with them, sort of like an existential detective'. Russell eventually put the cash towards *Spanking the Monkey* but, after *Three Kings*, he returned to the ideas that had been clouding in his brain for a decade. Writing with Wahlberg, Tomlin and

Schwartzman (whom he had befriended after seeing him in *Rushmore*) in mind, he penned a script about a Zendo master he had visited in Manhattan. 'I thought it was a great setting for an ensemble comedy, because you have all different kinds of people trying to investigate reality and consciousness, which was interesting and serious but also funny to me. As a Zen monk once said to me, "If you're not laughing, you're definitely not getting what's happening."'

But, with the (ultimately averted) actor's strike looming in 2000, Russell decided he didn't want to pursue the project further, believing it not yet ready to be rushed into production. It was at this point that he had a dream, involving a female detective. 'She was not following me for criminal reasons – but she was following me for spiritual and metaphysical reasons. I cracked up when I read that back – because I write my dreams down – and said, "That's going to be the story."' The only thing he pulled in from his Zendo script was the friendship between the characters played by Wahlberg and Schwartzman, which was 'really modelled on my own friendship with Mark'.

Undeniably, Tommy is Wahlberg's best role since he worked with Russell on *Three Kings*, and is also something of a continuation of the character of Troy Barlow. 'I like that he has another scene with Saïd Taghmaoui [who features as a translator for an Andalusian widow] who played the interrogator in *Three Kings*,' says Russell:

> I like that connection, the connections that people don't want to think about. It's a lot easier to say, 'Terror is bad. Kill terrorists.' Well, how did they get to be terrorists? I don't think you can ever justify terrorism, but we financed and trained the dictatorships in Saudi Arabia, Iraq and Syria, these countries that have no democracy. And the only kind of dissent that they tolerate is terrorists, who are Muslim Fundamentalists who direct their anger at Europe and the United States. So I think it's crazy not to talk about that. That all went into Mark's character.

Several of the actors, including Wahlberg, found Russell's script to be as personal as it was confusing. In the scene where Tommy mentions children going to prison, he concludes that 'Father Flavin doesn't have money to help them'. It was Russell who urged Wahlberg to mention 'his [real] parish priest who pulled him off the streets', the Rev. James Flavin of St Edward's Church in Brockton, Massachusetts. Still involved with his mentor, Wahlberg is as passionate about helping him aid inner city kids – notably in ensuring they are not tried in court as adults – as Tommy is about the petroleum crisis. 'It was a great asset to me to know him as well I did, because he had never put this kind of soulfulness into a comedy,' says Russell. 'It's unusual for a director to have that opportunity with a movie star.' A committed Christian – 'Spiritually he would see everything in the films in Christian terms, which is fine with me,' says Russell – Wahlberg evidently had no qualms about the centrepiece scene where Albert and Tommy have dinner with Steven's adopted Christian family and confront them over their evangelical beliefs.

In a rather revealing location report in *The New York Times*, Russell was shown up as a director who likes to intentionally destabilize his actors for the sake of their performances. It noted, 'Mr Russell did all he could to raise the level of tension on set, unapologetically goading, shocking and teasing his actors.'[135] No doubt, Russell loves to throw lines at his actors as they're performing, forcing them to improvise as he keeps the cameras rolling. From shouting 'Fuck! Start! Go! Serious!' instead of 'Action' to walking into frame during the shoot to explain what he wants, he's an eccentric who manages to instil his own hyperactive energy into his productions and onto film. Someone who thinks nothing of stripping off to his boxer shorts to exercise in the street in front of his cast and crew, Russell's innocent transgressions of social barriers are one thing, but there's no doubt he exploits his actors' inner psyches more than most. 'Jude was going through his own mini-breakdown at the time, with his marriage falling apart, and he took a lot of that energy and poured it into the part,' says Russell. 'I couldn't have been luckier. He calibrated that in the movie.'

Russell admits that Brad Stand – obsessed with such images of all-American perfection as Shania Twain and Pete Sampras – is a character he can identify with. 'At the same time he was derived from executives and alpha males that I know from the film industry,' adds Russell. 'There are so many businessmen who are like that, though I can identify with them.' Russell relishes Brad's collapse, as he loses his house in a fire and, far worse, his self-confidence with people. Guilt-ridden about his overweight gecko-obsessed brother, Brad finally cracks when he realizes what a bore he is, retelling the same mirthless anecdote about Shania Twain's food allergies over and over again. Snapped sobbing on his lawn after realising his beloved jet-skis have been torched, Brad later spies the Polaroid of himself at this low ebb and snarls: 'Nobody sees that picture.' As Russell surmises, 'I suppose this is what his character represents . . . We have all this shit going on inside us but nobody's supposed to see it.'

Much the same can be said for Dawn, Brad's trophy girlfriend and the face of Huckabees, who undergoes a crisis of her own. 'Stop looking at me,' she cries in Albert's meditation, hinting that she is sick of being a Barbie doll. Eventually swapping her bikini for dungarees and a milkmaid's bonnet – lending her the appearance of an 'Amish bag lady', as Vivian puts it – her transition makes a trenchant statement about the voyeuristic nature of cinema. The role was originally offered to Gwyneth Paltrow, who eventually dropped out. Nicole Kidman then briefly flirted with the part but, locked into an ironclad contract for *The Stepford Wives* (2004) remake, she was unable to commit. It eventually went to her friend Naomi Watts – like Kidman and Paltrow, an actress who strives hard to break free from the 'beauty' roles to which Hollywood readily wants to chain her.

Russell evidently delights in deconstructing his actors' images, forcing the Adonis-like Law to vomit into his own hand, Wahlberg to bash his own face with a red ball and the aloof Huppert to be covered in mud during an outdoor sexual encounter. Russell casts Schwartzman's mother, Talia Shire, as Albert's Jewish matriarch, recalling Mel Coplin's adoptive mother in *Flirting with Disaster*. When Caterine takes Albert back to his parents' house – telling him 'you were trained to betray yourself right here' – we discover that Albert was 'orphaned by indifference'. From ignoring him when his cat died when he was nine to berating him for losing his job with the Open Spaces Coalition, Albert's mother is chiefly responsible for her son's emotional problems. While casting Shire opposite her offspring smacks of a smug in-joke in line with those in *Ocean's Twelve*, it nevertheless adds a mischievous postmodern layer that reminds us we are watching actors in a movie. 'I gave my life to this selfish bastard,' says Shire at one point, although we're not sure if she's broken character.

Evidently in touch with his own sense of self, Russell regularly meditated with Wahlberg and Schwartzman at his house and on the set (near the catering table by all accounts). He even developed a meditation technique similar to the one practised by Albert, where he zips himself up in a body bag and hacks away at his demons with a machete. Russell also took Law on hikes into the hills and gave everyone tapes of Robert Thurman's overview of Tibetan Buddhism, *The*

Jewel Tree of Tibet. A Buddhist for over twenty-five years, Russell was taught by Thurman (the noted Tibetan scholar and father of Uma) when he was at Amherst College. The character of Bernard Jaffe is loosely based on his friend and mentor. 'Robert always had the rumpled suit but he's a serious scholar,' says Russell. 'He translates Chinese and Sanskrit and things that take an enormous amount of discipline.' In some infomercials Russell created to supplement the film (and appear on the film's DVD), Thurman appears with quantum physics expert Dr Joseph Rudnick on a television show hosted by the Jaffes.

It all points to the issue of identity, a key theme in Russell's films. Just as Ray struggled to define himself in the shadow of his parents in *Spanking the Monkey*, so Mel's search for his real parents represented a similar quest in *Flirting with Disaster*. Albert attempts to construct his own identity by planting eight by tens of himself in the archive shop where he first encounters Steven. And after Brad and Dawn question who they are, Russell sends the characters into a maelstrom of confusion in the final act. Dawn, in particular, is no longer the face of Huckabees, just the voice, replaced by the more malleable model, Heather. This splicing of identity reaches its peak when Steven and his adopted brother arrive to get her autograph, on an old photograph of Dawn. In another example, Brad and Albert's faces swap on a Polaroid, prompting Albert to think, 'I'm Brad and he's me.' In line with the Jaffes' thinking, it also recalls Téa Leoni's adoption researcher Tina from *Flirting with Disaster*, who notes, 'We can't help but feel that there's something out there that's going to make us feel complete, give us a sense of belonging, connectedness, if you will'.

Complementing the stark truths faced by the characters, Russell and DP Deming worked out a limited palette of whites, blacks and blues. Aside from the greens of the forest, flashes of red glimpsed with Tommy's ball and a painting in the Jaffes' office, and the Technicolor stars-and-stripes commercials filmed by Dawn, brighter colours are outlawed. Similarly, the costumes were drained of colour, while T-shirts and blue jeans were banned. 'I wanted it to have an organized look, like a later Buñuel film,' says Russell. 'While the ideas may be very destabilising, the environment is not.' Inspired by the monochromatic palette of Buñuel's *The Discreet Charm of the Bourgeoisie* (1972), Russell also 'looked at' Michelangelo Antonioni's *Blow-Up* (1966).

While Antonioni's film dealt with the manipulation of image in much the way Russell's film does, the backdrop of *I* ❤ *Huckabees* is like a shifting canvas. Think of the Escher-like corridors Albert heads down to find the Jaffes' office; the Cubist sequence where chunks of Brad's and Albert's faces float in the ether; the Magritte-inspired bowler hat on a stand in Bernard's room. The production designer K. K. Barrett's additional touches, such as the watermelon ornaments in Bernard's office, lend the set a surreal flavour that complements the moments when Russell delves into the characters' inner psyches – including the prize image of Brad breastfeeding Albert. Not content with putting our bodies under the microscope in *Three Kings*, Russell prizes open our souls in *I* ❤ *Huckabees*.

Splitting the critics, *I* ❤ *Huckabees* only took $12.7 million in the U.S. Overseas it fared little better, taking a particular pasting from the British critics. One of many detractors, Philip French interestingly identified the film's humour as part of a burgeoning movement comprised of other directors and writers under discussion here. 'David O. Russell's deeply disappointing *I* ❤ *Huckabees* is a lesser product of "the new whimsy", that school of surreal, absurdist comedy to which Charlie Kaufman, Spike Jonze, Wes Anderson and Paul Thomas Anderson belong . . . The picture is even less funny than *What's New, Pussycat?* which it resembles, and the actors, straining for effect, seem as embarrassed as the audience.'[136]

As derogatory as French's comment is, it does indicate that Russell and Co. are being seen as an unofficial group or 'school'. That said, their attempts at comedy are hardly whimsical. Surreal, maybe; absurdist, definitely. In Russell's case, *I* ❤ *Huckabees* is a film that reflects all of his work to date, retreating through the anti-war feeling of *Three Kings* to the introspective investigations of the self in his earlier films. Once again, Russell had burrowed his way into the studio system to say his piece.

I'm so insignificant, I can't even kill myself . . .
I'm a thumbprint on the window of a skyscraper.
   Miles, *Sideways*

Rather like Wes Anderson with *The Life Aquatic with Steve Zissou*, on the face of it, *Sideways* feels like Alexander Payne has got stuck in a groove – even if he has swapped Nebraska for the Californian vineyards. Another adaptation (of Rex Pickett's then-unpublished novel); another road-movie; another men-in-crisis story . . . one has to wonder if Payne was beginning his, in the words of *Sideways'* Maya, 'inevitable decline'. On the contrary, however, Payne – again in Maya's words – 'continues to evolve'. She, of course, is talking about wine, the perfect metaphor for people: part of a speech *Variety*'s Todd McCarthy called 'one of the great monologues in modern cinema'.[137]

Sideways is the story of two San Diego guys, Miles (Paul Giamatti) and Jack (Thomas Haden Church), who go on a wine-tasting week before the latter gets married. A wine connoisseur with a drinking problem, Miles is an English teacher and a would-be writer, whose sprawling novel *The Day After Yesterday* ('you mean "Today"?' as someone quips) is currently being touted around publishing houses. While the unscrupulous Jack, a one-time soap star, is out to get laid before he gets hitched, Miles is still recovering from his divorce two years ago. As Jack puts it, he has been 'officially depressed for, like, two years now'; and this week, he is determined to disperse the clouds around his former college roommate. On their hedonistic tour, they meet Maya (Virginia Madsen), a waitress acquaintance of Miles, and her friend Stephanie (Payne's real-life wife, Sandra Oh). Jack is soon enjoying carnal pleasures with single mother Stephanie, as Miles struggles to pluck up the courage to court Maya.

Sideways almost never came to be. As Pickett explained, in a highly entertaining account in *Premiere* magazine, his life had begun to mirror Miles's when he penned the novel out of sheer desperation. Divorced, broke and barely recognized as a writer (despite having done some uncredited work on David Fincher's *Alien3*), 'I was turning forty in a personal shambles,' he noted.[138] Like Miles, he had witnessed his mystery novel *La Purisima* die a slow death as publishing houses rejected it one by one. Deciding to write another screenplay, he came up with *Two Guys on Wine* – loosely based on a weekend wine jaunt to the Santa Ynez Valley – only to abandon it when it failed to gel. Forced to live hand to mouth, his only social life at the time centred on regular weekly tastings he attended at a Santa Monica wine shop named Epicurus.

It eventually inspired him to write a short story about a wine tasting which spirals out of control. In a flash of brilliance he decided to use it as the beginning of a first-person novel, with the story from *Two Guys on Wine* as the basis for the remainder. Despite enthusiasm from his agent – who worked for Endeavor, the company that also represented Payne – every publisher on the planet again shut the door on Pickett. By this point, penniless and with his electricity cut off, he was left literally in the dark with only his manuscript – now titled *Sideways* – for company. Even his agent, depressed with the business, departed. While another eventually picked him up, and agreed to represent the novel, Pickett was about to be made homeless, weeks behind with the rent. 'How had I sunk so low?' he wondered. 'I'm a proverbial Hollywood loser, the most banal cliché of all.'[139]

It was at this point that the phone rang. Impressed by *Citizen Ruth*, Pickett had always earmarked Payne as the first choice to direct an adaptation of his work. The director finally read the novel in galley form, while on a London to Los Angeles flight after he had been in Scotland with *Election* for the 1999 Edinburgh Film Festival. He immediately responded to it. '[I liked] those guys, how pathetic they are, how sad they are, their pathetic dreams, wrong self-images, comic set pieces and the lying. It's just all laid out. Anything that starts off being human and doesn't let you down by bringing up some contrivance – suddenly the gun comes out, there's a murder. I didn't want violence. I just want people. It didn't let me down that way.' He phoned Pickett, dubbing him 'Rex the King'. By the sounds of it, he saved his life. 'He gives me too much credit,' says a modest Payne. 'I just wanted to make a movie from his book.'

Not unexpectedly, Payne once again hooked up with Jim Taylor to help adapt the book. Their adjustments included altering the ending to Pickett's novel. In his finale, Miles – having met with his ex-wife Victoria at Jack's wedding reception, only to discover that she is pregnant – bumps into Maya. She has decided to turn up, despite being irked at Miles for not telling Stephanie that Jack was a groom-to-be. 'He gets together with Maya, which we thought was too much like a movie,' says Payne. 'We didn't go for that too much.' Their alternative has Miles meeting with Victoria and her new spouse outside the church – an encounter that causes him to skip the reception and head home. It's a desperate moment where it seems possible that Miles is about to kill himself, an act he had already talked about in relation to writers like Sylvia Plath and Ernest Hemingway. What he does, however, is tantamount to suicide: he unearths the precious bottle of 1961 Cheval Blanc that he was saving for his tenth wedding anniversary, takes it to a fast-food restaurant, and drinks it surreptitiously under the table. Slurping it from a Styrofoam cup, how much lower can a connoisseur go? But just as Payne and Taylor were unhappy with Miles living happily ever after with Maya, so they did not want to tip him over the edge in true clichéd Hollywood style. So the film concludes with Miles, having received a phone message from Maya several weeks later, heading back out to see her. He knocks on the door – just as a rap on the door woke him up at the film's outset – then the screen fades to black. We don't know if she'll answer, if she's even still there. And Payne certainly offers no hint that the pair will make it as a couple.

It's a fine example of the restraint Payne and Taylor are able to exercise in their writing. The joy of *Sideways*, as with their previous collaborations, is the humanizing detail, uncommon in most Hollywood movies. Take the manner in which we learn about Stephanie's past relationships. Stephanie, an Asian-American, has a Caucasian mother and a black daughter, both of whom are only briefly glimpsed. The diverse ethnicity of her family is made clear, adding an interesting dimension to her character without Payne and Taylor ever feeling the need to comment upon it in the script. It is, after all, rather unimportant to our understanding of her spiky character within the context of this story.

You can almost feel Payne leaving behind the more cartoon-like aspects of *About Schmidt* in the early scenes of *Sideways*; after visiting Miles's mother on the first day of their trip, Miles and Jack sneak out the door in the morning and leave her snoring in her red dressing gown on the couch. The camera pans away to show the television in the living room still on. There, on top of the set, are the cheap flowers Miles bought her for her birthday, forgotten and out of water. In the past Payne would have replaced the flowers, the perfect symbol of the wilting relationship between mother and son, with some hideous ornament for amusement value. Payne keeps many of these moments low key, thanks to Rolfe Kent's jazz-tinged score. Following on from his work on *About Schmidt*, where Payne suggested he listen to music by Nino Rota, for *Sideways* the director requested that Kent check out the score for Mario Monicelli's *Big Deal on Madonna Street*. 'I'm just always on the prowl for ideas, that's all,' admits Payne. 'From that film, I derive the idea of having a lot of jazz wafting over scenes, rather than concretely scoring moments.'

As for casting, after securing Jack Nicholson for *About Schmidt*, Payne could easily have found four stars to take the lead roles in his next film. But instead he wisely went down the other path: resurrecting careers, searching out newcomers and taking risks. He had 'never seen' Thomas Haden Church – best known for his Fox series *Ned and Stacey*, opposite Debra Messing. Virginia Madsen he was only dimly aware of; likewise Paul Giamatti. From his role as the documentary filmmaker Toby Oxman in Todd Solondz's *Storytelling*, to his karaoke salesman in Bruce Paltrow's *Duets* (2000) and the curmudgeonly comic creator Harvey Pekar in *American Splendor*, Giamatti has rather cornered the market in playing sad-sack losers. Payne claims this 'never occurred' to him, noting there was no one better to play Miles.

In many ways *Sideways* falls alongside other 'intellectual odd couple' movies – notably Dino Risi's *Il Sorpasso* (1962), Bruce Robinson's *Withnail and I* (1987) and Michael Cacoyannis's *Zorba the Greek* (1964). All three follow the same pattern – an outgoing sensualist and an introverted, paralysed neurotic are thrown together. Notably in *Il Sorpasso* and *Zorba the Greek*, the so-called 'intellectual' character, rather like Miles, does not have the wherewithal to go after the woman he desires. 'It's best done in *Zorba the Greek*,' says Payne. 'It's two sides of a single man's soul in conversation with each other. That's the basic idea with two characters like this. But I don't think it's successfully done – nor did we really care about it – in the screenplay for *Sideways*.'

If they're not in conversation exactly, Jack and Miles perfectly express the two all-too-predictable and pathetic sides of the male beast. An 'infant', according to Miles, with a total lack of concern for the moral consequences of his actions, Jack is defined by his base animal urges. 'All I have is my instinct,' he yells at Miles. Yet Haden Church never patronises his character or makes him feel malevolent in any way. When Jack falls for Stephanie's charms, he seems genuinely taken by her, even suggesting to Miles that they could move to the area and buy a vineyard. A fount of optimism, it's the same spirit that makes him believe he can still revive his fading career as a television star. If Jack acts like a predator, it's because he has a need to prove to himself that he's still a player. About to become domesticated, this is his one last hunt in the jungle. To be fair, he has already been tamed. When he realizes he may lose his bride, he breaks down. 'I can't lose Christine,' he sobs. 'I'm nothing.' The bravado is shot down – but rather than laugh at this wretched creature, thanks to Haden Church's ability to make Jack likeable despite all his flaws, we feel for him in this moment of self-pity.

Not unlike Payne's note to composer Kent during *About Schmidt* – to create music to help prop up one's smile – Miles is forever doing the same in *Sideways*, grinning and bearing his way through life. Giamatti walks a delicate tightrope with the character; while it might be easy to dismiss a man who goes to bed with a copy of *Barely Legal* for company, his earnest approach to Maya, noting how their time together has meant 'a big deal to him', elicits our sympathy. It shouldn't. After all, Miles is a prize snob – and not just about wine. 'I've completely underestimated Stephanie,' he says, as he learns she has an impressive bottle nestling in her cellar.

Much of the humour with Miles is derived from his appreciation of a good vintage. One particularly fruity concoction he describes as 'quaffable but far from transcendent'; another smells of both strawberries and cheese. As for Merlot, if anybody orders it, he's 'fucking leaving'. Compared to both Stephanie and Maya, he has an elitist view of the subject that makes laymen like Jack feel intimidated. Maya, for example, speaks about wine in a poetic, alluring, almost sexual way: 'A bottle of wine is actually alive,' she says – and when she says it, you believe her.

'I don't judge Miles's wine snobbery,' says Payne.

I think it's funny. I don't know how people read it but I didn't mean it to be a critique or mocking of it. There's something funny about it. What's more interesting to me, is that it's not about wine snobbery, it's about a guy who holds his self-esteem in something outside of self-knowledge. It's about knowledge of something outside of himself. There are so many people who are losers to some degree, but they're experts on this or that. They drive you crazy with how much they know about it! They are genuinely kind of failures in some way. All of us have this to some degree. I'm a film snob. I can be a bit pedantic about film knowledge and I'm quietly proud of it! I meet people who say, 'When I go to the movies I don't want to think. I think all day at work. I just want to let go and enjoy myself, so I put on an Adam Sandler movie.' I try to be patient but I have contempt.

It would be easy for Miles to become a caricature, a wine anorak, but what helps avoid this, are his visits to 'the dark side', as Jack puts it. While he's no barfly waking up with dozens of empty bottles around him, he's a binge drinker when things get tough. From drinking from a bottle while running full pelt down a hill after Jack tells him his ex-wife has remarried and will be at the wedding ceremony, to tipping a spittoon of wine dregs over himself when he finds out his novel has been rejected, Miles is no convivial fellow when he hits the booze. As Giamatti says, Miles 'really just wants to get hammered all the time'. Both he and Jack are 'drunk through the whole movie. It's not like they're stumble-drunks – they're guys who drink themselves into that weird sobriety. They are lucidly drunk, in the way a real hardcore alcoholic can be. You're so able to cope with it, you can function in some ways.'

As it stands, Payne draws out one of Giamatti's most heartbreaking performances to date. The crestfallen look on his face, when Victoria tells him she is pregnant, turns to total despair with barely a flicker. He earlier told Maya, 'It was the one unpolluted part of the divorce – no kids.' But to learn that his ex-spouse is expecting so soon after remarrying is a shattering moment that far outstrips having a manuscript rejected; he puts on that brave face, which only makes the whole scene even more painful to watch. Payne notes he put Giamatti through nine takes to get it right. 'It's only the last two or three that I suggested to him to keep smiling when she gives him the news. 'Cos he was doing a brilliant job the whole way. I thought "OK, that's good. But what else can we do? What else is out there? What other opportunities are there?" Basically, that was the only direction I gave him in that scene – keep smiling and stay chipper. Fighting the emotion rather than really encouraging it often brings the emotion out more.'

It's a direction that somewhat typifies the film and its characters, as they grimace their way through life's slings and arrows. Downbeat and melancholy it may be, but Payne's style is never overbearing, always in service of the story. Like the bee-sting in *Election* or the waterbed frolics in *About Schmidt*, the comic interludes remain broad. Miles fires back balls at rival golfers while Stephanie smashes Jack repeatedly with her motorbike helmet when she finds out he's engaged. Jack drives Miles's car into a tree to make it look as if the injuries he sustained from the beating were from an accident – only for the vehicle to miss the trunk. There's also the very angry and very naked husband of one of Jack's conquests chasing Miles down the street, after he has sneaked back in the man's house to retrieve his friend's wallet. Even the sight of President Bush on television as a couple copulate brings a smile.

Yet the timing of these hilarious moments never feels contrived, as they ebb and flow naturally through the story, puncturing the sadness. Here Payne isn't pandering to an actor's talents, as he did with Jack Nicholson, but deriving the comedy from the events that unfold. Interspersed between them are some real sweet and poignant touches. Note the scene where Miles and Maya finally head up to her apartment to (we assume) make love. The camera respectfully stays outside the front door as it shuts, panning around to settle on the nearby houses shaded in darkness. With the camera stationary, an invisible cut moves the narrative on to daybreak, as the sun comes up; the camera then swings back to the front door as Miles opens it to leave. It's a truly elegant sequence, to which a written description does little justice.

Despite its title, *Sideways* was most certainly a step forward for Payne – but also for his fellow Sundance Kids. It was one of the best-reviewed films of the year. In North America, the New York, Los Angeles, Chicago, Toronto and broadcast critics all voted it the best film of the year. Winning in all six categories it was nominated in at the Independent Spirit Awards, it also garnered seven Golden Globe nominations (more than any other film). Scooping Best Motion Picture – Musical or Comedy, Payne and Taylor also won the Best Screenplay award, repeating their success at the awards for *About Schmidt*.

The snowball effect began. Released on just four screens back in late October 2004, it reached a peak of 1,786 screens by early February 2005. A classic platform release, handled with true skill, the film eventually grossed $71 million, spurred on by its five 2005 Oscar nominations. In the ceremony, once again, Haden Church and Madsen represented the film in the Supporting Actor/Actress categories – though both were beaten. Up for Best Picture, *Sideways* also afforded Payne his first Best Director Oscar nomination. Both he and the film lost to Clint Eastwood's *Million Dollar Baby* (2004), but it didn't matter. As expected, Payne and Taylor instead picked up the first Oscar of their careers for Best Adapted Screenplay. After thanking their agents and their wives, Payne added, 'We love Fox Searchlight for letting us make a film with complete creative freedom.' With Charlie Kaufman winning the Original Screenplay award for *Eternal Sunshine of the Spotless Mind*, it was a defining moment. Soderbergh's success with *Traffic* was no longer a one-off; the Sundance Kids were no longer outlaws.

58 Paul Giamatti and Thomas Haden Church enjoy a glass in *Sideways*.

Epilogue: Bursting the *Bubble*

So, where does this leave us? It's not like this story ends with a huge bang. Neither are these Sundance Kids ready to hold Hollywood hostage. After all, F-64 failed before it began, Pizza Knights is just a club for fan boys and girls and, while companies like Propaganda are no more, the studios still make movies like 2004's *Catwoman*. While many of these directors are friends, colleagues or acquaintances – sharing actors, designers and DPs – they are no closer to proclaiming a movement than they ever were. Neither do they necessarily want to. But all are still united in a common goal: to make good films. 'I think we just cheer each other on, because we all make room for each other,' says David O. Russell. 'We want our films to succeed.'

But did the mavericks really take back Hollywood? Or was it more a case of being allowed entrance once again after years in the wilderness? Right now, the studios have read the numbers and they are starting to add up. 'They're just interested in money,' says Payne. 'I don't think they care about cachet. They like it when they take a risk and it pays off with good reviews. I hope that I can be optimistic in that they will continue doing this with me, and other filmmakers.' But, rather like baseball managers, after a few bad results studio heads will roll. Patronage only lasts as long as the films are making money.

In a town as fickle as Hollywood, you're only as good as your last box office gross. While Sofia Coppola and Alexander Payne were revered for *Lost in Translation* and *Sideways*, it doesn't mean they'll still be making studio-funded films in ten years' time. Only time will tell if they have the strength to keep producing the edgy and unconventional fare that established their reputations.

The danger of becoming too precious about committing to new projects is also a very real threat. After *Panic Room*, Fincher spent three years in a creative lull. After he quit both *MI:3* and *Lords of Dogtown*, his name was attached to numerous projects including a remake of Alfred Hitchcock's *Strangers on a Train* (1951) and a biopic of Herman J. Mankiewicz, the writer of *Citizen Kane*. There was also the long-gestating adaptation of Arthur C. Clarke's *Rendezvous with Rama* and a version of the F. Scott Fitzgerald story 'The Curious Case of Benjamin Button', a romance featuring a man who begins to age backwards. If anything, such procrastination works against the momentum the Sundance Kids have built up. Whatever you think of Soderbergh's diverse output, his desire to keep on making films is to be applauded.

'This is a very cyclical business,' says Soderbergh. 'I've been up, down and sideways. Everything changes. In the States, I think the movie business in the next five years will change a lot . . . *a lot!* It's an interesting time. On the independent side, something is going to have to change. First of all, the independent as we knew it ten years ago has disappeared. Attendance for independent films is down, for the most part, and they're going to have to do something to survive. I don't know what that is. Sometimes, interesting things come out of crisis.'

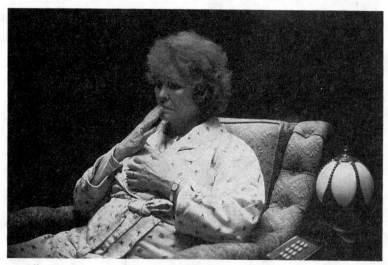

59 Ellen Burstyn as Sara Goldfarb in *Requiem for a Dream*.

If anything, fifteen years after *sex, lies, and videotape*, it is the beginning of a fruitful era in Hollywood. Yet it is foolhardy to think we're ever going to return to the freewheeling days of New Hollywood. The example of Darren Aronofsky proves that not all Sundance alumni find their way in the studio system. The Brooklyn-born filmmaker won the Best Director award at the 1998 festival for his $60,000 debut, *Pi*, a 'black and white movie about God, math and bad-ass Jews', as he puts it, that went on to make $3.2 million. After his second film – an adaptation of Hubert Selby Jr's novel about addiction, *Requiem for a Dream* (2000) – afforded Ellen Burstyn a Best Actress Oscar nomination, Aronofsky looked set to be a major player. Yet he has suffered from mainstream studios being unwilling to accommodate his vision. He expended considerable energy attempting to relaunch Warner Bros.' *Batman* franchise, adapting Frank Miller's 1987 graphic novel *Batman: Year One* with the author. It never made it beyond script stage – and with Christopher Nolan's *Batman Begins* now a reality, no doubt it never will.

More intriguing for fans of Aronofsky's work is his epic romance *The Fountain*, that spans three time periods. Only weeks away from shooting in 2002, the $75 million project fell apart when star Brad Pitt pulled out and financiers pulled the plug. '[In Hollywood] once you start playing with more money, you have to entertain more people,' Aronofsky reflects. 'You never get the same type of control as the money rises. It basically becomes a negotiation, about finding the best answer to make everyone feel safe with all the decisions made.' It took another three years before Warner Bros. was convinced to fund the project – this time with Hugh Jackman in the lead – at a lower cost of $40 million.

The good news is, the next generation is already forming. Leading the way is David Gordon Green; like so many of the directors in this book, he has managed his career with immense acumen, carefully selecting projects to match his growing ambitions. His story also underlines that Sundance is no longer the only option for American independent filmmakers. Born in 1975, the Arkansas native made his directorial debut in 2000 with *George Washington*. With its cast of unknowns, budget of just $50,000 and tale of teenage tragedy, it was perfect Sundance material – until it was rejected.

'I really do take pride in making the movie that didn't go there and was still able to succeed on its own terms,' he says:

When we didn't get in, I thought, 'How, as an American indie filmmaker, do you get your movie out there?' I had no idea, as it's the only thing you hear about. I was pretty devastated. But then I just thought, 'Fuck it. Let's go and get people to see it.' We premiered at Berlin and found great European audiences. It was more profitable in the UK than it was in America. Sundance is the gatekeeper of independent film; at least, that's what we're conditioned to think. People don't think about the New York Film Festival, the Newport Film Festival or even Toronto, which all helped launch an awareness of our movie.

60 Paul Schneider in *All the Real Girls*.

By contrast, Green's follow-up, *All the Real Girls*, was accepted for the 2003 Sundance festival, where it won a Special Jury Prize. A growing-pains love story starring Zooey Deschanel and set in a North Carolina town, it ebbed and flowed to the 'honest rhythm of Southern lifestyles', as Green claims, and was picked up by Sony Pictures Classics. Green did not want it merely playing in art house cinemas. 'I want to appeal to a certain demographic. I want eighteen-year-old girls to come, and that's not traditionally done. We're really trying to reach out and broaden the marketing and the potential demographic – and that's a challenge.'

They didn't succeed – but Green's awareness of how the industry works belies his youth. Already compared to Terrence Malick for the evocative sense of place in his work, his third film, *Undertow* (2003), confirmed it. 'A pretty strange twisted little movie' with shades of Charles Laughton's *The Night of the Hunter* (1955), it was produced by Malick, who had seen *George Washington* and felt Green was right to adapt a script an English-teacher friend of his had written. With its 'surreal dreamlike quality', this story of two brothers (Jamie Bell and Devon Alan) who are chased down river by their unhinged uncle (Josh Lucas) again represented a step up in terms of casting. Straying into genre territory, yet retaining the integrity of his earlier films, Green was spreading his wings that bit further. As he says, 'It's not like I'm avoiding Hollywood. I think I'm very interested in Hollywood. I just want Hollywood to grow up a little bit, and stop being whiny babies!'

Like Aronofsky, Green has already had his first negative brush with the system – with the long-gestating adaptation of John Kennedy Toole's *A Confederacy of Dunces*, a 1960s-set story about New Orleans–based would-be academic Ignatius J. Reilly. The project has been in development since 1980, when Harold Ramis was attached to direct. Soderbergh tried to get it made from the time of *King of the Hill*. Penning a script with Scott Kramer, he was then forced into a protracted legal battle with the producer Scott Rudin. Claiming he and Kramer were shut out of the project after Paramount studios had covertly purchased the rights on Rudin's behalf, the case was eventually settled before it went to trial. Miramax later purchased the rights for *A Confederacy of Dunces* from Paramount for $1.5 million, with Section Eight set to co-produce with Drew Barrymore's Flower Films, but by this point Soderbergh had slid off the director's chair.

Impressed by Section Eight and a long-term fan of the book, Green petitioned his agent to get him a meeting. 'You see the movies that Steven Soderbergh and George Clooney have been executive producing and making themselves; they're making challenging movies,' he says. '*Solaris* and *Confessions of a Dangerous Mind* are two of the most challenging, studio-backed films of the last twenty years – since the 1970s. Like them or not, they're unusual. It's great to have two people out there using their names, reputations and value for the benefit of pushing the system, and not just making cookie-cutter movies with a Top 40 soundtrack.' But after arguments over casting, *A Confederacy of Dunces* remains unmade. 'The politics and the paperwork of the studio system got in the way,' shrugs Green, who claims he owes it to the fans of the Pulitzer Prize–winning book to cast it properly.

With his contacts book already including Malick and Soderbergh, Green appears to be the link between the filmmakers of the 1970s, the Sundance Kids and the future. 'In watching the evolution of filmmakers I admired from the 1970s, they're getting more and more distant from an audience perspective; they're manufactured now because they're so pre-conceived,' he says. 'They're less about the struggles of life and movies and honest emotion. If you watch a movie like *Sugarland Express* . . . it's so full of life and energy. I just love that movie. Now, a comedy by Steven Spielberg is more test-marketed, where audience reaction is critical. Then, he was in touch with a naive aspect of an audience member; now he's in touch with the mechanics of success.'

Yet as long as the elder generation continues to act as patrons, it would seem there is a chance. Despite the demise of F-64, Alexander Payne was invited in 2004 to participate in a similar company called Buena Onda. Initiated by Mike Leigh's regular producer, Simon Channing-Williams, and Donald Ranvaud, who produced Walter Salles's *Central Station* (1998), again the idea was for filmmakers to keep direct ownership and control over their productions. Others involved in these early stages include *City of God* (2002) director Fernando Meirelles and writer Gabriel García Márquez. 'The idea was that ten directors would own this company,' explains Meirelles. 'We would create our projects and sell directly to the main territories to finance them. The last market would be the U.S.; when you bring the U.S. studios to projects, they want to control you. So this would be a way to have control and keep the profits of the film.' It may yet disprove Payne's belief that such companies are doomed to fail.

Could such an outfit freeze out Hollywood studios? It's hard to say. For the moment, whether they are indulged or merely tolerated, ambitious directors must seek shelter in the system. But the storm clouds are gathering; as blockbusters head towards the $200 million mark, making profit a thing of the past, something's going to give. Amid widespread panic in Hollywood, the U.S. box-office haul in the summer of 2005 saw a steep 13 percent drop in admissions from the previous year. 'I think you're going to see that plateau, and I think that's going to continue to some extent,' estimates Soderbergh. 'It'll find a new normal and I don't think we're there yet. They built too many theatres – there's between eight and ten thousand too many screens in the U.S. They've doubled the amount of screens in the last fifteen years.'

As pointed out by David Siegel, the studios are in a state of flux right now, notably about the tried-and-tested formula that Hollywood stars guarantee box-office. 'Alexander's experience with *Sideways* has left a lot of people in Hollywood scratching their heads. Nobody besides Fox Searchlight was going to step up and give him the amount of money he wanted with no stars in the movie at all – and yet it was super-super successful. I hope that has helped people think a little bit broader.' His filmmaking partner Scott McGehee concurs. 'Films like *Sideways* that make a lot of money increase people's belief that it's a good business to be in. It's all business. You can't fool yourself.' Ironically, their debut, *Suture*, would be almost impossible to make as an independent production in America today. 'So-called "difficult" or more avant-garde films are so hard to get made in the United States now," says Siegel. 'At the same time, the studios are doing more movies that would be considered independent films ten years ago . . . But I'm not sure if I understand what's going on exhibition-wise right now, because it's unusual.'

The signs indicate that the very nature of a theatrical release – cinemas to DVD to pay-TV to cable to networks – is set for extinction. In April 2005, it was announced that the Dallas-based 2929 Entertainment, run by Todd Wagner and Mark Cuban, plan to release six high-definition video films shot by Soderbergh for $2 million apiece. The idea is to unveil each film via a simultaneous same-day release in cinemas, on DVD and on pay cable and satellite TV, a radical notion that looks set to change the industry irreparably. As far-fetched as it sounds, 2929 Entertainment own a variety of companies to implement the idea: distribution arm Magnolia Pictures, the Landmark theatre chain, TV channels HDNet and HDNet Movies and so on. 'It's an idea that, to my mind, was in the air,' says Soderbergh. 'These windows, and what to do about them, it's been discussed since we started to see the revenue base shift from theatrical to DVD. I just felt it was inevitable. Mark Cuban and Todd Wagner had all of the distribution mechanisms to do it. I just went to them and said, "We should do this. Somebody is going to do this. Why don't we be the first?"'

The first of the six is *Bubble*, a murder mystery written by *Full Frontal*'s Coleman Haugh set in a wintry West Virginia town. Premiering at the Venice Film Festival in September 2005 to mixed reviews – *Variety* called it a 'likeable if unexciting little tale'[140] – *Bubble* is more likely to be remembered for the debate it will stir up within the industry than as a major addition to Soderbergh's canon. Exhibitors are already promising to boycott the film. In an article in *Premiere*, Dick Westerling, a spokesperson for Regal Cinemas, the largest theatre chain in the U.S., stated that any film given a simultaneous release on DVD or TV will not make it onto their screens 'to maintain the integrity of the theatrical release'. Others are also sceptical. 'I think it's a bad idea for the exhibition of movies,' says Siegel. 'It seems to be a way to drive DVD sales. I don't even understand it from a business point of view. It seems that having movies out in theatres is a way to create interest for DVDs.'

For Soderbergh, *Bubble* is less *Full Frontal* and more full circle. A tragic look at unrequited love and loneliness, the film centres on three workers in a doll factory: middle-aged Martha (Debbie Doebereiner), pot-smoking youngster Kyle (Dustin Ashley) and their new colleague, single-mother Rose (Misty Wilkins). While Martha considers Kyle her 'best friend', she is suspicious of the obnoxious Rose and her proclamations that 'you can't make money in this area – it's just poor'. A petty thief with no compunction about taking advantage of Martha, Rose asks her to babysit her daughter while she goes on a date – which turns out to be with Kyle. By the next morning, Rose is found dead in her home – though rather like the death of Gus Delario in *Full Frontal*, the event itself is almost incidental as far as the mechanics of the plot are concerned. The film is more about our inability to communicate. 'I thought I could talk to her like a daughter,' Martha says, referring to Rose. As both the title and the interludes where Martha is bathed in a white light suggest, the characters are isolated in their own worlds, through the crushing monotony of their work and life.

Shot over eighteen days in Belpre, Ohio, after the excess of its predecessor, *Bubble* was yet another self-prescribed vow of purity taken by Soderbergh. 'There can be times – certainly coming off *Ocean's Twelve* – where you want to make a cave-painting,' he says. 'You need to strip everything down and do something that's simple. It was a necessary step to cleanse my palate.' Much of this came through working with non-professionals, an experience Soderbergh had briefly enjoyed on 2003's HBO show *K Street*, a semi-improvised lobbyist satire he devised and directed. 'I was really intrigued by the scenes that we did on that show with people who were not actors. There was something there. The problem in that show was that there was a gap between the actors and the non-actors – you could feel the line between the two. So I felt we should do one where it's all non-actors. There's just a lack of self-awareness, which is very hard to fake.'

Just as Soderbergh and Hough shaped the story to fit the town, once it had been scouted, so the actors were encouraged to bring themselves to the parts, and not worry about hitting marks or remembering lines. 'In a sense, there was no wrong answer because we were designing it to fit them,' says Soderbergh, pointing out that Kyle's confession of panic attacks to Rose came from Ashley's own experience. As for the interrogation scene, where Martha is questioned by the frighteningly methodical Detective Taylor (real law-enforcer Decker Moody), the actress had no idea what was coming or that she would be shown photographs of Rose's bruised corpse. 'Afterwards, she said, "I got really freaked out",' remembers Soderbergh. 'You're trying to create this environment where the emotions are real.'

It can be no coincidence that the themes of *sex, lies, and videotape*, where characters similarly endured emotional solitary confinement, are recalled. Just as Soderbergh's debut launched a revolution, *Bubble* is set to do the same. Not only symbolising his ability to aesthetically reinvent himself with every new film, it also proves how he is not one to bow to the status quo. 'My whole life growing up before my first feature, all I wanted was some money to make a movie. So to have the opportunity and not take advantage of it, I'm surprised. Maybe that will change. But I certainly feel there are a lot of filmmakers that are still allowing the system to dictate what they do more than they should. We all have to, to a certain extent, because it's a business but there's more freedom out there for some filmmakers than I think they're taking advantage of.'

As *Bubble* shows, with the advent of digital video – not only for cameras but projection in theatres as well – the times they are a changing. 'In the next five years, when the digital changeover happens, the entire paradigm for the business is going to change,' says Soderbergh. 'So then you don't really need the studio anymore – except for films that require enormous amounts of money. For anything other than that you'll be able to do a deal directly with the theatres and cut the middleman out. The business is going to change radically. It's already starting to happen. For people like myself, who are self-motivated and like working on their own, it's going to be a godsend.'

With a shift to digital projection, which means the physical labour involved in shipping prints around the world is going to change, studios may become dinosaurs once again – just as they were in the mid-1960s, when epic visions of grandeur in the *Cleopatra* mould almost made them extinct. Says Soderbergh, 'It'll mean I can call up the theatre chain myself and say, "I'm downloading the movie right now." I can cut the studios out entirely.' If such a pattern catches on, directors will doubtless have no compunction about abandoning the Hollywood machine to regain their independence. The word might suddenly begin to mean something again.

Notes

1 Galloway, Stephen, *The Hollywood Reporter*, 'The Mild Bunch', 25 June–1 July 2002.
2 Biskind, Peter, *Premiere*, 'Promised Land', February 1991.
3 *New Oxford English Dictionary*, Oxford University Press (1998), p. 1144.
4 Galloway, Stephen, *The Hollywood Reporter*, 'The Mild Bunch', 25 June–1 July 2002.
5 Olsen, Mark, *Sight & Sound*, 'Cool and the Gang', January 2004.
6 Biskind, Peter, *Down and Dirty Pictures: Miramax, Sundance, and the Rise of Independent Film*, Simon & Schuster (2004), p. 387.
7 Thompson, Anne, *Empire*, 'The New Kid In Town', August 1989.
8 Salisbury, Mark, *Burton on Burton*, Faber & Faber (1995), p. 82.
9 Jacobson, Harlan, *Film Comment*, 'Truth or Consequences', July/August 1989.
10 Andrew, Geoff, *Time Out*, 'Whit and Wisdom', 21–28 November 1990.
11 Fried, John, *Cineaste*, 'Rise of an Indie: An Interview with Hal Hartley', March 1993.
12 For a fuller examination of Section Eight, see Chapter 17.
13 Biskind, Peter, *Vanity Fair*, 'The Return of Quentin Tarantino', October 2003.
14 Fuller, Graham, *Projections 3: Answers First, Questions Later*, Faber & Faber (1994), p. 174.
15 Olsen, Mark, *Sight & Sound*, 'Turning on a Dime', October 2003.
16 Smith, Adam, *Empire*, 'Bryan Singer: One on One', May 2001.
17 Johnston, Sheila, *Independent*, 'David O. Russell's folks saw *Spanking the Monkey* and weren't amused. Must have been the masturbation. Or the incest.' 9 August 1995.
18 ibid.
19 Bernstein, Paula S, *Filmmaker*, 'Obsession for Men', Summer 1994.
20 Minsky, Terry, *Rolling Stone*, 'Hot Phenom', 18 May 1989.
21 In the wake of 9/11 and the Iraq conflict, Soderbergh found himself pulling the script out of his cupboard. 'Now, the world the way it is, I don't know that it is irrelevant anymore,' he says. 'I thought if I was going to do this, I'd have to rewrite it as a black comedy. I don't think I could do it straight.' With the suggestion he might write it from the point of view of the captain of the USS *Nathan James*, 'but have him be a sort of Buck Turgidson figure', this could easily be Soderbergh's *Dr. Strangelove*. 'It's a really black comedy about a guy who, in the midst of global destruction, is very concerned about ego issues. [The captain is] someone whose opinion of himself is extremely elevated and in this awful set of circumstances is much more concerned with

how he will appear to posterity, and putting a positive spin on some really bad decisions.'

22 Travers, Peter, *Rolling Stone*, Issue 623.

23 In late 2003, Soderbergh received a call notifying him that the rights to *Kafka* had lapsed – 'which is a pretty good indication of how people felt about the movie'. Offered the opportunity to re-cut and re-score it, while he was on post-production on *Ocean's Twelve*, Soderbergh went back and did just that. 'It's a different movie,' he confirms. 'There's new material – stuff that I shot that never made the movie is now in there. I'm doing it for my own interest; to see if I can make something that I'm happier with. I think the goal, ultimately, is to put out a double DVD with the original version and the new version.'

24 Gilbey, Ryan, *It Don't Worry Me*, Faber & Faber (2003), p. 182.

25 Hoberman, J., *Village Voice*, 11 October 1994.

26 Andrew, Geoff, *Time Out*, 'Killing Joke', 21–28 September 1994.

27 Lippy, Tod, *Projections 11: in Conversation with David O. Russell*, Faber & Faber, pp. 323–332.

28 Norman, Neil, *The Times*, 'Yeah I spent $400m but we made some classics', 10 December 2004.

29 Hirsch, Foster, *Detours and Lost Highways: A Map of Neo-Noir*, Limelight Editions (1999), p. 5.

30 ibid, p. 7.

31 Lim, Dennis, *Village Voice*, 'Having Your Way with Hollywood, or the Further Adventures of Steven Soderbergh', 9 January 2001.

32 Andrew, Geoff, *Stranger Than Paradise*, Prion Books (1998), p. 273.

33 Floyd, Nigel, *Time Out*, 'Prime Suspects', 9–16 August 1995.

34 Hirsch, Foster, *Detours and Lost Highways: A Map of Neo-Noir*, Limelight Editions (1999), p. 286

35 Salisbury, Mark, *Empire*, 'Seventh Hell', February 1996. NB To date, the identity of the Zodiac Killer remains unsolved. Fincher is set to base the sixth film of his career, due for release in 2006, on Robert Graysmith's books, *Zodiac* and *Zodiac Unmasked*.

36 Thompson, Ben, *Saturday Telegraph: Weekend Magazine*, 'Blame It on the Boogie Man', 3 January 1998.

37 In 2005, P. T. Anderson got the chance to watch his idol work, after he volunteered to be a so-called 'pinch-hitter' on Altman's adaptation of Garrison Keillor's *A Prairie Home Companion*. As dictated by the insurance company, it meant that Anderson was on hand to complete the picture should the aged director fall ill. In the end, he was not required.

38 McManus, Kevin, *Washington Post*, 27 February 1997.

39 Jones, Kent, *Film Comment*, 'Family Romance', November/December 2001.

40 Scorsese, Martin, *Esquire*, 'Wes Anderson', March 2000.

41 Jordan, Geoff, *Creative Screenwriting*, '*Citizen Ruth*: Interview with Alexander Payne', Vol. 4, No. 3, Fall 1997.

42 In 1969, the pregnant Norma McCorvey, under Texan law, was not allowed to have an abortion, despite claiming it was a result of rape by her

boyfriend. Known as Jane Roe, to protect her identity, she became the centre of the 'Roe versus Wade' landmark case, when she and various pro-choice organizations took the case to the Supreme Court, who eventually ruled that all state laws restricting or limiting abortion were 'unconstitutional'. Yet in 1995, while working as marketing director at a Dallas abortion centre, McCorvey was converted by the pro-life group Operation Rescue and defected, amid much consternation, to the other side.

43 Lippy, Tod, *Scenario*, 'Writing and Directing *Citizen Ruth*', Winter 1996.

44 ibid.

45 Jordan, Geoff, *Creative Screenwriting*, '*Citizen Ruth*: Interview with Alexander Payne', Vol. 4, No. 3.

46 Lippy, Tod, *Scenario*, 'Writing and Directing *Citizen Ruth*', Winter 1996.

47 *Bottle Rocket* Production Notes, Columbia Pictures, 1996.

48 Figgis, Mike, *Projections 10: in conversation with Paul Thomas Anderson*, Faber & Faber (1999), p. 29.

49 ibid, p. 30.

50 Rooney, David, *Variety*, 5–11 February 1996.

51 Turan, Kenneth, *Los Angeles Times*, 11 February 1996.

52 Brooks, James L., *Rushmore*, 'Foreword', Faber & Faber (1999), p. xii.

53 Potter, Maximillian, *Premiere*, 'Do these men represent the future of Hollywood filmmaking . . . or the death of it?', February 1998.

54 Burman, Mark, *Starburst – Monster Special*, 'David Fincher's *Alien³*ation', Vol. 15.

55 Burke, Tristan, *Hotdog*, 'So Much for the City', February 2004.

56 Pulver, Andrew, *The Guardian: Guide*, 'Prince of Darkness', 10 October 1997.

57 Cooney, Jenny, *Empire*, 'The Head Master', November 1997.

58 Eimer, David, *Time Out*, 'Game Boy', 8–15 October 1997.

59 Blair, Iain, *Film and Video*, 'Motion Pictures: David Fincher', October 1997.

60 Smith, Ethan, *New York*, 'Spike Jonze Unmasked', 25 October 1999.

61 Andrew, Geoff, *Stranger Than Paradise*, Prion Books (1998), p. 277.

62 Soderbergh, Steven, *Getting Away with It. Or: The Further Adventures of the Luckiest Bastard You Ever Saw*, Faber & Faber (1999), pp. 27–8.

63 ibid, p. 215.

64 ibid, p. 183.

65 McKenna, Kristine, *Creative Screenwriting*, 'An Interview with Paul Thomas Anderson', Vol 5, No. 1.

66 Patterson, John, *Guardian*, 'Magnolia Maniac', 10 March 2000.

67 McKenna, Kristine, *Creative Screenwriting*, 'An Interview with Paul Thomas Anderson', Vol. 5, No. 1.

68 Fischer, Paul, *www.urbancinefile.com.au*, 'Turning Insecurities Into Acting'.

69 Anderson, Paul Thomas, *Neon*, '10 Films That Influenced Boogie Nights', August 1998.

70 Goldman, Steven, *Total Film*, 'Paul Thomas Anderson', March 2000.

71 Anderson, Paul Thomas, *Neon*, '10 Films That Influenced Boogie Nights', August 1998.

72 Figgis, Mike, *Projections 10: in Conversation with Paul Thomas Anderson*, Faber & Faber (1999), p.37.

73 Thompson, Ben, *Saturday Telegraph: Weekend Magazine*, 'Blame It on the Boogie Man', 3 January 1998.

74 Maslin, Janet, *New York Times*, 8 October 1997.

75 www.newline.com

76 Connolly, John, *Premiere*, 'Flirting with Disaster', July 1998.

77 ibid.

78 Cullum, Paul, *Fade In*, 'Deconstructing De Luca: The Man, the Myth, the Movies', Vol. 6, 2000.

79 ibid.

80 ibid.

81 Macnab, Geoffrey, *Sight & Sound*, October 1999.

82 Anderson, Wes, *Rushmore*, 'Introduction', Faber & Faber (1999), p. xvi.

83 Foundas, Scott, *L.A. Weekly*, 'Geek Implosion', 11–17 June 2004.

84 Kelly, Richard, *Sight & Sound*, September 1999.

85 Rosenbaum, Jonathan, *Chicago Reader*, 5 February 1998.

86 O'Sullivan, Charlotte, *Independent*, 'Extortion? Nazi Clubs? Welcome to an X-Man's World', 18 August 2000.

87 Jones, Alan, *Shivers*, 'The Evil That Men Do', Issue 61.

88 Smith, Adam, *Empire*, 'Bryan Singer: One on One', May 2001.

89 ibid.

90 French, Philip, *Observer*, 22 March 1998.

91 Haut, Woody, *Sight & Sound*, 'Maximum Elmore', April 2005.

92 Eimer, David, *Sunday Times*, 'Still Shooting from the Lip', 8 March 1998.

93 Coles, Joanna, *Guardian*, 'Making a New Fist of It', 21 December 1997.

94 Soderbergh, Steven, *Getting Away with It. Or: The Further Adventures of the Luckiest Bastard You Ever Saw*, Faber & Faber (1999), p. 190.

95 Haut, Woody, *Sight & Sound*, 'Maximum Elmore', April 2005.

96 Soderbergh, Steven, *Getting Away with It. Or: The Further Adventures of the Luckiest Bastard You Ever Saw*, Faber & Faber (1999), p. 190.

97 Lim, Dennis, *The Independent on Sunday*, 'Autobiography, or reel life', 22 November 1998.

98 *Guardian* interview with Adrian Wootton, NFT, 5 January 1998.

99 ibid.

100 ibid.

101 Eimer, David, *Sunday Times*, 'Still Shooting from the Lip', 8 March 1998.

102 Mackenzie, Suzie, *Guardian*, 'Death in the Family', 15 April 2000.

103 Charity, Tom, *Time Out*, 'The Crying Game', 29 March–5 April 2000.

104 Gill, Erin, *Diva*, 'A First Time Winner', April 2000.

105 O'Sullivan, Charlotte, *Independent*, 'Dear Daddy, I'm Doing Just Fine', 5 May 2000.

106 Zeman, Ned, *Vanity Fair*, 'The Admirable Clooney', October 2003.

107 ibid.

108 Divine, Christian, *Creative Screenwriting*, 'Flirting with Hollywood: An Interview with David O. Russell', January/February 2000.

109 Under the Bunker, *Three Kings* DVD, Warner Bros., 1999.
110 The title is deliberately without the apostrophe. As Russell says, 'To me it encapsulated what the film was about. They pay with their souls and their lives and their bodies. It also talked about "pay". How much are they getting paid? How much are the contractors getting paid? What is America getting paid out of this?'
111 Walker, Alexander, *Evening Standard*, 11 November 1999.
112 Linson, Art, *What Just Happened? Bitter Hollywood Tales from the Front Line*, Bloomsbury (2002), p. 143.
113 Thompson, Anne, *Premiere*, 'The System Is Broken', September 2000.
114 Hoberman, J., *Village Voice*, 11 December 2001.
115 Sloane, Judy, *Starburst*, 'X – The Unknown', May 2003.
116 Bradshaw, Peter, *Guardian*, 30 April 2004.
117 Soderbergh, Steven, *Getting Away with It. Or: The Further Adventures of the Luckiest Bastard You Ever Saw*, Faber & Faber (1999), p. 167.
118 Hoberman, J., *Village Voice*, 10–16 April 2002.
119 Olsen, Mark, *Sight & Sound*, May 2004.
120 Pope, Alexander, *Eloisa to Abelard* lines 207–12; *Poetical Works*, Oxford University Press (1990), pp. 115–16.
121 Wilson, Ben, *Arena*, 'A Beautiful Mind', May 2004.
122 Morris, Mark, *Observer*, 16 April 2000.
123 Sorensen, Holly, *Premiere*, 'The Unbearable Lightness of Being Marty Bowen', April 2004.
124 Feld, Rob, *WGA Written By*, 'The Voiceover Kings', March 2003.
125 Some of the temp music used by Payne as dummy tracks laid down before Kent's work was grafted on was from Paul Thomas Anderson's *Magnolia*.
126 Kidman can be heard in an uncredited cameo, as the voice of Stephen Altman's girlfriend on the phone when Meg makes her distress call.
127 Taylor, Ella, *Guardian*, 'I don't like being told what to do', 13 October 2003.
128 Hauser, Brooke, *Premiere*, 'Sea Shtick', December 2004/January 2005.
129 Edwards, Richard, *Hotdog*, 'What About Bill?', February 2005.
130 Gilbey, Ryan, *Sight & Sound*, March 2005.
131 Bradshaw, Peter, *Guardian*, 10 October 2003 (*Vol 1*); 23 April 2004 (*Vol 2*).
132 McCartney, Jenny, *Sunday Telegraph*, 12 October 2003.
133 Dinning, Mark, *Empire*, 'The Big Boss', November 2003.
134 Olsen, Mark, *Sight & Sound*, 'Turning on a Dime', October 2003.
135 Waxman, Sharon, *New York Times*, 'The Nudist Buddhist Borderline-Abusive Love In', 19 September 2004.
136 French, Philip, *Observer*, 28 November 2004.
137 McCarthy, Todd, *Variety*, 20 September 2004.
138 Pickett, Rex, *Premiere*, 'Blown "Sideways" Through Life', October 2004.
139 ibid.
140 Young, Deborah, *Variety*, 3 September 2005.

General Index

This index contains all entries other than those of film titles.
It includes titles of television programs, stage plays, novels and magazines.
Illustrations are denoted in **bold**.

A&M Records, 23
ABC, 9
Acord, Lance, 162–3, 388
Adams, Brooke, 35
Adams, Joey Lauren, 99
Affleck, Ben, 82, 99
Affleck, Casey, 294
Air, 251, 388
Alan, Devon, 440
Alda, Alan, 81
Aldrich, Robert, 76
Alfred Hitchcock Presents, 95
Allen, Karen, 62
Allen, Scott, 176
Allen, Woody, 18, 245, 320–1, 325
Allende, Salvador, 45
Almodóvar, Pedro, 92
Altman, Robert
    Andie MacDowell and, 12
    Julianne Moore and, xxvii
    a maverick?, xvii
    1970s, xviii
    P. T. Anderson and, xxviii, 128–9, 131,
        189, 258, 263, 448
    Palme d'Or, 7
    Peter Gallagher and, 13
    Richard Linklater and, 99
    Three Kings and, 269
    USA Films, 361
American Psycho (Bret Easton Ellis), 253
American Zoetrope, 97, 247
Amiel, Jon, 120, 410
Amis, Martin, 228
'And Death Shall Have No Dominion' (Dylan
    Thomas), 372
Anders, Alison, 29, 35, 36, 92, 94
Anderson, Brad, 82–3
Anderson, Ernie, 127
Anderson, J. Todd, 335
Anderson, Lindsay, 213, 279, 282

Anderson, Paul Thomas
    Alexander Payne and, 351
    as auteur, 338
    background, 136, 142
    Boogie Nights, 187–96, **191**, 344
    collaborators, regular, 143, 381, 420
    crime genre and, 107
    debut, 127
    families, depiction of, xxviii
    Hard Eight, 113, 127–31, 145
    Isabelle Huppert on, xxii
    Julianne Moore and, xxvii
    Magnolia, 143, 188, 257–66, 451
    Miramax, 82
    Punch-Drunk Love, 341, 353–6
    Robert Altman and, xxviii, 128–9, 131,
        189, 258, 263, 448
    Steven Soderbergh and, 6
    Sundance Institute and, xv
Anderson, Wes
    Bill Murray and, 381–3
    Bottle Rocket, 132–6, **134**, 146–7
    budgets for his movies, xxviii
    collaborators, regular, 143–4, 338
    crime genre and, 107
    debut, 127
    Henry Selick and, 172
    Life Aquatic with Steve Zissou, The, 136,
        389–95
    Miramax, 82
    originality of, 337
    Owen Wilson and, 133, 338, 351, 382,
        394
    Pizza Knights, xv
    Royal Tenenbaums, The, 77, 341, 342–8,
        343
    Rushmore, 211–19
    on Scorsese, xxviii
    Scott Rudin and, 103, 420
Anonymous Content, 156

Antonioni, Michelangelo, 61, 141, 424
Araki, Greg, 22, 29
Aranofsky, Darren, 438–9, 441
Arau, Alfonso, 90
Armitage, George, 238
Arnold, William, 143
Arquette, David, 91, 92
Arquette, Patricia, 322
Artisan Entertainment, 238
Ashby, Hal, xix, 44, 141, 348
Ashley, Dustin, 443
Ashmore, Shawn, 311
Astaire, Fred, 355
Attanasio, Paul, 63
August, Bille, 79
Austen, Jane, 18
Austin Film Society, 98
Austin Studios, 98
Avary, Roger, 31, 32, 70–1, 254

Baena, Jeff, 420
Baker Hall, Philip, 126, 128–31, 190, 194, 259, 261–2, 265
Baldwin, Alec, 342, 344
Baldwin, Stephen, 106, 114
Balk, Fairuza, 35
Ball, Alan, 320, 327
Ballard, J. G., 14, 279
Baltimore Pictures, 53, 63
Banderas, Antonio, 92, 93, 94, 96
Barrett, K. K., 420, 425
Barris, Chuck, 319, 336
Barrymore, Drew, 247, 333, 441
Bass, Ron, 319–20
Bates, Kathy, 351
Baumbach, Noah, 393
Bava, Mario, 70
Bay, Michael, 151, 155, 156
Beach Boys, The, 273
Bean, Henry, 40
Beastie Boys, 160
Beatles, The, 57, 176, 177, 260, 344
Beatty, Warren, 199, 258, 276, 400
Beckinsale, Kate, 20
Begley, Louis, 137, 348, 352
Belber, Stephen, 102
Bell, Jamie, 440
Bender, Lawrence, 32, 41, 94
Bening, Annette, 13
Bergman, Ingmar, 348
Berkeley, Busby, 160
Berlin Film Festival, 272, 298, 334
Berman, Shari Springer, 40

Bernstein, Charles, 404
Berri, Claude, 400
Berry, Halle, 308, 313
Betrayal (Harold Pinter), 331
Bickford, Laura, 296
Bielinsky, Fabián, 302
Bienen, Andy, 248
Big Bounce, The (Elmore Leonard), 227
Bing, Christopher, 166
Binoche, Juliette, 39
Bishop, Joey, 293
Biskind, Peter, xvi, xxv
Bismuth, Pierre, 328
Björk, 160, 163, 322
Black, Shane, 198, 319
Black Mask, 75
Blackman, Jeremy, 261–2
Blanchett, Cate, xxvii, 392
blockbusters, xix, 10
Bludhorn, Charles, xviii
B movies, 5, 23, 75, 113–14
Bobbitt, John Wayne, 278
Bobbitt, Lorena, 278
Bocquet, Gavin, 54
Bogart, Humphrey, xx
Bogdanovich, Peter, xviii, xxviii, 59, 132, 245, 389–90
Bogosian, Eric, 100
Bondarchuk, Natalya, 370
Bonham Carter, Helena, 278, 279
Bono, 270
Book of the Damned, The (Charles Fort), 264
Boorman, John, 76, 176–7, 239
Borden, Lizzie, 78
Borg, Björn, 344
Bornedal, Ole, 172
Bounty Hunters, The (Elmore Leonard), 227
Bowen, Marty, 337–8
Bowie, David, 391, 394
Boyce, Brandon, 45, 220, 314
Bradford, Jesse, 52, 60
Brando, Marlon, 189
Branson, Richard, 8, 158
Brantley, Betsy, 175, 176
Brantley, Duncan, 62
Brat Pack, 14
Breillat, Catherine, 253
Bremer, Arthur, 177
Brinkley, William, 53
Brion, Jon, 143, 263, 356, 420
British Board of Film Classification, 29
Broderick, Matthew, 206, 207
Brody, Adrien, 60, 62, 303, 327

Brolin, James, 288
Brolin, Josh, 172
Brooks, Albert, 230
Brooks, Dina, 48
Brooks, James L., 144
Broomfield, Nick, 180, 181
Bruce, Lenny, 320, 321
Buckeye Entertainment, 47
Buena Onda, 442
Buena Vista, 219
Bui, Tony, 40
Bulger, Jamie, 29
Bunker, Eddie, 32
Buñuel, Luis, 140, 424
Burgess, Anthony, 277
Burke, Robert John, 19
Burns, Edward, 40, 417
Burroughs, William, 54
Burstyn, Ellen, **438**, 439
Burton, Tim, 9, 10, 171, 294, 382, 415
Burwell, Carter, 163, 269
Buscemi, Steve, **28**, 32, 35, 36, 94, 96
Bush, George H.W., 208
Bush, George W., 83, 272, 299, 417
Byrd, Jim, 333
Byrne, Gabriel, **106**, 114, 115, 116, 223
Byrne, Michael, 222

Caan, James, **134**, 135
Caan, Scott, 294
Cage, Nicolas, 155, 218, 307, **318**, 319, 327
Cagney, James, 33
Cahiers du Cinéma, xx
Cain, James M., 227
Calderon, Paul, 75, 95
Cameron, James, 153, 275, 369
Campbell, Jessica, 206
Cannes Film Festival
    About Schmidt, 341
    Hard Eight, 145
    Henry Fool, 20
    King of the Hill, 63
    Lost in Translation, 388
    Pulp Fiction, 69
    Punch-Drunk Love, 341
    Safe, 24
    Usual Suspects, The, 117
    Virgin Suicides, The, 252
Cannon Films, 138, 201
Canonero, Milena, 394
Canterbury Tales, The (Geoffrey Chaucer), 119
Capote, Truman, 247
Capra, Frank, 347

Carlisle, Belinda, 8
Carpenter, John, 199
Carpenter, Richard, 23
Carradine, David, 72, 400
Carradine, John, 400
Carrey, Jim, 197, 276, 329, 333, 382
Carson, L. M. Kit, 143
Carter, Rubin, 290
Caruso, D. J., 120
Cassavetes, John, xx, 9, 14, 131, 217
Cassel, Seymour, 35, 213, 391–2
Cassell, Vincent, 409
Castle, The (Franz Kafka), 54
Castle Rock Entertainment, 100, 197
Catcher in the Rye, The (J. D. Salinger), 213
Caton-Jones, Michael, 60, 78
Cavazos, Lumi, 135
Chambers, Marilyn, 193
Chandler, Raymond, 77, 227, 319
Channel 4, 20
Channing-Williams, Simon, 442
Chaplin, Charlie, 58
Chaucer, Geoffrey, 76, 119, 120
Chayefsky, Paddy, 320
Che Guevara, 240
Cheadle, Don, xvii, 187, 236, 288, 294, 381
Cheh, Chang, 403
Chemical Brothers, 388
Chernin, Peter, 275–6
Chiba, Sonny, 30, 72, 400, 406
Chicago (band), 269
Chinn, Bob, 193
Christensen, Erika, **286**, 288, 298
Christie, Julie, 20, 177, 234
Christmas Carol, A (Charles Dickens), 157
Christopher, Mark, 20
Church, Thomas Haden, 426, 429, 432, **433**
Cimino, Michael, xix
Cinebeam, 46
Cinema Libre, 274
Clark, Dick, 336
Clark, Larry, 81, 138
Clarke, Arthur C., 437
'Clementine's Loop' (Michael Penn and
    Patrick Warren), 130
Clinton, Bill, 11, 146, 208, 273
Clinton, Hillary, 146
Clooney, George
    Confessions of a Dangerous Mind, 319,
        333–5
    Good Night, and Good Luck., 303
    loyalty and admiration for directors, xxvii,
        258, 301, 381

Clooney, George (*cont.*)
  Ocean's Eleven, 293–5
  Ocean's Twelve, 410
  Out of Sight, 229, 230, 234, 238
  Section Eight, xxiv
  Solaris, 361, 369, 372–3
  Spy Kids, 96
  Steven Soderbergh and, xxiv, 381, 441
  Three Kings, 266–8, **269**
  Welcome to Collinwood, 302
Clooney, Nick, 335
Clooney, Rosemary, 335
Close, Glenn, 13
Coen Brothers, xvi, 32, 69, 114, 131, 133,
  335, 362
Columbia Pictures, xxix, 7, 92, 144, 146,
  147, 219
comic books, 307–8
Commodores, The, 208
Communism, 53
Condon, Bill, 416
Confederacy of Dunces, A (John Kennedy
  Toole), 441
Cooper, Chris, 325
Coppola, Francis Ford
  Alexander Payne and, xxviii, 140
  Directors Company and, xviii
  Godfather, The, xix, 218
  a maverick?, xvii, 19
  P. T. Anderson meets, 258
  Palme d'Or, 7
  Rushmore and, 218
  Sofia Coppola and, 245–6, 384
  Steven Soderbergh and, 300
  Zoetrope, 97
Coppola, Roman, 246
Coppola, Sofia, 244–7
  Isabelle Huppert on, xxii
  Lance Acord and, 162
  Lost in Translation, 381–9, 410, 420, 437
  on the new generation of film directors, xxi
  Sundance and, xv
  Virgin Suicides, The, 249–53
Corbucci, Sergio, 211
Cort, Bud, 392
Costner, Kevin, 384
Cotten, Joseph, 56
Coupland, Douglas, 22
Cousteau, Jacques, 394
Cox, Brian, 214, 310
Cox, James, 193
Crash (J. G. Ballard), 279
Craven, Wes, 197
Cronenberg, David, 14, 54, 55, 193

Cronenweth, Jeff, 280
Crow, Sheryl, 290
Crowe, Cameron, 230, 287
Crowe, Russell, 365
Cruise, Tom, 59, 249, 258, **259**, 261, 287
Cuban, Mark, 443
Cumming, Alan, 309
Cummings, Howard, 112, 116
Cure, The 251
'The Curious Case of Benjamin Button'
  (F. Scott Fitzgerald), 437
Curtis, Cliff, 270
Curtiz, Michael, 287
Cusack, John, 81, 150, 164

Dafoe, Willem, 391
Dahl, John, 152
Dahl, Roald, 95
Daldry, Stephen, 287
Damiano, Gerard, 194
Damon, Matt, 82, 293, 294, 295, 410
Dante Alighieri, 119
Dante, Joe, 45
Dassin, Jules, 33
David Copperfield (Charles Dickens), 167
Davies, Jeremy, 38, 44, 369
Davis, Elliot, 8, 61, 112, 180, 182, 234, 254
Davis, Hope, 83, 350
Davis, Sammy Jr, 293
Davis, Tamra, 162
Davis, Viola, 369
Davison, Bruce, 311
Dawson's Creek, 320
Day-Lewis, Daniel, 79
Day Today, The (BBC), 178
De Laurentiis, Dino, 201
De Luca, Mike, xxvi, 199–200, 201, 264
de Medeiros, Maria, 71
De Niro, Robert, 60, 118, 189, 231, 233,
  341
De Palma, Brian, 34, 70, 77
De Sica, Vittorio, 61
Death Row Records, xxii
Debussy, Claude, 292
DeCillo, Tom, 36
Del Toro, Benicio, 97, 106, 114, **286**, 297,
  298, 299
del Toro, Guillermo, 171
Delpy, Julie, 100, 100, 102
Deming, Peter, 420, 424
Demme, Jonathan, 131, 157, 180
Demme, Ted, 140, 230
Denis, Claire, 253
Depp, Johnny, 333

Deren, Nancy, 143
Dern, Laura, 139, 141, 146
DeSanto, Tom, 309
Deschanel, Zooey, 440
Deutchman, Ira, 197
Devane, William, 95
DeVito, Danny, 71, 249
Devo, 144
di Bonaventura, Lorenzo, xxvi, 267
Diaz, Cameron, 164, 387
DiCaprio, Leonardo, 60, 192
Dick, Nigel, 151, 152
Dick, Philip K., 104
Dickens, Charles, 157
Dickinson, Angie, 294
Dickinson, Emily, 43, 167
Dignan, Stephen, 217
Diller, Barry, xxiv, 156, 361, 362
Dillon, Melinda, 261
Dimension, 84, 87, 172
Directors Company, xxiv
Directors Guild of America, 97
Disney, xxvi, xxix, 7, 80, 83–4, 201, 219,
     341, 415
Divine Comedy, The (Dante Alighieri), 119
Dobbs, Lem, 53–6, 58, 238
Doebereiner, Debbie, 443
Dogme95, 174, 374
Dollard, Pat, 8, 53
Donner, Richard, 308
Donovan, Martin, 16
Dougherty, Michael, 314–15, 316
Douglas, Kirk, 141
Douglas, Michael, 157, 288, 298, 299
Down and Dirty Pictures (Peter Biskind),
     xxv
Downey, Robert Jr, 104
Downey, Robert Sr, 189–90
DreamWorks SKG, 199, 416
Dreyfuss, Julie, 401
Duchovny, David, 374
Dukakis, Michael, 11
Dunst, Kirsten, 249, 332, 383–4, 388

Eastwood, Clint, 41, 69, 432
Eckhart, Aaron, 289
Edinburgh Film Festival, 427
Edwards, Blake, 355
Egoyan, Atom, 12
Eichhorn, Lisa, 60
Eisner, Michael, 83–4
Elliott, Alison, 110
Ellis, Bret Easton, 253
Ellroy, James, 227

Eloisa to Abelard (Alexander Pope), 328
Elswit, Robert, 143
Emery, R. Lee, 154
Eminem, 237
Endeavor, 426
ER, 335
Esposito, Giancarlo, 114
Esposito, John, 93
Eszterhas, Joe, 199, 319
Eugenides, Jeffrey, 245, 247
Evans, Robert, 205
Excalibur Films, 81
Executioner's Song, The (Norman Mailer),
     247

F-64, xvi, xxiv, xxv, 361, 362, 437, 442
Faces, The, 216, 218
Fallen Angels, 59
Farina, Dennis, 231
Farrelly, Bobby, 205
Farrelly, Peter, 205
Farris, Anna, 387
Fatboy Slim, 161
Fellini, Federico, 375, 386
Ferguson, Larry, 153
Ferrara, Abel, 29, 228
Ferrell, Will, 416
Ferris, Michael, 157
Fichtner, William, 110
Figgis, Mike, 199
film noir, 107–8, 111, 116, 117, 119, 122
Finch, Nigel, 22
Fincher, David
     Alien³, 10, 152–5, 426
     box office hits, xxvii, 415
     collaborators, regular, 338, 381
     crime genre, xxviii, 107, 205
     F-64, xxiv, 361
     Fight Club, xxvi, 275–82, 420
     Game, The, 156–60
     Lords of Dogtown, 254
     Miramax and, 82
     miscellaneous projects, 437
     Panic Room, 363–8, 410, 420
     Pizza Knights, xv
     Propaganda, 151–2, 155–6
     Se7en, 108, 117, 120–2, 130, 197
     Steven Soderbergh and, 6, 296
     2006 film release, 448
     uncredited acting roles, 166, 373
     Wes Anderson and, 132
Fine Line Features, 47, 197, 323
Finney, Albert, 287, 410
First Look (USC), 45

Fitzgerald, F. Scott, xvii, 18, 135, 347, 437
Flack, Sarah, 239
Fleder, Gary, 113
Flower Films, 441
Focus Features, xxix, 362, 415
Fonda, Bridget, 233
Fonda, Peter, 240
Ford, John, 22, 61, 403
Ford, Harrison, 60
Forman, Milos, 195
Forster, Robert, 230, 231, 233
Fort, Charles, 264
Foster, Jodie, 118, 362, 363, 365, 367
Foster, Stephen, 118
Foundas, Scott, 212
Fox, Vivica A., 401
Fox Filmed Entertainment, xxv, 275
Fox Searchlight, 39–40, 102, 180, 411,
    415–17, 420, 432, 442
Fox TV, 47
Frank, Scott, 129, 228, 232, 235, 238
Frankenheimer, John, 199
Fraser, Brendan, 59
Frears, Stephen, 33
Freeman, Morgan, 118, 122, 123
French New Wave, xviii, xx, 75
Fricker, Brenda, 79
Friedberg, Mark, 392
Friedkin, William, xvii, xviii, 24, 297,
    300, 347
Fukasaku, Kinji, 403
Fujita, Toshiya, 403
Funky Bunch, 192
Fuqua, Antoine, 151

Gaghan, Stephen, 287, 296–7, 302
Gallagher, Peter, 11, 13, 59, 110, 112
Gallardo, Carlos, 86, 89–90, 92
Galloway, Stephen, xxi, xxv
Gamble, Mason, 212
Garofalo, Janeane, 81
Garcia, Andy, 292, 293
García Márquez, Gabriel, 442
Gardiner, Greg, 39
Gates, Bill, 157
Genet, Jean, 23
Gere, Richard, 39
German Expressionism, 55, 56
Getting Away With It, 176
Ghoulardi Films, 127
Giamatti, Paul, xxvii, 426, 429, 430, 431, 433
Gibson, Mel, 365
Gibson, William, 153
Giler, David, 153

Gilliam, Terry, xxiii, 33, 55, 75, 109, 280
Gittes, Harry, 352
Gladstein, Richard, 32
Glenn, Scott, 249
Glennon, James, 143, 350
Glover, Danny, 345
Godard, Jean-Luc, xx, 77, 196, 231, 388
Godfrey, Arthur, 265
Goebbels, Joseph, 219
Goldberg, Myla, 39
Goldberg, Whoopi, 80
Goldblum, Jeff, 392
Goldman, William, 320
Golin, Steve, 151, 152, 156
Gómez, Consuelo, 90, 92
Gondry, Michel, 155, 321–2, 323–4,
    328, 420
Gonzales, Mark, 162
Good Machine, 362
Goodall, Jane, 391
Goodis, David, 59
Gould, Elliott, 240, 293
Grace, April, 265
Grace, Topher, 288, 294, 298
Gracie Films, 144
Graff, Todd, 129
Graham, Heather, 187, 191
Gramercy Pictures, 25, 99, 108, 361
Grand Jury Prize (Sundance), xvi, 35, 40, 43,
    47, 50, 253
Grant, Cary, 408
Grant, Susannah, 287, 289
Gray, F. Gary, 228, 238
Gray, James, 301
Gray, Spalding, 60, 62, 180–3
Graysmith, Robert, 448
Green, David Gordon, 439–41
Greenaway, Peter, 78
Greene, Peter, 71
Greenstein, Scott, 25
Grey, Joel, 56
Grier, Pam, 226, 230–3, 235
Griffin, Ted, 293, 302
Griffith, D. W., xxviii
Grosbard, Ulu, xv
Grossmith, George, 349
Grossmith, Weedon, 349
Gugino, Carla, 96
Guinness, Alec, 56
Gulf Wars, xxvi, 257
Guzmán, Luis, 187, 192, 239, 288, 302

Hackford, Taylor, 7
Hackman, Gene, 342, 343, 347, 356, 357

Hall, Conrad L., 366
Hall, Conrad W., 366
Hallström, Lasse, 83
Hamann, Craig, 31
Hammett, Dashiell, 227, 229, 419
Hamsher, Jane, 32, 220
Hannah, Daryl, 403
Hanson, Curtis, 227, 333
Hardwicke, Catherine, 253–4, 267, 271, 416
Harlin, Renny, 153
Harrelson, Woody, 104
Harris, Dan, 314, 315
Harron, Mary, 253
Hartley, Hal, xxii, 17–20, 21, 25, 53
Hartnett, Josh, 250
Harwood, Ronald, 327
Haskin, Sam, 251
Hauer, Rutger, 236, 334
Hawke, Ethan, 45, 46, 100, 100, 101, 102
Hawkes, John, 92
Hawks, Howard, xviii, xx, 22, 227
Hayashi, Fumihiro, 388
Hayek, Salma, 92, 93
Hayes, Isaac, 404
Hayman, Stephanie, 246
Haynes, Todd, 20–5, 29, 301
Haysbert, Dennis, 26
Hayter, David, 314
Hayward, Charles, 137
Heart (band), 251
Hedaya, Dan, 114
Hedren, Tippi, 140
Helfgott, David, 197
Hellman, Monte, 32
Hemingway, Ernest, 154, 427
Hendrickson, Benjamin, 44
Herrmann, Bernard, 404
Herskovitz, Marshall, 297
Herz, Adam, 205
Heslov, Grant, 303
Hess, Jared, 212
Hicks, Scott, 197
Hill, Lauryn, 62
Hill, Walter, 153, 199, 347
Hinckley, John, 118, 177
Hirsch, Foster, 116, 122
Hitchcock, Alfred
    Fincher's project, 437
    Game, The and, 157
    influence, xviii, 22
    Kafka and, 56
    Kill Bill and, 403

Ocean's Twelve and, 408
Panic Room and, 368
Pulp Fiction and, 76
Hoberman, J., 76
Hodges, Mike, 238
Hoffman, Dustin, xv, 232, 419
Hoffman, Philip Seymour, xxvii, 190, 192, 262, 265, 354, 381
Hollies, The, 241
Holm, Ian, 54, 55
Holmes, David, 292
Holmes, John, 193, 195
Holocaust, 219–20, 221
Hombre (Elmore Leonard), 161
Hooper, Tobe, 197
Hope, Ted, 362
Hopper, Dennis, 7
Hopper, Edward, 61
Horace, 76
Hotchner, A. E., 53
Hough, Coleman, 373, 443, 444
Hough, John, 237
Houston, Whitney, 261
Hu, Kelly, 310
Hughes, Carol, 171
Hughes, John, 206, 212
'Human Behaviour' (Björk and Michel Gondry), 322
Hunter, Holly, 253
Huppert, Isabelle, xxii, 420
Huston, Angelica, 342, 383, 392, 395
Huston, John, xviii, 33, 132–3, 227, 229, 268, 346
Hyde-Pierce, David, 321

Ice Cube, 266, 269, **269**
ICM, xix
Ifans, Rhys, 323
IFC Films, 83
In Cold Blood (Truman Capote), 247
Incubus, 218
Independent Digital Entertainment (InDigEnt), 102
Independent Film Channel, 102, 274
Independent Spirit Awards, 218
Industrial Light and Magic (ILM), 152
Inferno (Dante Alighieri), 119
Irons, Jeremy, 54
Ita, Shuyna, 403
Italian neo-realism, xviii

Jackman, Hugh, 308, 310, 439
Jackson, Joshua, 294
Jackson, Peter, 88, 198, 264

Jackson, Samuel L., 69, **74,** 75, 145, 230, 234, 237, 381
Jacksons, 162
Jacobs, Greg, 302–3
Jacobs, Marc, 246
Jagger, Mick, 217
James, Henry, 390, 394
James Best Acting School, 31
Jane, Thomas, 190, 192
Janssen, Famke, 312
Jarmusch, Jim, xxii, 9, 18, 19, 382
Jaymes, Cathryn, 31
Jefferson Airplane, 158
Jemison, Eddie, 176, 294
Jensen, David, 176, 182
Jeremy, Ron, 194
Jersey Films, 71, 93, 229, 289
Jesus and Mary Chain, 388
Jeunet, Jean-Pierre, 366
Jewison, Norman, 290
Joanou, Phil, 156
Johansson, Scarlett, xvii, 380, 384, 388
Johnson, Mark, 53, 63
Johnston, Joe, 341
Jolie, Angelina, 249, 417
Jones, Leslie, 143
Jones, Quincy, 404
Jones, Robert, 113, 115
Jones, Spike, 161
Jonze, Spike
    Adaptation, 324, 362
    Being John Malkovich, 160–7, 321, 387, 420
    Charlie Kaufman and, xxviii, 163, 165–7, 324, 333, 338
    F-64, xxiv, 361
    genre and, 107
    Isabelle Huppert on, xxii
    Miramax and, 82
    Philip French on, 425
    Pizza Knights, xv
    Sofia Coppola and, 246, 386
    Steven Soderbergh and, 6–7
    Three Kings, 270
Jordan, Gregor, 268
Jordan, Neil, 79, 249
Jorge, Seu, 391
Jovovich, Milla, 99
Judge, Mike, 98

Kael, Pauline, xviii, 211
Kafka, Franz, 53–6
Kalin, Tom, 22
Kamen, Michael, 315

Karen Sisco (ABC), 231
Karlson, Phil, 33, 131
Kasdan, Lawrence, 107
Katt, Nicky, 99, 240, 374
Katzenberg, Jeffrey, 80
Kaufman, Charlie, 319–21, 337–8
    Adaptation, 324–7
    Being John Malkovich, 160, 165–7
    Confessions of a Dangerous Mind, 333–6
    Eternal Sunshine of the Spotless Mind, 328–33
    Human Nature, 321–4
    Spike Jonze and, xxviii, 163, 165–7, 324, 333, 338
    Steven Soderbergh and, 229
Kaufman, Philip, 292
Kavanaugh, Charles, 48
Kaye, Tony, 200
Kazan, Elia, 189
Keaton, Michael, 231
Keener, Catherine, 150, 163, 374, 376
Keillor, Garrison, 448
Keitel, Harvey, 28, 32, 34, 75, 76
Kelly, Richard, 21
Kent, Rolfe, 143, 352, 428, 430, 451
Kerrigan, Lodge, 40
Khondji, Darius, 121, 364, 366
Kidman, Nicole, 365, 423, 451
Kieslowski, Krzysztof, 69
Killer Films, 20
Kim, Helen, 407
King, Stephen, 219–20
King of the Hill (A. E. Hotchner), 53
Kinks, The, 218
Kitaj, R. B., 54
Klein, Chris, 206–7
Kloves, Steve, 130
KNB EFX, 93
Knightley, Keira, 303
Koepp, David, 320, 362, 368
Kokin, Kenneth, 48
Kopelson, Arnold, 154
Korchek, Jeff, 361
Korine, Harmony, 138, 247, 301
Koteas, Elias, 220
Krabbé, Jeroen, 60
Kramer, Scott, 441
Kramer, Stanley, 53
Kubrick, Stanley
    David Fincher and, xxviii, 153, 366
    Eyes Wide Shut, 257, 265
    Paths of Glory, 273
    Quentin Tarantino and, 29, 31, 33
    Solaris and, 369, 372

Kuriyama, Chiaki, 403
Kurosawa, Akira, 348, 404
Kurtz, Swoosie, 140
Kurtzman, Bob, 93
Kusama, Karyn, 40, 253
Kussman, Dylan, 113
Kwon-taek, Im, 341

La Motta, Jake, 189
LaBute, Neil, 156
LaChapelle, David, 160
Lachman, Ed, 25, 249, 291
LaGravenese, Richard, xxvi, xxix, 129, 140, 289, 415
Lakeshore Entertainment, 156
Lam, Ringo, 33, 404
Lancaster, Burt, 110
Landau, Jon, 153
Larkin, Philip, 44
Laughton, Charles, 440
Laurel Canyon, 193
Law, Jude, 301, 417, **418**, 419, 423
Lawrence, Martin, 80
Ledger, Heath, 254
Lee, Ang, 10, 287, 308, 362
Lee, Bruce, 403
Lee, Spike, xxvi, 9, 18, 19, 75, 237
Lee, Stan, 310
Leigh, Janet, 76
Leigh, Jennifer Jason, 303
Leigh, Mike, 361, 442
Lem, Stanislaw, 368, 369
Lemmon, Jack, 45, 141, 348
Leonard, Elmore, 77, 227–3, 238, 321, 368
Leonard, Robert Sean, 102
Leone, Sergio, 34, 93, 399
Leoni, Téa, 424
Lester, Richard, xxviii, 56, 57, 176, 183, 400
Leto, Jared, 279, 363
Levinson, Barry, 9, 53
Lewinsky, Monica, 11, 209
Ligeti, György, 372
Lightstorm Entertainment, 369
Linklater, Richard, xxiii, 17, 21–2, 29, 86, 98–104
Linson, Art, 276, 280
Liotta, Ray, 189
Lipsky, Jeff, 361
Liu, Gordon, 403
Liu, Lucy, 382, 401
Live Entertainment, 32
Livingston, Jennie, 22
Livingston, Ron, 337

Lloyd, Walt, 8, 55
Loach, Ken, 240
Logan, John, 319
London, Jason, 99
London Film Festival, 179
'Lonely Boy' (Andrew Gold), 194
Lonergan, Kenneth, 40, 253
Lopez, Jennifer, 230, 238
Lorre, Peter, 95
Lovecraft, H. P., 199
Lowe, Rob, 11
Lubitsch, Ernst, 132
Lucas, George
  American Graffiti, 99, 152
  cinema's roots and, 18
  film schools, 128
  Francis Ford Coppola and, xviii
  M. Night Shyamalan and, xxii
  Star Wars films, xix, 257, 282, 313
Lucas, Josh, 440
Luhrmann, Baz, 365
Lumet, Sidney, 263
Lurie, Rod, xv
Lynch, David, 23, 43, 47, 69, 107, 139, 179, 420
Lyne, Adrian, 9
Lynne, Michael, 197

Mac, Bernie, 294
MacDowell, Andie, **4**, 11, 12–13
Macy, William H., xxvii, **186**, 188, 192, 262, 265
Madden, John, 83
Madonna, 21, 30, 79, 94
Madsen, Michael, 32, 34, 381, 399
Madsen, Virginia, 426, 429, 432
'Magic Man' (Heart), 251
Mailer, Norman, 247
Malick, Terrence, 31, 133, 251, 257, 392, 399, 440–1
Malkovich, John, 150, 164–7
Malle, Louis, 213
Malone, Mike, 176
Mamet, David, 192
'Man from the South' (Alfred Hitchcock Presents), 95
Mangold, James, 95, 327
Manhattan Beach, 31
Mankiewicz, Herman J., 437
Mann, Aimee, 260, 261, 263
Mann, Michael, 257
Mantegna, Joe, 59
Mao Zedung, 240

Marquette, Ron, 43
Marsden, James, 312
Martinez, Cliff, 8, 57, 372
Marvel Comics, 224, 307, 309–10
Marvin, Lee, 34
Marx Brothers, 320–1
Mason, Morgan, 8
Max, Arthur, 121
Maxwell, Larry, 48
Maybury, John, 301, 303
Mayers, Michael, 44
McCarey, Leo, 136
McCarthy, Cormac, 344
McCarthy, Joseph, 303
McCartney, Jenny, 402
McComb, Heather, 221
McConaughey, Matthew, 99, 101
McCormack, Mary, 374
McCorvey, Norma, 139, 448–9
McDowell, Alex, 280
McElhone, Natasha, 369, 370, 372
McGehee, Scott, 39, 442
McGovern, Elizabeth, 62
McGregor, Ewan, 172, 301
McKay, Adam, 416
McKee, Robert, 320, 326–7
McKellen, Ian, xxvii, 219, 308, 309, 311,
    316, 381
McNaughton, John, 120
McQuarrie, Christopher, 48, 108, 113, 115,
    116, 314, 338
McQueen, Steve, 95
McTiernan, John, 293, 296
Meat Loaf, 278
Mechanic, Bill, xvii, 275–7, 297, 307
Meirelles, Fernando, 442
Melville, Herman, 391
Melville, Jean-Pierre, 130
Mendes, Sam, xxiv, 82, 366
Messina, Philip, 371
Messing, Debra, 429
Metamorphosis, The (Franz Kafka), 54
Microsoft, 157
Mikel, Ted V., 404
Mild Bunch, The (Hollywood Reporter), xvi
Milestone, Lewis, 33, 288, 292, 293, 295
Miller, Frank, 97, 439
Milton, John, 76, 119
Minghella, Anthony, 83
Minnelli, Vincente, 355
Miramax, 77–84
    Alexander Payne and, 145–6
    Disney and, 415

Elmore Leonard rights, 227
George Clooney and, 333
New Line and, 80, 196
New York and, 200
Pulp Fiction, 197, 401
Quentin Tarantino and, 400–1
rise of, xxix
Robert Rodriguez and, 87
Rolling Thunder, 95
Samuel L. Jackson, 75
Steven Soderbergh and, 171–2, 361, 373, 441
Sundance and, 9
Todd Haynes and, 24, 25
see also Weinstein, Harvey
Mirren, Helen, 20
Mirrione, Stephen, 287, 334
Mitchell, John Cameron, 22
Moby-Dick (Herman Melville), 391
Molina, Alfred, 190, 192
Monicelli, Mario, 302, 428
Moody, Decker, 444
Moon Safari (Air), 251
Moore, Demi, 7
Moore, Julianne, xxvii, 24, 187, 192, 262
Moore, Mary Tyler, 81
Moore, Michael, 49, 83, 145
Moore, Simon, 296
Moore, Thurston, 246
Morricone, Ennio, 71, 211, 352, 404
Morris, Chris, 178
Morris, Errol, 82
Mothersbaugh, Mark, 144, 254
Motion Picture Association of America, 79
Mottola, Greg, 173
MTV, 206
Mulroney, Dermot, 350
Murdoch, Rupert, 275, 416
Murnau, F. W., 55, 56, 58
Murphy, Brittany, 42
Murphy, Don, 31, 220
Murray, Bill, 381–5
    Life Aquatic with Steve Zissou, The,
        389, 392
    Lost in Translation, 380
    loyalty to directors, xxvii
    mid-life crises and, 410
    Rushmore, 214, 215
    Royal Tenenbaums, The, 344
Murrow, Edward R., 303
Museum of Modern Art, New York, 419
Musgrave, Robert, 133, 134
Myatt, Major General Michael, 274
Myers, Mike, 198, 333

Naked Lunch (William Burroughs), 54, 60
National Endowment for the Arts, 23, 47
National Film Theatre, London, 30
National Third Coast Film and Video
    Festival, 89
Natural Nylon, 301
Needful Things (Stephen King), 219
New Line, 196–201
    David O. Russell and, 47, 416
    Miramax and, 80, 196
    rise of, xxix
    Se7en, 108, 154, 362
New Regency, 416
Newell, Mike, 230
Newman, Bob, 241
Newman, Thomas, 291
News Corporation, 275
Nichols, Mike, xxviii, 9, 44, 81, 213, 301, 372
Nicholson, Jack, 232, 348, 352, 357, 362,
    428, 432
9/11, xxvi, 417
Noé, Gaspar, 279
Nolan, Christopher, 301–2, 308, 331, 439
Nolfi, George, 408
Nolte, Nick, 172
Norrington, Stephen, 307
Northam, Jeremy, 173
Northern Arts, 180
Norton, Edward, 275, 282
Noyce, Philip, 120
Nunez, Victor, 43
NYPD Blue, 297

October Films, 362
O'Donnell, Peter, 71
Once and Future King, The (T. H. White),
    312
Operation Desert Storm, 272
Ophüls, Max, 131
Orchid Thief, The (Susan Orlean), 324,
    328, 338
Orion Pictures, 152
Orlean, Susan, 324
Oshima, Yukari, 98
Ottman, John, 46–7, 49–50, 115, 116, 220,
    221, 315, 316
Otto, Miranda, 323
Owen, Clive, 97
Ozu, Yasujiro, 98, 348

Pacino, Al, 232, 302
Pakula, Alan J., 301
Palace Pictures, 78, 79, 113

Palahniuk, Chuck, 277
Pallana, Deepak, 217
Pallana, Kumar, 217
Palme d'Or, 7, 13, 69, 140, 152
Palminteri, Chazz, 114
Paltrow, Bruce, 429
Paltrow, Gwyneth, 121, 129–30, 130, 131,
    145, 344, 346, 423
Paquin, Anna, 310
Paradise Lost (John Milton), 119
Paramount, xviii, 220, 361, 415, 416, 441
Parker, Alan, 155
Parks, Michael, 405
Pasolini, Pier Paolo, 98
Passer, Ivan, 138
Payne, Alexander, 136–41
    About Schmidt, 341, 348–52, 362
    collaborators, regular, 338
    debut, 127
    Election, 205–11, 337
    F-64, xxiv, xxv, 361, 442
    Francis Ford Coppola and, xxviii, 140
    genre and, 107
    on Hollywood, xxvii, 417, 437
    Pizza Knights, xv
    Sideways, 395, 411, 416, 425–32
    Steven Soderbergh and, 6
Pearce, Guy, 330
Peckinpah, Sam, xxi, 33, 98, 368
Peirce, Kimberly, xv, xxiii, 22, 200,
    245–53, 301
Penn, Arthur, xix
Penn, Chris, 33–4
Penn, Michael, 130, 143
Penn, Sean, 157, 165, 365, 383
Peralta, Stacey, 254
Perot, Ross, 208
Perrotta, Tom, 208
Phantom Planet (band), 218
Phoenix Pictures, 223, 314
Pickett, Rex, 425, 426, 427
Pierce, David Hyde, 374, 376
Pinter, Harold, 331
Pitt, Brad
    cameo appearance, 165
    Darren Aronofsky and, 439
    Fight Club, 276, **282**
    Full Frontal, 373, 375
    Kirsten Dunst and, 249
    new directors and, xxvii, 258, 381
    Ocean's Eleven, 293
    Ocean's Twelve, 410
    Se7en, 118, 122, 123

Pixar, 80
'Pizza Knights', xv, 253, 254, 437
Place, Mary Kay, 140
Plath, Sylvia, 427
Playboy, 251
Playboy Video Enterprises, 138
Plummer, Amanda, 72
Polanski, Roman, 132, 133
Pollack, Sydney, xvi, xix, 7, 53, 59, 62–3, 230
Pollak, Kevin, 106, 114, 115
Pollock, Jackson, 174
PolyGram, 152
Pope, Alexander, 76, 328
Populist Pictures, 40
Posey, Parker, 99
Poster, Randy, 218
Postlethwaite, Pete, 115
Powell, Michael, 12, 132, 251
Powell, Nik, 78
Prairie Home Companion, A (Garrison Keillor), 448
Presley, Elvis, 292, 293
Pressburger, Emeric, 132
Preston, Kelly, 140
'Professional Man, The' (*Fallen Angels* episode), 59
Propaganda Films, 151–6, 416, 437
Proyas, Alex, 155
Pryce, Jonathan, 109
Public Enemy, 269
Pulcini, Robert, 40
Pullman, Philip, 198
Purgatory (Dante Alighieri), 119

Qin, Shaobo, 293
Quaid, Dennis, 24, 130, 288
Quaser cameras, 89
'Quiet Room, The' (*Fallen Angels* episode), 59

Rafelson, Bob, xix, 19, 44
Raimi, Sam, 32, 45
Rambone, Dirk, 193
Ramis, Harold, 382, 441
Ranvaud, Donald, 442
Ratner, Brett, 316
Ray, Bingham, 361
RCA, 7, 8
RCA-Columbia, 9
Reagan, Ronald, 22, 48, 208
Red Hot Chili Peppers, 57
Redford, Robert, xv, xvi, 46, 53, 63, 147, 156, 295
Reed, Carol, 55

Reed, Nikki, 253
Reeve, Christopher, 316
Reeves, Keanu, 104
Reilly, John C., 129–31, 130, 145, 187, 190, 259, 260, 303
Reiner, Carl, 294
Reiner, Rob, 61, 197, 237, 302
Reitzell, Brian, 388
Rendezvous with Rama (Arthur C. Clarke), 437
Renfro, Brad, 219
Renoir, Jean, xx, 131, 136, 342
Resnais, Alain, 238
Reynolds, Burt, 140, 186, 187, 193, 228
Rhames, Ving, 69, 230
Ribisi, Giovanni, 249, 384
Ribisi, Marissa, 99
Rice, Peter, 416
Richardson, Robert, 407
Richardson, Tony, 213
Ridgley, Robert, 190
Rifkin, Arnold, 199
Risi, Dino, 429
Ritchie, Guy, 30, 294
Ritchie, Michael, 132
Rivette, Jacques, xx
RKO, xxi
Roach, Jay, 341
Robards, Jason, 259, 262
Robbins, Tim, 82, 322
Roberts, Julia, xxvii, 287–91, 294, 360, 361, 374, 381, 409
Robinson, Bruce, 429
Rockwell, Alexandre, 35, 36, 94
Rodman, Howard, 59
Rodriguez, Robert, 86–98
   crime genre and, 107
   inclusion of, xxiii,
   Mariachi, El, 7, 39
   Quentin Tarantino and, 404
   Sundance and, 29, 35
Roeg, Nicholas, 176, 234
Rogers, Ginger, 355
Rohmer, Eric, xx
Rolling Thunder, 95
Rolling Stones, 217
Romanek, Mark, 155, 416
Romijn-Stamos, Rebecca, 313
Ross, Gary, 173
Rossellini, Roberto, 60
Rota, Nino, 352, 428
Roth, Joe, 219
Roth, Tim, 29, 72, 94
Rothman, Tom, xxv, 416

Rotoscoping, 101
Rotterdam Film Festival, 147
Routh, Brandon, 316
Roxy Music, 388
Rudd, David, 137
Rudin, Scott, 103, 420, 441
Ruffalo, Mark, 329
Rum Punch (Elmore Leonard), 229
Russell, David O.
   Flirting with Disaster, 81–2, 127, 381
   genre and, 107
   I ❤ Huckabees, 395, 410–11, 416–25, 418
   'independents' and, xxii
   Mike Nichols and, xxviii
   9/11 and, xxvi
   photograph, 256
   Spanking the Monkey, 43–5, 47, 49
   Spike Jonze and, 160
   Steven Soderbergh and, 6
   Sundance and, xv, xvii, 39, 53, 437
   Three Kings, 253, 257, 266–70, 272–4
Russell, Theresa, 54
Russo, Anthony, 302
Russo, Joe, 302
Russo, Kathleen, 182
Ryan, Meg, 130, 365
Ryder, Winona, 245
Rysher Entertainment, 130, 145

Salinger, J. D., 135, 213, 342, 347, 391
Salisbury, Mark, 10
Salles, Walter, 442
Salt, Waldo, 320
San Giacomo, Laura, 11, 12
Sandler, Adam, 199, 340, 353, 357
Sargent, Joseph, 3
Sarsgaard, Peter, 251
Sartre, Jean-Paul, xx
Satter, Michelle, 129
Savides, Harris, 156–7
Sayles, John, 9, 40–1
Scanner Darkly, A (Philip K. Dick), 104
Schamus, James, 314, 362
Schneider, Paul, 440
Schrader, Paul, 228
Schroeder, Ricky, 220
Schumacher, Joel, 307
Schwartzman, Jack, 218
Schwartzman, Jason
   I ❤ Huckabees, 381, 418, 418, 419,
     421, 423
   Rushmore, 204, 212, 215, 218
Schwimmer, David, 224

Scorsese, Martin
   After Hours, 157
   on *Bottle Rocket*, 136, 147
   Casino, 292
   film schools, 128
   Gangs of New York, 341, 400
   Goodfellas, 187, 194
   influence of, xxviii, 70
   a maverick?, xvii,
   1970s, xviii
   P. T. Anderson and, 131, 196
   Palme d'Or, 7
   Raging Bull, 189
   shorts, 245
   Steven Soderbergh and, 300
   Taxi Driver, 6
   on Wes Anderson, 136
Scott, Dougray, 308
Scott, George C., 176
Scott, Ridley, 155, 287
Scott, Tony, 32, 95, 231
Selby, Hubert Jr, 438
Selick, Henry, 171–2, 391, 393
Selleck, Tom, 193
Sellers, Peter, 355
Sena, Dominic, 151, 156
Sevigny, Chloë, 20, 247
Sex Pistols, 388
Sexton, Brendan III, 251
Seymour, Cara, 327
Shainberg, Steven, 14
Shaw Brothers, 402–3
Shaye, Robert, 196–200
Sheen, Charlie, 166
Shelly, Adrienne, 19
Sheridan, Jim, 79
Sherwood, Bill, 23
Shields, Kevin, 388
Shire, Talia, 218, 423
Showtime, 6, 59
Shue, Elisabeth, 110
Shyamalan, M. Night, xxii, 75, 200
Siegel, David, 39, 442, 443
Siegel, Don, 75
Sigel, Newton Thomas, 116, 220, 272,
     316, 334
Sighvatsson, Joni, 151, 156
Sillitoe, Alan, 213
Silver, Casey, 229–30
Simon and Garfunkel, 260
Simpsons, The, 144
Sinatra, Frank, 293
Sinatra, Nancy, 404

Singer, Bryan
  Apt Pupil, 205, 219–24
  collaborators, regular, 338, 381
  crime genre and, 107
  David O. Russell and, 44
  Miramax, 82
  on 9/11, xxvi
  Public Access and, 45–50
  rise of, 127
  Steven Soderbergh and, 7, 53
  Steven Spielberg and, xxviii, 42–3, 308
  Sundance and, xv, xxvii, 39
  Usual Suspects, The, 108, 112–17, 122
  X-Men, 306, 307–11, 313–16, 409
Siodmak, Robert, 109, 110
Sirk, Douglas, 24, 25
Six Feet Under, 320
Skjoldbjærg, Erik, 301
Skye, Ione, 35
Slamdance, 180
Smith, Frank E., 59
Smith, Kevin, xxiii, 14, 30, 39, 82
Smith, Kurtwood, 140
Soderbergh, Charley, 180
Soderbergh, Steven, 5–14
  Bubble, 443–5
  on cinema, xxv
  George Clooney and, xxiv, 381, 441
  collaborations, 338, 381
  crime genre and, 107, 122, 132, 205
  Erin Brockovich, 287–92
  F-64, xxiv, 361, 362
  Full Frontal, 175, 373–7, 420
  Gray's Anatomy, 180–3
  Human Nature, 321
  Jaws and, 42
  Kafka, 56–8, 448
  King of the Hill, 59–63
  Last Ship, 53–4
  Limey, The, 238–41
  miscellaneous projects, 171–2
  9/11 and, 447
  Ocean's Eleven, 292–6, 308, 420
  Ocean's Twelve, 407–11
  Out of Sight, 104, 228–35
  photographs, xiv, 170
  Populist Pictures, 40
  Richard Lester and, xxviii
  Schizopolis, 173–80
  Section Eight, 25, 104, 300–4, 415
  sex, lies, and videotape, 5–14, 17, 79
  Solaris, 369–73
  Sundance and, xv

  Suture and, 39
  Traffic, 296–300, 432
  Underneath, The, 108–12
Solondz, Todd, xxii, 40, 81, 200, 361, 429
Sonic Youth, 162, 246
Sonnenfeld, Barry, 228, 231
Sonny and Cher, 404
Sony Pictures, 93, 341, 362, 363
Sony Pictures Classics, xxix, 415, 440
Sorvino, Mira, 173
Spacey, Kevin
  Se7en, 122, 123, 154
  Swimming with Sharks, 82
  Usual Suspects, The, 47, 106, 108, 114,
    116, 118
Spader, James, 5, 7, 13, 14
Spenser, Edmund, 76
Spiegel, Scott, 32
Spielberg, Steven
  Bryan Singer and, xxviii, 42–3, 308
  Duel, 131
  film school, 128
  Jaws, xix, 415
  Saving Private Ryan, 82, 399
  Steven Soderbergh and, 296
  Sugarland Express, The, 441
Springer, Jerry, 335
Springfield, Rick, 152, 190
St James, Jessie, 193
St Vincent, Julia, 193
Stallone, Sylvester, 96
Stamp, Terence, 56, 238, 239–40, 376
Stanford, Aaron, 311
Star Trek, 30, 316
Star Trek: The Next Generation, 308
Steinbeck, John, 61
Stevens, Cat, 218, 260
Stewart, Jane Ann, 143
Stewart, Kristen, 363
Stewart, Patrick, xxvii, 308, 309
Stiffed (Susan Faludi), 278
Stiller, Ben, xxvii, 341, 344, 381
Stillman, Whit, 17–20, 25, 53
Stone, Oliver, 32, 176, 407
Strathairn, David, 303
Streep, Meryl, 326
Streets of San Francisco, 159
Studio 54, 20
Sturges, John, 404
Sturges, Preston, 81, 132
Sundance Film Festival
  All the Real Girls, 2003, 440
  Cigarettes and Coffee, 1993, 129

on feature films, 41
John Sayles on, 40–1
Next Stop Wonderland, 1998, 82
Quentin Tarantino, 1992, 25, 29
Reservoir Dogs overlooked, 70
sex, lies, and videotape, 7
Stillman and Hartley, 1990, 17
Virgin Suicides, The, 2000, 253
Sundance Filmmakers Lab, 129, 248
Sundance Institute, xvi, 9, 39, 46, 53, 87, 127, 437
Sutherland, Donald, 234
Sutherland, Kiefer, 59
Svevo, Italo, 332
Swank, Hilary, xxvii, 248, 249
Swinton, Tilda, 337

Taghmaoui, Saïd, 270
Tarantino, Quentin
    Austin Film Society, 98
    crime genre and, 107, 108
    Elmore Leonard and, 227–9, 231–2
    favourite actors, 381
    favourite movies, 6
    Four Rooms, 94–5
    Jackie Brown, 230–1, 233–8
    Kill Bill, 399–407
    Miramax, 197
    photograph, 68
    Pulp Fiction, 69–77, 197, 231
    Reservoir Dogs, 29–35, 79, 131
    Richard Linklater and, 21
    rise of, 127
    Robert Rodriguez and, 87–8, 93
    Sundance and, xv, 25, 29
Tarkovsky, Andrei, 36, 58, 369–72
Tati, Jacques, 355
Taylor, Jim
    About Schmidt, 341, 348
    Citizen Ruth, 140
    Election, 206, 208–9
    Payne meets, 137–8, 348
    Payne's collaborator, 338, 351
    Sideways, 427, 428, 432
Technicolor, 25, 323
Telluride, 39, 91
Tenenbaum, Brian, 217
Tenenbaum, Nancy, 173
Tent, Kevin, 143
thirtysomething (ABC), 9
This Be the Verse (Philip Larkin), 44
Thomas, Dylan, 372
Thornton, Billy Bob, 103

3:10 to Yuma (Elmore Leonard), 227
'Three Times a Lady' (The Commodores), 208
Thurman, Uma, 70, 73, 102, 381, 398, 399
Tierney, Lawrence, 32, 34
Time-Warner, 198, 199
Tokuma Corporation, 46
Tokyo International Film Corporation, 46
Tolkien, J.R.R., 88, 198
Tomei, Marisa, 321
Tomlin, Lily, 81, 419, 420
Toole, John Kennedy, 441
Tornatore, Giuseppe, 79
Toronto Film Festival, 39, 91, 92
Touchstone Pictures, 219, 341
Towne, Robert, 320
Traffik (Channel 4), 296
Travers, Peter, 55
Travolta, John, 69, 72, 73, 228, 233, 399
Trial, The (Franz Kafka), 54
TriStar, 7, 71, 91, 160
Troche, Rose, 22
Troublemaker Studios, 89, 97
Truffaut, François, xx, 61, 131, 213, 344, 375
Tucker, Chris, 233
Tukur, Ulrich, 369
Tulliver, Barbara, 143
Turner, Ted, 197
Turner Broadcasting Systems, 197–8
Turturro, John, 410
Twain, Mark, 61
Twentieth Century Fox
    Alien, 152
    Boys Don't Cry, 252
    Bryan Singer and, 307
    Elmore Leonard and, 227
    Newton Boys, The, 101
    Solaris, 361, 373
    Traffic, 297
    2929 Entertainment, 443
Twilight Zone, The, 76
Twohy, David, 153

Uhls, Jim, 277, 282
Underwood, Blair, 360, 374
Unger, Deborah Kara, 159
United States Film Festival, xvi
Universal, xxix, 53, 62, 99, 137–8, 174–5, 415
USA Films, xxiv, 25, 156, 361, 362
USC School of Cinema-Television, 42, 48

Vachon, Christine, 9, 20, 22–3, 24
Van Damme, Jean-Claude, 75

Van Sant, Gus, 44, 81, 138, 144, 251
Vargas, Jacob, **286**, 299
Vaughn, Matthew, 316
Vega, Alexa, 96
Venice Film Festival, 96, 275, 388, 443
Verdi, Giuseppe, 163
Vibenius, Bo Arne, 403
Video Archives, 31
Vietnam, xxvi, 417
Vigo, Jean, xx
Vinterberg, Thomas, 197
Virgin Vision, 8
Visconti, Luchino, 394
Vitale, Ruth, 197
Vivendi Universal Entertainment, 362
von Sydow, Max, 79
von Trier, Lars, 174, 361

Wachowski Brothers, 308
Wagner, Todd, 443
Wahlberg, Mark,
    Boogie Nights, 187, **192**, 381
    I ❤ Huckabees, 417, 419–22, **419**
    Planet of the Apes, 294
    Three Kings, 266, **269**, 270, 381
Walker, Alexander, 275
Walker, Andrew Kevin, 118–20, 154
Walters, Melora, 190, 193, 260, 354
Ward, Vincent, 153
Warner Bros.
    art house division, xxix, 415
    Batman, 9
    Bryan Singer and, 316
    David O. Russell and, xxvi
    Fountain, The, 439
    Insomnia, 301
    New Line and, 198
    Section Eight and, 300, 303, 408
    Three Kings, 266, 272–4, 416
Warren, Lesley Ann, 239
Wasco, David, 144, 406
Washington, Denzel, 41
Watergate, xxvi
Waters, John, 9, 196
Watson, Alberta, **38**, 44
Watson, Emily, **340**, 353
Watts, Naomi, **414**, 417, 423
Weinstein, Bob, 71, 77–84, 87, 95–6
Weinstein, Harvey, 77–84, *see also* Miramax
    Cary Woods and, 139
    Citizen Ruth, 145–6
    Four Rooms, 94
    Kill Bill, 400–1

Pulp Fiction, 71
    Quentin Tarantino and, 71, 94, 400–1
    Samuel L. Jackson and, 75
    Todd Haynes and, 24, 25
Weintraub, Jerry, 293, 376, 408
Welles, Orson, xxi, 7, 55, 161, 342
Wenders, Wim, 13, 35
West, Simon, 151, 155
West Wing, The, 300
Westerling, Dick, 443
Wharton, Edith, 135, 347
Whitaker, Forest, 363, 364, 368
White, Mike, 103, 320, 338
White, T. H., 312
'White Rabbit' (Jefferson Airplane), 158
Who, The, 218
Wiene, Robert, 55
Wiggins, Wiley, 102
Wilde, Oscar, 18
Wilder, Billy, 141, 211, 227, 273
Wilkins, Misty, 444
Wilkinson, Tom, 329
Willard, Fred, 321
William Morris Agency, xix, 156, 199, 338
Williams, Burt, 43
Williams, John, 356
Williams, Olivia, 214
Williamson, Kevin, 95, 320
Williamson, Nicol, 220
Willis, Bruce, 69, **74**, 75, 95
Wilson, Andrew, 133, 217
Wilson, Luke, 133, **134**, 217, 294, 344
Wilson, Owen
    Bottle Rocket, 133–5, **134**, 143
    Life Aquatic with Steve Zissou, The, 391
    loyalty to directors, xxvii
    Ocean's Eleven, 294
    Royal Tenenbaums, The, 341, 344
    Rushmore, 212, 213, 217, 337
    Wes Anderson meets, 133
    Wes Anderson's collaborator, 338, 351,
        382, 394
Winslet, Kate, 329
Winterbottom, Michael, 408
Wise, Robert, 131
Witherspoon, Reese, 206, 207
Wolff, Tobias, 60
Womack, Bobby, 235
Wong Kar-Wai, 95
Woo, John, 236, 308, 408
Wood, Elijah, 96, 329
Wood, Evan Rachel, 253
Woods, Cary, 138–9

Woods, James, 60, 249
Woolley, Steven, 78, 79
Wo-Ping, Yuen, 404

Yakin, Boaz, 41–2
Yeoman, Robert, 144
Yoakam, Dwight, 363, 365

Zahn, Steve, 236
Zaillian, Steven, 319
Zaldívar, Juan Carlos, 274

Zane, Lisa, 137
Zeno's Conscience (Italo Svevo), 332
Zeta-Jones, Catherine, 288, 327, 408,
      409, 410
Ziembicki, Bob, 143
Ziskin, Laura, 280
Zodiac (Robert Graysmith), 448
Zodiac Unmasked (Robert Graysmith),
      448
Zwick, Ed, 272, 297
Zwigoff, Terry, 213

Index of Films

This index contains only titles of films.
Illustrations are denoted in **bold**.

À bout de souffle (Jean-Luc Godard), 388
About Schmidt (Alexander Payne), 348–53
  Cannes Film Festival, 341
  cinematographer, 143
  origins of, 137
  Panic Room and, 367
  Sideways and, 417, 428, 430, 431, 432
  Sony and, 362
Abyss, The (James Cameron), 369
Ace in the Hole (Billy Wilder), 141
Adaptation (Spike Jonze), 318, 324–8
  approval seeking in, 336
  entertainment industry in, 337
  Eternal Sunshine of the Spotless Mind
    and, 333
  Kaufman and Jonze, 163
  Kaufman's role in, 320
  Kaufman's stature after, 319
  romantic comedy elements in, 329
  Sony and, 362
Adventures of Sharkboy and Lavagirl (Robert
  Rodriguez), 96
Aeon Flux (Karyn Kusama), 40, 253
After Hours (Martin Scorsese), 157
Airport 75 (Jack Smight), xxv
Aladdin (Disney), 80
Alien (Ridley Scott), 152
Alien: Resurrection (Jean-Pierre Jeunet), 366
Alien³ (David Fincher), 10, 108, 152–5, 157,
  276, 279, 362–3, 426
Aliens (James Cameron), 153
All That Heaven Allows (Douglas Sirk), 25
All That Jazz (Bob Fosse), 194
All the President's Men (Alan J. Pakula), 6
All the Real Girls (David Gordon Green),
  440, **440**
Almost Famous (Cameron Crowe), 287
Altered States (Ken Russell), 5
Amanda by Night (Robert McCallum),
  188, 195

Ambition (Hal Hartley), 19
American Beauty (Sam Mendes), 13, 327
American Graffiti (George Lucas), 99, 152
American History X (Tony Kaye), 200, 277
American Pie (Paul Weitz), 205, 206, 208
American President, The (Rob Reiner), 237
American Splendor (Shari Springer Berman
  and Robert Pulcini), 40, 429
Anchorman: The Legend of Ron Burgundy
  (Adam McKay), 416
Angels With Dirty Faces (Michael Curtiz), 287
Animal House (John Landis), 205
Anna and the King (Andy Tennant), 276
Annie Hall (Woody Allen), 6
Any Given Sunday (Oliver Stone), 302
Apartment, The (Billy Wilder), 141
Apocalypse Now (Francis Ford Coppola),
  218, 245
Apt Pupil (Bryan Singer), 43, 45, 205,
  219–24, 307, 309, 311, 319
Armageddon (Michael Bay), 151
As Good As It Gets (James L. Brooks), 144
Asphalt Jungle, The (John Huston), 33
Austin Powers (Jay Roach), 198
Austin Stories (Robert Rodriguez), 89
Awful Truth, The (Leo McCarey), 136

Bad Boys (Michael Bay), 30, 155
Bad Lieutenant (Abel Ferrara), 29
Bad News Bears (Richard Linklater), 103, 132
Bad Timing (Nicholas Roeg), 177
Badlands (Terrence Malick), 31, 251
Ballad of Bettie Page, The (Mary Harron), 253
Band Wagon, The (Vincente Minelli), 355
Barcelona (Whit Stillman), 20
Barton Fink (Coen Brothers), 69, 94
Basic Instinct (Paul Verhoeven), 319
Basketball Diaries, The (Scott Kalvert), 192
Batman (Tim Burton), 9, 10, 307, 415
Batman Begins (Christopher Nolan), 308, 439

Battle Royale (Kinju Fukasaku), 403

Be Cool (F. Gary Gray), 228, 238

Beat of the Live Drum (David Fincher), 152

Bedhead (Robert Rodriguez), 89

Bee Season (Scott McGehee and David Siegel), 39

Before Sunrise (Richard Linklater), 100, 100, 102

Before Sunset (Richard Linklater), 103, 104

Being John Malkovich (Spike Jonze), 150, 160–7, 319–22, 336–8
  Adaptation and, 324–6
  approval seeking in, 336
  Eternal Sunshine of the Spotless Mind and, 328–9, 331
  identity theme, 162
  Jonze receives script, 160–1
  K. K. Barrett, 420
  musical score, 269
  Propaganda Films and, 156
  unique qualities of, 167
  Venice Film Festival, 275

Being There (Hal Ashby), 141

Best Laid Plans (Mike Barker), 293

Beverly Hills Cop II (Tony Scott), 32

Big Bounce, The (George Armitage), 238

Big City Nights (Spike Jonze), 160

Big Deal on Madonna Street (Mario Moncelli), 302, 428

Bingo Inferno (David O. Russell), 45

Black Hawk Down (Ridley Scott), 373

Black Sabbath (Mario Bava), 70

Blade (Stephen Norrington), 307

Blood Simple (Coen brothers), xvi, 78, 131

Blow-Up (Michelangelo Antonioni), 424

Blue Velvet (David Lynch), 23, 43, 139

Bob le Flambeur (Jean-Pierre Melville), 130

Body Heat (Lawrence Kasdan), 107

Bone Collector, The (Philip Noyce), 120

Bonfire of the Vanities, The (Brian De Palma), 75

Bonnie and Clyde (Arthur Penn), 31

Boogie Nights (Paul Thomas Anderson), 186, 187–96, 191, 192
  'Clementine's Loop', 130
  establishing sequence, 344
  gross take, 264
  influences on, 131
  Julianne Moore and, xxvii,
  Magnolia and, 266, 353
  Mark Wahlberg in, 381
  music and, 130, 260
  origins of, 128

  Punch-Drunk Love and, 353, 355
  timespan, 258
  Tom Cruise and, 265

Border Radio (Allison Anders, Dean Lent, Kurt Voss), 35

Born to Kill (Robert Wise), 131

Bottle Rocket (Wes Anderson), 132–6, 134, 142–4, 146–7, 212, 216–19, 346

Boxer from Shantung, The (Chang Cheh), 403

Boys Don't Cry (Kimberly Peirce), 22, 200, 245, 248, 249, 251–3

Boyz N the Hood (John Singleton), 41

Brainscan (John Flynn), 119

Brazil (Terry Gilliam), xxiii, 55, 56, 109

Breakfast Club, The (John Hughes), 212

Breaking the Waves (Lars von Trier), 361

Breathless (Jim McBride), 141

Brief Encounter (David Lean), 385

Bringing Out the Dead (Martin Scorsese), 257

Broadcast News (James L. Brooks), 144

Broken Flowers (Jim Jarmusch), 382

Brothers McMullen, The (Edward Burns), 40

Bubble (Steven Soderbergh), 443–5

Buffalo Soldiers (Gregor Jordan), 268

Bulworth (Warren Beatty), 276

Butch Cassidy and the Sundance Kid (George Roy Hill), xvi, 320

Cabinet of Dr. Caligari, The (Robert Wiene), 55

California Split (Robert Altman), 131

Carnal Knowledge (Mike Nichols), 9, 30, 44

Casino (Martin Scorsese), 292

Casualties of War (Brian de Palma), 129

Cat Chaser (Abel Ferrara), 228

Catch-22 (Mike Nichols), 372

Catwoman (Jean-Christophe 'Pitof' Comar), xxv, 437

Central Station (Walter Salles), 442

Charley Varrick (Don Siegel), 75

Charlie's Angels (McG), 382

Chasing Amy (Kevin Smith), xxiii

Chicago (Rob Marshall), 327

Chihwaseon (Im Kwon-taek), 341

Chinatown (Roman Polanski), 205, 320, 352

Chuck and Buck (Miguel Arteta), 103

Chungking Express (Wong Kar-Wai), 95

Cigarettes and Coffee (Paul Thomas Anderson), 128, 129

Cinema Paradiso (Giuseppe Tornatore), 79

Citizen Kane (Orson Welles), xxi, 7, 277, 437

Citizen Ruth (Alexander Payne), 82, 127, 138–43, 145–6, 208, 351, 427

City of God (Fernando Meirelles), 442

City on Fire (Ringo Lam), 33, 404

Claire Dolan (Lodge Kerrigan), 40

Clean, Shaven (Lodge Kerrigan), 40

Clerks (Kevin Smith), xxiii, 14, 21, 39, 50, 80

Clockwork Orange, A (Stanley Kubrick), 29, 70, 276, 277

Close Encounters of the Third Kind (Steven Spielberg), 43, 356

Clueless (Amy Heckerling), 208

Coffee and Cigarettes (Jim Jarmusch), 382

Con Air (Simon West), 151, 155

Confessions of a Dangerous Mind (George Clooney), 301, 319, 333–6, 337

Conversation, The (Francis Ford Coppola), xviii, xix, 6, 141

Cook, the Thief, His Wife and Her Lover, The (Peter Greenaway), 78

Cookie's Fortune (Robert Altman), xxvii, 257

Cop Land (James Mangold), 96

Copycat (Jon Amiel), 120

Cotton Club, The (Francis Ford Coppola), 246, 252

Courage Under Fire (Ed Zwick), 272

Crash (David Cronenberg), 14

Criminal (Greg Jacobs), 302, 303

Crimson Tide (Tony Scott), 95

Criss Cross (Robert Siodmak), 109–12

Crouching Tiger, Hidden Dragon (Ang Lee), 404

Cruising (William Friedkin), 23

Crying Game, The (Neil Jordan), 79–80, 117

Cutter's Way, (Ivan Passer), 138

Dad (Gary David Goldberg), 45

Daisy Miller (Peter Bogdanovich), xviii, 390

Day for Night (François Truffaut), 375

Day the Earth Stood Still, The (Robert Wise), 309

Daytrippers, The (Greg Mottola), 173

Dazed and Confused (Richard Linklater), 22, 86, 99, 100, 101, 104

Dead Poets Society (Peter Weir), 46

Decade Under the Influence, A (Ted Demme and Richard LaGravenese), 140

Deconstructing Harry (Woody Allen), 325

Deep End, The (Scott McGehee and David Siegel), 39

Deep Throat (Gerard Damiano), 194

Deliverance (John Boorman), 30, 76, 193

Desperado (Robert Rodriguez), 87, 92, 93, 94

Desperate Living (John Waters), 196

Destiny Turns on the Radio (Jack Baran), 95

Devil in Miss Jones, The (Paul Thomas), 194

Devil's Own, The (Alan J. Pakula), 219

Dick Tracy (Warren Beatty), 302

Die Hard (John McTiernan), 75

Dillinger (Max Nosseck), 32

Dirk Diggler Story, The (Paul Thomas Anderson), 128

Dirty Dancing: Havana Nights (Guy Ferland), 41

Dirty Dozen, The (Robert Aldrich), 293

Dirty Mary, Crazy Larry (John Hough), 237

Disclosure (Barry Levinson), 9

Discreet Charm of the Bourgeoisie, The (Luis Buñuel), 424

Do the Right Thing (Spike Lee), 9

Dogma (Kevin Smith), xxiii

Dogtown and the Z-Boys (Stacey Peralta), 254

Dolce vita, La (Federico Fellini), 386

Doll Squad, The (Ted V. Mikel), 404

Donnie Brasco (Mike Newell), 230

Donnie Darko (Richard Kelly), 21

Don't Look Now (Nicholas Roeg), 177, 234

Dr. Strangelove (Stanley Kubrick), 276, 447

Drugstore Cowboy (Gus Van Sant), 144

Dude, Where's My Car (Danny Leiner), 205

Duel (Steven Spielberg), 43, 131

Duets (Bruce Paltrow), 429

Dumb and Dumber (Peter Farrelly and Bobby Farrelly), 197

Easy Rider (Dennis Hopper), 7

Ed Wood (Tim Burton), 382

Edward Scissorhands (Tim Burton), 10

8½ (Federico Fellini), 375

Election (Alexander Payne), 205–11
The Apartment and, 141
cinematographer, 143
comedy in, 431
Edinburgh Film Festival, 427
music score, 352
politics and, 139
theme, 348

Empire Strikes Back, The (Irvin Kershner), 152, 313

End of Violence, The (Wim Wenders), 13

English Patient, The (Anthony Minghella), 78

Entrapment (Jon Amiel), 410

Erin Brockovich (Steven Soderbergh), xxvi, 58, 287–92, 296, 297, 361, 409

E.T. the Extra-Terrestrial (Steven Spielberg), 42

Eternal Sunshine of the Spotless Mind (Michel Gondry), 319, 324, 328–34, 336, 362, 420, 432

Explorers (Joe Dante), 45, 96
Eyes Wide Shut (Stanley Kubrick), 257, 265

Faculty, The (Robert Rodriguez), 87, 92, 95, 320
Fahrenheit 9/11 (Michael Moore), 83, 145
Falling Down (Joel Schumacher), 159
Falling in Love (Ulu Grosbard), 60
Family Viewing (Atom Egoyan), 12
Far from Heaven (Todd Haynes), 301
Fast Times at Ridgemont High (Amy Heckerling), 208
Fatal Attraction (Adrian Lyne), 9
Female Convict Scorpion: Jailhouse 41 (Shuyna Ita), 403
Female Trouble (John Waters), 196
Femme Nikita, La (Luc Besson), 76
Ferris Bueller's Day Off (John Hughes), 206
Fight Club (David Fincher), 275–82, 282
  Bill Mechanic and, 307
  Brad Pitt and, 122
  Game, The and, 157
  Nicole Kidman and, 365
  Panic Room and, 366, 368, 420
  theme, xxvi, 157
5 Against the House (Phil Karlson), 131
Five Easy Pieces (Bob Rafelson), 44
Flesh and Bone (Steve Kloves), 130
Flirting with Disaster (David O. Russell), 81, 127, 266, 418, 423, 424
Flora Plum (Jodie Foster), 365
Forrest Gump (Robert Zemeckis), 69
Fountain, The (Darren Aronofsky), 439
Four Daughters (Michael Curtiz), 287
Four Rooms (Allison Anders, Robert Rodriguez, Alexandre Rockwell, Quentin Tarantino), 36, 87, 94–5
400 Blows, The (François Truffaut), 78, 213
Foxy Brown (Jack Hill), 232
Frank Miller's Sin City (Robert Rodriguez), 97
Freddy's Dead: The Final Nightmare (Rachel Talalay), 199
French Connection, The (William Friedkin), xviii, 347
Fresh (Boaz Yakin), 41, 75
From Dusk Till Dawn (Robert Rodriguez), 92, 93
From Dusk Till Dawn 2: Texas Blood Money (Scott Spiegel), 41, 405
Full Frontal (Steven Soderbergh), 360, 373–7
  betrayal in, 291
  Bubble and, 443, 444
  commerciality of, 361

  Ocean's Twelve and, 409
  Sarah Flack and, 239
  Steven Soderbergh in, 175
  still from, 360
  videotape used in, 12
Funny Girl (William Wyler), 194

Game, The (David Fincher), 156–60, 280, 281, 368
Game of Death (Robert Clouse), 403
Game Over (Robert Rodriguez), 96
Gangs of New York (Martin Scorsese), 341, 400
Garden State (Zach Braff), 415
Gas Food Lodging (Allison Anders), 35
General's Daughter, The (Simon West), 151
Generation X (Douglas Coupland), 22
George Washington (David Gordon Green), 439, 440
Get Carter (Mike Hodges), 238
Get Shorty (Barry Sonnenfeld), 228, 230, 231
Ghost World (Terry Zwigoff), 213
Ghostbusters (Ivan Reitman), 382
Girl from Monday, The (Hal Hartley), 20
Girl, Interrupted (James Mangold), 249
Girlfight (Karyn Kusama), 40, 253
Gladiator (Ridley Scott), 287, 319
Godfather, The (Francis Ford Coppola), xviii, xix, 6, 205, 218, 252, 352
Godfather Part II, The (Francis Ford Coppola), xix, 246
Godfather Part III, The (Francis Ford Coppola), 245
Gone in Sixty Seconds (Dominic Sena), 151
Good Girl, The (Miguel Arteta), 103
Good Night, and Good Luck. (George Clooney), 303
Good, the Bad and the Ugly, The (Sergio Leone), 399
Good Will Hunting (Gus Van Sant), 78, 82
Goodfellas (Martin Scorsese), 187, 189, 194
Goonies, The (Richard Donner), 96
Gosford Park (Robert Altman), 361
Grace of My Heart (Allison Anders), 35
Graduate, The (Mike Nichols), 44, 213, 260
Grapes of Wrath, The (John Ford), 61
Gray's Anatomy (Steven Soderbergh), 62, 109, 171, 179–83, 229, 234, 241
Greystoke: The Legend of Tarzan (Hugh Hudson), 13
Grifters, The (Stephen Frears), 164
Grosse Pointe Blank (George Armitage), 164
Groundhog Day (Harold Ramis), 382
Gunsmog (Steven Spielberg), 42

Hairspray (John Waters), 196

Happiness (Todd Solondz), xxii, 361

Hard Day's Night, A (Richard Lester), 57

Hard Eight (Paul Thomas Anderson), **126**, 127–32, **130**, 142–3, 145, 187–8, 190, 264

Harold and Maude (Hal Ashby), 44, 141, 260, 348

Heat (Michael Mann), 302

Heaven's Gate (Michael Cimino), xxii

Heaven's Prisoners (Phil Joanou), 156

Hedwig and the Angry Inch (John Cameron Mitchell), 22

Help! (Richard Lester), 57

Henry Fool (Hal Hartley), 20

Henry: Portrait of a Serial Killer (John McNaughton), 120

Hideaway (Brett Leonard), 119

High Fidelity (Stephen Frears), 164

Hit, The (Stephen Frears), 33

Hitcher, The (Robert Harmon), 153

Hot Rock, The (Peter Yates), 295

Hours, The (Stephen Daldry), 103

House of Wax (André deToth), 96

Hulk (Ang Lee), 10, 308

Human Nature (Michel Gondry), 321–4, 420

Hurricane, The (Norman Jewison), 257, 290

I ♥ Huckabees (David O. Russell), **414**, 416–25, **418**, **419**
  Isabelle Huppert and, xxii
  Jason Schwartzman and, 381
  9/11 and, xxvi
  Scott Rudin and, 103

I Shot Andy Warhol (Mary Harron), 253

Identity (James Mangold), 327

If . . . (Lindsay Anderson), 213, 282

Ikiru (Akira Kurosawa), 348

Iguana (Monte Hellman), 32

Imitation of Life (Douglas Sirk), 25

In the Mouth of Madness (H. P. Lovecraft), 199

In the Name of the Father (Jim Sheridan), 79

In the Soup (Alexandre Rockwell), 35

Independence Day (Roland Emmerich), 275

Inside Out (Playboy Video Enterprises), 138

Insider, The (Michael Mann), 257

Insomnia (Christopher Nolan), 301, 302

Interview with the Vampire (Neil Jordan), 249

Intruder (Scott Spiegel), 32

Invasion of the Body Snatchers (Don Siegel), 92

Island of Dr. Moreau (John Frankenheimer), 199

It's a Wonderful Life (Frank Capra), 277

Jackass: The Movie (Jeff Tremaine), 161

Jacket, The (John Maybury), 301, 303

Jackie Brown (Quentin Tarantino), 72, **226**, 229–38, 401, 406

Jade Pussycat, The (Bob Chinn), 193

Janitor (Steven Soderbergh), 6

Jaws (Steven Spielberg), xix, 6, 42, 43, 308, 356, 415

Jay and Silent Bob Strike Back (Kevin Smith), xxiii

Jean de Florette (Claude Berri), 400

Jersey Girl (Kevin Smith), xxiii

Journey to Fear (Orson Welles), xxi

Ju Dou (Yimou Zhang), 82

Juice (Ernest R. Dickerson), 41

Jules et Jim (François Truffaut), 344

Jungle Fever (Spike Lee), 75

Jurassic Park (Steven Spielberg), 10

Jurassic Park III (Joe Johnston), 341

Kafka (Steven Soderbergh), 8, 53–61, 63, 182, 291, 373, 448

Kalifornia (Dominic Sena), 154

Kansas City Confidential (Phil Karlson), 33

Keane (Lodge Kerrigan), 40

Kids (Larry Clark), 81, 83, 138–9

Kill Bill (Quentin Tarantino), 33, 72, 88, 238, 398, 399–407

Kill Me Again (John Dahl), 152

Killing, The (Stanley Kubrick), 33

Killing Zoe (Roger Avary), 71

King Arthur (Antoine Fuqua), 151

King of Marvin Gardens (Bob Rafelson), 44

King of the Hill (Steven Soderbergh), **52**, 58–63, 109, 240, 289, 302, 372

Kingpin (Peter and Bobby Farrelly), 205

Kinsey (Bill Condon), 416

Kiss Me Deadly (Robert Aldrich), 76

Kiss of the Spiderwoman (Hector Babenko), 78

L.A. Confidential (Curtis Hanson), 227

Lady Snowblood (Toshiya Fujita), 403–4

Lady Vanishes, The (Alfred Hitchcock), 56

Last Good Breath, The (Kimberly Peirce), 246

Last Man Standing (Walter Hill), 199

Last Picture Show, The (Peter Bogdanovich), xviii, 245, 389–90

Last Tango in Paris (Bernardo Bertolucci)

Last Year at Marienbad (Alain Resnais), 238

Lawrence of Arabia (David Lean), 271

Less Than Zero (Marek Kanievska), 14

Life Aquatic with Steve Zissou, The (Wes Anderson), 389–95, **393**
  Anderson shooting, 136

Life Aquatic with Steve Zissou, The (cont.)
  Bill Murray and, 381
  David Moritz and, 144
  Henry Selick and, 172
  Scott Rudin and, 103, 420
  Sideways and, 425
Life, or Something Like It (Stephen Herek), 417
Life Without Zoe (Francis Ford Coppola), 245, 254
Like Water for Chocolate (Alfonso Arau), 90
Limey, The (Steven Soderbergh), 238–41
  crime genre, 107
  flashback in, 177
  Full Frontal and, 376
  Kafka and, 56
  structural experiments in, 109, 289
  videotape used in, 12
Lion's Den (Bryan Singer), 45, 113
Little Nicky (Adam Sandler), 199
Living End, The (Greg Araki), 22
Living in Oblivion (Tom DeCillo), 36
Lock, Stock and Two Smoking Barrels (Guy Ritchie), 30
Loneliness of the Long Distance Runner, The (Alan Sillitoe), 213
Long Goodbye, The (Robert Altman), 240
Long Kiss Goodnight, The (Renny Harlin), 198, 199, 319
Longest Day, The (Ken Annakin), 293
Look Who's Talking (Amy Heckerling), 72
Lord of the Rings (Peter Jackson), 88, 198, 264, 308
Lords of Dogtown (Catherine Hardwicke), 253–4, 437
Lost Highway (David Lynch), 107
Lost in Translation (Sofia Coppola), 162, 246, 253, 380, 381–9, 420, 437
Lost Weekend (Billy Wilder), 141
Love & Sex (Valerie Breiman), 253
Love Is the Devil (John Maybury), 301

Macbeth (Orson Welles), xxi
Magnificent Ambersons, The (Orson Welles), xxi, 342
Magnificent Seven, The (John Sturges), 404
Magnolia (Paul Thomas Anderson), 257–66, 259, 353–6
  Anderson's description, 188
  Anderson's team, 143
  'Clementine's Loop', 130
  Michael De Luca and, 200
  music from, 451
  Robert Altman and, 131
  theme, 142

Make Way for Tomorrow (Leo McCarey), 136
Mala Noche (Gus Van Sant), 44
Mallrats (Kevin Smith), xxiii
Maltese Falcon, The (John Huston), 157, 229
Man Who Wasn't There, The (Coen brothers), 362
Manon des Sources (Claude Berri), 400
Mariachi, El (Robert Rodriguez), 7, 39, 86, 87, 89–92, 94, 96, 98
Marnie (Alfred Hitchcock), 403
M*A*S*H (Robert Altman), 269, 273, 300
Mask, The (Charles Russell), 164
Mask of Zorro, The (Martin Campbell), 87
Matrix, The (Wachowski Brothers), 308, 313, 404
Maverick (Richard Donner), 365
Meet the Parents (Jay Roach), 341
Memento (Christopher Nolan), 330, 331
Men in Black (Barry Sonnenfeld), 229
Menace II Society (Allen Hughes, Albert Hughes), 41
Metropolitan (Whit Stillman), 17–20
M:I-2 (John Woo), 308
Mi vida loca (Allison Anders), 35, 92
Midnight Cowboy (John Schlesinger), 320
Miller's Crossing (Coen brothers), 114, 410
Million Dollar Baby (Clint Eastwood), 432
Mimic (Guillermo del Toro), 171, 172–3
Mission: Impossible (Brian De Palma), 362
Mission: Impossible 3 (J. J. Abrams), 156
Modern Times (Charlie Chaplin), 58
Monster in a Box (Nick Broomfield), 180
Moulin Rouge (Baz Luhrmann), 365
Murmur of the Heart (Louis Malle), 213
My Best Friend's Wedding (P. J. Hogan), 164
My Left Foot (Jim Sheridan), 79
My Secret Moments (Alexander Payne and Jim Taylor), 138, 143

Naked Lunch (William Burroughs), 54, 60
Napoleon Dynamite (Jared Hess), 212, 415
Nashville (Robert Altman), xix, 131, 189, 263
Natural Born Killers (Oliver Stone), 31, 93, 405, 407
Navajo Joe (Sergio Corbucci), 211
Network (Sidney Lumet), 263, 320
New York Stories, 245
Newton Boys, The (Richard Linklater), 101, 103, 104
Next Stop Wonderland (Brad Anderson), 82
Night in Tunisia, A (Wes Anderson), 133
Night of the Hunter, The (Charles Laughton), 440

7839

Nightmare Before Christmas, The (Tim Burton), 171
Nightmare on Elm Street (Wes Craven), 197
Nightwatch (Ole Bernedal), 172
Nine Queens (Fabián Bielinsky), 302
9012 Live (Steven Soderbergh), 7
No Such Thing (Hal Hartley), 20
Nosferatu (F. W. Murnau), 55

O Lucky Man (Lindsay Anderson), 279
Ocean's Eleven (Lewis Milestone), 33, 288
Ocean's Eleven (Steven Soderbergh), 288, 289, 292–6, 334, 361, 376, 408–9
Ocean's Twelve (Steven Soderbergh), 178, 303–4, 407–11, 423, 448
Office Space (Mike Judge), 98
Old School (Todd Phillips), 205
On the Beach (Stanley Kramer), 53
On the Waterfront (Elia Kazan), 189
Once Upon a Time in Mexico (Robert Rodriguez), 87, 93
One Hour Photo (Mark Romanek), 416
One Night Stand (Mike Figgis), 199
Opening of Misty Beethoven (Henri Paris), 188
Out of Sight (Steven Soderbergh), 228–35
  action sequences, 295
  Erin Brockovich and, 289
  fate as theme, 179
  Limey, The and, 238–41, 289
  preparation for, 183
  Quentin Tarantino and, 236
  Soderbergh's opportunity, 104,
  structural experiments, 109
Outsiders, The (Francis Ford Coppola), 246

Panic Room (David Fincher), 362–8, 369, 373, 420
Paper Moon (Peter Bogdanovich), xviii, 390
Paris Is Burning (Jennie Livingston), 22
Paris, Texas (Wim Wenders), 35
Parting Glances (Bill Sherwood), 23
Passion of Martin, The (Alexander Payne), 137, 138
Paths of Glory (Stanley Kubrick), 273
Patton (Franklin J. Schaffner), 383
Pearl Harbor (Michael Bay), 151
Peeping Tom (Michael Powell), 12
Peggy Sue Got Married (Francis Ford Coppola), 246
Pelican Brief, The (Alan J. Pakula), 376
Pelle the Conqueror (Bille August), 79
People vs. Larry Flynt, The (Milos Forman), 195

Perfect Couple, A (Robert Altman), 131
Performance (Nicholas Roeg), 177
Petulia (Richard Lester), 176, 177
Pi (Darren Aronofsky), 438
P.I. Private Investigations (Nigel Dick), 152
Pianist, The (Roman Polanski), 46, 311, 327
Pieces (Anthony and Joe Russo), 302
Pink Flamingos (John Waters), 196
Pink Panther, The (Blake Edwards), 132, 355
Pitch Black (David Twohy), 153
Planet of the Apes (Tim Burton), 294
Play It Again, Sam (Herbert Ross), 320
Player, The (Robert Altman), 13, 82, 131, 197
Playing for Keeps (Bob and Harvey Weinstein), 78
Pleasantville (Gary Ross), 173
Point Blank (John Boorman), 176, 239
Point of No Return (John Badham), 76
Poison (Todd Haynes), 21, 22, 23–4
Polyester (John Waters), 196
Poor Cow (Ken Loach), 240
Porky's (Bob Clark), 205
Presumed Innocent (Alan J. Pakula), 60
Pretty Woman (Garry Marshall), 12, 288
Price Above Rubies, A (Boaz Yakin), 41
Psycho (Alfred Hitchcock), 76
Public Access (Bryan Singer), 43–50, 113, 219, 220
Pulp Fiction (Quentin Tarantino), 69–78, 73, 74
  Bob Kurtzman and, 93
  Elmore Leonard and, 227–30
  importance of, 29, 401
  influences on, 31
  Jackie Brown and, 235, 236
  John Travolta and, 233
  Kill Bill and, 405
  Miramax and, 197, 401
  prequel planned, 399
  success of, 231
  Underneath and, 111
Punch-Drunk Love (Paul Thomas Anderson), 340, 353–7
  award for, 341
  family theme, 142, 342, 367
  Robert Altman's influence, 131
  team for, 143, 381
Putney Swope (Robert Downey Sr), 189–90

Quiz Show (Robert Redford), 63

Raging Bull (Martin Scorsese), 70, 189, 276
Rain Man (Barry Levinson), 320
Rapid Eye Movement (Steven Soderbergh), 6

Rear Window (Alfred Hitchcock), 368
Rebel Without a Cause (Nicholas Ray), 91
Red Rock West (John Dahl), 152
Reefer Madness (Louis J. Gasnier), 196
Règle du Jeu, La (Jean Renoir), 342
Remember the Titans (Boaz Yakin), 41
Replacement Killers, The (Antoine
   Fuqua), 151
Requiem for a Dream (Darren Aronofsky),
   438, 439
Reservoir Dogs (Quentin Tarantino), 28,
   29–35
   Bob Kurtzman and, 93
   borrowings for, 404
   Harvey Weinstein and, 79
   Jackie Brown and, 235, 236
   Kill Bill and, 402, 405
   prequel planned, 399
   Pulp Fiction and, 71, 72, 75, 77
   Royal Tenenbaums, The and, 77
   Sundance and, 70
Return of the Jedi (George Lucas), 152
Return of the King (Peter Jackson), 198, 415
Reversal of Fortune (Barbet Schroeder), 54
Rififi (Jules Dassin), 33, 295
Right Stuff, The (Phil Kaufman), 292
Road to Perdition (Sam Mendes), 366
Road Trip (Todd Phillips), 205
Roadracers (Robert Rodriguez), 91, 91
Rock, The (Michael Bay), 151, 155
Roger and Me (Michael Moore), 49
Rookie, The (Clint Eastwood), 41
Royal Tenenbaums, The (Wes Anderson),
   342–8, 343
   Angelica Huston in, 392
   Ben Stiller in, 381
   Bill Murray in, 382
   name choice, 217
   Reservoir Dogs and, 77
   Scott Rudin and, 420
   success of, 390
   Wes Anderson after, 394
   a Wes Anderson movie, 132
Ruby in Paradise (Victor Nunez), 43
Rules of Engagement (William Friedkin), 297
Rumble Fish (Francis Ford Coppola), 246
Rumor Has It (Rob Reiner), 302
Rushmore (Wes Anderson), 204, 211–19, 215
   actors for, 381
   Bill Murray in, 381, 382
   death in, 346
   director promotes, 345
   Disney and, 201

   teen theme, 205
   theatrical origins, 342, 391
   a Wes Anderson movie, 132

Safe (Todd Haynes), 24
Sarafina (Darrell Roodt), 80
Saturday Night Fever (John Badham), 72
Saving Private Ryan (Steven Spielberg),
   82, 399
Scandal (Michael Caton-Jones), 78, 79
Schindler's List (Steven Spielberg), 311, 319
Schizopolis (Steven Soderbergh), 170, 173–80
   Beatles' films and, 57
   budget, 109
   Full Frontal and, 377
   Limey, The and, 239, 240, 241
   Out of Sight and, 234
   Soderbergh works on, 171
   Solaris and, 369
   themes, 56, 58, 291
   Traffic and, 289
School of Rock (Richard Linklater), 101, 103
Scream (Wes Craven), 87, 95
Secret Honor (Robert Altman), 128
Secretary (Steven Shainberg), 14
Secrets and Lies (Mike Leigh), 361
Serpico (Sidney Lumet), 218
Se7en, 117–22, 123
   crime genre and, 107
   Fight Club and, 276
   Gwyneth Paltrow and, 130
   New Line and, 108, 362
   script, 154
   success of, 197, 364
Seven Samurai, The (Akira Kurosawa), 404
sex, lies, and videotape (Steven Soderbergh),
   4, 5–14
   awards, 69, 79
   betrayal in, 291
   Hal Hartley and, 19
   importance of, 17, 63
   Richard Linklater and, 21
   Solaris and, 369
   Sundance and, xvi
   themes, 178, 445
Shakespeare in Love (John Madden), 78,
   82, 196
Shine (Scott Hicks), 197
Short Cuts (Robert Altman), xxvii, 12, 99,
   131, 263
Sideways (Alexander Payne), 425–32, 433
   Fox Searchlight and, 415–16, 417
   hailed as masterpiece, xxix, 437

Lost Weekend and, 141
   success of, 442
   team for, 143
Silence of the Lambs, The (Jonathan Demme), 365
Sin City (Robert Rodriguez and Frank Miller), 87, 97–8, 104
Singin' in the Rain (Gene Kelly and Stanley Donen), 194
Sixth Sense, The (M. Night Shyamalan), 75, 200
Slacker (Richard Linklater), 21, 30, 99, 101, 102, 103
Sleepy Hollow (Tim Burton), 257
Small Change (François Truffaut), 213
Smokey and the Bandit (Hal Needham), 193
Solaris (Steven Soderbergh), 179, 291, 296, 361, 368–72, 408
Soldiers Pay (David O. Russell), 273,274
Something Wild (Jonathan Demme), 157
Sorpasso, Il (Dino Risi), 429
Spanking the Monkey (David O. Russell), 38
   archetypes, 418
   award, 50
   Flirting with Disaster and, 81, 424
   production history, 47
   Russell's family's view, 447
   Russell's sense of humour, 45
   script, 44
   themes, 49
   Three Kings and, 266
Speed (Jan de Bont), 229
Spider-Man (Sam Raimi), 320, 362, 415
Spy Kids (Robert Rodriguez), 87, 94, 95–6, 98
Squid and the Whale, The (Noah Baumbach), 393
Stalag 17 (Billy Wilder), 273
Stalker (Andrei Tarkovsky), 36, 58
Stand By Me (Rob Reiner), 61
Star Is Born, A (George Cukor), 194
Star Trek: Nemesis (Stuart Baird), 46
Star Wars: Episode 1- The Phantom Menace (George Lucas), 257
Star Wars: Episode IV- A New Hope (George Lucas), xix, , 120, 313
Stepford Wives, The (Frank Oz), 423
Stick (Burt Reynolds), 228
Sting, The (George Roy Hill), 295
Stonewall (Nigel Finch), 22
Storytelling (Todd Solonz), 200, 429
Straight Time (Ulu Grosbard), xv
Stranger Than Paradise (Jim Jarmusch), 9
Strangers on a Train (Alfred Hitchcock), 437

Straw Dogs (Sam Peckinpah), 368
Strictly Ballroom (Baz Luhrmann), 80
SubUrbia (Richard Linklater), 100, 102
Sugar Town (Allison Anders), 35
Sugarland Express (Steven Spielberg), 43, 308, 441
Summer of Sam (Spike Lee), 257
Superman (Richard Donner), 308
Superman Returns (Bryan Singer), 316
Superstar: The Karen Carpenter Story (Todd Haynes), 23
Surviving Desire (Hal Hartley), **16**, 19
Suture (Scott McGehee and David Siegel), 39, 173,442
Swimming to Cambodia (Jonathan Demme), 180
Swimming with Sharks (George Huang), 82
Swoon (Tom Kalin), 22
Swordfish (Dominic Sena), 151
Sympathy for the Devil (Jean-Luc Godard), 196
Syriana (Stephen Gaghan), 302

Taking Lives (John Caruso), 120
Taking of Pelham 123 (Joseph Sargent), 33
Tape (Richard Linklater), 101, 102, 104
Targets (Peter Bogdanovich), 389
Taxi Driver (Martin Scorsese), xix, 6, 70, 177, 276
Tears of the Sun (Antoine Fuqua), 151
Teenage Mutant Ninja Turtles (Steve Barron), 197
Terms of Endearment (James L. Brooks), 144
Texas Chainsaw Massacre, The (Tobe Hooper), 82, 197
Theory of Achievement (Hal Hartley), 19
There's Something About Mary (Bobby Farrelly and Peter Farrelly), 164
Thin Blue Line, The (Errol Morris), 82
Thin Red Line, The (Terrence Malick), 257, 276
Things to Do in Denver When You're Dead (Gary Fleder), 113
Third Man, The (Carol Reed), 55, 56, 57
Thirteen (Catherine Hardwicke), 253, 416
36th Chamber of Shaolin (Lau Kar-leung), 403
This Boy's Life (Michael Caton-Jones), 60
Thomas Crown Affair, The (John McTiernan), 293
Three Kings (David O. Russell), 266–74, **269**
   Fight Club and, 275, 276, 282
   Gulf War theme, xxvi, 257
   Mark Wahlberg in, 381
   Russell and Warner Bros. after, 416

Three Seasons (Tony Bui), 40

3:10 to Yuma (Delmar Daves), 227

Thriller: En Grym Film (Bo Arne Vibenius), 403

Titan AE, (Don Bluth), 276

Titanic (James Cameron), xxvi, 275

To Catch a Thief (Alfred Hitchcock), 408

Tokyo Story (Yasujiro Ozu), 348

Tomb Raider (Simon West), 151

Top Gun (Tony Scott), 32

Touch (Paul Schrader), 228

Touch of Evil (Orson Welles), xxi

Town and Country (Peter Chelsom), 199

Traffic (Steven Soderbergh), 296–300
  awards, xxiv, 171, 287, 334, 361
  filters used in, 109, 291
  social issues in, xxvi,
  Soderbergh's greatest achievement, 289
  structural experiments, 109
  uncommercial nature, 288

Training Day (Antoine Fuqua), 151

Trainspotting (Danny Boyle), 70

Treasure of the Sierra Madre, The (John Huston), 268

Trois couleurs: Rouge (Krzysztof Kieslowski), 69

True Romance (Tony Scott), 31–2, 72, 93, 229, 231, 405

Truman Show, The (Peter Weir), 219

Trust (Hal Hartley), 21

Truth or Dare (Alek Keshishian), 79

Tunel, El (Ernesto Sabato), 137

Twelve Monkeys (Terry Gilliam), 75, 280

Two Lane Blacktop (Monte Hellman), 32

2001: A Space Odyssey (Stanley Kubrick), 369, 372

Unbelievable Truth, The (Hal Hartley), 17, 18–19, 43

Underneath, The, (Steven Soderbergh), 108–12
  cinematography, 254
  crime genre and, 107
  filters used in, 299
  gross take, 171
  Peter Gallagher and, 59
  Populist Pictures and, 40
  themes, 122, 178

Undertow (David Gordon Green), 440

Uptown Girls (Boaz Yakin), 42

Urban Legends: Final Cut (John Ottman), 315

Usual Suspects, The (Bryan Singer), 106, 112–18
  Christopher McQuarrie and, 48
  crime genre and, 107
  Gabriel Byrne and, 223
  Gramercy and, 108
  Marvel Comics, 310
  Ottman's montage, 49, 222
  Public Access and, 47, 50
  Se7en and, 122
  Stephen King and, 220

Velvet Goldmine (Todd Haynes), 20, 25

Vertigo (Alfred Hitchcock), 157

Virgin Suicides, The (Sofia Coppola), 244, 245, 247, 249–53, 383–4, 385, 386

Viridiana (Luis Buñuel), 140

Waking Life (Richard Linklater), 101, 104

Wall Street (Oliver Stone), 14, 159

Warriors, The (Walter Hill), 347

Welcome to Collinwood (Anthony Russo and Joe Russo), 302, 303

Welcome to the Dollhouse (Todd Solondz), 40, 81

What's New, Pussycat? (Clive Donner), 425

What's Up, Doc? (Peter Bogdanovich), 390

Who's That Knocking at My Door? (Martin Scorsese), 131

Wild at Heart (David Lynch), 69, 139, 152

Wild Bunch, The (Sam Peckinpah), xxi, 30

Wild Strawberries (Ingmar Bergman), 348

Withnail and I (Bruce Robinson), 429

Wizard of Oz, The (Victor Fleming), 21, 58

Wonderland (James Cox), 193

Working Girls (Lizzie Borden), 78

X-Men (Bryan Singer), xxvi, 43, 108, 224, 306, 307–16

Yards, The (James Gray), 301

You Can Count On Me (Kenneth Lonergan), 40, 253

You Can't Take It with You (Frank Capra), 347

Your Friends and Neighbors (Neil LaBute), 156

Zoolander (Ben Stiller), 103

Zorba the Greek (Michael Cacoyannis), 429